NAOKI URASAWA Volume. 2

◆MONSTER◆

Perfect Edition

NAOKI URASAWA † Volume 2

MONSTER

Perfect Edition

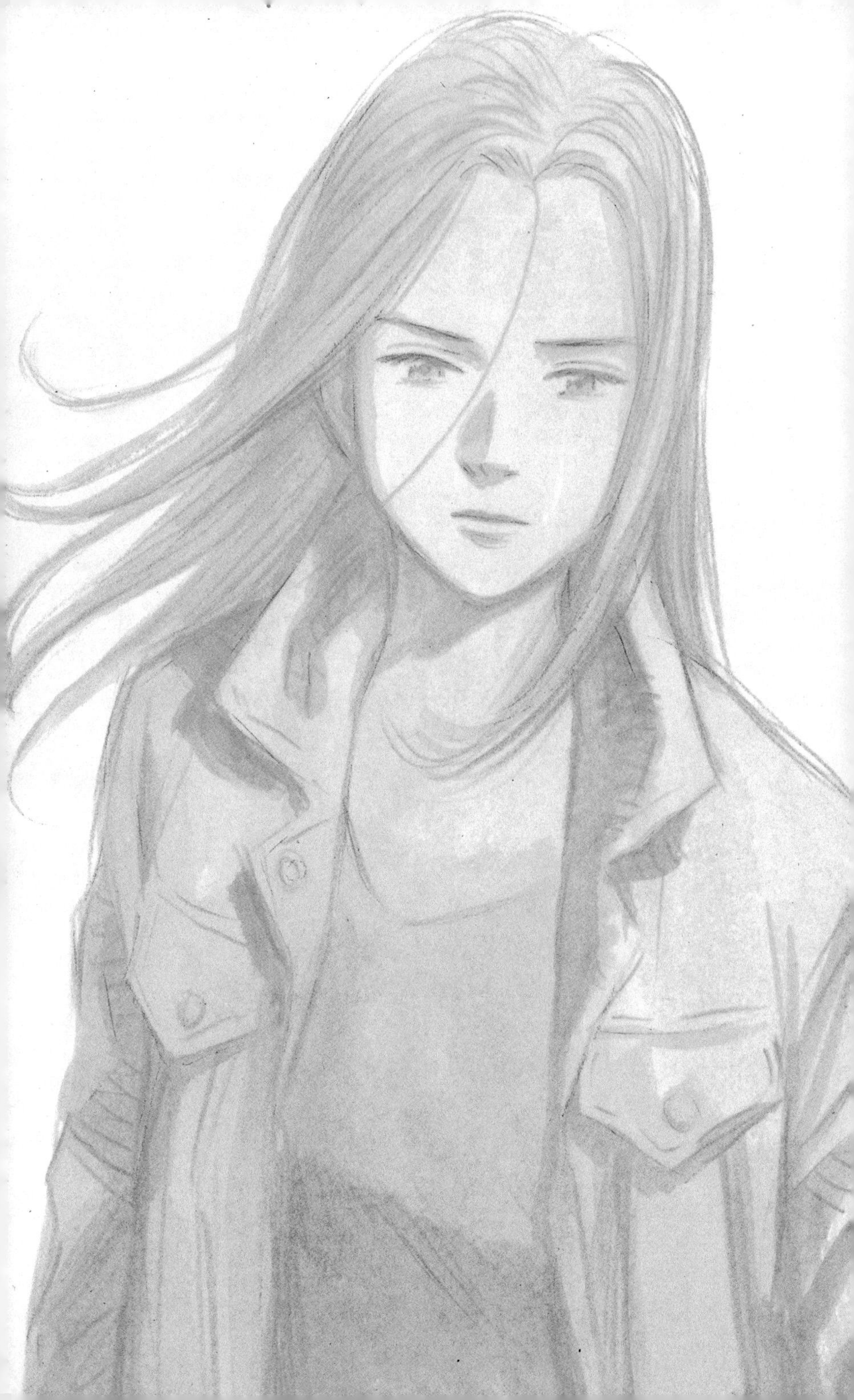

Contents

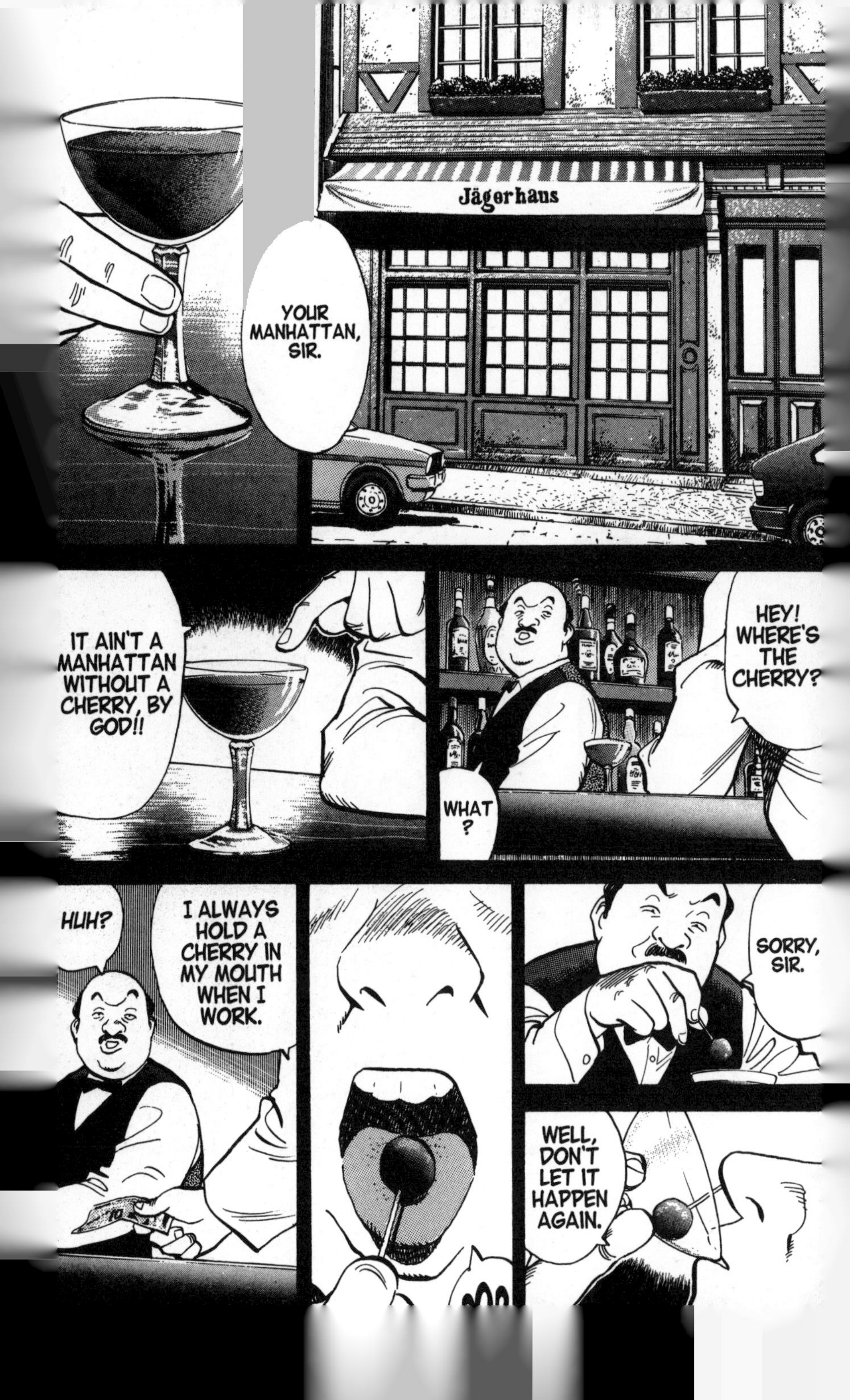
Jägerhaus
YOUR MANHATTAN, SIR.
HEY! WHERE'S THE CHERRY?
WHAT?
IT AIN'T A MANHATTAN WITHOUT A CHERRY, BY GOD!!
SORRY, SIR.
WELL, DON'T LET IT HAPPEN AGAIN.
I ALWAYS HOLD A CHERRY IN MY MOUTH WHEN I WORK.
HUH?

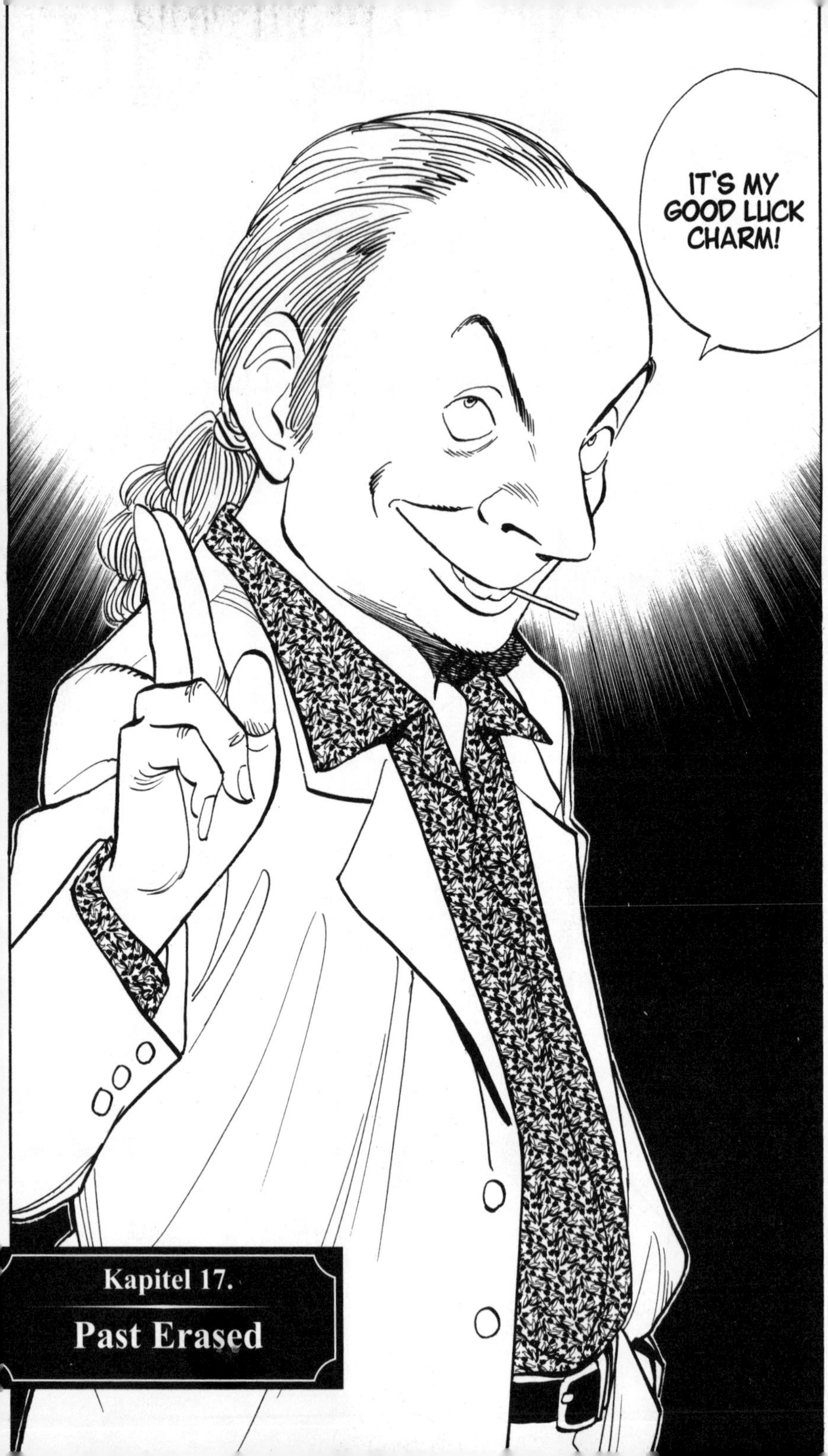
IT'S MY GOOD LUCK CHARM!

Kapitel 17.

Past Erased

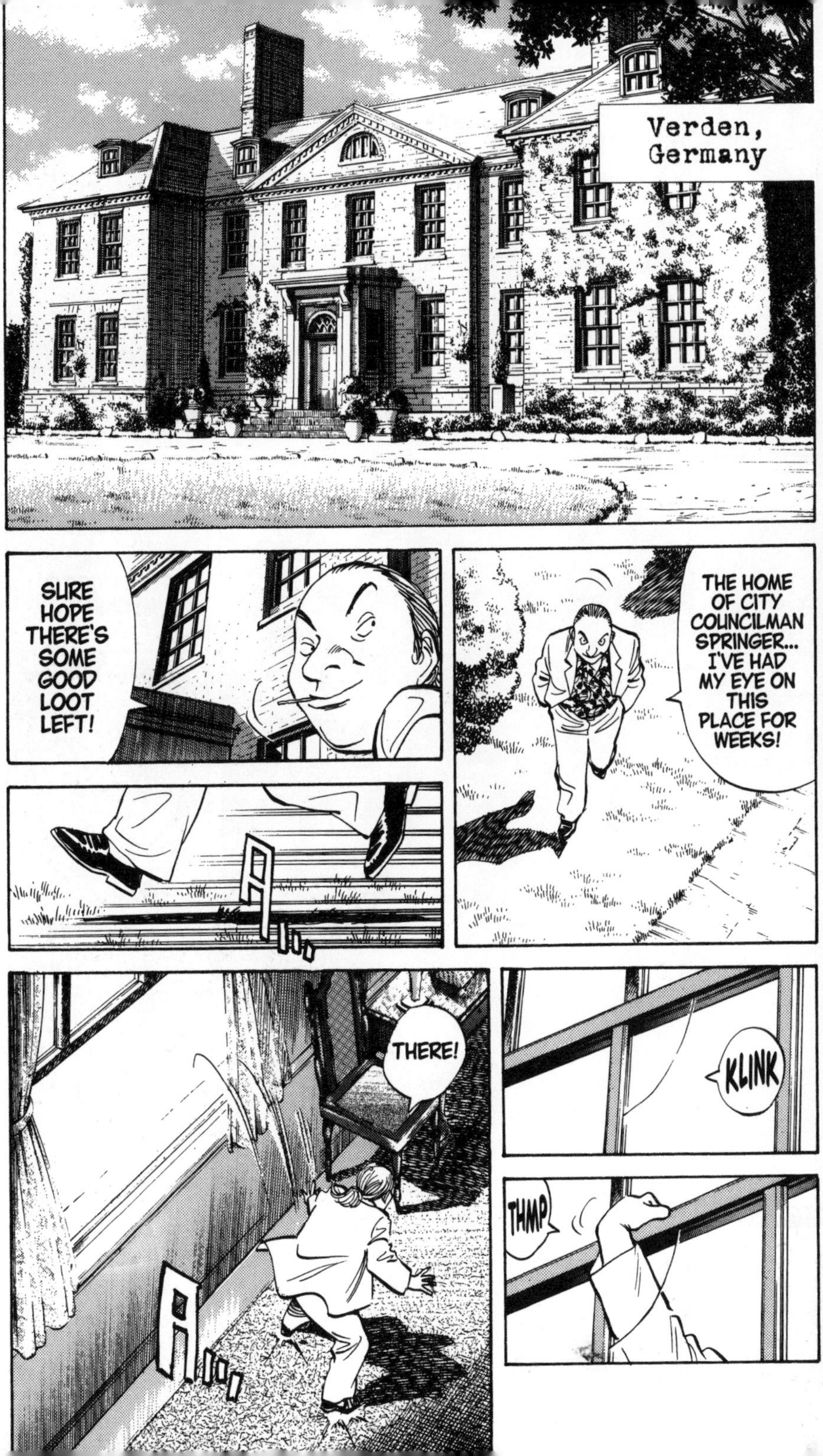
Verden, Germany
THE HOME OF CITY COUNCILMAN SPRINGER... I'VE HAD MY EYE ON THIS PLACE FOR WEEKS!
SURE HOPE THERE'S SOME GOOD LOOT LEFT!
KLINK
THMP
THERE!

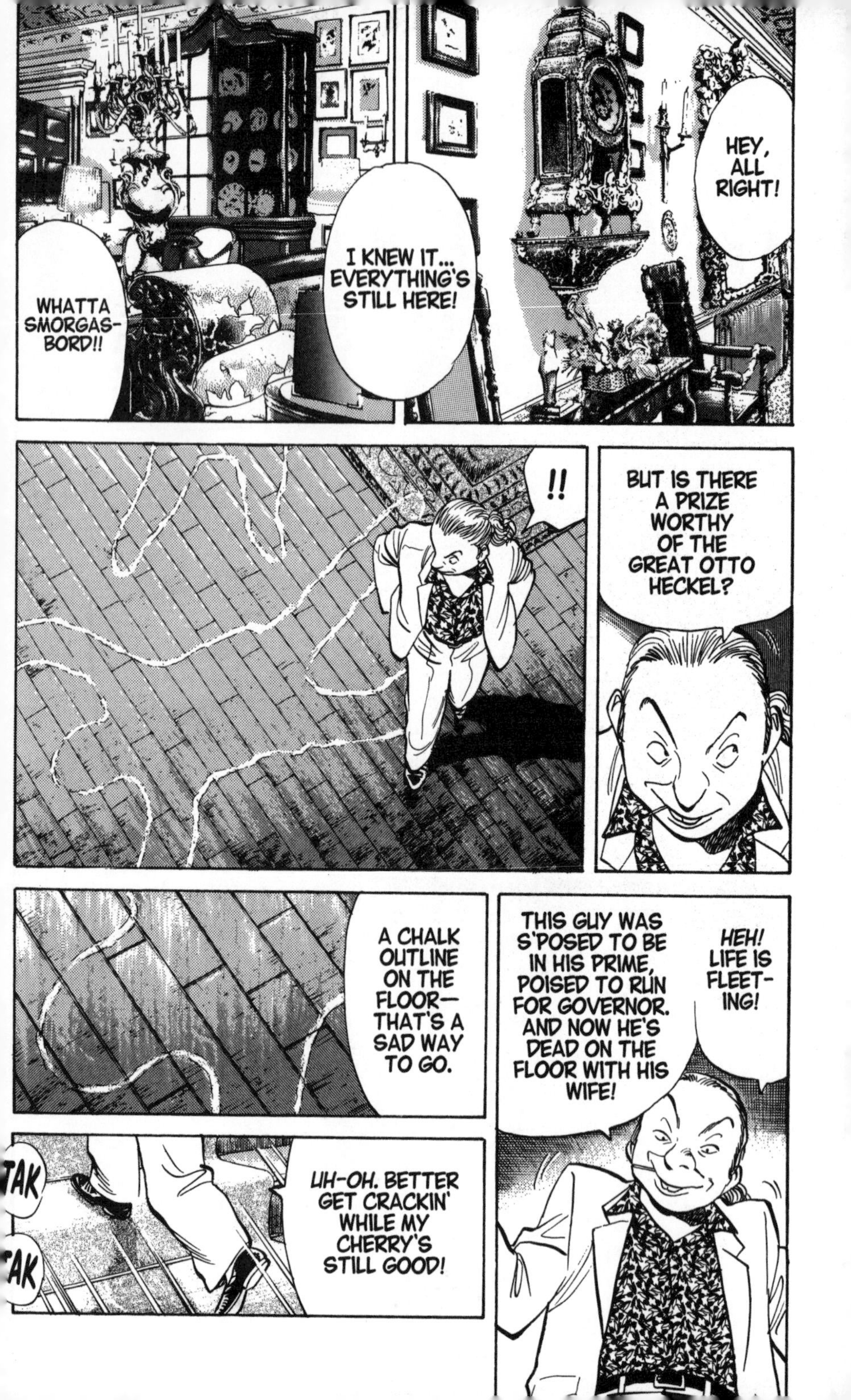
HEY, ALL RIGHT!
I KNEW IT... EVERYTHING'S STILL HERE!
WHATTA SMORGAS-BORD!!
BUT IS THERE A PRIZE WORTHY OF THE GREAT OTTO HECKEL?
!!
HEH! LIFE IS FLEET-ING!
THIS GUY WAS S'POSED TO BE IN HIS PRIME, POISED TO RUN FOR GOVERNOR. AND NOW HE'S DEAD ON THE FLOOR WITH HIS WIFE!
A CHALK OUTLINE ON THE FLOOR— THAT'S A SAD WAY TO GO.
UH-OH. BETTER GET CRACKIN' WHILE MY CHERRY'S STILL GOOD!
TAK
TAK

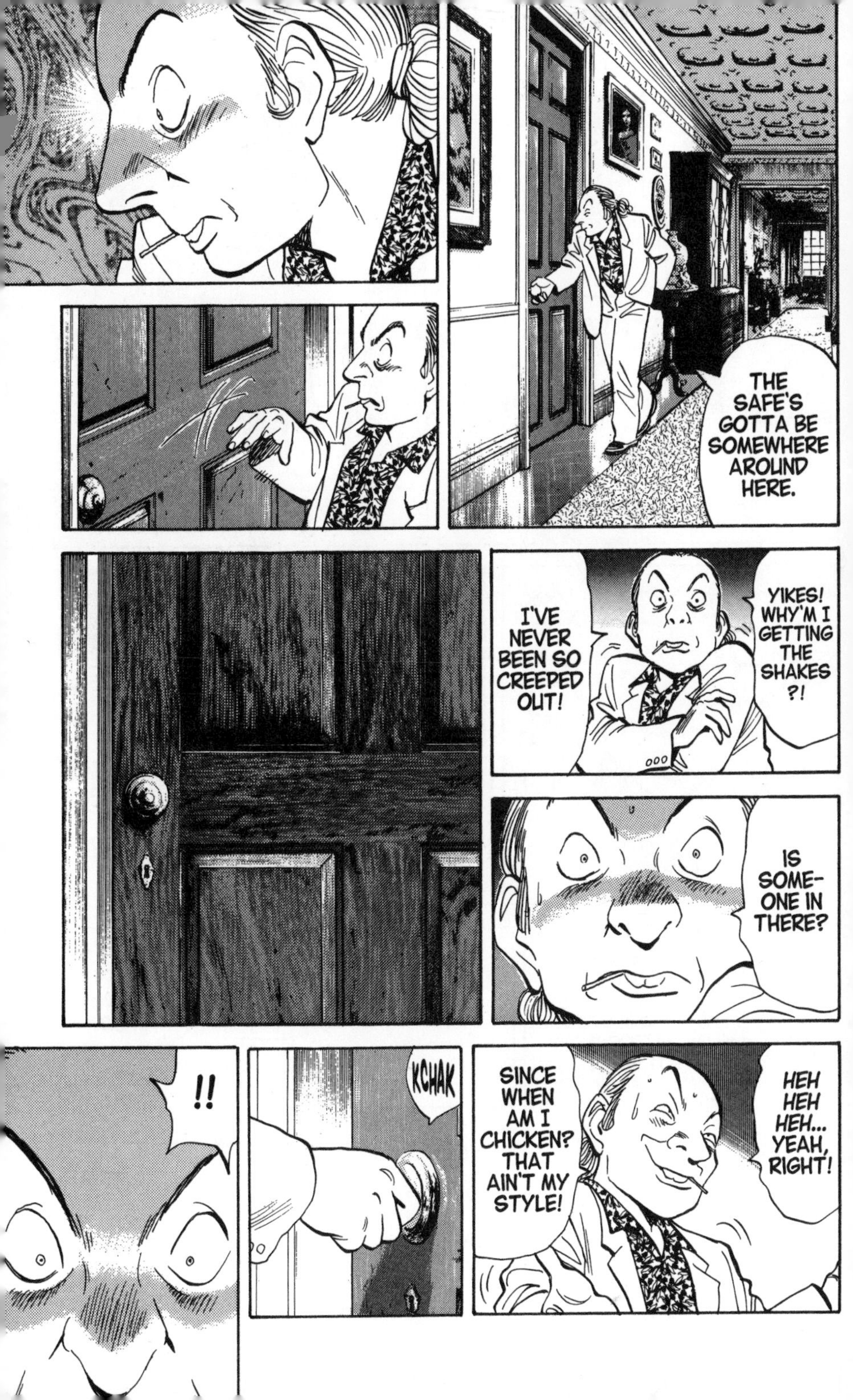
THE SAFE'S GOTTA BE SOMEWHERE AROUND HERE.
YIKES! WHY'M I GETTING THE SHAKES ?!
I'VE NEVER BEEN SO CREEPED OUT!
IS SOME-ONE IN THERE?
HEH HEH HEH... YEAH, RIGHT!
SINCE WHEN AM I CHICKEN? THAT AIN'T MY STYLE!
KCHAK
!!

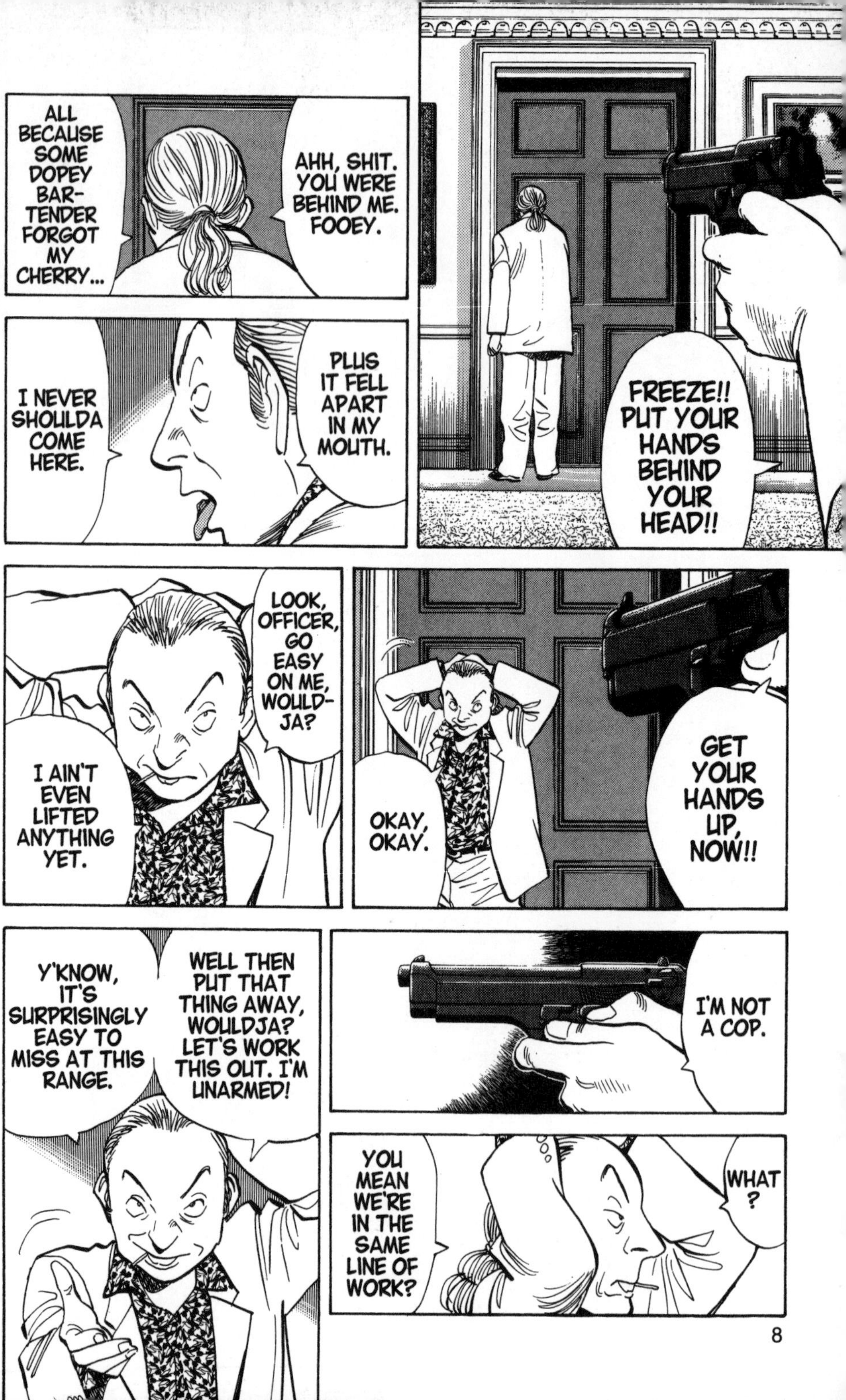
FREEZE!! PUT YOUR HANDS BEHIND YOUR HEAD!!
AHH, SHIT. YOU WERE BEHIND ME. FOOEY.
ALL BECAUSE SOME DOPEY BAR-TENDER FORGOT MY CHERRY...
PLUS IT FELL APART IN MY MOUTH.
I NEVER SHOULDA COME HERE.
GET YOUR HANDS UP, NOW!!
OKAY, OKAY.
LOOK, OFFICER, GO EASY ON ME, WOULDJA?
I AIN'T EVEN LIFTED ANYTHING YET.
I'M NOT A COP.
WHAT?
YOU MEAN WE'RE IN THE SAME LINE OF WORK?
WELL THEN PUT THAT THING AWAY, WOULDJA? LET'S WORK THIS OUT. I'M UNARMED!
Y'KNOW, IT'S SURPRISINGLY EASY TO MISS AT THIS RANGE.

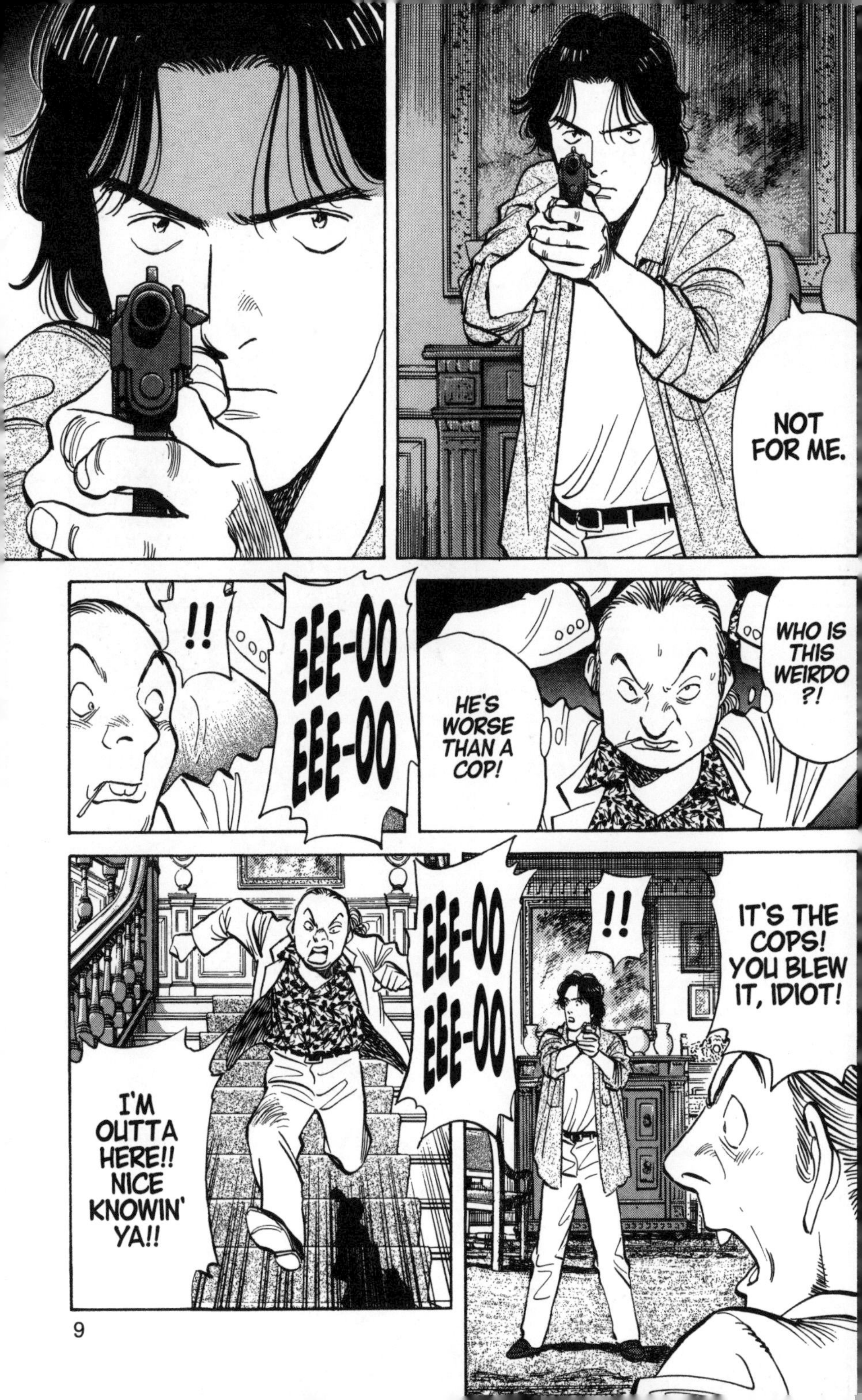
NOT FOR ME.
WHO IS THIS WEIRDO ?!
HE'S WORSE THAN A COP!
EEE-OO EEE-OO
!!
IT'S THE COPS! YOU BLEW IT, IDIOT!
!!
EEE-OO EEE-OO
I'M OUTTA HERE!! NICE KNOWIN' YA!!

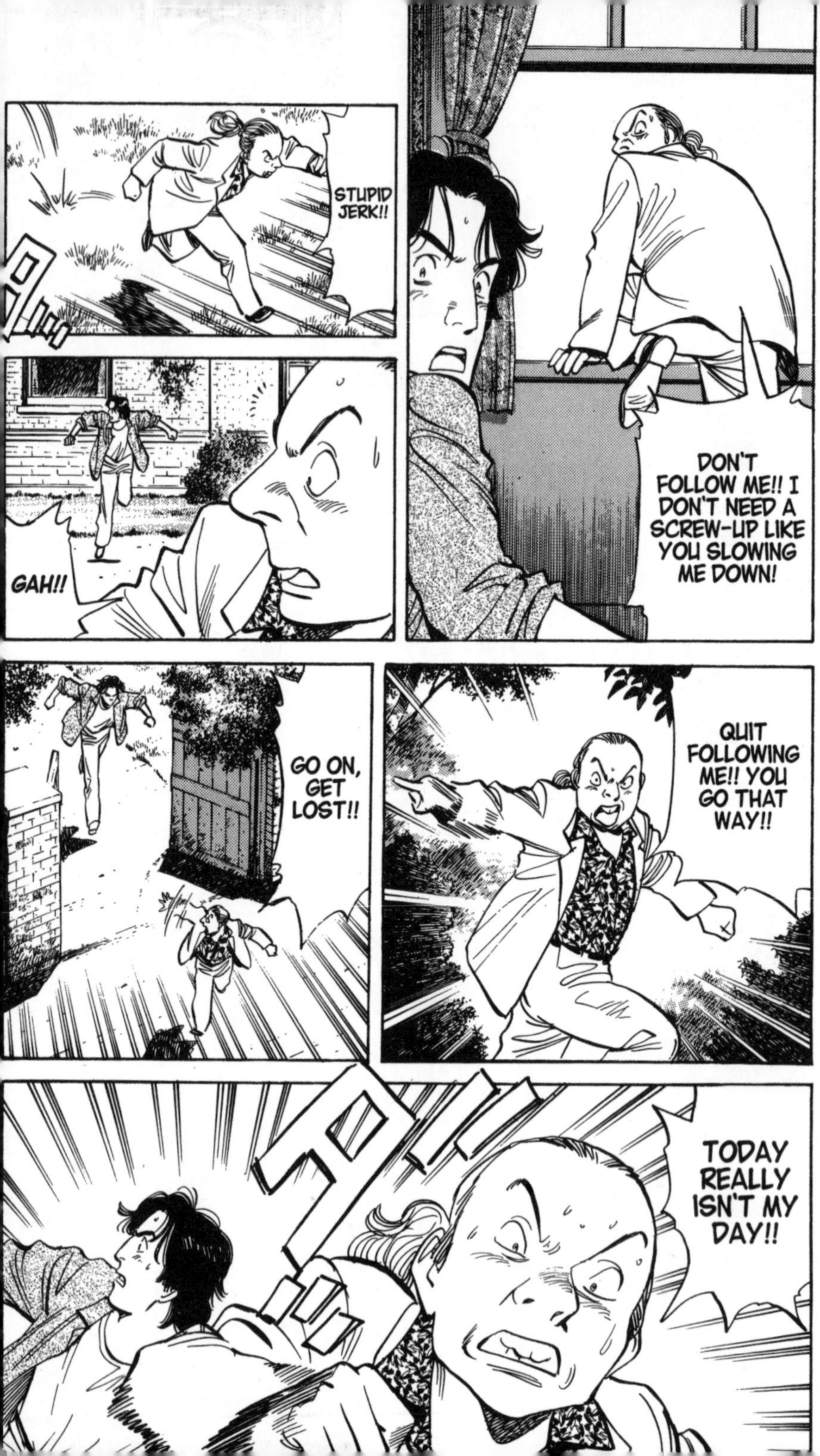
DON'T FOLLOW ME!! I DON'T NEED A SCREW-UP LIKE YOU SLOWING ME DOWN!
STUPID JERK!!
GAH!!
QUIT FOLLOWING ME!! YOU GO THAT WAY!!
GO ON, GET LOST!!
TODAY REALLY ISN'T MY DAY!!

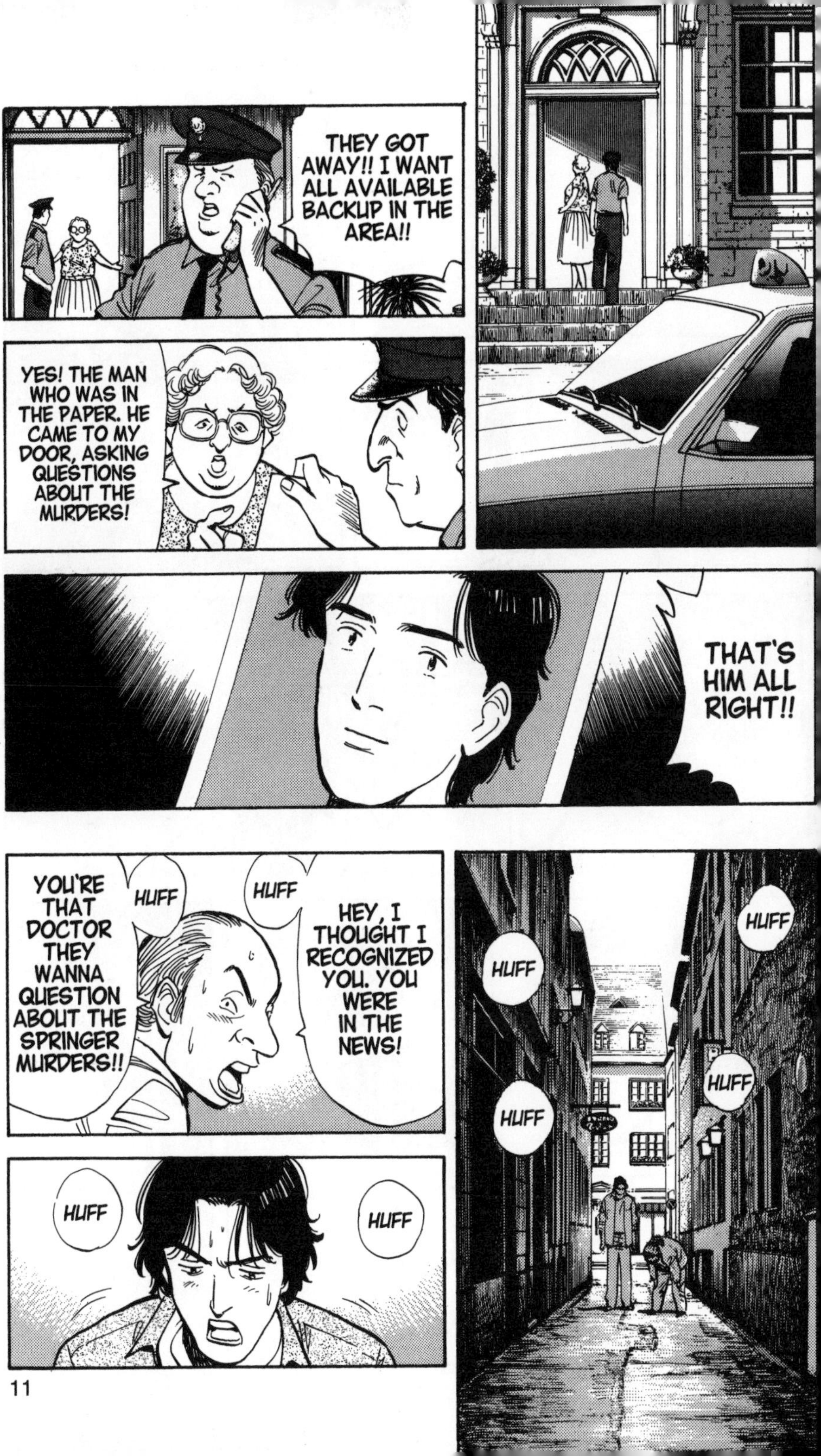
THEY GOT AWAY!! I WANT ALL AVAILABLE BACKUP IN THE AREA!!
YES! THE MAN WHO WAS IN THE PAPER. HE CAME TO MY DOOR, ASKING QUESTIONS ABOUT THE MURDERS!
THAT'S HIM ALL RIGHT!!
HUFF
HUFF
HUFF
HUFF
HUFF
HEY, I THOUGHT I RECOGNIZED YOU. YOU WERE IN THE NEWS!
HUFF
YOU'RE THAT DOCTOR THEY WANNA QUESTION ABOUT THE SPRINGER MURDERS!!
HUFF
HUFF

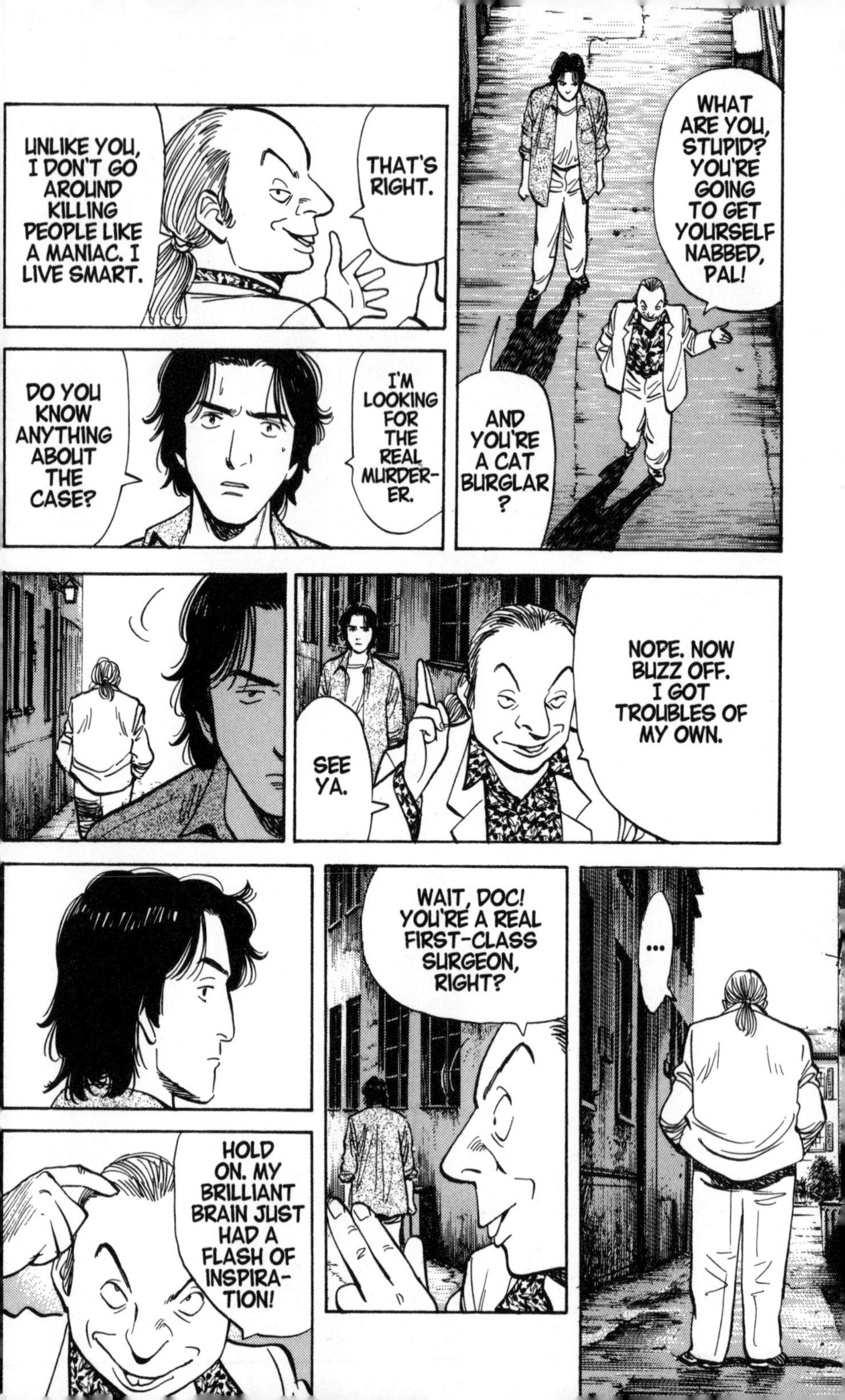
WHAT ARE YOU, STUPID? YOU'RE GOING TO GET YOURSELF NABBED, PAL!
AND YOU'RE A CAT BURGLAR?
THAT'S RIGHT.
UNLIKE YOU, I DON'T GO AROUND KILLING PEOPLE LIKE A MANIAC. I LIVE SMART.
I'M LOOKING FOR THE REAL MURDERER.
DO YOU KNOW ANYTHING ABOUT THE CASE?
NOPE. NOW BUZZ OFF. I GOT TROUBLES OF MY OWN.
SEE YA.
...
WAIT, DOC! YOU'RE A REAL FIRST-CLASS SURGEON, RIGHT?
HOLD ON. MY BRILLIANT BRAIN JUST HAD A FLASH OF INSPIRATION!

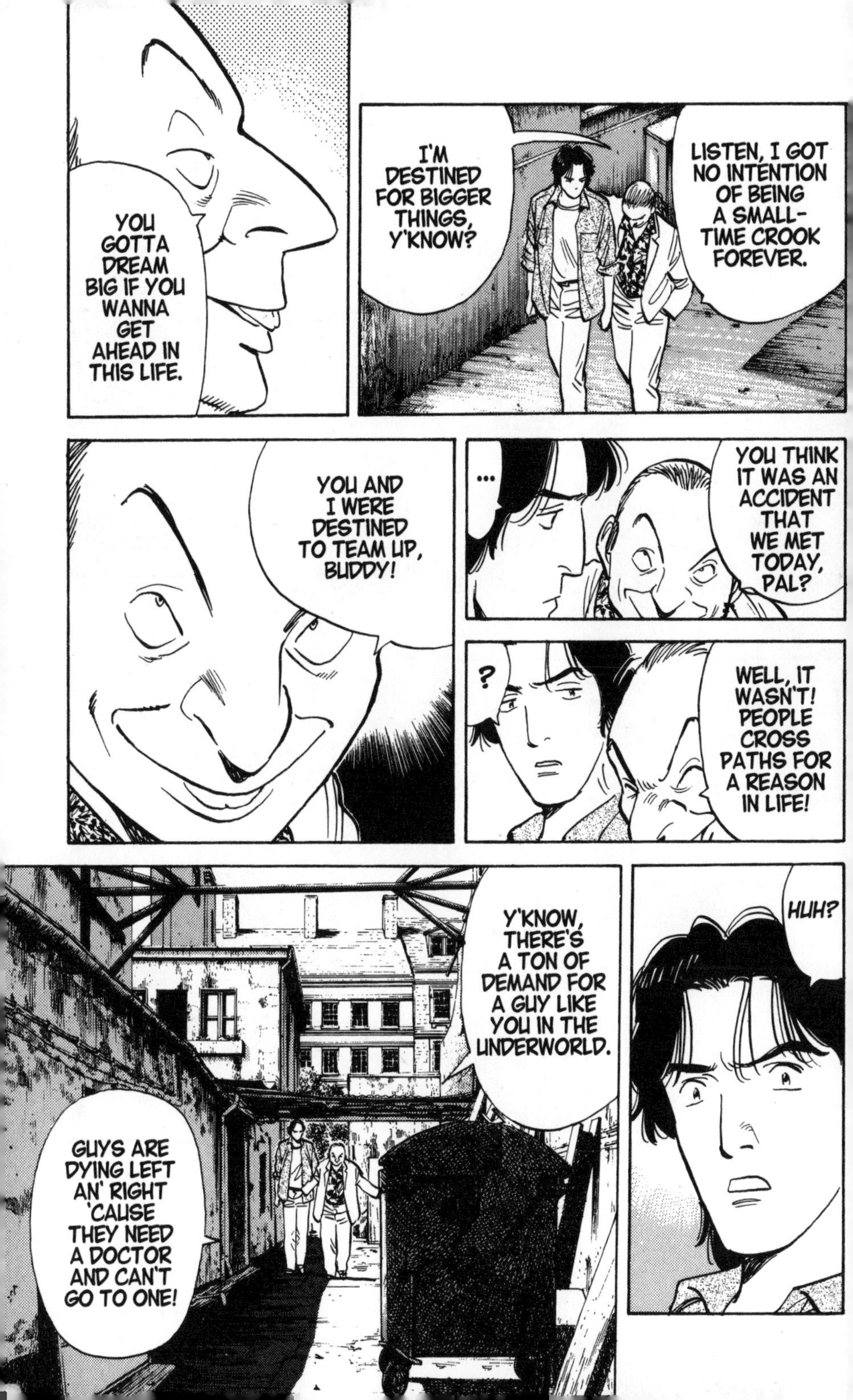
LISTEN, I GOT NO INTENTION OF BEING A SMALL-TIME CROOK FOREVER.
I'M DESTINED FOR BIGGER THINGS, Y'KNOW?
YOU GOTTA DREAM BIG IF YOU WANNA GET AHEAD IN THIS LIFE.
YOU THINK IT WAS AN ACCIDENT THAT WE MET TODAY, PAL?
...
WELL, IT WASN'T! PEOPLE CROSS PATHS FOR A REASON IN LIFE!
?
YOU AND I WERE DESTINED TO TEAM UP, BUDDY!
HUH?
Y'KNOW, THERE'S A TON OF DEMAND FOR A GUY LIKE YOU IN THE UNDERWORLD.
GUYS ARE DYING LEFT AN' RIGHT 'CAUSE THEY NEED A DOCTOR AND CAN'T GO TO ONE!

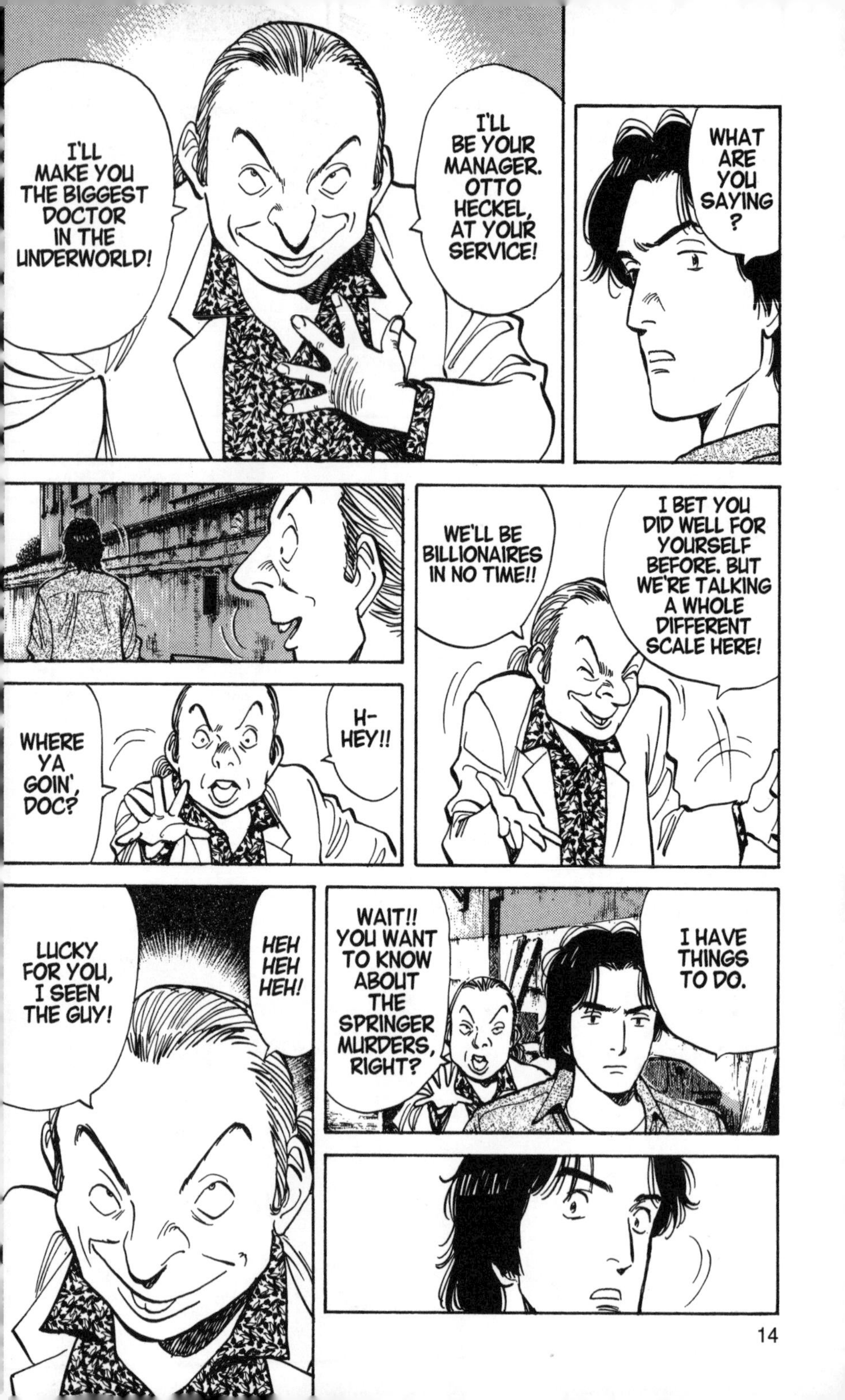
WHAT ARE YOU SAYING?
I'LL BE YOUR MANAGER. OTTO HECKEL, AT YOUR SERVICE!
I'LL MAKE YOU THE BIGGEST DOCTOR IN THE UNDERWORLD!
I BET YOU DID WELL FOR YOURSELF BEFORE. BUT WE'RE TALKING A WHOLE DIFFERENT SCALE HERE!
WE'LL BE BILLIONAIRES IN NO TIME!!
H- HEY!!
WHERE YA GOIN', DOC?
I HAVE THINGS TO DO.
WAIT!! YOU WANT TO KNOW ABOUT THE SPRINGER MURDERS, RIGHT?
HEH HEH HEH!
LUCKY FOR YOU, I SEEN THE GUY!

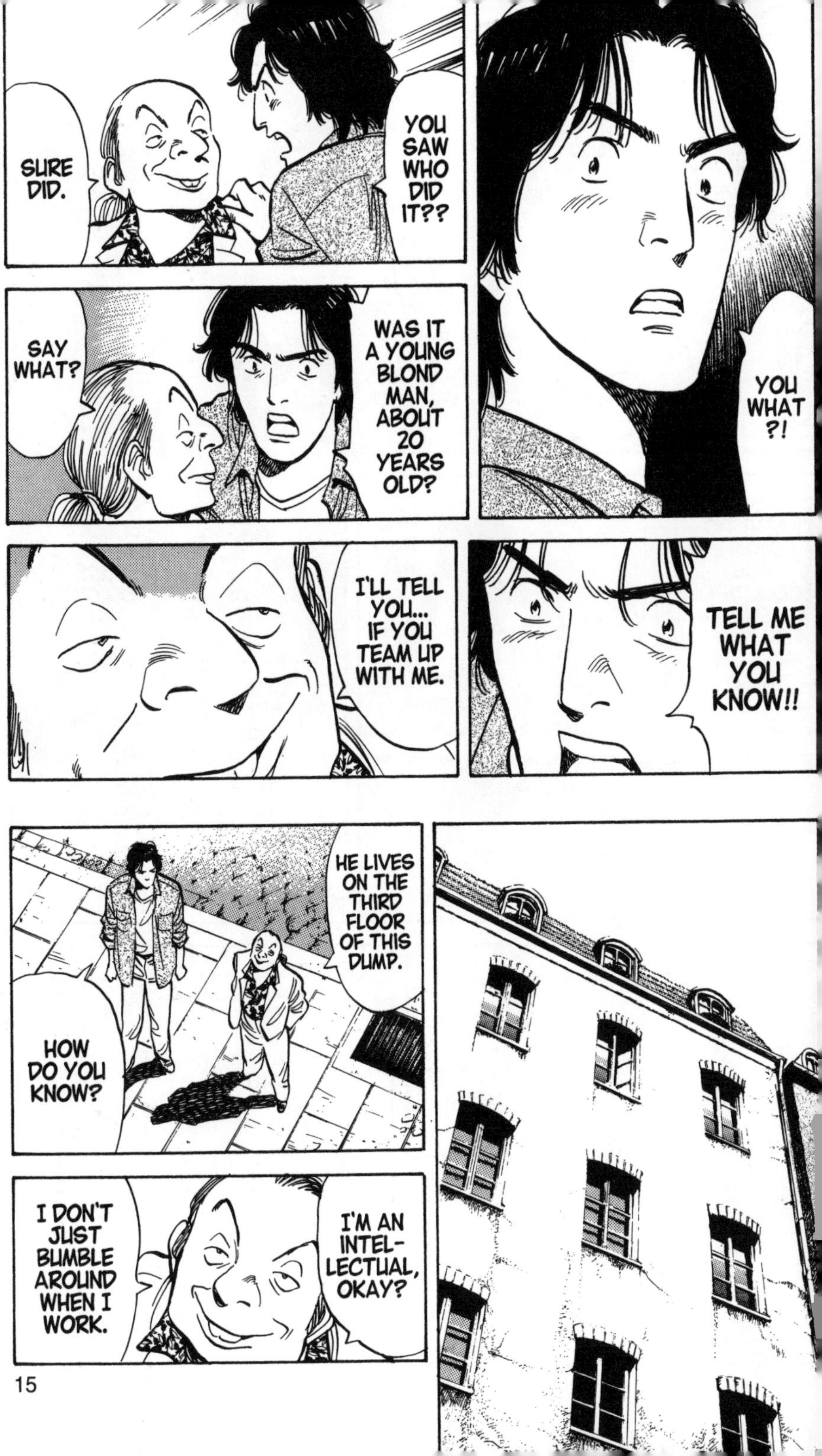
YOU WHAT?!
YOU SAW WHO DID IT??
SURE DID.
WAS IT A YOUNG BLOND MAN, ABOUT 20 YEARS OLD?
SAY WHAT?
TELL ME WHAT YOU KNOW!!
I'LL TELL YOU... IF YOU TEAM UP WITH ME.
HE LIVES ON THE THIRD FLOOR OF THIS DUMP.
HOW DO YOU KNOW?
I'M AN INTEL-LECTUAL, OKAY?
I DON'T JUST BUMBLE AROUND WHEN I WORK.

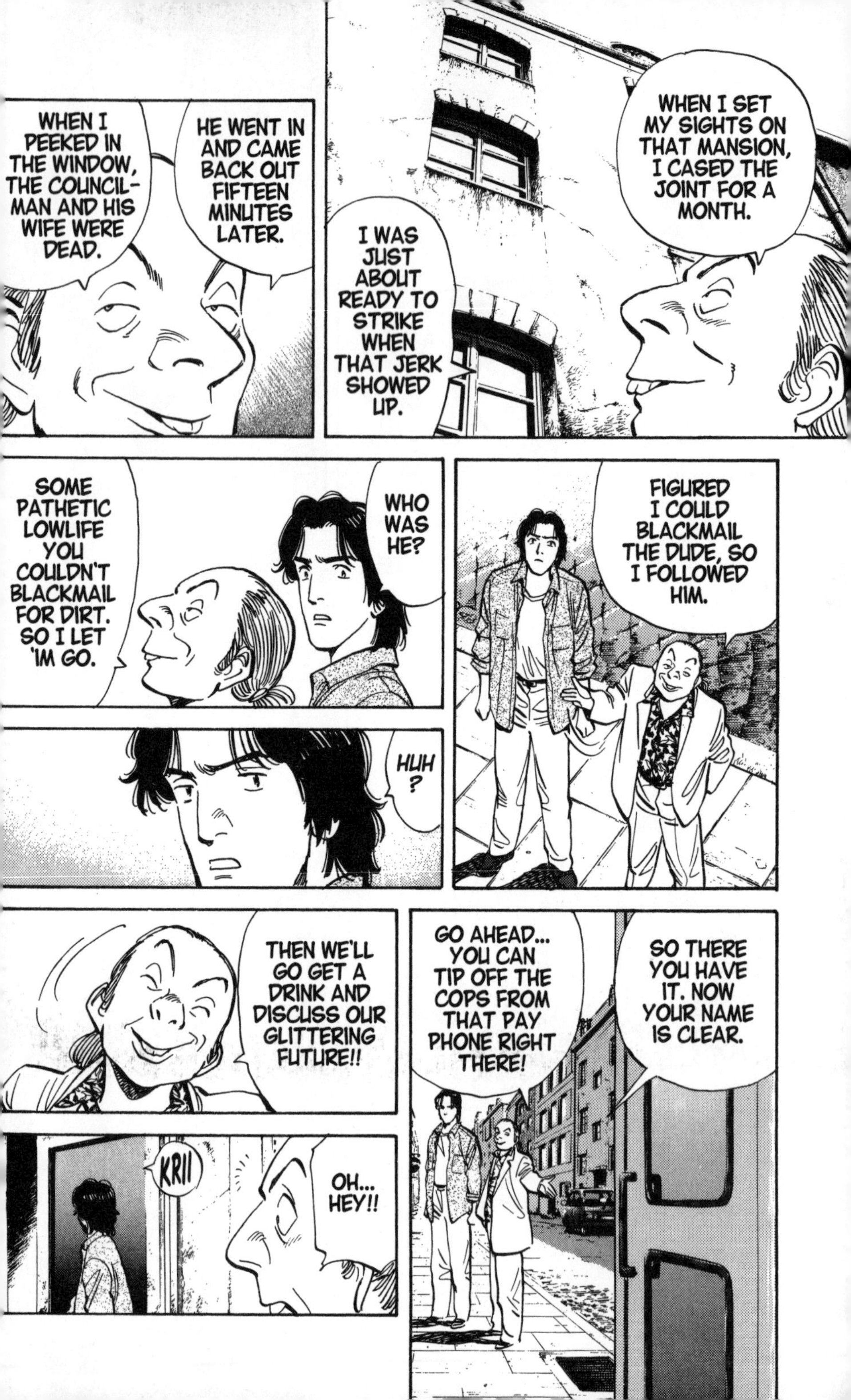
WHEN I SET MY SIGHTS ON THAT MANSION, I CASED THE JOINT FOR A MONTH.
I WAS JUST ABOUT READY TO STRIKE WHEN THAT JERK SHOWED UP.
HE WENT IN AND CAME BACK OUT FIFTEEN MINUTES LATER.
WHEN I PEEKED IN THE WINDOW, THE COUNCILMAN AND HIS WIFE WERE DEAD.
FIGURED I COULD BLACKMAIL THE DUDE, SO I FOLLOWED HIM.
WHO WAS HE?
SOME PATHETIC LOWLIFE YOU COULDN'T BLACKMAIL FOR DIRT. SO I LET 'IM GO.
HUH?
SO THERE YOU HAVE IT. NOW YOUR NAME IS CLEAR.
GO AHEAD... YOU CAN TIP OFF THE COPS FROM THAT PAY PHONE RIGHT THERE!
THEN WE'LL GO GET A DRINK AND DISCUSS OUR GLITTERING FUTURE!!
OH... HEY!!
KRII

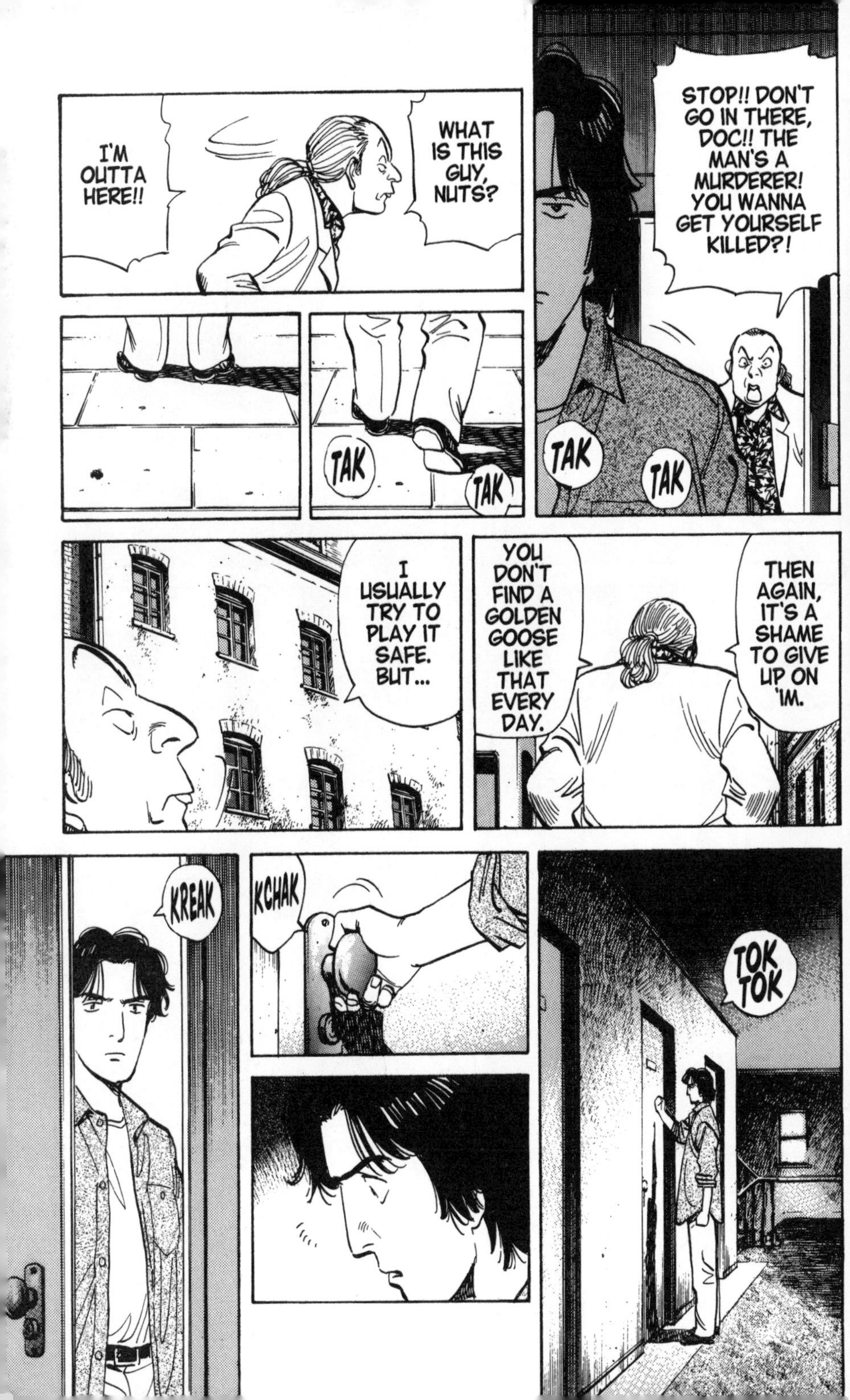
STOP!! DON'T GO IN THERE, DOC!! THE MAN'S A MURDERER! YOU WANNA GET YOURSELF KILLED?!
TAK
TAK
WHAT IS THIS GUY, NUTS?
I'M OUTTA HERE!!
TAK
TAK
THEN AGAIN, IT'S A SHAME TO GIVE UP ON 'IM.
YOU DON'T FIND A GOLDEN GOOSE LIKE THAT EVERY DAY.
I USUALLY TRY TO PLAY IT SAFE. BUT...
TOK TOK
KCHAK
KREAK

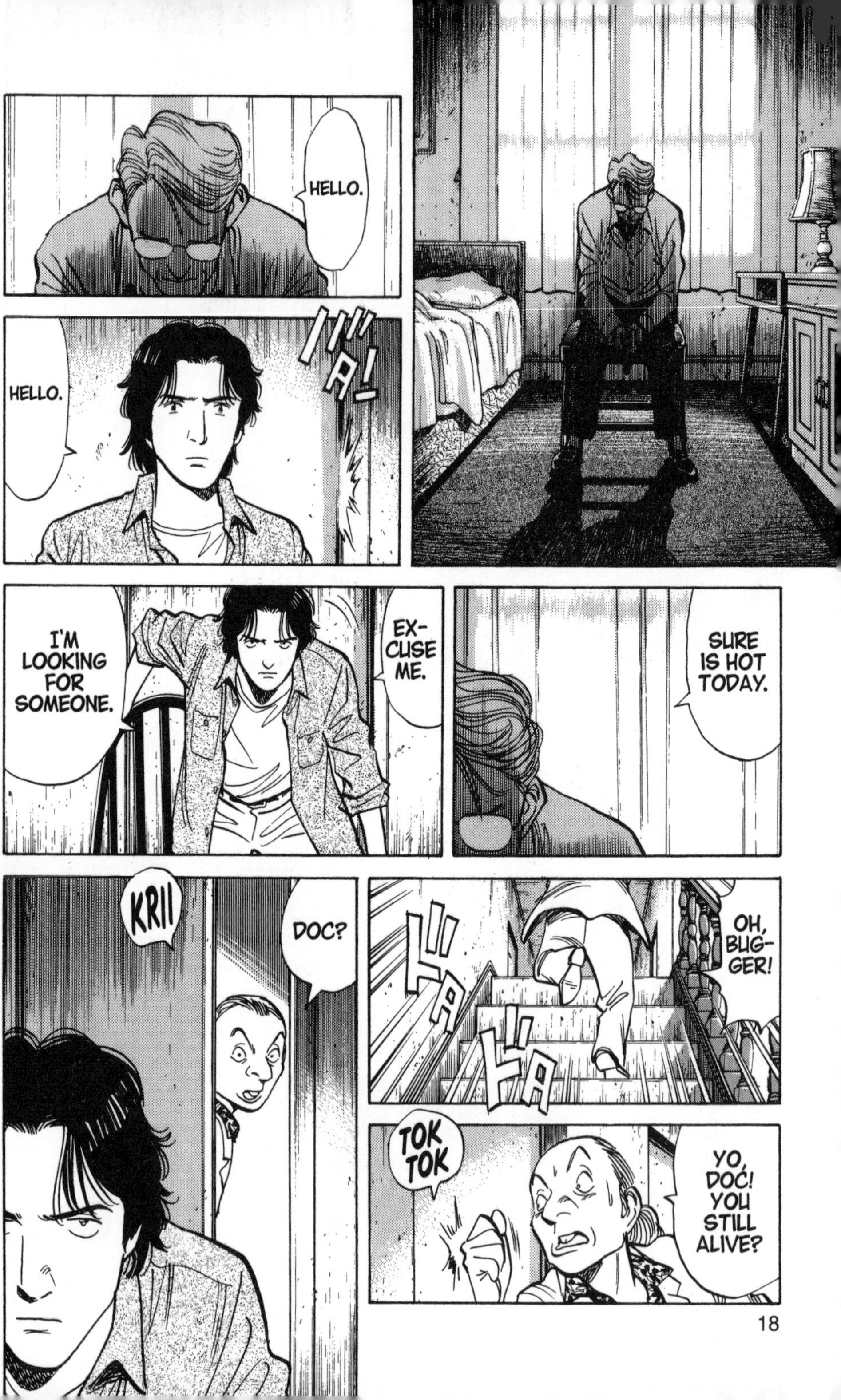
HELLO.
HELLO.
SURE IS HOT TODAY.
EX-CUSE ME.
I'M LOOKING FOR SOMEONE.
OH, BUG-GER!
YO, DOC! YOU STILL ALIVE?
TOK TOK
DOC?
KRII

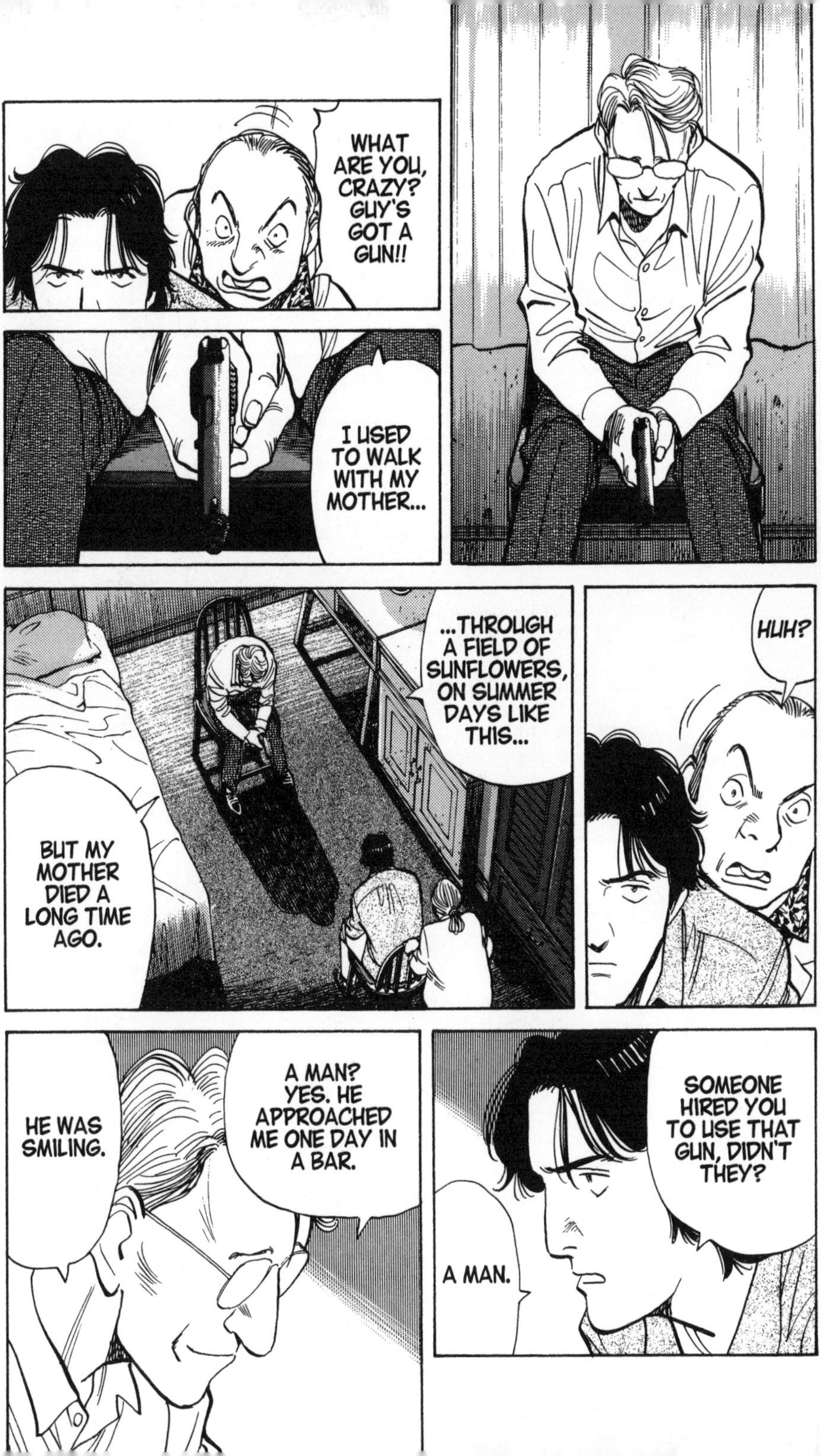
WHAT ARE YOU, CRAZY? GUY'S GOT A GUN!!
I USED TO WALK WITH MY MOTHER...
HUH?
...THROUGH A FIELD OF SUNFLOWERS, ON SUMMER DAYS LIKE THIS...
BUT MY MOTHER DIED A LONG TIME AGO.
SOMEONE HIRED YOU TO USE THAT GUN, DIDN'T THEY?
A MAN.
A MAN? YES. HE APPROACHED ME ONE DAY IN A BAR.
HE WAS SMILING.

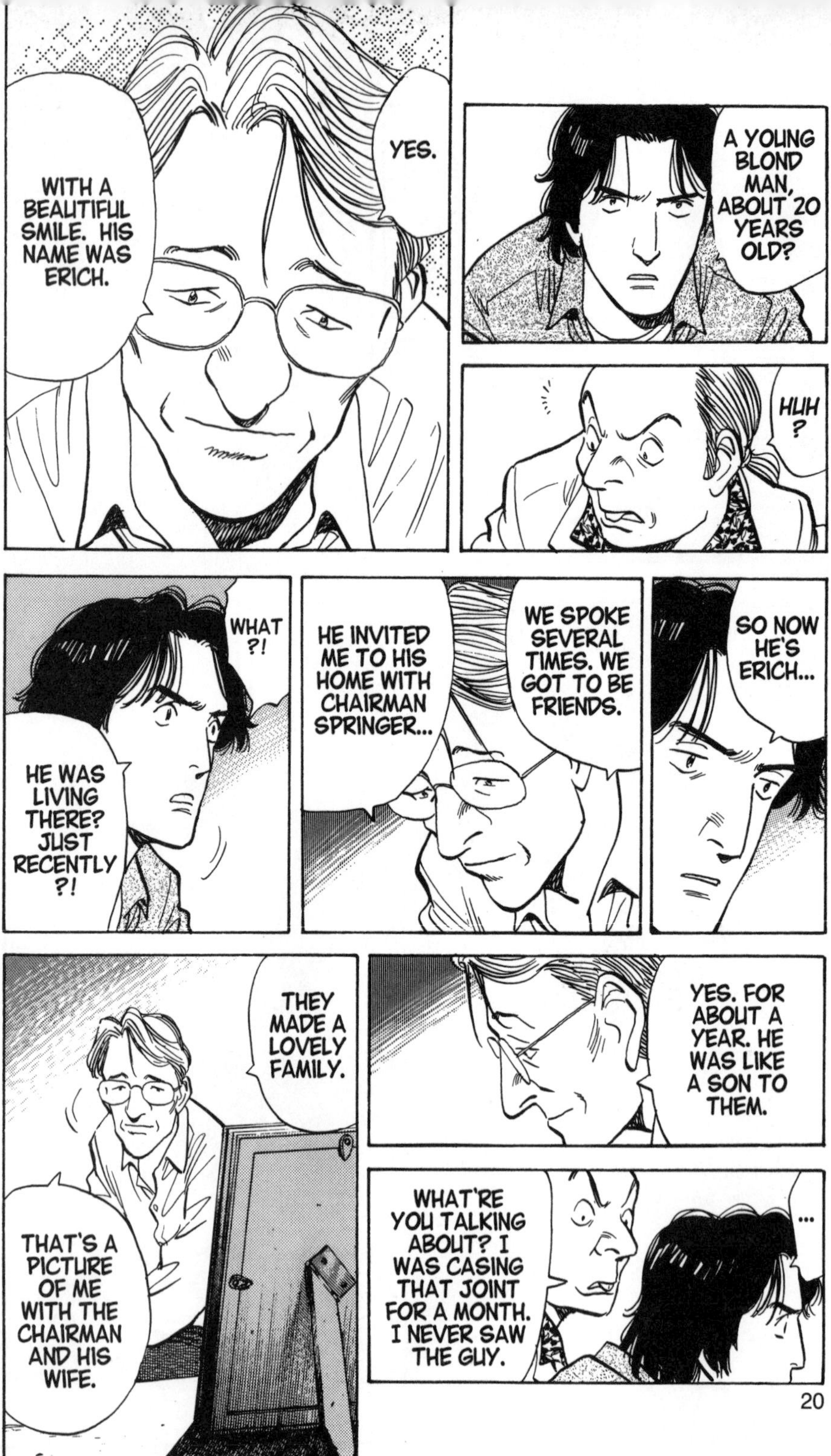
A YOUNG BLOND MAN, ABOUT 20 YEARS OLD?
HUH?
YES.
WITH A BEAUTIFUL SMILE. HIS NAME WAS ERICH.
SO NOW HE'S ERICH...
WE SPOKE SEVERAL TIMES. WE GOT TO BE FRIENDS.
HE INVITED ME TO HIS HOME WITH CHAIRMAN SPRINGER...
WHAT?!
HE WAS LIVING THERE? JUST RECENTLY?!
YES. FOR ABOUT A YEAR. HE WAS LIKE A SON TO THEM.
...
WHAT'RE YOU TALKING ABOUT? I WAS CASING THAT JOINT FOR A MONTH. I NEVER SAW THE GUY.
THEY MADE A LOVELY FAMILY.
THAT'S A PICTURE OF ME WITH THE CHAIRMAN AND HIS WIFE.

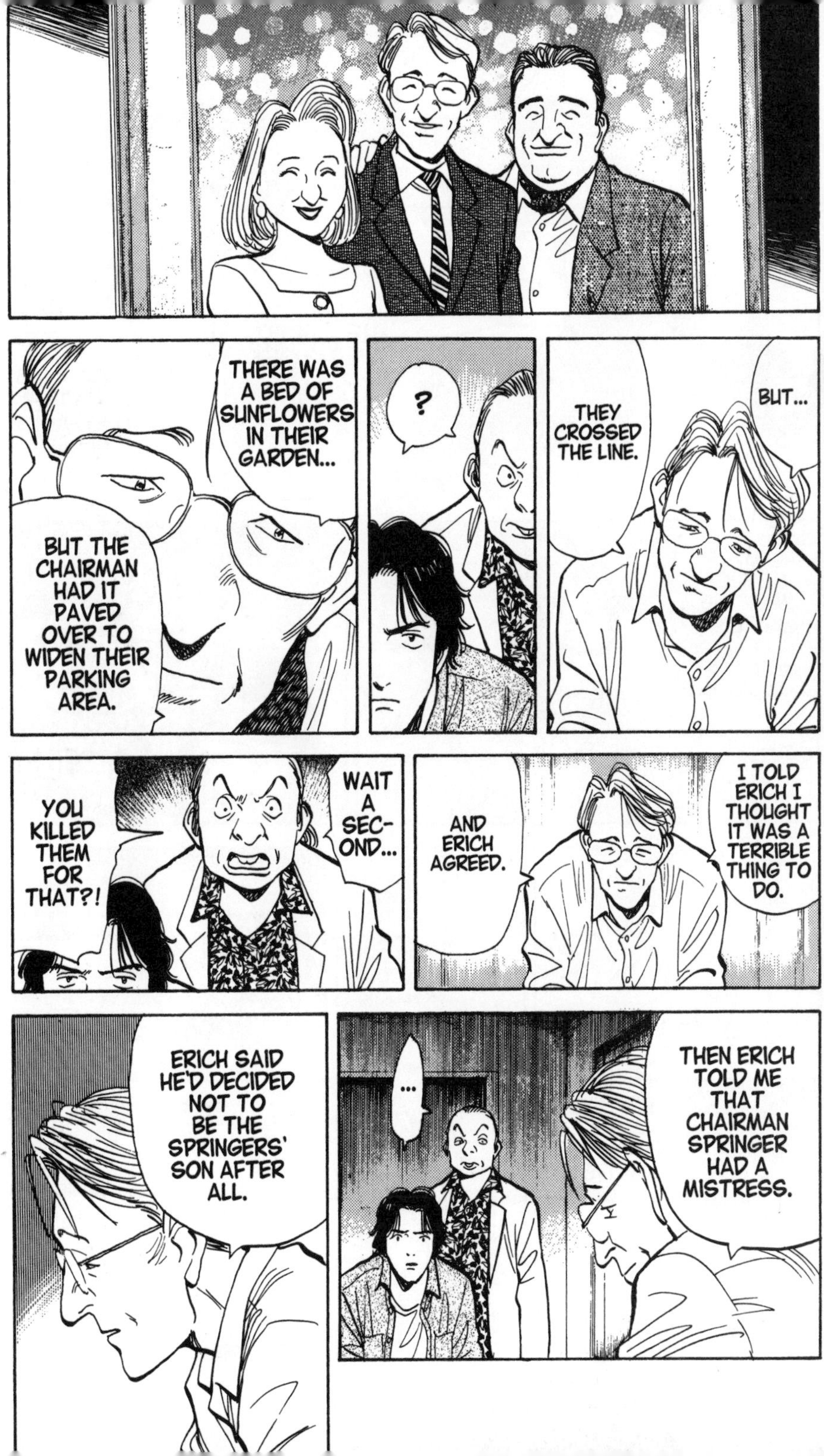
BUT...
THEY CROSSED THE LINE.
?
THERE WAS A BED OF SUNFLOWERS IN THEIR GARDEN...
BUT THE CHAIRMAN HAD IT PAVED OVER TO WIDEN THEIR PARKING AREA.
I TOLD ERICH I THOUGHT IT WAS A TERRIBLE THING TO DO.
AND ERICH AGREED.
WAIT A SEC-OND...
YOU KILLED THEM FOR THAT?!
THEN ERICH TOLD ME THAT CHAIRMAN SPRINGER HAD A MISTRESS.
...
ERICH SAID HE'D DECIDED NOT TO BE THE SPRINGERS' SON AFTER ALL.

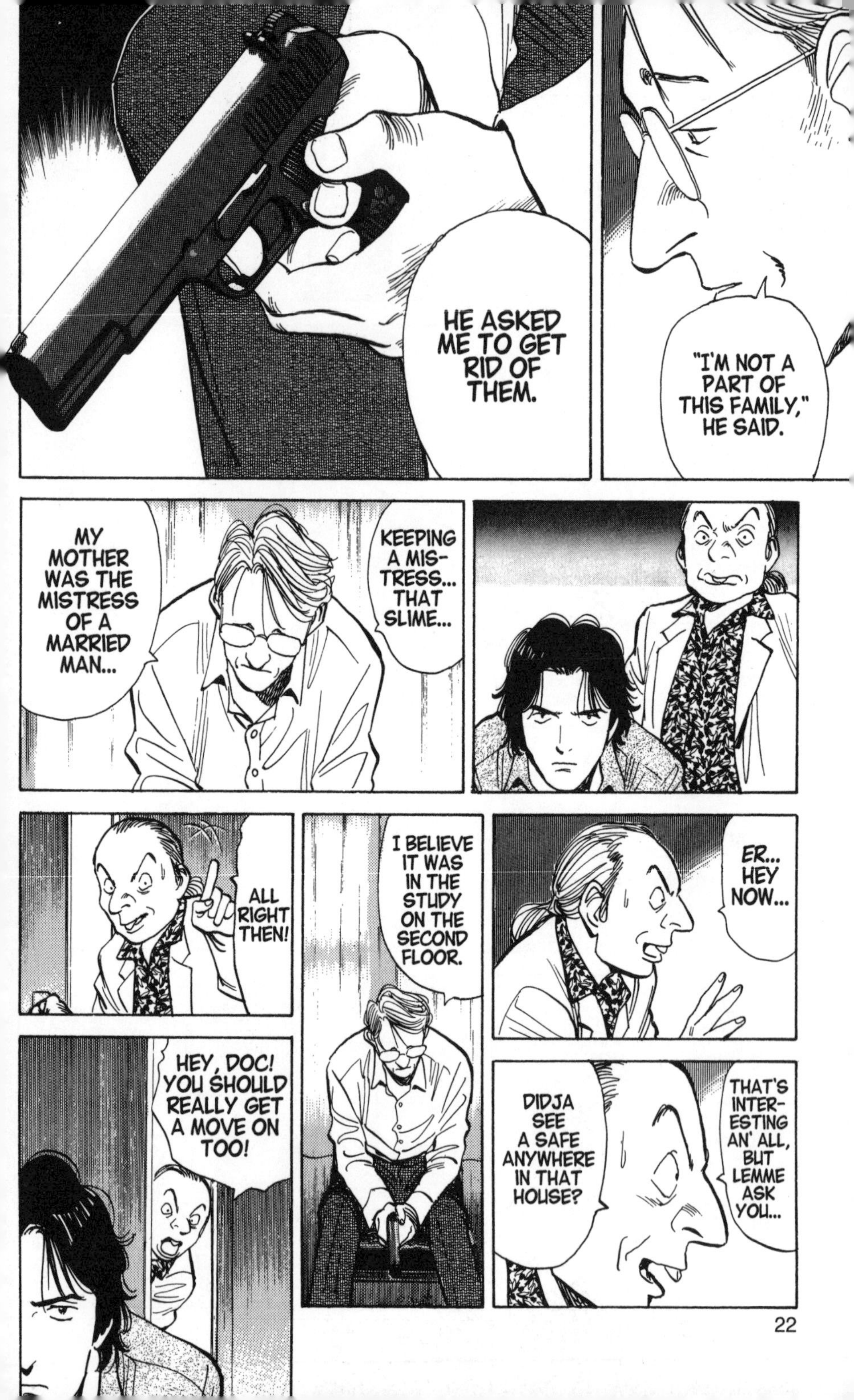
"I'M NOT A PART OF THIS FAMILY," HE SAID.
HE ASKED ME TO GET RID OF THEM.
KEEPING A MIS-TRESS... THAT SLIME...
MY MOTHER WAS THE MISTRESS OF A MARRIED MAN...
ER... HEY NOW...
THAT'S INTER-ESTING AN' ALL, BUT LEMME ASK YOU...
DIDJA SEE A SAFE ANYWHERE IN THAT HOUSE?
I BELIEVE IT WAS IN THE STUDY ON THE SECOND FLOOR.
ALL RIGHT THEN!
HEY, DOC! YOU SHOULD REALLY GET A MOVE ON TOO!

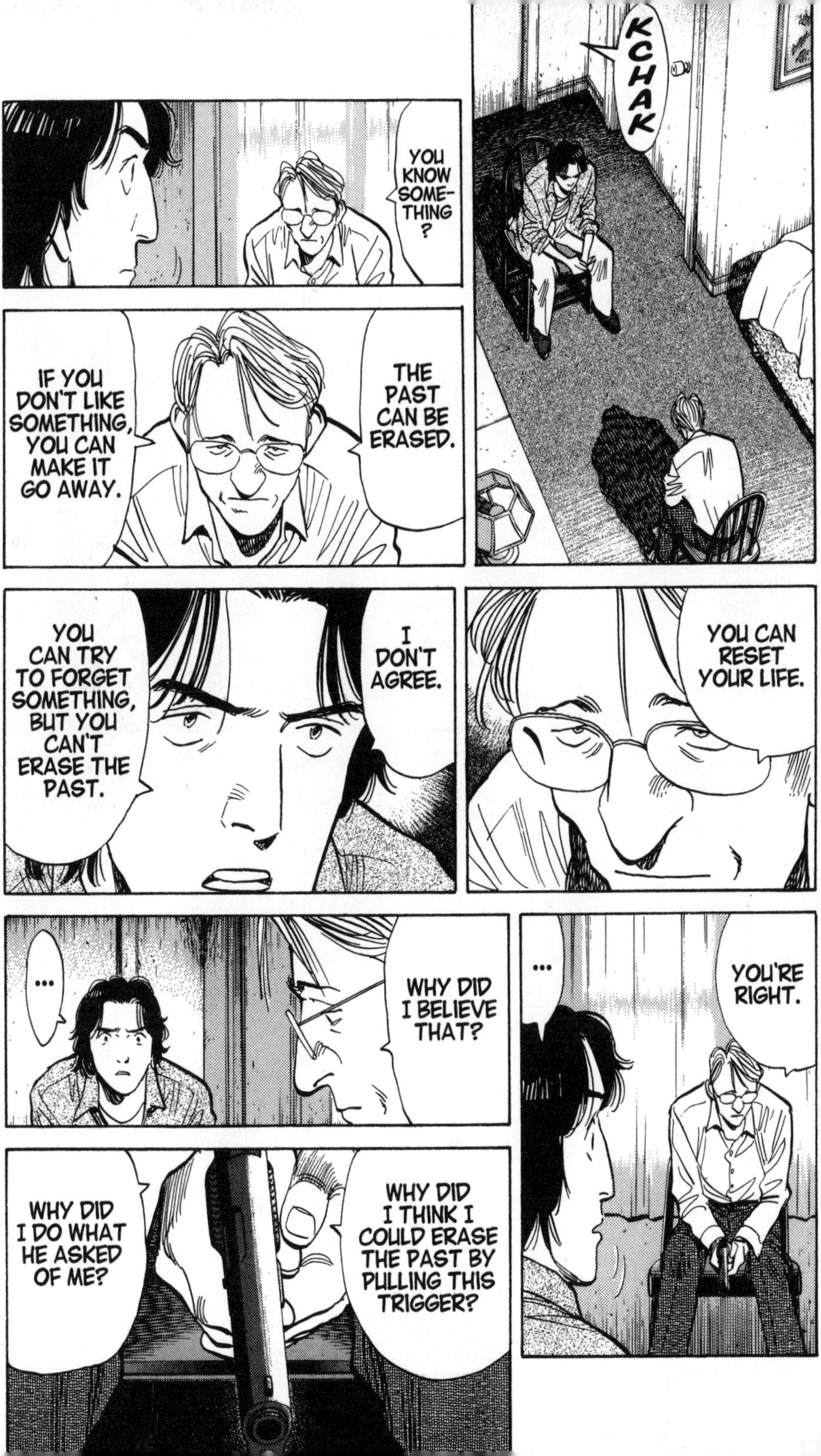
KCHAK
YOU KNOW SOME-THING?
THE PAST CAN BE ERASED.
IF YOU DON'T LIKE SOMETHING, YOU CAN MAKE IT GO AWAY.
YOU CAN RESET YOUR LIFE.
I DON'T AGREE.
YOU CAN TRY TO FORGET SOMETHING, BUT YOU CAN'T ERASE THE PAST.
YOU'RE RIGHT.
...
WHY DID I BELIEVE THAT?
...
WHY DID I THINK I COULD ERASE THE PAST BY PULLING THIS TRIGGER?
WHY DID I DO WHAT HE ASKED OF ME?

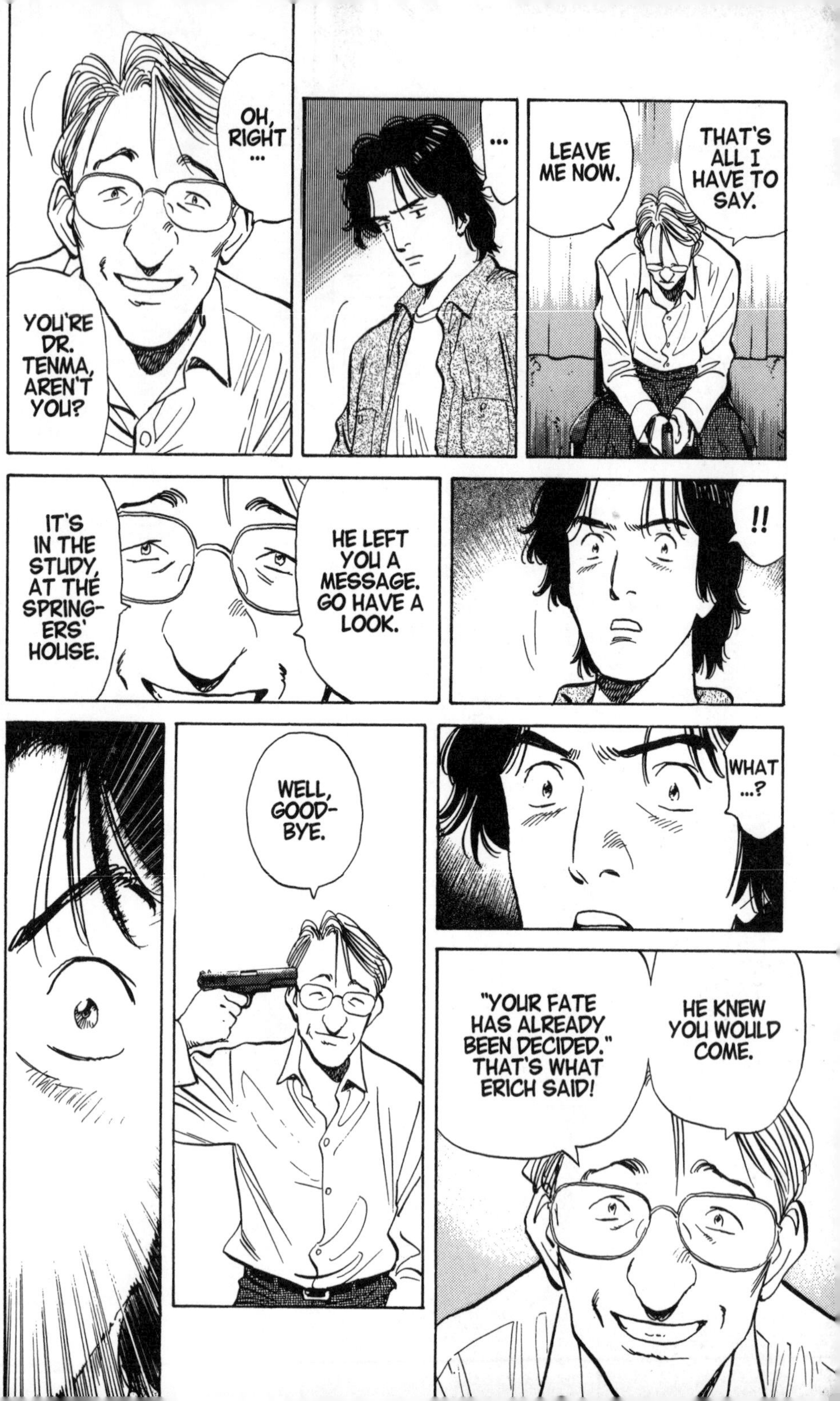
THAT'S ALL I HAVE TO SAY.
LEAVE ME NOW.
...
OH, RIGHT ...
YOU'RE DR. TENMA, AREN'T YOU?
!!
HE LEFT YOU A MESSAGE. GO HAVE A LOOK.
IT'S IN THE STUDY, AT THE SPRING-ERS' HOUSE.
WHAT ...?
HE KNEW YOU WOULD COME.
"YOUR FATE HAS ALREADY BEEN DECIDED." THAT'S WHAT ERICH SAID!
WELL, GOOD-BYE.

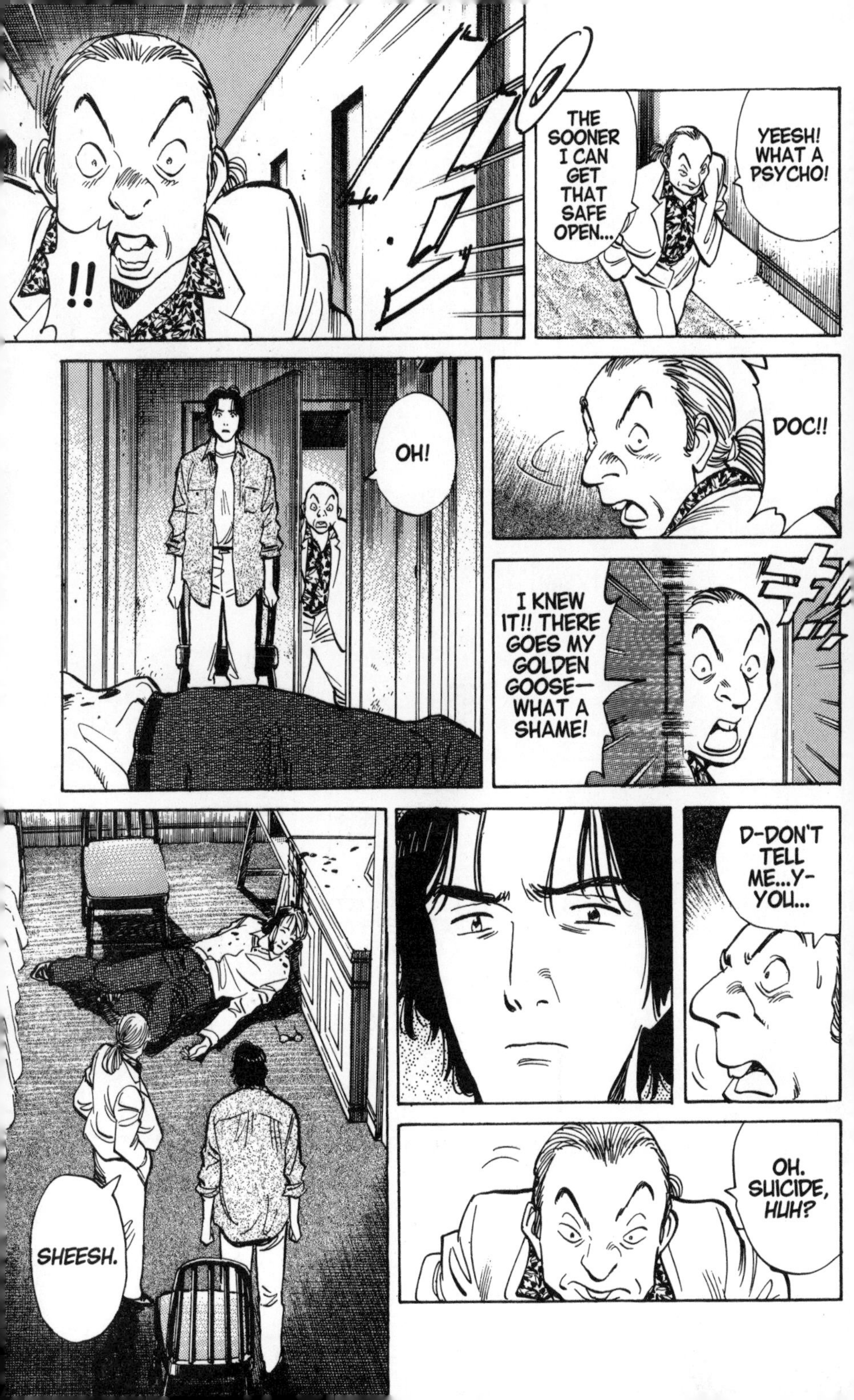
YEESH! WHAT A PSYCHO!
THE SOONER I CAN GET THAT SAFE OPEN...
!!
DOC!!
I KNEW IT!! THERE GOES MY GOLDEN GOOSE—WHAT A SHAME!
OH!
D-DON'T TELL ME...Y-YOU...
OH. SUICIDE, HUH?
SHEESH.

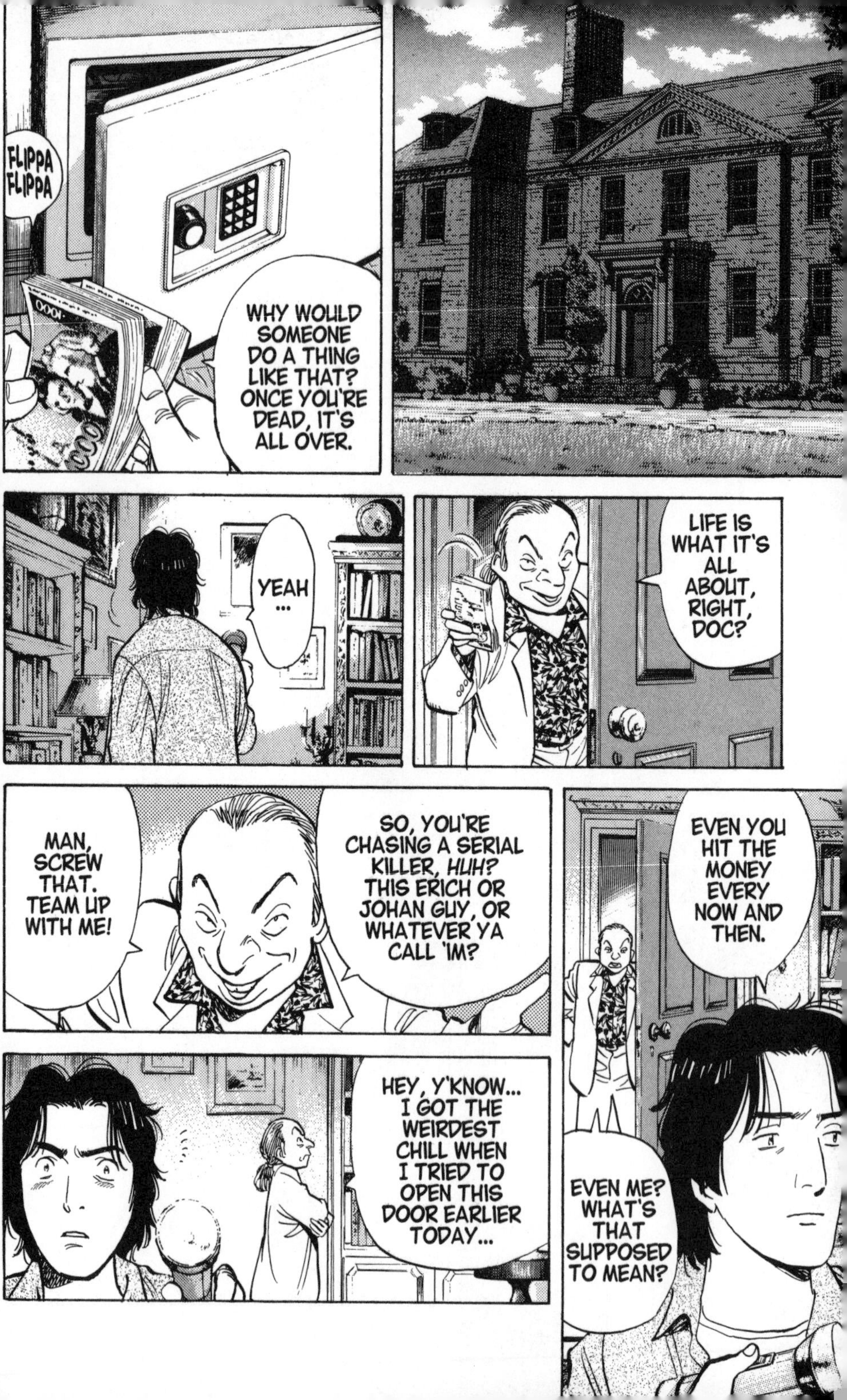
FLIPPA FLIPPA
WHY WOULD SOMEONE DO A THING LIKE THAT? ONCE YOU'RE DEAD, IT'S ALL OVER.
LIFE IS WHAT IT'S ALL ABOUT, RIGHT, DOC?
YEAH ...
EVEN YOU HIT THE MONEY EVERY NOW AND THEN.
EVEN ME? WHAT'S THAT SUPPOSED TO MEAN?
SO, YOU'RE CHASING A SERIAL KILLER, HUH? THIS ERICH OR JOHAN GUY, OR WHATEVER YA CALL 'IM?
MAN, SCREW THAT. TEAM UP WITH ME!
HEY, Y'KNOW... I GOT THE WEIRDEST CHILL WHEN I TRIED TO OPEN THIS DOOR EARLIER TODAY...

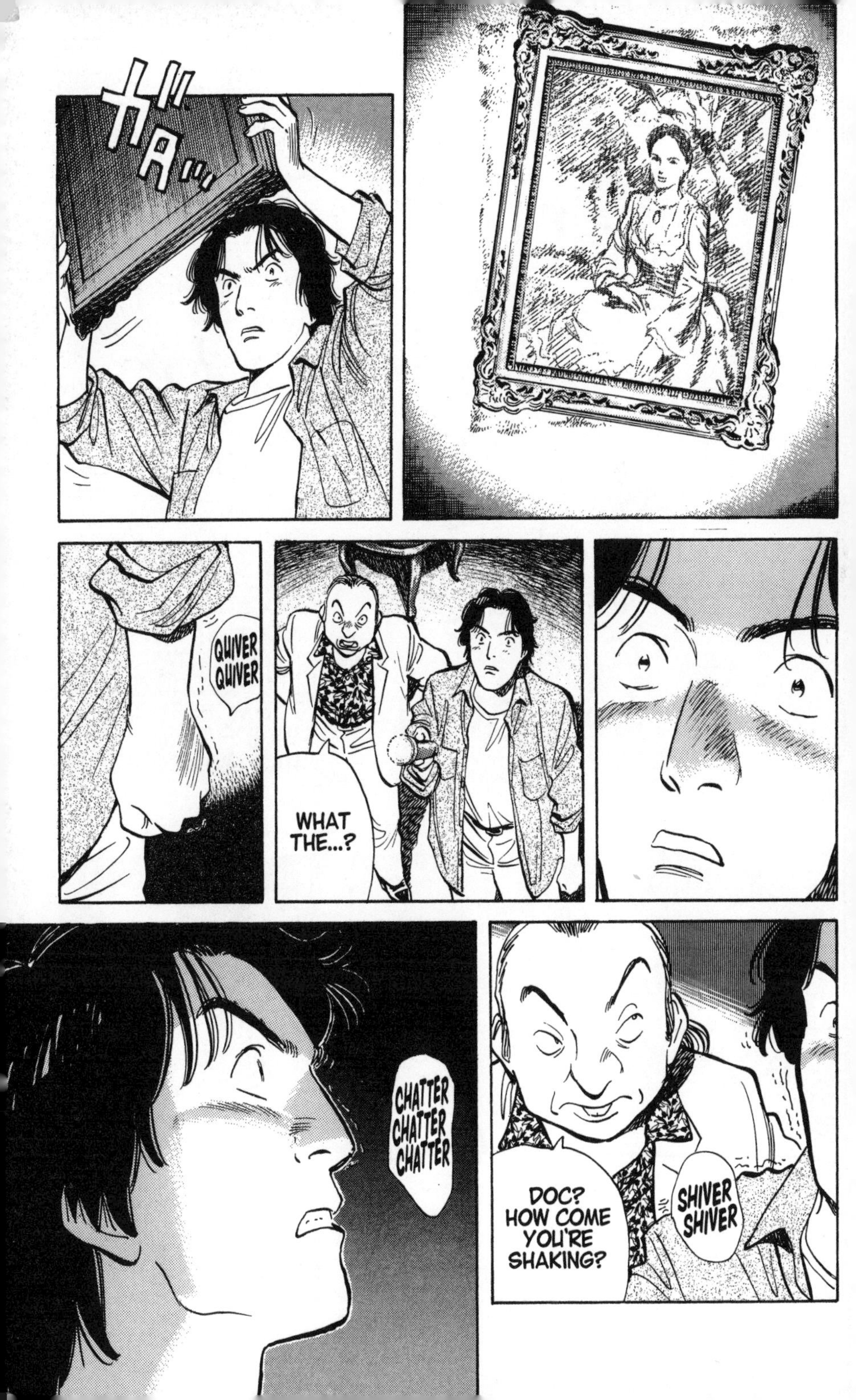
ガバッ
WHAT THE...?
QUIVER QUIVER
SHIVER SHIVER
DOC? HOW COME YOU'RE SHAKING?
CHATTER CHATTER CHATTER

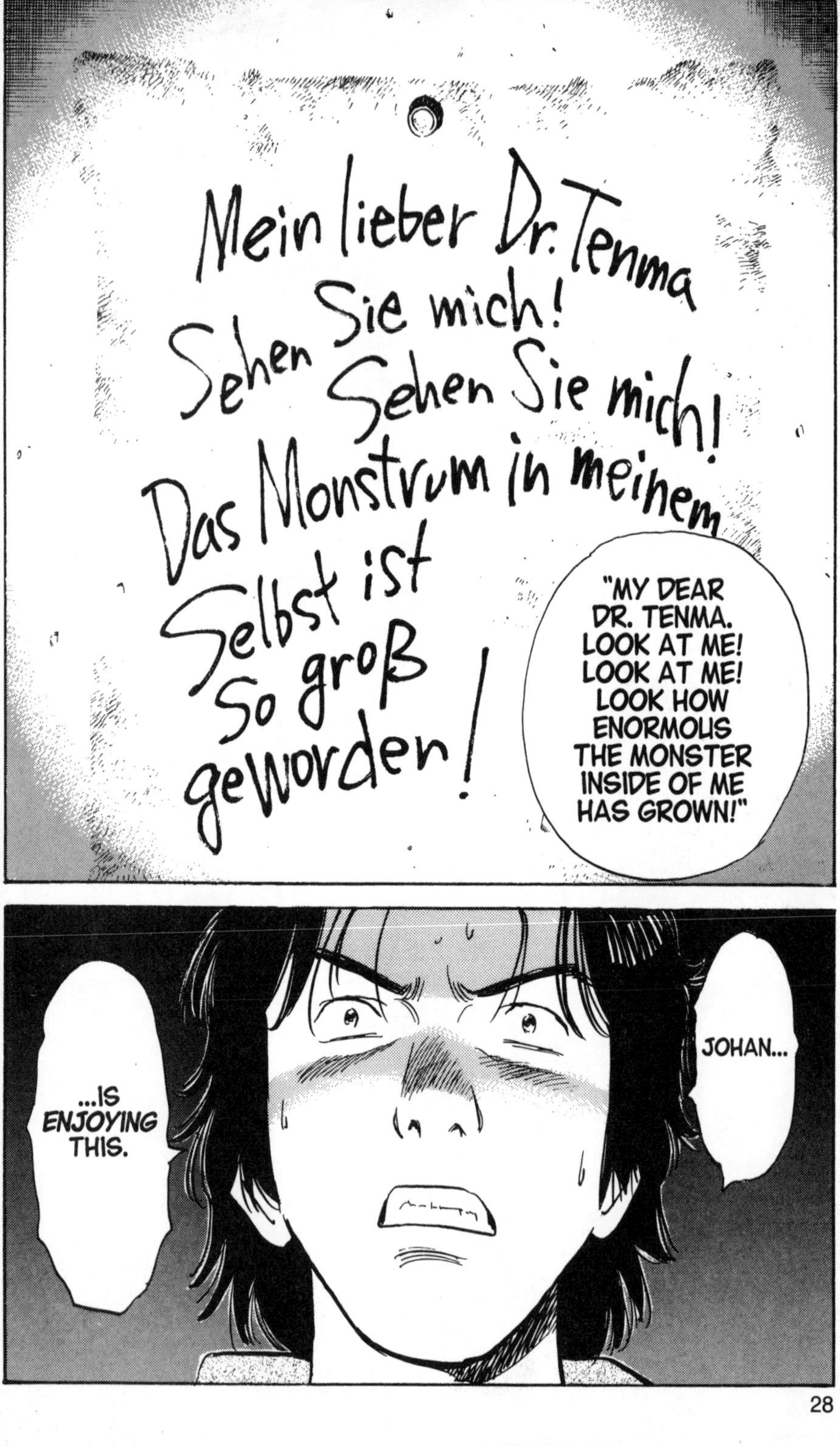
Mein lieber Dr. Tenma
Sehen Sie mich! Sehen Sie mich!
Das Monstrum in meinem Selbst ist So groß geworden!
"MY DEAR DR. TENMA. LOOK AT ME! LOOK AT ME! LOOK HOW ENORMOUS THE MONSTER INSIDE OF ME HAS GROWN!"
JOHAN...
...IS ENJOYING THIS.

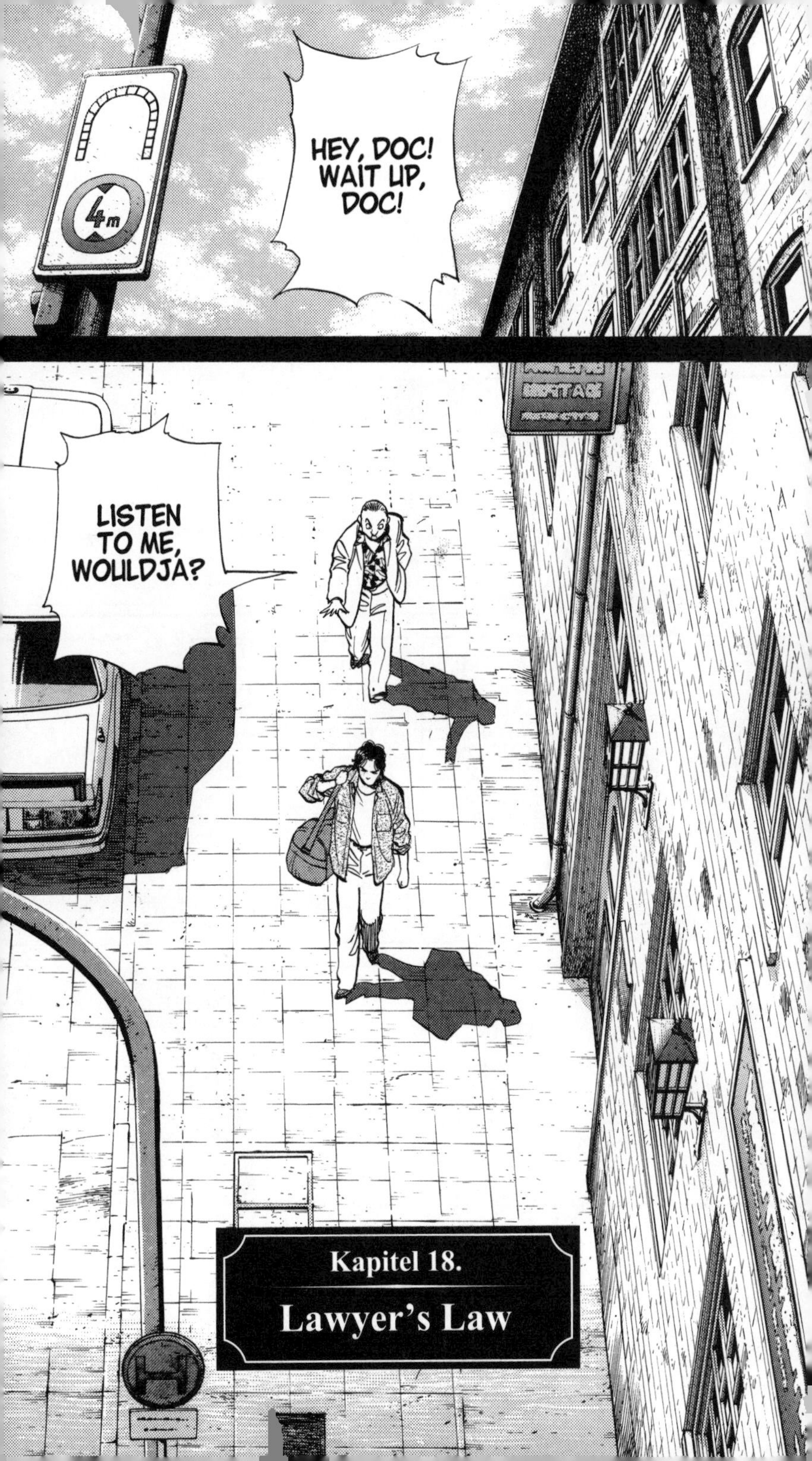
HEY, DOC! WAIT UP, DOC!
LISTEN TO ME, WOULDJA?
Kapitel 18.
Lawyer's Law

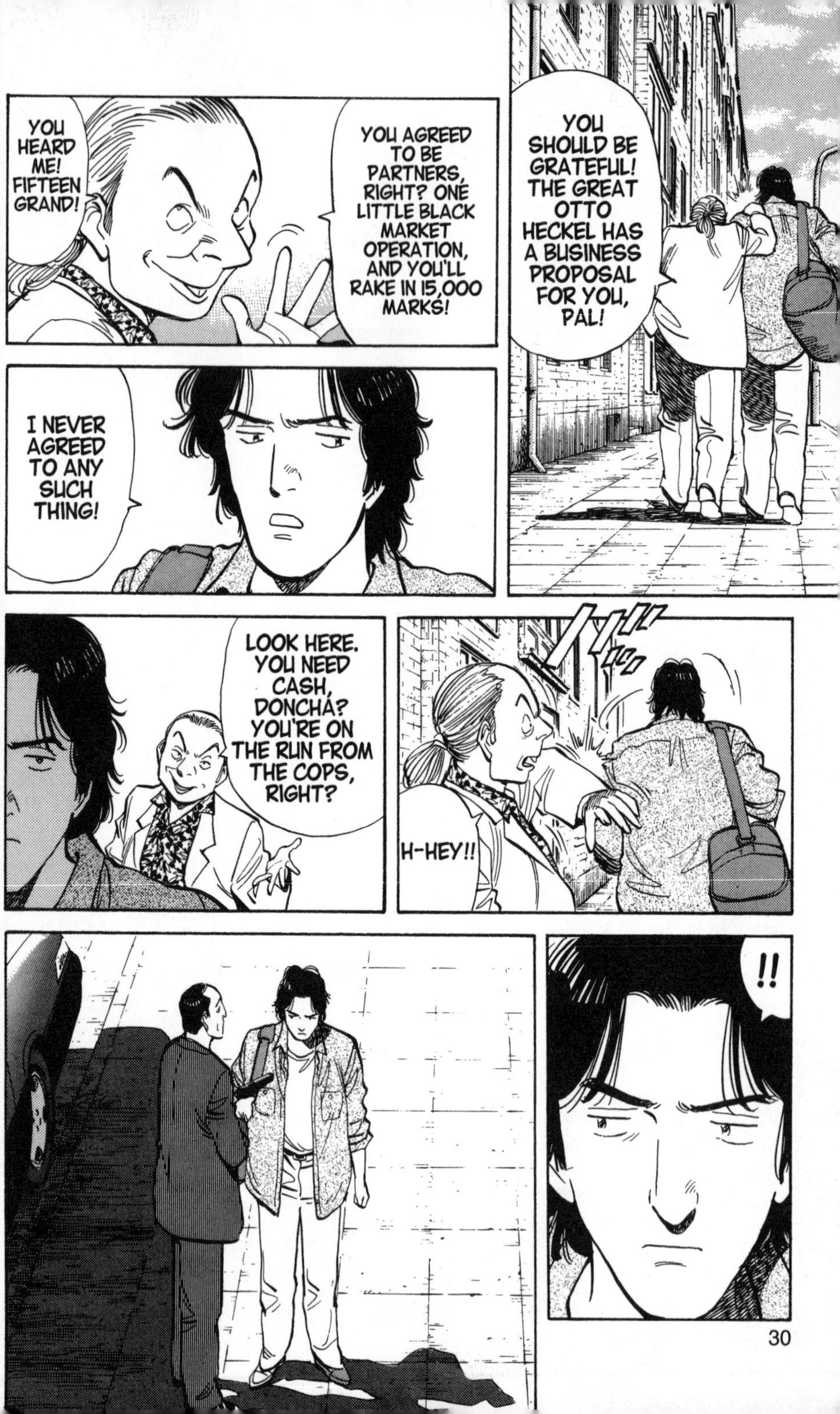
YOU SHOULD BE GRATEFUL! THE GREAT OTTO HECKEL HAS A BUSINESS PROPOSAL FOR YOU, PAL!
YOU AGREED TO BE PARTNERS, RIGHT? ONE LITTLE BLACK MARKET OPERATION, AND YOU'LL RAKE IN 15,000 MARKS!
YOU HEARD ME! FIFTEEN GRAND!
I NEVER AGREED TO ANY SUCH THING!
H-HEY!!
LOOK HERE. YOU NEED CASH, DONCHA? YOU'RE ON THE RUN FROM THE COPS, RIGHT?
!!

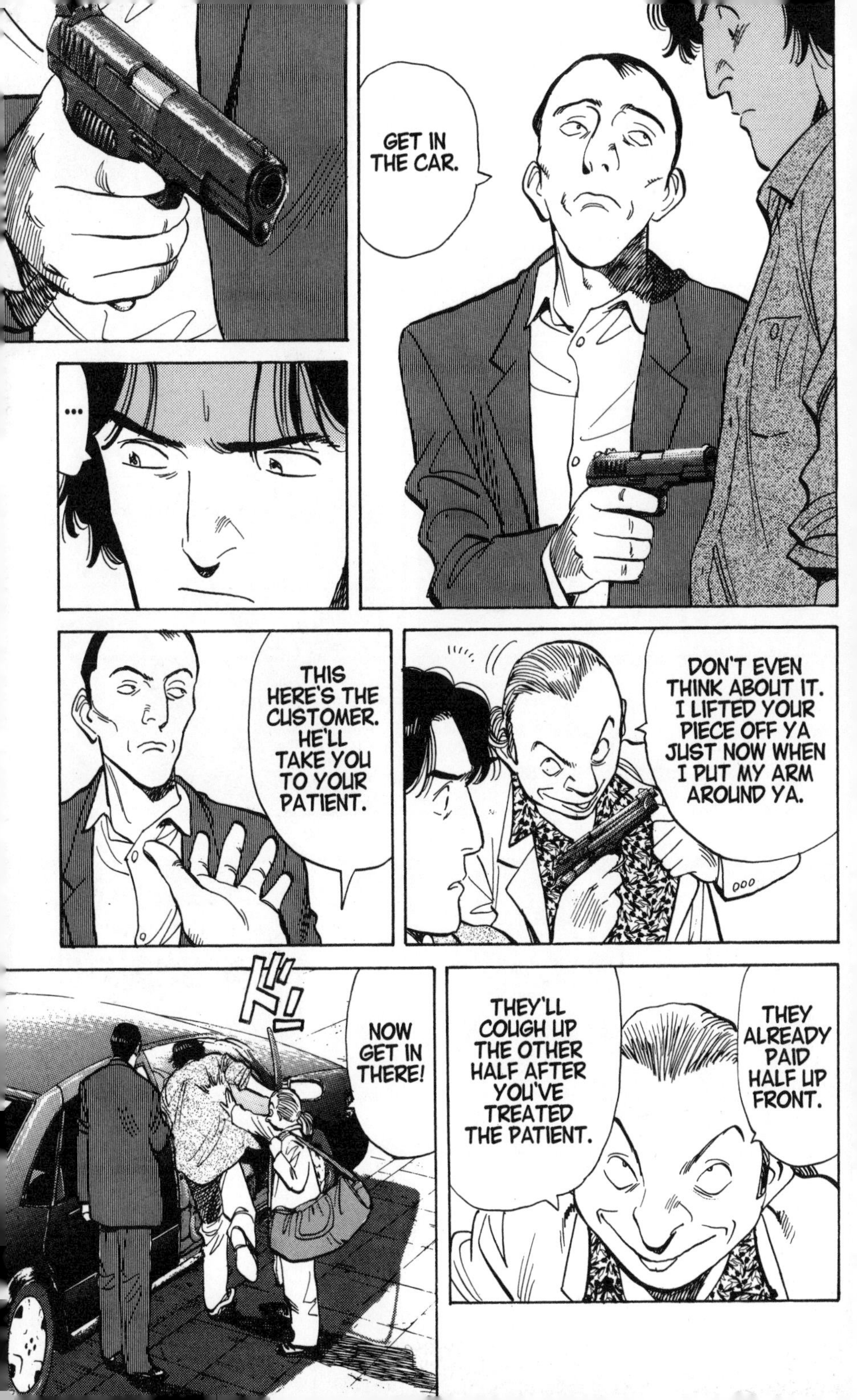
GET IN THE CAR.
...
DON'T EVEN THINK ABOUT IT. I LIFTED YOUR PIECE OFF YA JUST NOW WHEN I PUT MY ARM AROUND YA.
THIS HERE'S THE CUSTOMER. HE'LL TAKE YOU TO YOUR PATIENT.
THEY ALREADY PAID HALF UP FRONT.
THEY'LL COUGH UP THE OTHER HALF AFTER YOU'VE TREATED THE PATIENT.
NOW GET IN THERE!
ドン

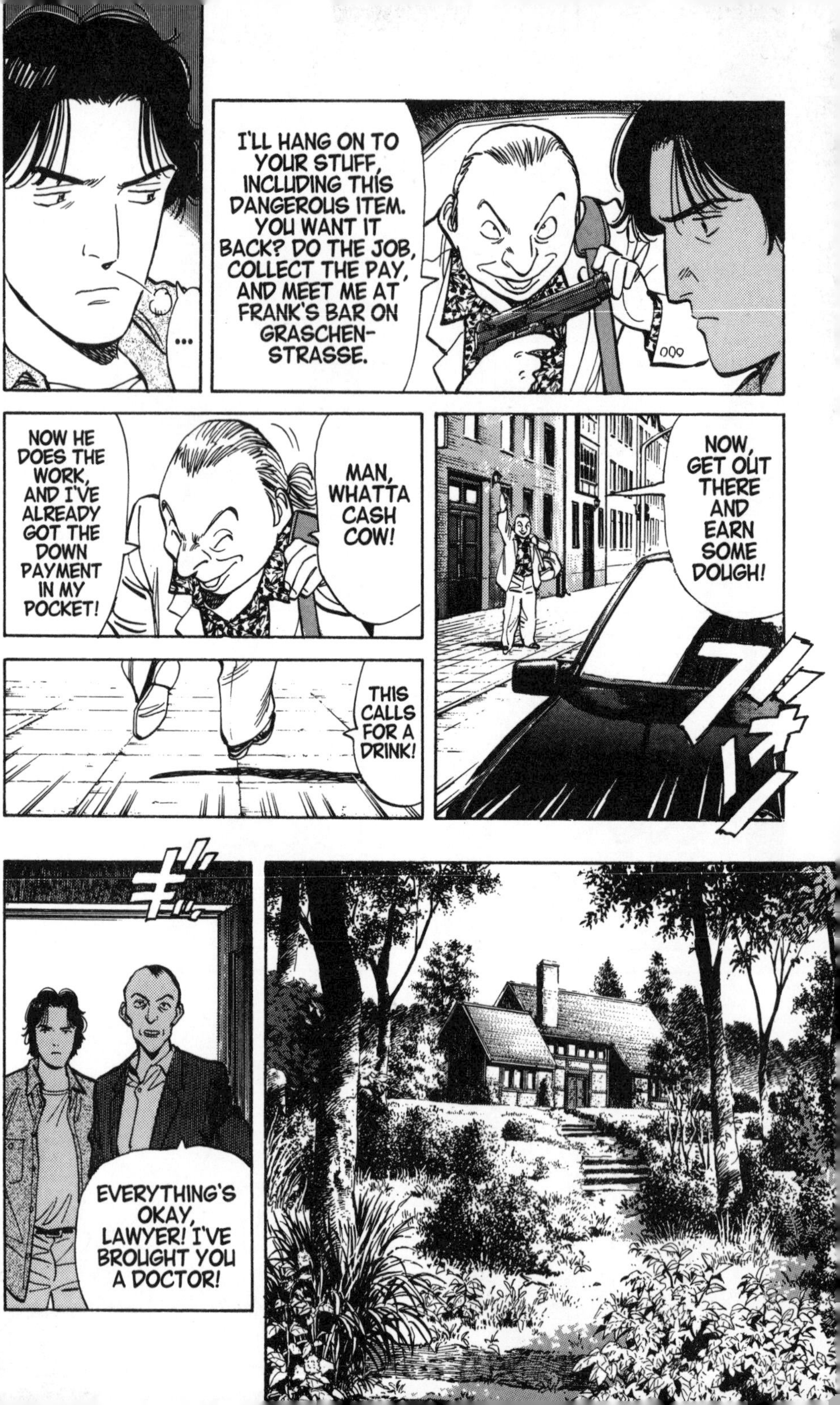
I'LL HANG ON TO YOUR STUFF, INCLUDING THIS DANGEROUS ITEM. YOU WANT IT BACK? DO THE JOB, COLLECT THE PAY, AND MEET ME AT FRANK'S BAR ON GRASCHEN-STRASSE.
...
NOW, GET OUT THERE AND EARN SOME DOUGH!
MAN, WHATTA CASH COW!
NOW HE DOES THE WORK, AND I'VE ALREADY GOT THE DOWN PAYMENT IN MY POCKET!
THIS CALLS FOR A DRINK!
EVERYTHING'S OKAY, LAWYER! I'VE BROUGHT YOU A DOCTOR!

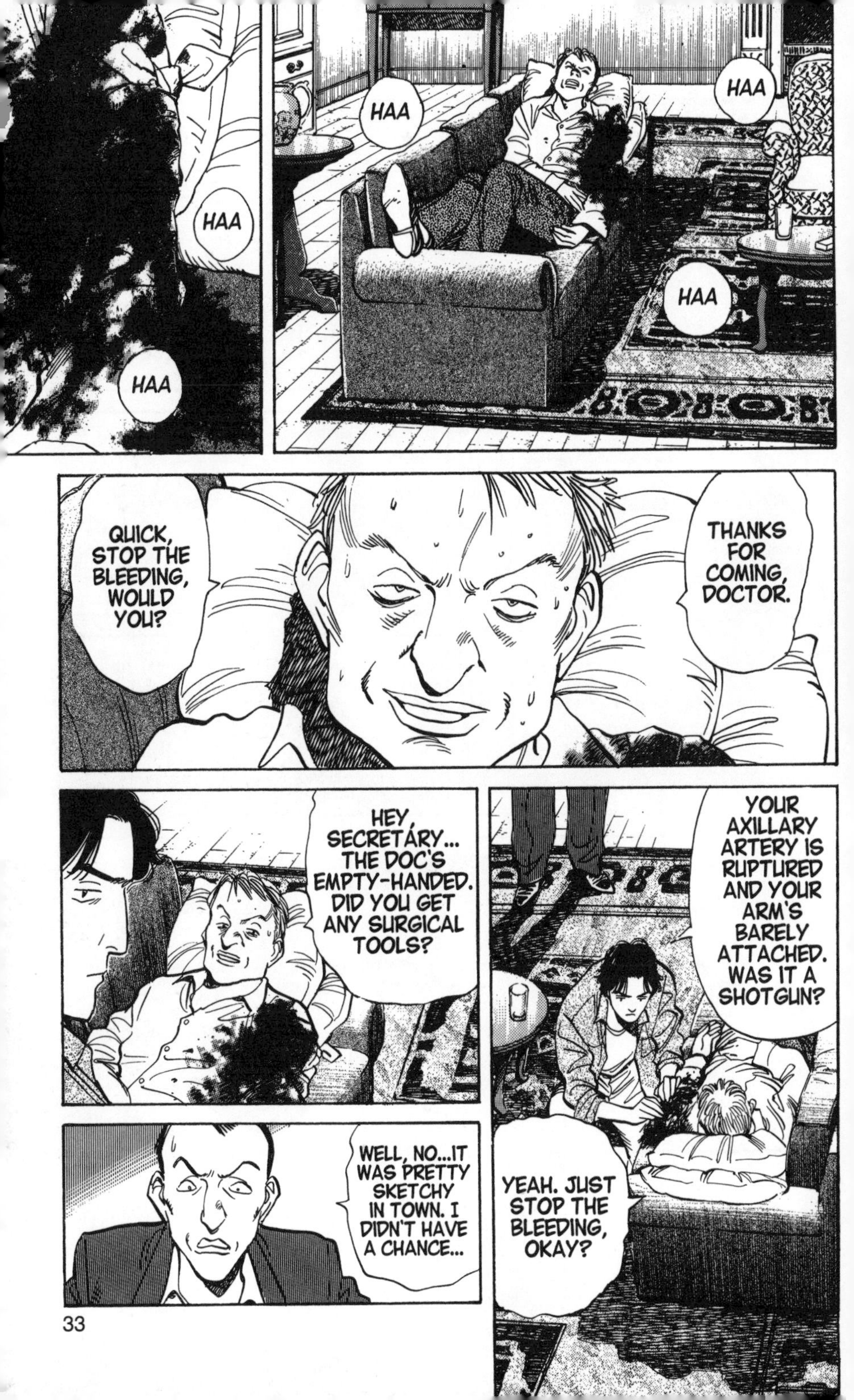
HAA
HAA
HAA
HAA
HAA
THANKS FOR COMING, DOCTOR.
QUICK, STOP THE BLEEDING, WOULD YOU?
YOUR AXILLARY ARTERY IS RUPTURED AND YOUR ARM'S BARELY ATTACHED. WAS IT A SHOTGUN?
YEAH. JUST STOP THE BLEEDING, OKAY?
HEY, SECRETARY... THE DOC'S EMPTY-HANDED. DID YOU GET ANY SURGICAL TOOLS?
WELL, NO...IT WAS PRETTY SKETCHY IN TOWN. I DIDN'T HAVE A CHANCE...

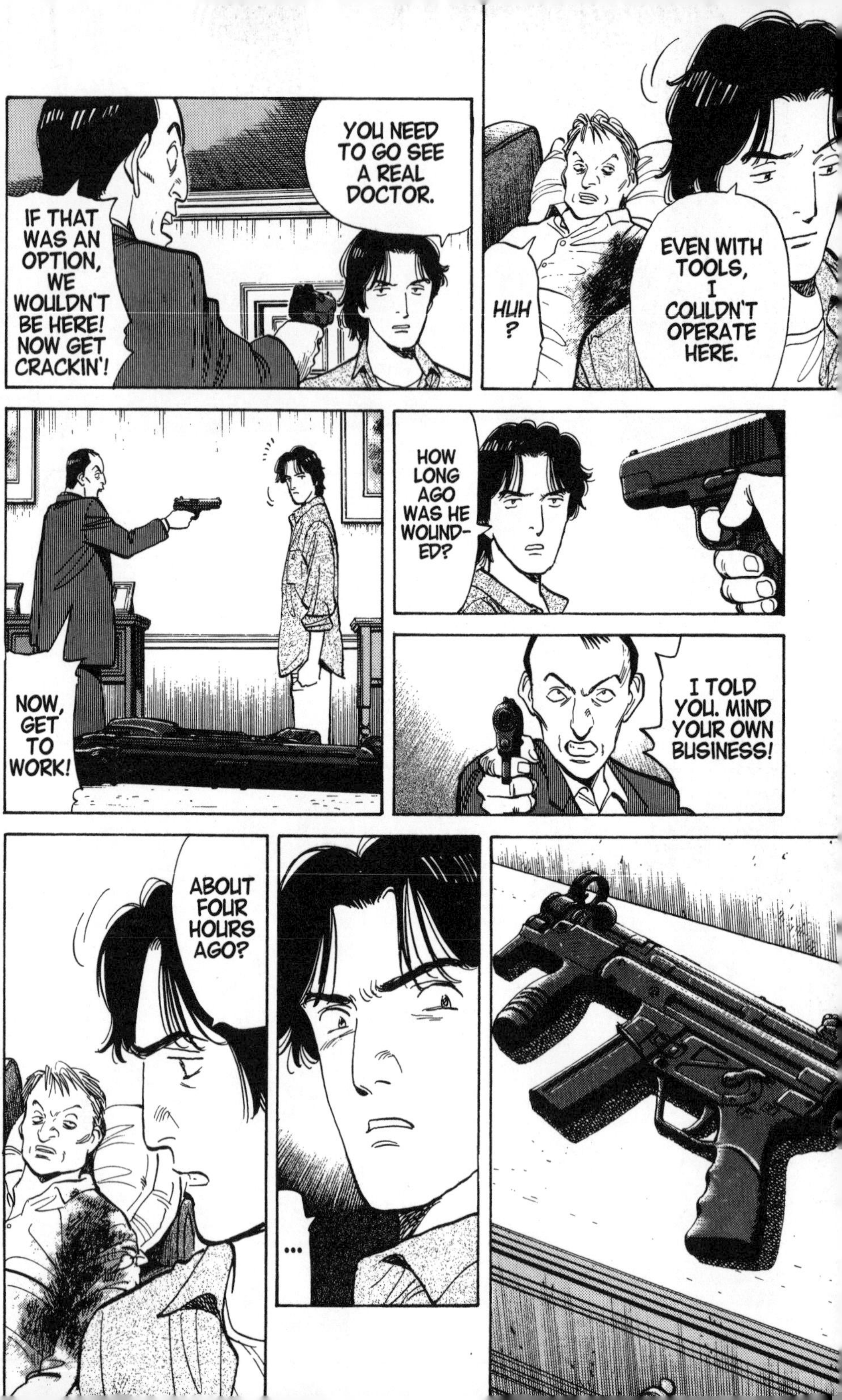
EVEN WITH TOOLS, I COULDN'T OPERATE HERE.
HUH?
YOU NEED TO GO SEE A REAL DOCTOR.
IF THAT WAS AN OPTION, WE WOULDN'T BE HERE! NOW GET CRACKIN'!
HOW LONG AGO WAS HE WOUND-ED?
I TOLD YOU. MIND YOUR OWN BUSINESS!
NOW, GET TO WORK!
...
ABOUT FOUR HOURS AGO?

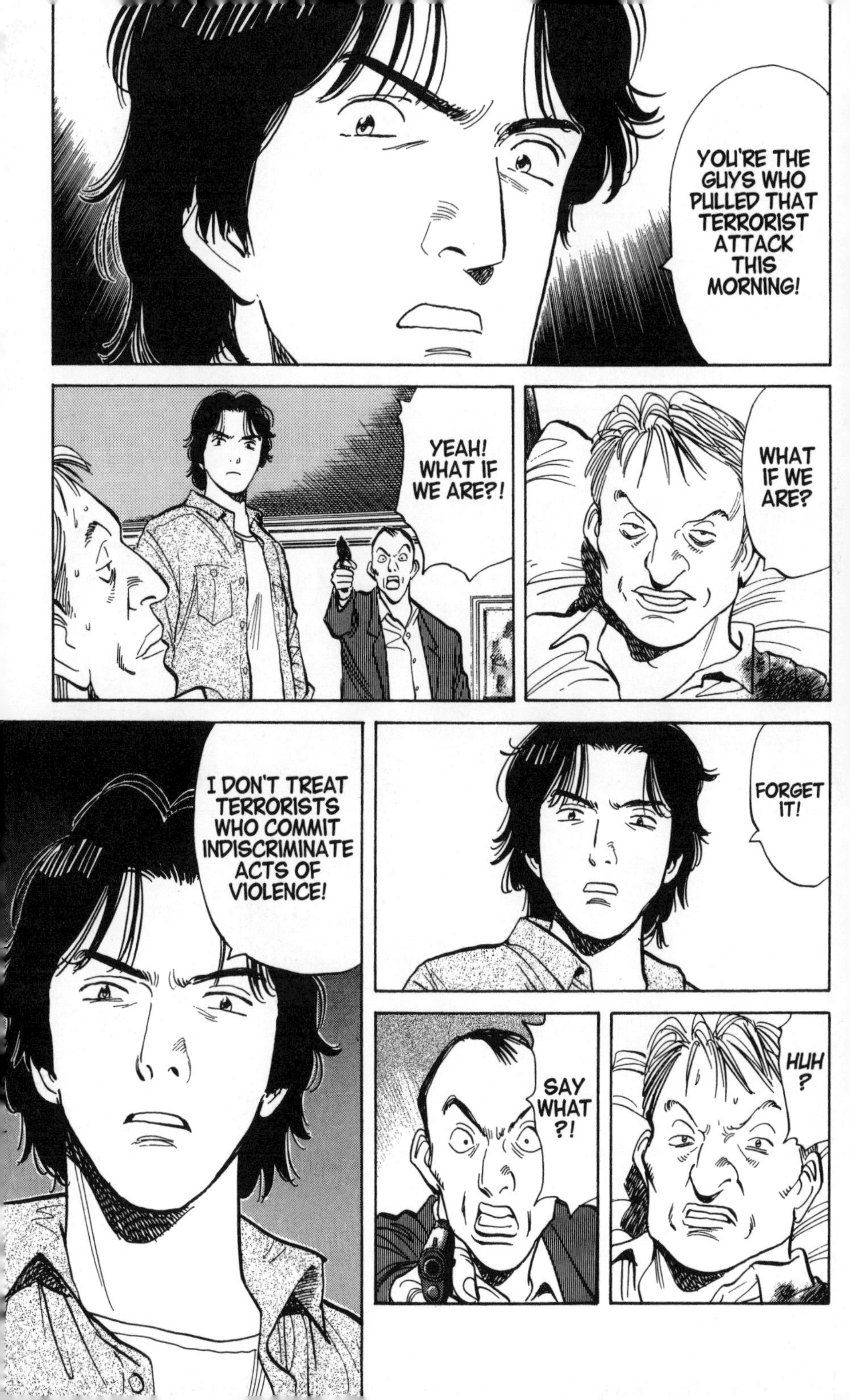
YOU'RE THE GUYS WHO PULLED THAT TERRORIST ATTACK THIS MORNING!
WHAT IF WE ARE?
YEAH! WHAT IF WE ARE?!
FORGET IT!
HUH?
SAY WHAT?!
I DON'T TREAT TERRORISTS WHO COMMIT INDISCRIMINATE ACTS OF VIOLENCE!

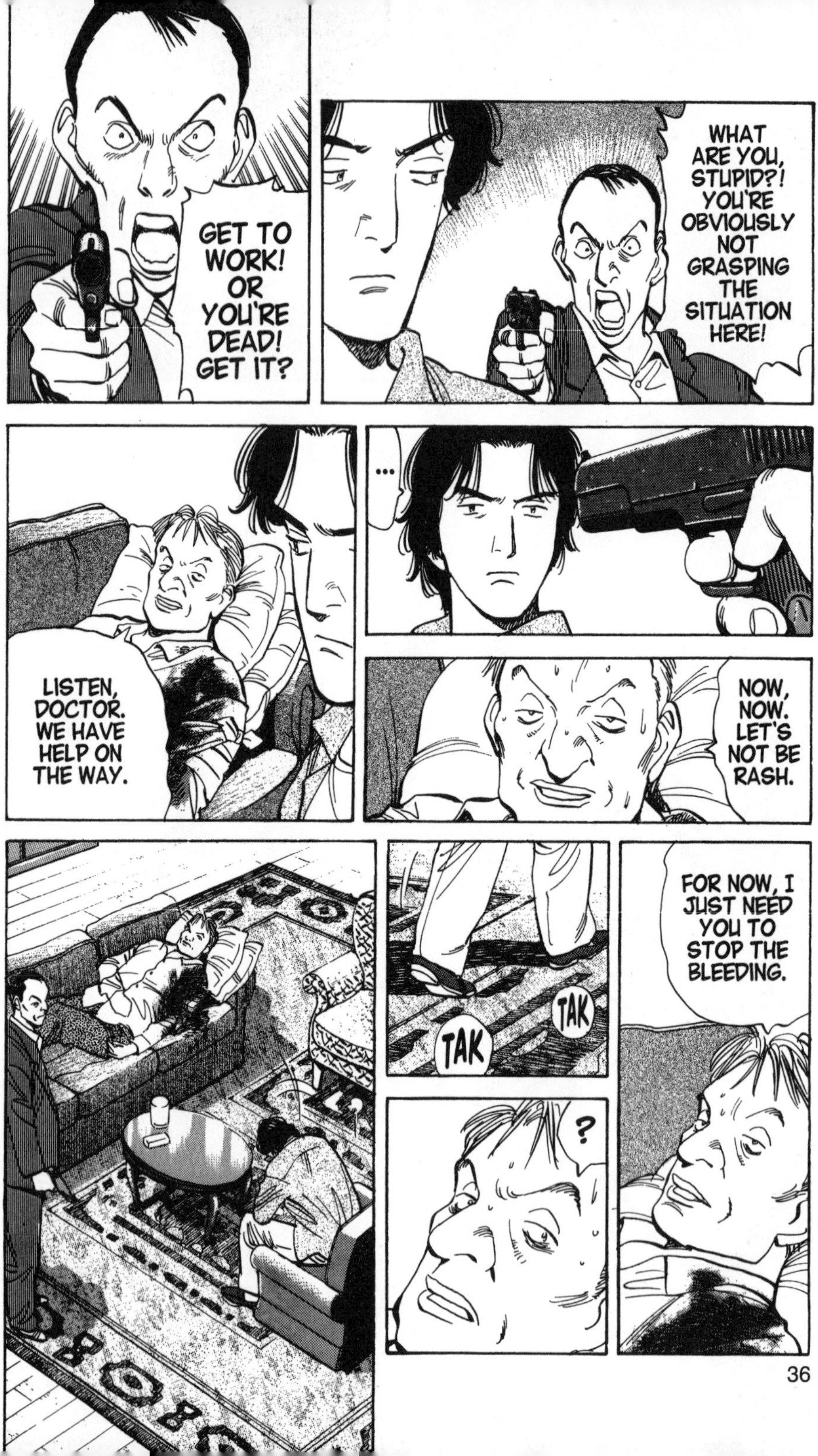
WHAT ARE YOU, STUPID?! YOU'RE OBVIOUSLY NOT GRASPING THE SITUATION HERE!
GET TO WORK! OR YOU'RE DEAD! GET IT?
...
NOW, NOW. LET'S NOT BE RASH.
LISTEN, DOCTOR. WE HAVE HELP ON THE WAY.
FOR NOW, I JUST NEED YOU TO STOP THE BLEEDING.
TAK
TAK
?

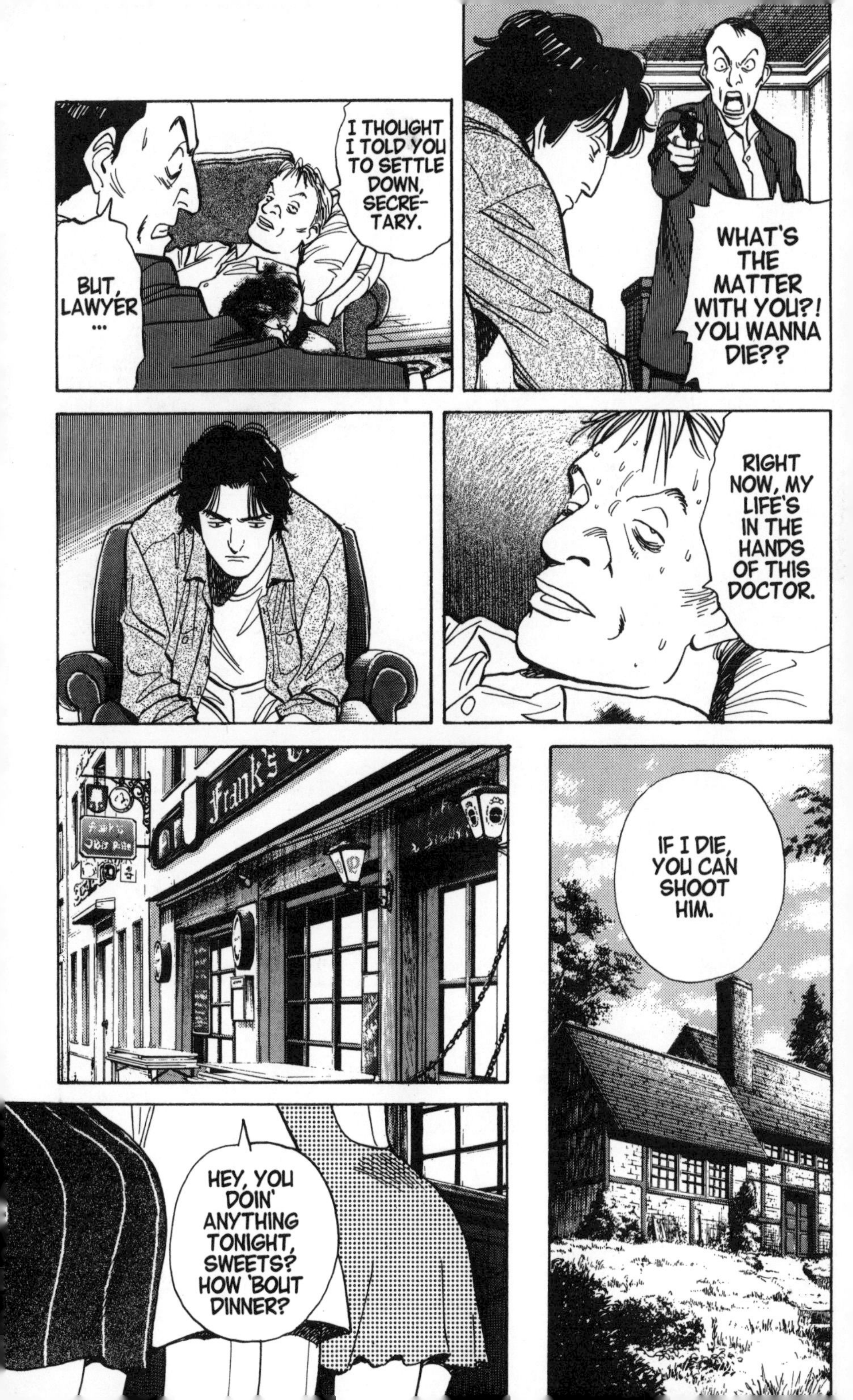
WHAT'S THE MATTER WITH YOU?! YOU WANNA DIE??
I THOUGHT I TOLD YOU TO SETTLE DOWN, SECRETARY.
BUT, LAWYER...
RIGHT NOW, MY LIFE'S IN THE HANDS OF THIS DOCTOR.
IF I DIE, YOU CAN SHOOT HIM.
Frank's
HEY, YOU DOIN' ANYTHING TONIGHT, SWEETS? HOW 'BOUT DINNER?

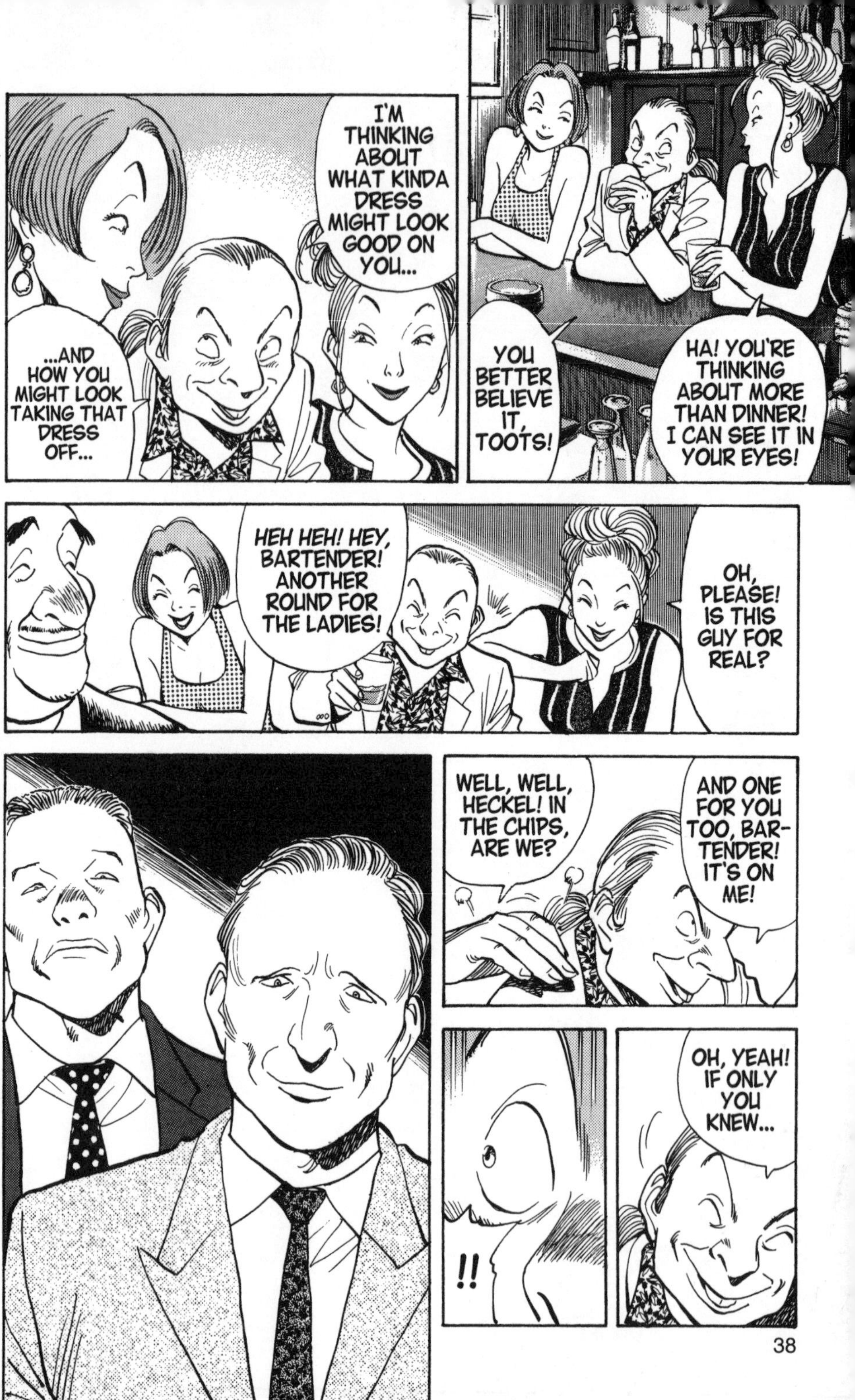
HA! YOU'RE THINKING ABOUT MORE THAN DINNER! I CAN SEE IT IN YOUR EYES!
YOU BETTER BELIEVE IT, TOOTS!
I'M THINKING ABOUT WHAT KINDA DRESS MIGHT LOOK GOOD ON YOU...
...AND HOW YOU MIGHT LOOK TAKING THAT DRESS OFF...
OH, PLEASE! IS THIS GUY FOR REAL?
HEH HEH! HEY, BARTENDER! ANOTHER ROUND FOR THE LADIES!
AND ONE FOR YOU TOO, BAR-TENDER! IT'S ON ME!
WELL, WELL, HECKEL! IN THE CHIPS, ARE WE?
OH, YEAH! IF ONLY YOU KNEW...
!!

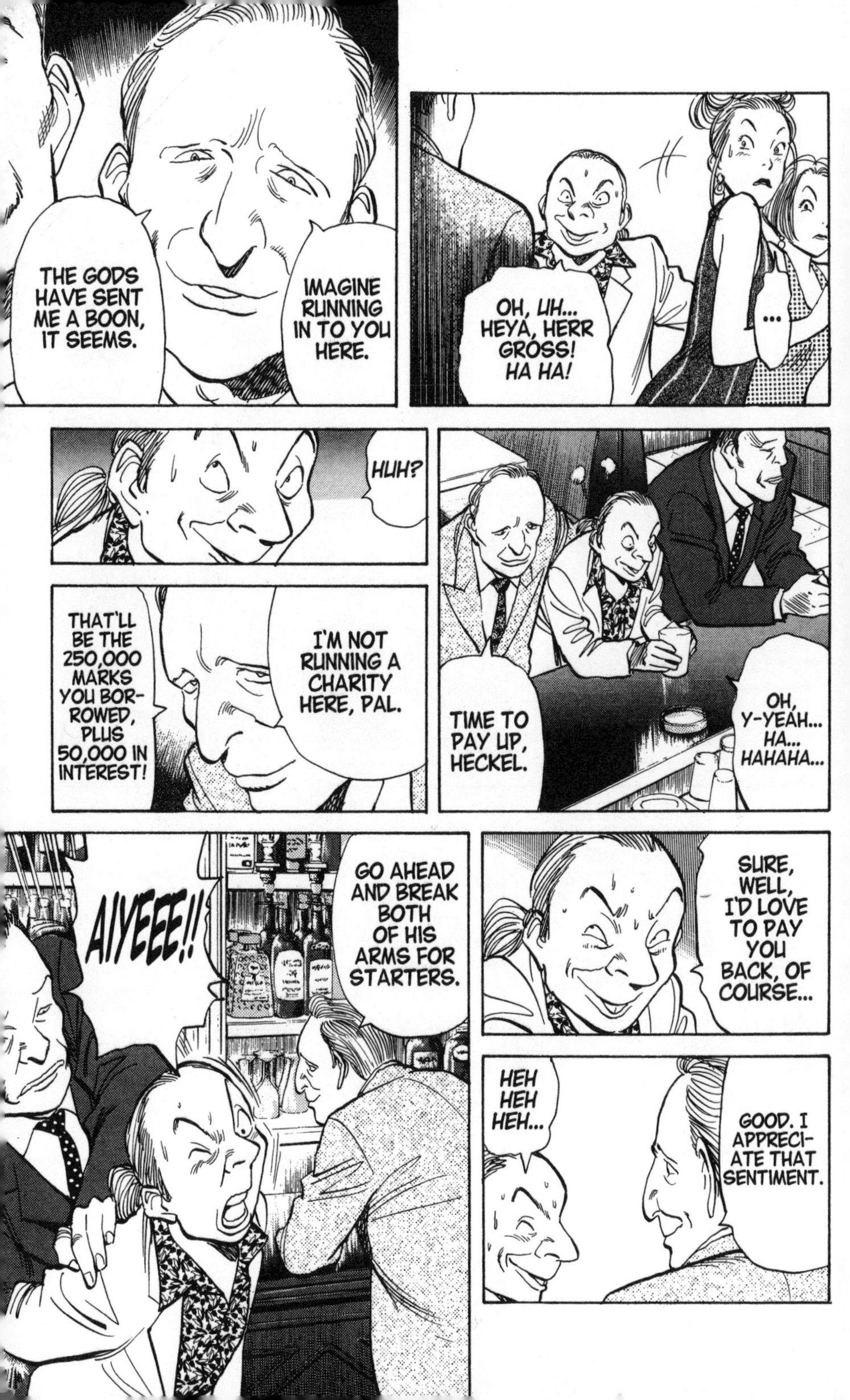
...
OH, UH... HEYA, HERR GROSS! HA HA!
IMAGINE RUNNING IN TO YOU HERE.
THE GODS HAVE SENT ME A BOON, IT SEEMS.
OH, Y-YEAH... HA... HAHAHA...
TIME TO PAY UP, HECKEL.
HUH?
I'M NOT RUNNING A CHARITY HERE, PAL.
THAT'LL BE THE 250,000 MARKS YOU BOR-ROWED, PLUS 50,000 IN INTEREST!
SURE, WELL, I'D LOVE TO PAY YOU BACK, OF COURSE...
GOOD. I APPRECI-ATE THAT SENTIMENT.
HEH HEH HEH...
GO AHEAD AND BREAK BOTH OF HIS ARMS FOR STARTERS.
AIYEEE!!

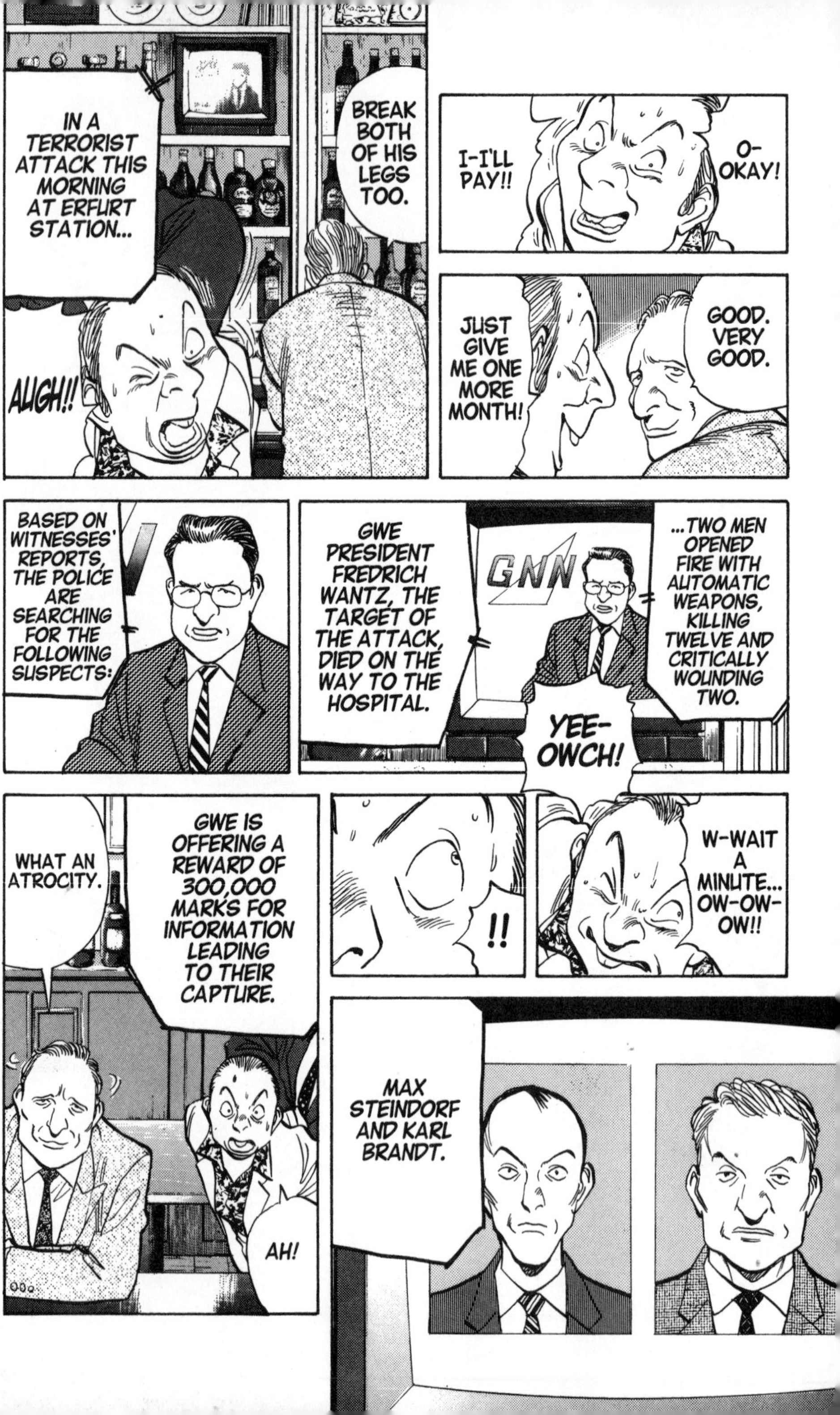
O-OKAY!
I-I'LL PAY!!
GOOD. VERY GOOD.
JUST GIVE ME ONE MORE MONTH!
BREAK BOTH OF HIS LEGS TOO.
IN A TERRORIST ATTACK THIS MORNING AT ERFURT STATION...
AUGH!!
...TWO MEN OPENED FIRE WITH AUTOMATIC WEAPONS, KILLING TWELVE AND CRITICALLY WOUNDING TWO.
GNN
GWE PRESIDENT FREDRICH WANTZ, THE TARGET OF THE ATTACK, DIED ON THE WAY TO THE HOSPITAL.
YEE-OWCH!
BASED ON WITNESSES' REPORTS, THE POLICE ARE SEARCHING FOR THE FOLLOWING SUSPECTS:
W-WAIT A MINUTE... OW-OW-OW!!
!!
MAX STEINDORF AND KARL BRANDT.
GWE IS OFFERING A REWARD OF 300,000 MARKS FOR INFORMATION LEADING TO THEIR CAPTURE.
WHAT AN ATROCITY.
AH!

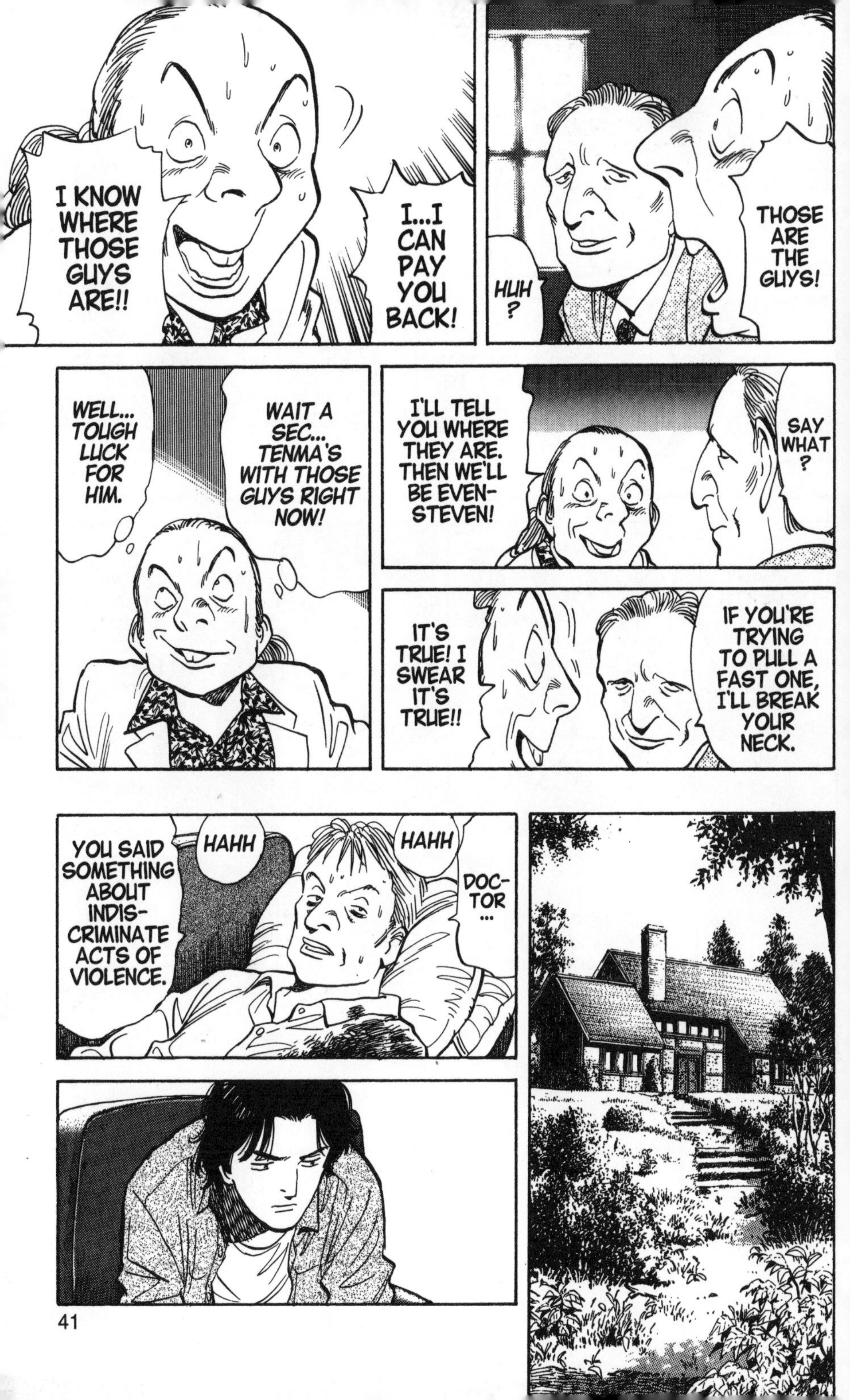
THOSE ARE THE GUYS!
HUH?
I...I CAN PAY YOU BACK!
I KNOW WHERE THOSE GUYS ARE!!
SAY WHAT?
I'LL TELL YOU WHERE THEY ARE. THEN WE'LL BE EVEN-STEVEN!
IF YOU'RE TRYING TO PULL A FAST ONE, I'LL BREAK YOUR NECK.
IT'S TRUE! I SWEAR IT'S TRUE!!
WAIT A SEC... TENMA'S WITH THOSE GUYS RIGHT NOW!
WELL... TOUGH LUCK FOR HIM.
HAHH
DOC-TOR...
HAHH
YOU SAID SOMETHING ABOUT INDIS-CRIMINATE ACTS OF VIOLENCE.

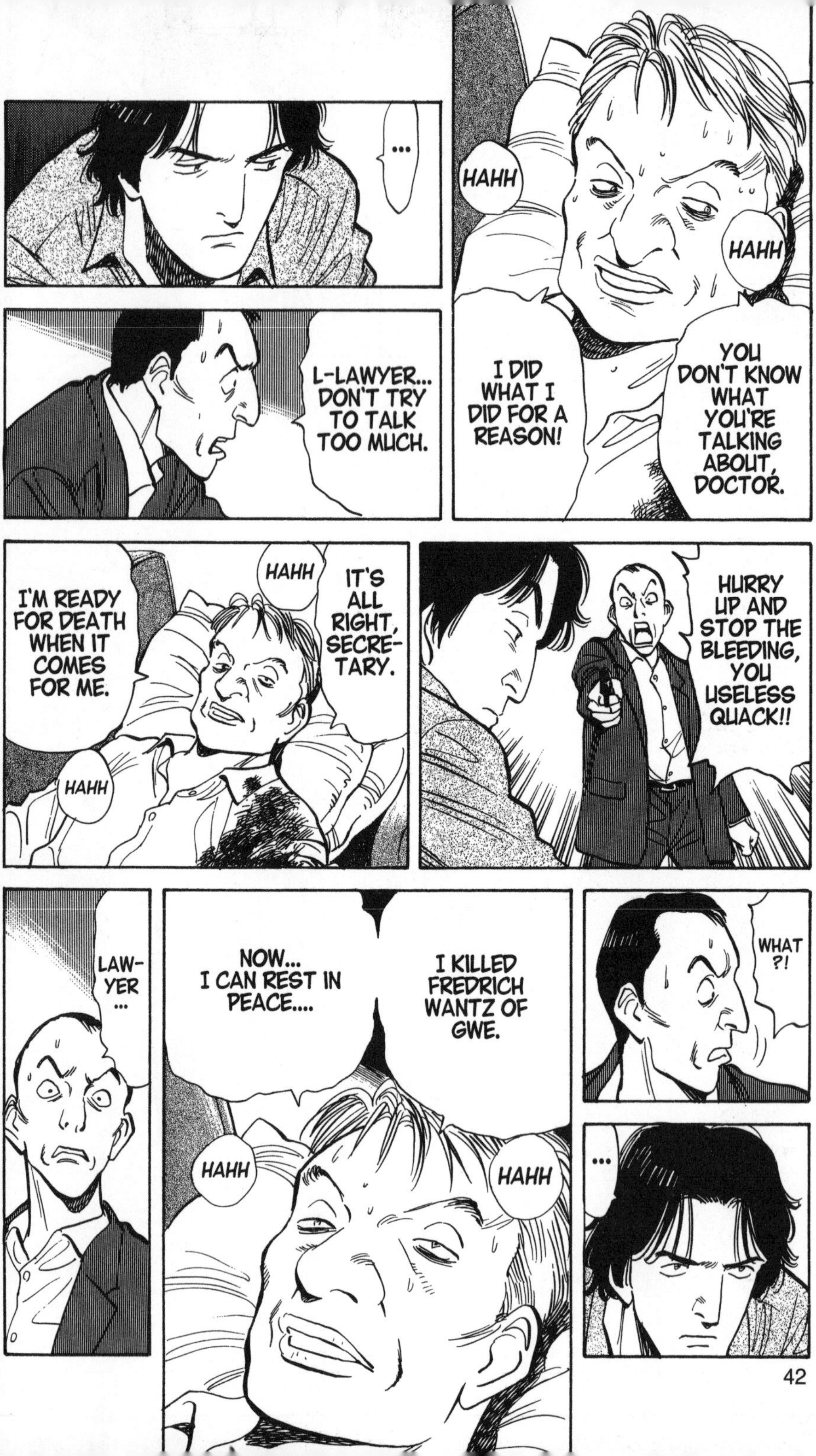

HAHH
HAHH
YOU DON'T KNOW WHAT YOU'RE TALKING ABOUT, DOCTOR.
I DID WHAT I DID FOR A REASON!
...
L-LAWYER... DON'T TRY TO TALK TOO MUCH.
HURRY UP AND STOP THE BLEEDING, YOU USELESS QUACK!!
IT'S ALL RIGHT, SECRETARY.
HAHH
I'M READY FOR DEATH WHEN IT COMES FOR ME.
HAHH
WHAT ?!
...
I KILLED FREDRICH WANTZ OF GWE.
HAHH
NOW... I CAN REST IN PEACE....
HAHH
LAW-YER ...

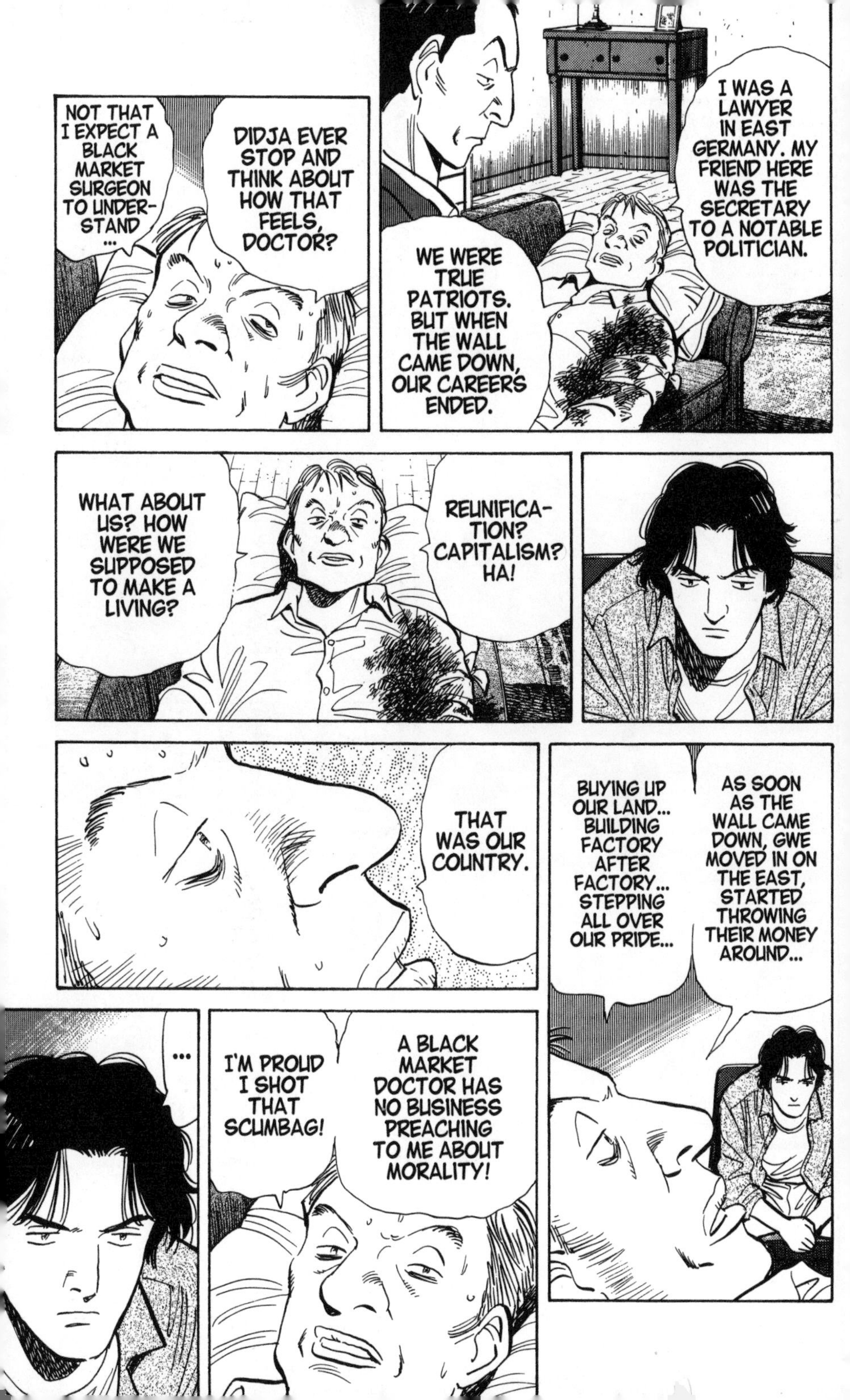
I WAS A LAWYER IN EAST GERMANY. MY FRIEND HERE WAS THE SECRETARY TO A NOTABLE POLITICIAN.
WE WERE TRUE PATRIOTS. BUT WHEN THE WALL CAME DOWN, OUR CAREERS ENDED.
DIDJA EVER STOP AND THINK ABOUT HOW THAT FEELS, DOCTOR?
NOT THAT I EXPECT A BLACK MARKET SURGEON TO UNDERSTAND...
REUNIFICATION? CAPITALISM? HA!
WHAT ABOUT US? HOW WERE WE SUPPOSED TO MAKE A LIVING?
AS SOON AS THE WALL CAME DOWN, GWE MOVED IN ON THE EAST, STARTED THROWING THEIR MONEY AROUND...
BUYING UP OUR LAND... BUILDING FACTORY AFTER FACTORY... STEPPING ALL OVER OUR PRIDE...
THAT WAS OUR COUNTRY.
A BLACK MARKET DOCTOR HAS NO BUSINESS PREACHING TO ME ABOUT MORALITY!
I'M PROUD I SHOT THAT SCUMBAG!
...

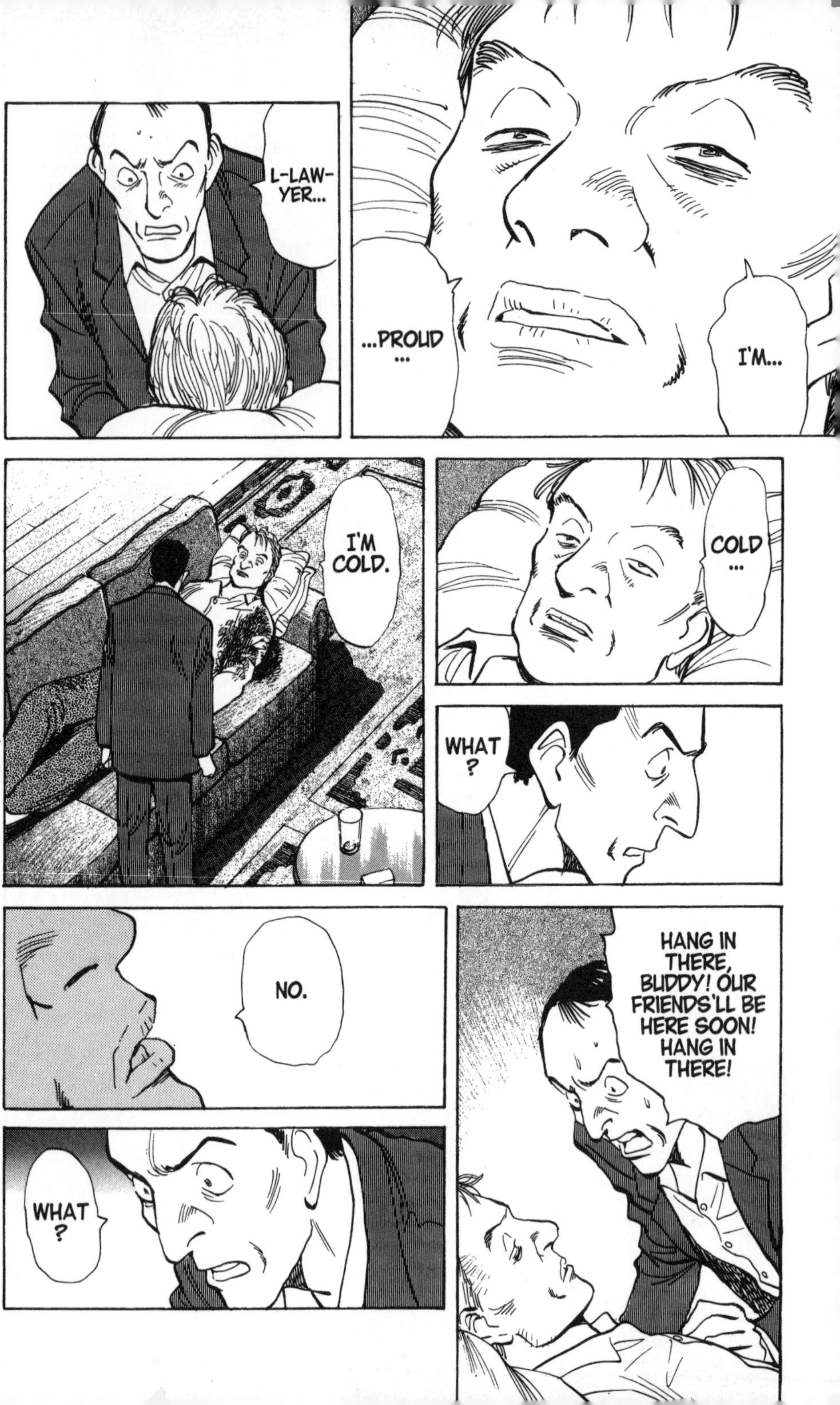
I'M...
...PROUD ...
L-LAW-YER...
COLD ...
WHAT ?
I'M COLD.
HANG IN THERE, BUDDY! OUR FRIENDS'LL BE HERE SOON! HANG IN THERE!
NO.
WHAT ?

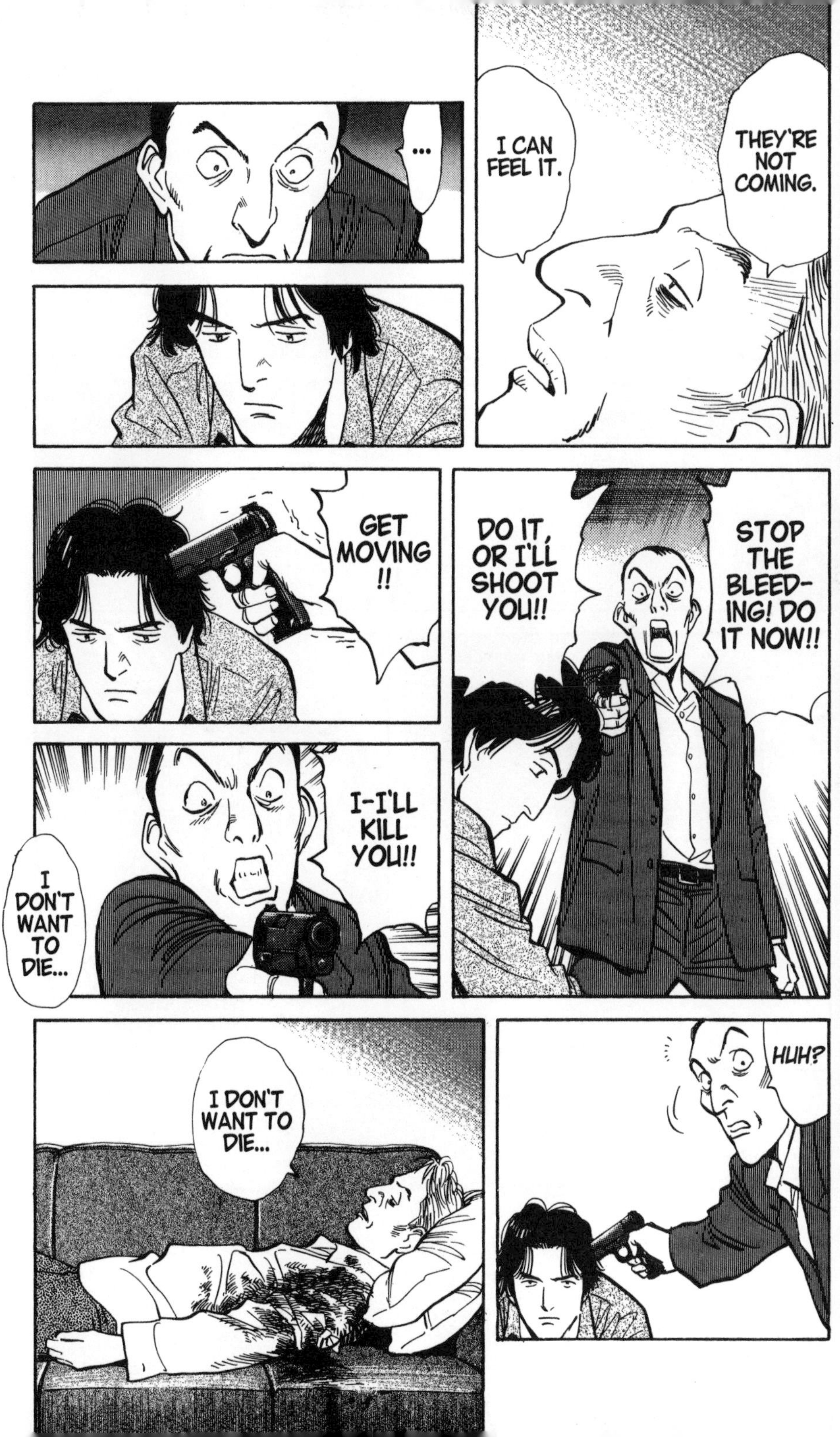
THEY'RE NOT COMING.
I CAN FEEL IT.
...
STOP THE BLEEDING! DO IT NOW!!
DO IT, OR I'LL SHOOT YOU!!
GET MOVING!!
I-I'LL KILL YOU!!
I DON'T WANT TO DIE...
HUH?
I DON'T WANT TO DIE...

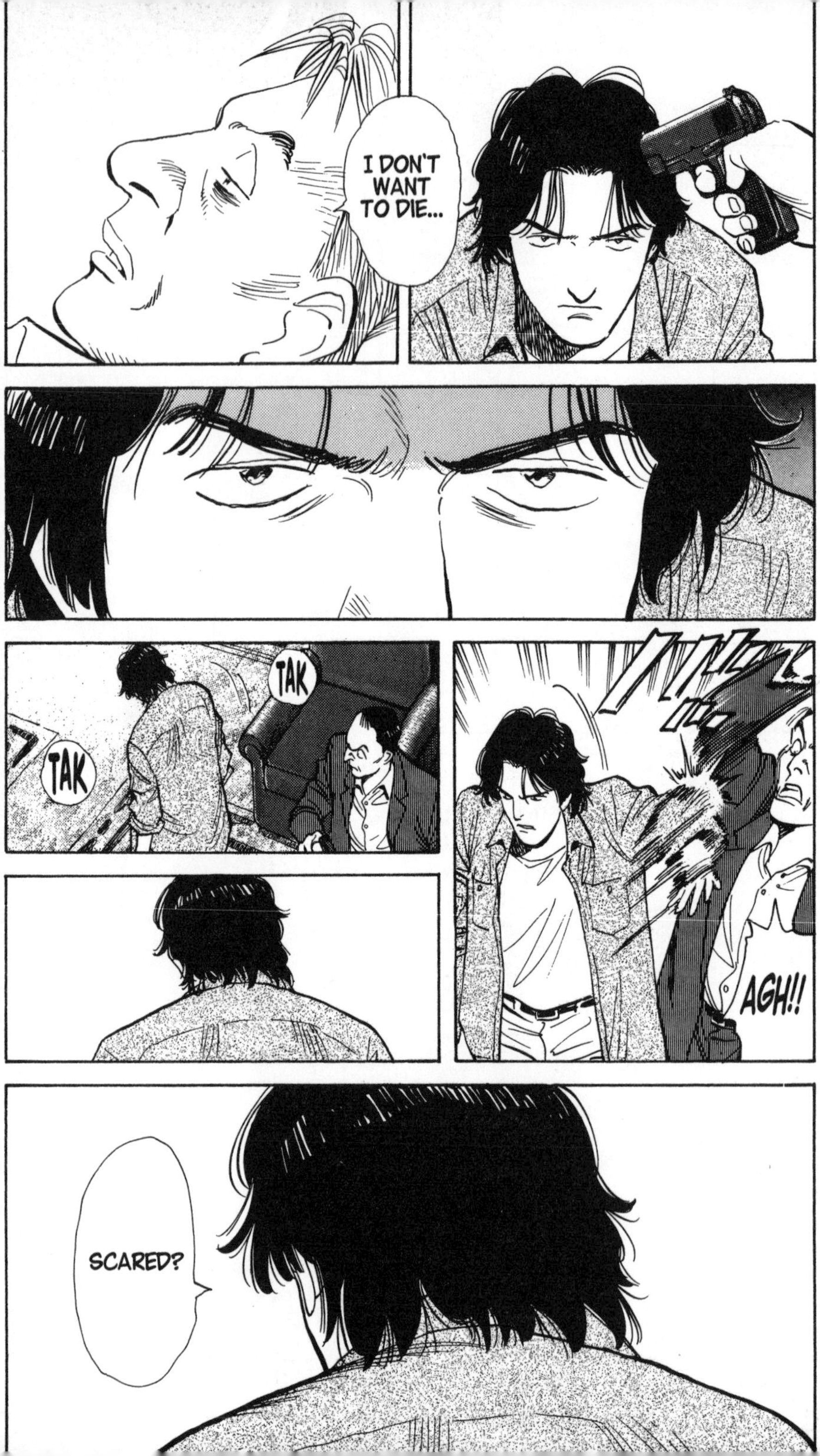
I DON'T WANT TO DIE...
AGH!!
TAK
TAK
SCARED?

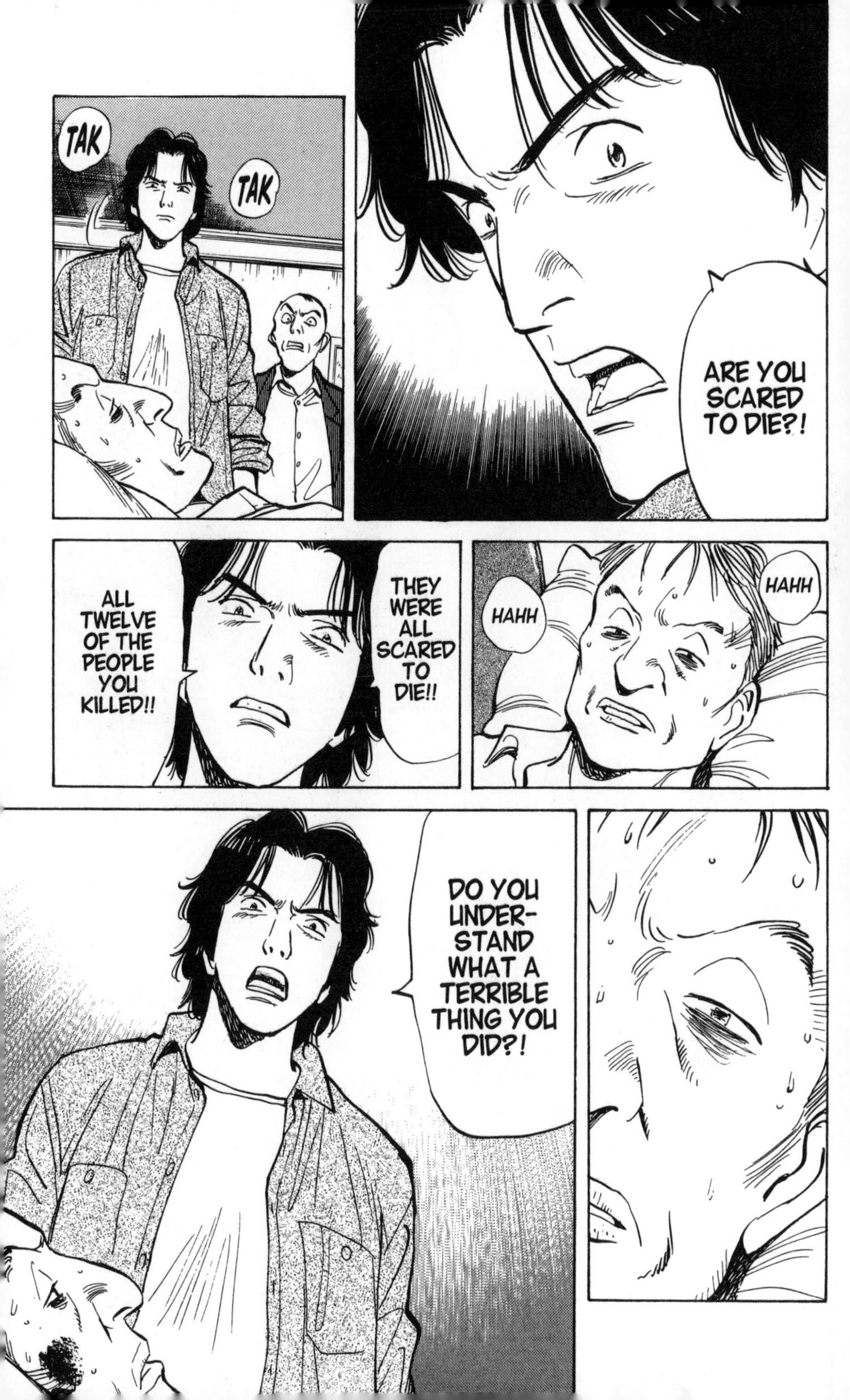
ARE YOU SCARED TO DIE?!
TAK
TAK
HAHH
HAHH
THEY WERE ALL SCARED TO DIE!!
ALL TWELVE OF THE PEOPLE YOU KILLED!!
DO YOU UNDER-STAND WHAT A TERRIBLE THING YOU DID?!

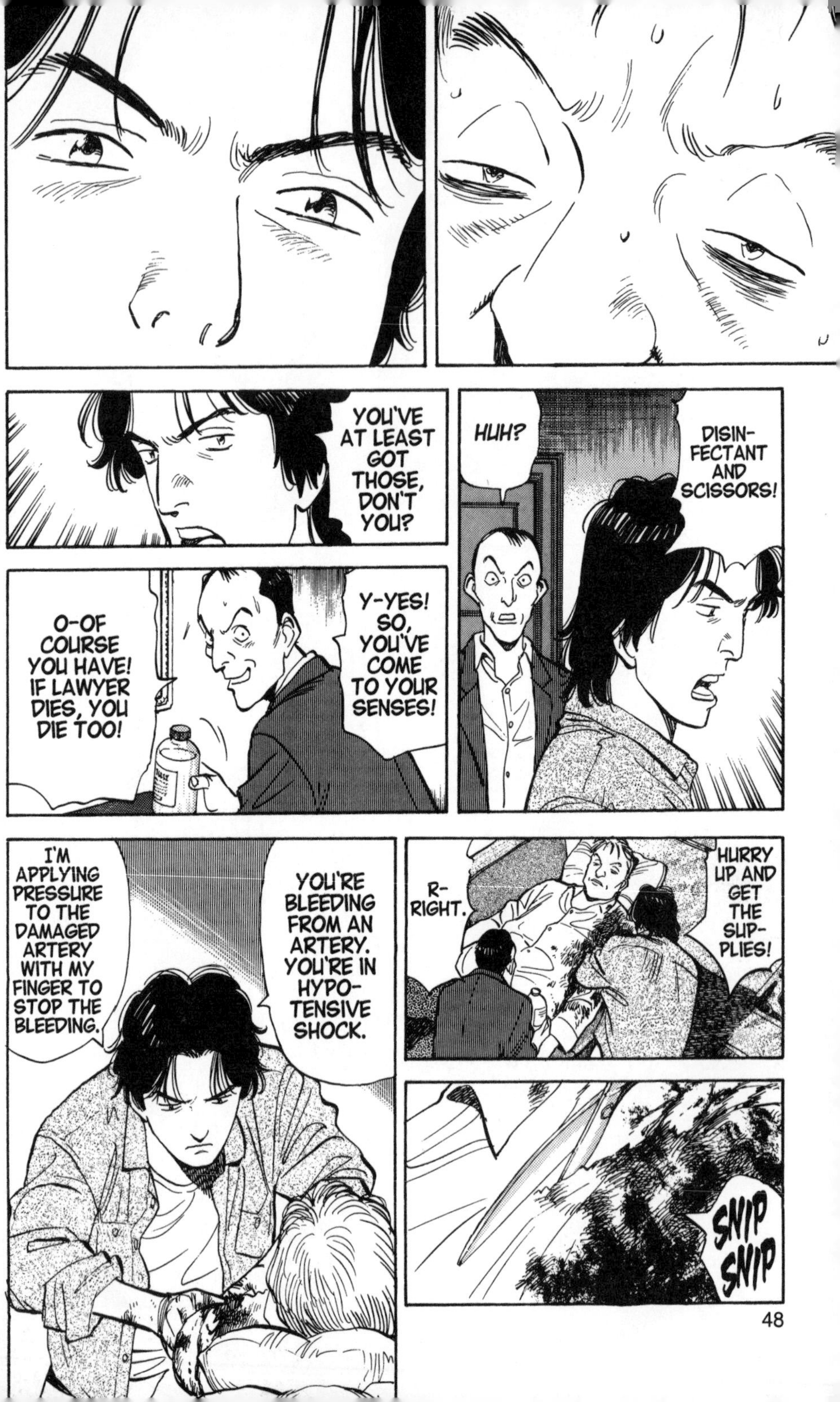
DISIN-FECTANT AND SCISSORS!
HUH?
YOU'VE AT LEAST GOT THOSE, DON'T YOU?
Y-YES! SO, YOU'VE COME TO YOUR SENSES!
O-OF COURSE YOU HAVE! IF LAWYER DIES, YOU DIE TOO!
HURRY UP AND GET THE SUP-PLIES!
R-RIGHT.
SNIP SNIP
YOU'RE BLEEDING FROM AN ARTERY. YOU'RE IN HYPO-TENSIVE SHOCK.
I'M APPLYING PRESSURE TO THE DAMAGED ARTERY WITH MY FINGER TO STOP THE BLEEDING.

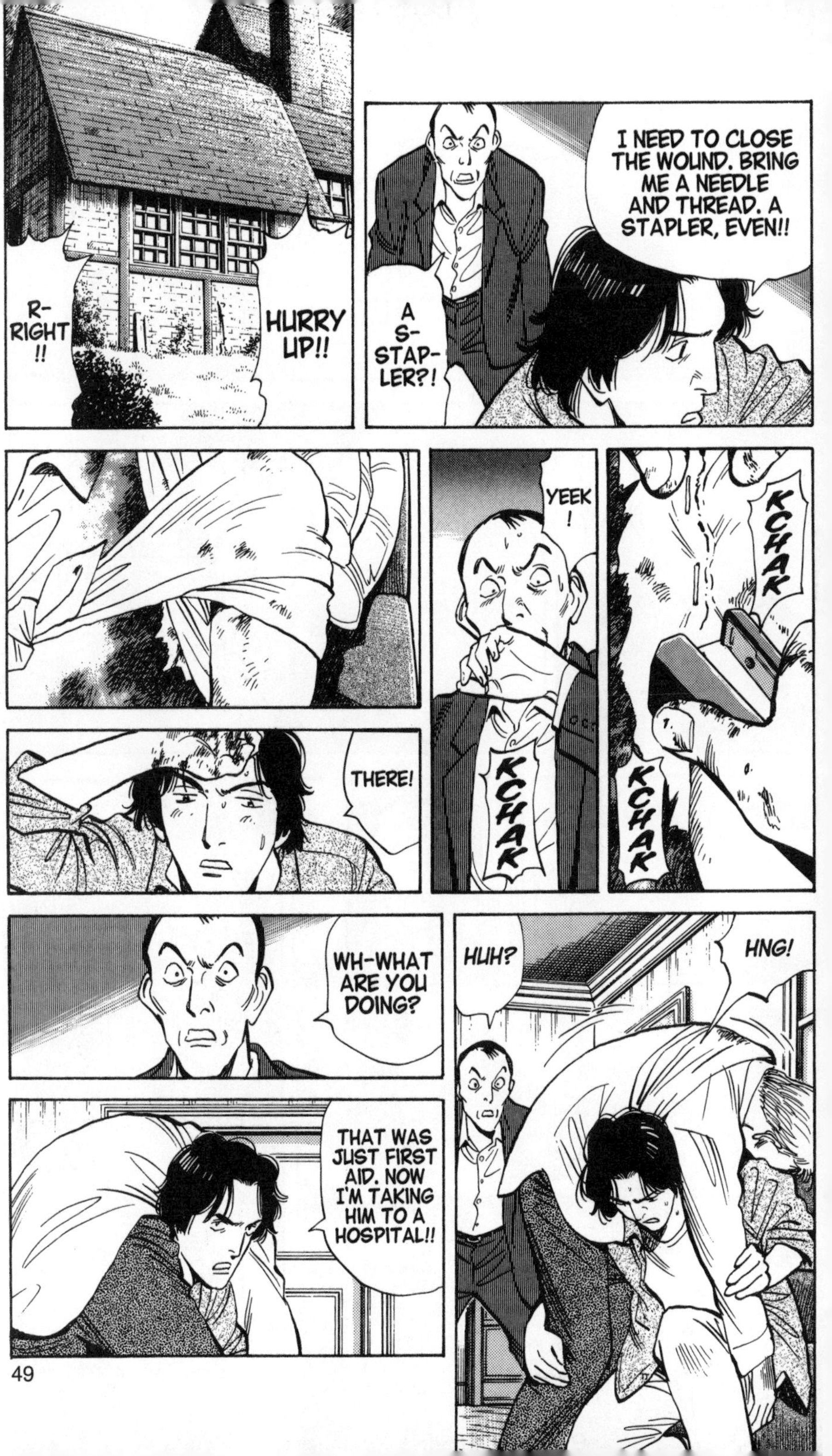
I NEED TO CLOSE THE WOUND. BRING ME A NEEDLE AND THREAD. A STAPLER, EVEN!!
A S-STAP-LER?!
HURRY UP!!
R-RIGHT!!
KCHAK
KCHAK
YEEK!
KCHAK
THERE!
HNG!
HUH?
WH-WHAT ARE YOU DOING?
THAT WAS JUST FIRST AID. NOW I'M TAKING HIM TO A HOSPITAL!!

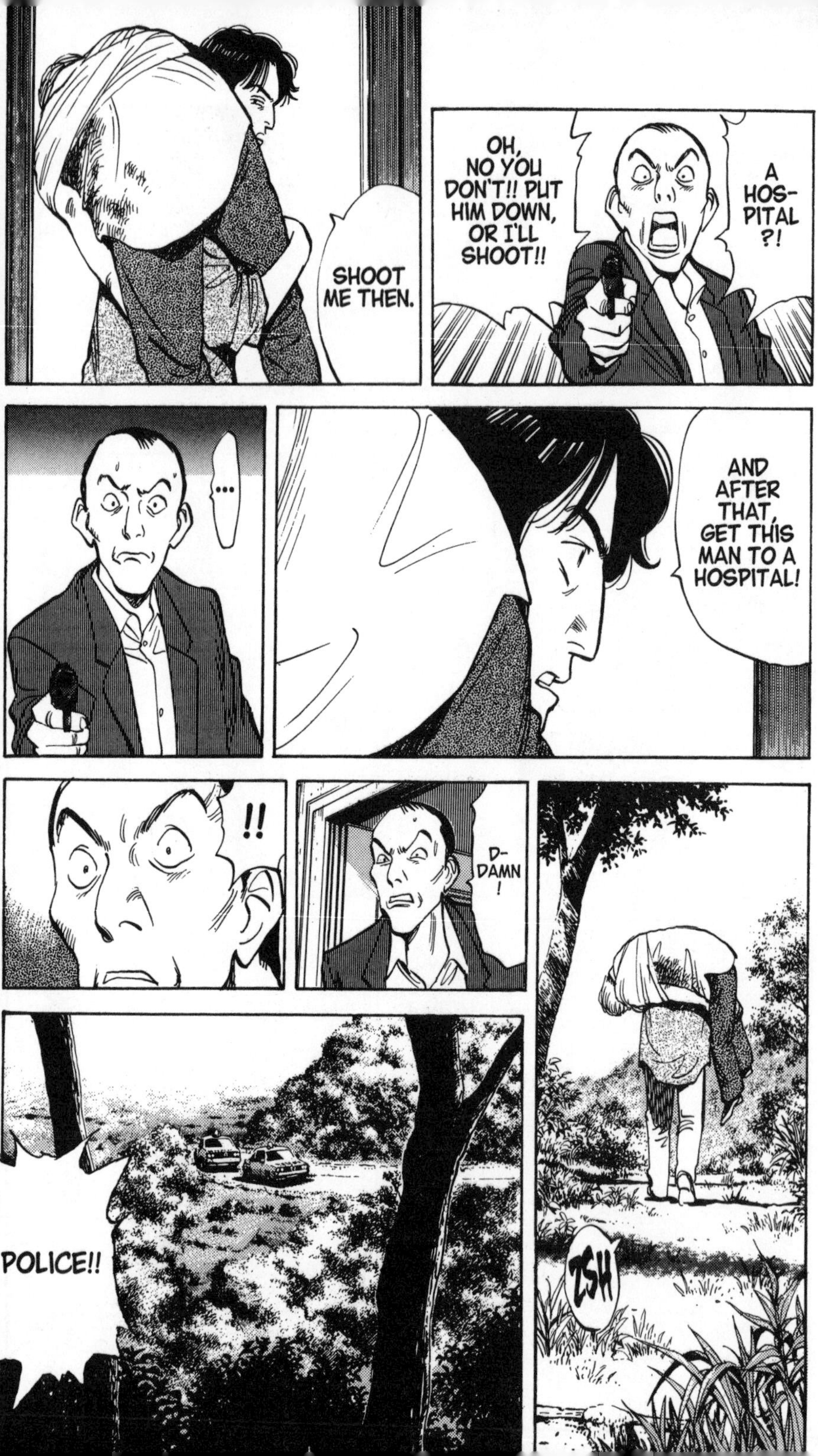
A HOS-PITAL?!
OH, NO YOU DON'T!! PUT HIM DOWN, OR I'LL SHOOT!!
SHOOT ME THEN.
AND AFTER THAT, GET THIS MAN TO A HOSPITAL!
...
ZSH
D-DAMN!
!!
POLICE!!

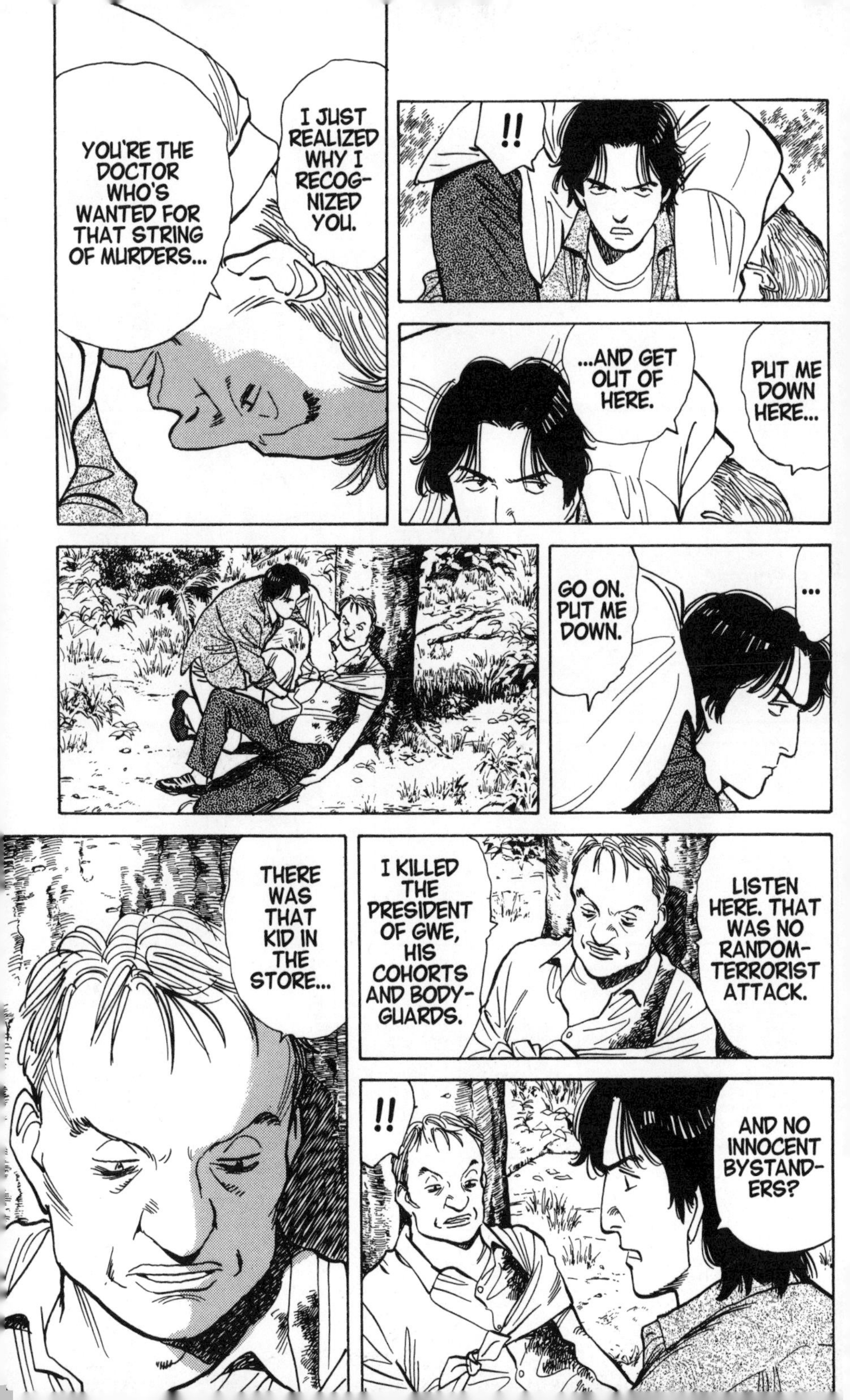
!!
PUT ME DOWN HERE...
...AND GET OUT OF HERE.
I JUST REALIZED WHY I RECOGNIZED YOU.
YOU'RE THE DOCTOR WHO'S WANTED FOR THAT STRING OF MURDERS...
...
GO ON. PUT ME DOWN.
LISTEN HERE. THAT WAS NO RANDOM-TERRORIST ATTACK.
I KILLED THE PRESIDENT OF GWE, HIS COHORTS AND BODY-GUARDS.
AND NO INNOCENT BYSTANDERS?
!!
THERE WAS THAT KID IN THE STORE...

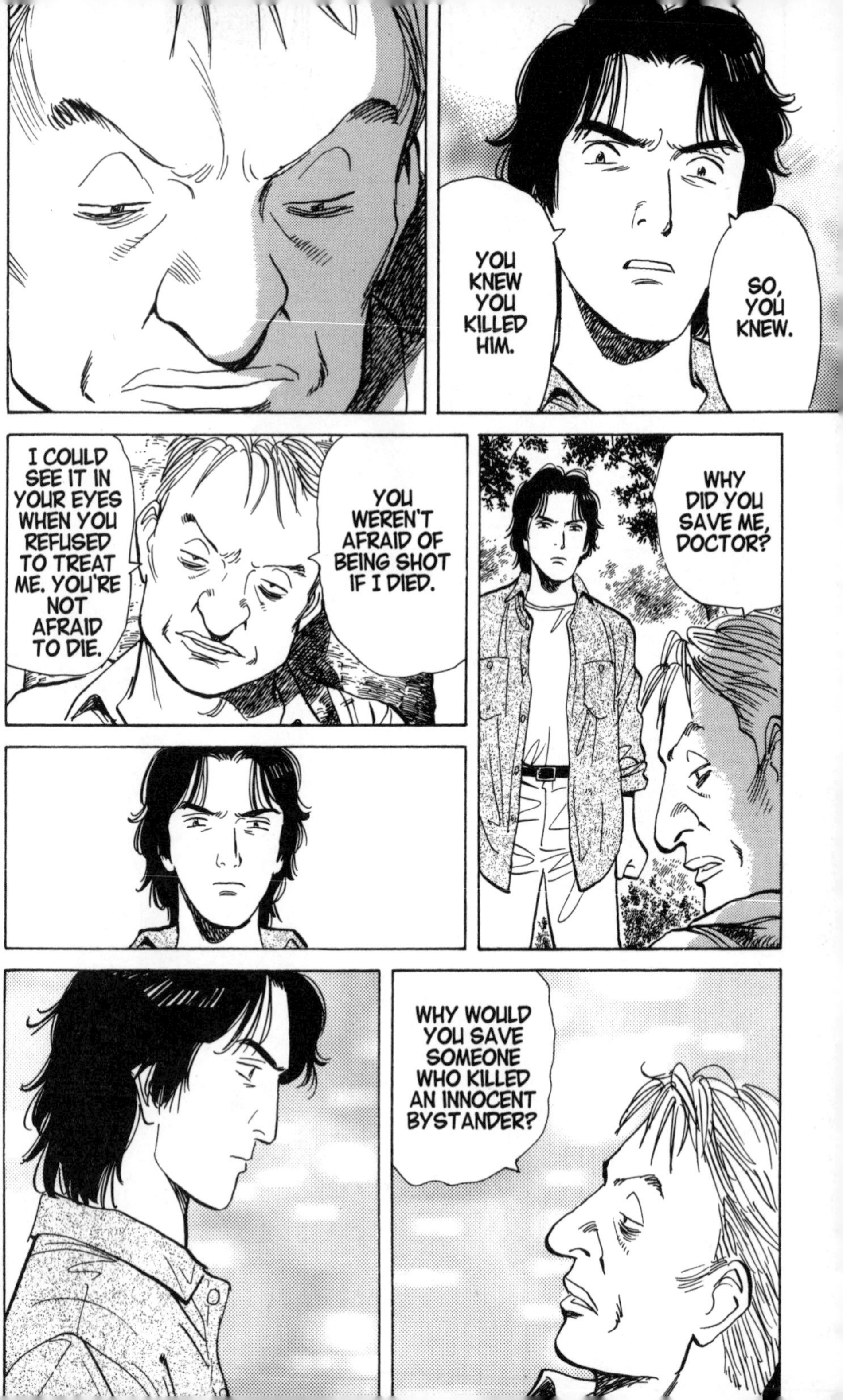
SO, YOU KNEW.
YOU KNEW YOU KILLED HIM.
WHY DID YOU SAVE ME, DOCTOR?
YOU WEREN'T AFRAID OF BEING SHOT IF I DIED.
I COULD SEE IT IN YOUR EYES WHEN YOU REFUSED TO TREAT ME. YOU'RE NOT AFRAID TO DIE.
WHY WOULD YOU SAVE SOMEONE WHO KILLED AN INNOCENT BYSTANDER?

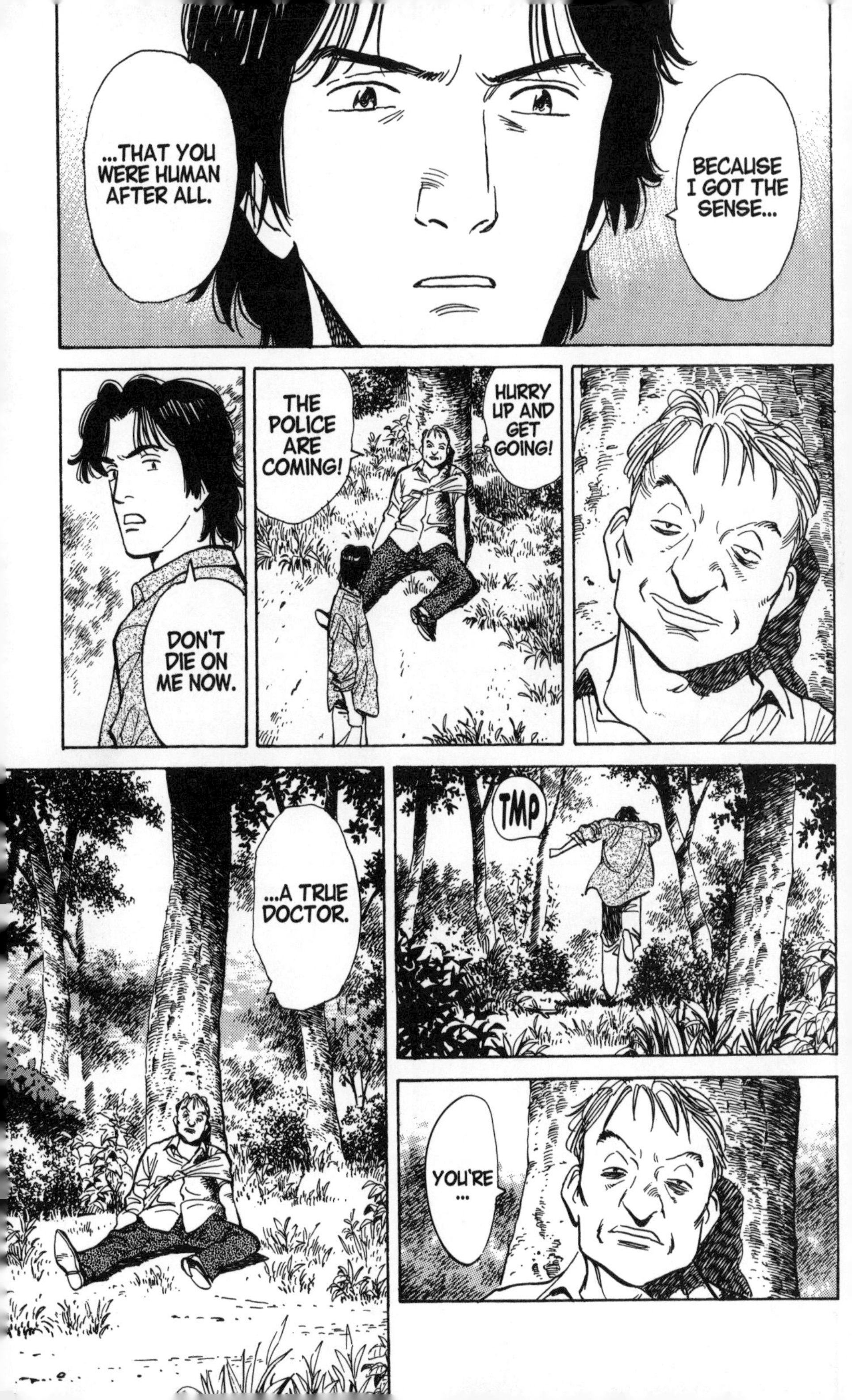
BECAUSE I GOT THE SENSE...
...THAT YOU WERE HUMAN AFTER ALL.
HURRY UP AND GET GOING!
THE POLICE ARE COMING!
DON'T DIE ON ME NOW.
TMP
YOU'RE ...
...A TRUE DOCTOR.

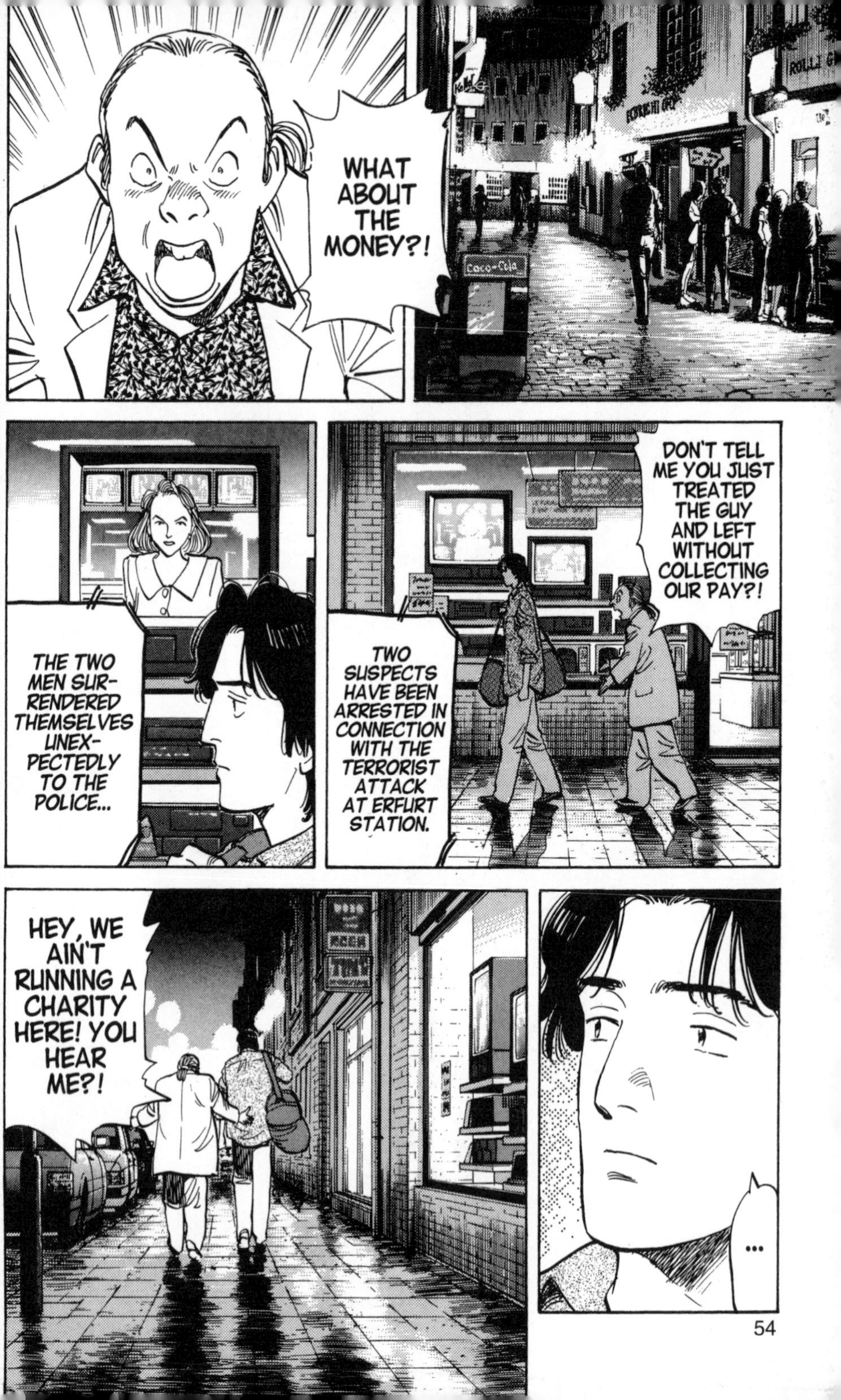
WHAT ABOUT THE MONEY?!
DON'T TELL ME YOU JUST TREATED THE GUY AND LEFT WITHOUT COLLECTING OUR PAY?!
TWO SUSPECTS HAVE BEEN ARRESTED IN CONNECTION WITH THE TERRORIST ATTACK AT ERFURT STATION.
THE TWO MEN SUR-RENDERED THEMSELVES UNEX-PECTEDLY TO THE POLICE...
...
HEY, WE AIN'T RUNNING A CHARITY HERE! YOU HEAR ME?!

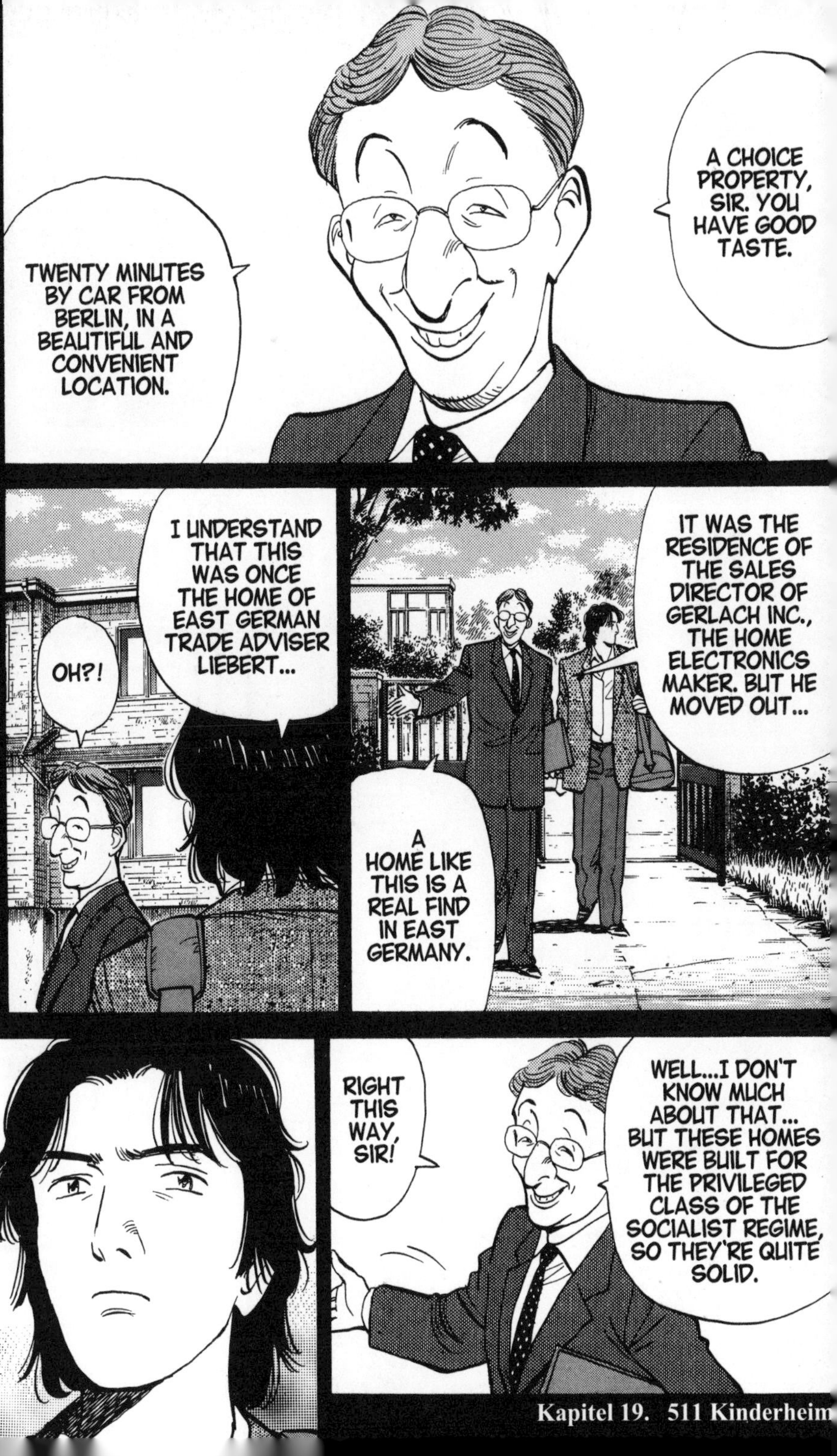
A CHOICE PROPERTY, SIR. YOU HAVE GOOD TASTE.
TWENTY MINUTES BY CAR FROM BERLIN, IN A BEAUTIFUL AND CONVENIENT LOCATION.
IT WAS THE RESIDENCE OF THE SALES DIRECTOR OF GERLACH INC., THE HOME ELECTRONICS MAKER. BUT HE MOVED OUT...
A HOME LIKE THIS IS A REAL FIND IN EAST GERMANY.
I UNDERSTAND THAT THIS WAS ONCE THE HOME OF EAST GERMAN TRADE ADVISER LIEBERT...
OH?!
WELL...I DON'T KNOW MUCH ABOUT THAT... BUT THESE HOMES WERE BUILT FOR THE PRIVILEGED CLASS OF THE SOCIALIST REGIME, SO THEY'RE QUITE SOLID.
RIGHT THIS WAY, SIR!

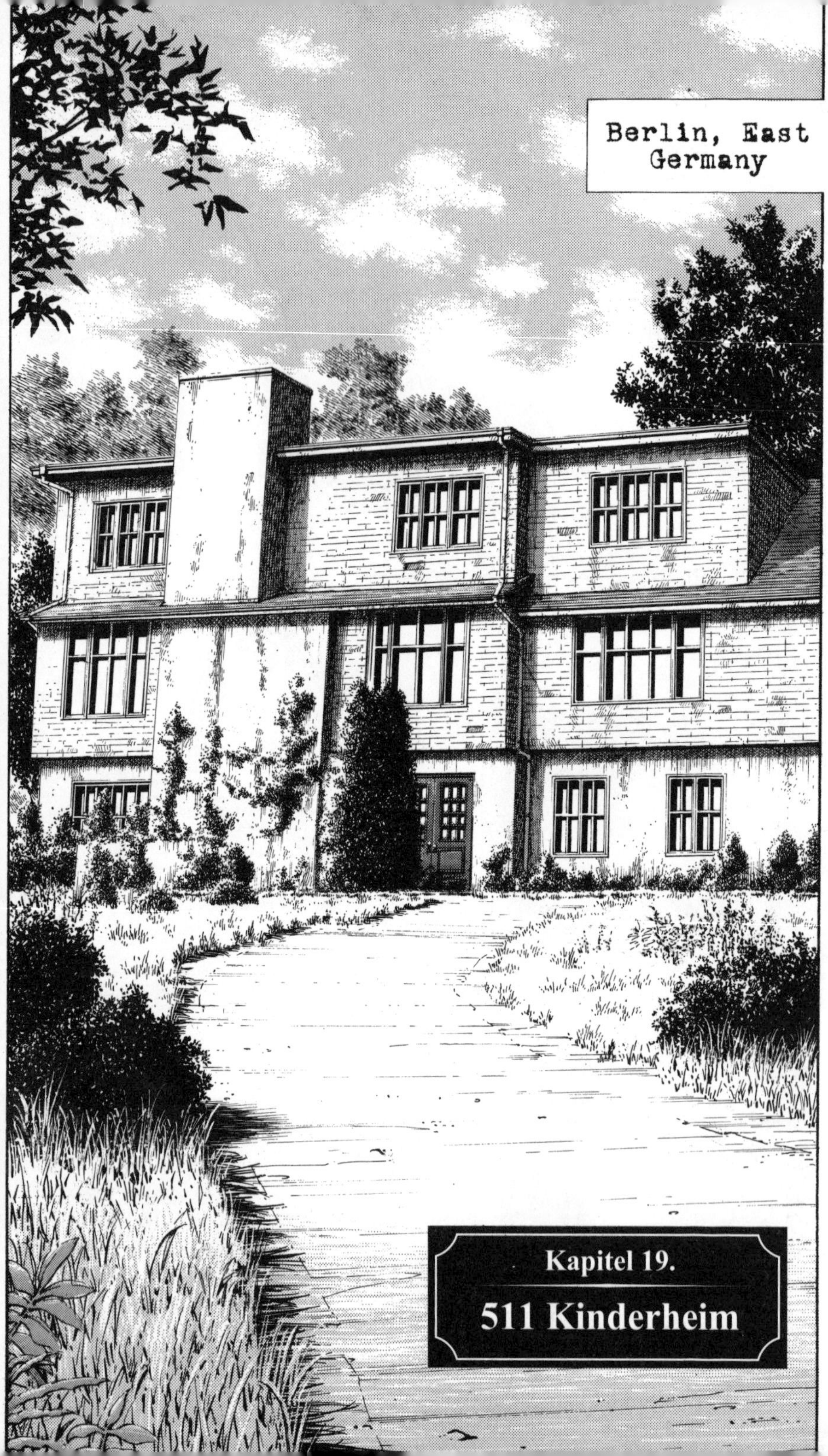
Berlin, East Germany
Kapitel 19.
511 Kinderheim

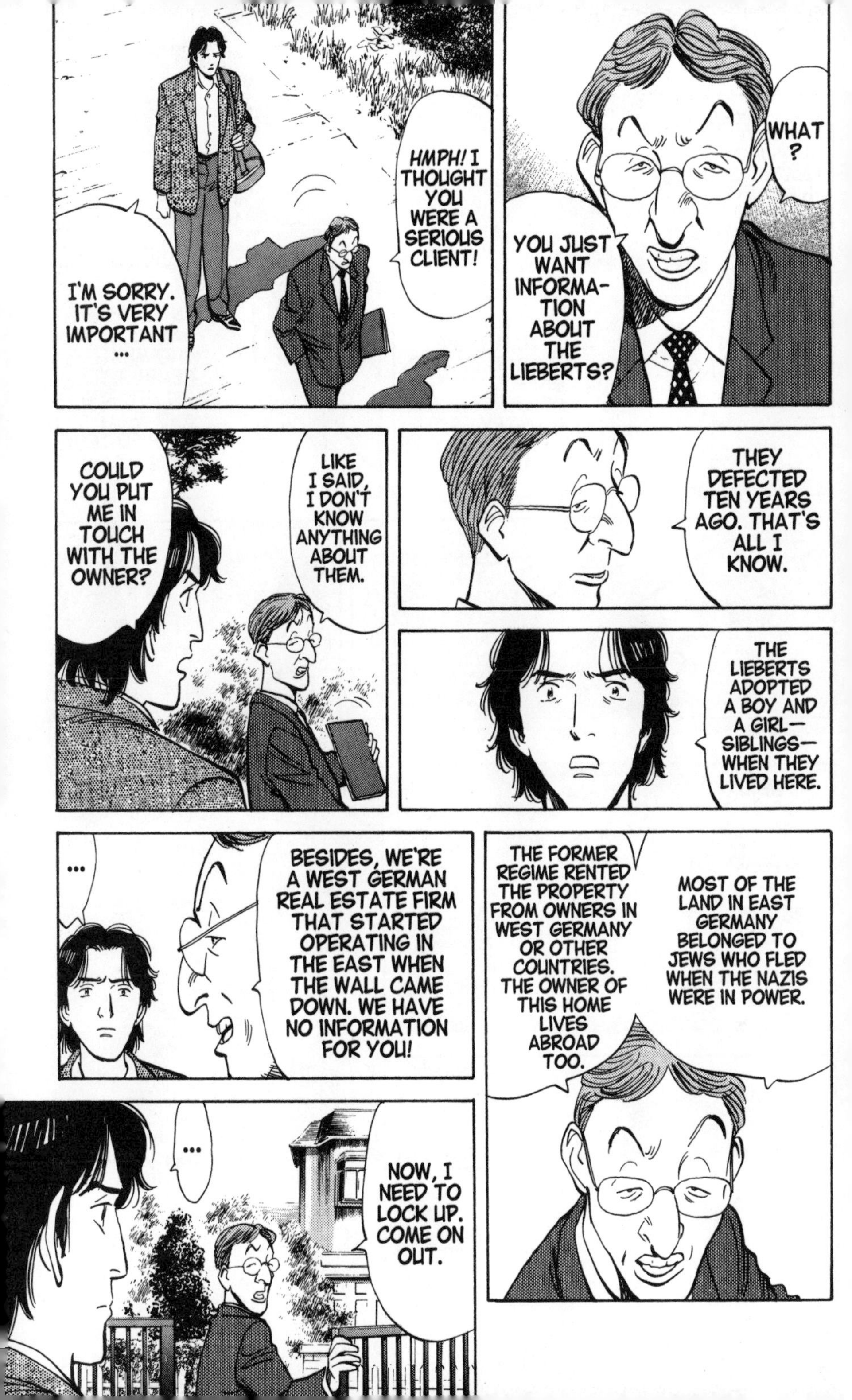
HMPH! I THOUGHT YOU WERE A SERIOUS CLIENT!
I'M SORRY. IT'S VERY IMPORTANT...
YOU JUST WANT INFORMATION-TION ABOUT THE LIEBERTS?
WHAT?
COULD YOU PUT ME IN TOUCH WITH THE OWNER?
LIKE I SAID, I DON'T KNOW ANYTHING ABOUT THEM.
THEY DEFECTED TEN YEARS AGO. THAT'S ALL I KNOW.
THE LIEBERTS ADOPTED A BOY AND A GIRL—SIBLINGS—WHEN THEY LIVED HERE.
BESIDES, WE'RE A WEST GERMAN REAL ESTATE FIRM THAT STARTED OPERATING IN THE EAST WHEN THE WALL CAME DOWN. WE HAVE NO INFORMATION FOR YOU!
...
MOST OF THE LAND IN EAST GERMANY BELONGED TO JEWS WHO FLED WHEN THE NAZIS WERE IN POWER.
THE FORMER REGIME RENTED THE PROPERTY FROM OWNERS IN WEST GERMANY OR OTHER COUNTRIES. THE OWNER OF THIS HOME LIVES ABROAD TOO.
NOW, I NEED TO LOCK UP. COME ON OUT.
...

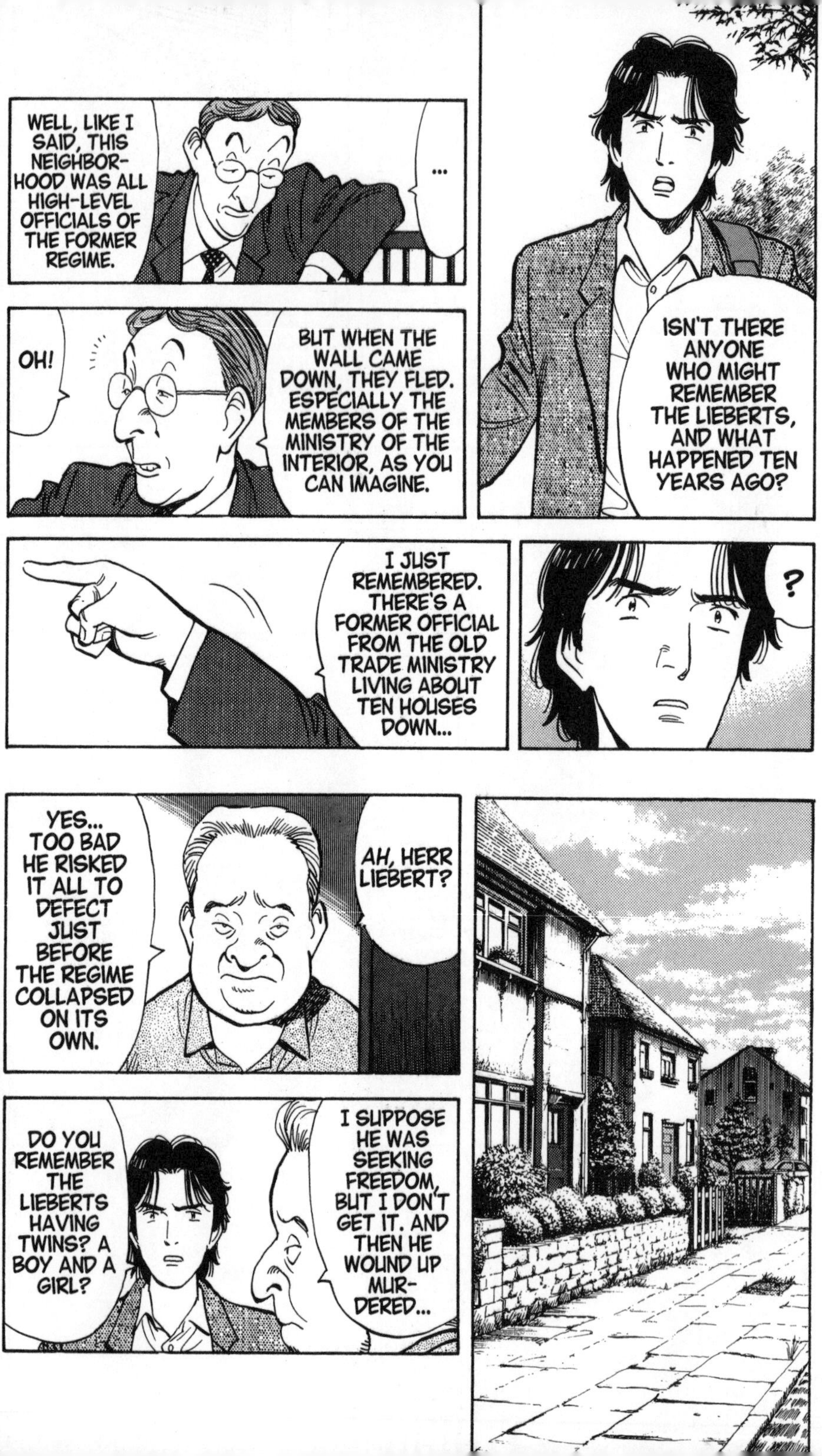
ISN'T THERE ANYONE WHO MIGHT REMEMBER THE LIEBERTS, AND WHAT HAPPENED TEN YEARS AGO?
WELL, LIKE I SAID, THIS NEIGHBOR-HOOD WAS ALL HIGH-LEVEL OFFICIALS OF THE FORMER REGIME.
...
BUT WHEN THE WALL CAME DOWN, THEY FLED. ESPECIALLY THE MEMBERS OF THE MINISTRY OF THE INTERIOR, AS YOU CAN IMAGINE.
OH!
?
I JUST REMEMBERED. THERE'S A FORMER OFFICIAL FROM THE OLD TRADE MINISTRY LIVING ABOUT TEN HOUSES DOWN...
AH, HERR LIEBERT?
YES... TOO BAD HE RISKED IT ALL TO DEFECT JUST BEFORE THE REGIME COLLAPSED ON ITS OWN.
I SUPPOSE HE WAS SEEKING FREEDOM, BUT I DON'T GET IT. AND THEN HE WOUND UP MUR-DERED...
DO YOU REMEMBER THE LIEBERTS HAVING TWINS? A BOY AND A GIRL?

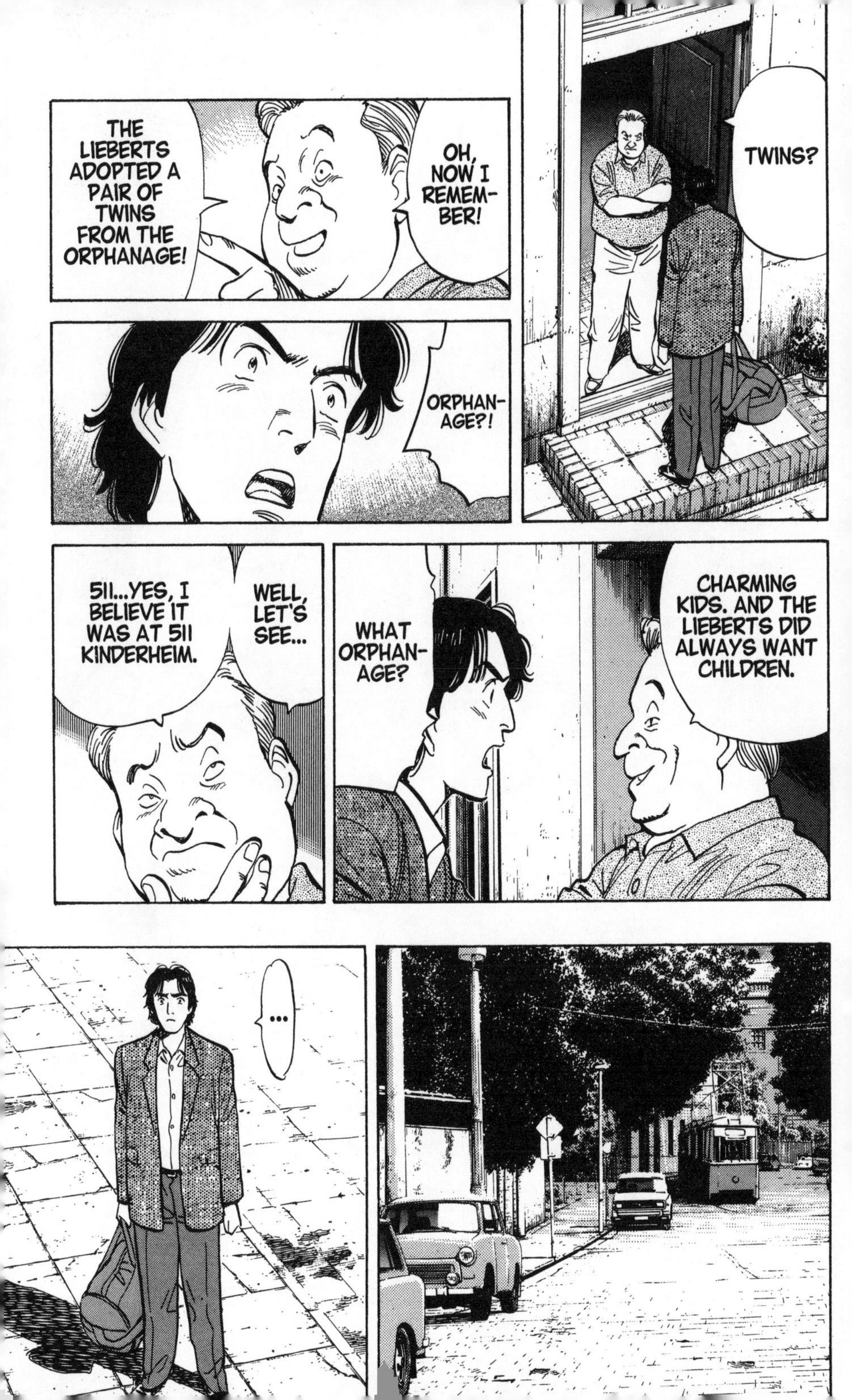
TWINS?
OH, NOW I REMEMBER!
THE LIEBERTS ADOPTED A PAIR OF TWINS FROM THE ORPHANAGE!
ORPHANAGE?!
CHARMING KIDS. AND THE LIEBERTS DID ALWAYS WANT CHILDREN.
WHAT ORPHANAGE?
WELL, LET'S SEE...
511...YES, I BELIEVE IT WAS AT 511 KINDERHEIM.
...

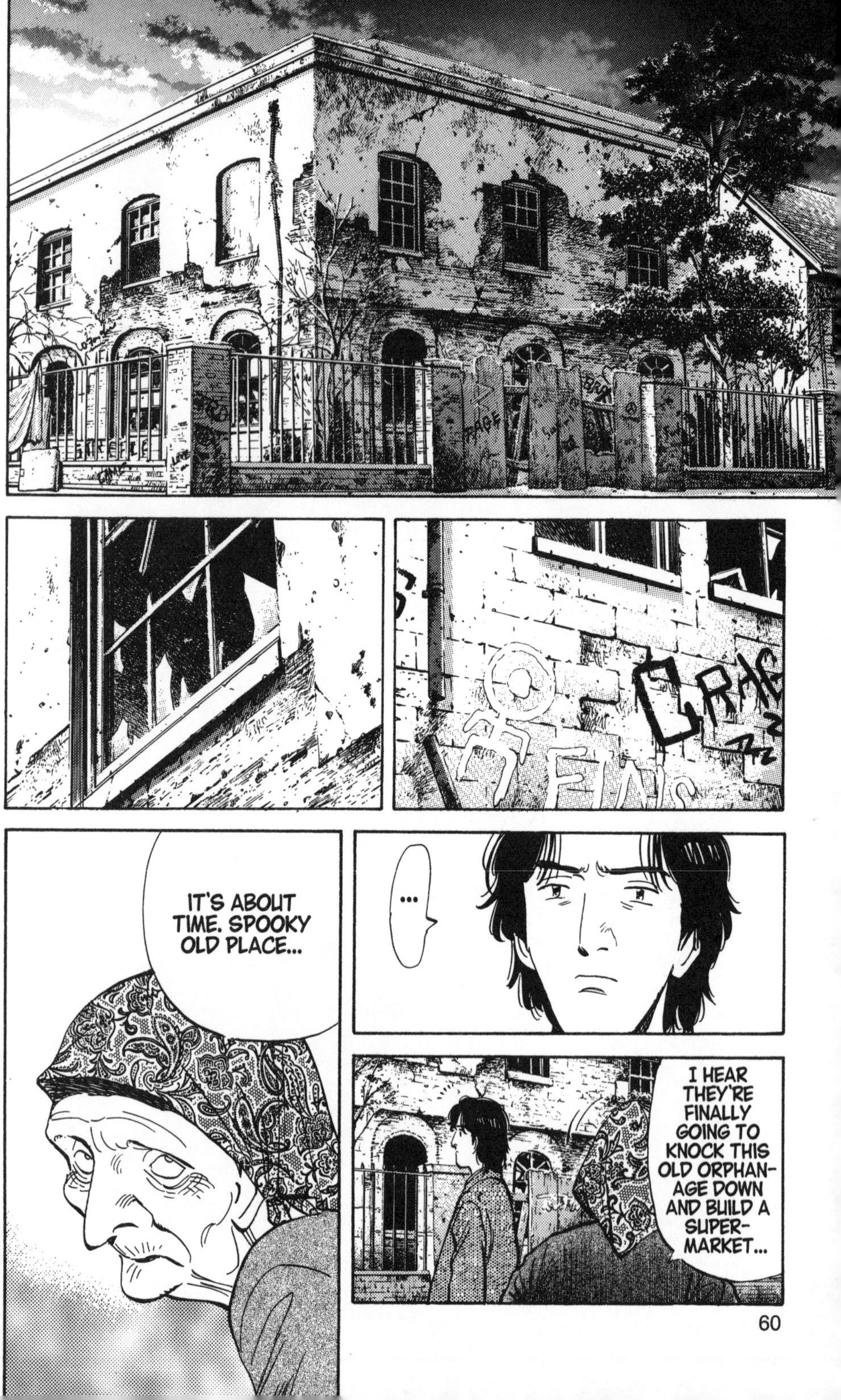
...
I HEAR THEY'RE FINALLY GOING TO KNOCK THIS OLD ORPHANAGE DOWN AND BUILD A SUPERMARKET...
IT'S ABOUT TIME. SPOOKY OLD PLACE...

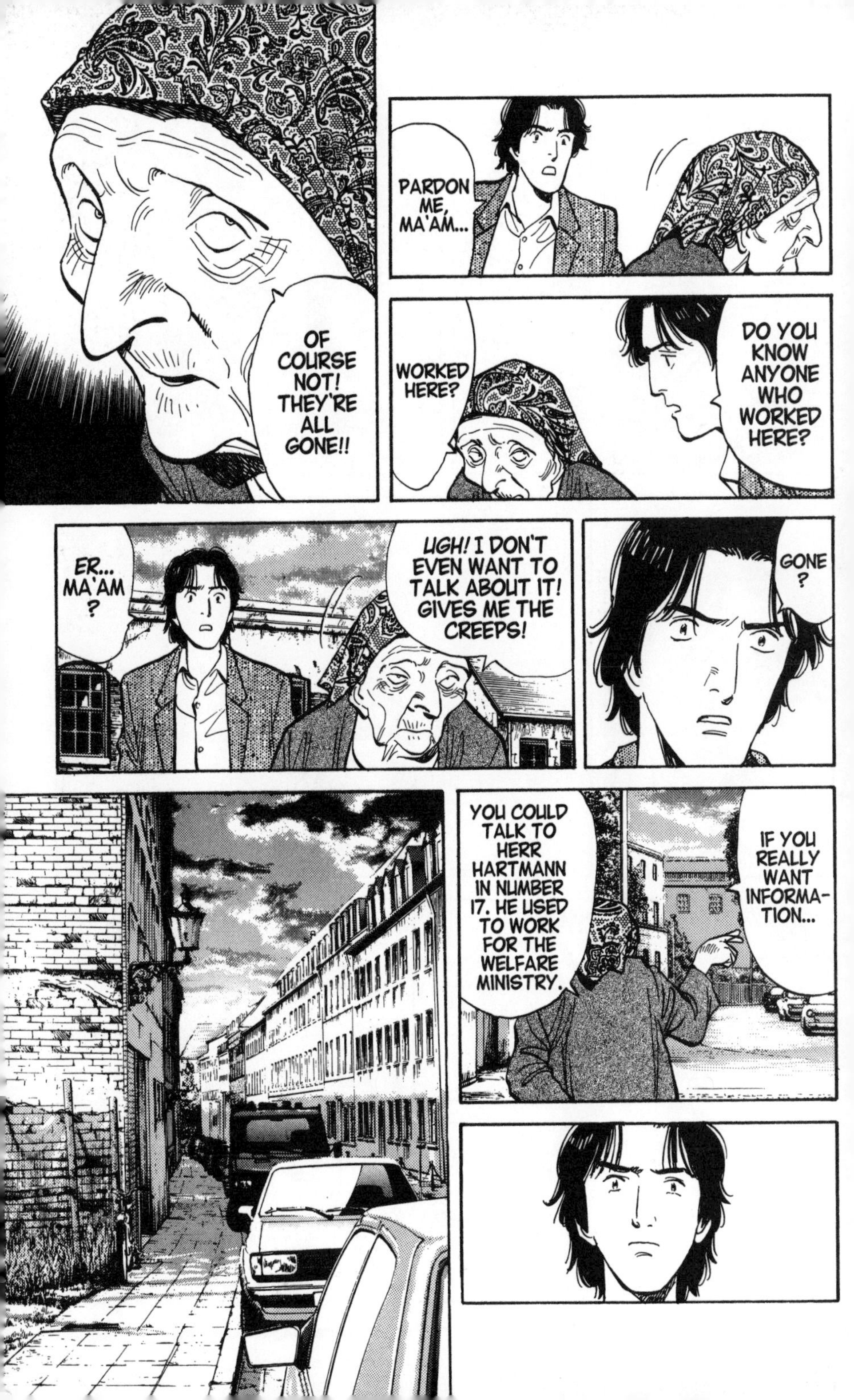
PARDON ME, MA'AM...
DO YOU KNOW ANYONE WHO WORKED HERE?
WORKED HERE?
OF COURSE NOT! THEY'RE ALL GONE!!
GONE?
UGH! I DON'T EVEN WANT TO TALK ABOUT IT! GIVES ME THE CREEPS!
ER... MA'AM?
IF YOU REALLY WANT INFORMATION...
YOU COULD TALK TO HERR HARTMANN IN NUMBER 17. HE USED TO WORK FOR THE WELFARE MINISTRY.

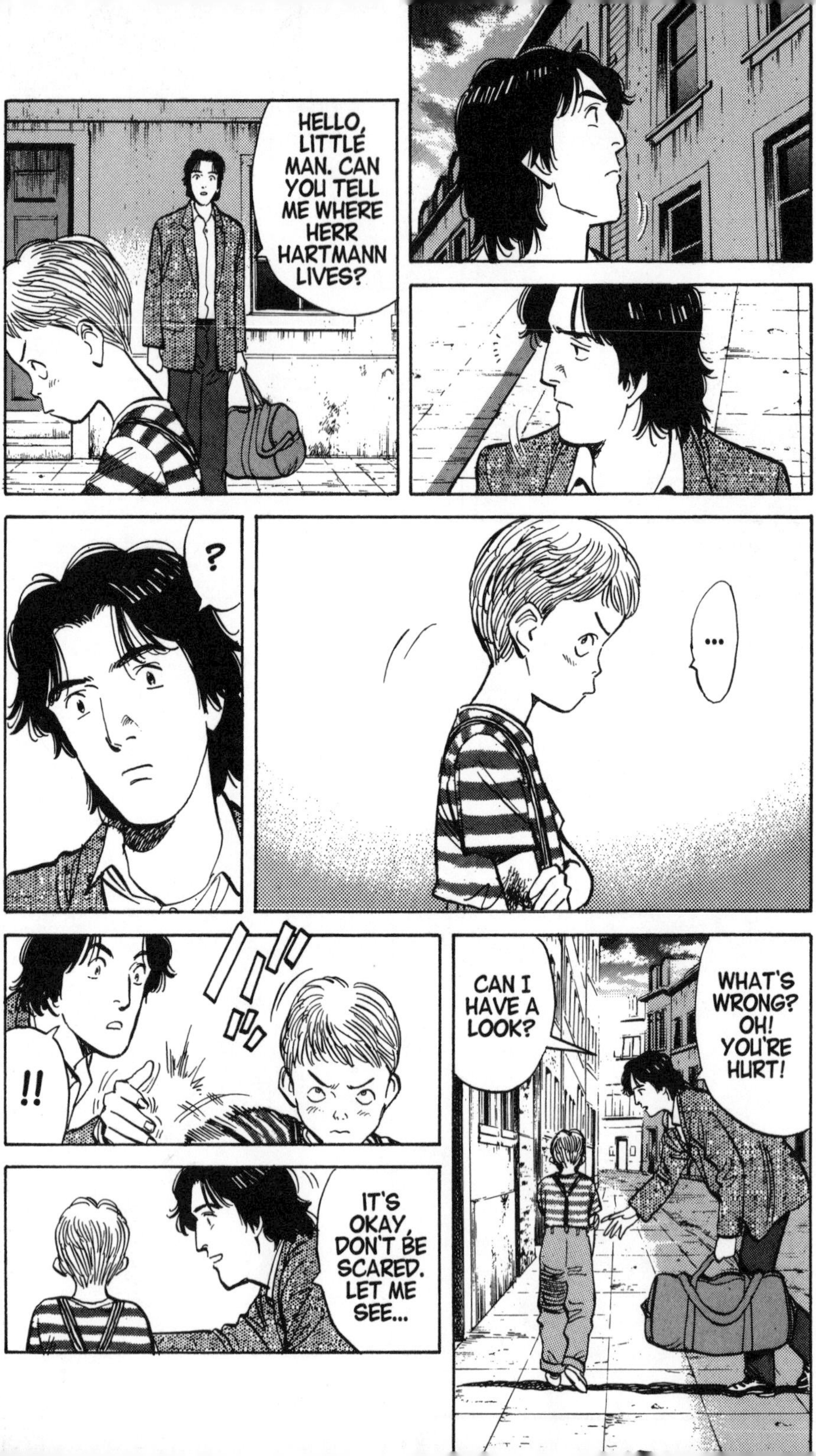
HELLO, LITTLE MAN. CAN YOU TELL ME WHERE HERR HARTMANN LIVES?
...
?
WHAT'S WRONG? OH! YOU'RE HURT!
CAN I HAVE A LOOK?
!!
IT'S OKAY, DON'T BE SCARED. LET ME SEE...

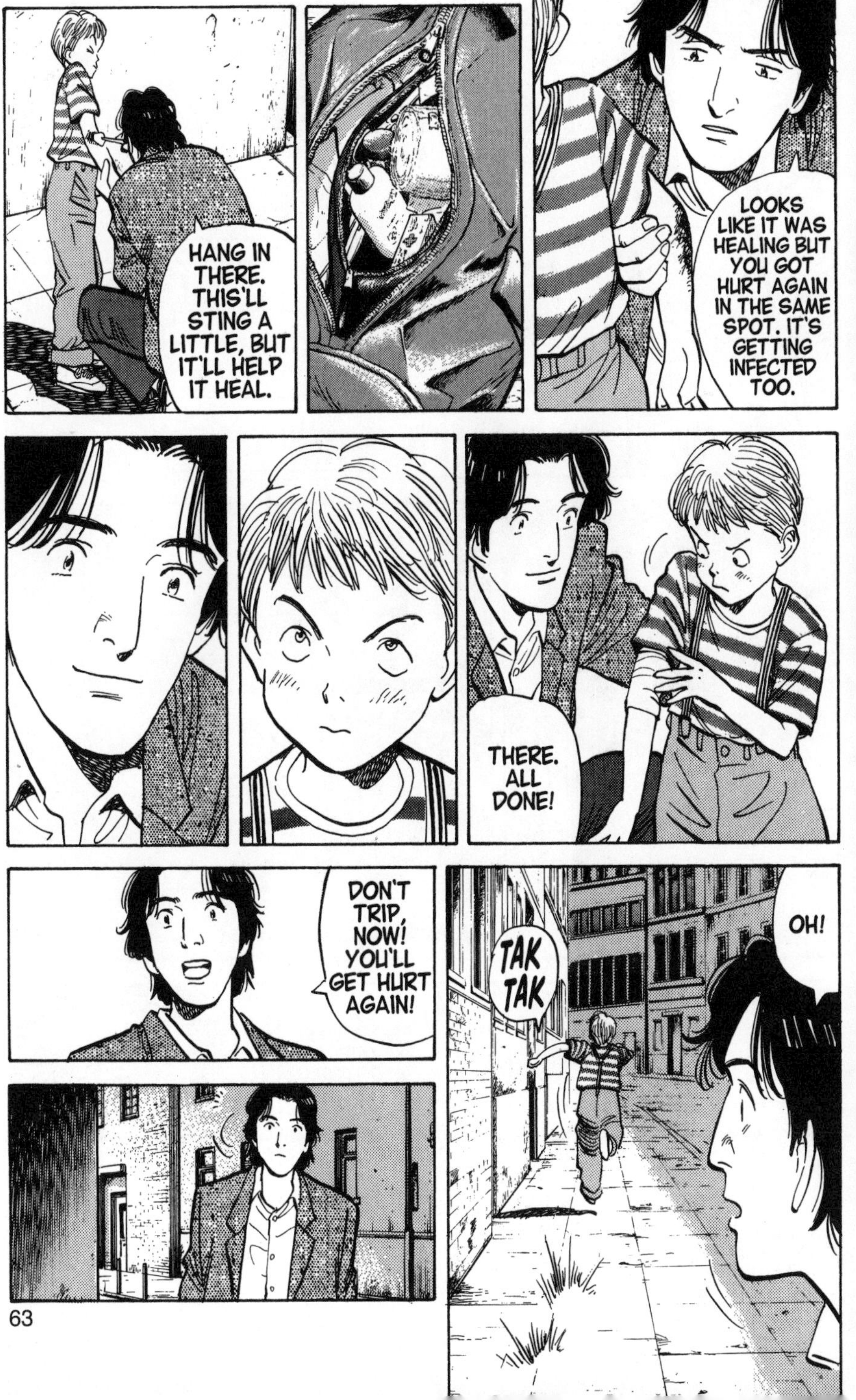
LOOKS LIKE IT WAS HEALING BUT YOU GOT HURT AGAIN IN THE SAME SPOT. IT'S GETTING INFECTED TOO.
HANG IN THERE. THIS'LL STING A LITTLE, BUT IT'LL HELP IT HEAL.
THERE. ALL DONE!
OH!
TAK TAK
DON'T TRIP, NOW! YOU'LL GET HURT AGAIN!

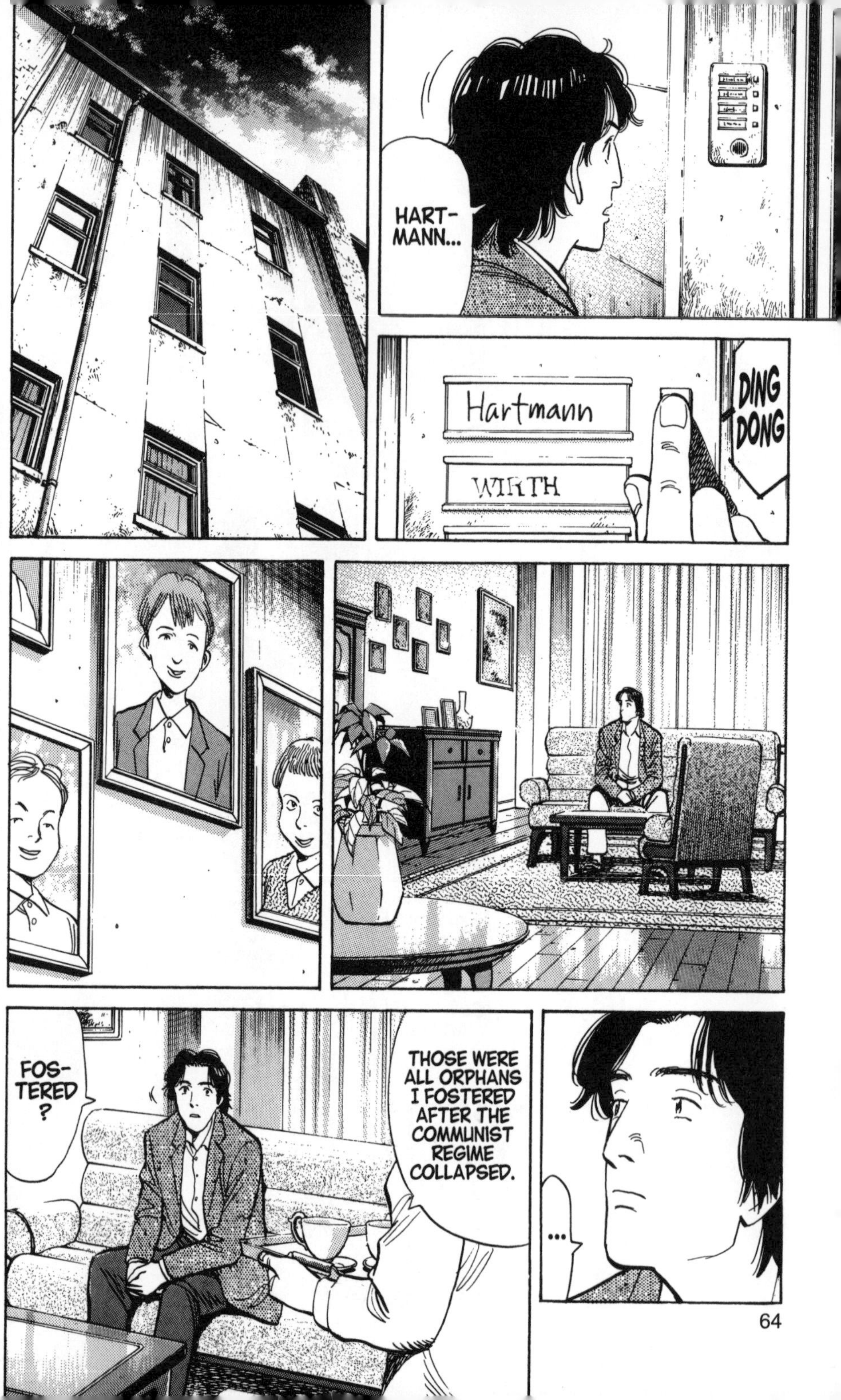
HART-MANN...
Hartmann
WIRTH
DING DONG
...
THOSE WERE ALL ORPHANS I FOSTERED AFTER THE COMMUNIST REGIME COLLAPSED.
FOS-TERED?

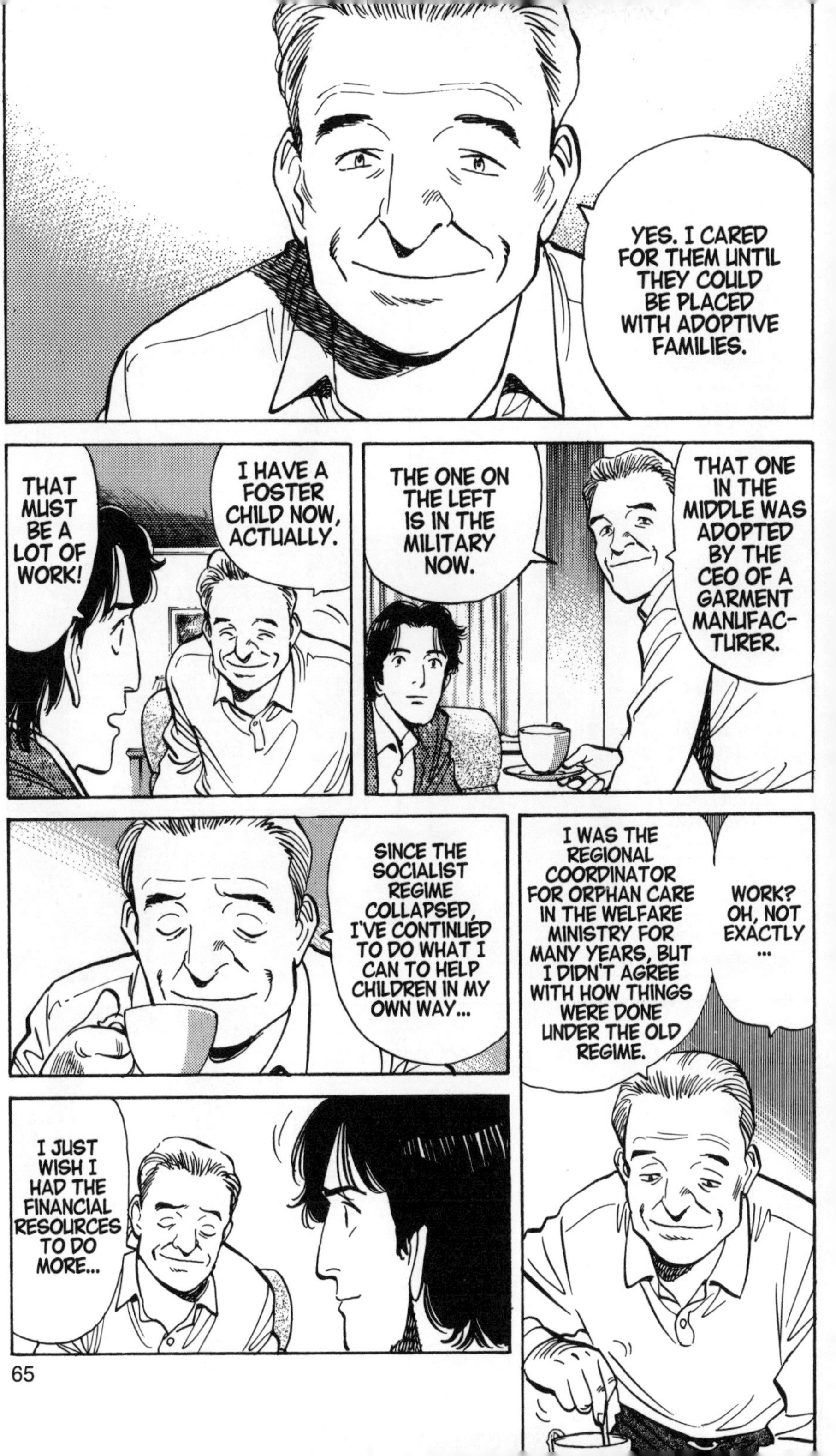
YES. I CARED FOR THEM UNTIL THEY COULD BE PLACED WITH ADOPTIVE FAMILIES.
THAT ONE IN THE MIDDLE WAS ADOPTED BY THE CEO OF A GARMENT MANUFAC-TURER.
THE ONE ON THE LEFT IS IN THE MILITARY NOW.
I HAVE A FOSTER CHILD NOW, ACTUALLY.
THAT MUST BE A LOT OF WORK!
WORK? OH, NOT EXACTLY ...
I WAS THE REGIONAL COORDINATOR FOR ORPHAN CARE IN THE WELFARE MINISTRY FOR MANY YEARS, BUT I DIDN'T AGREE WITH HOW THINGS WERE DONE UNDER THE OLD REGIME.
SINCE THE SOCIALIST REGIME COLLAPSED, I'VE CONTINUED TO DO WHAT I CAN TO HELP CHILDREN IN MY OWN WAY...
I JUST WISH I HAD THE FINANCIAL RESOURCES TO DO MORE...

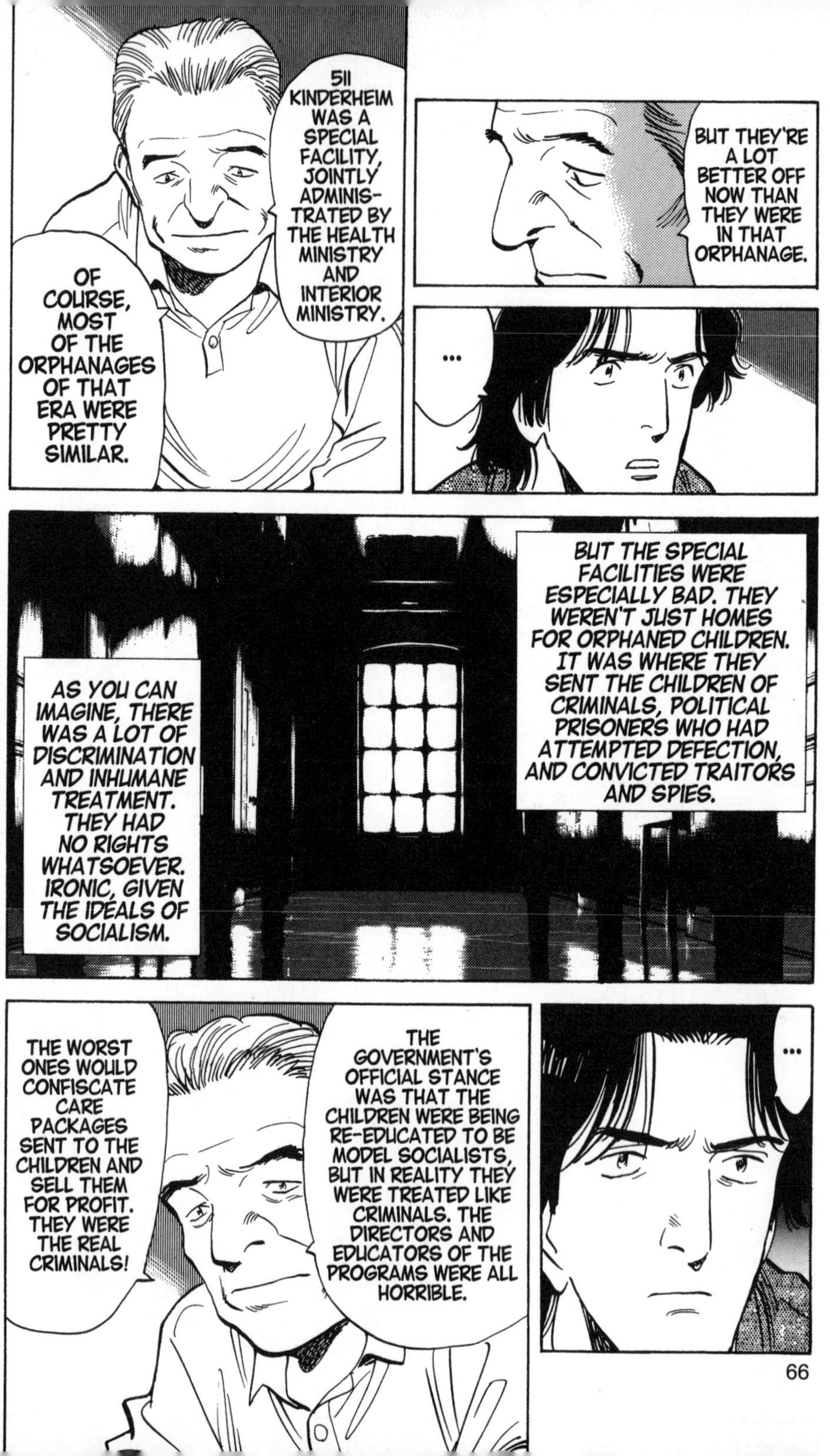
BUT THEY'RE A LOT BETTER OFF NOW THAN THEY WERE IN THAT ORPHANAGE.
...
511 KINDERHEIM WAS A SPECIAL FACILITY, JOINTLY ADMINIS-TRATED BY THE HEALTH MINISTRY AND INTERIOR MINISTRY.
OF COURSE, MOST OF THE ORPHANAGES OF THAT ERA WERE PRETTY SIMILAR.
BUT THE SPECIAL FACILITIES WERE ESPECIALLY BAD. THEY WEREN'T JUST HOMES FOR ORPHANED CHILDREN. IT WAS WHERE THEY SENT THE CHILDREN OF CRIMINALS, POLITICAL PRISONERS WHO HAD ATTEMPTED DEFECTION, AND CONVICTED TRAITORS AND SPIES.
AS YOU CAN IMAGINE, THERE WAS A LOT OF DISCRIMINATION AND INHUMANE TREATMENT. THEY HAD NO RIGHTS WHATSOEVER. IRONIC, GIVEN THE IDEALS OF SOCIALISM.
...
THE GOVERNMENT'S OFFICIAL STANCE WAS THAT THE CHILDREN WERE BEING RE-EDUCATED TO BE MODEL SOCIALISTS, BUT IN REALITY THEY WERE TREATED LIKE CRIMINALS. THE DIRECTORS AND EDUCATORS OF THE PROGRAMS WERE ALL HORRIBLE.
THE WORST ONES WOULD CONFISCATE CARE PACKAGES SENT TO THE CHILDREN AND SELL THEM FOR PROFIT. THEY WERE THE REAL CRIMINALS!

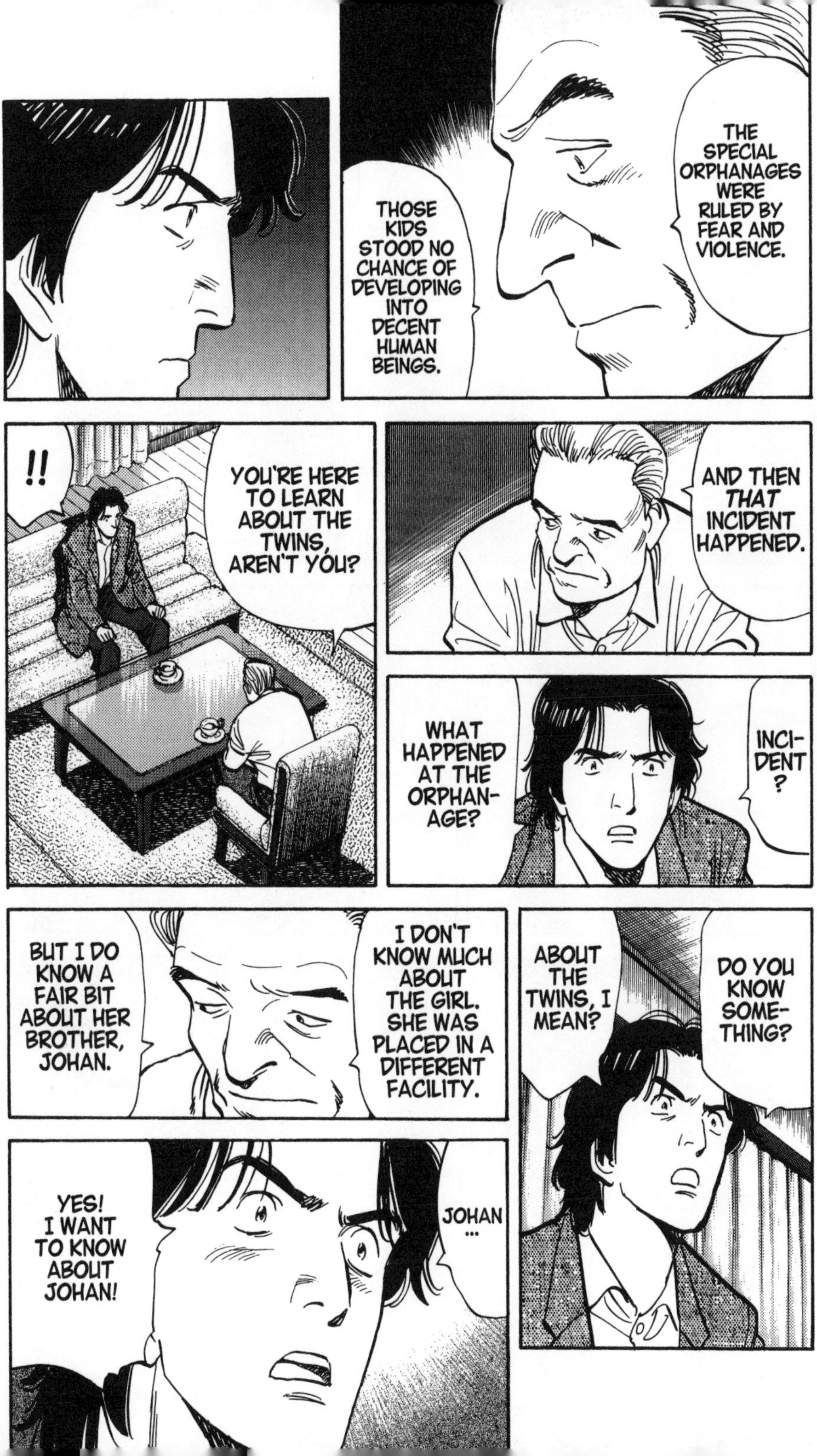
THE SPECIAL ORPHANAGES WERE RULED BY FEAR AND VIOLENCE.
THOSE KIDS STOOD NO CHANCE OF DEVELOPING INTO DECENT HUMAN BEINGS.
AND THEN *THAT* INCIDENT HAPPENED.
INCI-DENT?
WHAT HAPPENED AT THE ORPHAN-AGE?
YOU'RE HERE TO LEARN ABOUT THE TWINS, AREN'T YOU?
!!
DO YOU KNOW SOME-THING?
ABOUT THE TWINS, I MEAN?
I DON'T KNOW MUCH ABOUT THE GIRL. SHE WAS PLACED IN A DIFFERENT FACILITY.
BUT I DO KNOW A FAIR BIT ABOUT HER BROTHER, JOHAN.
JOHAN...
YES! I WANT TO KNOW ABOUT JOHAN!

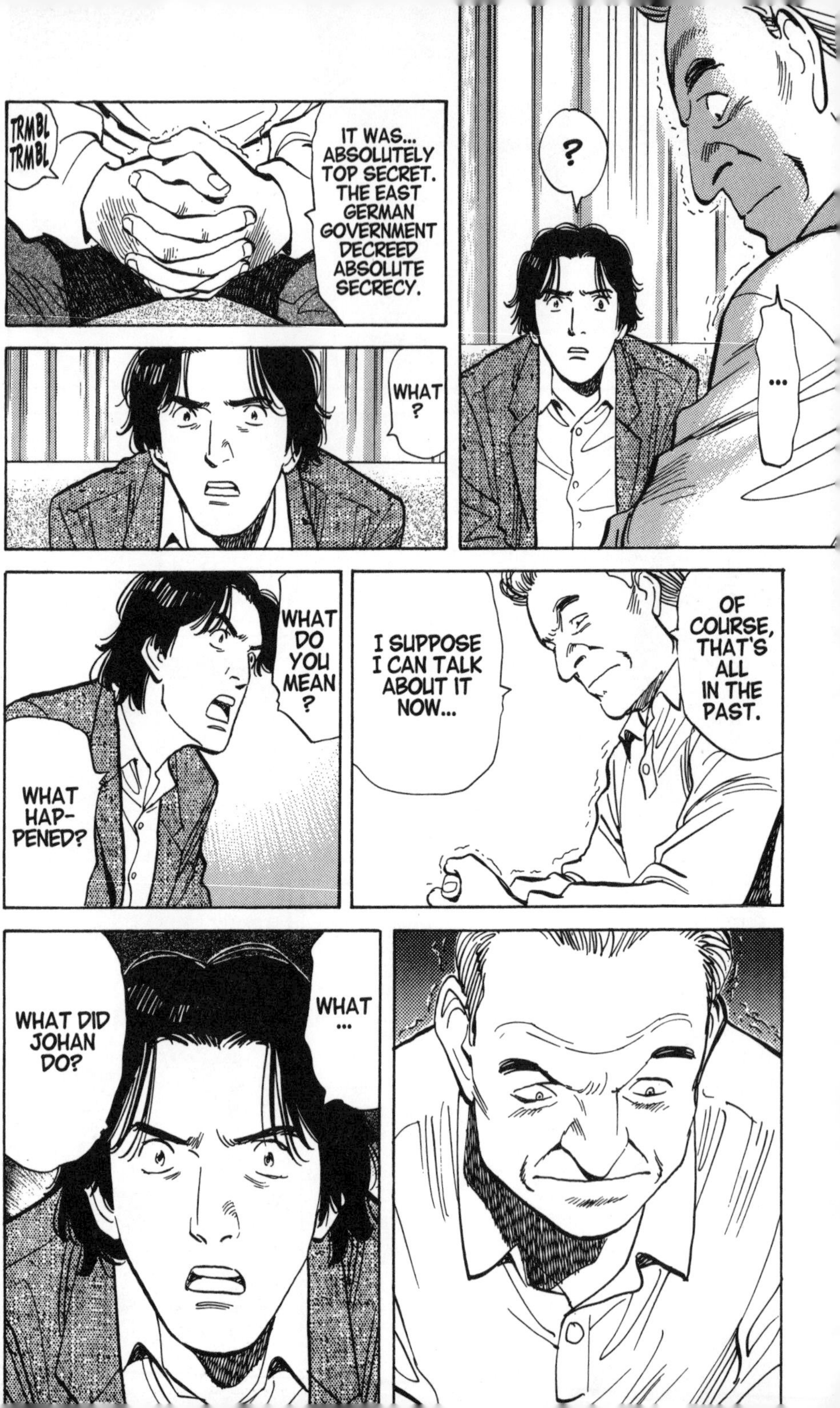
?
...
IT WAS... ABSOLUTELY TOP SECRET. THE EAST GERMAN GOVERNMENT DECREED ABSOLUTE SECRECY.
TRMBL TRMBL
WHAT?
OF COURSE, THAT'S ALL IN THE PAST.
I SUPPOSE I CAN TALK ABOUT IT NOW...
WHAT DO YOU MEAN?
WHAT HAPPENED?
WHAT...
WHAT DID JOHAN DO?

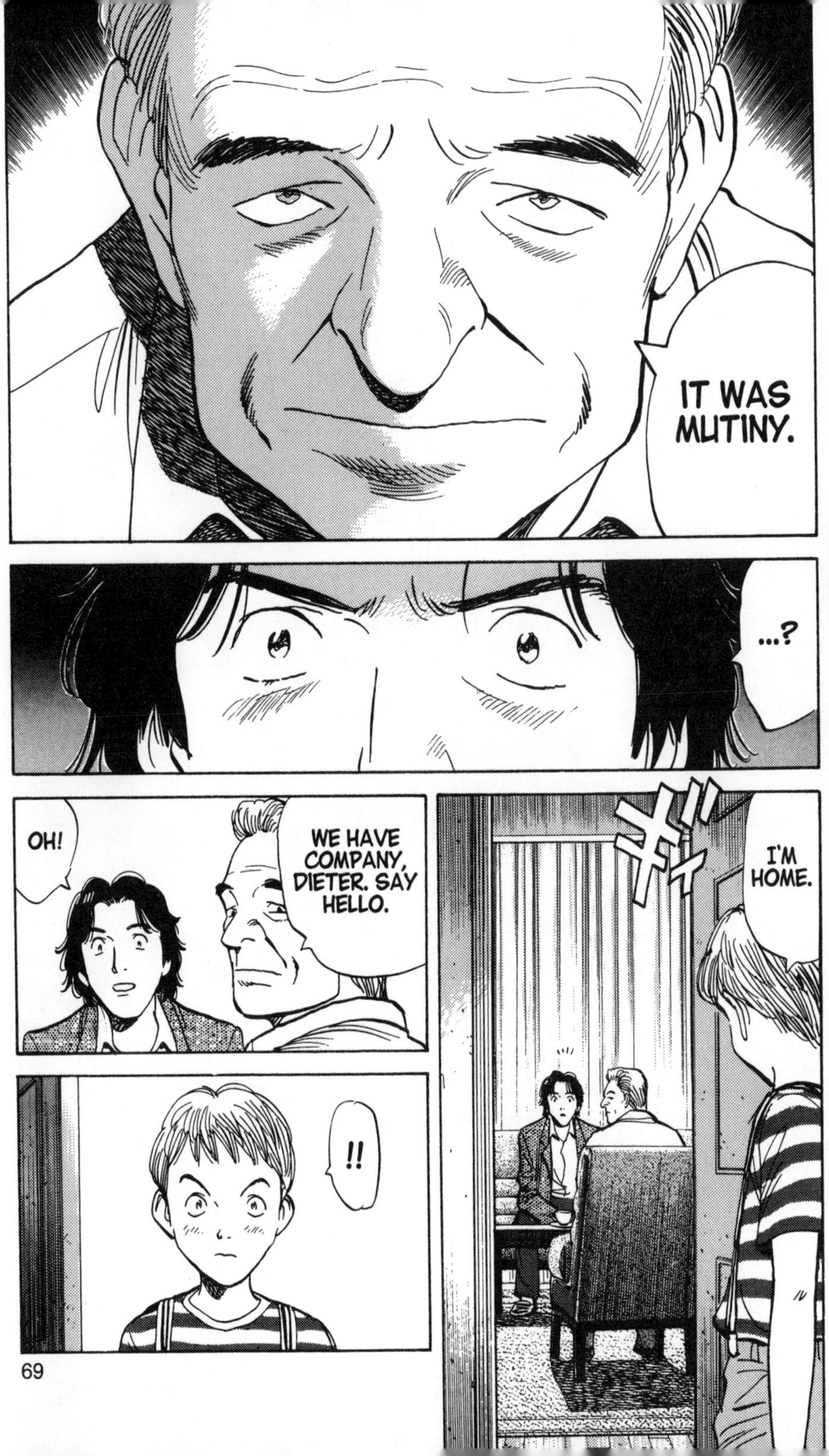
IT WAS MUTINY.
...?
ギィ
I'M HOME.
WE HAVE COMPANY, DIETER. SAY HELLO.
OH!
!!

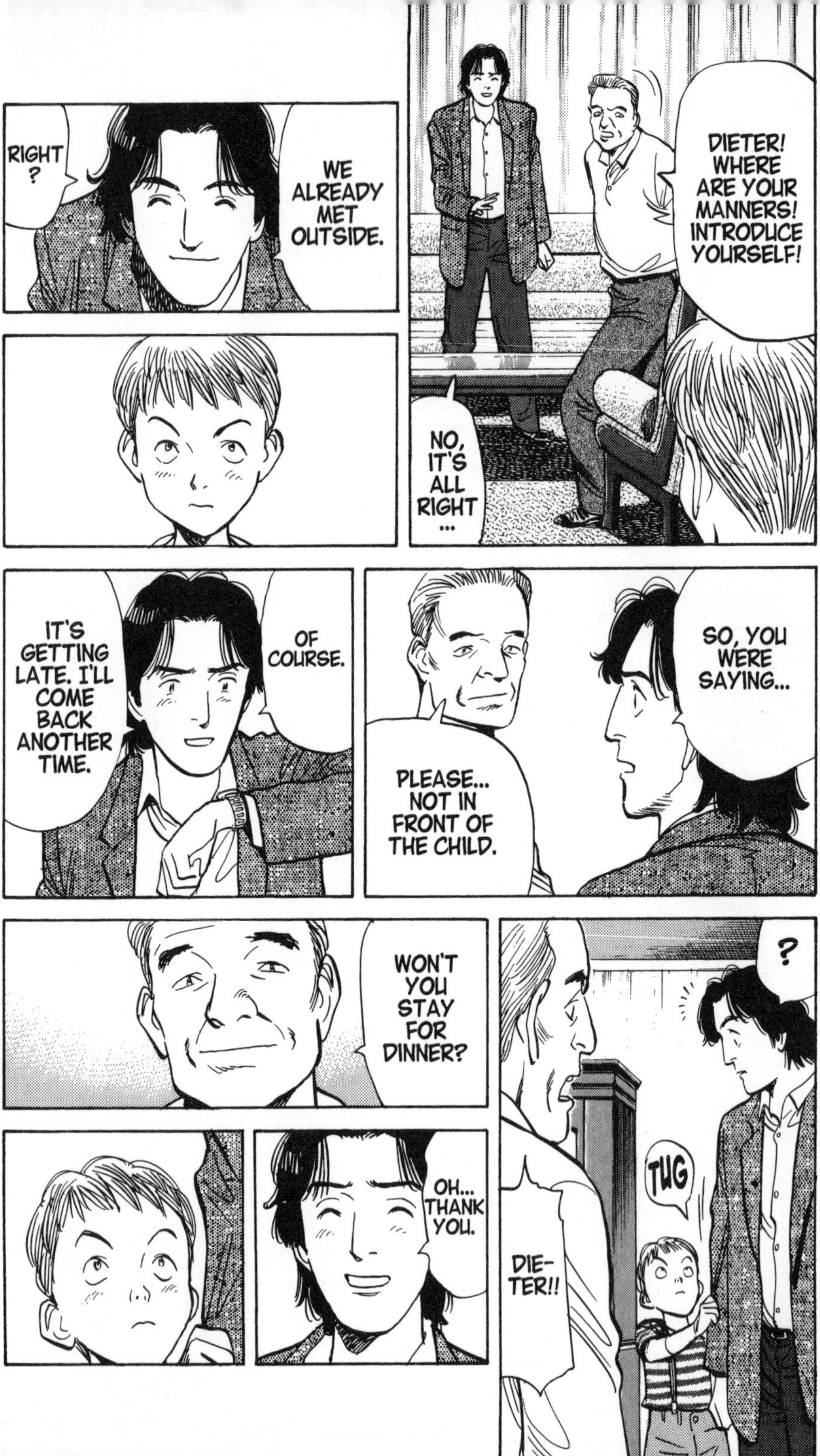
DIETER! WHERE ARE YOUR MANNERS! INTRODUCE YOURSELF!
NO, IT'S ALL RIGHT...
WE ALREADY MET OUTSIDE.
RIGHT?
SO, YOU WERE SAYING...
PLEASE... NOT IN FRONT OF THE CHILD.
OF COURSE.
IT'S GETTING LATE. I'LL COME BACK ANOTHER TIME.
?
TUG
DIE-TER!!
WON'T YOU STAY FOR DINNER?
OH... THANK YOU.

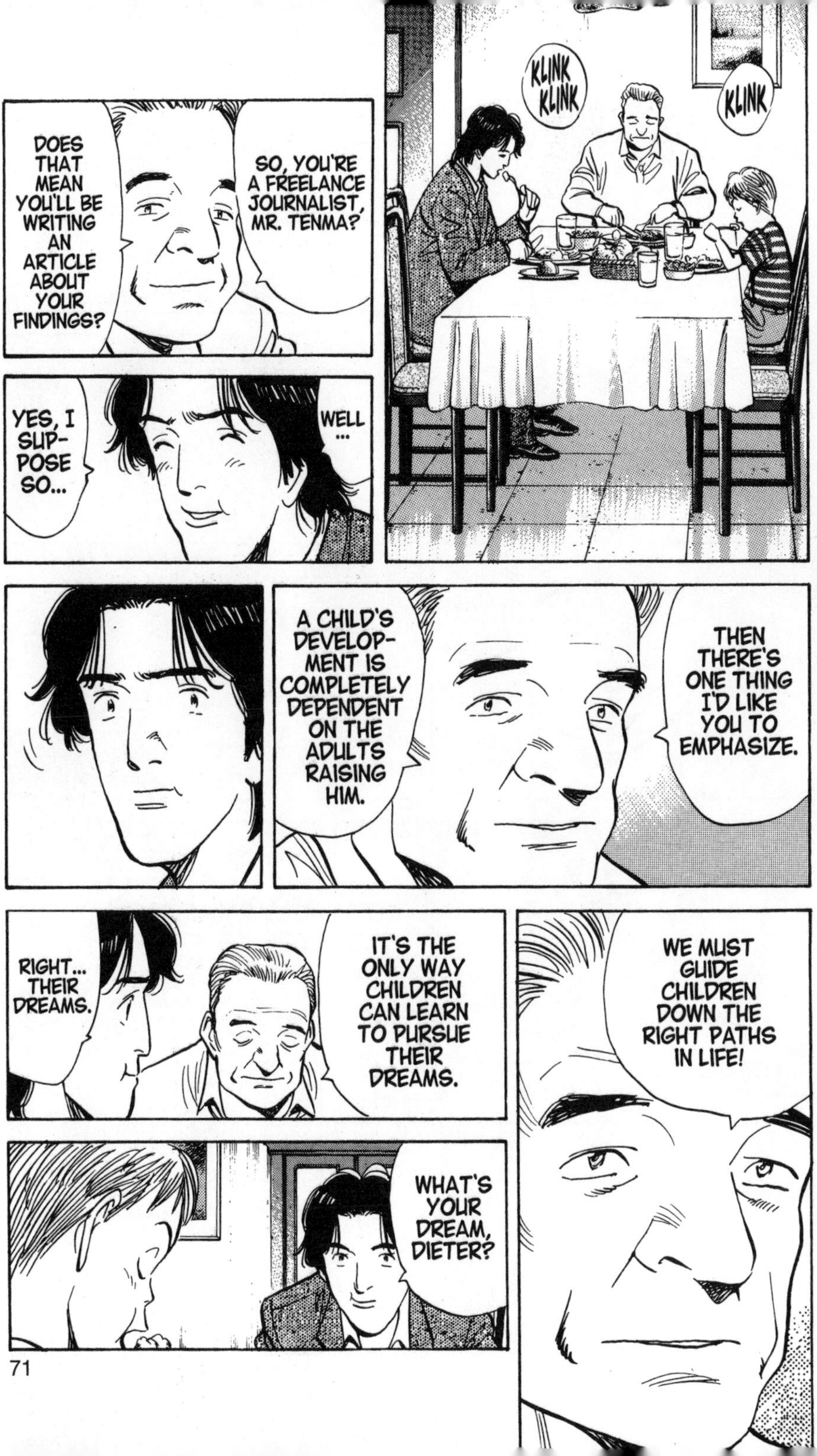
KLINK KLINK
KLINK
SO, YOU'RE A FREELANCE JOURNALIST, MR. TENMA?
DOES THAT MEAN YOU'LL BE WRITING AN ARTICLE ABOUT YOUR FINDINGS?
WELL...
YES, I SUPPOSE SO...
THEN THERE'S ONE THING I'D LIKE YOU TO EMPHASIZE.
A CHILD'S DEVELOPMENT IS COMPLETELY DEPENDENT ON THE ADULTS RAISING HIM.
WE MUST GUIDE CHILDREN DOWN THE RIGHT PATHS IN LIFE!
IT'S THE ONLY WAY CHILDREN CAN LEARN TO PURSUE THEIR DREAMS.
RIGHT... THEIR DREAMS.
WHAT'S YOUR DREAM, DIETER?

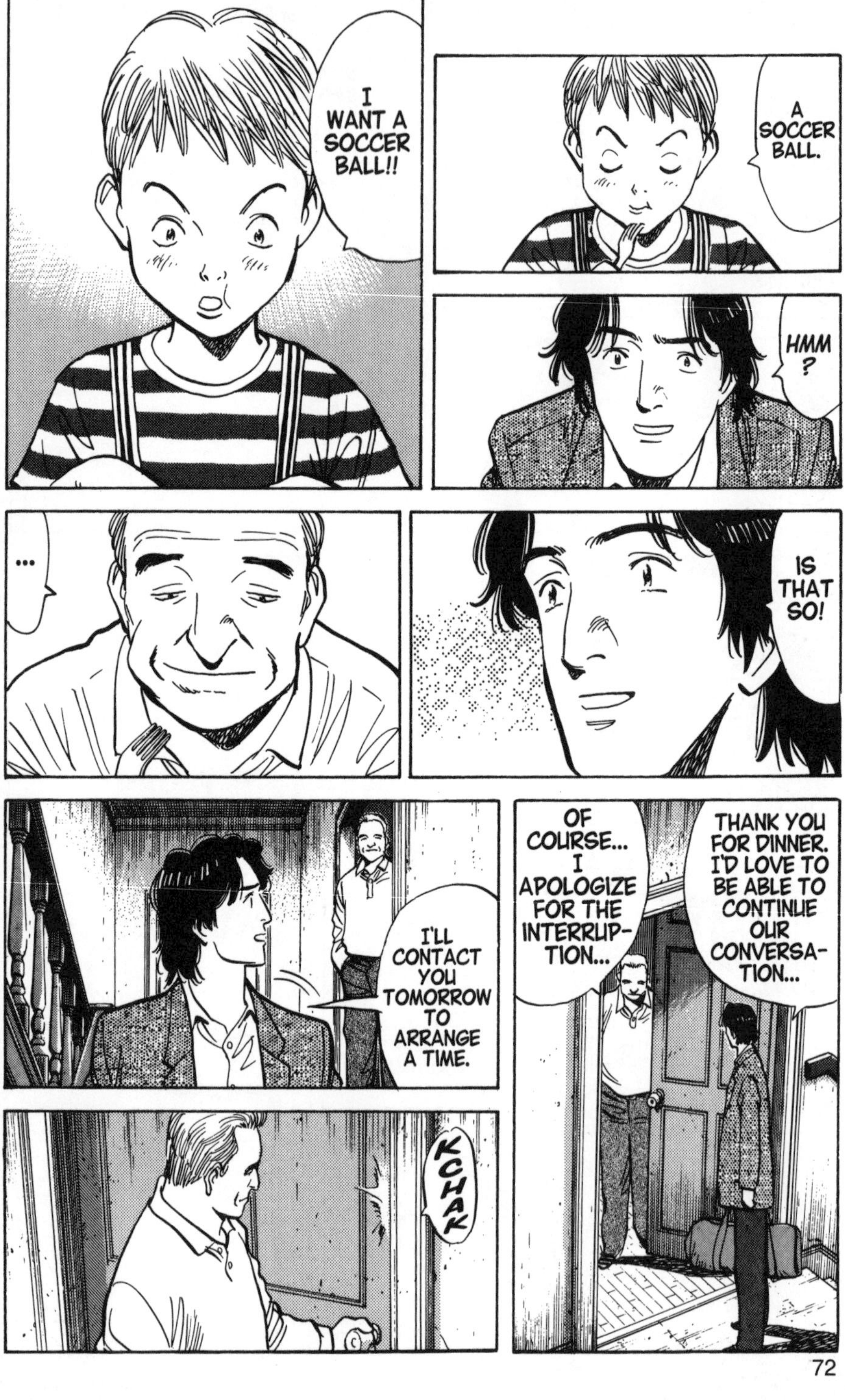
A SOCCER BALL.
HMM ?
I WANT A SOCCER BALL!!
IS THAT SO!
...
THANK YOU FOR DINNER. I'D LOVE TO BE ABLE TO CONTINUE OUR CONVERSA-TION...
OF COURSE... I APOLOGIZE FOR THE INTERRUP-TION...
I'LL CONTACT YOU TOMORROW TO ARRANGE A TIME.
KCHAK

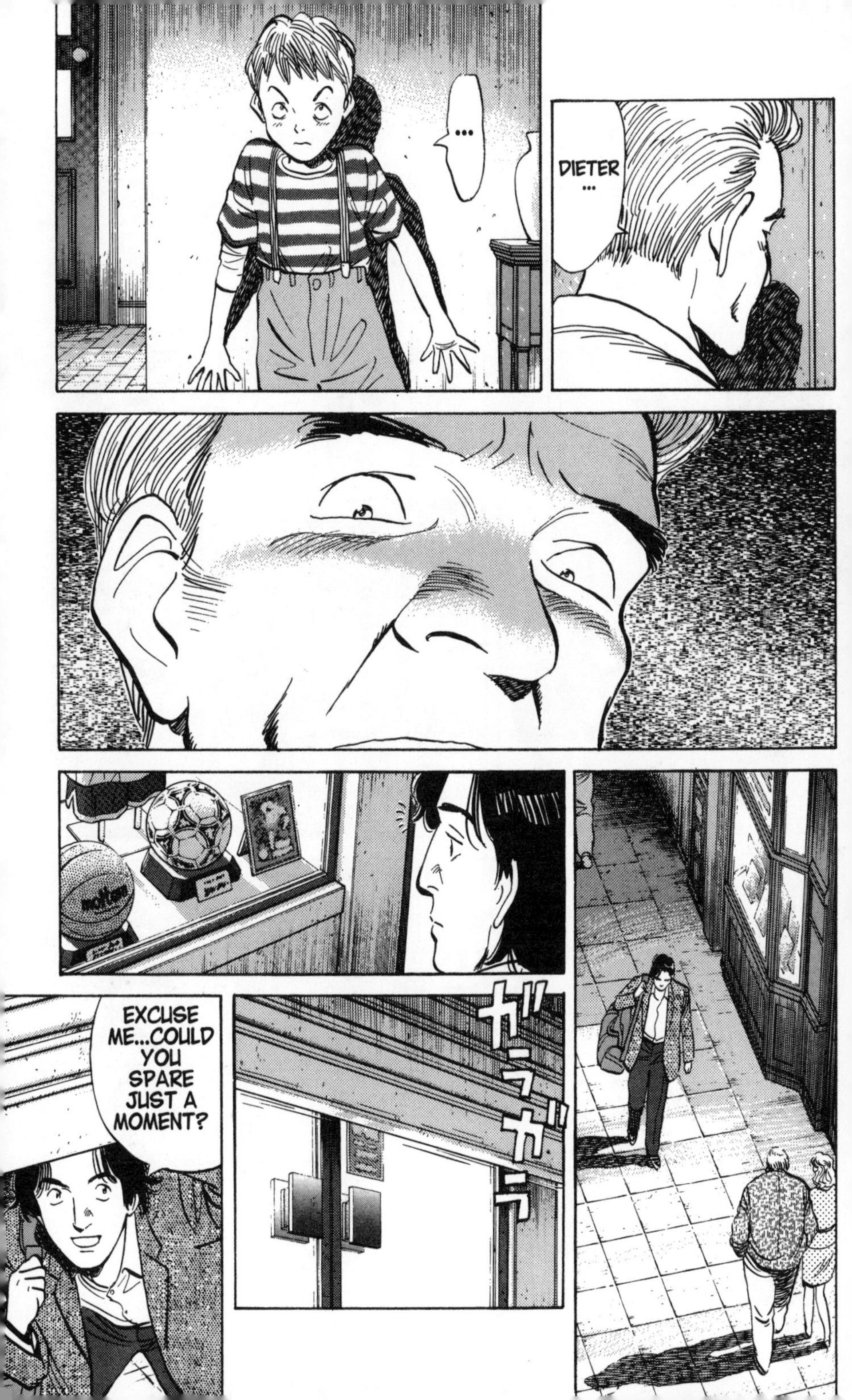
DIETER ...
...
ガラガラ
EXCUSE ME...COULD YOU SPARE JUST A MOMENT?

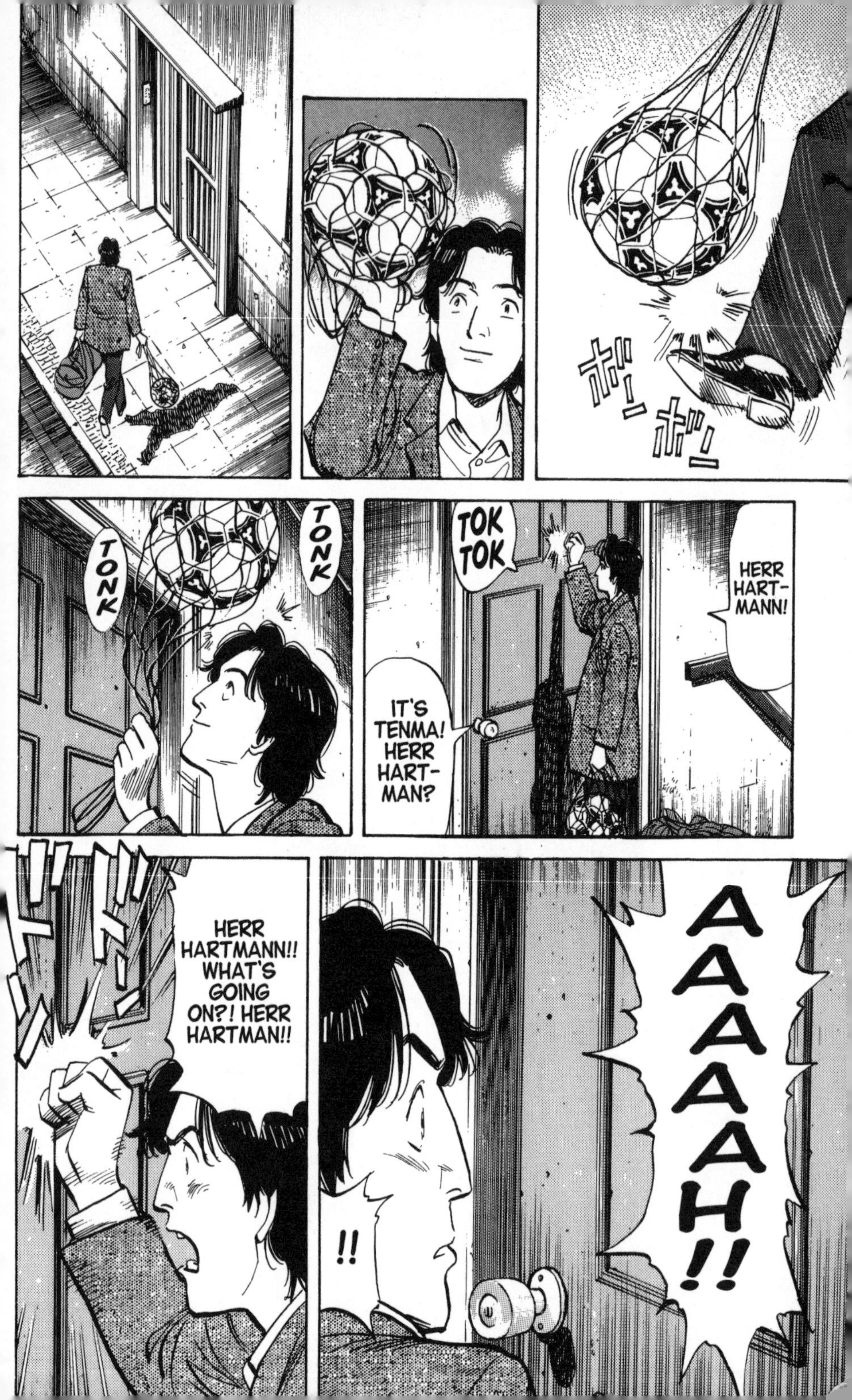
HERR HART-MANN!
TOK TOK
IT'S TENMA! HERR HART-MAN?
TONK
TONK
AAAAAH!!
!!
HERR HARTMANN!! WHAT'S GOING ON?! HERR HARTMAN!!

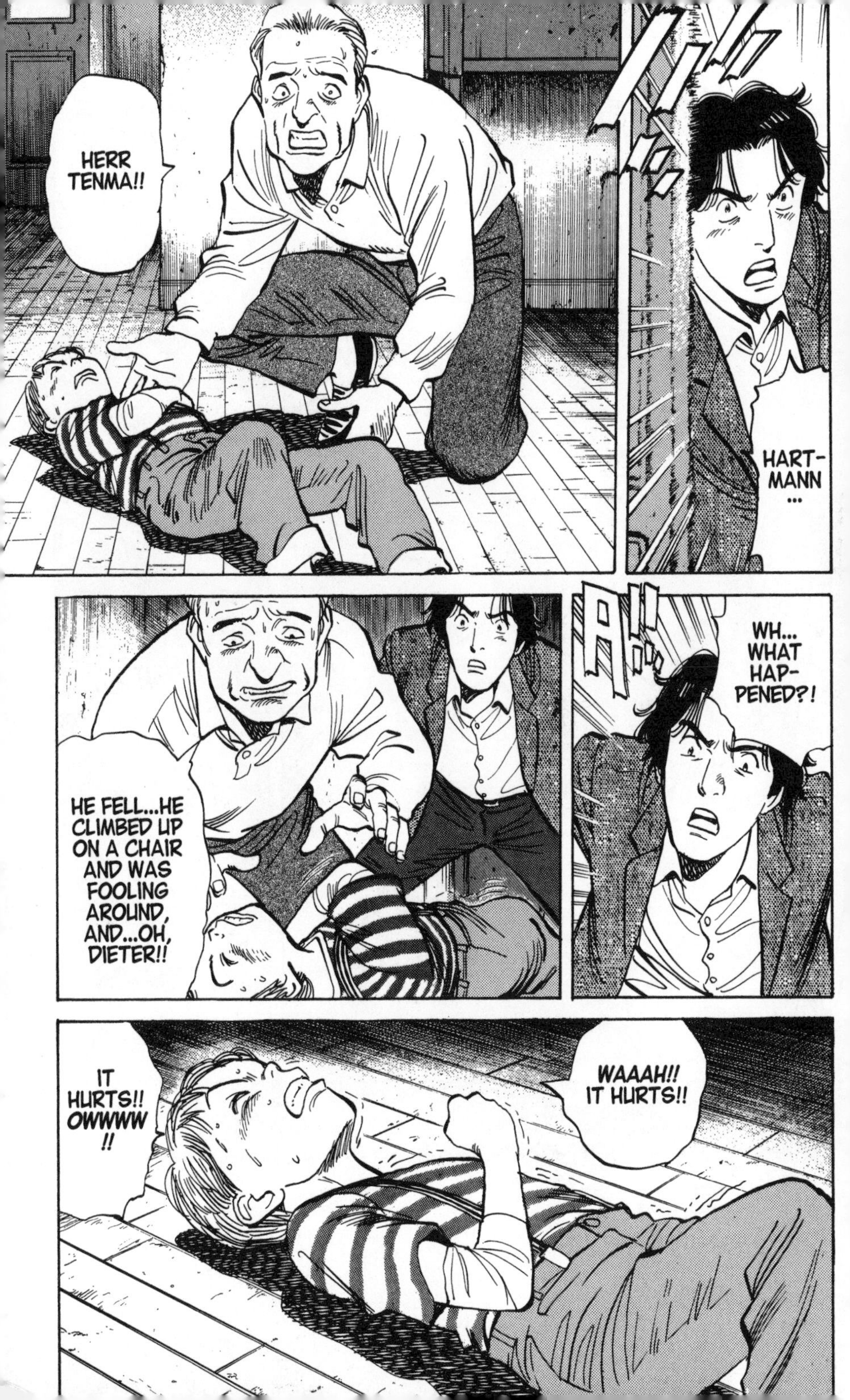
HART-MANN...
HERR TENMA!!
WH... WHAT HAPPENED?!
HE FELL...HE CLIMBED UP ON A CHAIR AND WAS FOOLING AROUND, AND...OH, DIETER!!
WAAAH!! IT HURTS!!
IT HURTS!! OWWWW!!

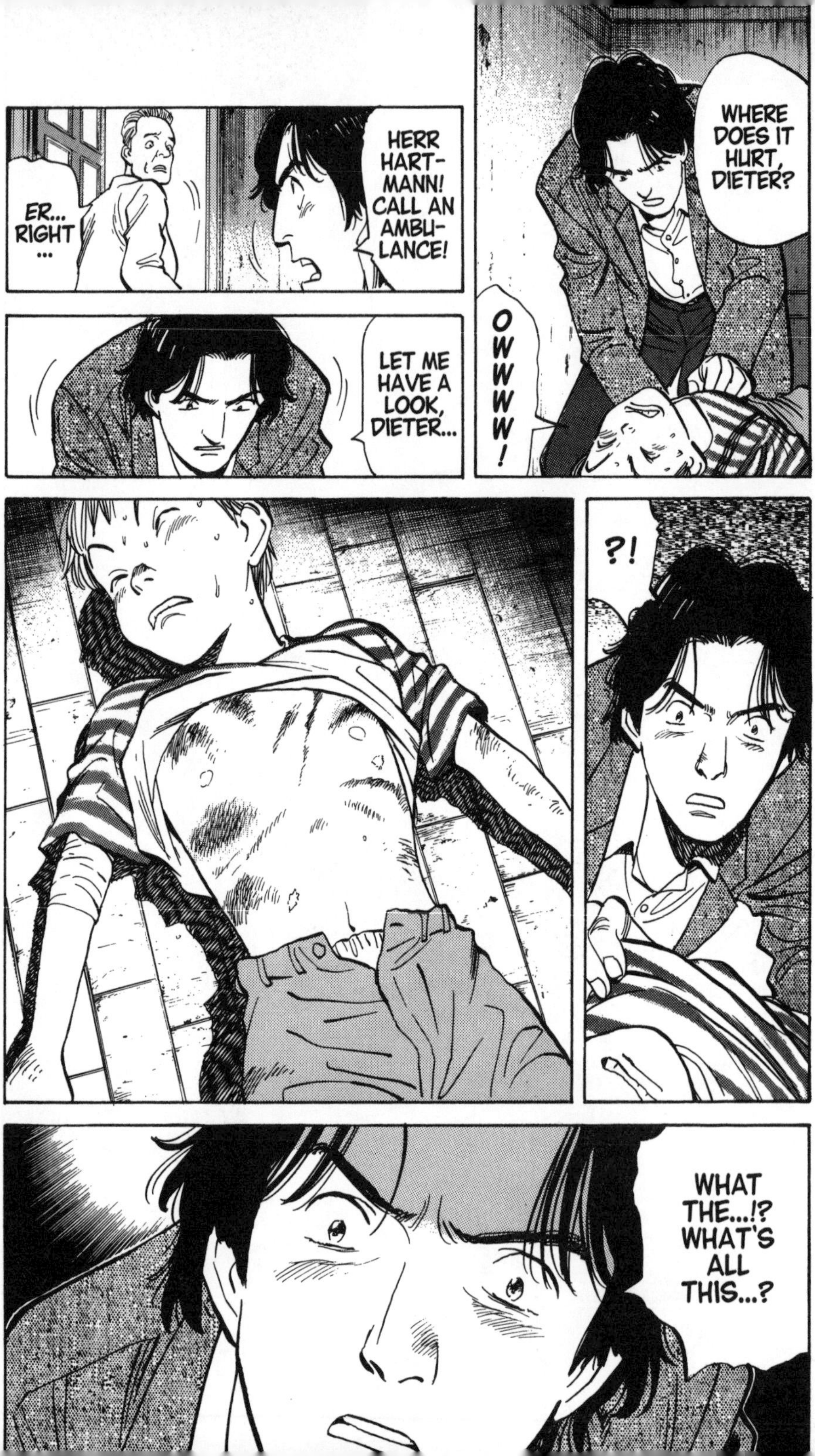
WHERE DOES IT HURT, DIETER?
OWWWWW!
HERR HART-MANN! CALL AN AMBU-LANCE!
ER... RIGHT ...
LET ME HAVE A LOOK, DIETER...
?!
WHAT THE...!? WHAT'S ALL THIS...?

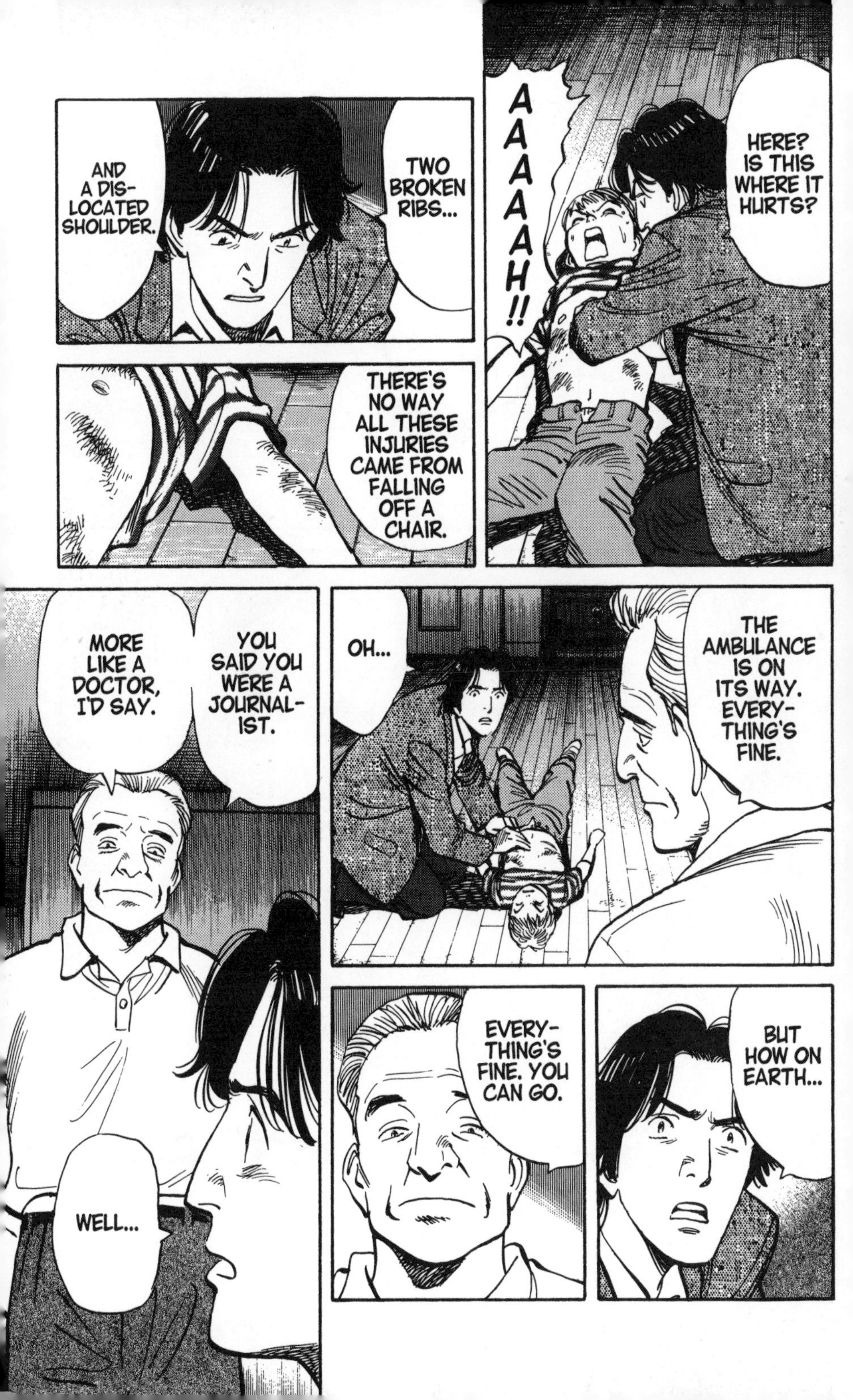
HERE? IS THIS WHERE IT HURTS?
AAAAAAH!!
TWO BROKEN RIBS...
AND A DIS-LOCATED SHOULDER.
THERE'S NO WAY ALL THESE INJURIES CAME FROM FALLING OFF A CHAIR.
THE AMBULANCE IS ON ITS WAY. EVERY-THING'S FINE.
OH...
BUT HOW ON EARTH...
EVERY-THING'S FINE. YOU CAN GO.
YOU SAID YOU WERE A JOURNAL-IST.
MORE LIKE A DOCTOR, I'D SAY.
WELL...

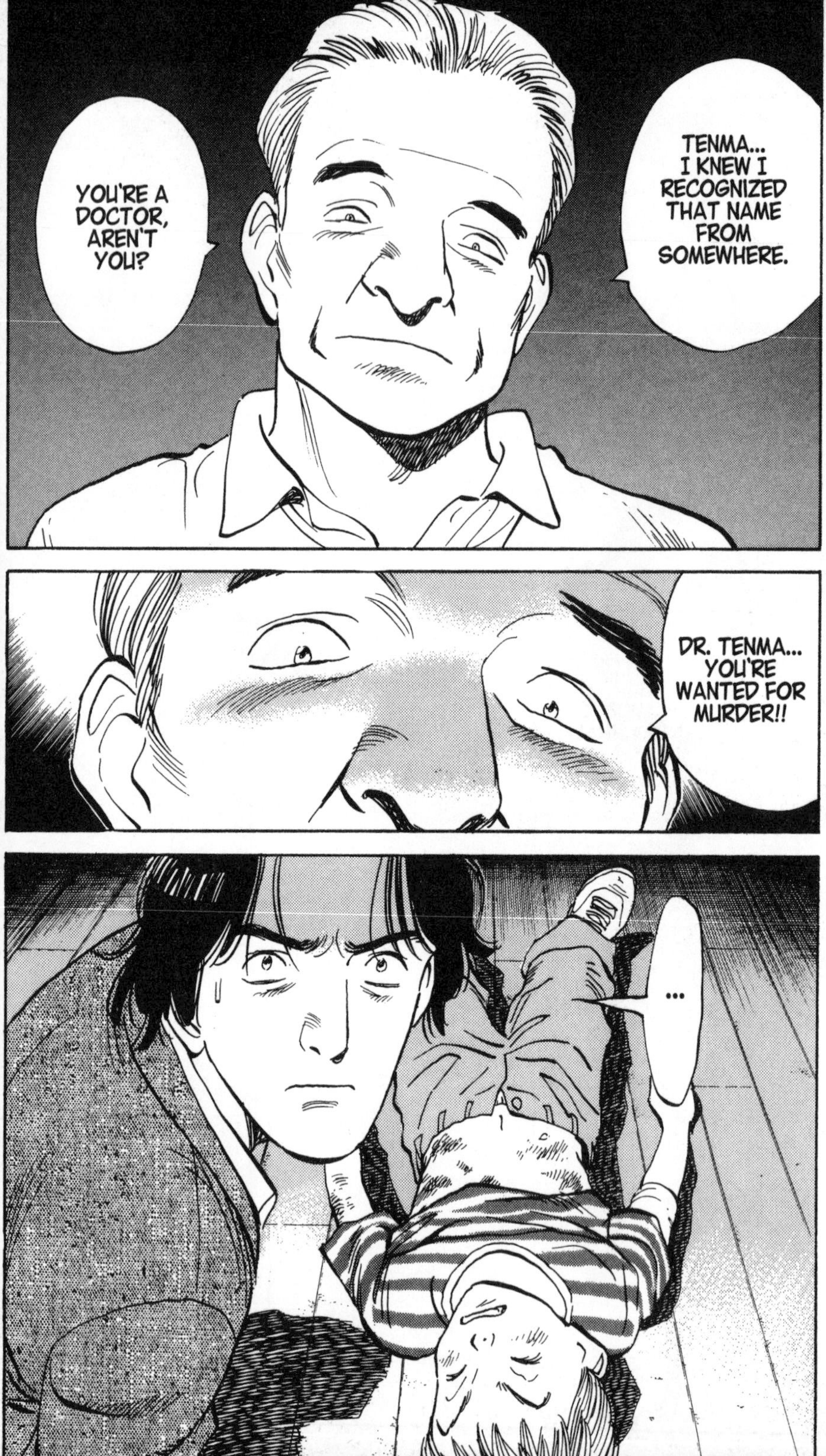
TENMA... I KNEW I RECOGNIZED THAT NAME FROM SOMEWHERE.
YOU'RE A DOCTOR, AREN'T YOU?
DR. TENMA... YOU'RE WANTED FOR MURDER!!
...

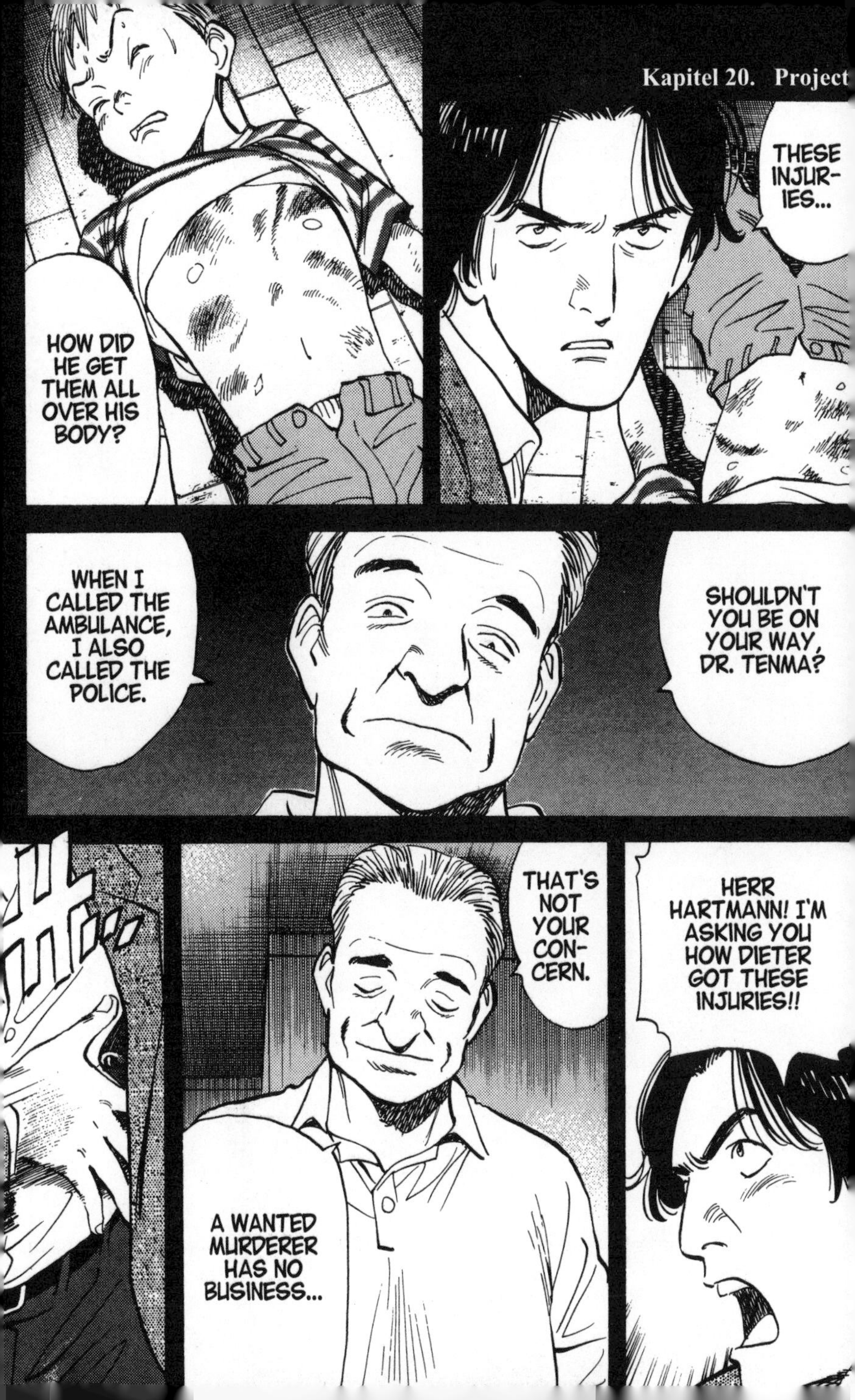
THESE INJURIES...
HOW DID HE GET THEM ALL OVER HIS BODY?
SHOULDN'T YOU BE ON YOUR WAY, DR. TENMA?
WHEN I CALLED THE AMBULANCE, I ALSO CALLED THE POLICE.
HERR HARTMANN! I'M ASKING YOU HOW DIETER GOT THESE INJURIES!!
THAT'S NOT YOUR CONCERN.
A WANTED MURDERER HAS NO BUSINESS...

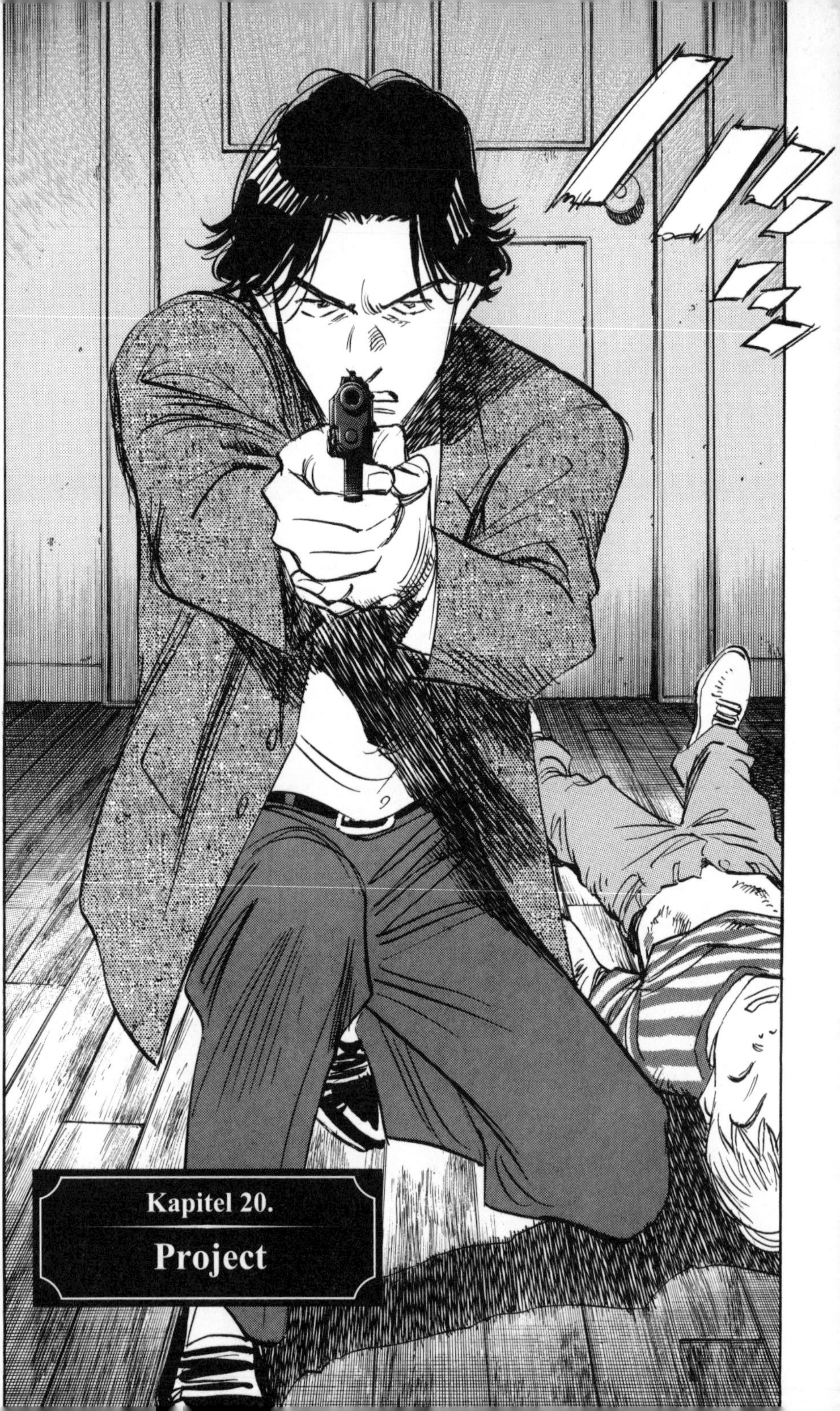
Kapitel 20.
Project

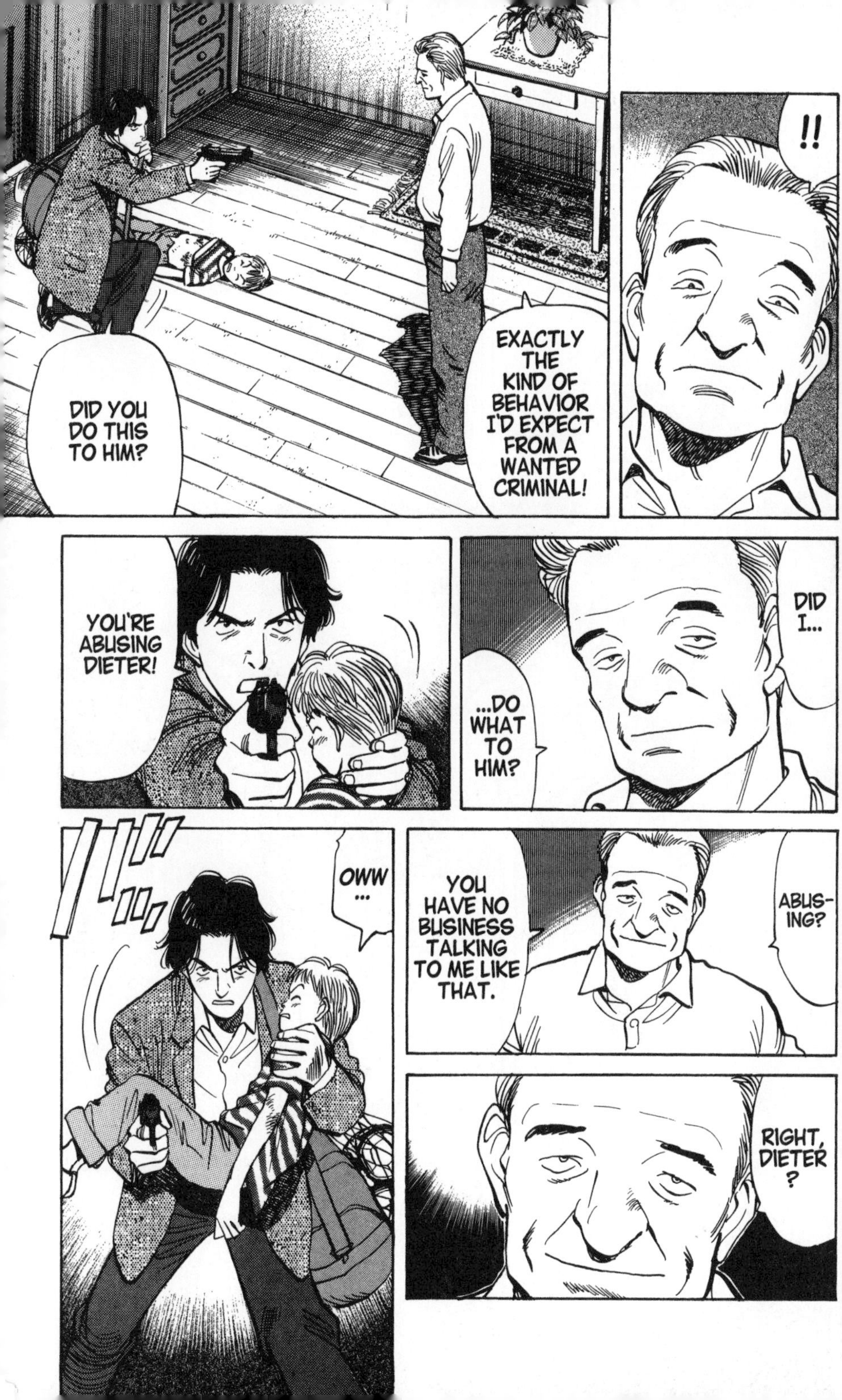
!!
EXACTLY THE KIND OF BEHAVIOR I'D EXPECT FROM A WANTED CRIMINAL!
DID YOU DO THIS TO HIM?
DID I...
...DO WHAT TO HIM?
YOU'RE ABUSING DIETER!
ABUS-ING?
YOU HAVE NO BUSINESS TALKING TO ME LIKE THAT.
RIGHT, DIETER?
OWW...

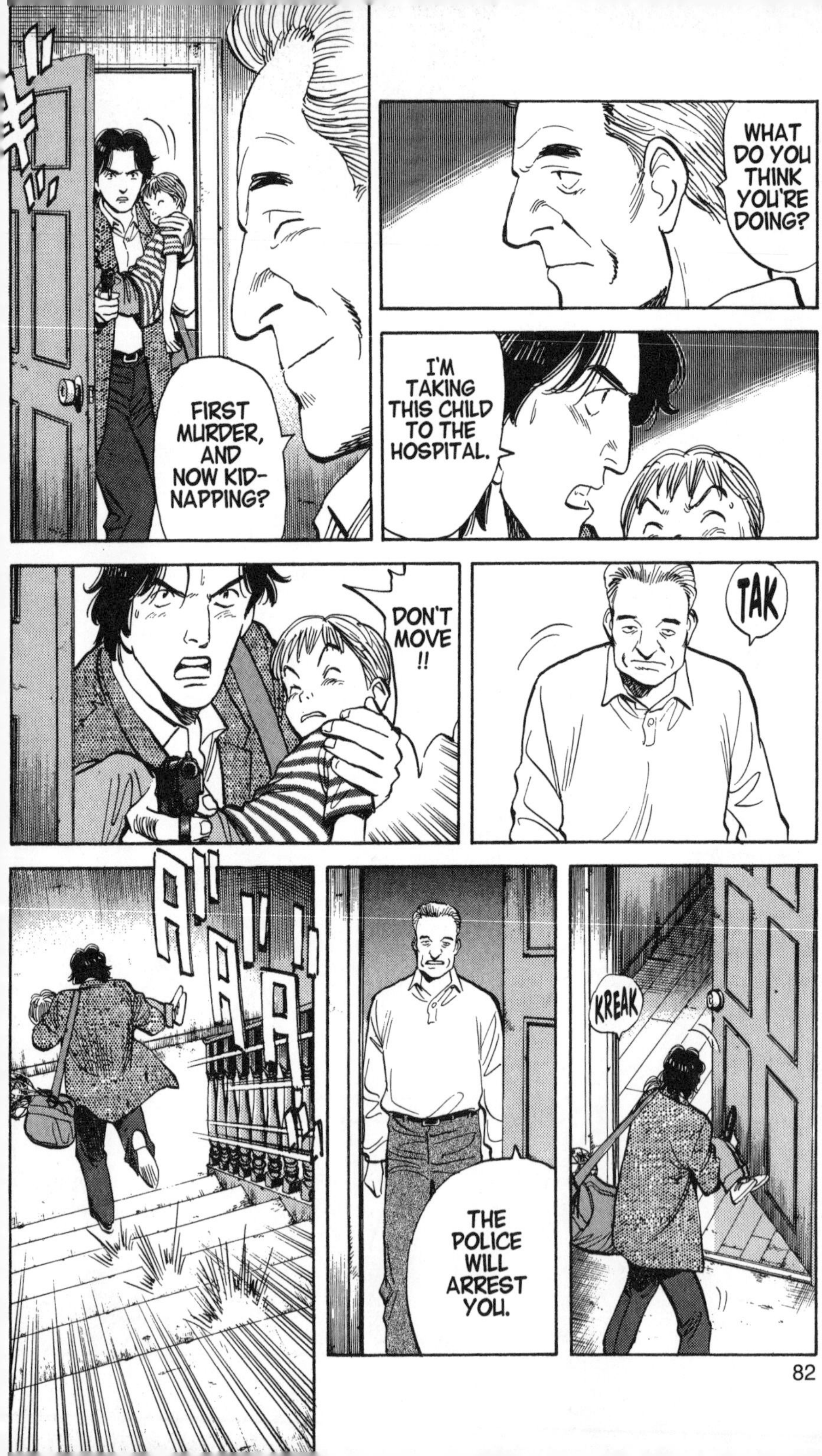
WHAT DO YOU THINK YOU'RE DOING?
I'M TAKING THIS CHILD TO THE HOSPITAL.
FIRST MURDER, AND NOW KID-NAPPING?
TAK
DON'T MOVE !!
KREAK
THE POLICE WILL ARREST YOU.

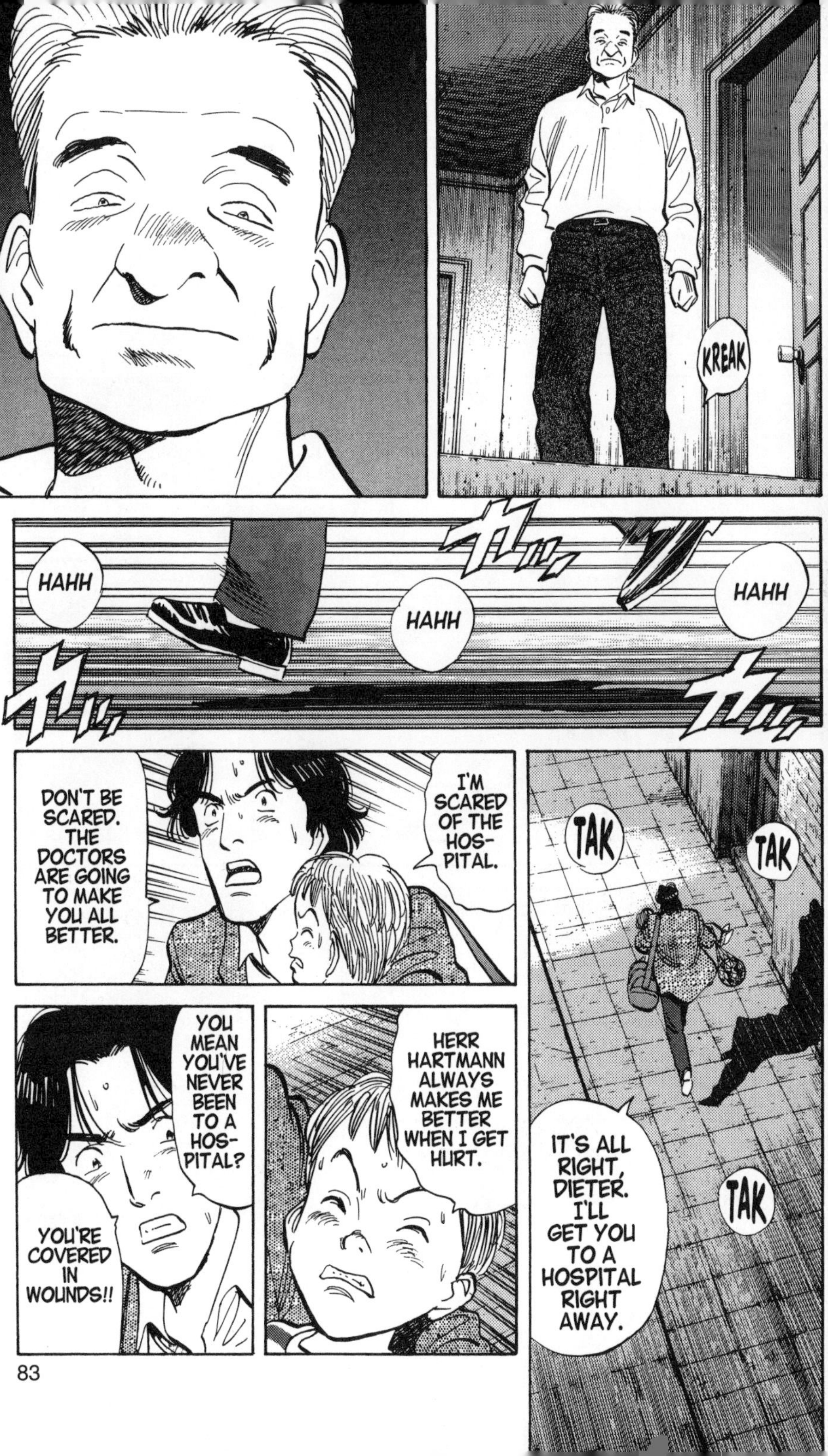
KREAK
HAHH
HAHH
HAHH
TAK
TAK
IT'S ALL RIGHT, DIETER. I'LL GET YOU TO A HOSPITAL RIGHT AWAY.
TAK
I'M SCARED OF THE HOS-PITAL.
DON'T BE SCARED. THE DOCTORS ARE GOING TO MAKE YOU ALL BETTER.
HERR HARTMANN ALWAYS MAKES ME BETTER WHEN I GET HURT.
YOU MEAN YOU'VE NEVER BEEN TO A HOS-PITAL?
YOU'RE COVERED IN WOUNDS!!

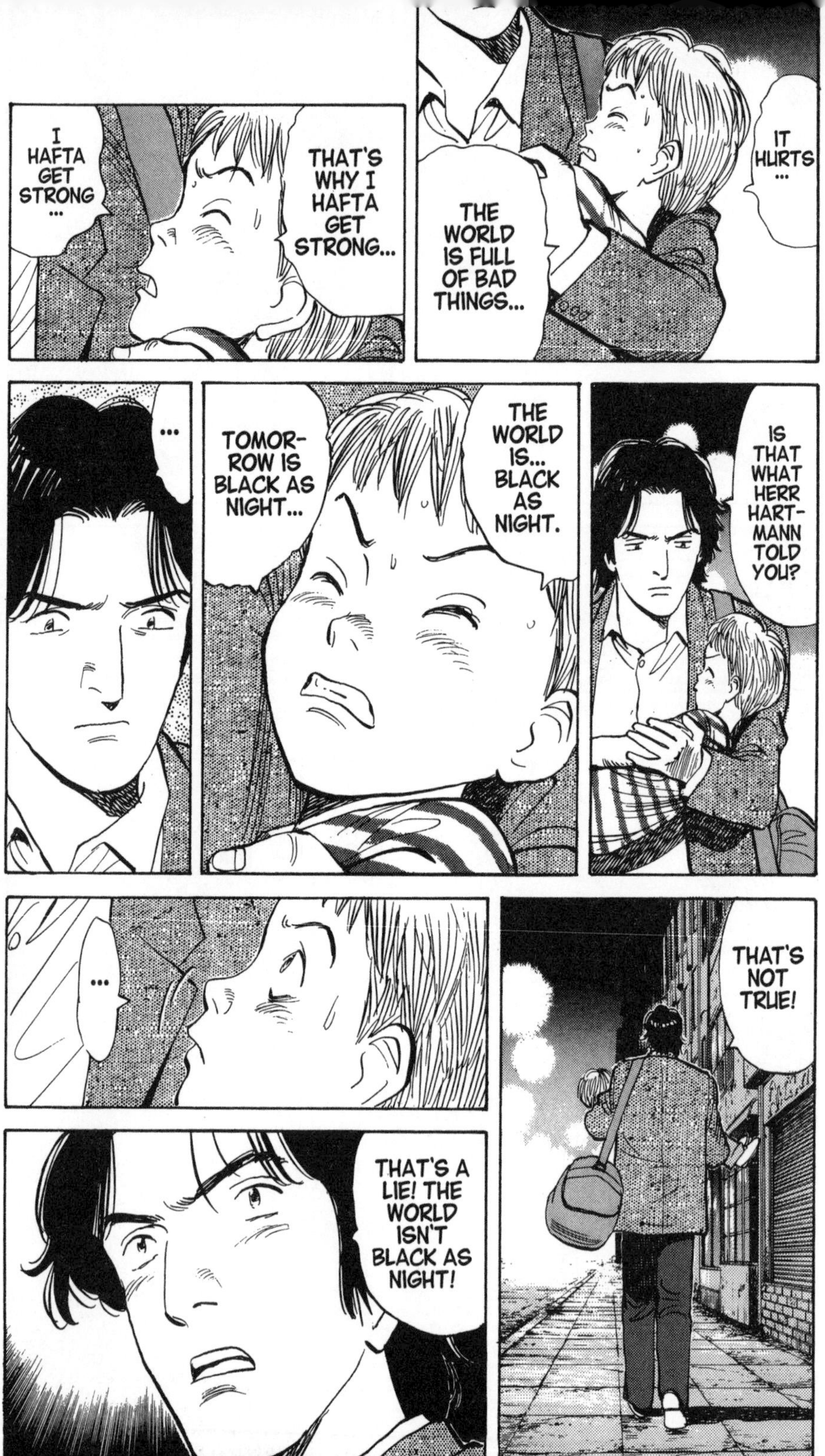
IT HURTS...
THE WORLD IS FULL OF BAD THINGS...
THAT'S WHY I HAFTA GET STRONG...
I HAFTA GET STRONG...
IS THAT WHAT HERR HARTMANN TOLD YOU?
THE WORLD IS... BLACK AS NIGHT.
TOMORROW IS BLACK AS NIGHT...
...
THAT'S NOT TRUE!
...
THAT'S A LIE! THE WORLD ISN'T BLACK AS NIGHT!

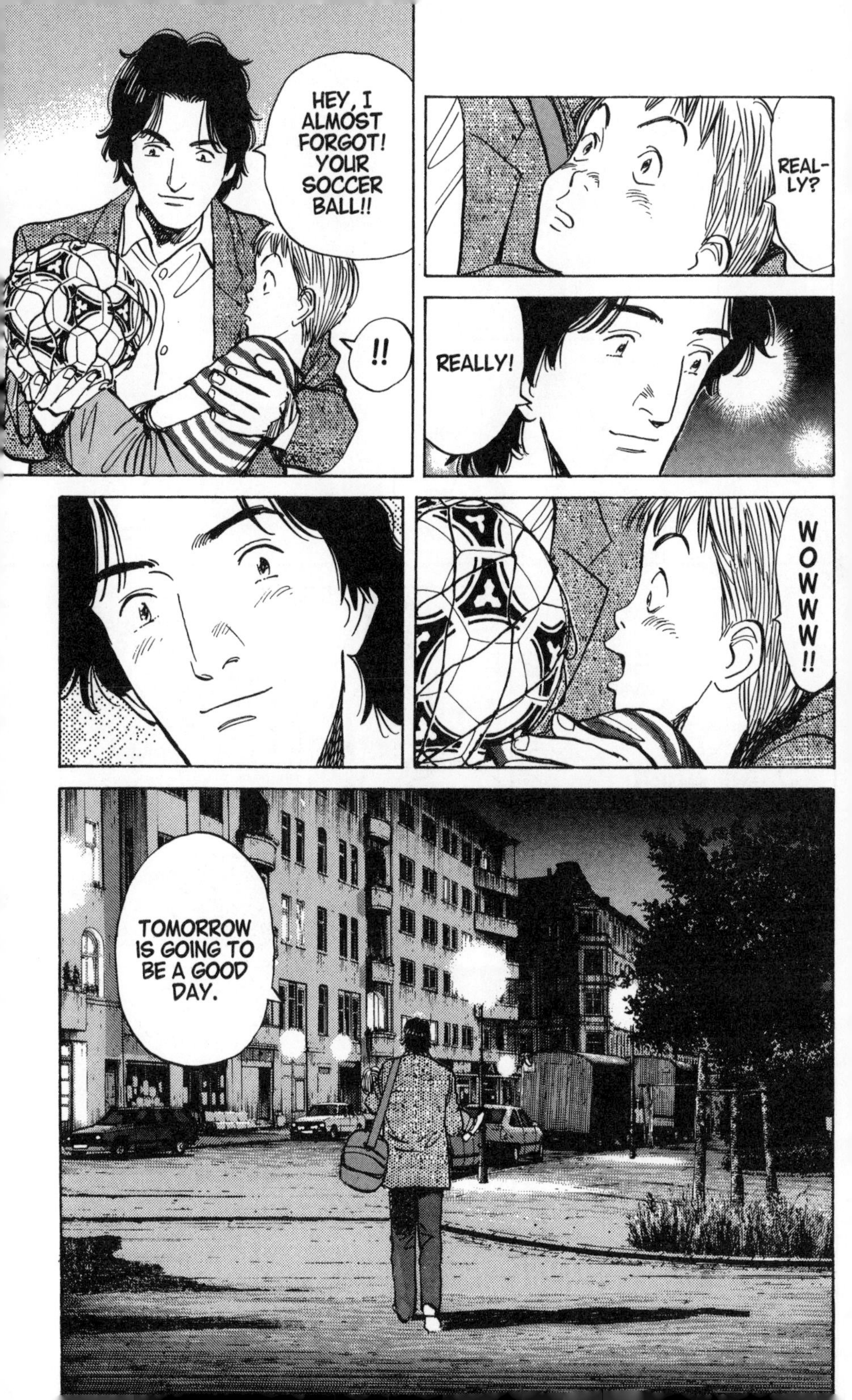
REAL-LY?
REALLY!
HEY, I ALMOST FORGOT! YOUR SOCCER BALL!!
!!
WOWWW!!
TOMORROW IS GOING TO BE A GOOD DAY.

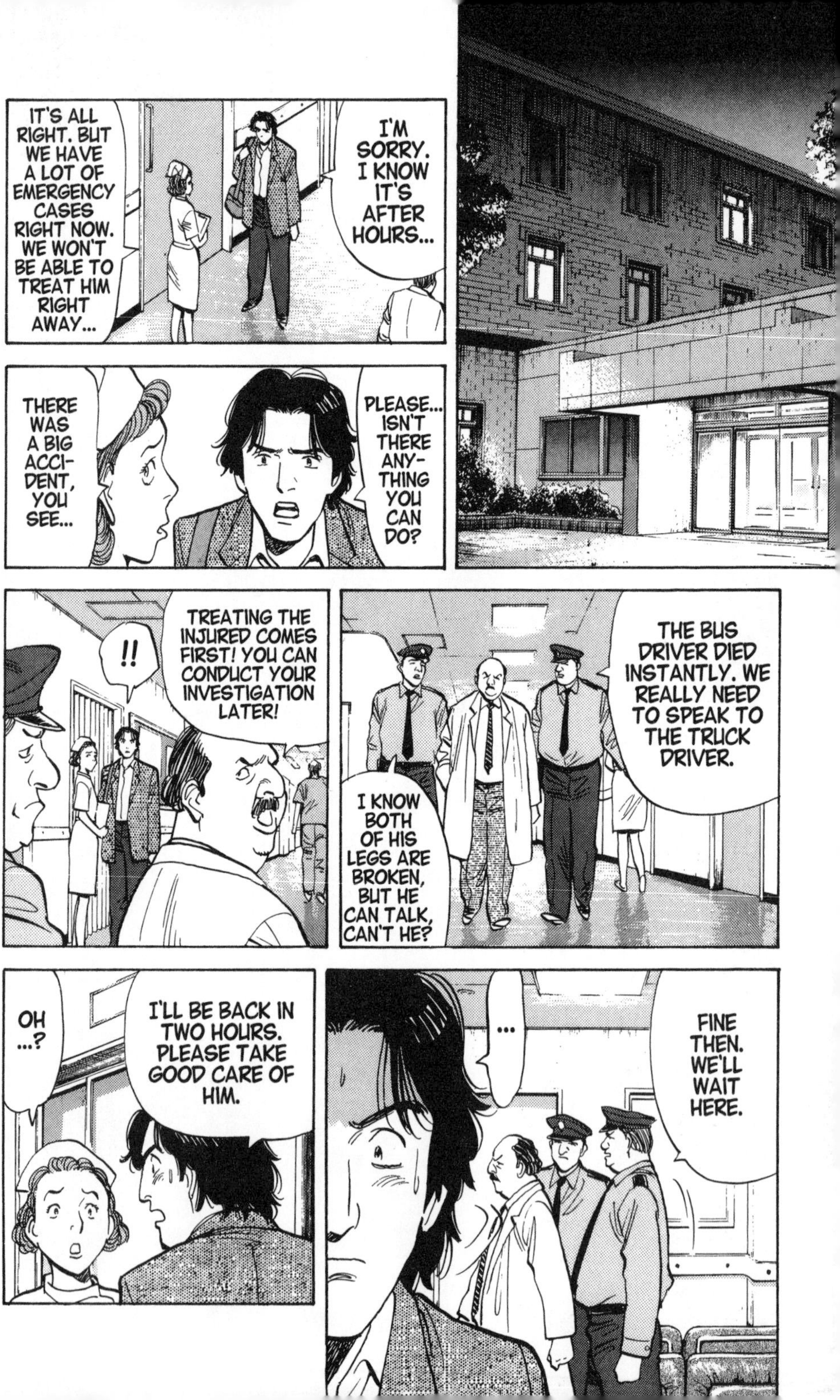
I'M SORRY. I KNOW IT'S AFTER HOURS...
IT'S ALL RIGHT. BUT WE HAVE A LOT OF EMERGENCY CASES RIGHT NOW. WE WON'T BE ABLE TO TREAT HIM RIGHT AWAY...
PLEASE... ISN'T THERE ANYTHING YOU CAN DO?
THERE WAS A BIG ACCIDENT, YOU SEE...
THE BUS DRIVER DIED INSTANTLY. WE REALLY NEED TO SPEAK TO THE TRUCK DRIVER.
I KNOW BOTH OF HIS LEGS ARE BROKEN, BUT HE CAN TALK, CAN'T HE?
TREATING THE INJURED COMES FIRST! YOU CAN CONDUCT YOUR INVESTIGATION LATER!
!!
FINE THEN. WE'LL WAIT HERE.
...
I'LL BE BACK IN TWO HOURS. PLEASE TAKE GOOD CARE OF HIM.
OH ...?

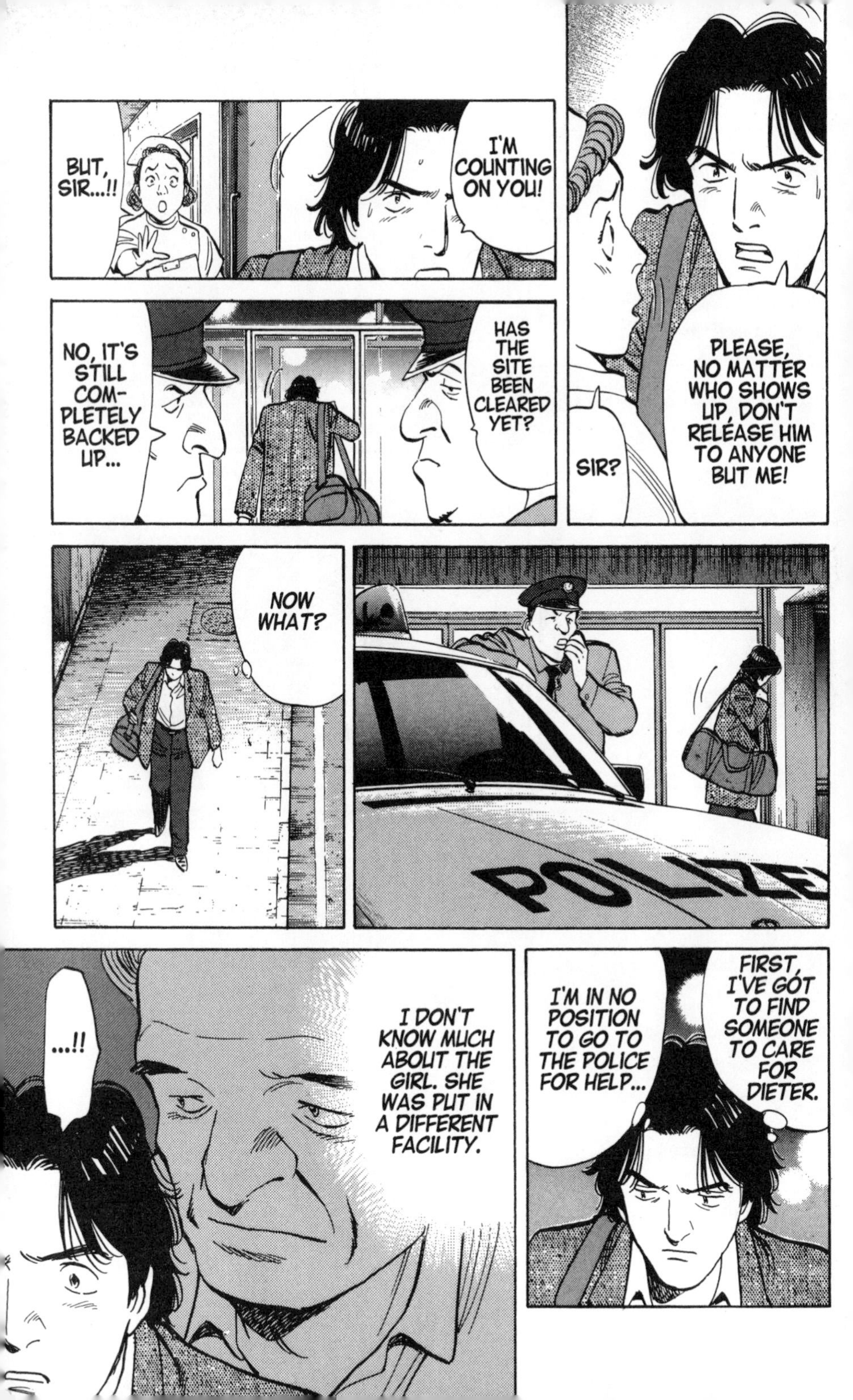
PLEASE, NO MATTER WHO SHOWS UP, DON'T RELEASE HIM TO ANYONE BUT ME!
SIR?
I'M COUNTING ON YOU!
BUT, SIR...!!
HAS THE SITE BEEN CLEARED YET?
NO, IT'S STILL COM-PLETELY BACKED UP...
POLIZE
NOW WHAT?
FIRST, I'VE GOT TO FIND SOMEONE TO CARE FOR DIETER.
I'M IN NO POSITION TO GO TO THE POLICE FOR HELP...
I DON'T KNOW MUCH ABOUT THE GIRL. SHE WAS PUT IN A DIFFERENT FACILITY.
...!!

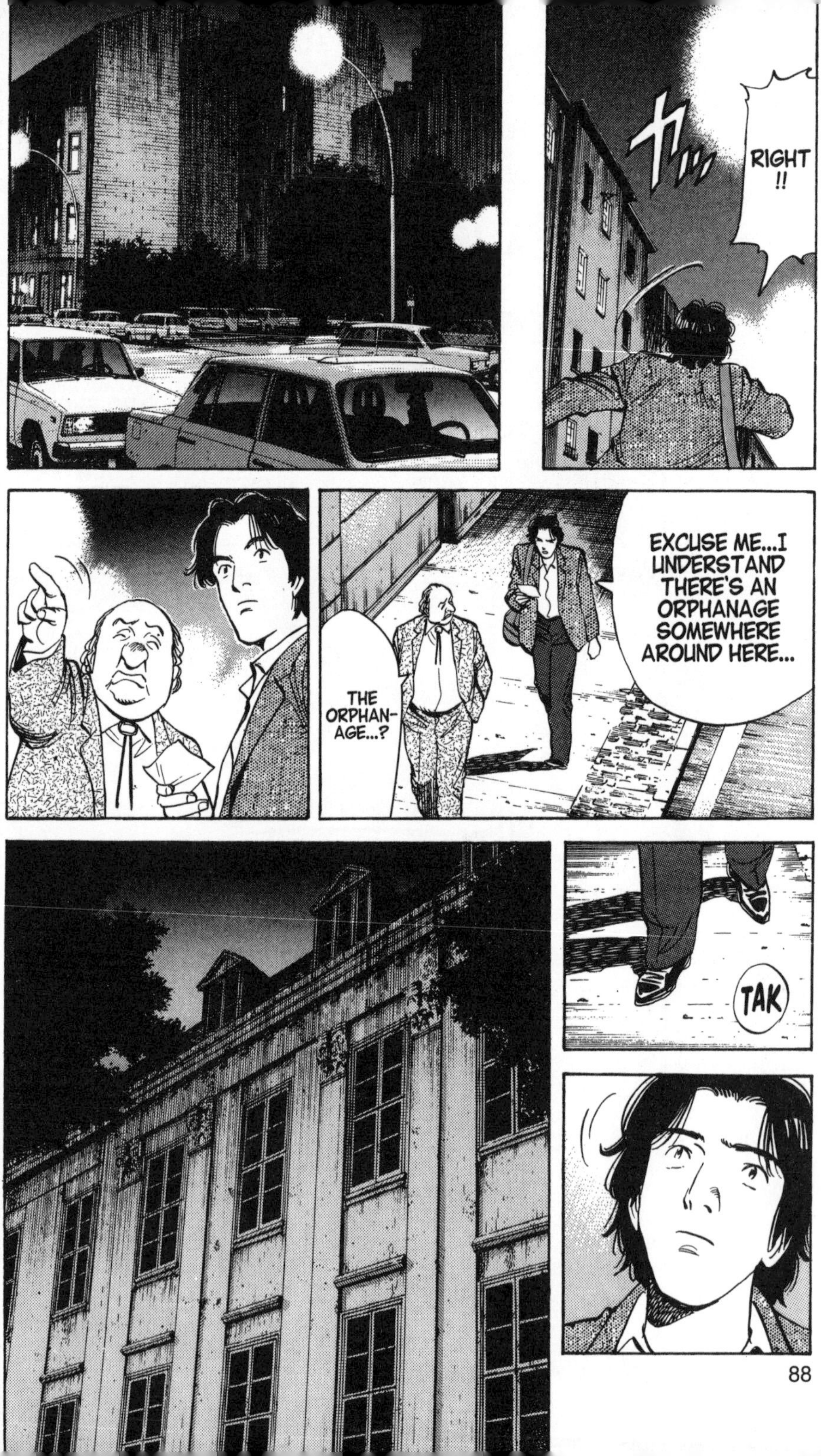
RIGHT !!
EXCUSE ME...I UNDERSTAND THERE'S AN ORPHANAGE SOMEWHERE AROUND HERE...
THE ORPHAN-AGE...?
TAK

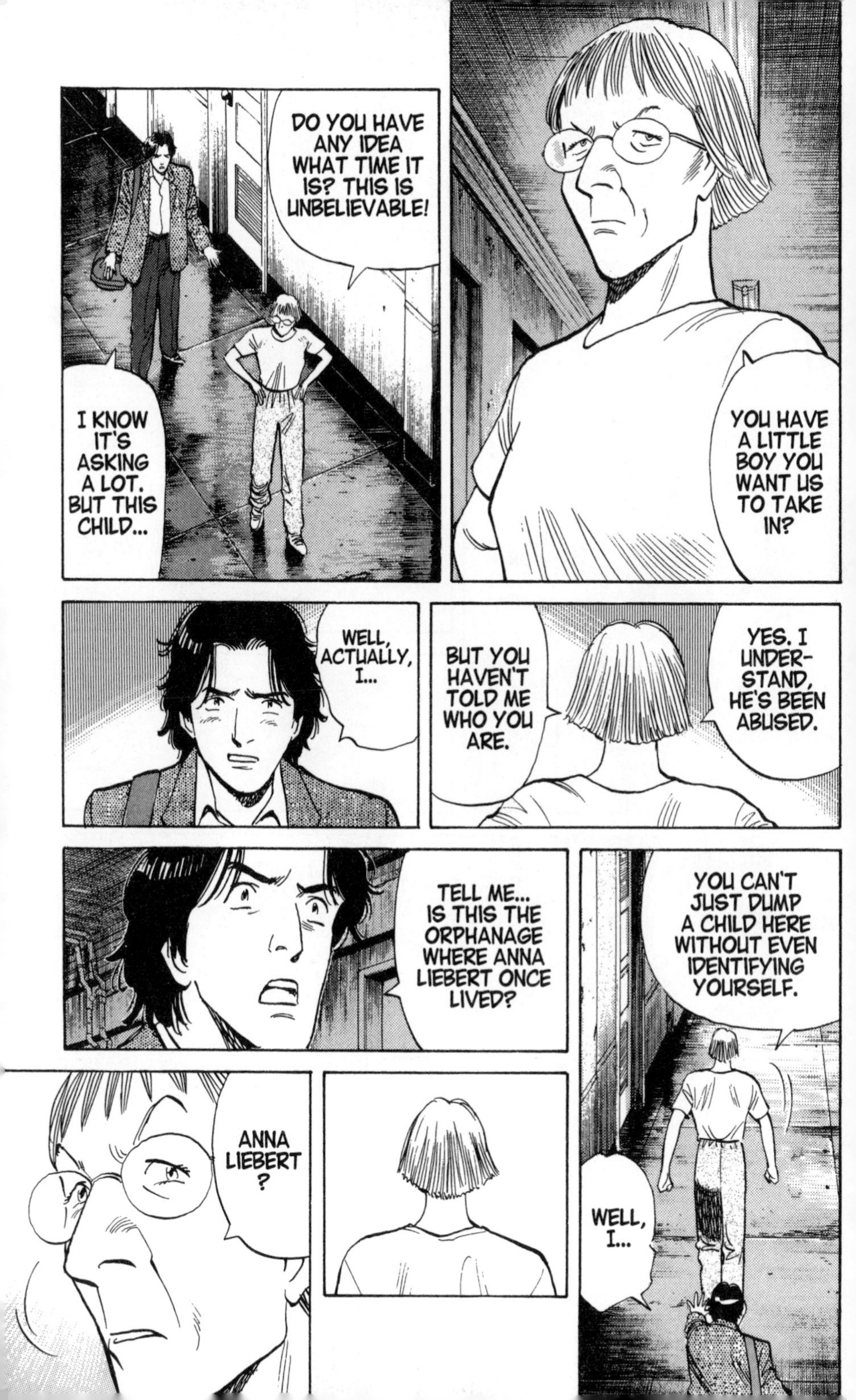
YOU HAVE A LITTLE BOY YOU WANT US TO TAKE IN?
DO YOU HAVE ANY IDEA WHAT TIME IT IS? THIS IS UNBELIEVABLE!
I KNOW IT'S ASKING A LOT. BUT THIS CHILD...
YES. I UNDERSTAND, HE'S BEEN ABUSED.
BUT YOU HAVEN'T TOLD ME WHO YOU ARE.
WELL, ACTUALLY, I...
YOU CAN'T JUST DUMP A CHILD HERE WITHOUT EVEN IDENTIFYING YOURSELF.
WELL, I...
TELL ME... IS THIS THE ORPHANAGE WHERE ANNA LIEBERT ONCE LIVED?
ANNA LIEBERT?

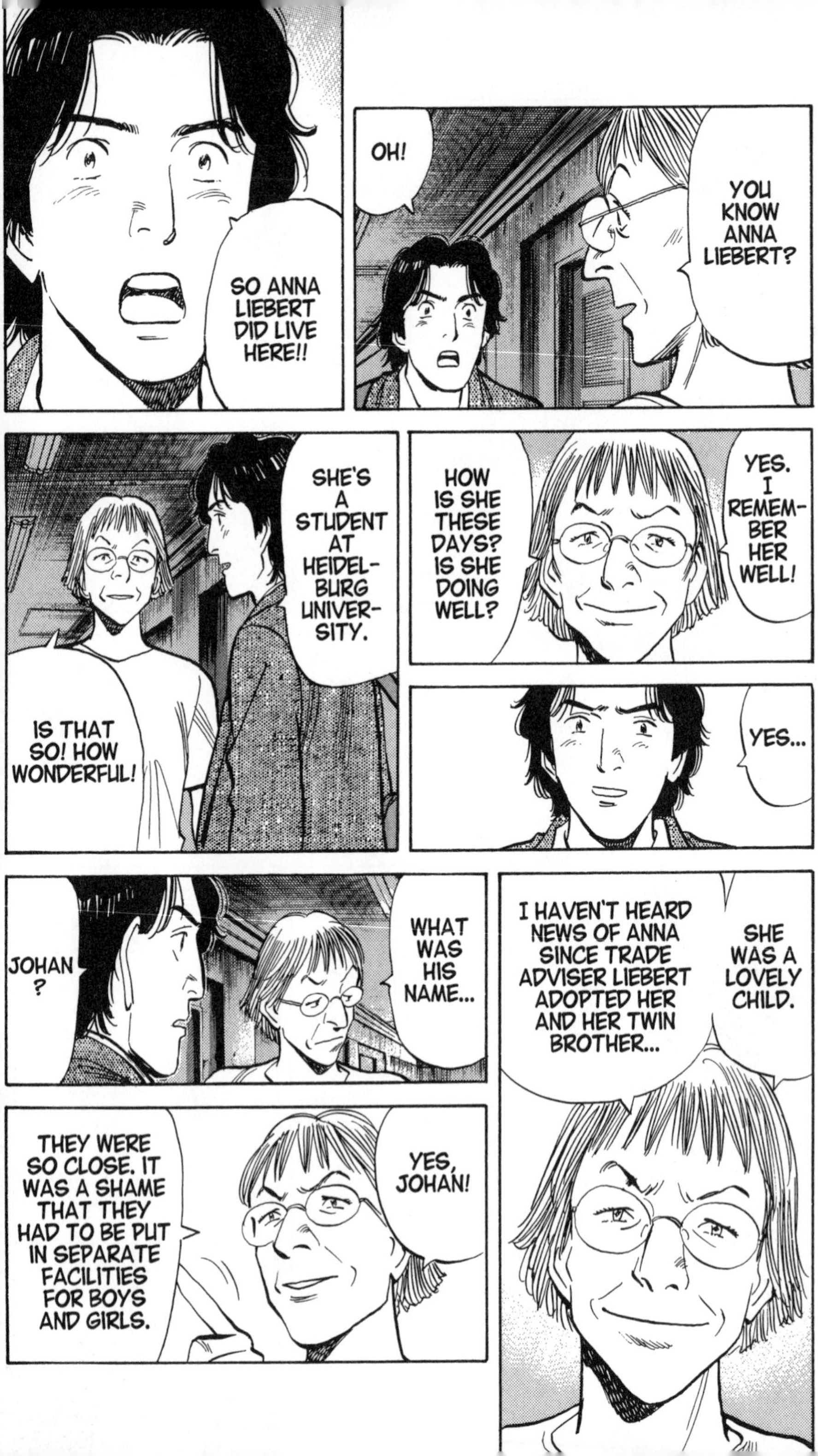
YOU KNOW ANNA LIEBERT?
OH!
SO ANNA LIEBERT DID LIVE HERE!!
YES. I REMEMBER HER WELL!
HOW IS SHE THESE DAYS? IS SHE DOING WELL?
YES...
SHE'S A STUDENT AT HEIDELBURG UNIVERSITY.
IS THAT SO! HOW WONDERFUL!
SHE WAS A LOVELY CHILD.
I HAVEN'T HEARD NEWS OF ANNA SINCE TRADE ADVISER LIEBERT ADOPTED HER AND HER TWIN BROTHER...
WHAT WAS HIS NAME...
JOHAN?
YES, JOHAN!
THEY WERE SO CLOSE. IT WAS A SHAME THAT THEY HAD TO BE PUT IN SEPARATE FACILITIES FOR BOYS AND GIRLS.

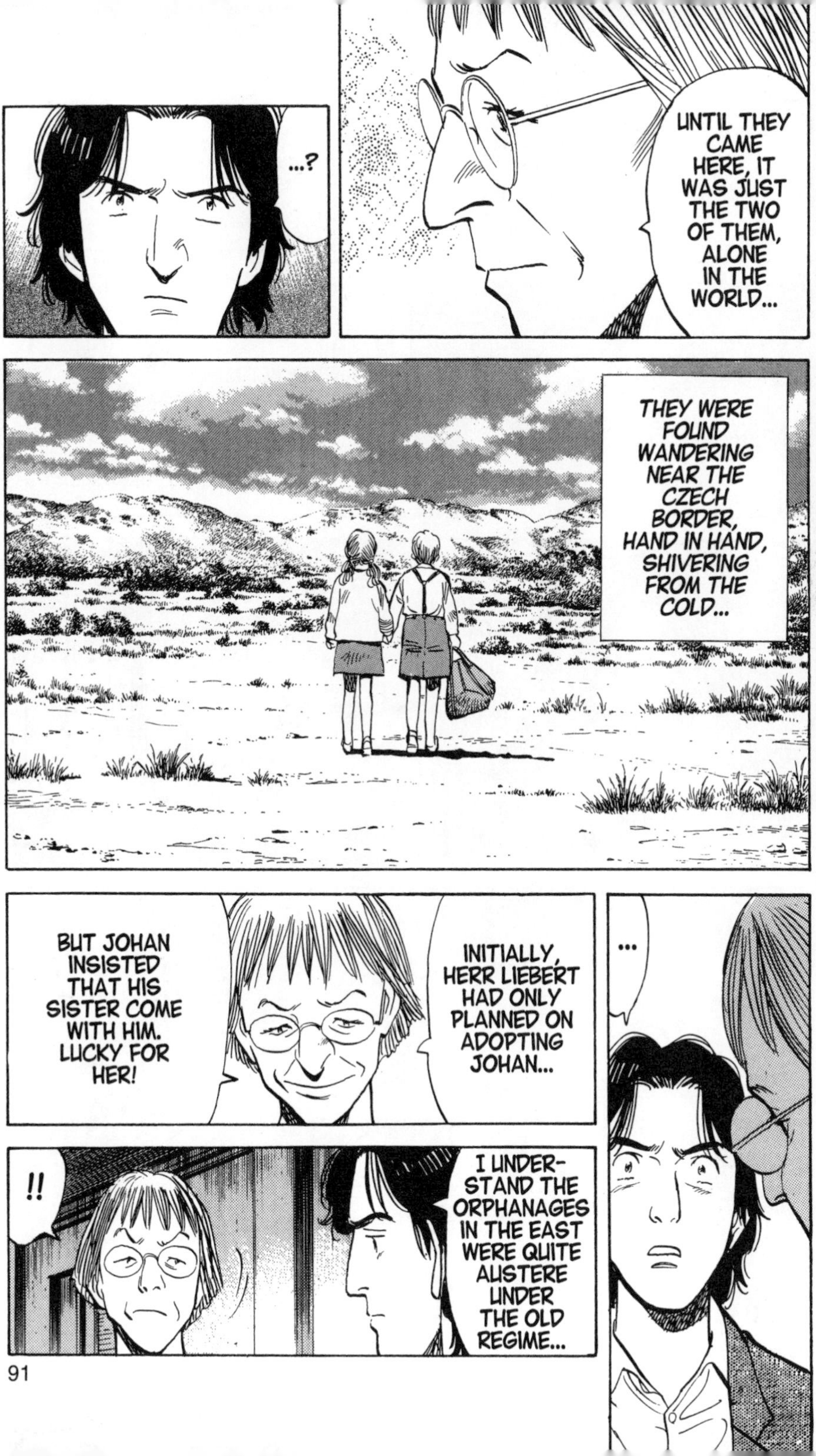
UNTIL THEY CAME HERE, IT WAS JUST THE TWO OF THEM, ALONE IN THE WORLD...
...?
THEY WERE FOUND WANDERING NEAR THE CZECH BORDER, HAND IN HAND, SHIVERING FROM THE COLD...
...
INITIALLY, HERR LIEBERT HAD ONLY PLANNED ON ADOPTING JOHAN...
BUT JOHAN INSISTED THAT HIS SISTER COME WITH HIM. LUCKY FOR HER!
I UNDER-STAND THE ORPHANAGES IN THE EAST WERE QUITE AUSTERE UNDER THE OLD REGIME...
!!

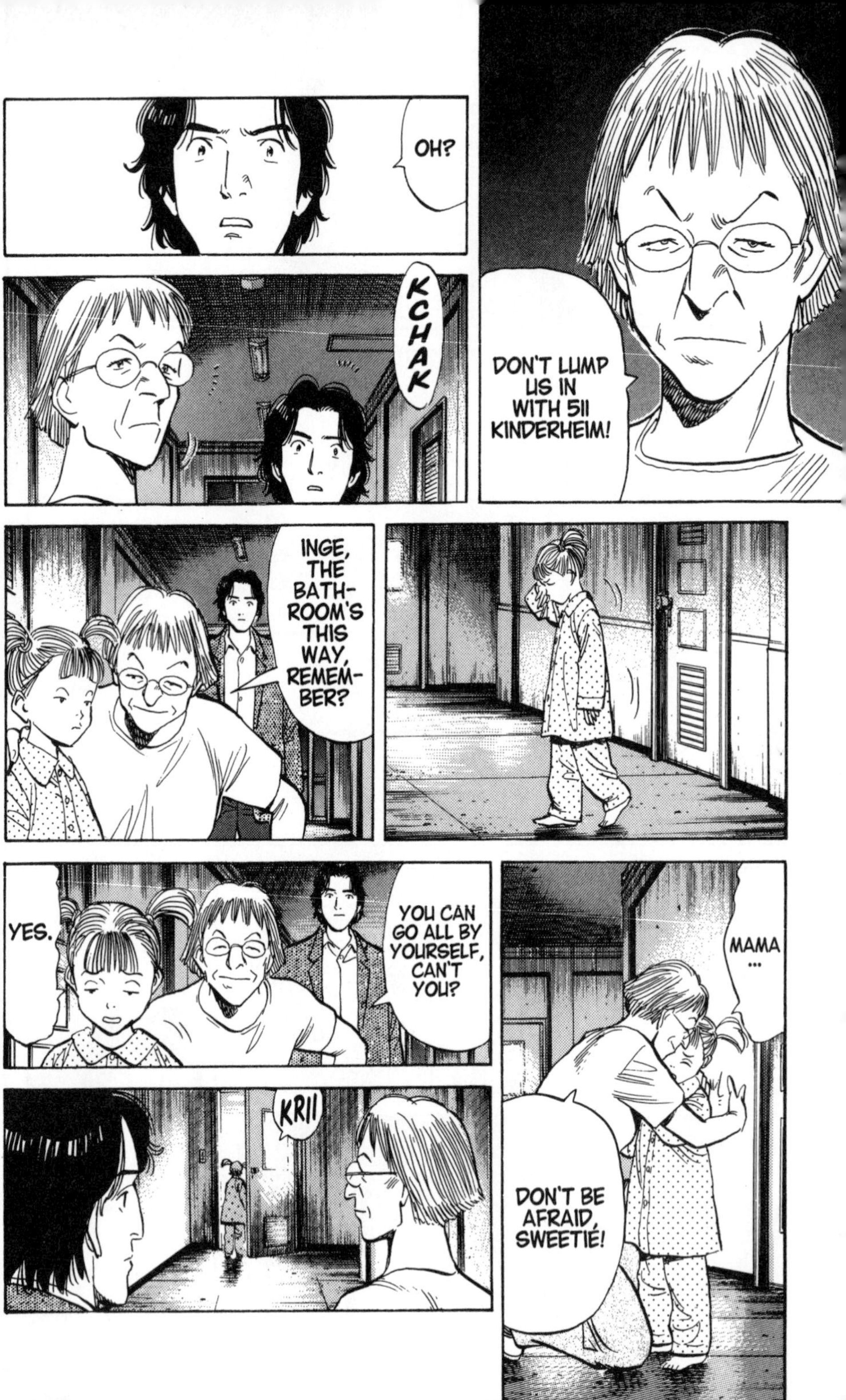
DON'T LUMP US IN WITH 511 KINDERHEIM!
OH?
KCHAK
INGE, THE BATH-ROOM'S THIS WAY, REMEM-BER?
MAMA ...
DON'T BE AFRAID, SWEETIÉ!
YOU CAN GO ALL BY YOURSELF, CAN'T YOU?
YES.
KRII

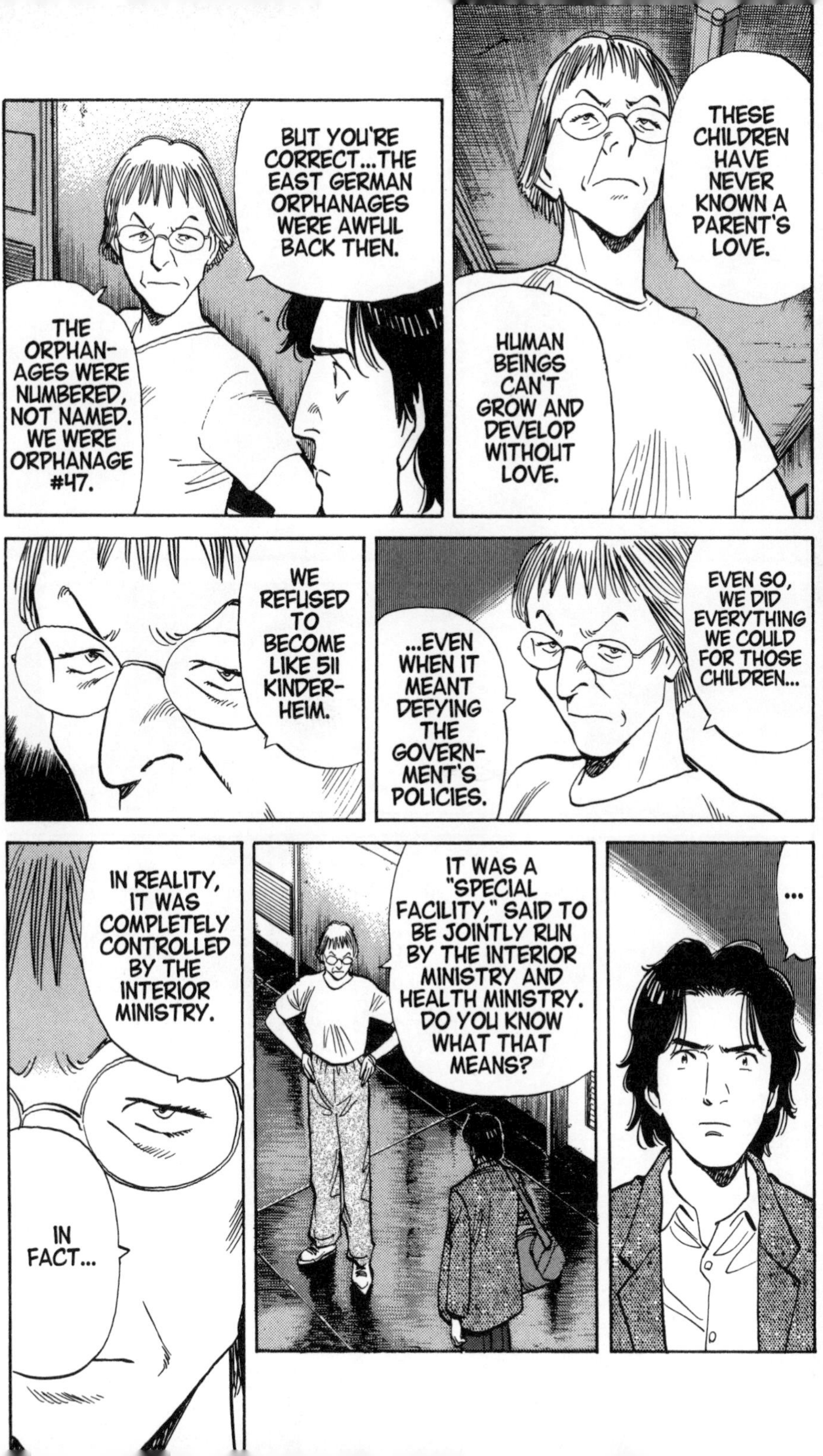
THESE CHILDREN HAVE NEVER KNOWN A PARENT'S LOVE.
HUMAN BEINGS CAN'T GROW AND DEVELOP WITHOUT LOVE.
BUT YOU'RE CORRECT...THE EAST GERMAN ORPHANAGES WERE AWFUL BACK THEN.
THE ORPHANAGES WERE NUMBERED, NOT NAMED. WE WERE ORPHANAGE #47.
EVEN SO, WE DID EVERYTHING WE COULD FOR THOSE CHILDREN...
...EVEN WHEN IT MEANT DEFYING THE GOVERNMENT'S POLICIES.
WE REFUSED TO BECOME LIKE 511 KINDERHEIM.
...
IT WAS A "SPECIAL FACILITY," SAID TO BE JOINTLY RUN BY THE INTERIOR MINISTRY AND HEALTH MINISTRY. DO YOU KNOW WHAT THAT MEANS?
IN REALITY, IT WAS COMPLETELY CONTROLLED BY THE INTERIOR MINISTRY.
IN FACT...

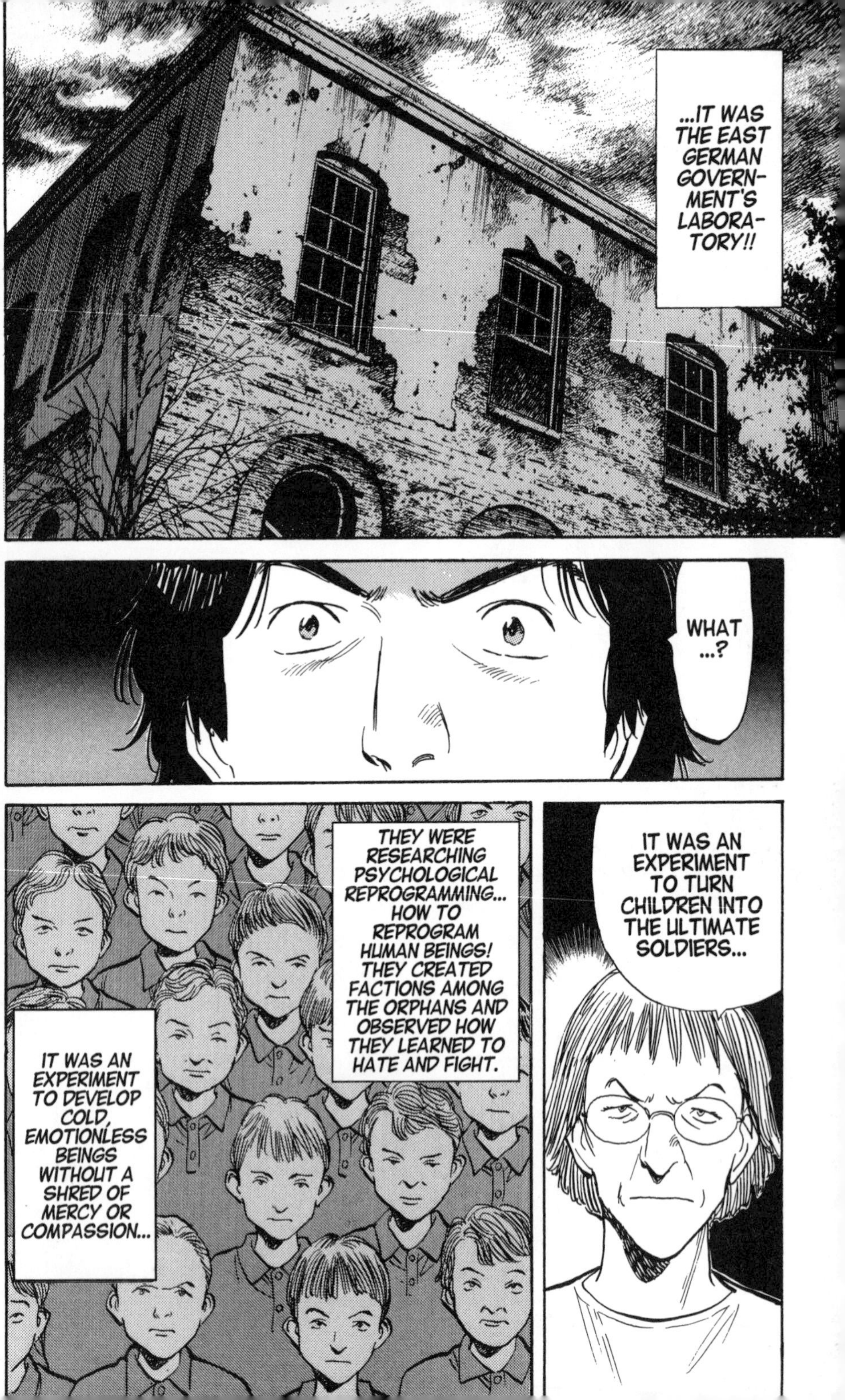
...IT WAS THE EAST GERMAN GOVERNMENT'S LABORATORY!!
WHAT ...?
IT WAS AN EXPERIMENT TO TURN CHILDREN INTO THE ULTIMATE SOLDIERS...
THEY WERE RESEARCHING PSYCHOLOGICAL REPROGRAMMING... HOW TO REPROGRAM HUMAN BEINGS! THEY CREATED FACTIONS AMONG THE ORPHANS AND OBSERVED HOW THEY LEARNED TO HATE AND FIGHT.
IT WAS AN EXPERIMENT TO DEVELOP COLD, EMOTIONLESS BEINGS WITHOUT A SHRED OF MERCY OR COMPASSION...

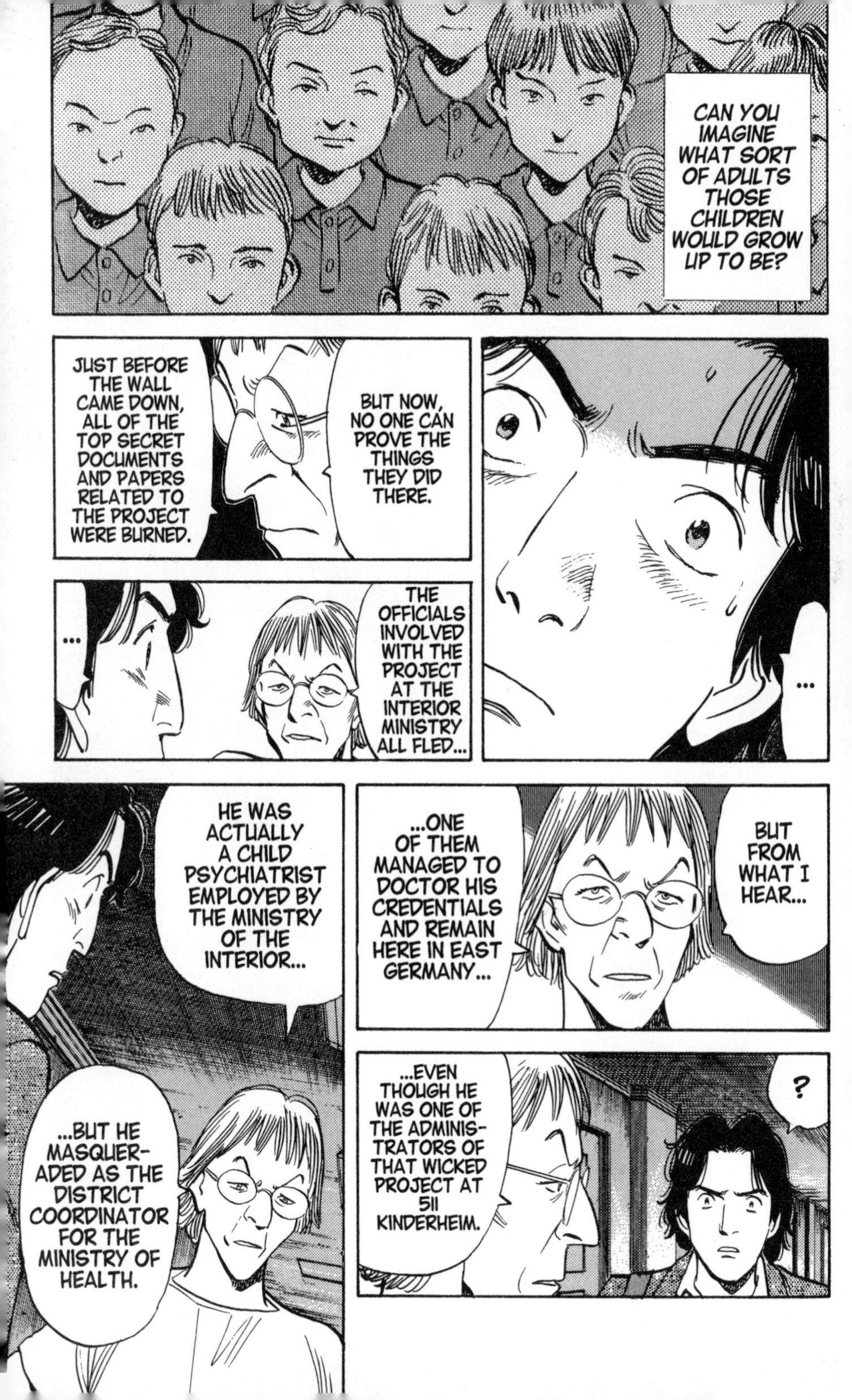
CAN YOU IMAGINE WHAT SORT OF ADULTS THOSE CHILDREN WOULD GROW UP TO BE?
...
BUT NOW, NO ONE CAN PROVE THE THINGS THEY DID THERE.
JUST BEFORE THE WALL CAME DOWN, ALL OF THE TOP SECRET DOCUMENTS AND PAPERS RELATED TO THE PROJECT WERE BURNED.
THE OFFICIALS INVOLVED WITH THE PROJECT AT THE INTERIOR MINISTRY ALL FLED...
...
BUT FROM WHAT I HEAR...
...ONE OF THEM MANAGED TO DOCTOR HIS CREDENTIALS AND REMAIN HERE IN EAST GERMANY...
?
...EVEN THOUGH HE WAS ONE OF THE ADMINIS-TRATORS OF THAT WICKED PROJECT AT 511 KINDERHEIM.
HE WAS ACTUALLY A CHILD PSYCHIATRIST EMPLOYED BY THE MINISTRY OF THE INTERIOR...
...BUT HE MASQUER-ADED AS THE DISTRICT COORDINATOR FOR THE MINISTRY OF HEALTH.

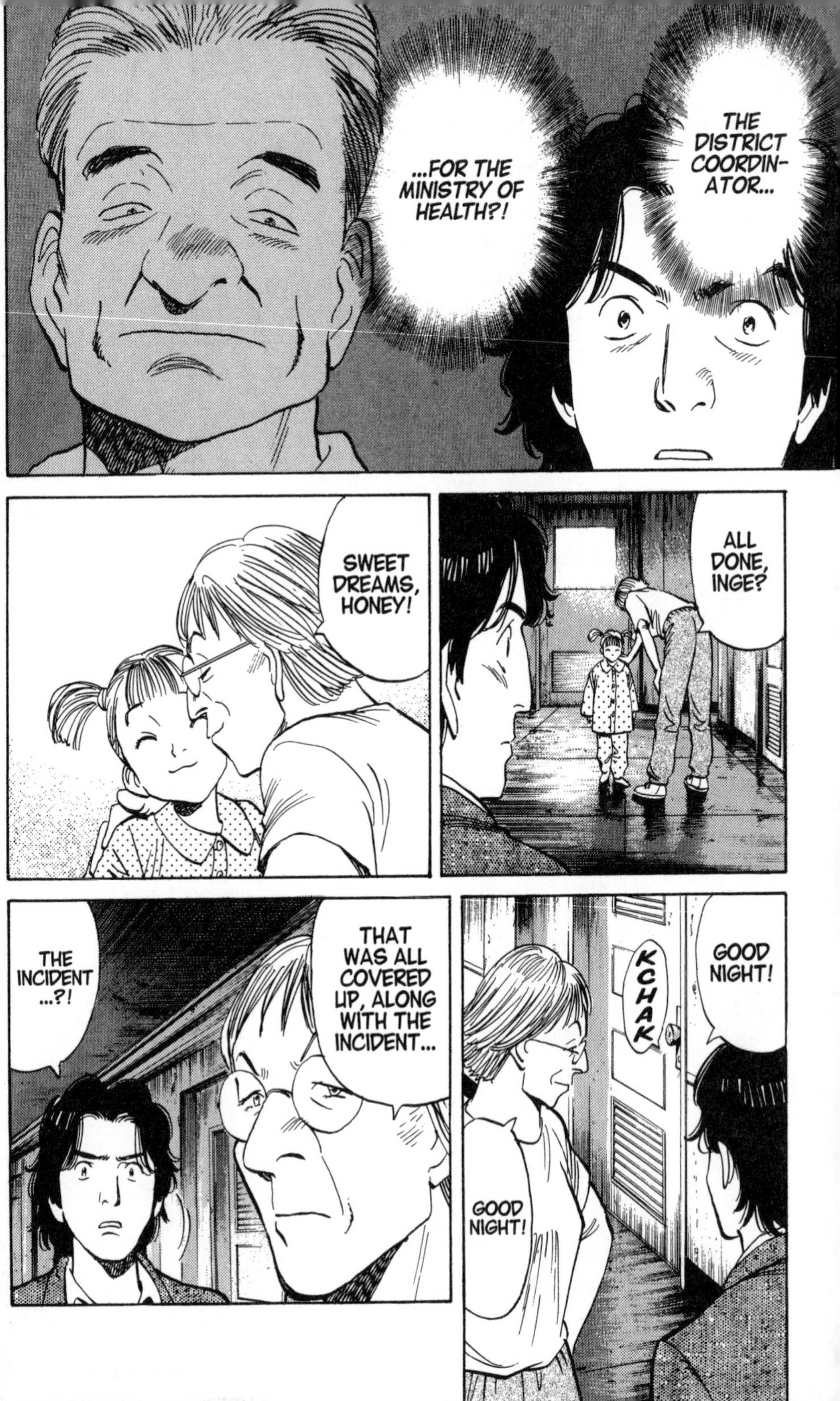
THE DISTRICT COORDIN-ATOR...
...FOR THE MINISTRY OF HEALTH?!
ALL DONE, INGE?
SWEET DREAMS, HONEY!
GOOD NIGHT!
KCHAK
GOOD NIGHT!
THAT WAS ALL COVERED UP, ALONG WITH THE INCIDENT...
THE INCIDENT ...?!

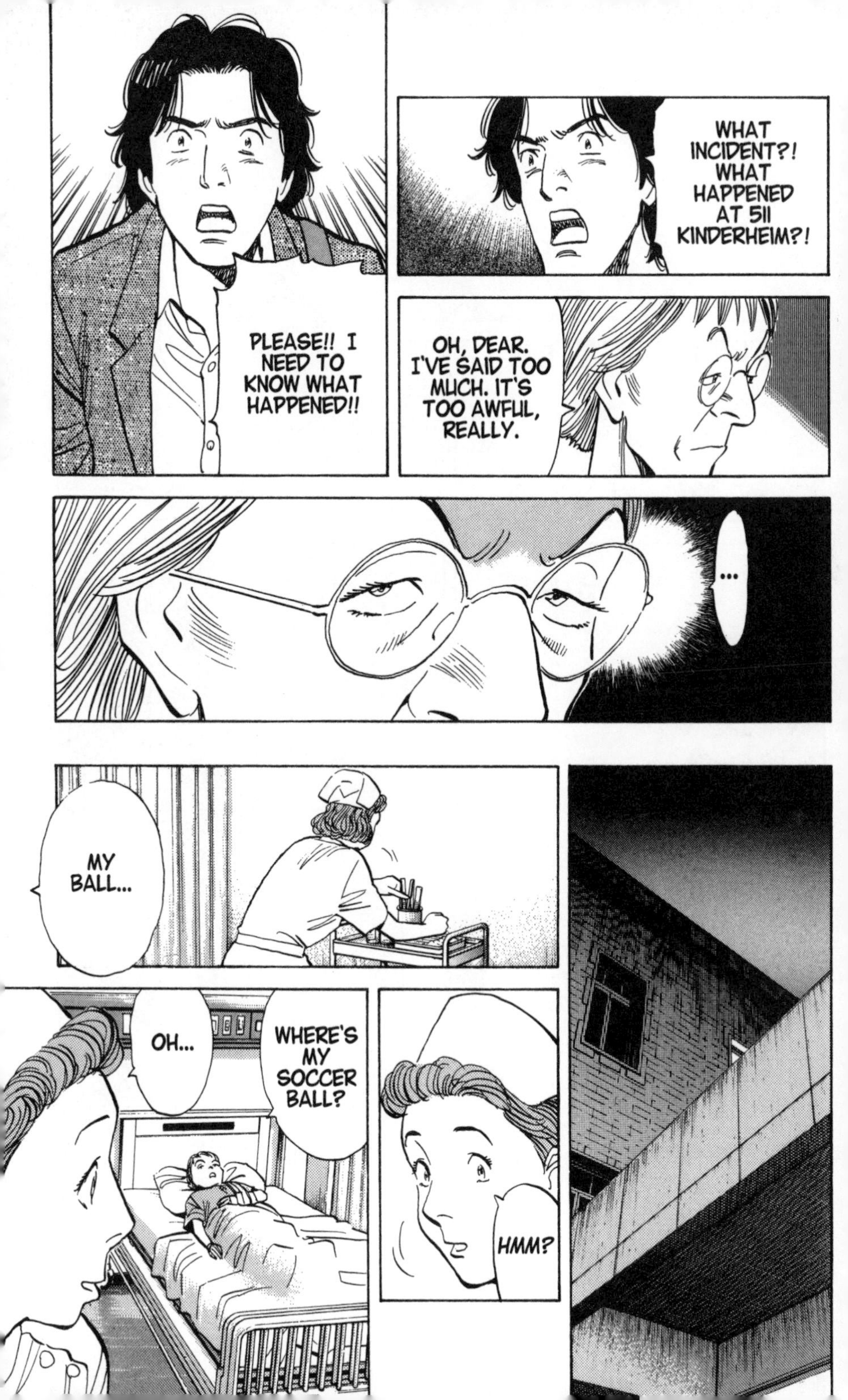
WHAT INCIDENT?! WHAT HAPPENED AT 511 KINDERHEIM?!
OH, DEAR. I'VE SAID TOO MUCH. IT'S TOO AWFUL, REALLY.
PLEASE!! I NEED TO KNOW WHAT HAPPENED!!
...
MY BALL...
HMM?
WHERE'S MY SOCCER BALL?
OH...

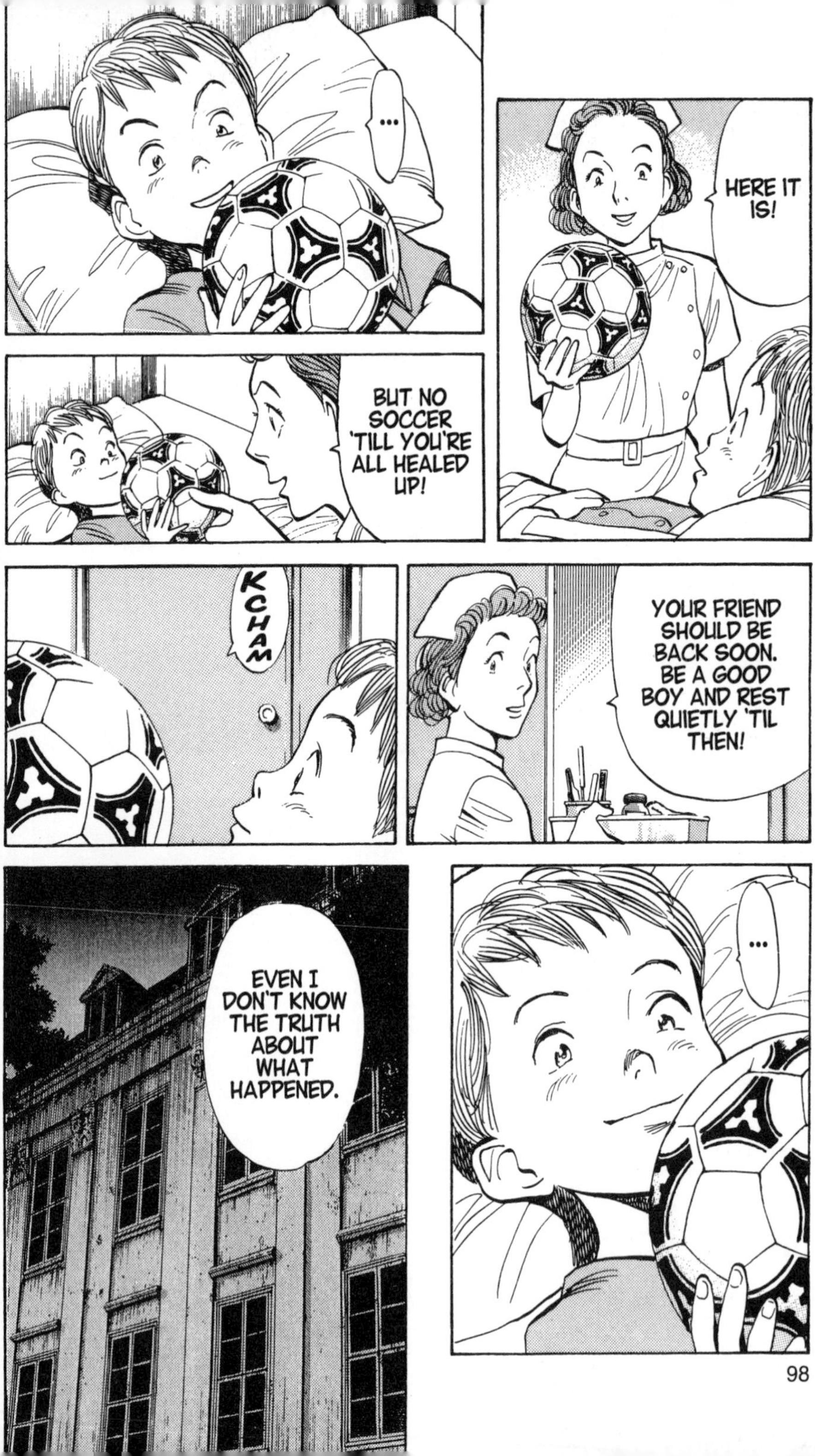
HERE IT IS!
...
BUT NO SOCCER 'TILL YOU'RE ALL HEALED UP!
YOUR FRIEND SHOULD BE BACK SOON. BE A GOOD BOY AND REST QUIETLY 'TIL THEN!
KCHAM
...
EVEN I DON'T KNOW THE TRUTH ABOUT WHAT HAPPENED.

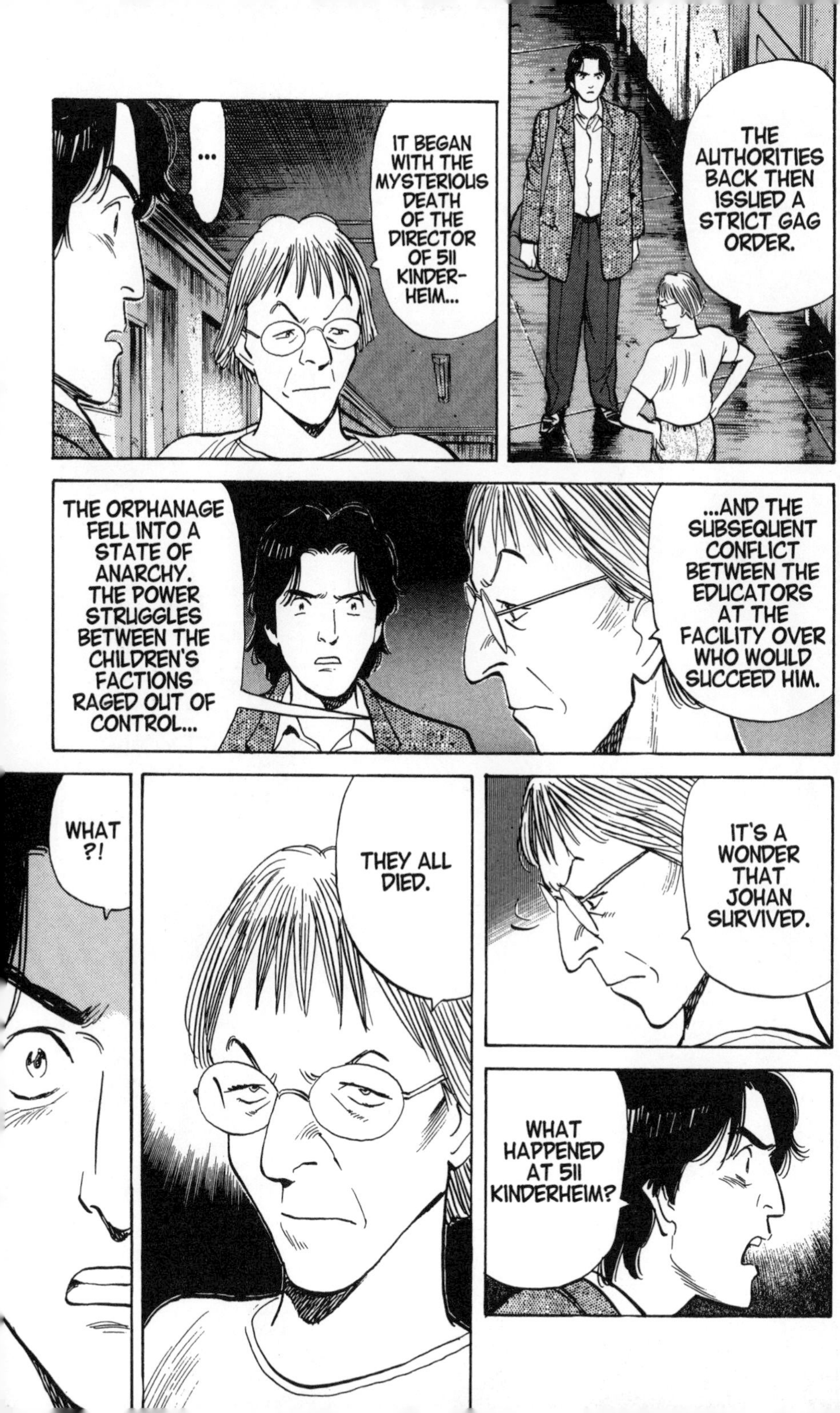
THE AUTHORITIES BACK THEN ISSUED A STRICT GAG ORDER.
IT BEGAN WITH THE MYSTERIOUS DEATH OF THE DIRECTOR OF 511 KINDER-HEIM...
...
...AND THE SUBSEQUENT CONFLICT BETWEEN THE EDUCATORS AT THE FACILITY OVER WHO WOULD SUCCEED HIM.
THE ORPHANAGE FELL INTO A STATE OF ANARCHY. THE POWER STRUGGLES BETWEEN THE CHILDREN'S FACTIONS RAGED OUT OF CONTROL...
IT'S A WONDER THAT JOHAN SURVIVED.
WHAT HAPPENED AT 511 KINDERHEIM?
THEY ALL DIED.
WHAT?!

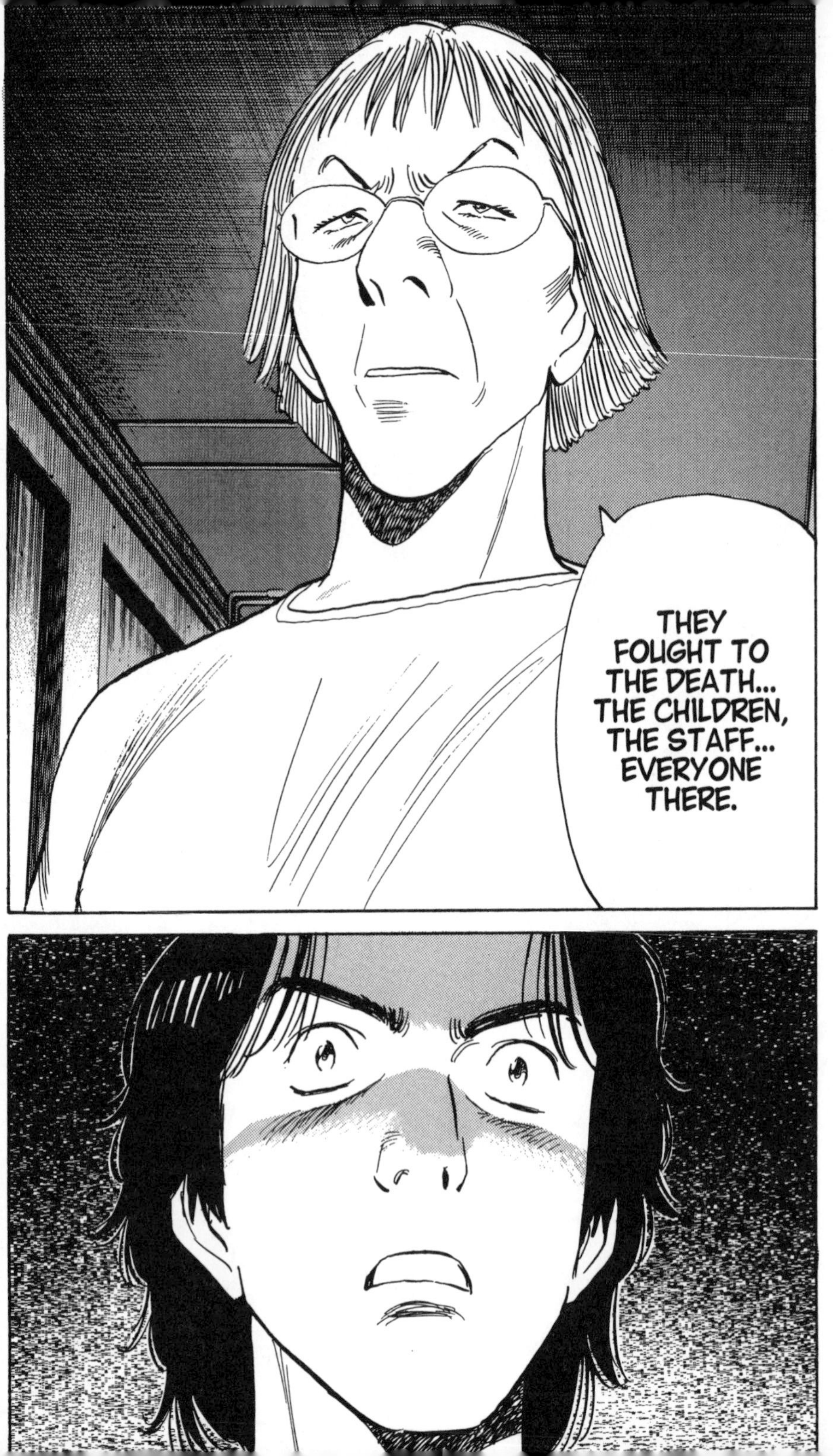
THEY FOUGHT TO THE DEATH... THE CHILDREN, THE STAFF... EVERYONE THERE.

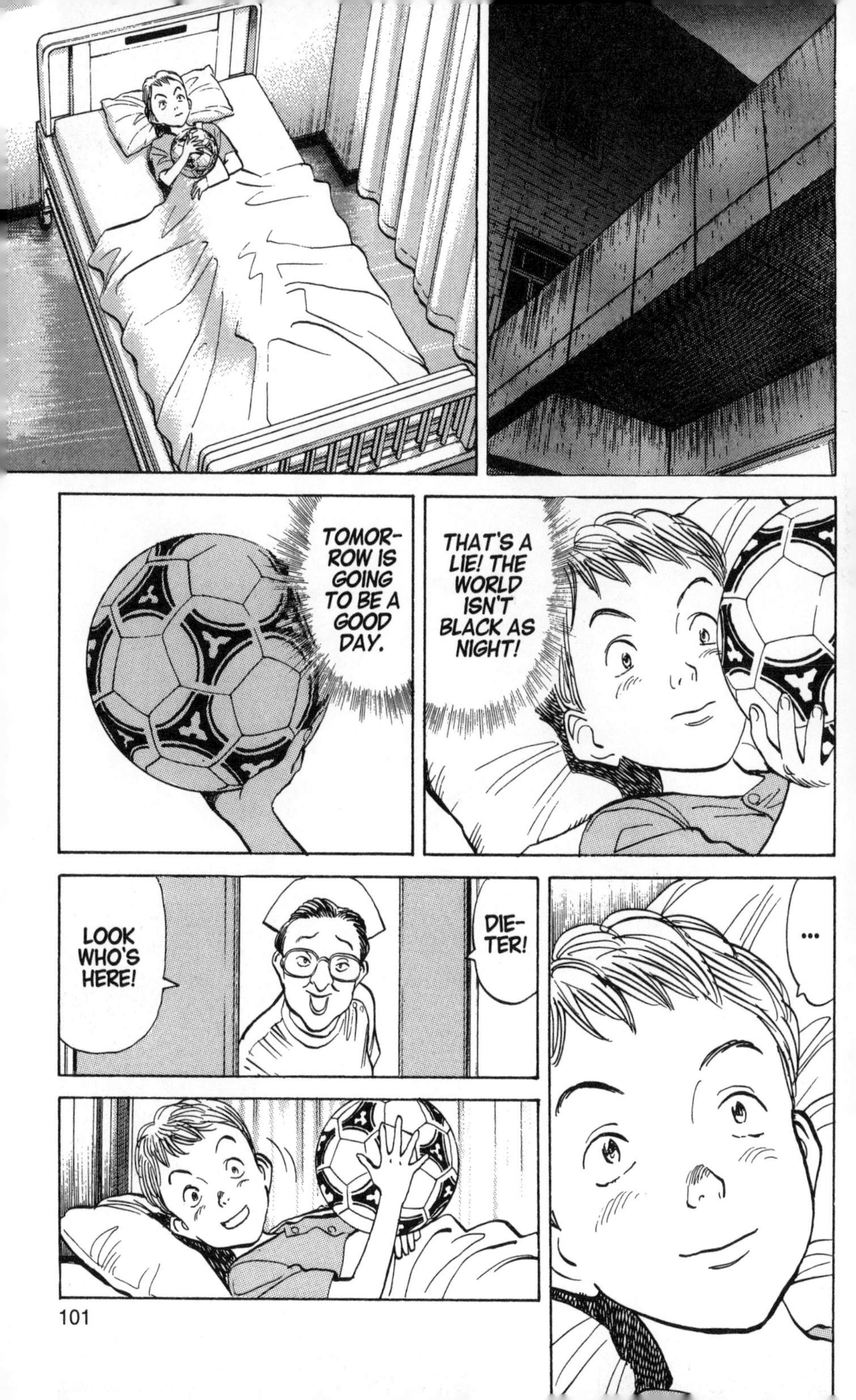
THAT'S A LIE! THE WORLD ISN'T BLACK AS NIGHT!
TOMOR-ROW IS GOING TO BE A GOOD DAY.
...
DIE-TER!
LOOK WHO'S HERE!

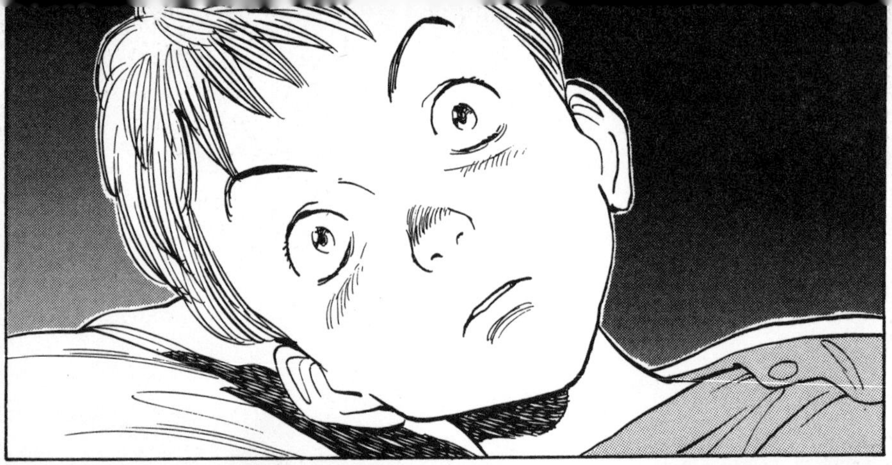
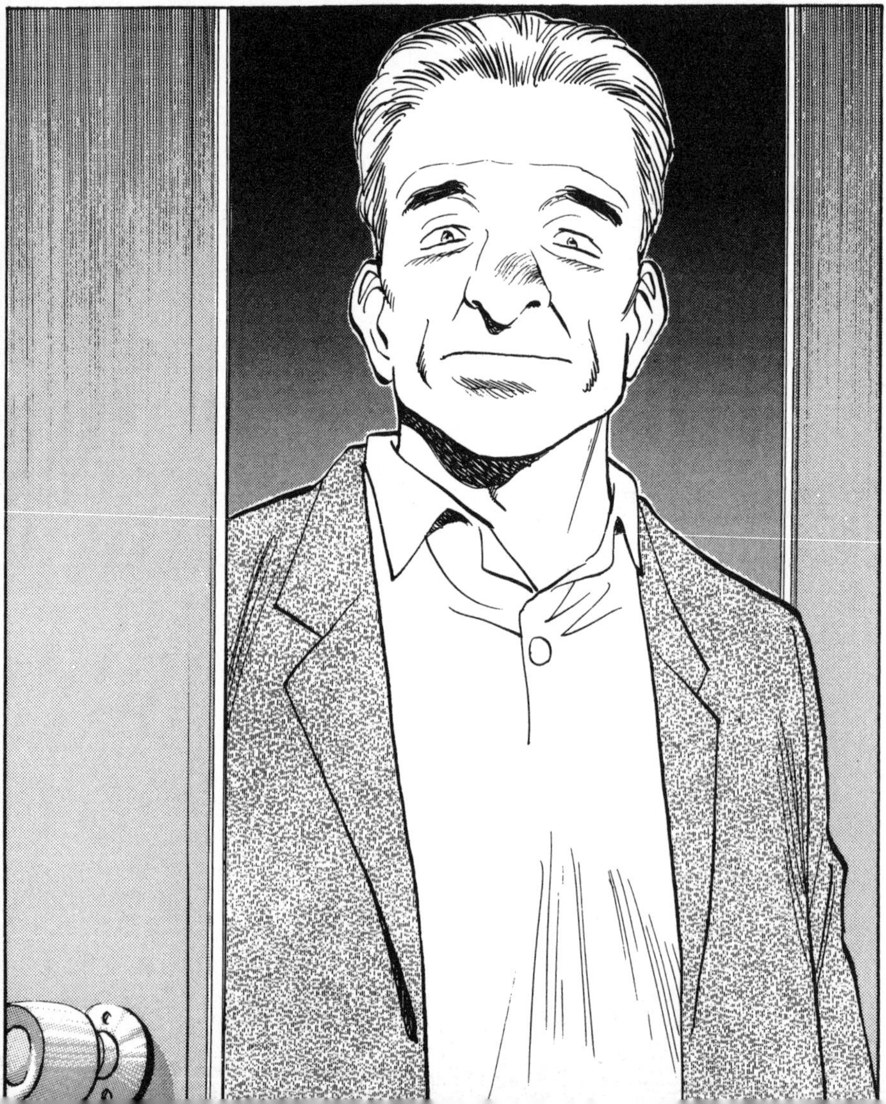

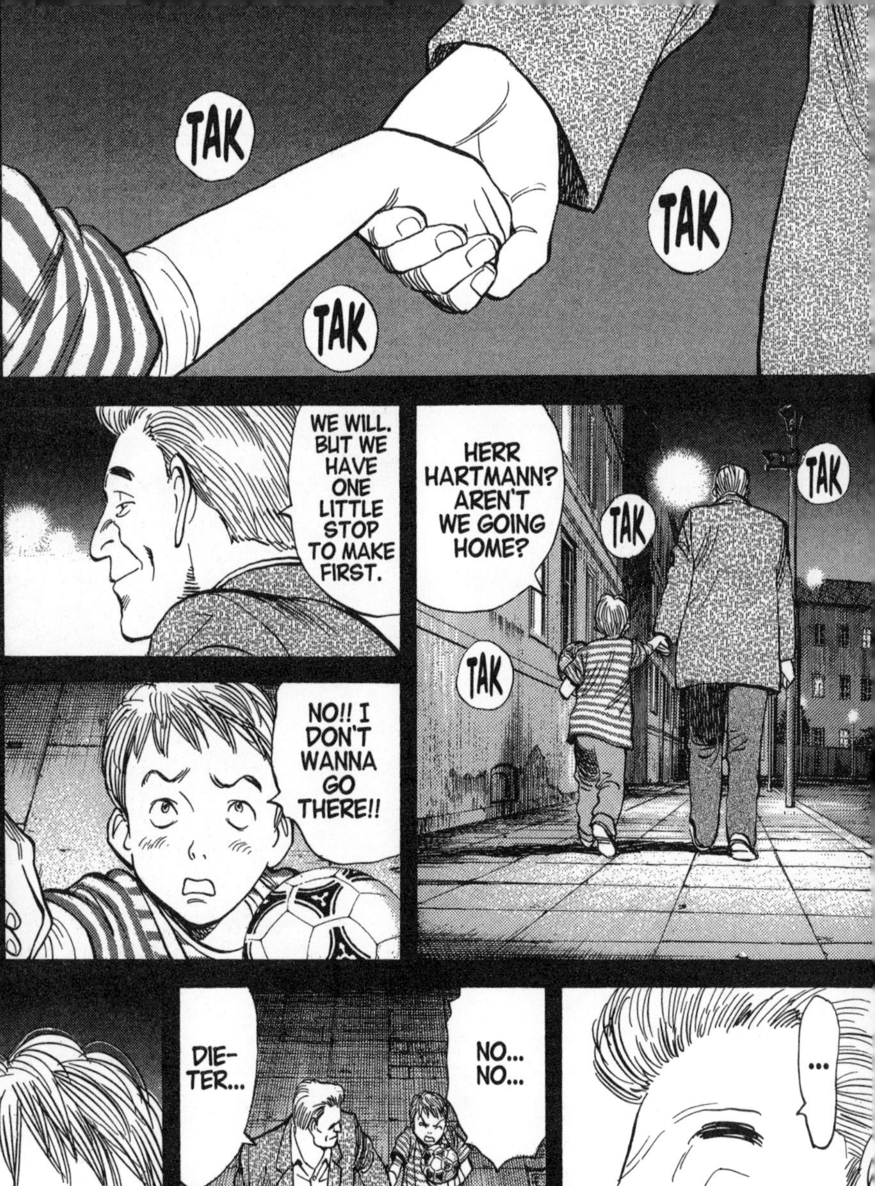
TAK
TAK
TAK
TAK
HERR HARTMANN? AREN'T WE GOING HOME?
TAK
TAK
WE WILL. BUT WE HAVE ONE LITTLE STOP TO MAKE FIRST.
NO!! I DON'T WANNA GO THERE!!
...
NO... NO...
DIE-TER...

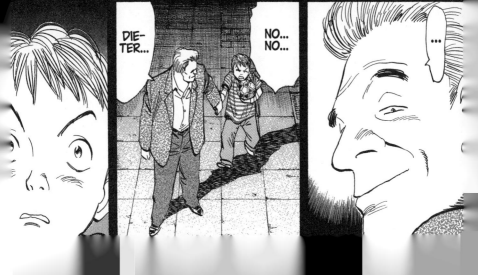

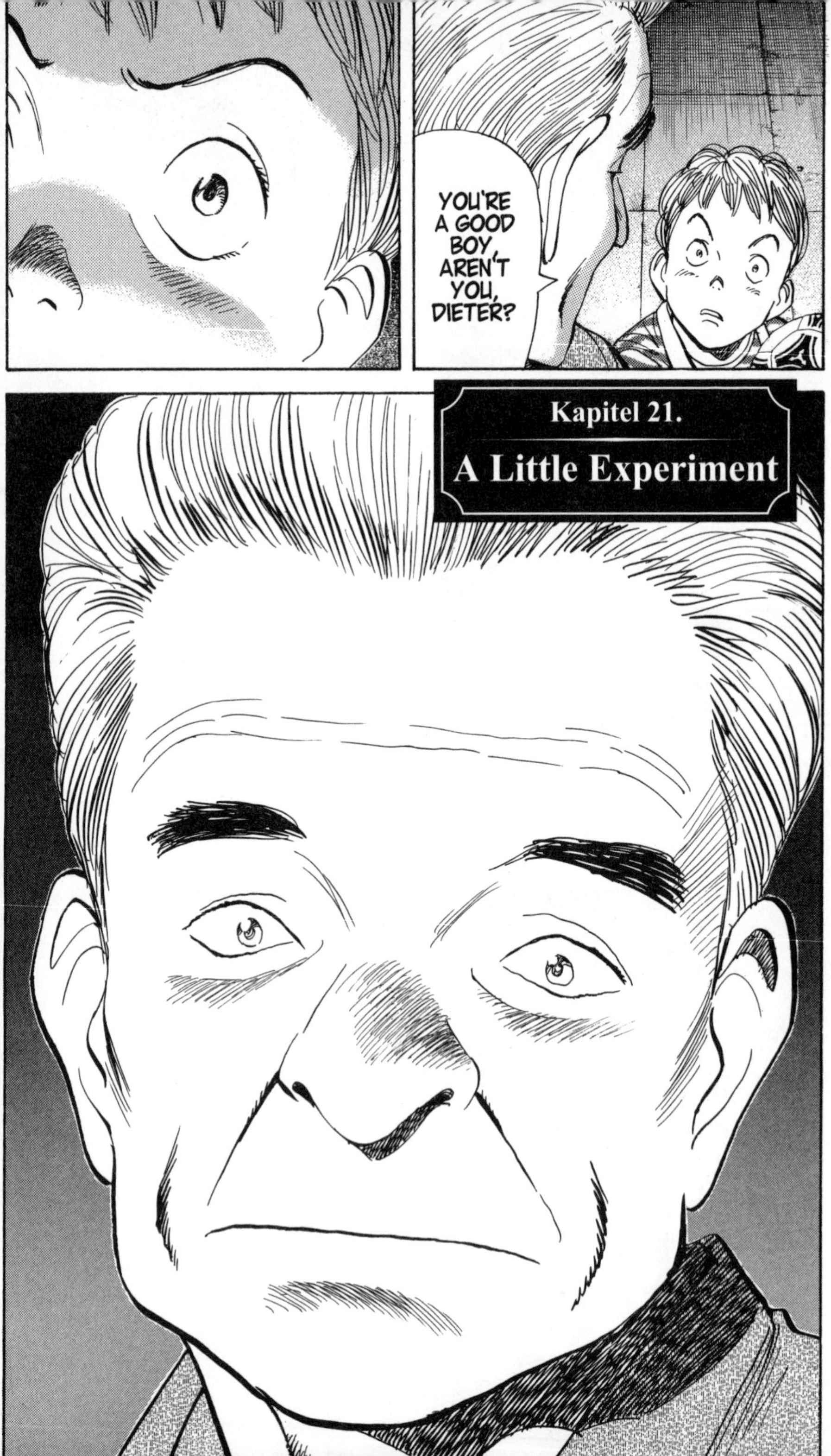
YOU'RE A GOOD BOY, AREN'T YOU, DIETER?
Kapitel 21.
A Little Experiment

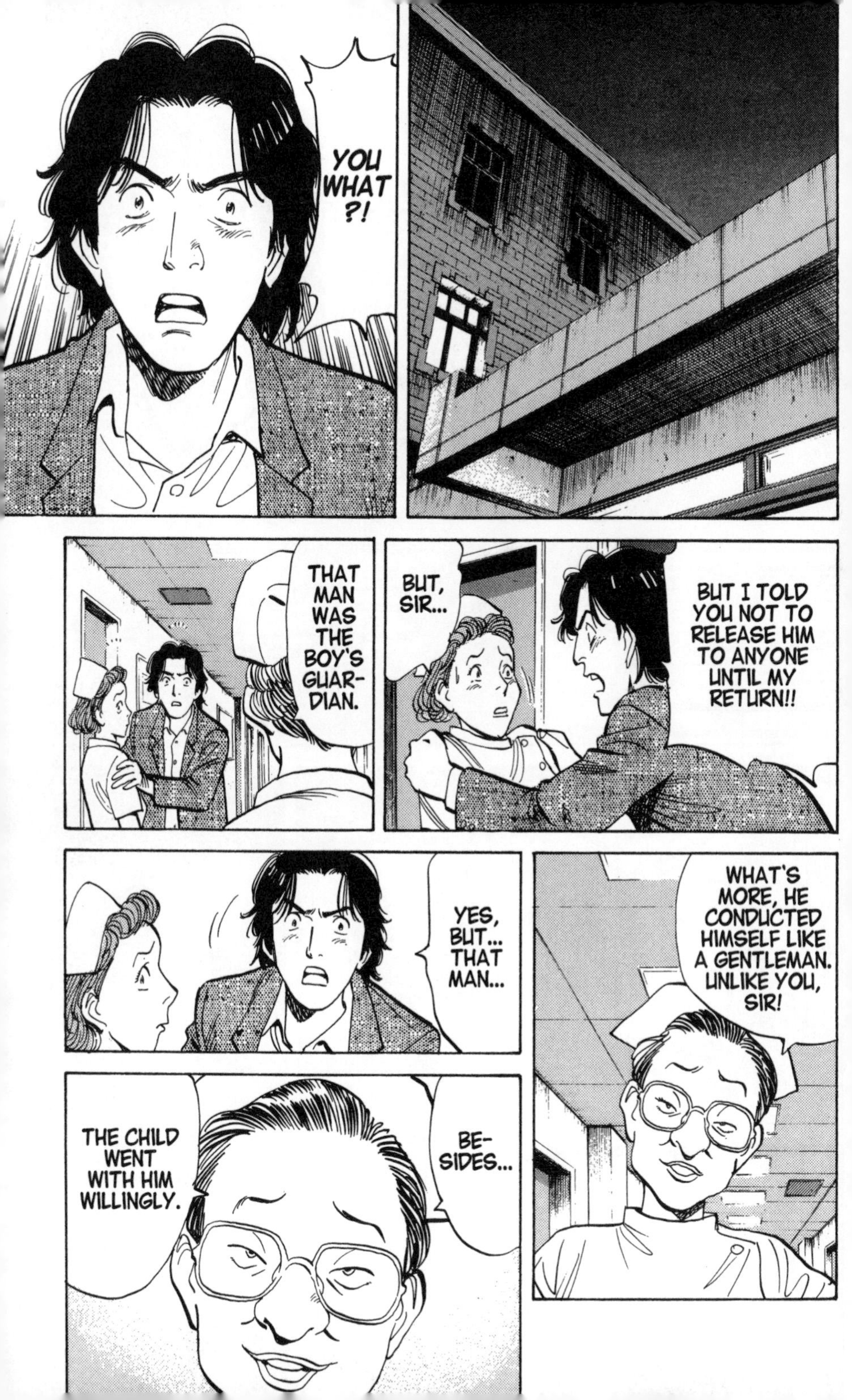
YOU WHAT?!
BUT I TOLD YOU NOT TO RELEASE HIM TO ANYONE UNTIL MY RETURN!!
BUT, SIR...
THAT MAN WAS THE BOY'S GUAR-DIAN.
WHAT'S MORE, HE CONDUCTED HIMSELF LIKE A GENTLEMAN. UNLIKE YOU, SIR!
YES, BUT... THAT MAN...
BE-SIDES...
THE CHILD WENT WITH HIM WILLINGLY.

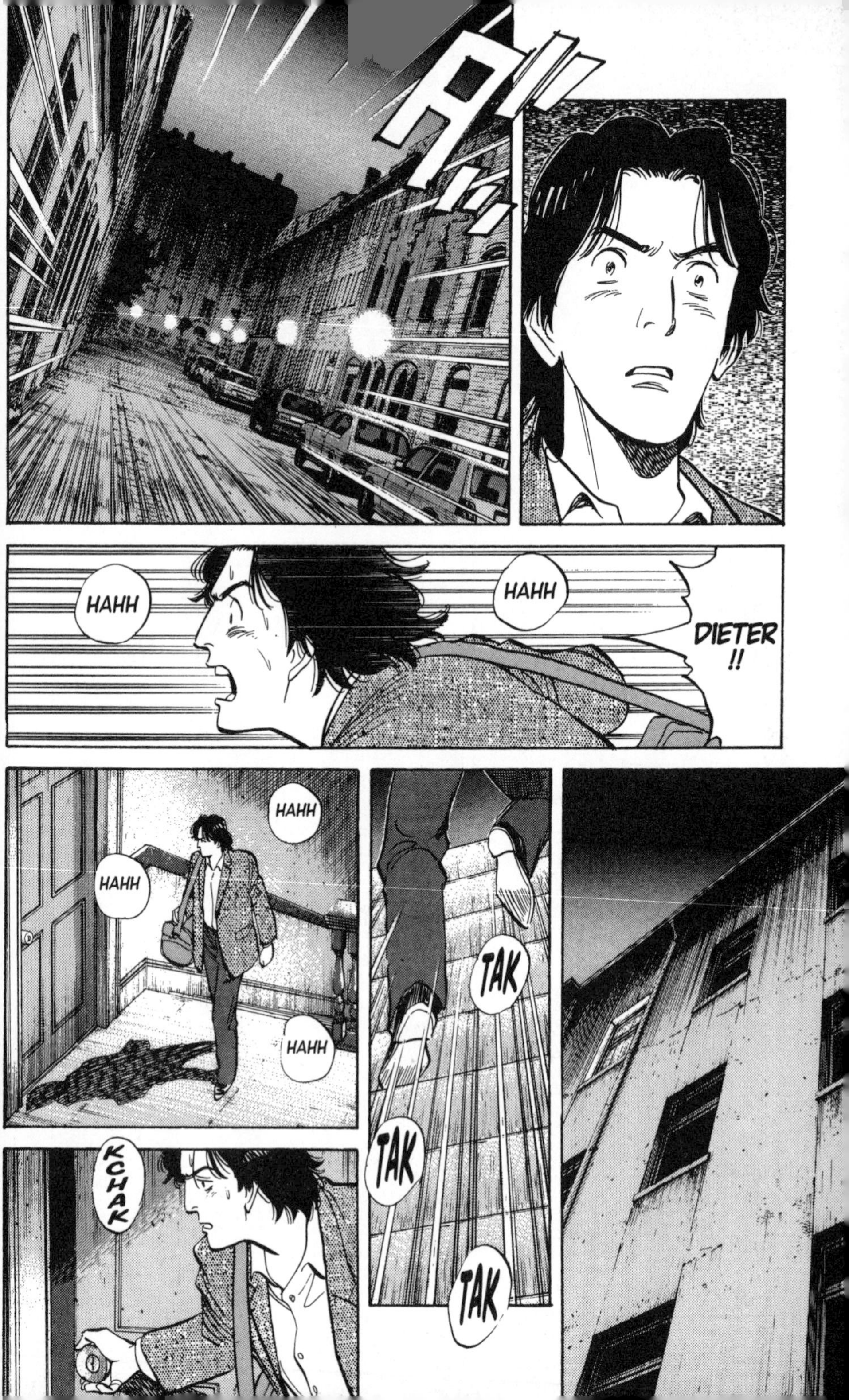
DIETER !!
HAHH
HAHH
TAK
TAK
TAK
HAHH
HAHH
HAHH
KCHAK

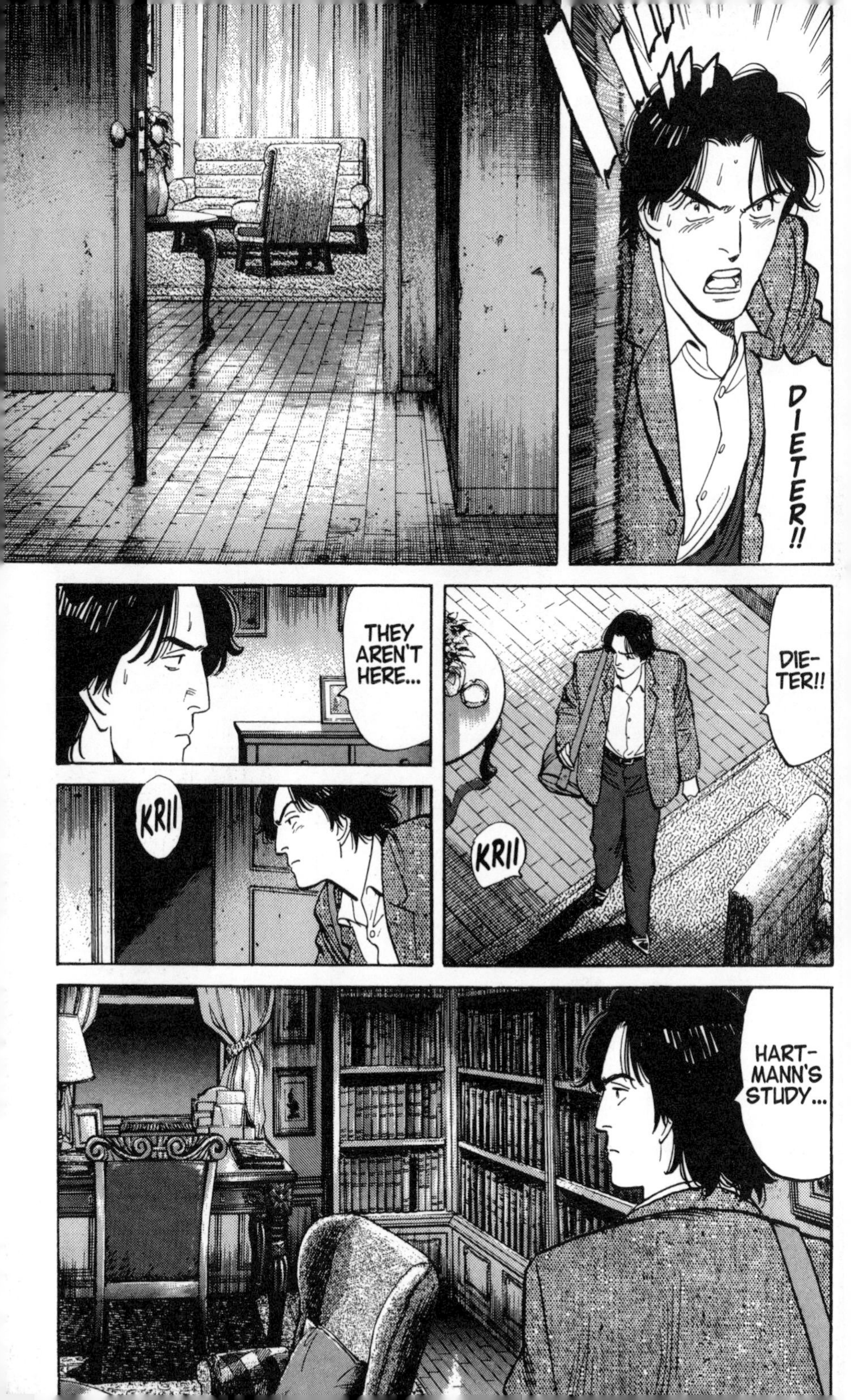
DIETER!!
DIE-TER!!
KRII
THEY AREN'T HERE...
KRII
HART-MANN'S STUDY...

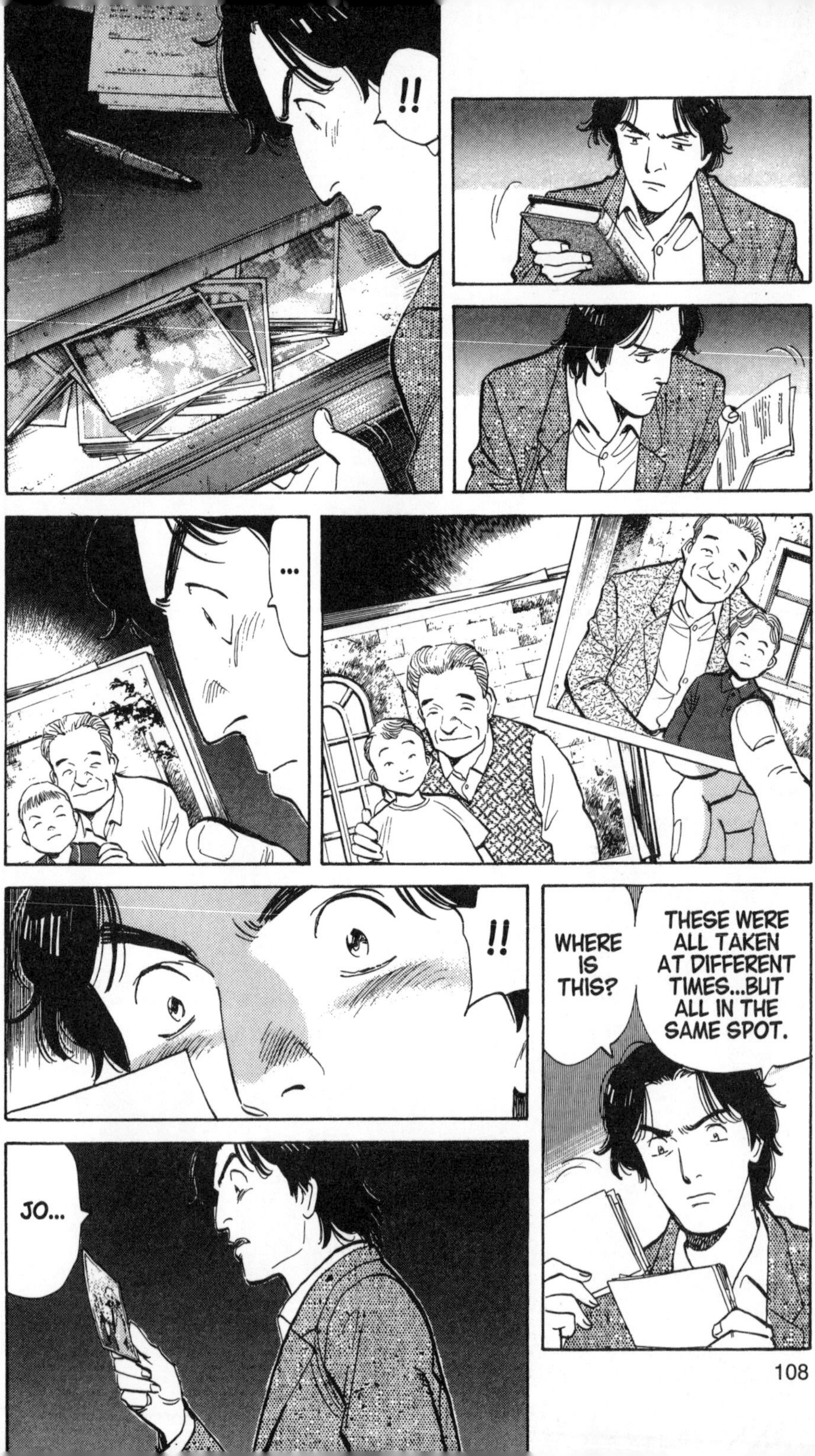
!!
...
THESE WERE ALL TAKEN AT DIFFERENT TIMES...BUT ALL IN THE SAME SPOT.
WHERE IS THIS?
!!
JO...

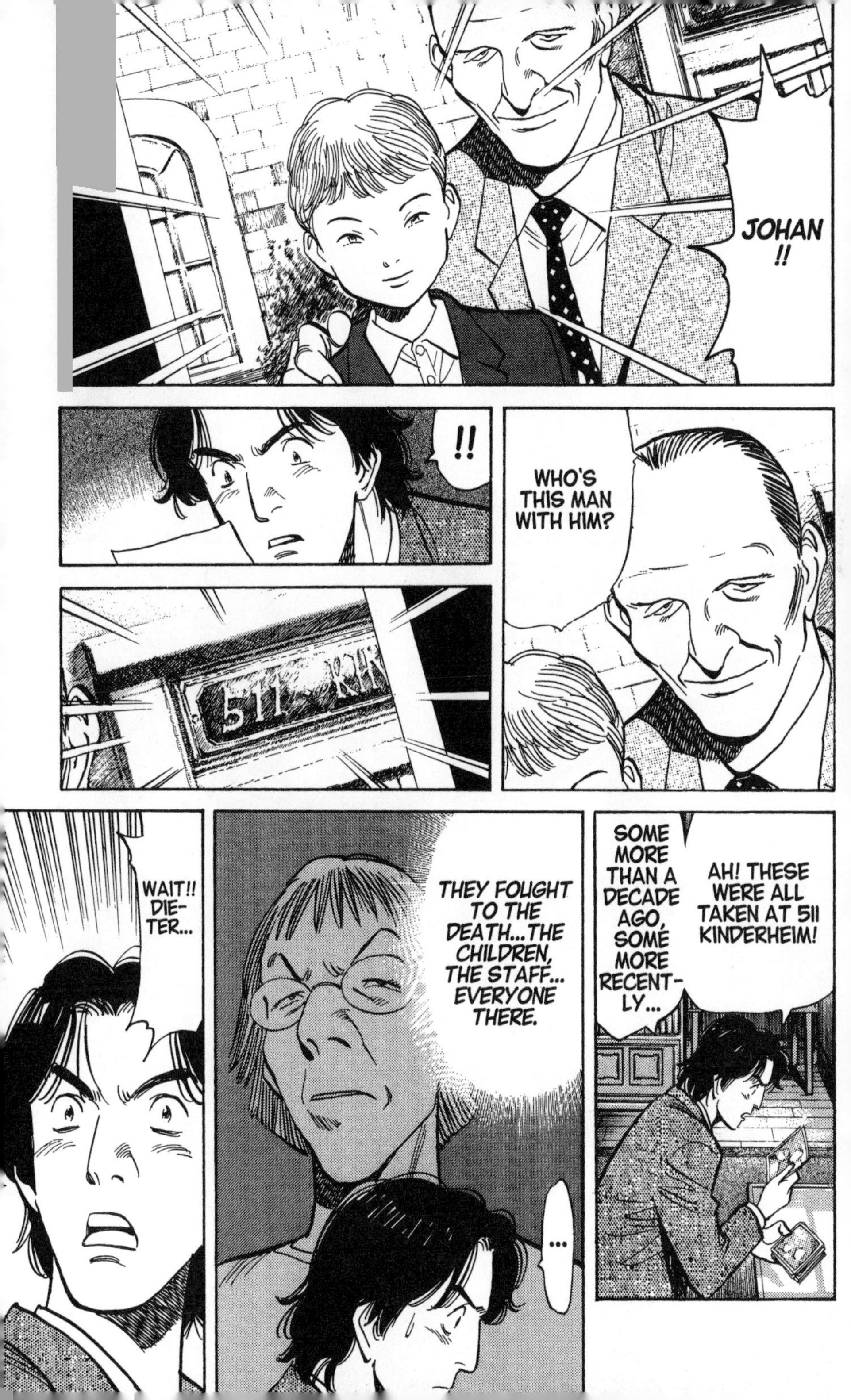
JOHAN !!
WHO'S THIS MAN WITH HIM?
!!
511
AH! THESE WERE ALL TAKEN AT 511 KINDERHEIM!
SOME MORE THAN A DECADE AGO, SOME MORE RECENTLY...
THEY FOUGHT TO THE DEATH...THE CHILDREN, THE STAFF... EVERYONE THERE.
...
WAIT!! DIETER...

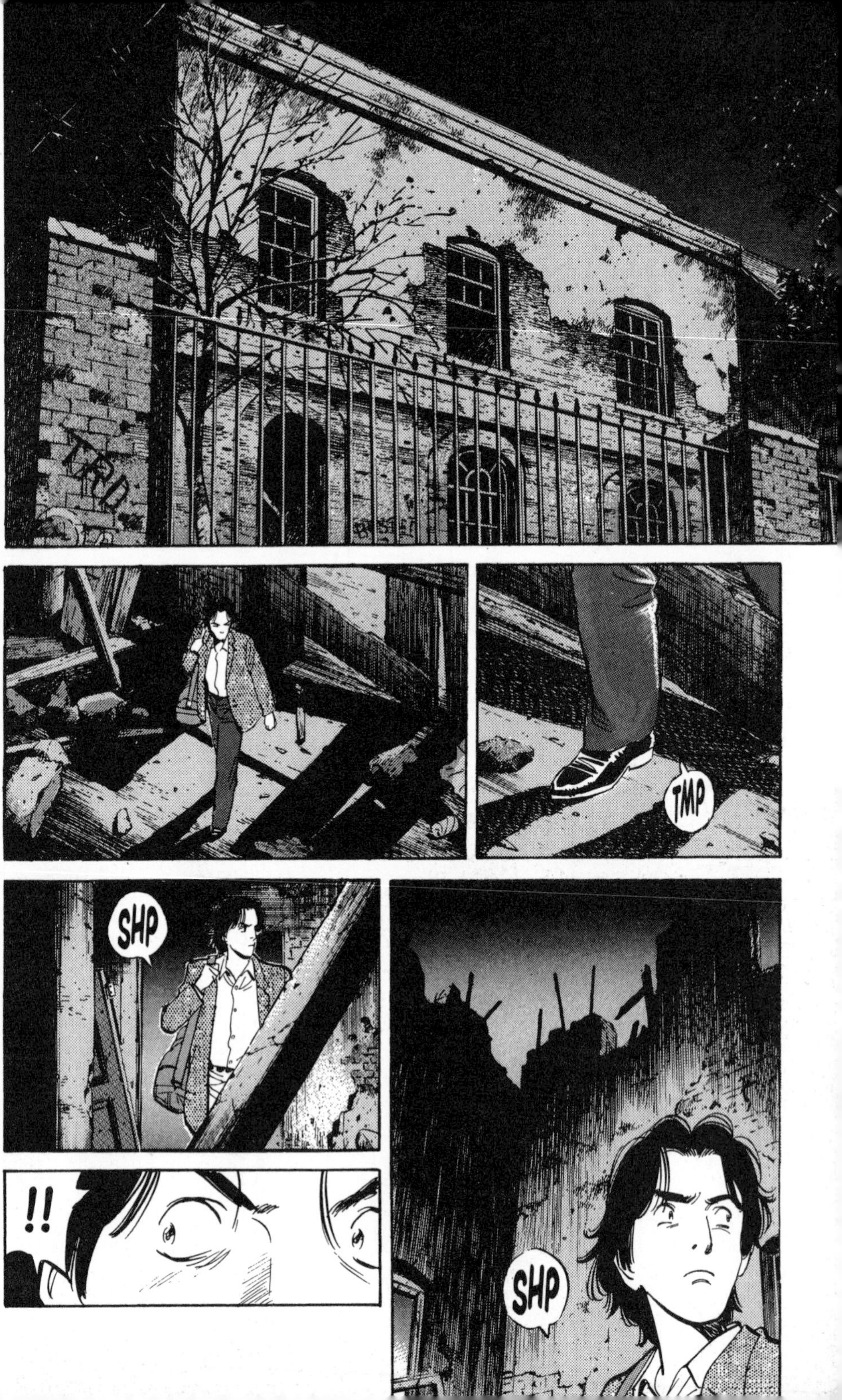
TMP
SHP
SHP
!!

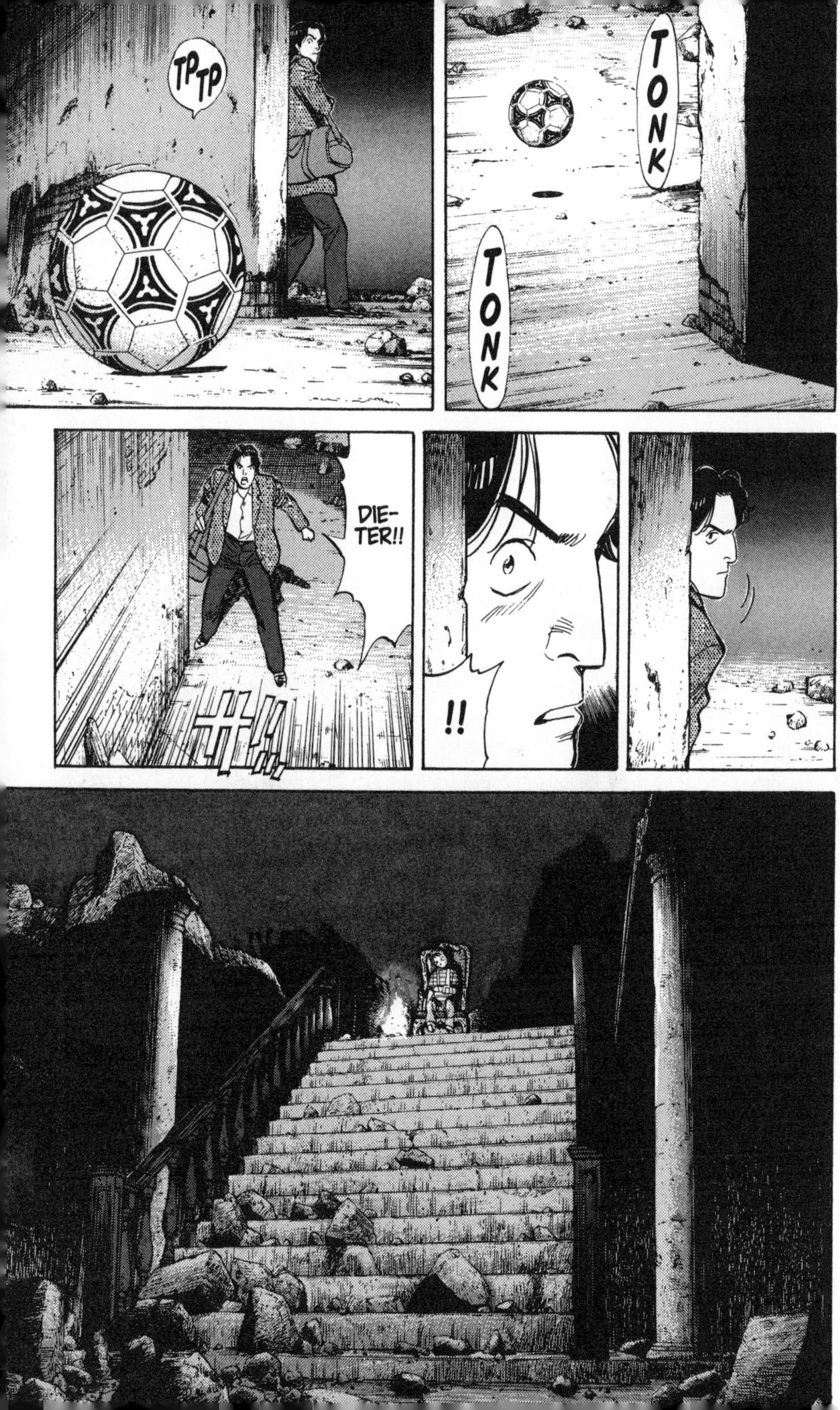
TONK
TONK
TP TP
!!
DIE-
TER!!

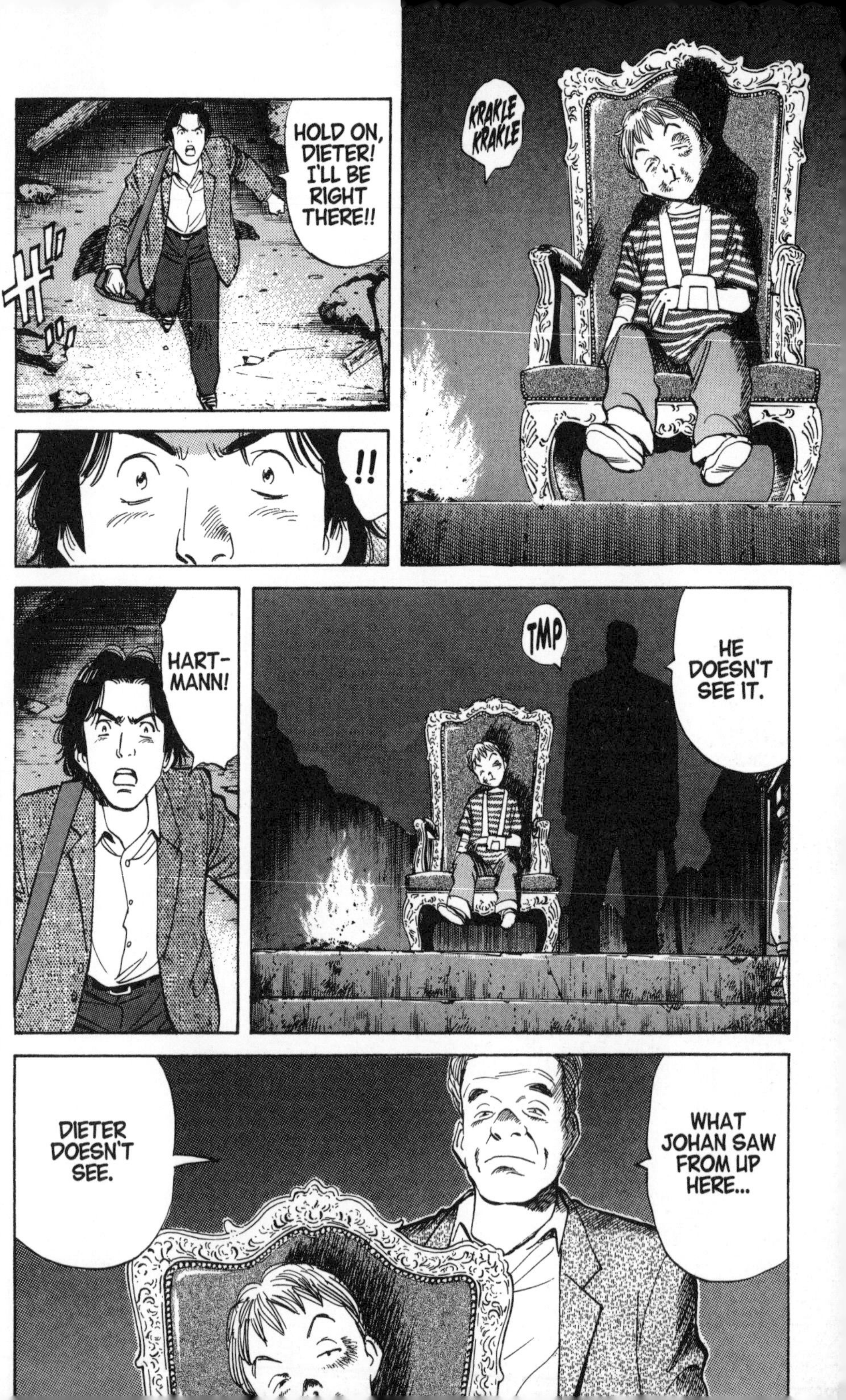
KRAKLE KRAKLE
HOLD ON, DIETER! I'LL BE RIGHT THERE!!
!!
TMP
HE DOESN'T SEE IT.
HART-MANN!
WHAT JOHAN SAW FROM UP HERE...
DIETER DOESN'T SEE.

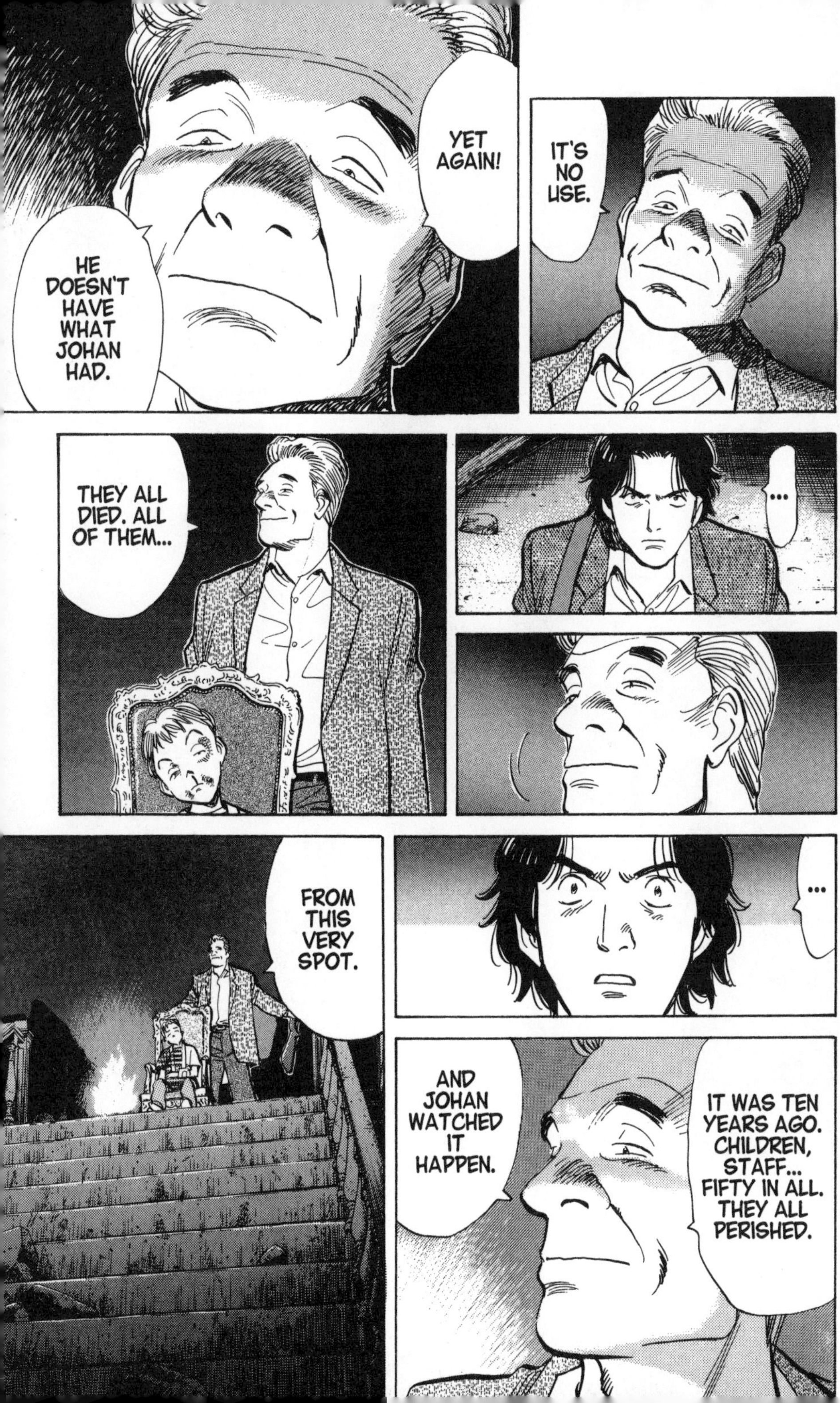
IT'S NO USE.
YET AGAIN!
HE DOESN'T HAVE WHAT JOHAN HAD.
...
THEY ALL DIED. ALL OF THEM...
...
IT WAS TEN YEARS AGO. CHILDREN, STAFF... FIFTY IN ALL. THEY ALL PERISHED.
AND JOHAN WATCHED IT HAPPEN.
FROM THIS VERY SPOT.

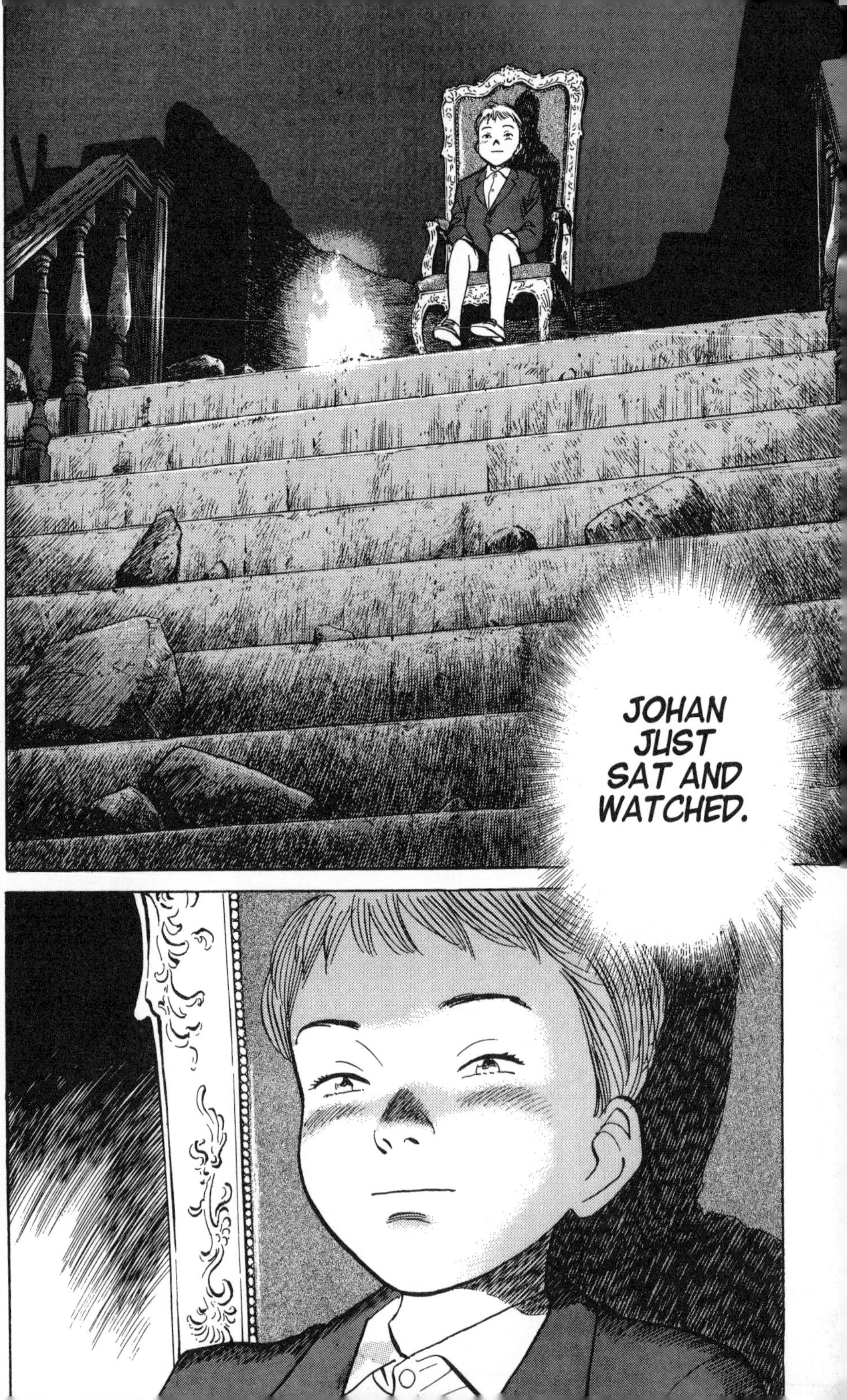
JOHAN JUST SAT AND WATCHED.

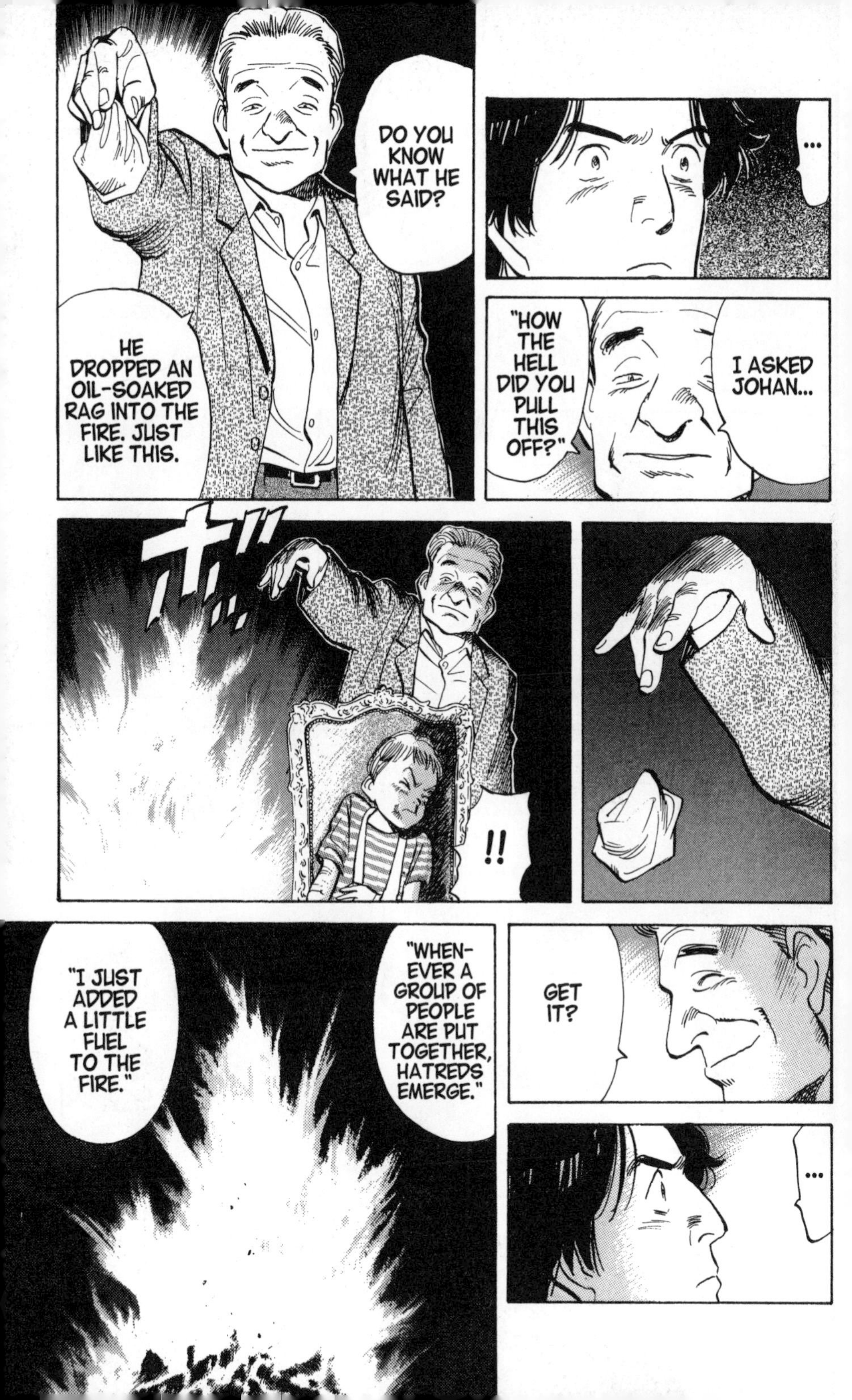
...
I ASKED JOHAN...
"HOW THE HELL DID YOU PULL THIS OFF?"
DO YOU KNOW WHAT HE SAID?
HE DROPPED AN OIL-SOAKED RAG INTO THE FIRE. JUST LIKE THIS.
!!
GET IT?
...
"WHEN-EVER A GROUP OF PEOPLE ARE PUT TOGETHER, HATREDS EMERGE."
"I JUST ADDED A LITTLE FUEL TO THE FIRE."

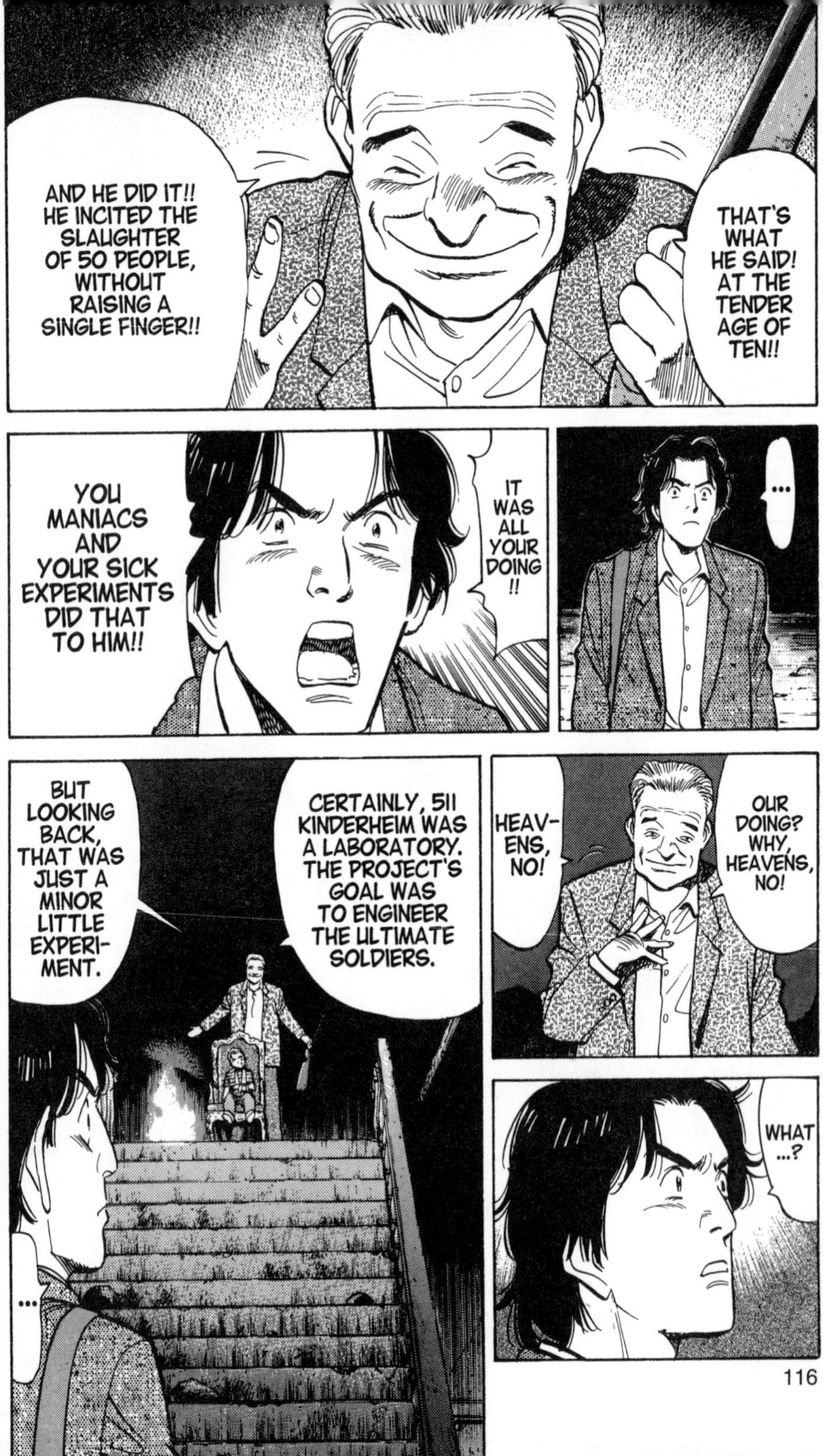
THAT'S WHAT HE SAID! AT THE TENDER AGE OF TEN!!
AND HE DID IT!! HE INCITED THE SLAUGHTER OF 50 PEOPLE, WITHOUT RAISING A SINGLE FINGER!!
...
IT WAS ALL YOUR DOING!!
YOU MANIACS AND YOUR SICK EXPERIMENTS DID THAT TO HIM!!
OUR DOING? WHY, HEAVENS, NO!
HEAV-ENS, NO!
WHAT ...?
CERTAINLY, 511 KINDERHEIM WAS A LABORATORY. THE PROJECT'S GOAL WAS TO ENGINEER THE ULTIMATE SOLDIERS.
BUT LOOKING BACK, THAT WAS JUST A MINOR LITTLE EXPERI-MENT.
...

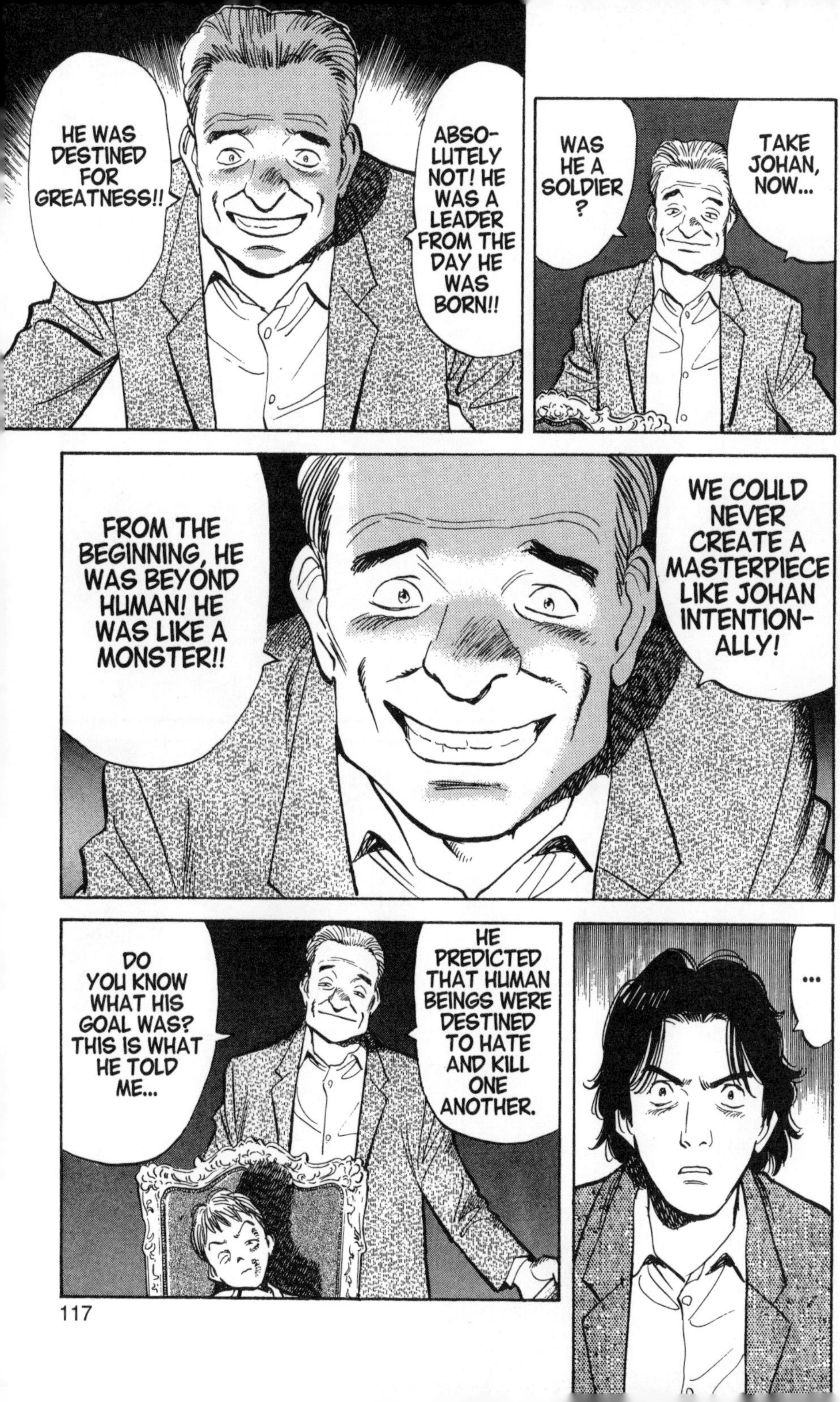

TAKE JOHAN, NOW...
WAS HE A SOLDIER?
ABSOLUTELY NOT! HE WAS A LEADER FROM THE DAY HE WAS BORN!!
HE WAS DESTINED FOR GREATNESS!!
WE COULD NEVER CREATE A MASTERPIECE LIKE JOHAN INTENTIONALLY!
FROM THE BEGINNING, HE WAS BEYOND HUMAN! HE WAS LIKE A MONSTER!!
...
HE PREDICTED THAT HUMAN BEINGS WERE DESTINED TO HATE AND KILL ONE ANOTHER.
DO YOU KNOW WHAT HIS GOAL WAS? THIS IS WHAT HE TOLD ME...

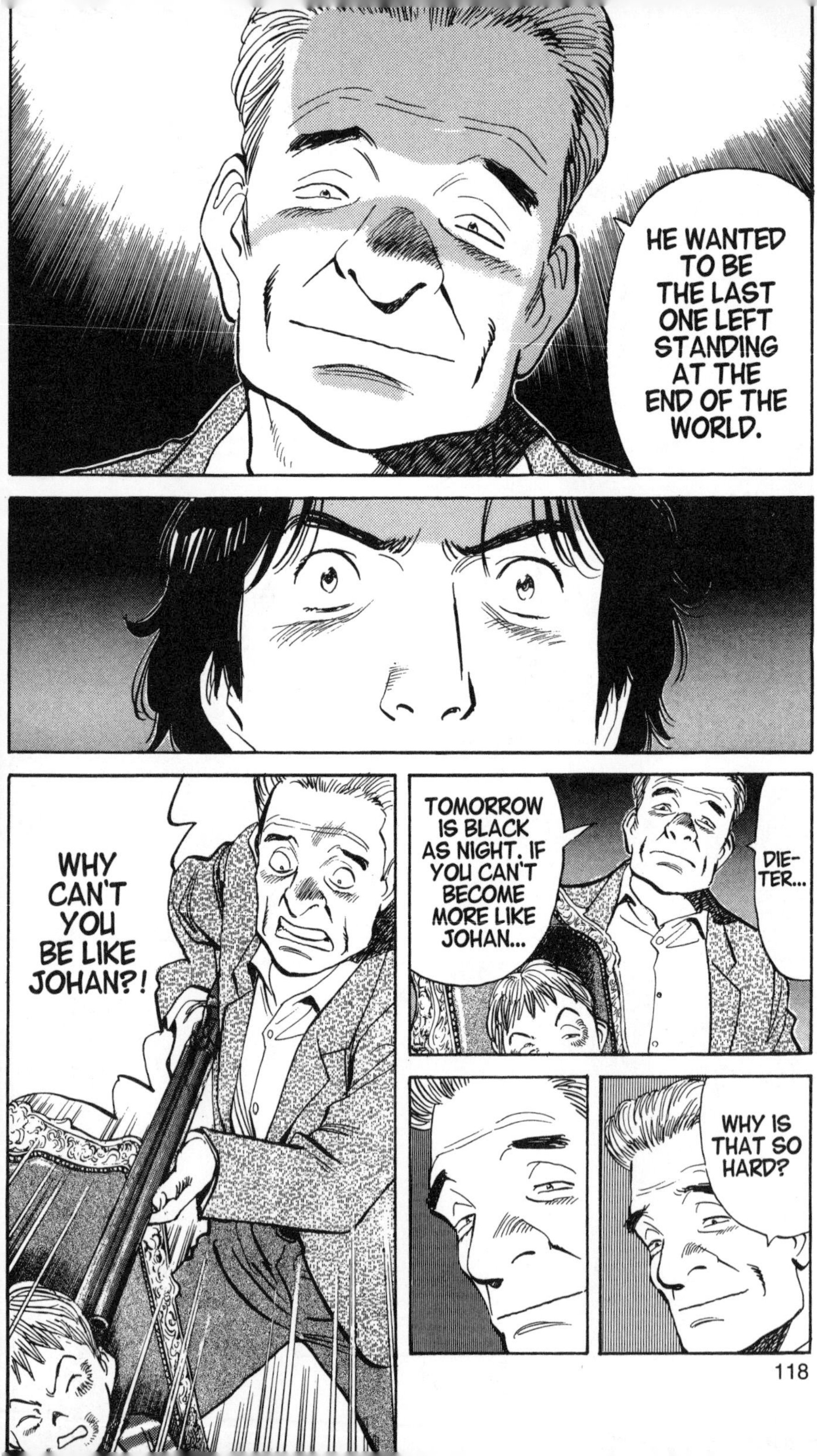
HE WANTED TO BE THE LAST ONE LEFT STANDING AT THE END OF THE WORLD.
DIE-TER...
TOMORROW IS BLACK AS NIGHT. IF YOU CAN'T BECOME MORE LIKE JOHAN...
WHY IS THAT SO HARD?
WHY CAN'T YOU BE LIKE JOHAN?!

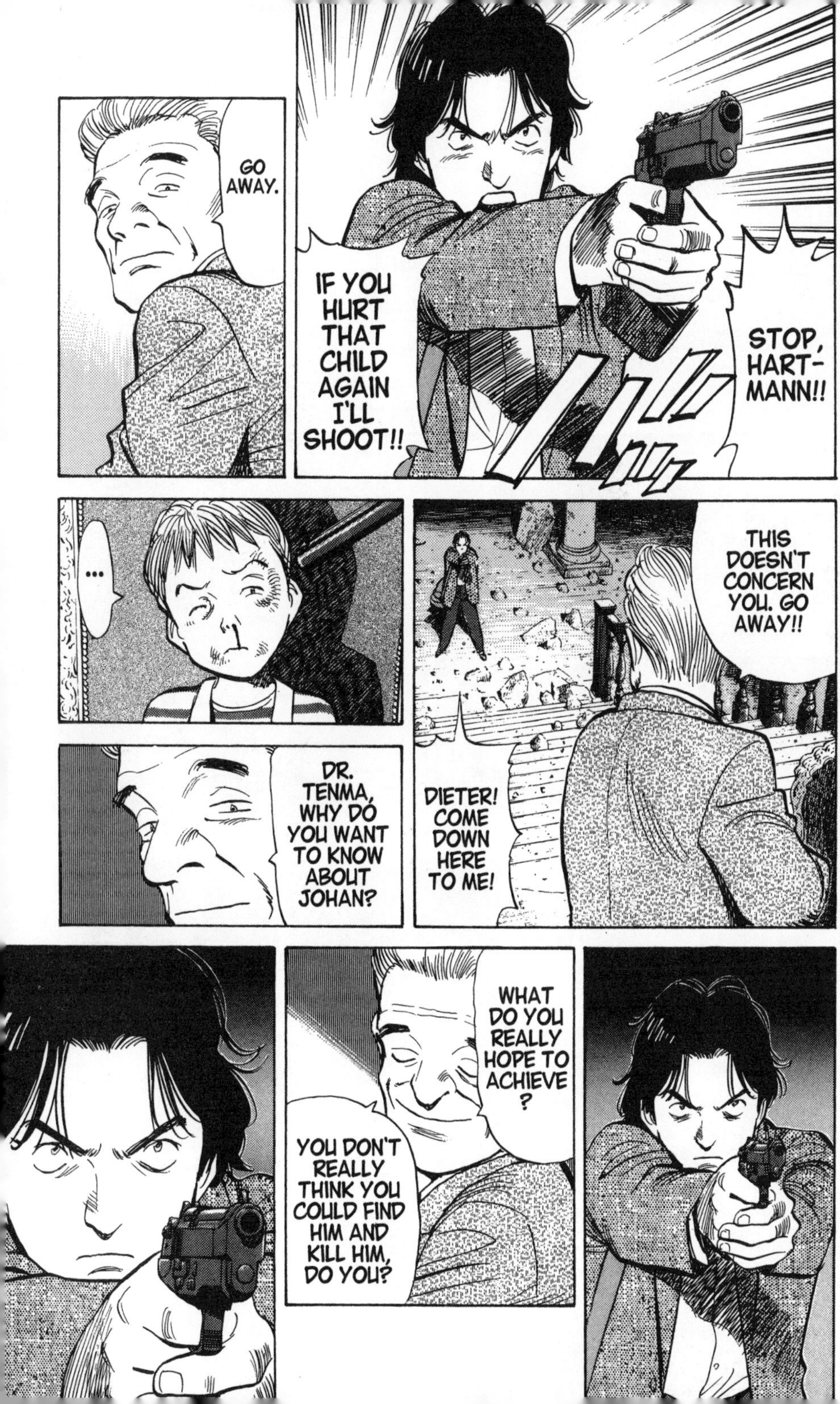
STOP, HART-MANN!!
IF YOU HURT THAT CHILD AGAIN I'LL SHOOT!!
GO AWAY.
THIS DOESN'T CONCERN YOU. GO AWAY!!
DIETER! COME DOWN HERE TO ME!
...
DR. TENMA, WHY DO YOU WANT TO KNOW ABOUT JOHAN?
WHAT DO YOU REALLY HOPE TO ACHIEVE?
YOU DON'T REALLY THINK YOU COULD FIND HIM AND KILL HIM, DO YOU?

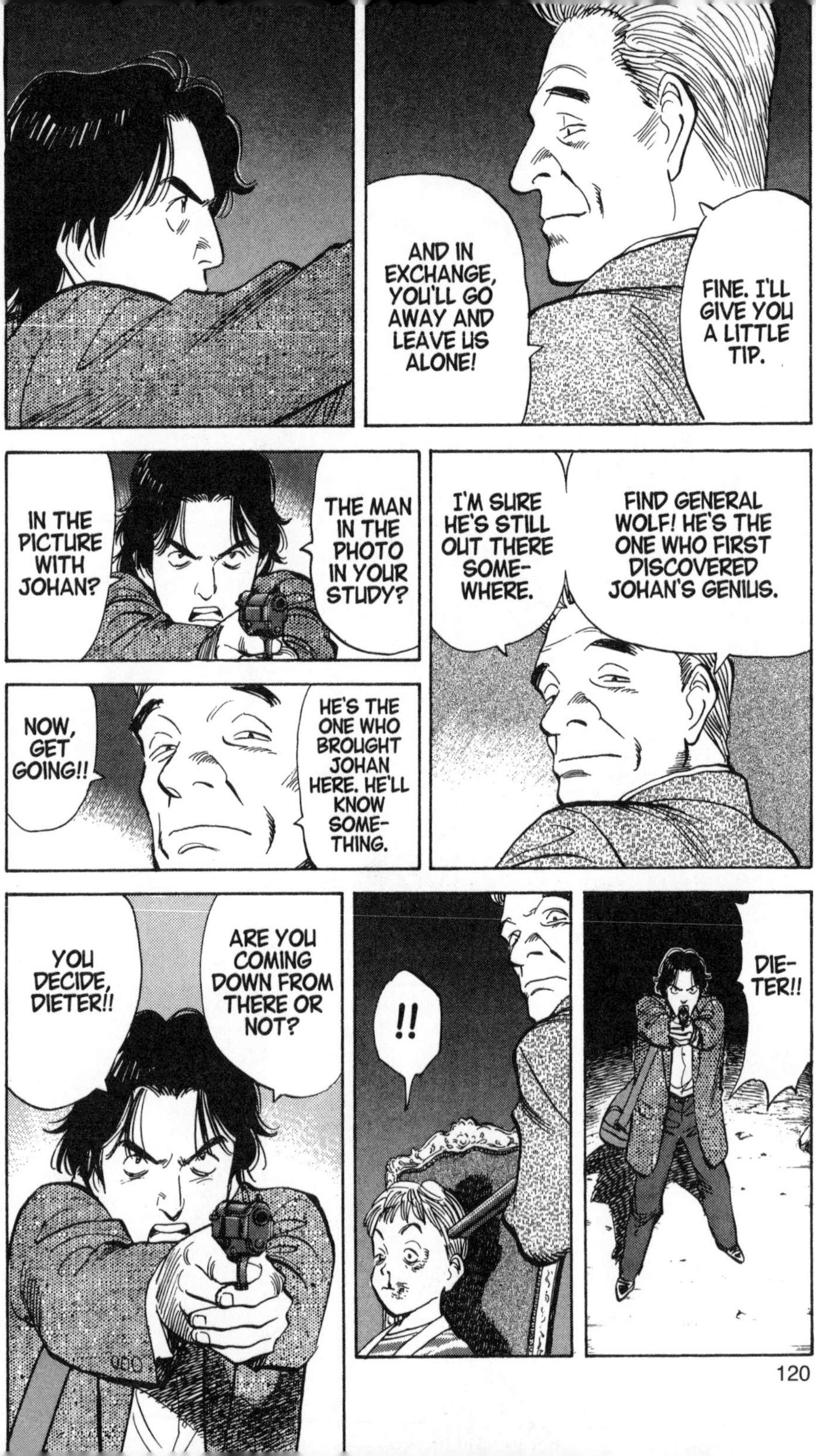

FINE. I'LL GIVE YOU A LITTLE TIP.
AND IN EXCHANGE, YOU'LL GO AWAY AND LEAVE US ALONE!
FIND GENERAL WOLF! HE'S THE ONE WHO FIRST DISCOVERED JOHAN'S GENIUS.
I'M SURE HE'S STILL OUT THERE SOME-WHERE.
THE MAN IN THE PHOTO IN YOUR STUDY?
IN THE PICTURE WITH JOHAN?
HE'S THE ONE WHO BROUGHT JOHAN HERE. HE'LL KNOW SOME-THING.
NOW, GET GOING!!
DIE-TER!!
!!
ARE YOU COMING DOWN FROM THERE OR NOT?
YOU DECIDE, DIETER!!

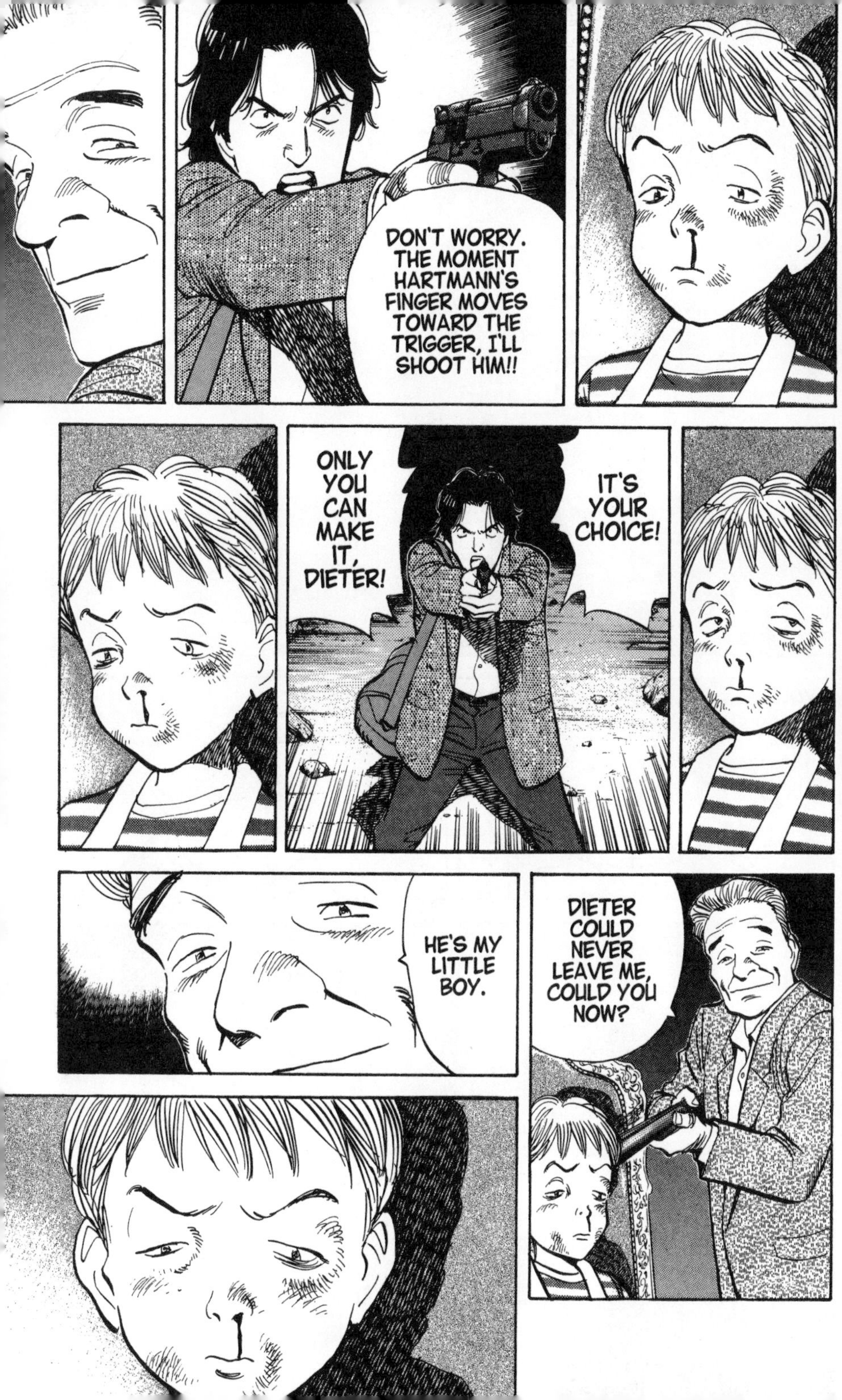
DON'T WORRY. THE MOMENT HARTMANN'S FINGER MOVES TOWARD THE TRIGGER, I'LL SHOOT HIM!!
IT'S YOUR CHOICE!
ONLY YOU CAN MAKE IT, DIETER!
DIETER COULD NEVER LEAVE ME, COULD YOU NOW?
HE'S MY LITTLE BOY.

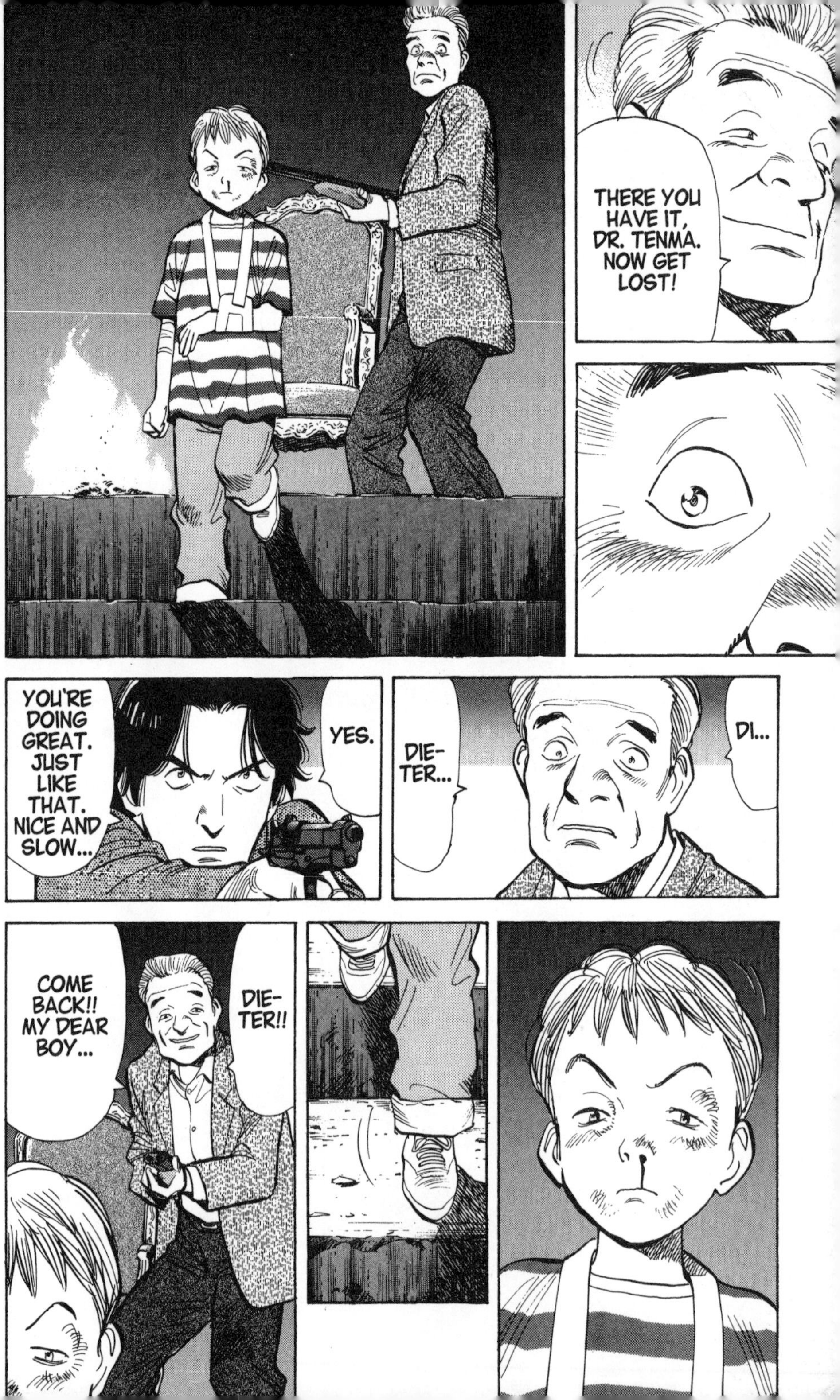
THERE YOU HAVE IT, DR. TENMA. NOW GET LOST!
DI...
DIE-TER...
YES.
YOU'RE DOING GREAT. JUST LIKE THAT. NICE AND SLOW...
DIE-TER!!
COME BACK!! MY DEAR BOY...

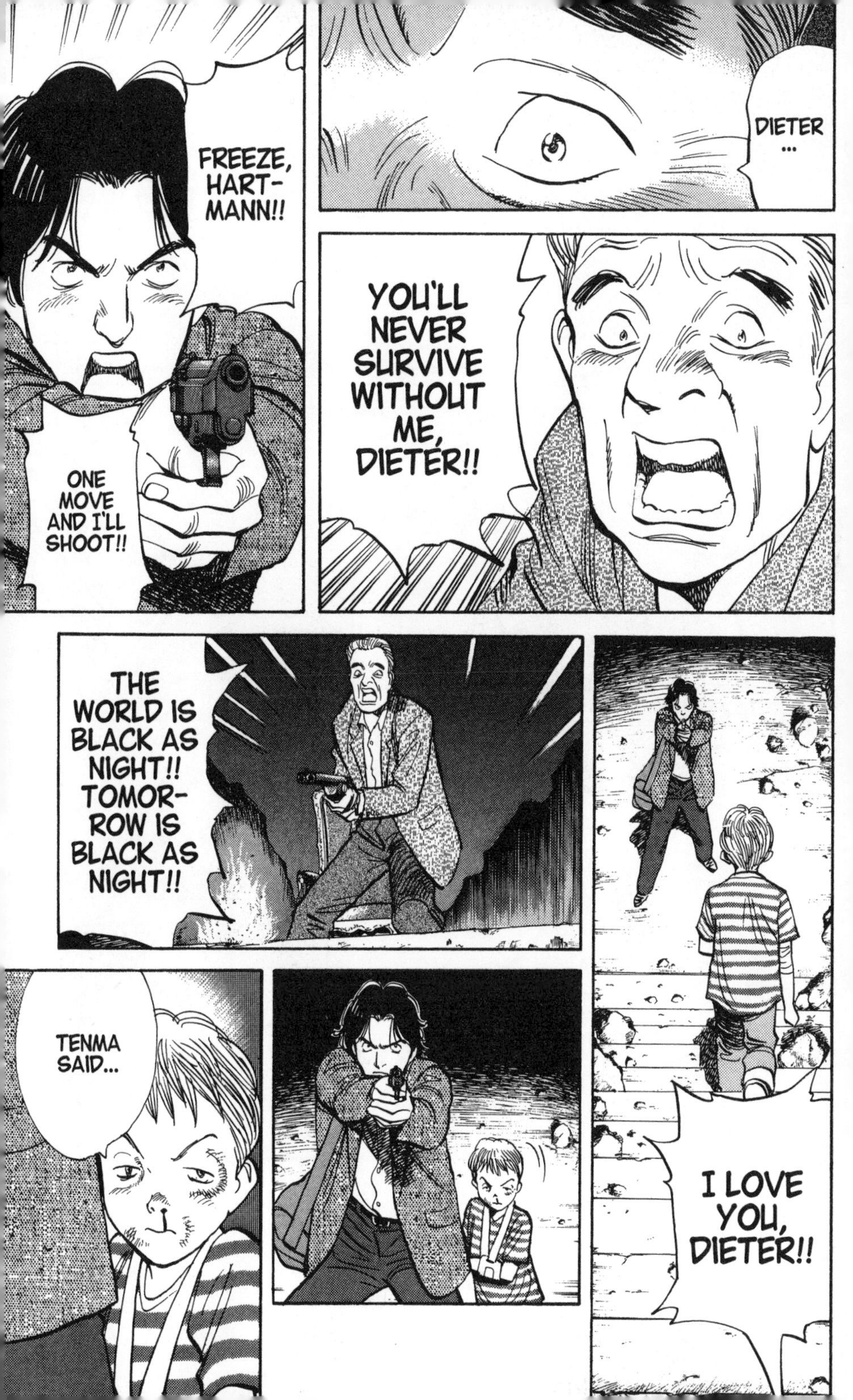
DIETER ...
YOU'LL NEVER SURVIVE WITHOUT ME, DIETER!!
FREEZE, HART-MANN!!
ONE MOVE AND I'LL SHOOT!!
I LOVE YOU, DIETER!!
THE WORLD IS BLACK AS NIGHT!! TOMOR-ROW IS BLACK AS NIGHT!!
TENMA SAID...

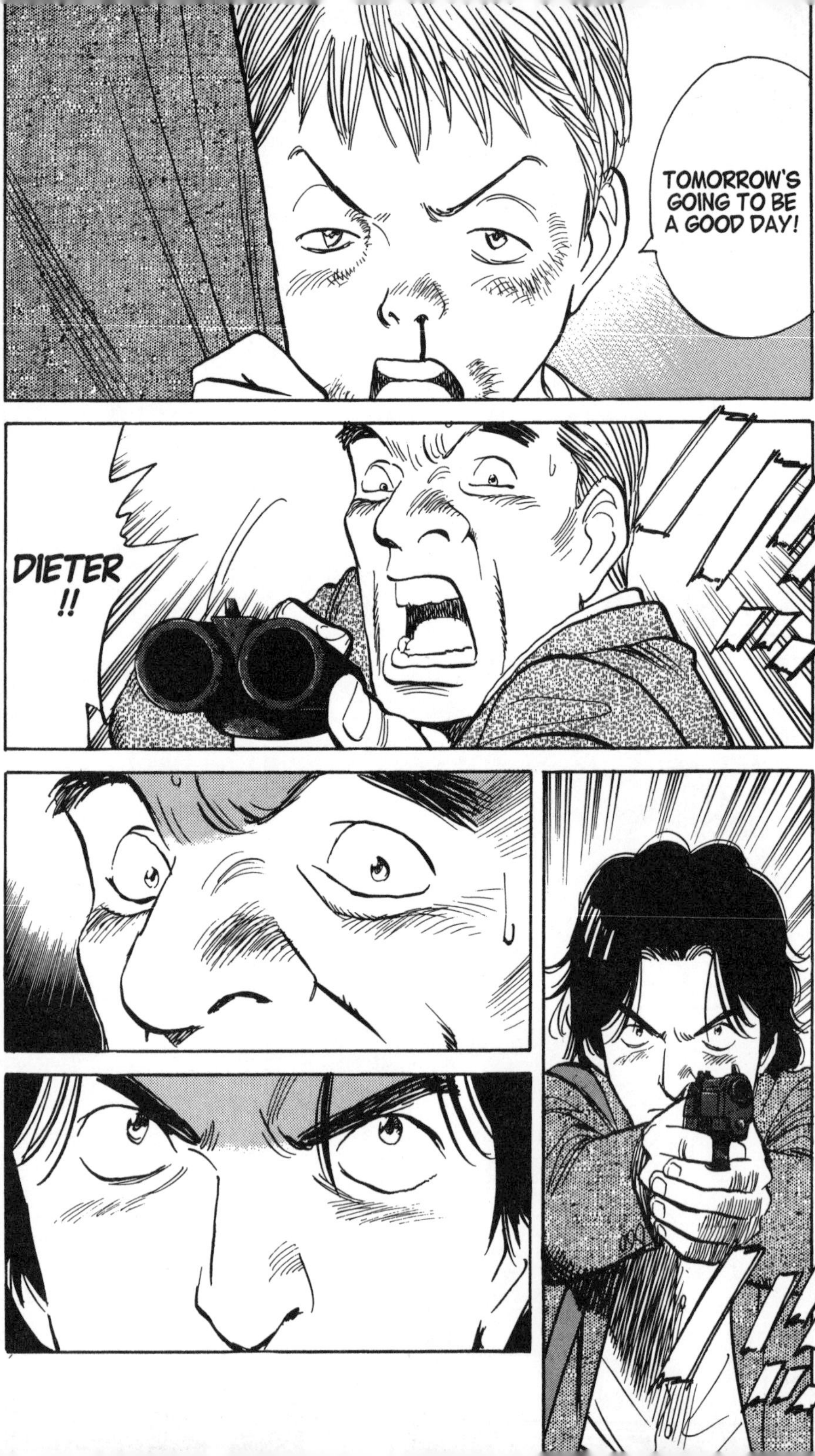
TOMORROW'S GOING TO BE A GOOD DAY!
DIETER !!

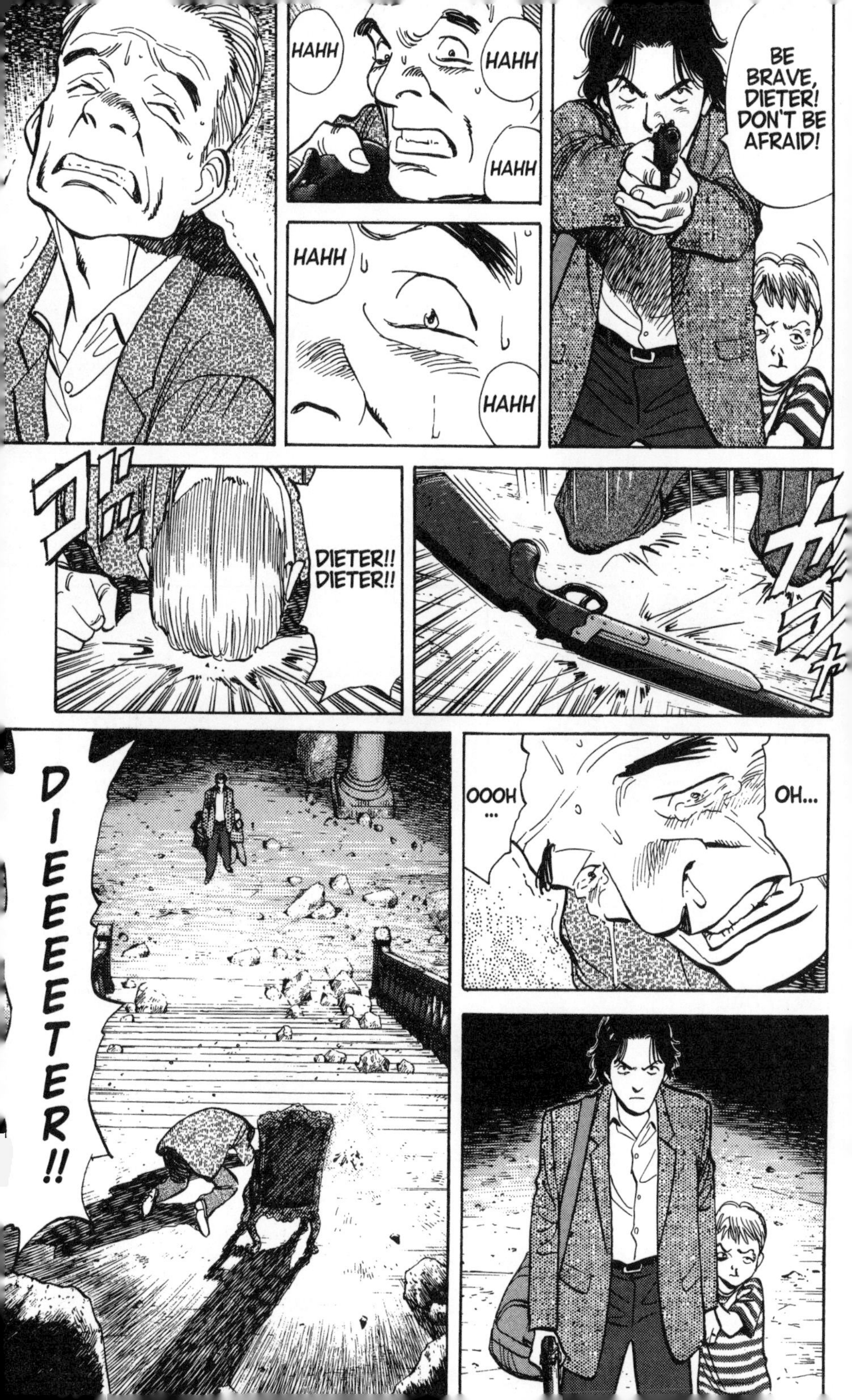
BE BRAVE, DIETER! DON'T BE AFRAID!
HAHH
HAHH
HAHH
HAHH
HAHH
DIETER!! DIETER!!
OH...
OOOH ...
DIEEEEETER!!

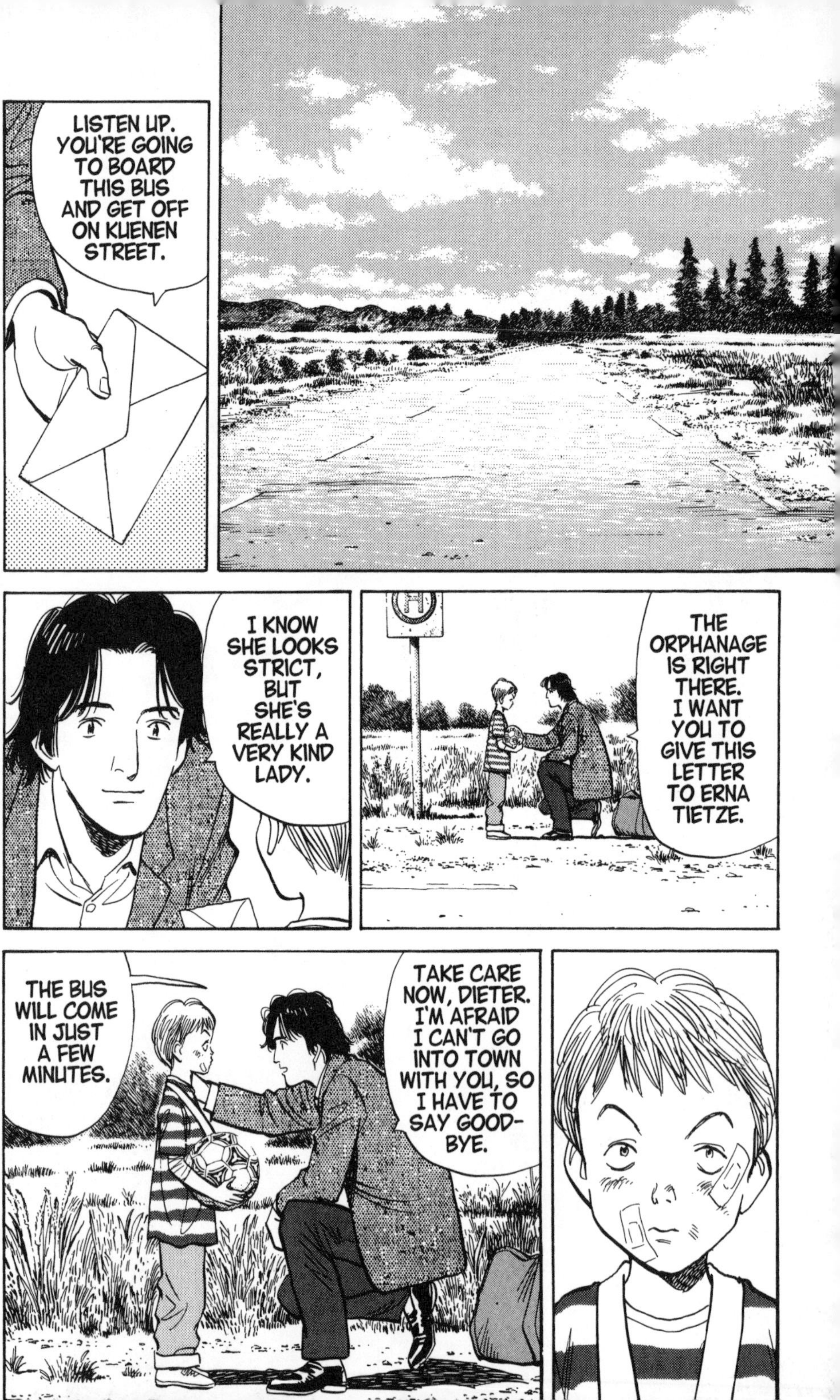
LISTEN UP. YOU'RE GOING TO BOARD THIS BUS AND GET OFF ON KUENEN STREET.
THE ORPHANAGE IS RIGHT THERE. I WANT YOU TO GIVE THIS LETTER TO ERNA TIETZE.
I KNOW SHE LOOKS STRICT, BUT SHE'S REALLY A VERY KIND LADY.
TAKE CARE NOW, DIETER. I'M AFRAID I CAN'T GO INTO TOWN WITH YOU, SO I HAVE TO SAY GOOD-BYE.
THE BUS WILL COME IN JUST A FEW MINUTES.

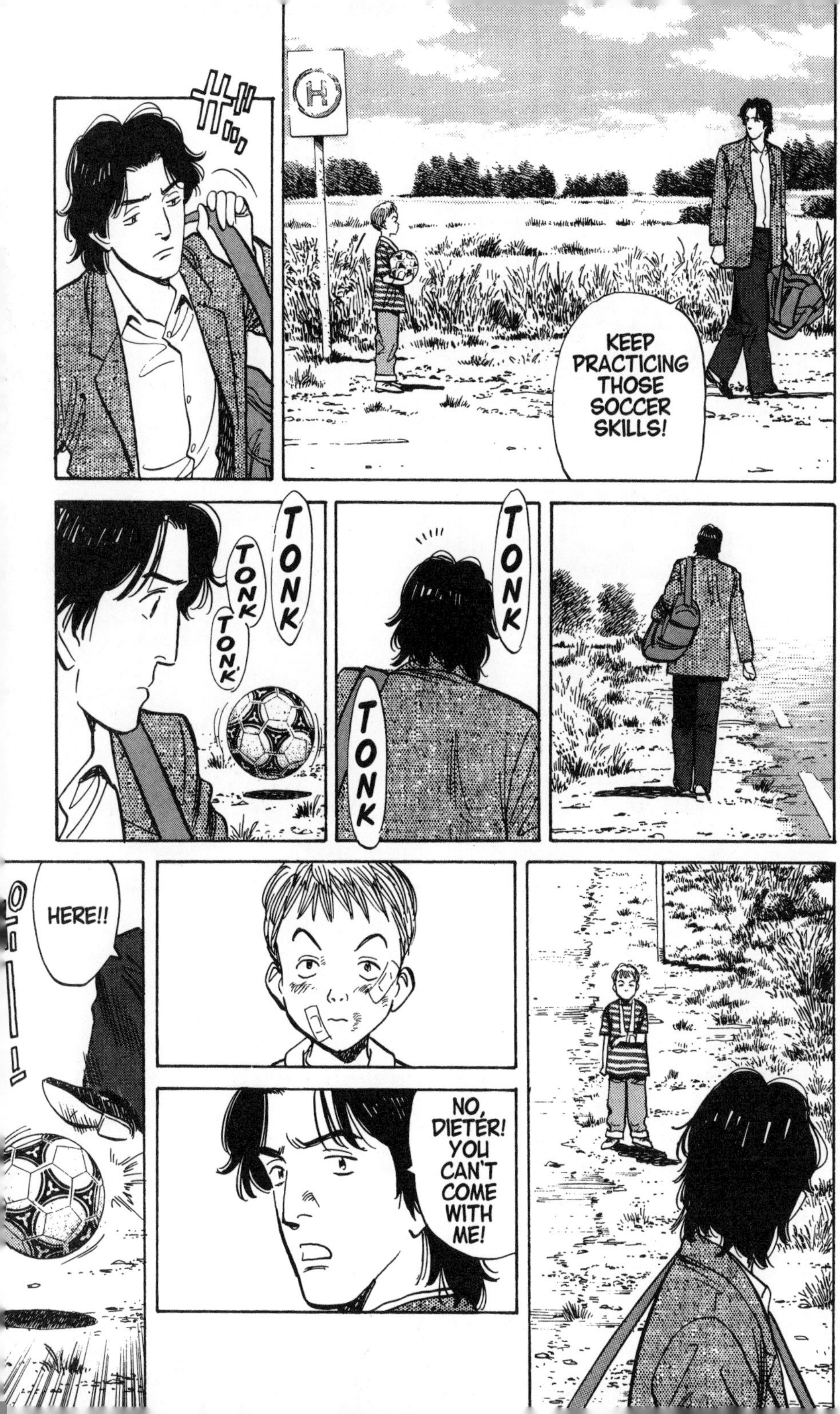
KEEP PRACTICING THOSE SOCCER SKILLS!
TONK
TONK
TONK
TONK
TONK
NO, DIETER! YOU CAN'T COME WITH ME!
HERE!!

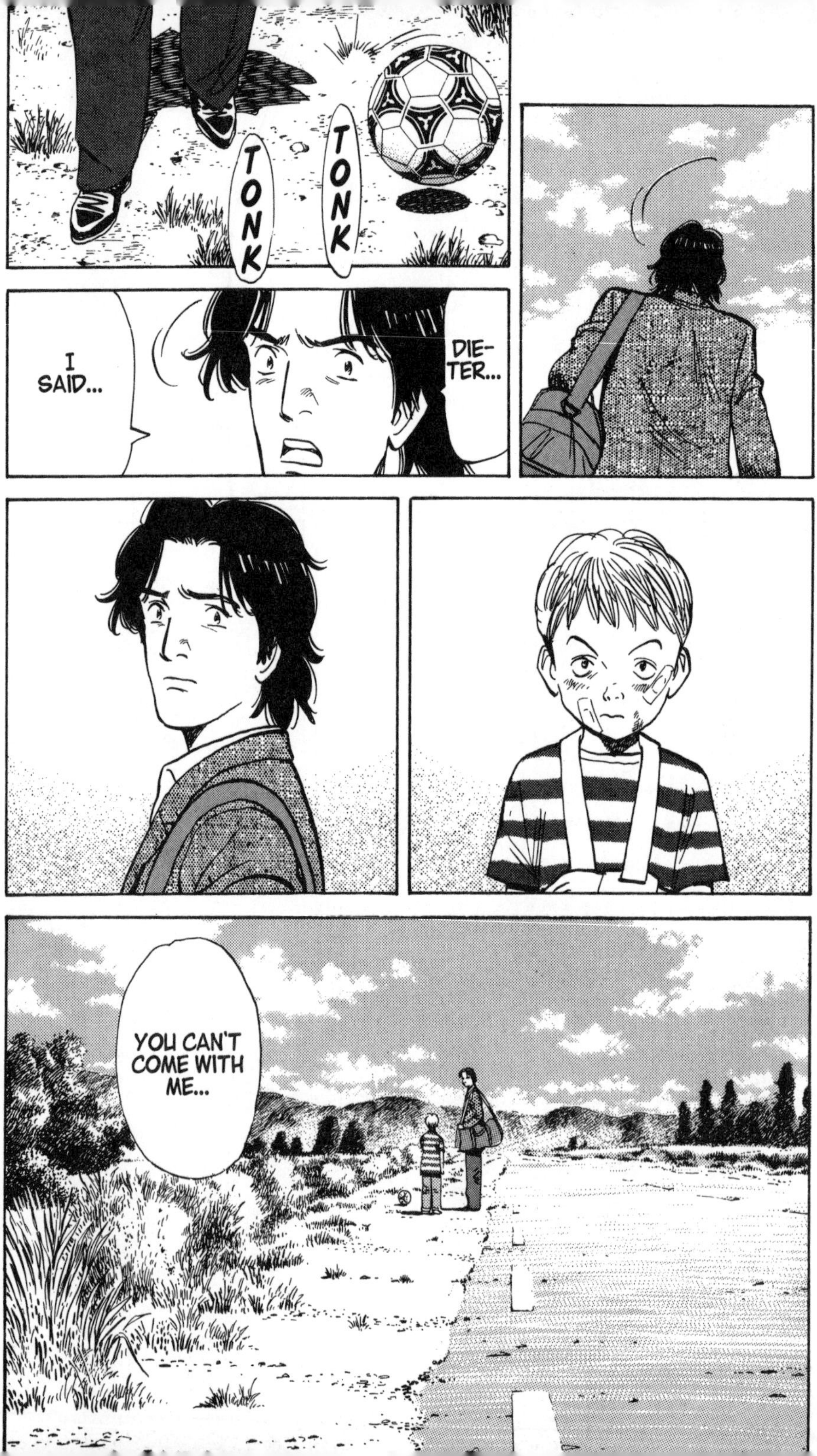
TONK
TONK
DIE-TER...
I SAID...
YOU CAN'T COME WITH ME...

Kapitel 22.
Petra and Schumann

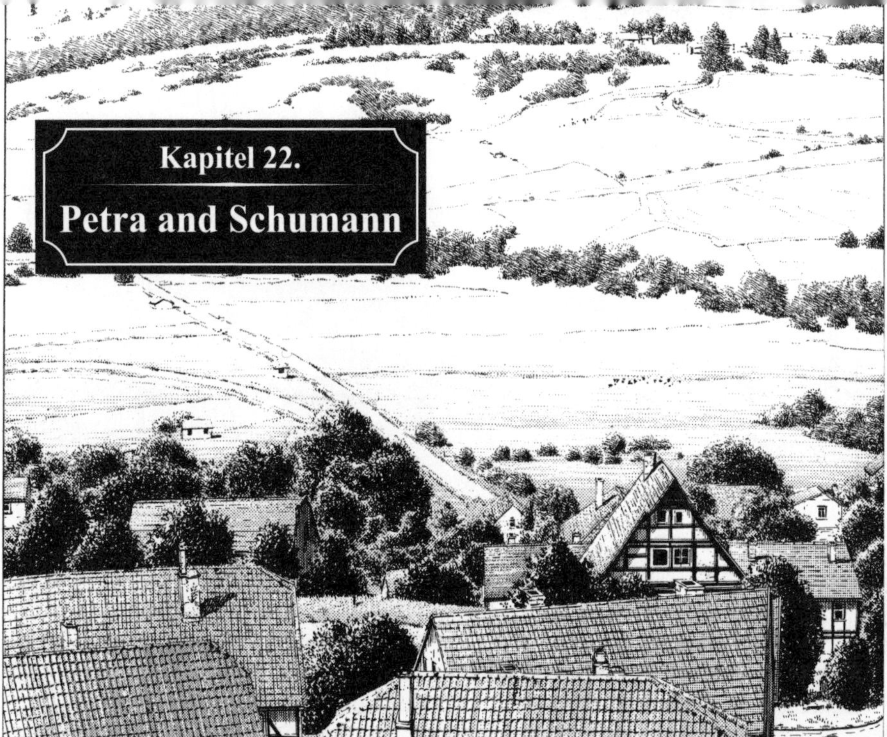

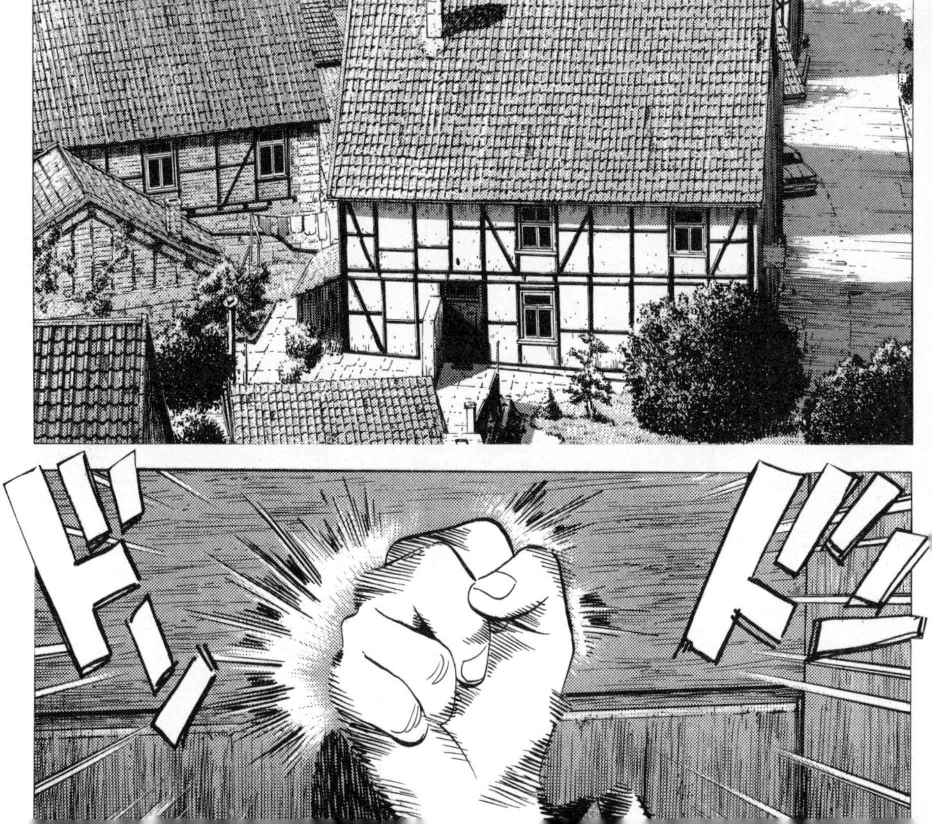

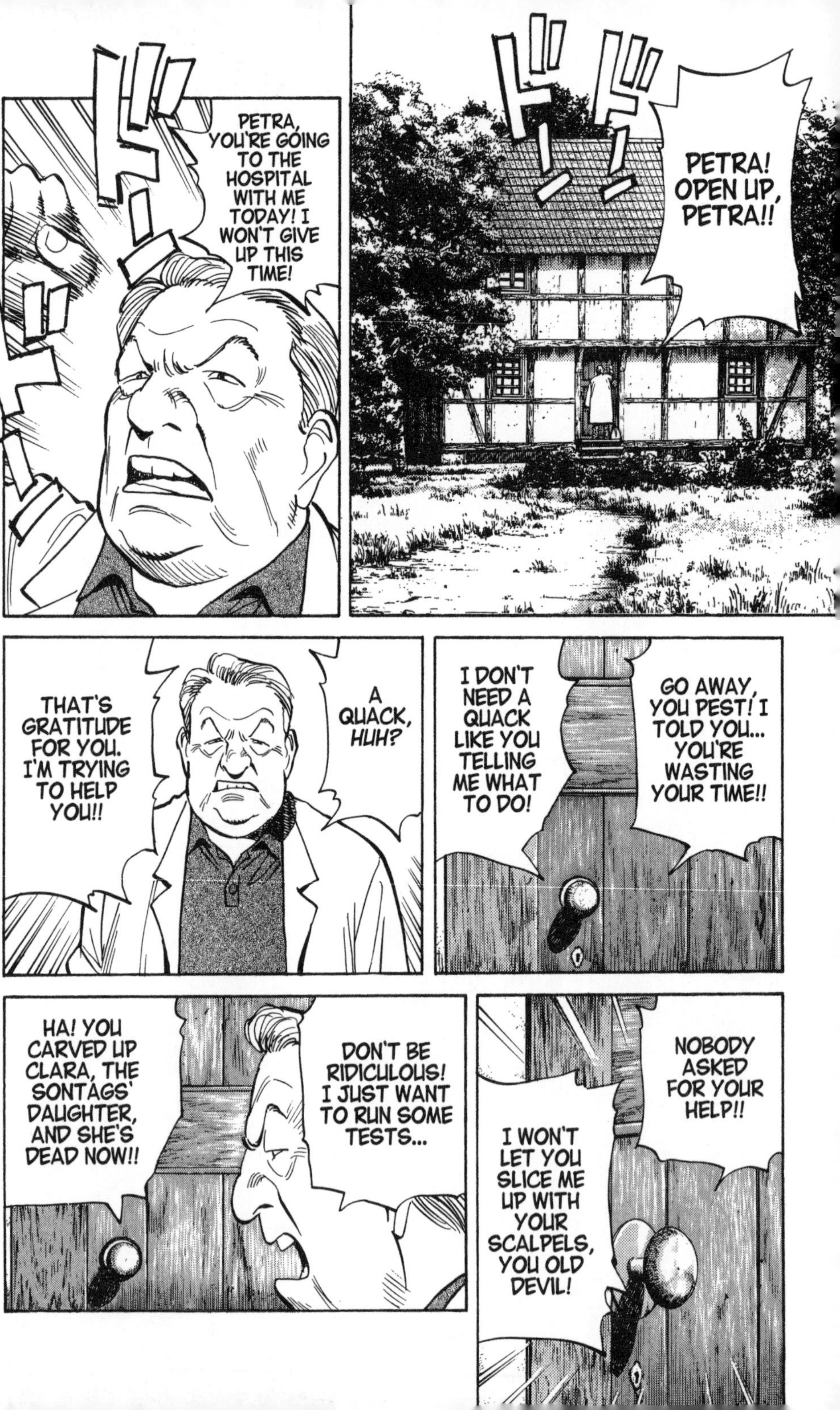
PETRA! OPEN UP, PETRA!!
PETRA, YOU'RE GOING TO THE HOSPITAL WITH ME TODAY! I WON'T GIVE UP THIS TIME!
GO AWAY, YOU PEST! I TOLD YOU... YOU'RE WASTING YOUR TIME!!
I DON'T NEED A QUACK LIKE YOU TELLING ME WHAT TO DO!
A QUACK, HUH?
THAT'S GRATITUDE FOR YOU. I'M TRYING TO HELP YOU!!
NOBODY ASKED FOR YOUR HELP!!
I WON'T LET YOU SLICE ME UP WITH YOUR SCALPELS, YOU OLD DEVIL!
DON'T BE RIDICULOUS! I JUST WANT TO RUN SOME TESTS...
HA! YOU CARVED UP CLARA, THE SONTAGS' DAUGHTER, AND SHE'S DEAD NOW!!

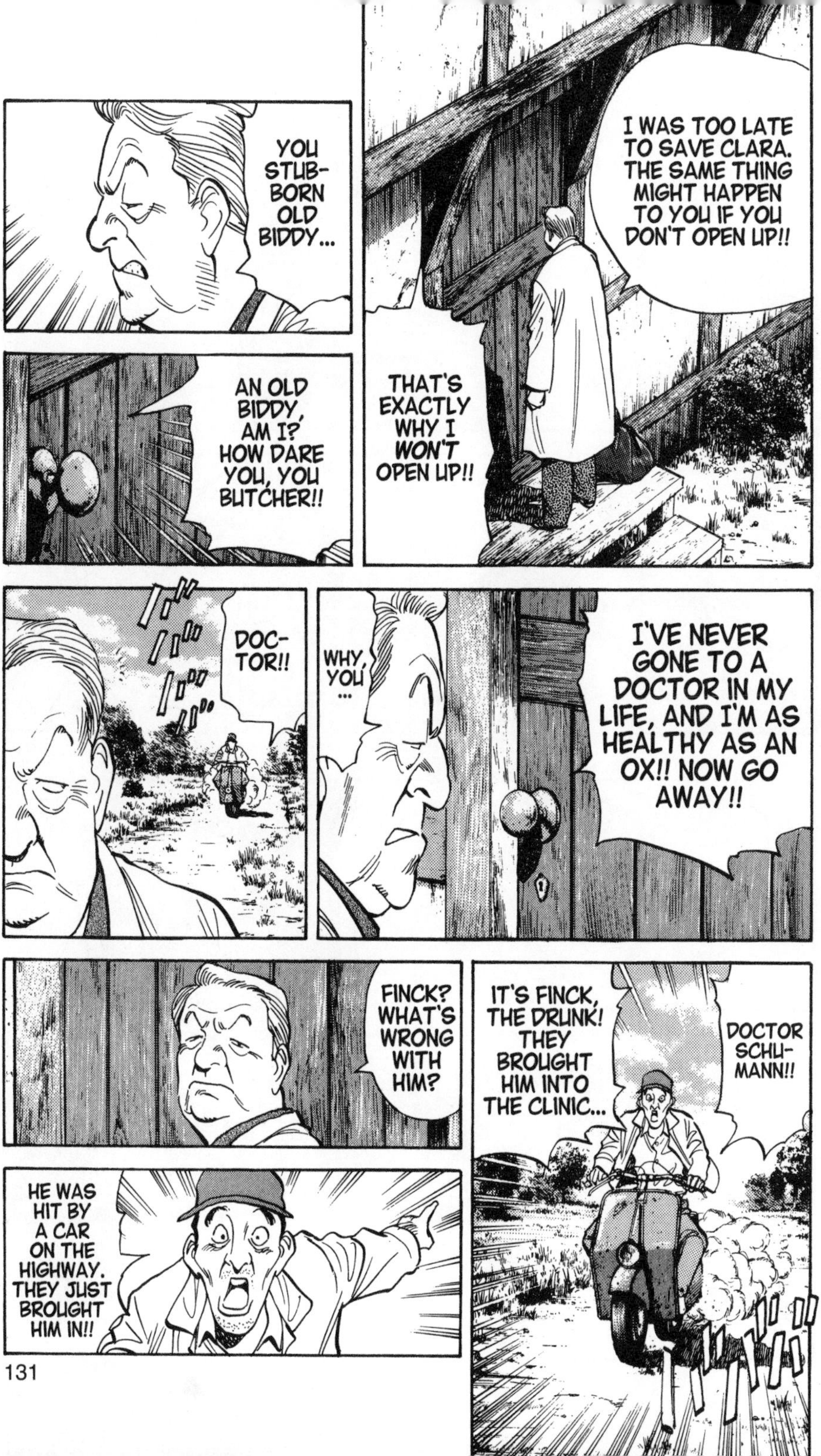
I WAS TOO LATE TO SAVE CLARA. THE SAME THING MIGHT HAPPEN TO YOU IF YOU DON'T OPEN UP!!
THAT'S EXACTLY WHY I *WON'T* OPEN UP!!
YOU STUBBORN OLD BIDDY...
AN OLD BIDDY, AM I? HOW DARE YOU, YOU BUTCHER!!
I'VE NEVER GONE TO A DOCTOR IN MY LIFE, AND I'M AS HEALTHY AS AN OX!! NOW GO AWAY!!
WHY, YOU ...
DOCTOR!!
DOCTOR SCHUMANN!!
IT'S FINCK, THE DRUNK! THEY BROUGHT HIM INTO THE CLINIC...
FINCK? WHAT'S WRONG WITH HIM?
HE WAS HIT BY A CAR ON THE HIGHWAY. THEY JUST BROUGHT HIM IN!!

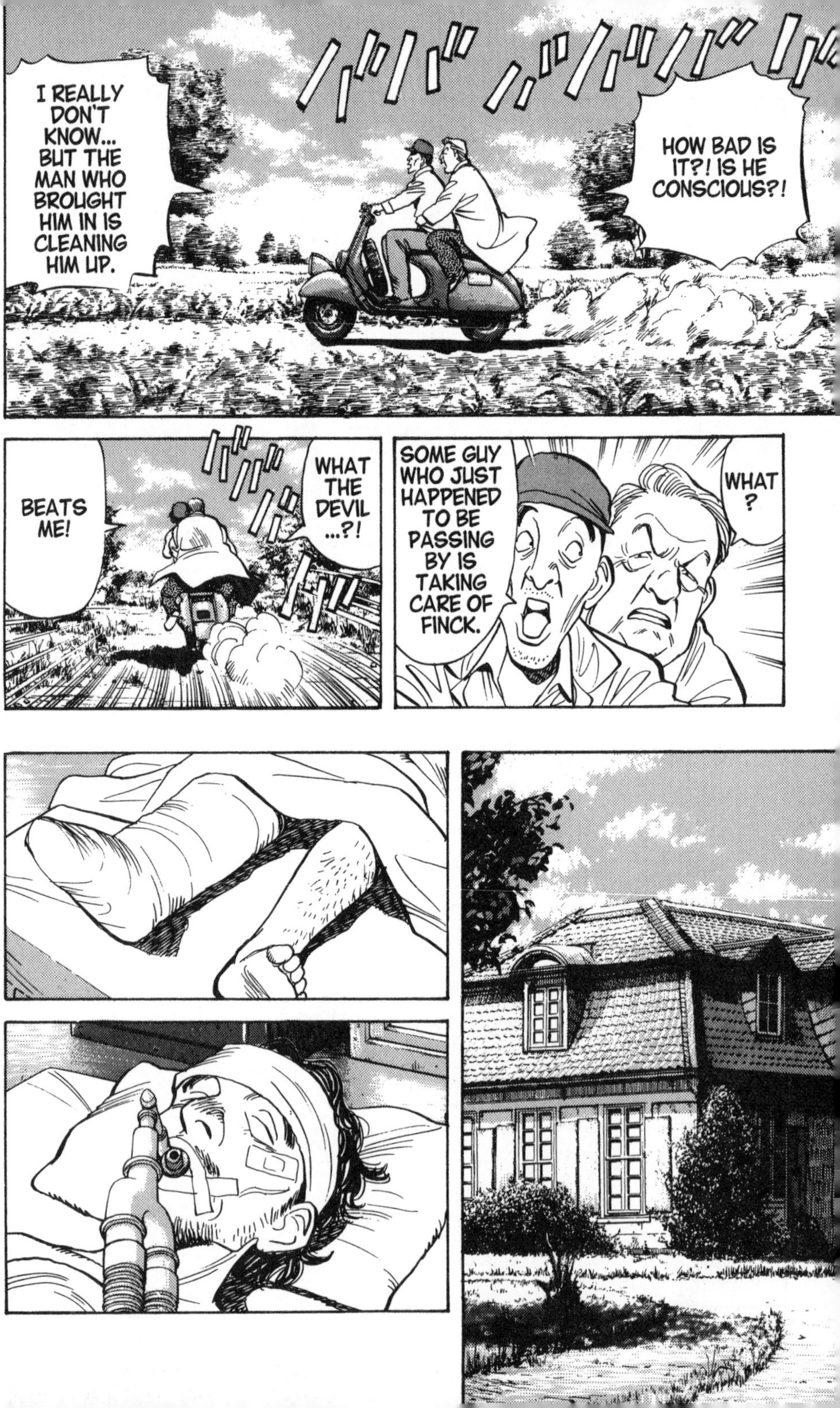
HOW BAD IS IT?! IS HE CONSCIOUS?!
I REALLY DON'T KNOW... BUT THE MAN WHO BROUGHT HIM IN IS CLEANING HIM UP.
WHAT?
SOME GUY WHO JUST HAPPENED TO BE PASSING BY IS TAKING CARE OF FINCK.
WHAT THE DEVIL ...?!
BEATS ME!

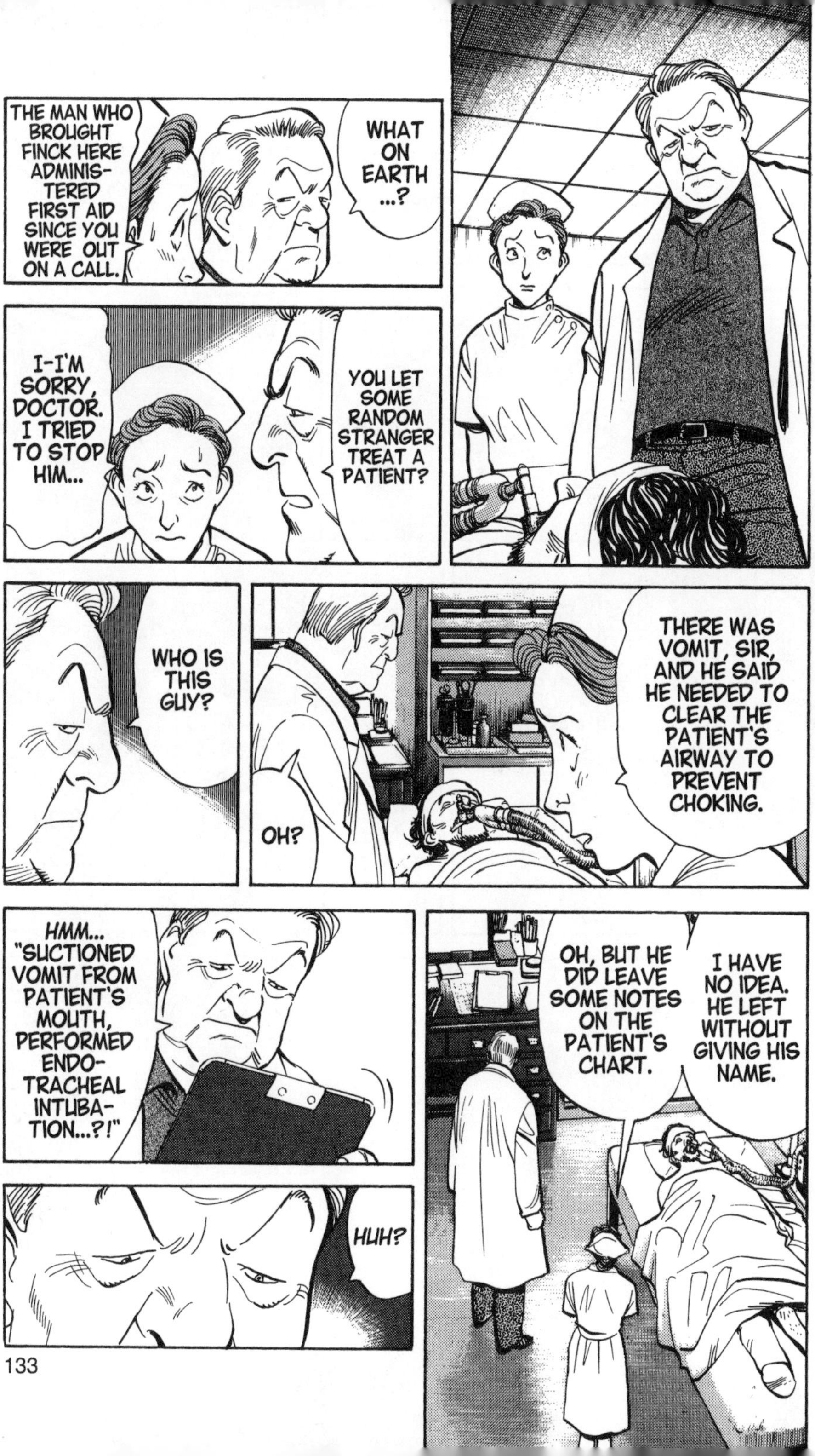
WHAT ON EARTH ...?
THE MAN WHO BROUGHT FINCK HERE ADMINISTERED FIRST AID SINCE YOU WERE OUT ON A CALL.
YOU LET SOME RANDOM STRANGER TREAT A PATIENT?
I-I'M SORRY, DOCTOR. I TRIED TO STOP HIM...
THERE WAS VOMIT, SIR, AND HE SAID HE NEEDED TO CLEAR THE PATIENT'S AIRWAY TO PREVENT CHOKING.
OH?
WHO IS THIS GUY?
I HAVE NO IDEA. HE LEFT WITHOUT GIVING HIS NAME.
OH, BUT HE DID LEAVE SOME NOTES ON THE PATIENT'S CHART.
HMM... "SUCTIONED VOMIT FROM PATIENT'S MOUTH, PERFORMED ENDOTRACHEAL INTUBATION...?!"
HUH?

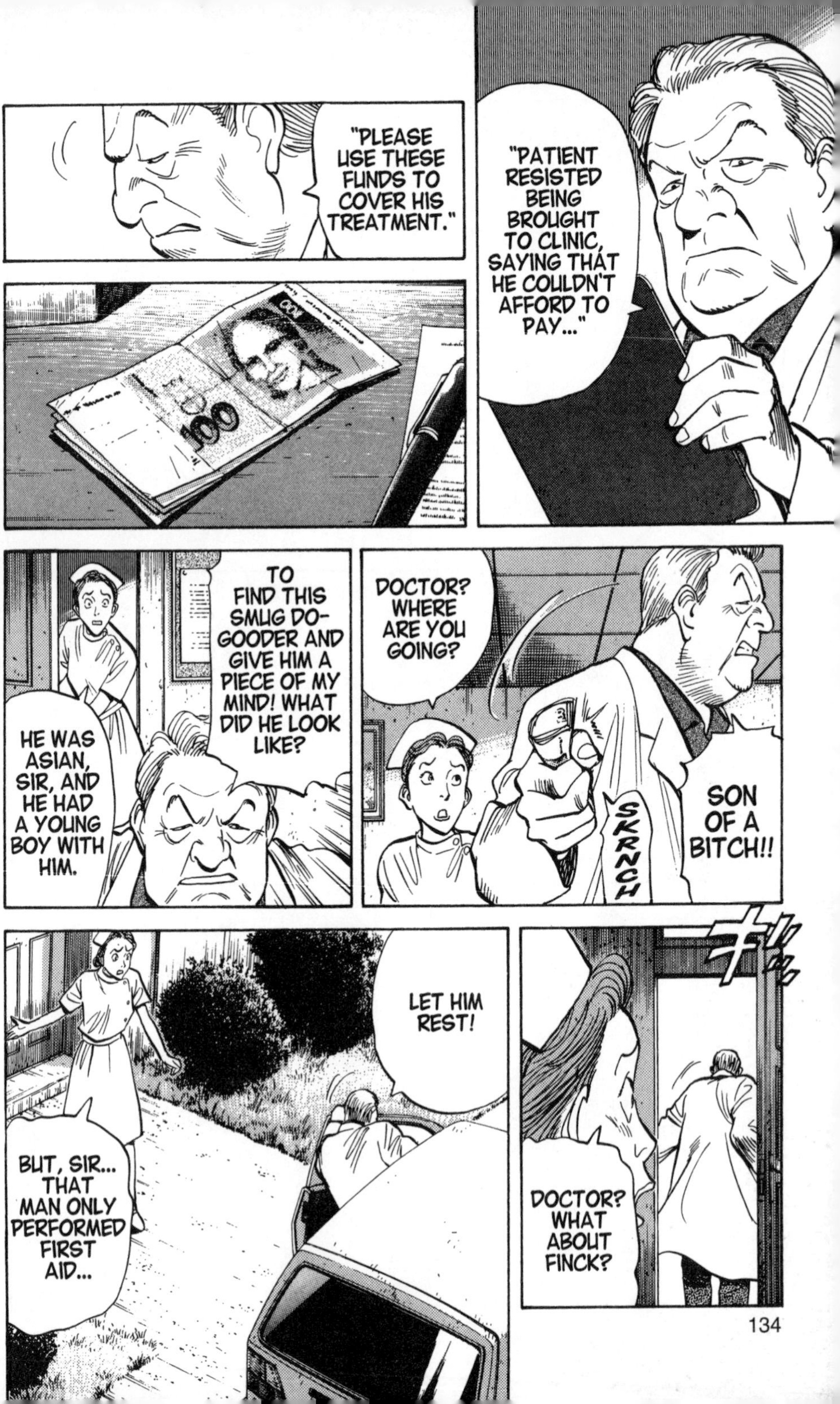
"PATIENT RESISTED BEING BROUGHT TO CLINIC, SAYING THAT HE COULDN'T AFFORD TO PAY..."
"PLEASE USE THESE FUNDS TO COVER HIS TREATMENT."
SKRNCH
SON OF A BITCH!!
DOCTOR? WHERE ARE YOU GOING?
TO FIND THIS SMUG DO-GOODER AND GIVE HIM A PIECE OF MY MIND! WHAT DID HE LOOK LIKE?
HE WAS ASIAN, SIR, AND HE HAD A YOUNG BOY WITH HIM.
DOCTOR? WHAT ABOUT FINCK?
LET HIM REST!
BUT, SIR... THAT MAN ONLY PERFORMED FIRST AID...

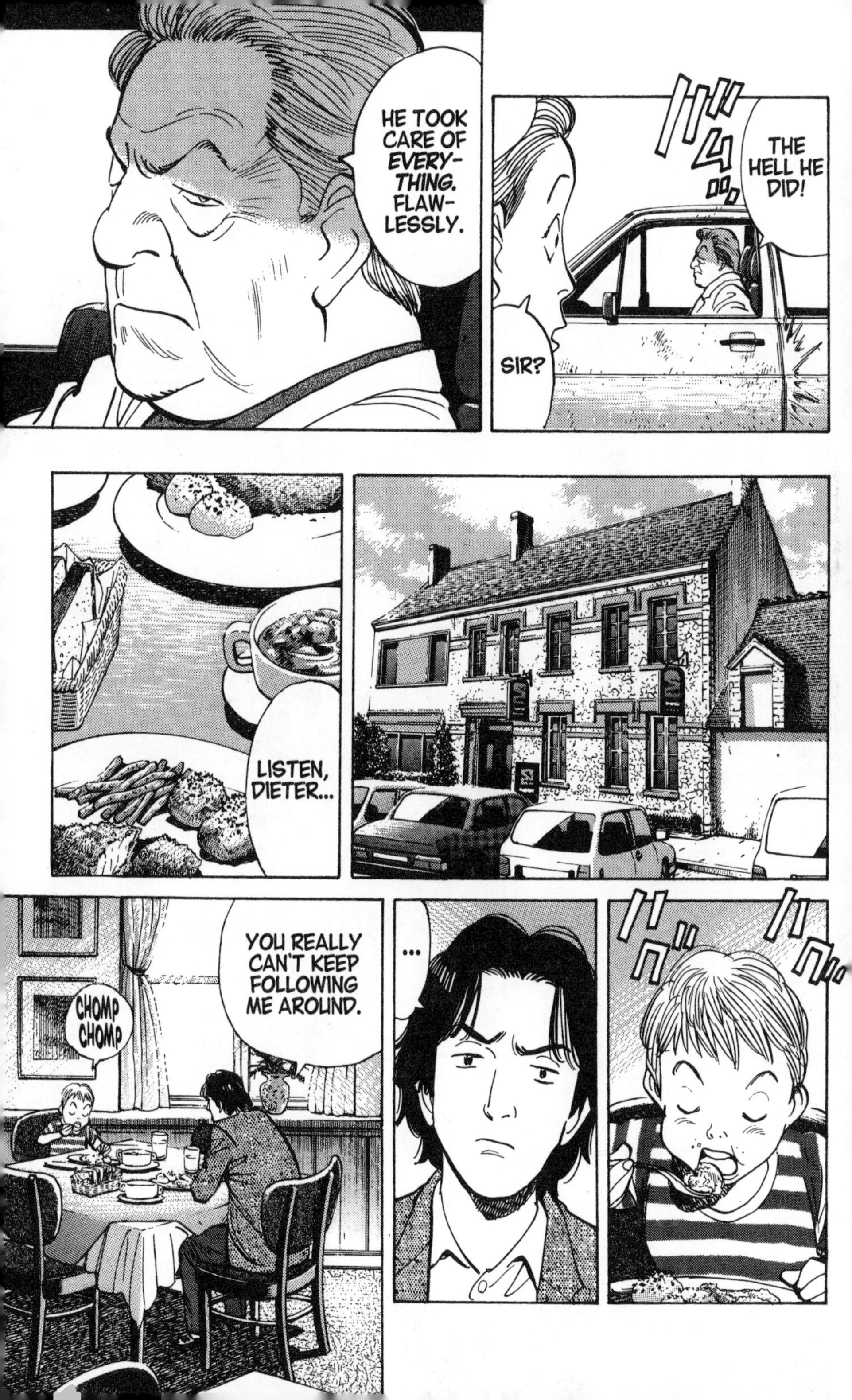
HE TOOK CARE OF EVERYTHING. FLAWLESSLY.
THE HELL HE DID!
SIR?
LISTEN, DIETER...
CHOMP CHOMP
YOU REALLY CAN'T KEEP FOLLOWING ME AROUND.
...

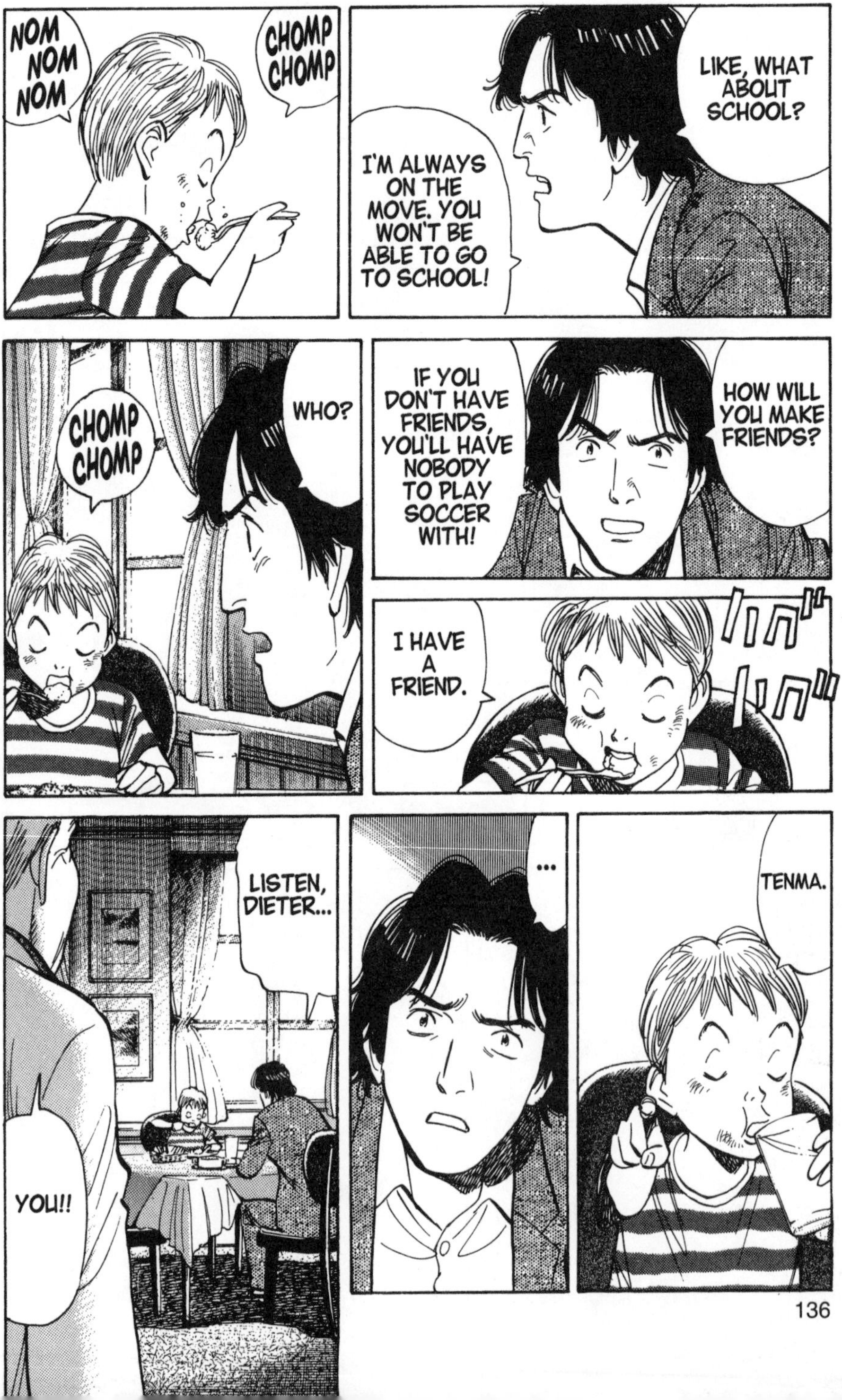
LIKE, WHAT ABOUT SCHOOL?
I'M ALWAYS ON THE MOVE. YOU WON'T BE ABLE TO GO TO SCHOOL!
CHOMP CHOMP
NOM NOM NOM
HOW WILL YOU MAKE FRIENDS?
IF YOU DON'T HAVE FRIENDS, YOU'LL HAVE NOBODY TO PLAY SOCCER WITH!
ハグハグ
I HAVE A FRIEND.
WHO?
CHOMP CHOMP
TENMA.
...
LISTEN, DIETER...
YOU!!

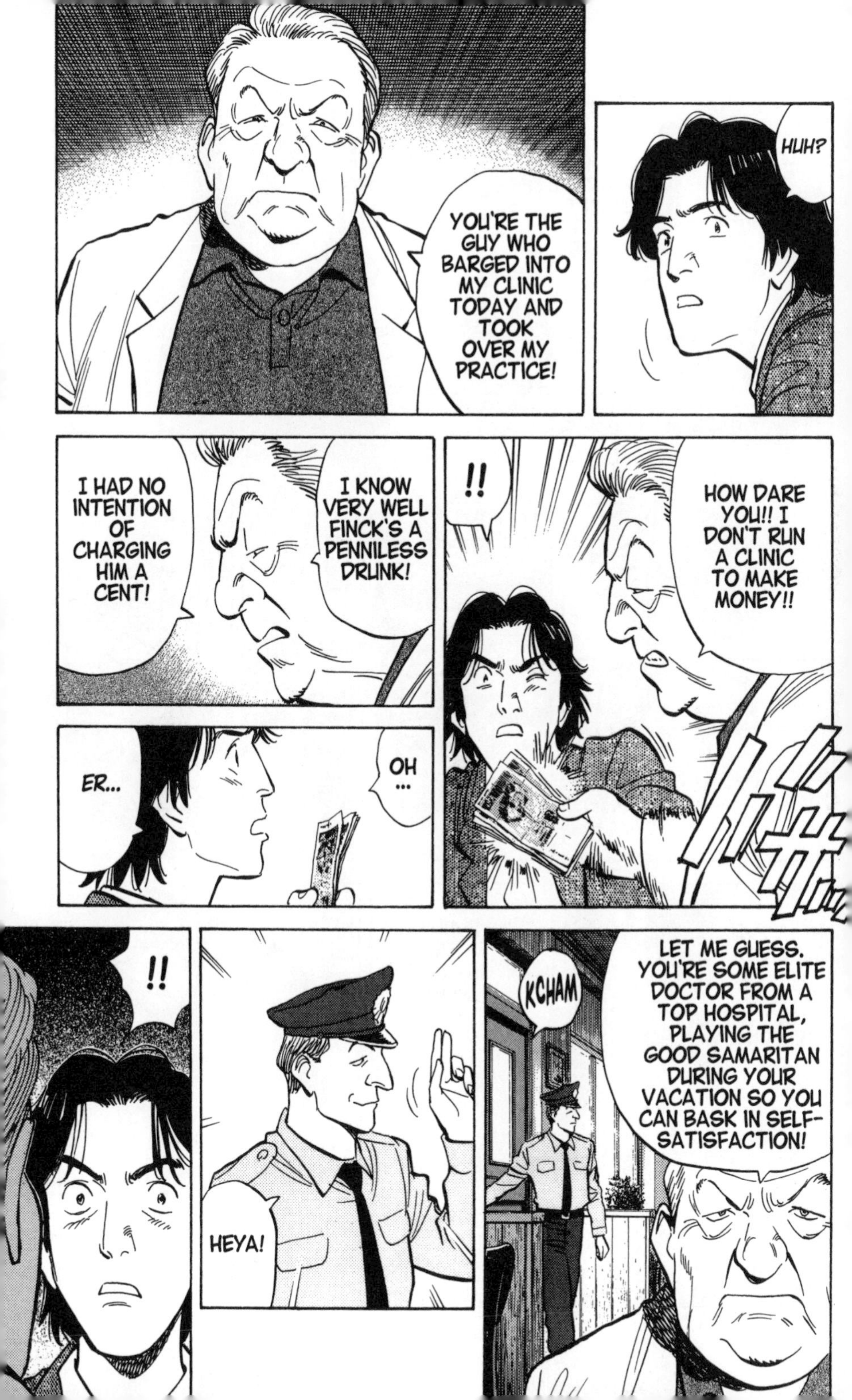
HUH?
YOU'RE THE GUY WHO BARGED INTO MY CLINIC TODAY AND TOOK OVER MY PRACTICE!
HOW DARE YOU!! I DON'T RUN A CLINIC TO MAKE MONEY!!
!!
I KNOW VERY WELL FINCK'S A PENNILESS DRUNK!
I HAD NO INTENTION OF CHARGING HIM A CENT!
OH ...
ER...
LET ME GUESS. YOU'RE SOME ELITE DOCTOR FROM A TOP HOSPITAL, PLAYING THE GOOD SAMARITAN DURING YOUR VACATION SO YOU CAN BASK IN SELF-SATISFACTION!
KCHAM
HEYA!
!!

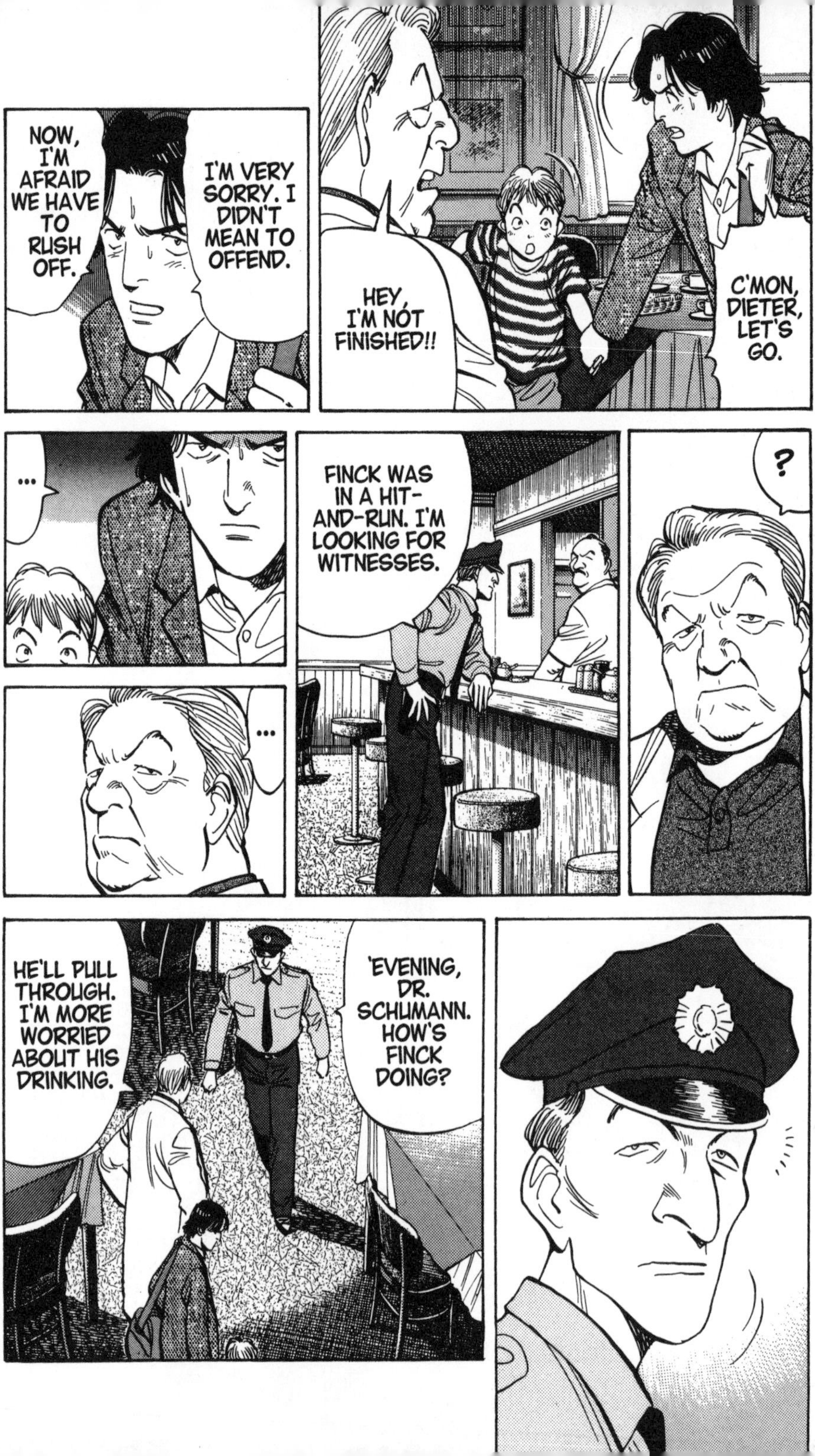
C'MON, DIETER, LET'S GO.
HEY, I'M NOT FINISHED!!
I'M VERY SORRY. I DIDN'T MEAN TO OFFEND.
NOW, I'M AFRAID WE HAVE TO RUSH OFF.
?
FINCK WAS IN A HIT-AND-RUN. I'M LOOKING FOR WITNESSES.
...
...
'EVENING, DR. SCHUMANN. HOW'S FINCK DOING?
HE'LL PULL THROUGH. I'M MORE WORRIED ABOUT HIS DRINKING.

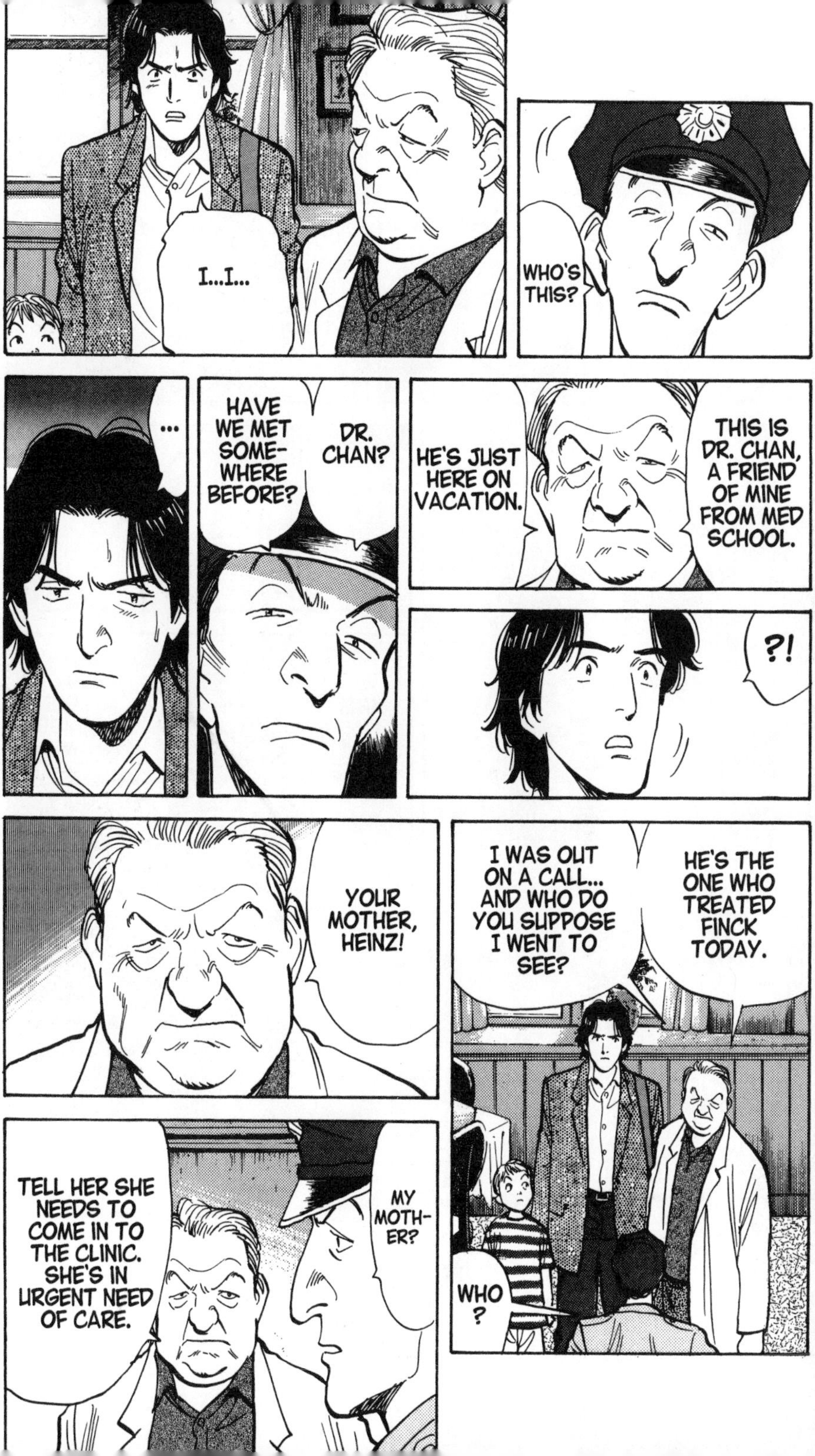
WHO'S THIS?
I...I...
THIS IS DR. CHAN, A FRIEND OF MINE FROM MED SCHOOL.
HE'S JUST HERE ON VACATION.
?!
DR. CHAN?
HAVE WE MET SOMEWHERE BEFORE?
...
HE'S THE ONE WHO TREATED FINCK TODAY.
I WAS OUT ON A CALL... AND WHO DO YOU SUPPOSE I WENT TO SEE?
WHO?
YOUR MOTHER, HEINZ!
MY MOTHER?
TELL HER SHE NEEDS TO COME IN TO THE CLINIC. SHE'S IN URGENT NEED OF CARE.

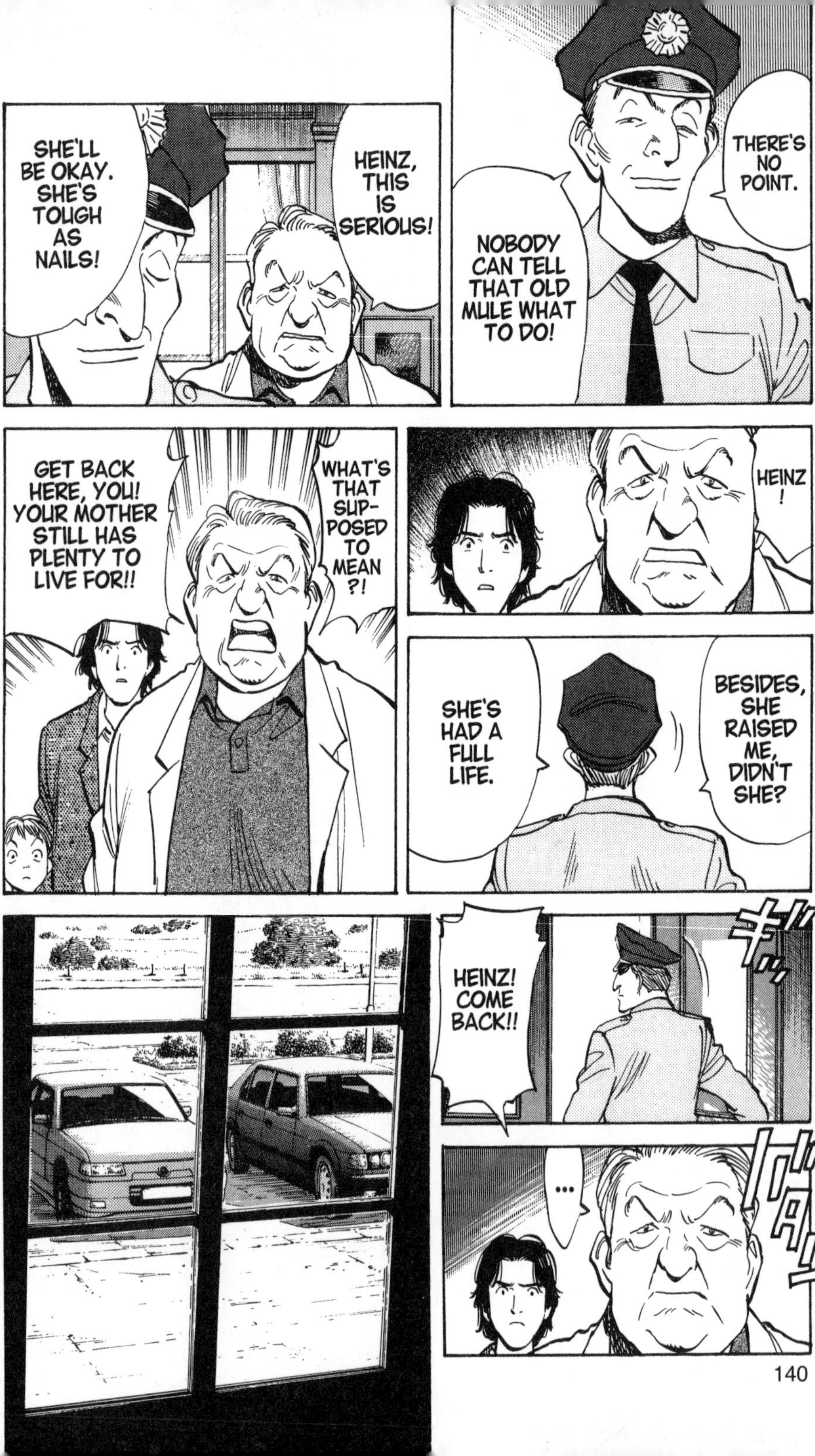
THERE'S NO POINT.
NOBODY CAN TELL THAT OLD MULE WHAT TO DO!
HEINZ, THIS IS SERIOUS!
SHE'LL BE OKAY. SHE'S TOUGH AS NAILS!
HEINZ!
BESIDES, SHE RAISED ME, DIDN'T SHE?
SHE'S HAD A FULL LIFE.
WHAT'S THAT SUP-POSED TO MEAN?!
GET BACK HERE, YOU! YOUR MOTHER STILL HAS PLENTY TO LIVE FOR!!
ギッ
HEINZ! COME BACK!!
バタン
...

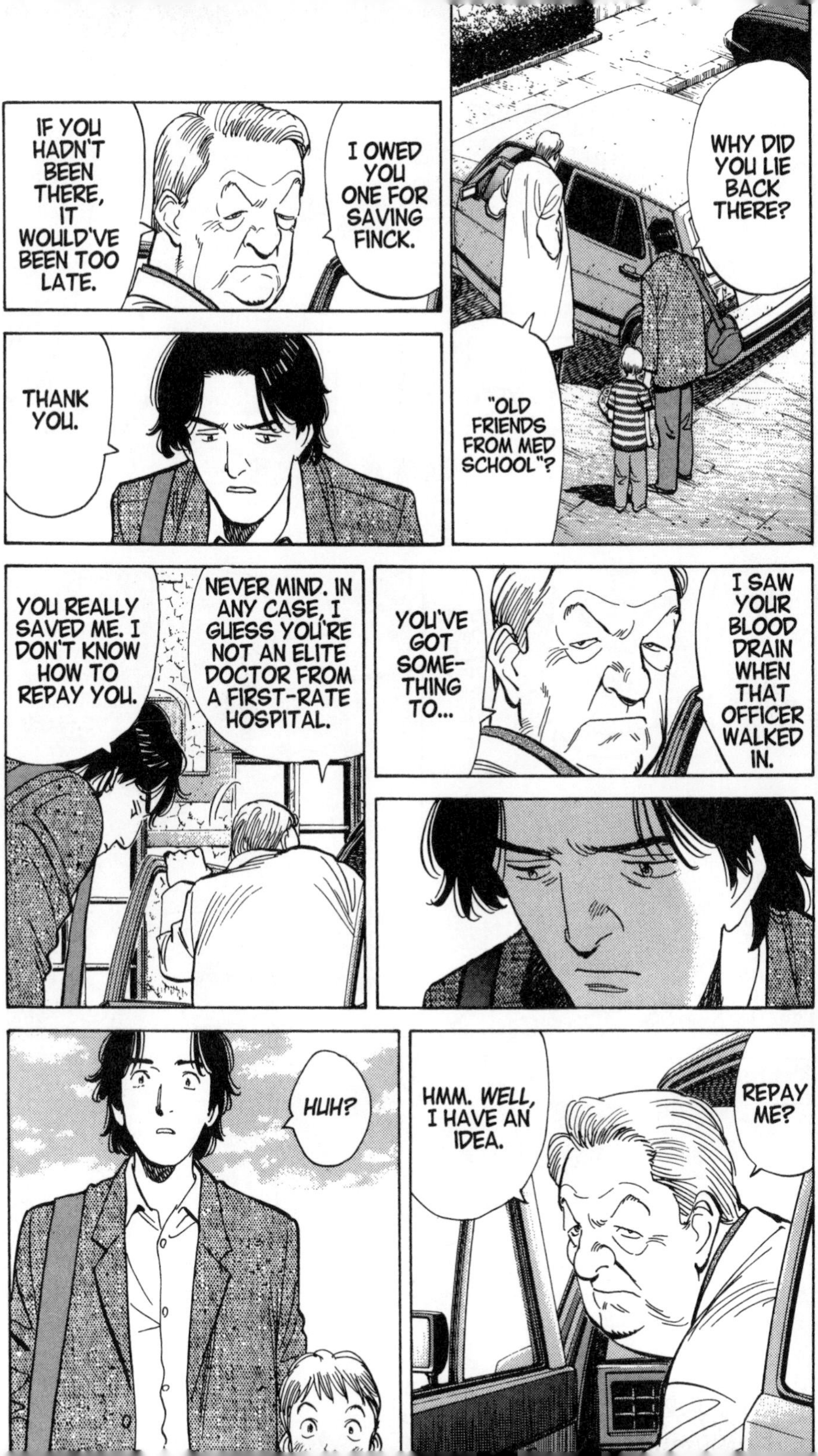
WHY DID YOU LIE BACK THERE?
"OLD FRIENDS FROM MED SCHOOL"?
I OWED YOU ONE FOR SAVING FINCK.
IF YOU HADN'T BEEN THERE, IT WOULD'VE BEEN TOO LATE.
THANK YOU.
I SAW YOUR BLOOD DRAIN WHEN THAT OFFICER WALKED IN.
YOU'VE GOT SOME-THING TO...
NEVER MIND. IN ANY CASE, I GUESS YOU'RE NOT AN ELITE DOCTOR FROM A FIRST-RATE HOSPITAL.
YOU REALLY SAVED ME. I DON'T KNOW HOW TO REPAY YOU.
REPAY ME?
HMM. WELL, I HAVE AN IDEA.
HUH?

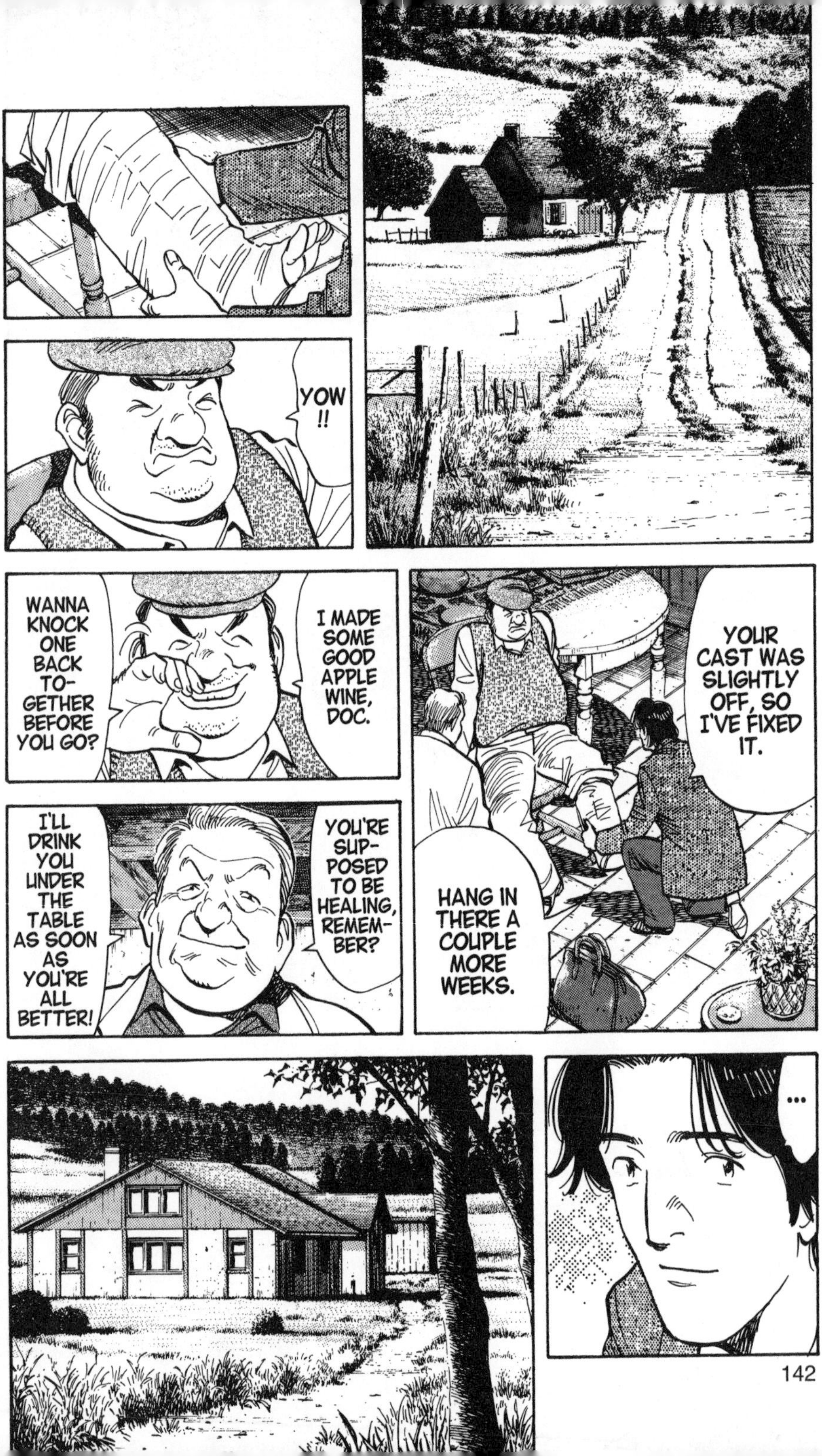
YOW!!
YOUR CAST WAS SLIGHTLY OFF, SO I'VE FIXED IT.
HANG IN THERE A COUPLE MORE WEEKS.
I MADE SOME GOOD APPLE WINE, DOC.
WANNA KNOCK ONE BACK TOGETHER BEFORE YOU GO?
YOU'RE SUPPOSED TO BE HEALING, REMEMBER?
I'LL DRINK YOU UNDER THE TABLE AS SOON AS YOU'RE ALL BETTER!
...

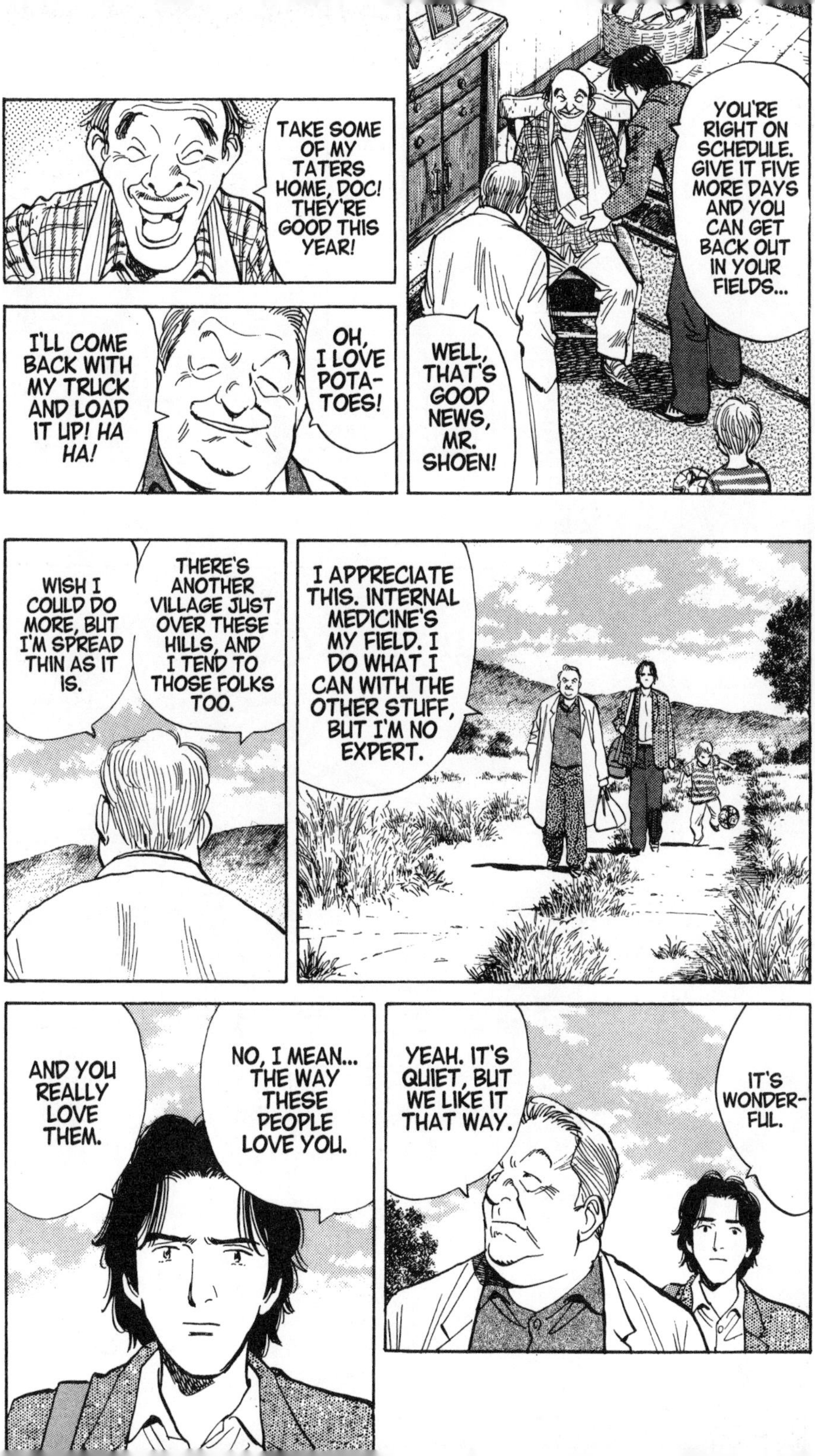
YOU'RE RIGHT ON SCHEDULE. GIVE IT FIVE MORE DAYS AND YOU CAN GET BACK OUT IN YOUR FIELDS...
WELL, THAT'S GOOD NEWS, MR. SHOEN!
TAKE SOME OF MY TATERS HOME, DOC! THEY'RE GOOD THIS YEAR!
OH, I LOVE POTA-TOES!
I'LL COME BACK WITH MY TRUCK AND LOAD IT UP! HA HA!
I APPRECIATE THIS. INTERNAL MEDICINE'S MY FIELD. I DO WHAT I CAN WITH THE OTHER STUFF, BUT I'M NO EXPERT.
THERE'S ANOTHER VILLAGE JUST OVER THESE HILLS, AND I TEND TO THOSE FOLKS TOO.
WISH I COULD DO MORE, BUT I'M SPREAD THIN AS IT IS.
IT'S WONDER-FUL.
YEAH. IT'S QUIET, BUT WE LIKE IT THAT WAY.
NO, I MEAN... THE WAY THESE PEOPLE LOVE YOU.
AND YOU REALLY LOVE THEM.

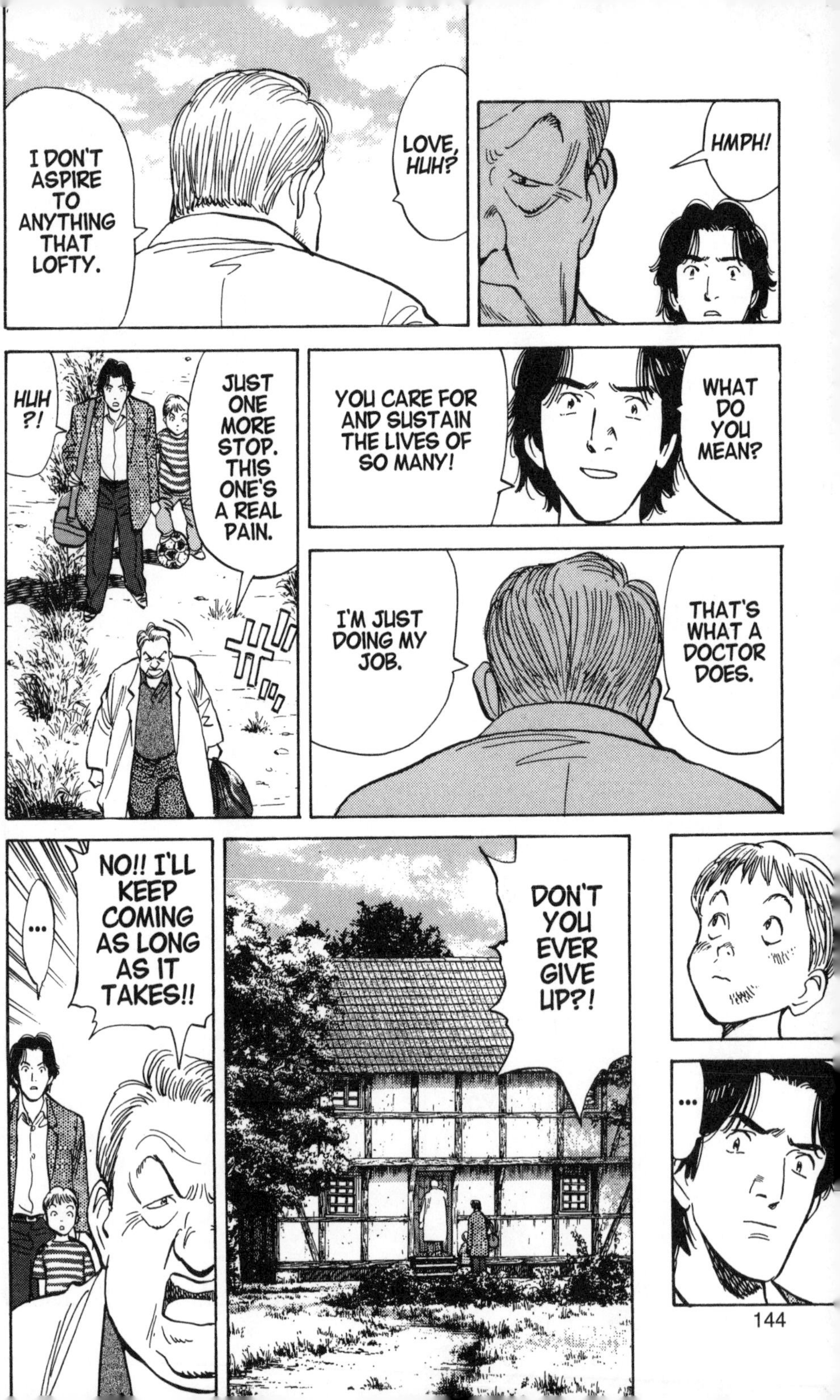
HMPH!
LOVE, HUH?
I DON'T ASPIRE TO ANYTHING THAT LOFTY.
WHAT DO YOU MEAN?
YOU CARE FOR AND SUSTAIN THE LIVES OF SO MANY!
THAT'S WHAT A DOCTOR DOES.
I'M JUST DOING MY JOB.
JUST ONE MORE STOP. THIS ONE'S A REAL PAIN.
HUH?!
...
DON'T YOU EVER GIVE UP?!
NO!! I'LL KEEP COMING AS LONG AS IT TAKES!!
...

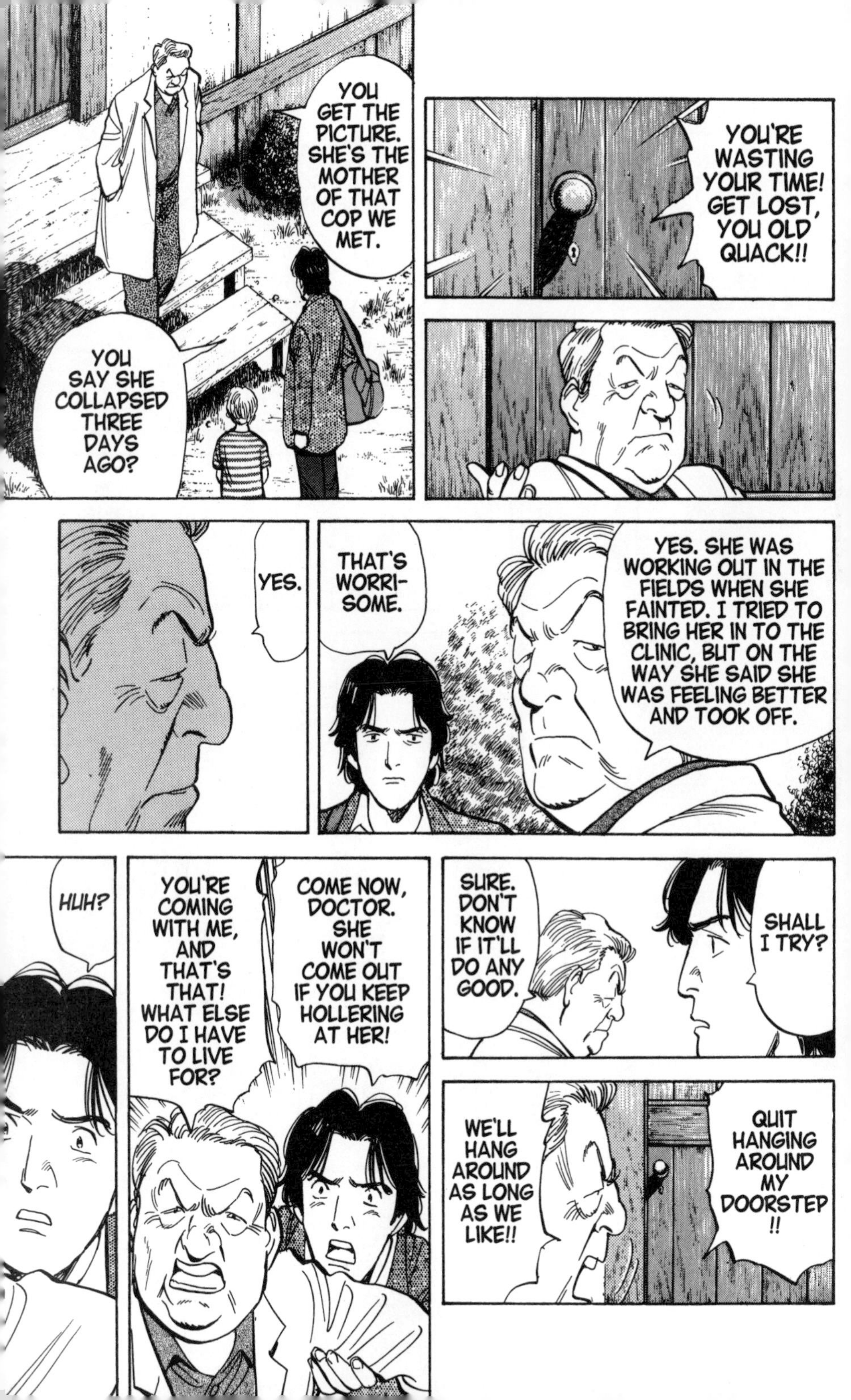
YOU'RE WASTING YOUR TIME! GET LOST, YOU OLD QUACK!!
YOU GET THE PICTURE. SHE'S THE MOTHER OF THAT COP WE MET.
YOU SAY SHE COLLAPSED THREE DAYS AGO?
YES. SHE WAS WORKING OUT IN THE FIELDS WHEN SHE FAINTED. I TRIED TO BRING HER IN TO THE CLINIC, BUT ON THE WAY SHE SAID SHE WAS FEELING BETTER AND TOOK OFF.
THAT'S WORRI-SOME.
YES.
SHALL I TRY?
SURE. DON'T KNOW IF IT'LL DO ANY GOOD.
QUIT HANGING AROUND MY DOORSTEP!!
WE'LL HANG AROUND AS LONG AS WE LIKE!!
COME NOW, DOCTOR. SHE WON'T COME OUT IF YOU KEEP HOLLERING AT HER!
YOU'RE COMING WITH ME, AND THAT'S THAT! WHAT ELSE DO I HAVE TO LIVE FOR?
HUH?

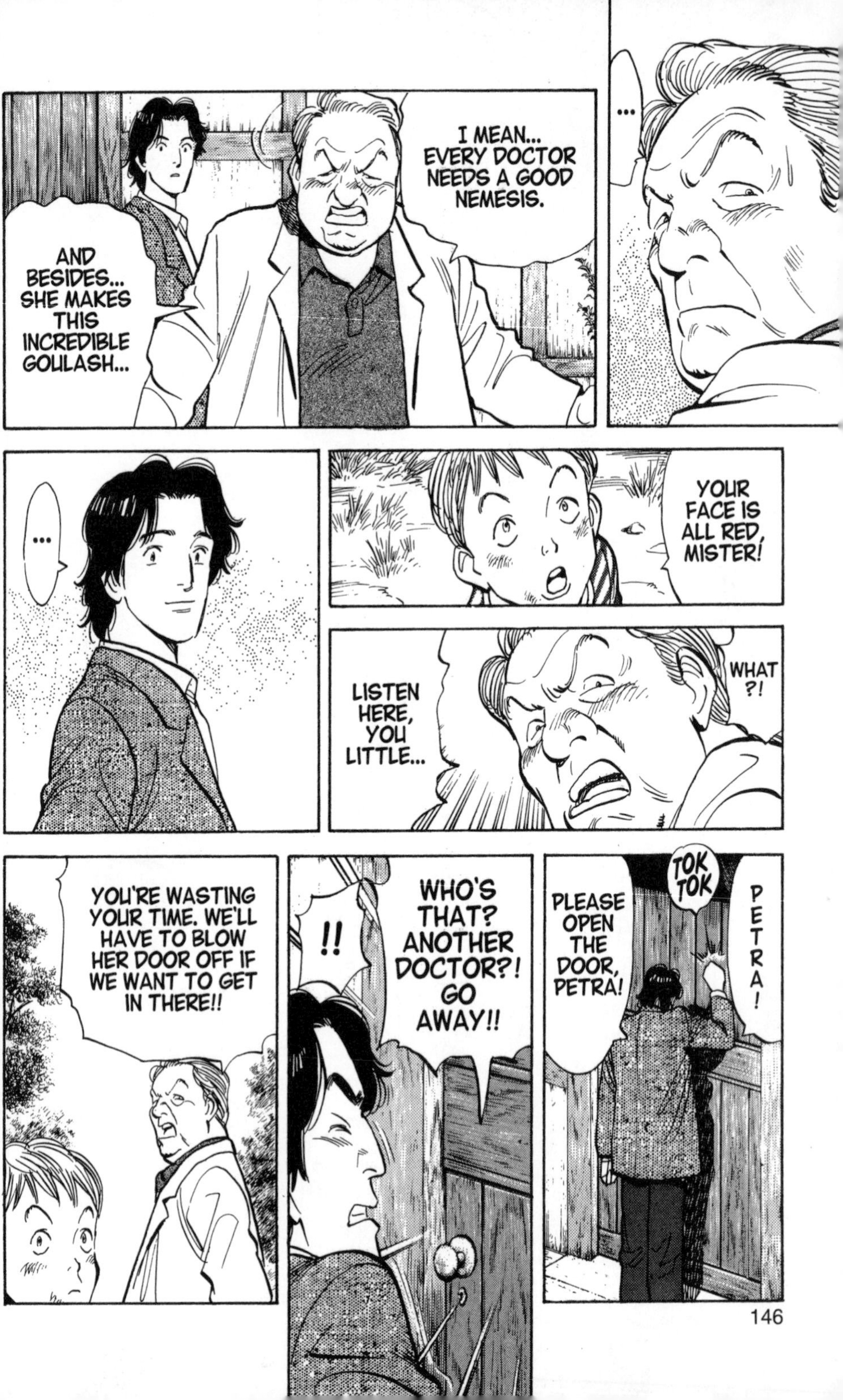
...
I MEAN... EVERY DOCTOR NEEDS A GOOD NEMESIS.
AND BESIDES... SHE MAKES THIS INCREDIBLE GOULASH...
YOUR FACE IS ALL RED, MISTER!
WHAT?!
LISTEN HERE, YOU LITTLE...
...
PETRA!
TOK TOK
PLEASE OPEN THE DOOR, PETRA!
WHO'S THAT? ANOTHER DOCTOR?! GO AWAY!!
!!
YOU'RE WASTING YOUR TIME. WE'LL HAVE TO BLOW HER DOOR OFF IF WE WANT TO GET IN THERE!!

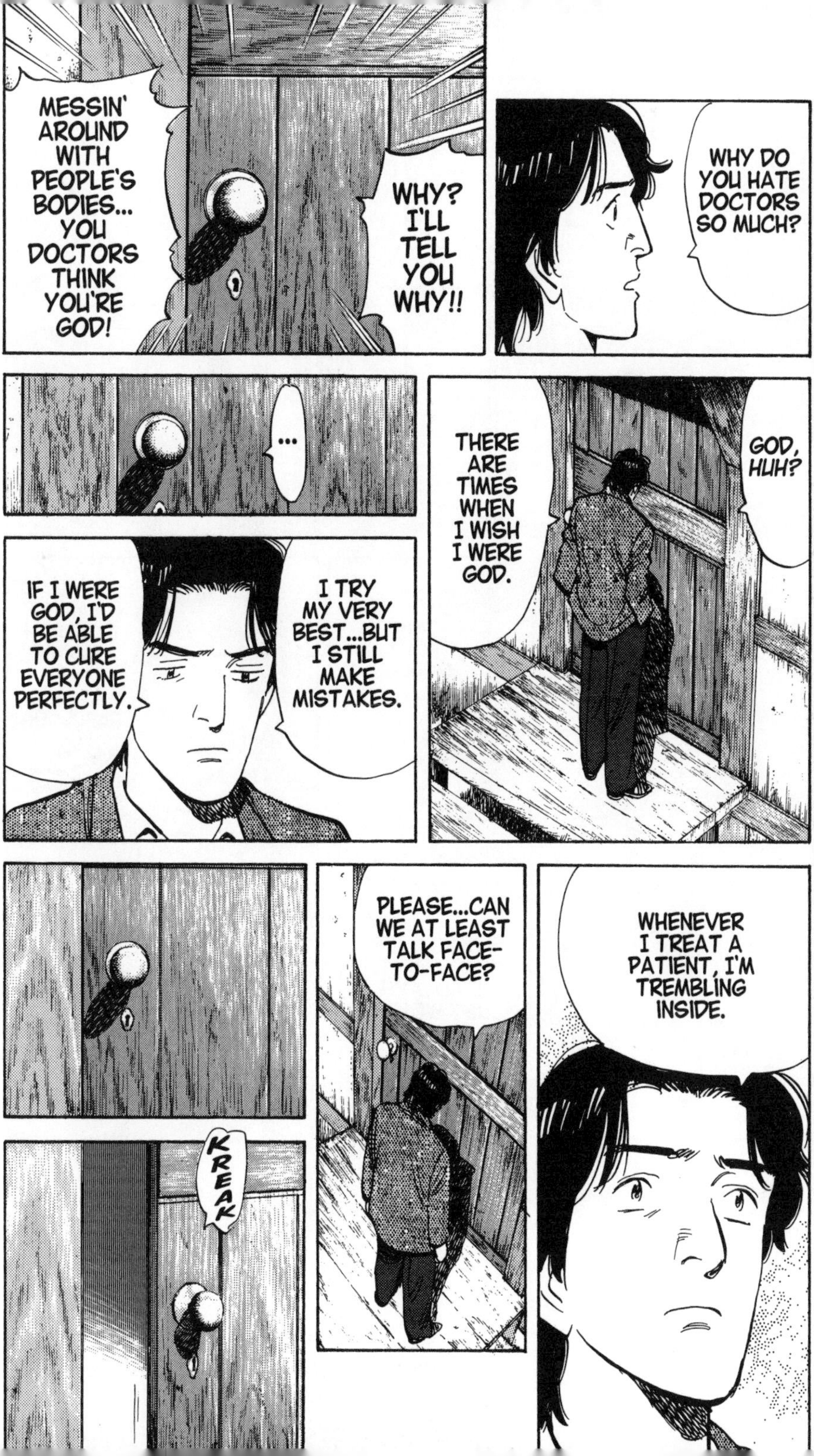
WHY DO YOU HATE DOCTORS SO MUCH?
WHY? I'LL TELL YOU WHY!!
MESSIN' AROUND WITH PEOPLE'S BODIES... YOU DOCTORS THINK YOU'RE GOD!
GOD, HUH?
THERE ARE TIMES WHEN I WISH I WERE GOD.
...
I TRY MY VERY BEST...BUT I STILL MAKE MISTAKES.
IF I WERE GOD, I'D BE ABLE TO CURE EVERYONE PERFECTLY.
WHENEVER I TREAT A PATIENT, I'M TREMBLING INSIDE.
PLEASE...CAN WE AT LEAST TALK FACE-TO-FACE?
KREAK

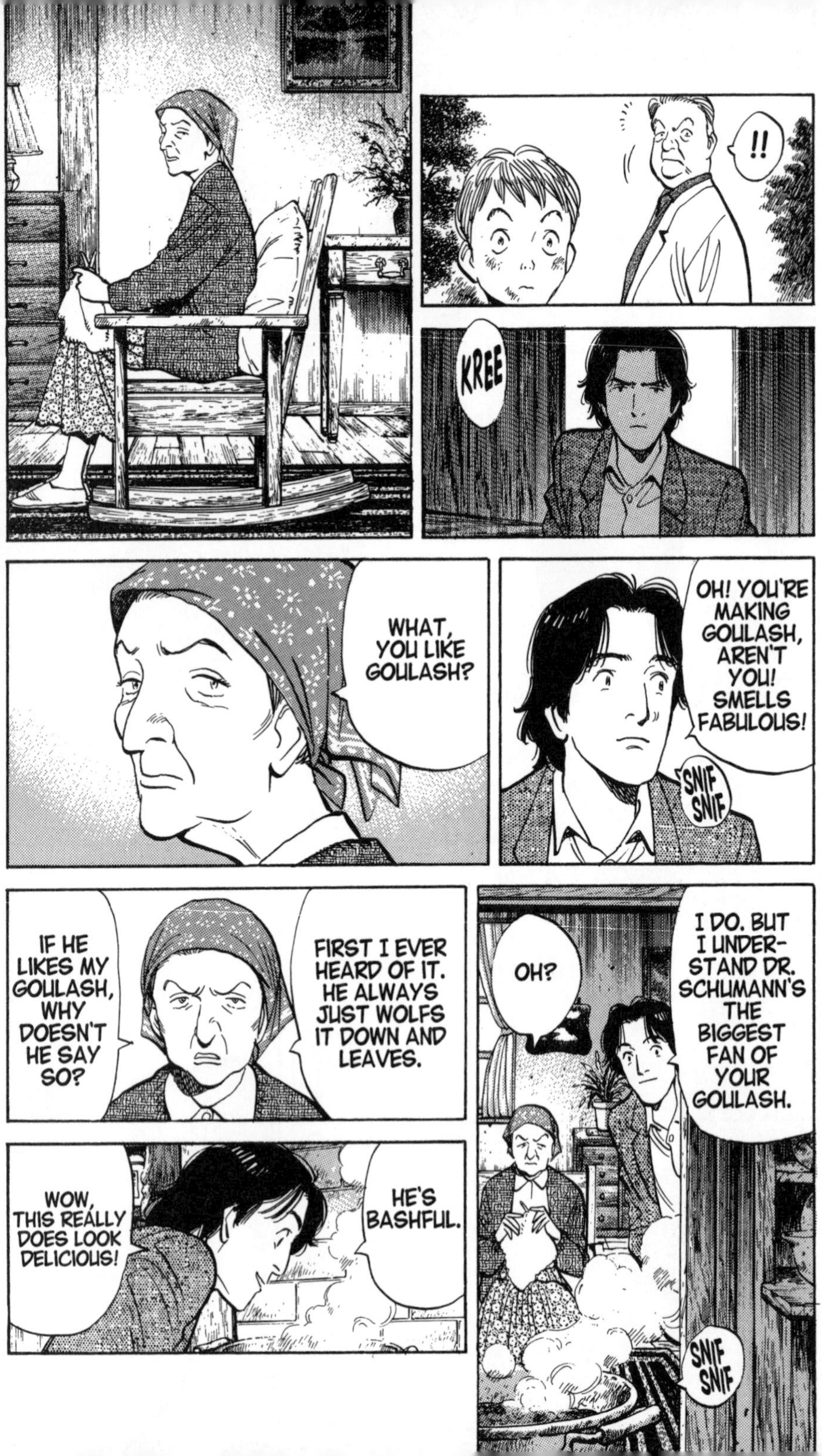
!!
KREE
OH! YOU'RE MAKING GOULASH, AREN'T YOU! SMELLS FABULOUS!
SNIF SNIF
WHAT, YOU LIKE GOULASH?
I DO. BUT I UNDER-STAND DR. SCHUMANN'S THE BIGGEST FAN OF YOUR GOULASH.
OH?
SNIF SNIF
FIRST I EVER HEARD OF IT. HE ALWAYS JUST WOLFS IT DOWN AND LEAVES.
IF HE LIKES MY GOULASH, WHY DOESN'T HE SAY SO?
HE'S BASHFUL.
WOW, THIS REALLY DOES LOOK DELICIOUS!

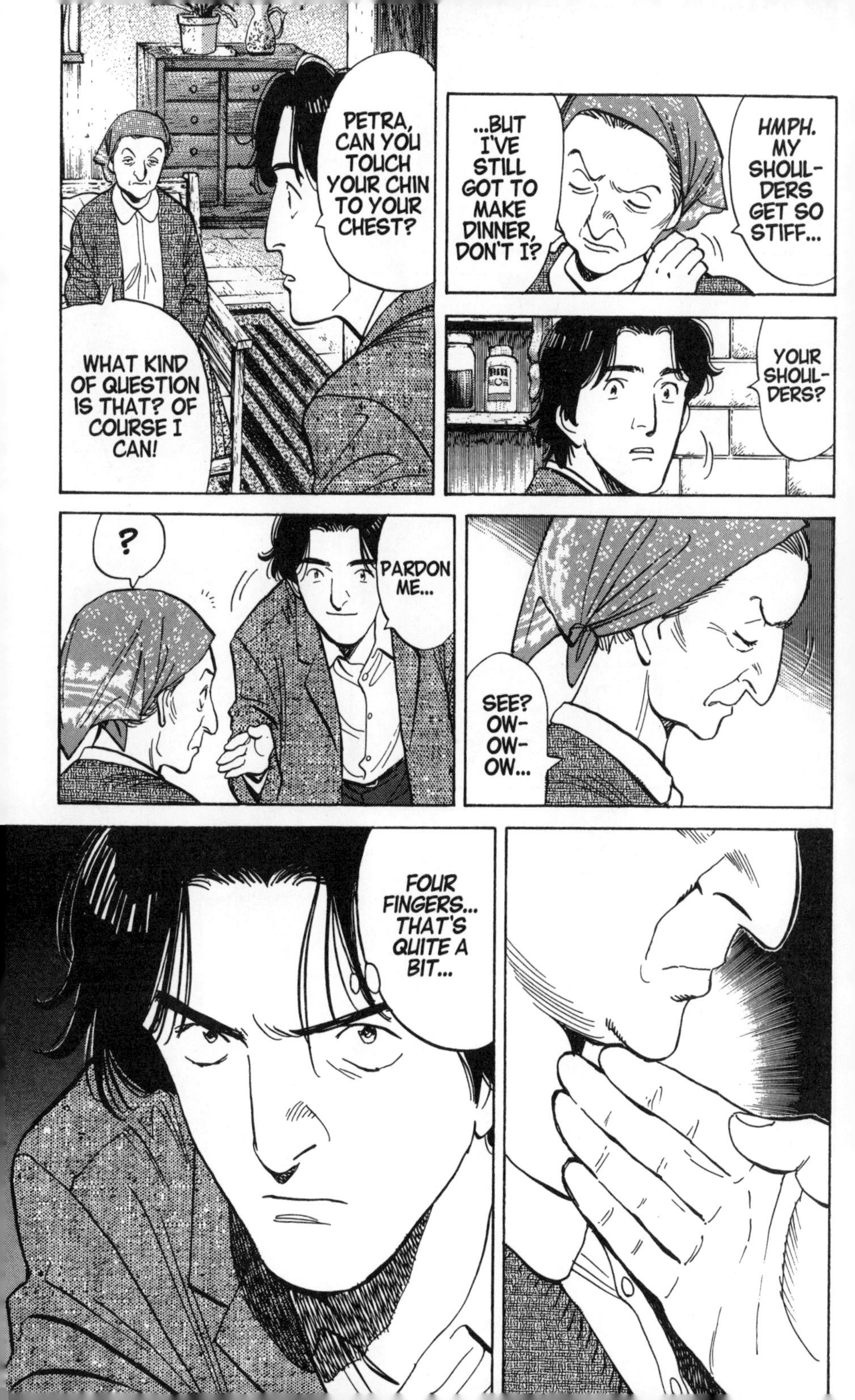
HMPH. MY SHOULDERS GET SO STIFF...
...BUT I'VE STILL GOT TO MAKE DINNER, DON'T I?
YOUR SHOULDERS?
PETRA, CAN YOU TOUCH YOUR CHIN TO YOUR CHEST?
WHAT KIND OF QUESTION IS THAT? OF COURSE I CAN!
SEE? OW-OW-OW...
PARDON ME...
?
FOUR FINGERS... THAT'S QUITE A BIT...

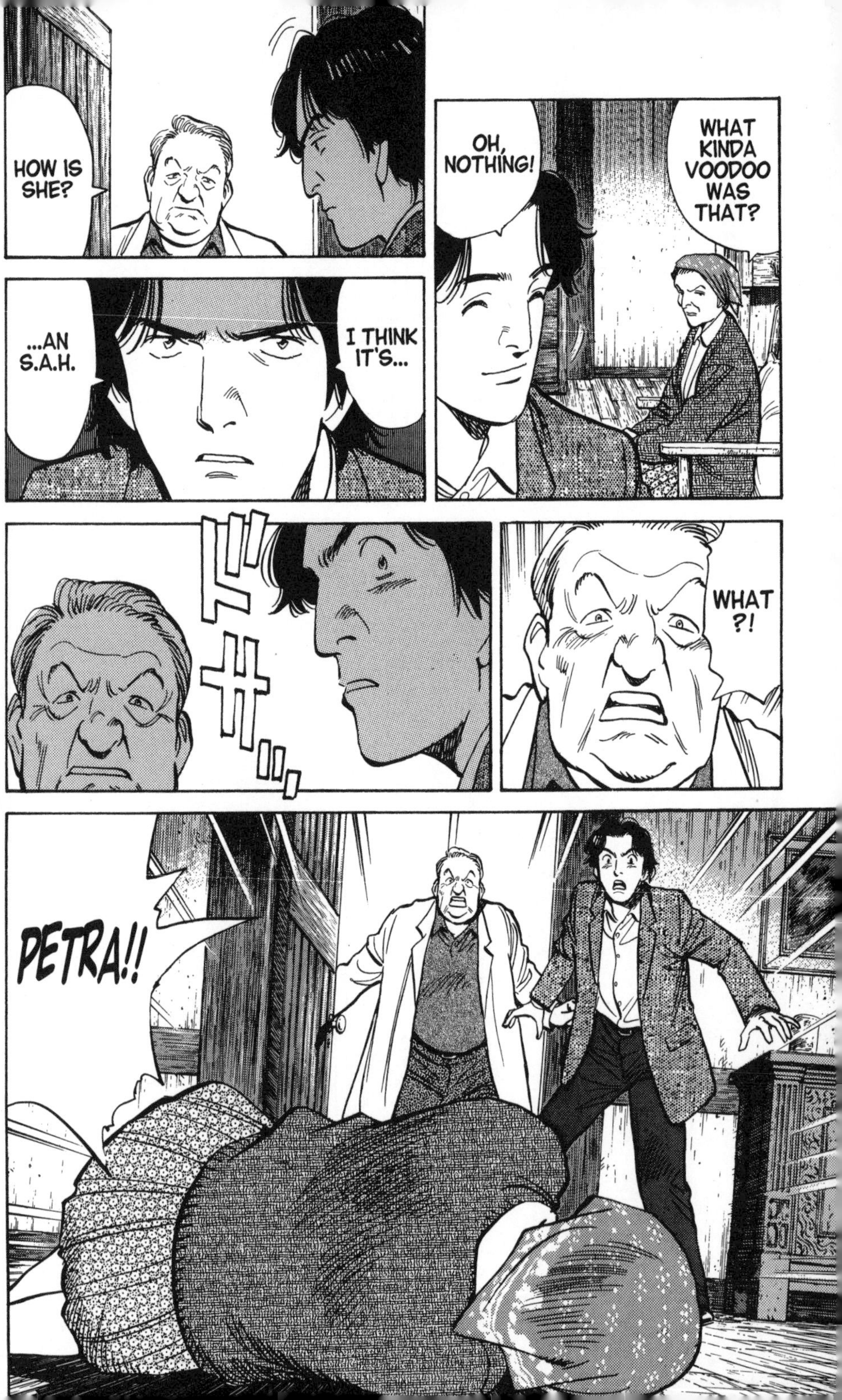
WHAT KINDA VOODOO WAS THAT?
OH, NOTHING!
HOW IS SHE?
I THINK IT'S...
...AN S.A.H.
WHAT?!
ドサ
PETRA!!

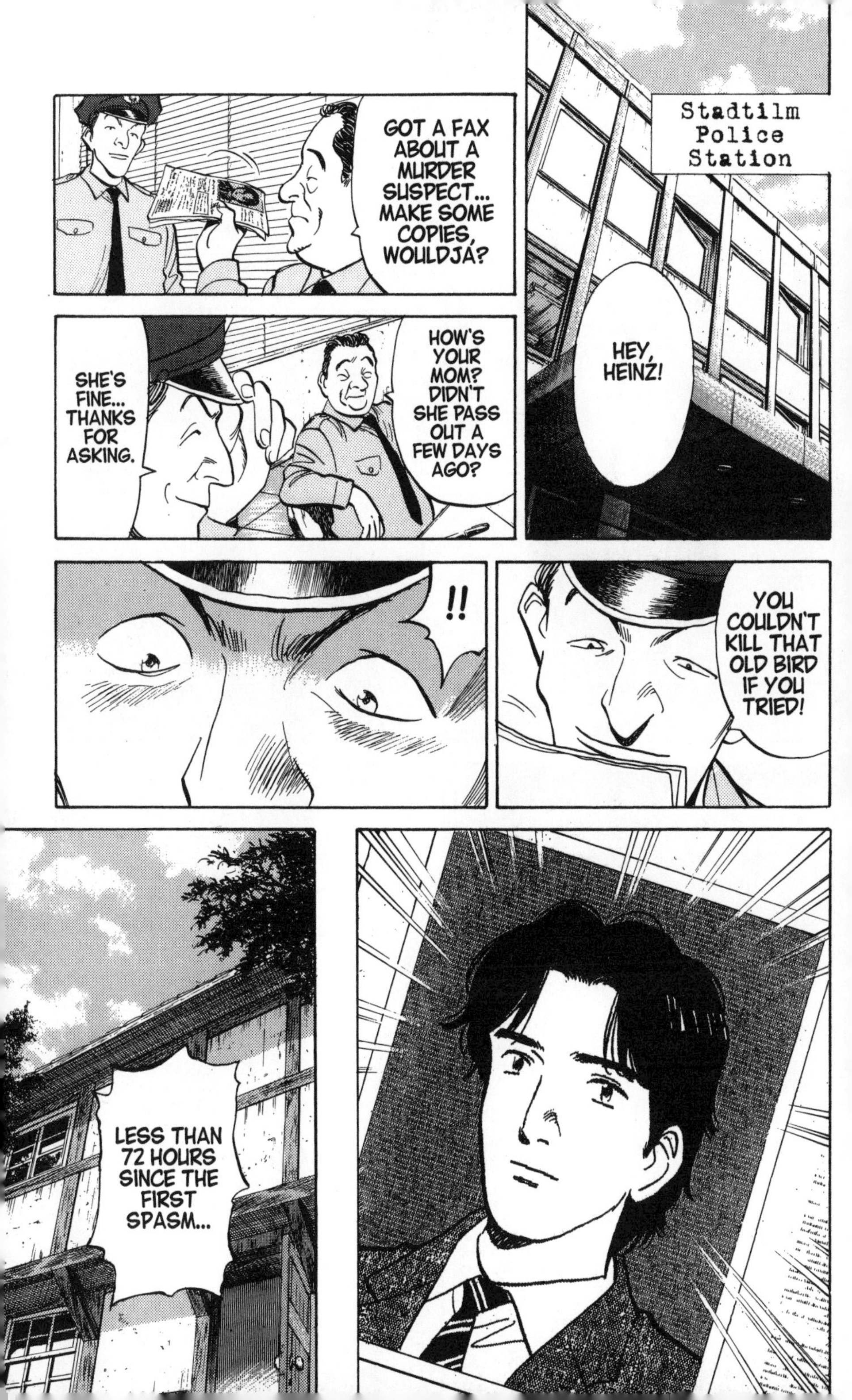
Stadtilm Police Station
HEY, HEINZ!
GOT A FAX ABOUT A MURDER SUSPECT... MAKE SOME COPIES, WOULDJA?
HOW'S YOUR MOM? DIDN'T SHE PASS OUT A FEW DAYS AGO?
SHE'S FINE... THANKS FOR ASKING.
YOU COULDN'T KILL THAT OLD BIRD IF YOU TRIED!
!!
LESS THAN 72 HOURS SINCE THE FIRST SPASM...

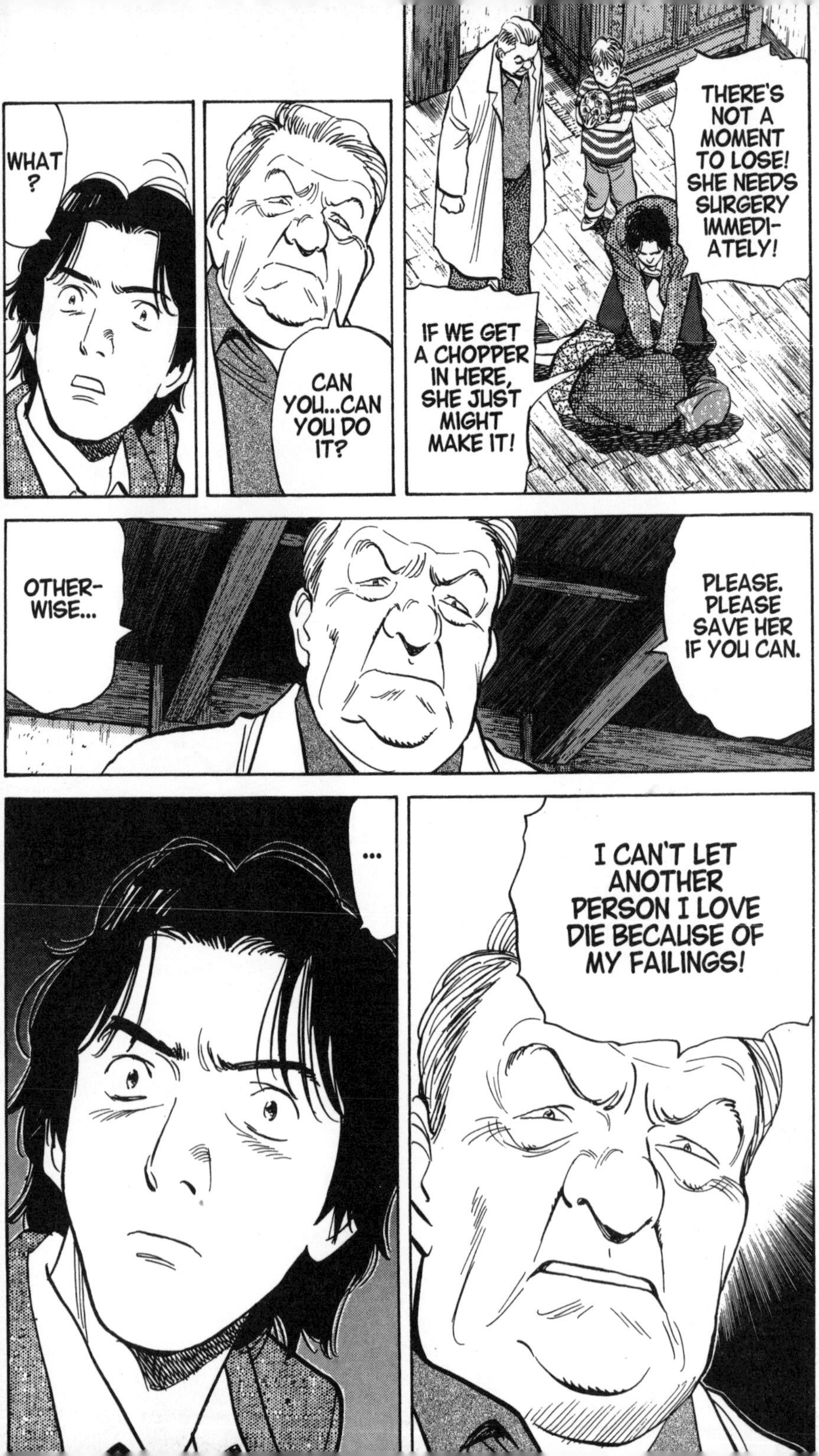
THERE'S NOT A MOMENT TO LOSE! SHE NEEDS SURGERY IMMEDI-ATELY!
IF WE GET A CHOPPER IN HERE, SHE JUST MIGHT MAKE IT!
CAN YOU...CAN YOU DO IT?
WHAT?
PLEASE. PLEASE SAVE HER IF YOU CAN.
OTHER-WISE...
I CAN'T LET ANOTHER PERSON I LOVE DIE BECAUSE OF MY FAILINGS!
...

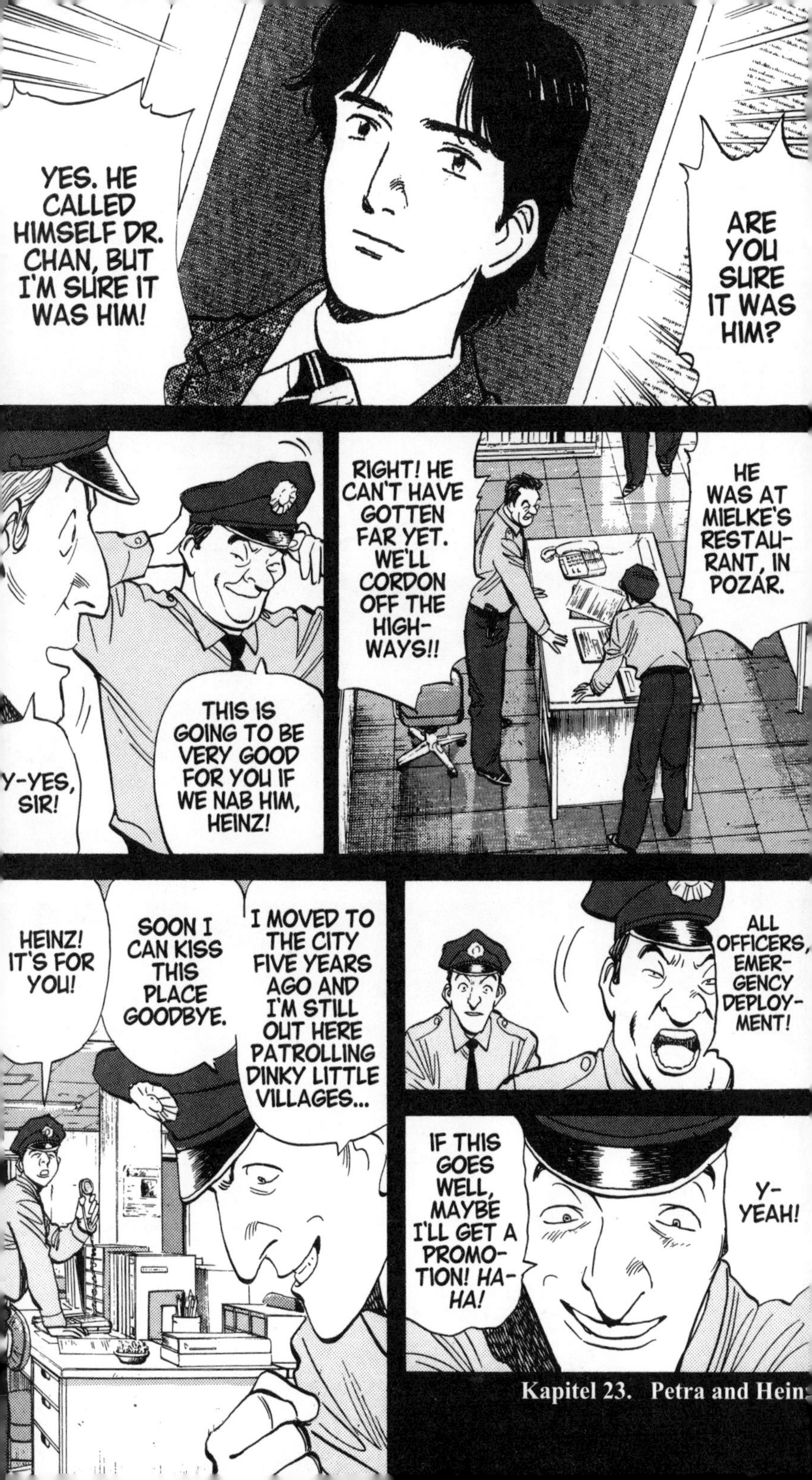
ARE YOU SURE IT WAS HIM?
YES. HE CALLED HIMSELF DR. CHAN, BUT I'M SURE IT WAS HIM!
HE WAS AT MIELKE'S RESTAURANT, IN POZÁR.
RIGHT! HE CAN'T HAVE GOTTEN FAR YET. WE'LL CORDON OFF THE HIGHWAYS!!
THIS IS GOING TO BE VERY GOOD FOR YOU IF WE NAB HIM, HEINZ!
Y-YES, SIR!
ALL OFFICERS, EMERGENCY DEPLOYMENT!
IF THIS GOES WELL, MAYBE I'LL GET A PROMOTION! HA-HA!
Y-YEAH!
I MOVED TO THE CITY FIVE YEARS AGO AND I'M STILL OUT HERE PATROLLING DINKY LITTLE VILLAGES...
SOON I CAN KISS THIS PLACE GOODBYE.
HEINZ! IT'S FOR YOU!
Kapitel 23. Petra and Hein

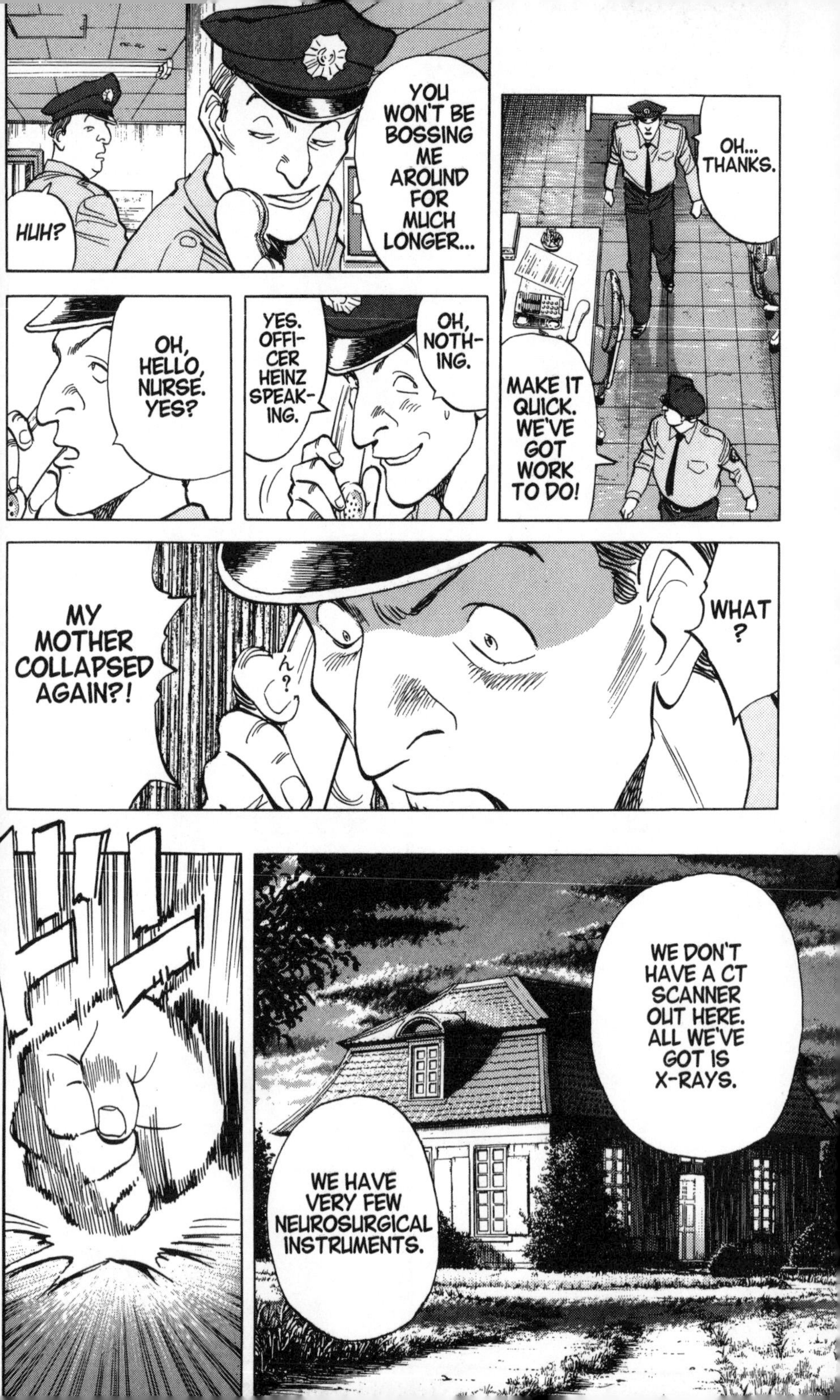
OH... THANKS.
MAKE IT QUICK. WE'VE GOT WORK TO DO!
YOU WON'T BE BOSSING ME AROUND FOR MUCH LONGER...
HUH?
OH, NOTHING.
YES. OFFICER HEINZ SPEAKING.
OH, HELLO, NURSE. YES?
WHAT?
ん?
MY MOTHER COLLAPSED AGAIN?!
WE DON'T HAVE A CT SCANNER OUT HERE. ALL WE'VE GOT IS X-RAYS.
WE HAVE VERY FEW NEUROSURGICAL INSTRUMENTS.

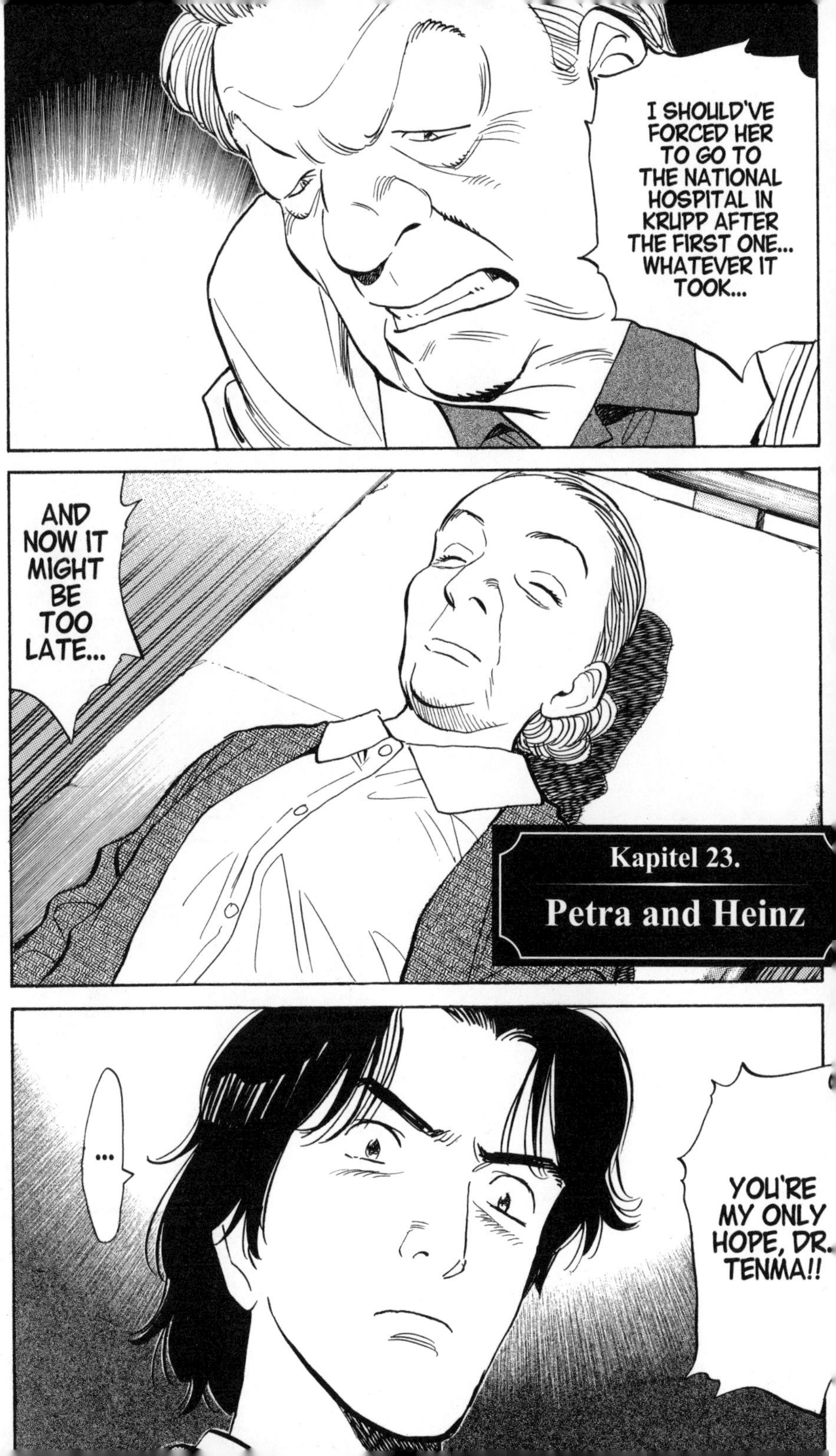
I SHOULD'VE FORCED HER TO GO TO THE NATIONAL HOSPITAL IN KRUPP AFTER THE FIRST ONE... WHATEVER IT TOOK...
Kapitel 23.
Petra and Heinz
AND NOW IT MIGHT BE TOO LATE...
YOU'RE MY ONLY HOPE, DR. TENMA!!
...

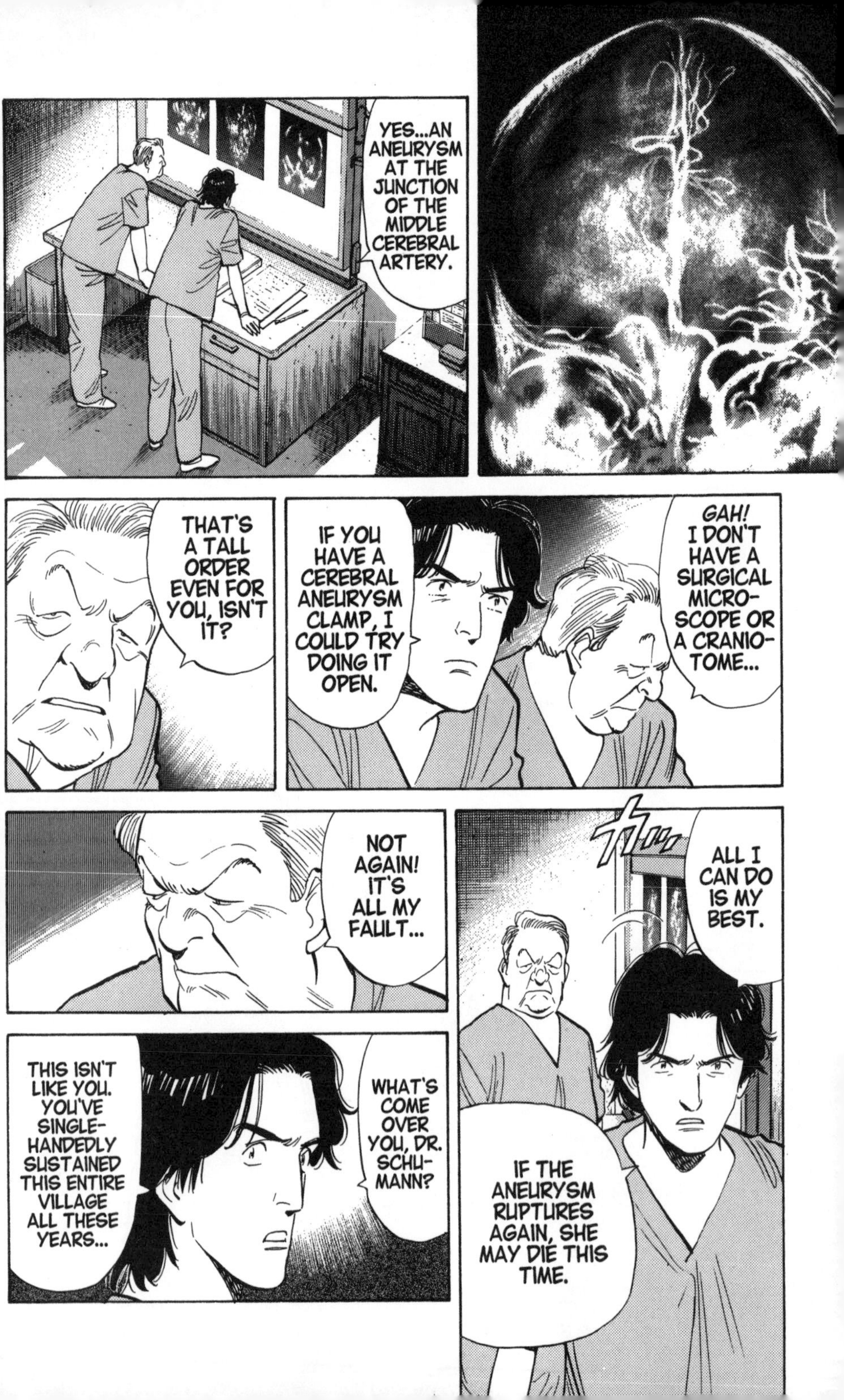
YES...AN ANEURYSM AT THE JUNCTION OF THE MIDDLE CEREBRAL ARTERY.
GAH! I DON'T HAVE A SURGICAL MICRO-SCOPE OR A CRANIO-TOME...
IF YOU HAVE A CEREBRAL ANEURYSM CLAMP, I COULD TRY DOING IT OPEN.
THAT'S A TALL ORDER EVEN FOR YOU, ISN'T IT?
ALL I CAN DO IS MY BEST.
IF THE ANEURYSM RUPTURES AGAIN, SHE MAY DIE THIS TIME.
NOT AGAIN! IT'S ALL MY FAULT...
WHAT'S COME OVER YOU, DR. SCHU-MANN?
THIS ISN'T LIKE YOU. YOU'VE SINGLE-HANDEDLY SUSTAINED THIS ENTIRE VILLAGE ALL THESE YEARS...

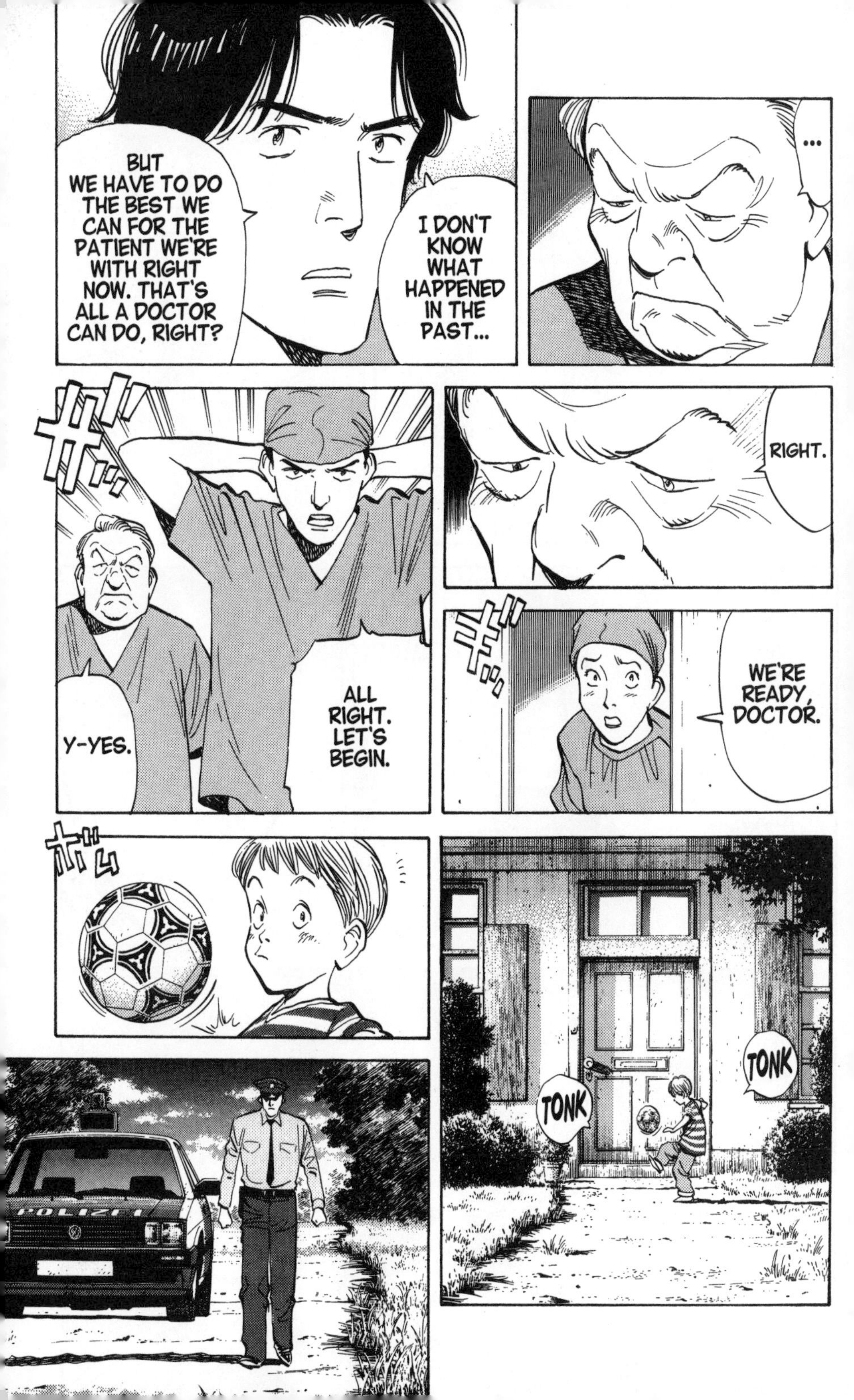
...
I DON'T KNOW WHAT HAPPENED IN THE PAST...
BUT WE HAVE TO DO THE BEST WE CAN FOR THE PATIENT WE'RE WITH RIGHT NOW. THAT'S ALL A DOCTOR CAN DO, RIGHT?
RIGHT.
ギッ
WE'RE READY, DOCTOR.
ガッ
ALL RIGHT. LET'S BEGIN.
Y-YES.
TONK
TONK
ボム
POLIZEI

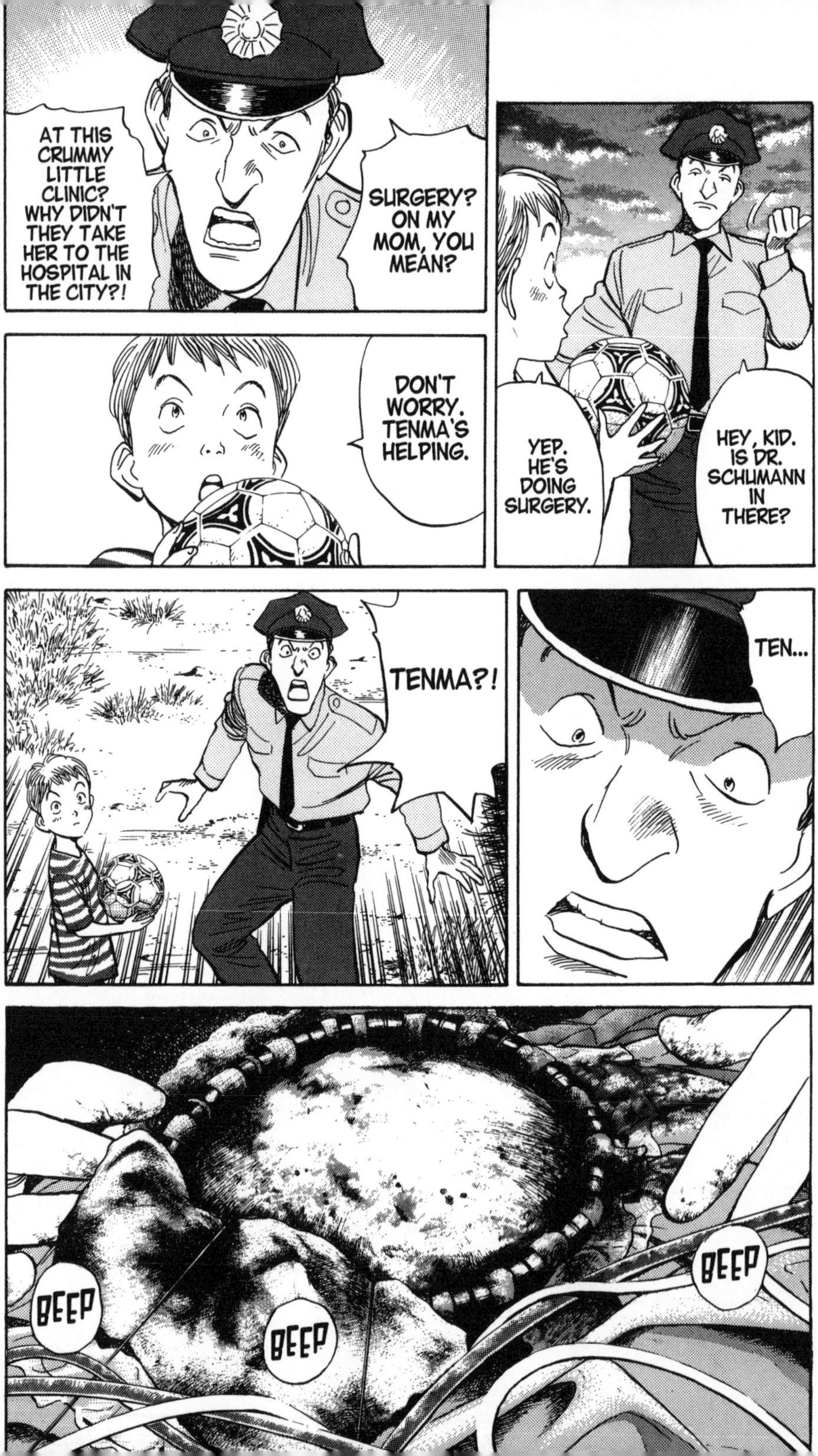
HEY, KID. IS DR. SCHUMANN IN THERE?
YEP. HE'S DOING SURGERY.
SURGERY? ON MY MOM, YOU MEAN?
AT THIS CRUMMY LITTLE CLINIC? WHY DIDN'T THEY TAKE HER TO THE HOSPITAL IN THE CITY?!
DON'T WORRY. TENMA'S HELPING.
TEN...
TENMA?!
BEEP
BEEP
BEEP

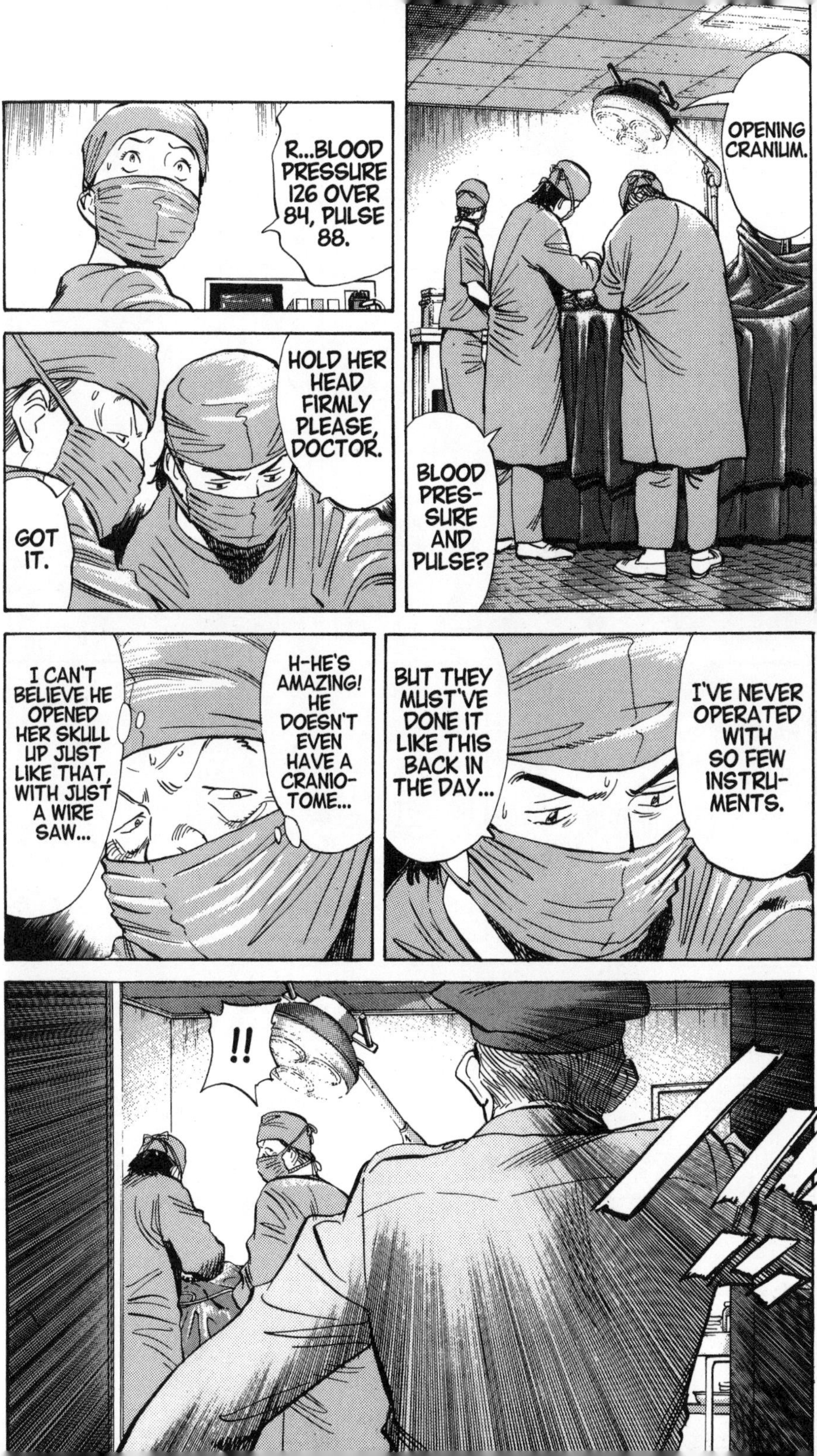
OPENING CRANIUM.
BLOOD PRESSURE AND PULSE?
R...BLOOD PRESSURE 126 OVER 84, PULSE 88.
HOLD HER HEAD FIRMLY PLEASE, DOCTOR.
GOT IT.
I'VE NEVER OPERATED WITH SO FEW INSTRUMENTS.
BUT THEY MUST'VE DONE IT LIKE THIS BACK IN THE DAY...
H-HE'S AMAZING! HE DOESN'T EVEN HAVE A CRANIOTOME...
I CAN'T BELIEVE HE OPENED HER SKULL UP JUST LIKE THAT, WITH JUST A WIRE SAW...
!!

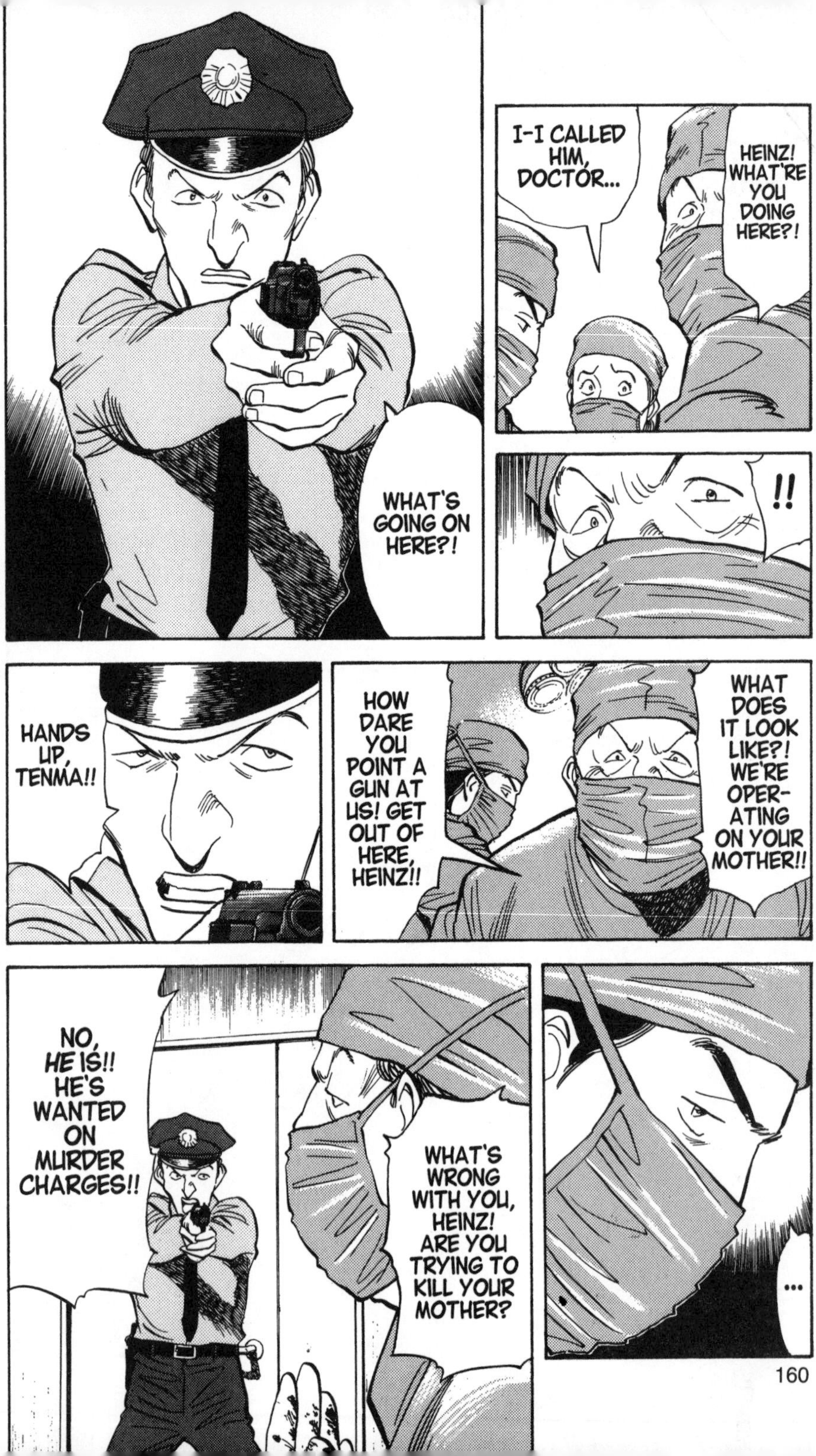
HEINZ! WHAT'RE YOU DOING HERE?!
I-I CALLED HIM, DOCTOR...
!!
WHAT'S GOING ON HERE?!
WHAT DOES IT LOOK LIKE?! WE'RE OPER-ATING ON YOUR MOTHER!!
HOW DARE YOU POINT A GUN AT US! GET OUT OF HERE, HEINZ!!
HANDS UP, TENMA!!
...
WHAT'S WRONG WITH YOU, HEINZ! ARE YOU TRYING TO KILL YOUR MOTHER?
NO, *HE* IS!! HE'S WANTED ON MURDER CHARGES!!

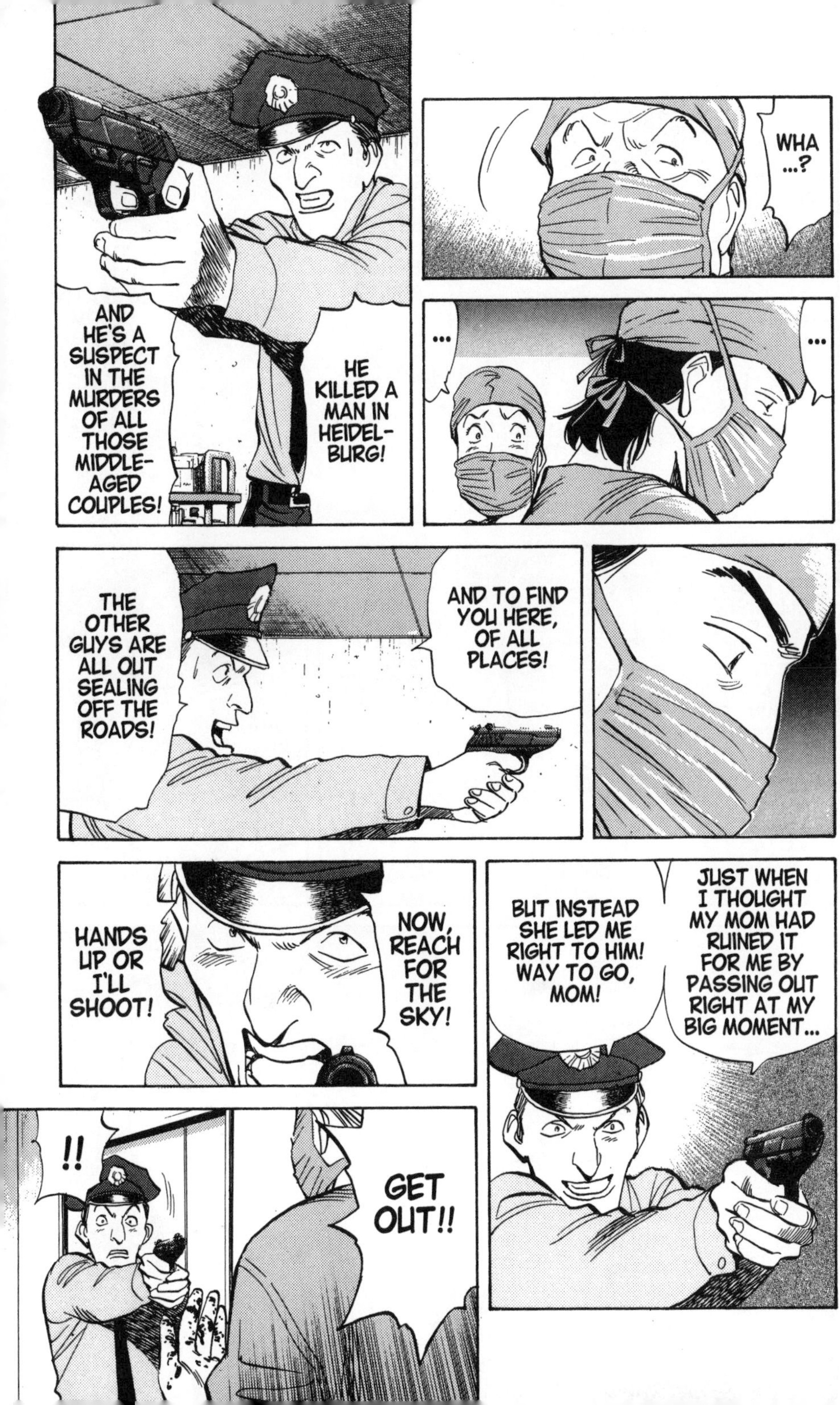
WHA ...?
...
...
HE KILLED A MAN IN HEIDEL-BURG!
AND HE'S A SUSPECT IN THE MURDERS OF ALL THOSE MIDDLE-AGED COUPLES!
AND TO FIND YOU HERE, OF ALL PLACES!
THE OTHER GUYS ARE ALL OUT SEALING OFF THE ROADS!
JUST WHEN I THOUGHT MY MOM HAD RUINED IT FOR ME BY PASSING OUT RIGHT AT MY BIG MOMENT...
BUT INSTEAD SHE LED ME RIGHT TO HIM! WAY TO GO, MOM!
NOW, REACH FOR THE SKY!
HANDS UP OR I'LL SHOOT!
GET OUT!!
!!

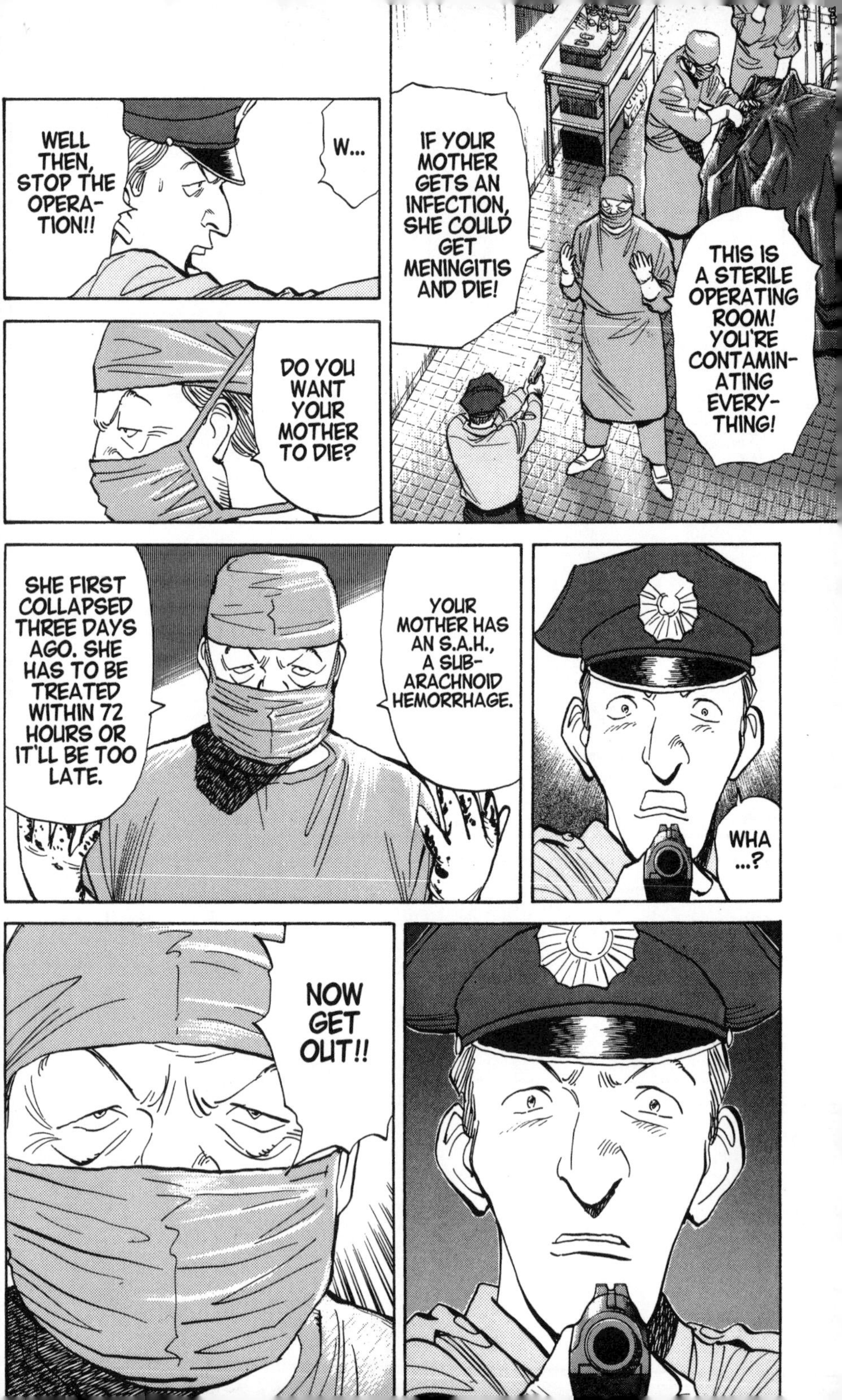
THIS IS A STERILE OPERATING ROOM! YOU'RE CONTAMINATING EVERYTHING!
IF YOUR MOTHER GETS AN INFECTION, SHE COULD GET MENINGITIS AND DIE!
W...
WELL THEN, STOP THE OPERATION!!
DO YOU WANT YOUR MOTHER TO DIE?
WHA ...?
YOUR MOTHER HAS AN S.A.H., A SUB-ARACHNOID HEMORRHAGE.
SHE FIRST COLLAPSED THREE DAYS AGO. SHE HAS TO BE TREATED WITHIN 72 HOURS OR IT'LL BE TOO LATE.
NOW GET OUT!!

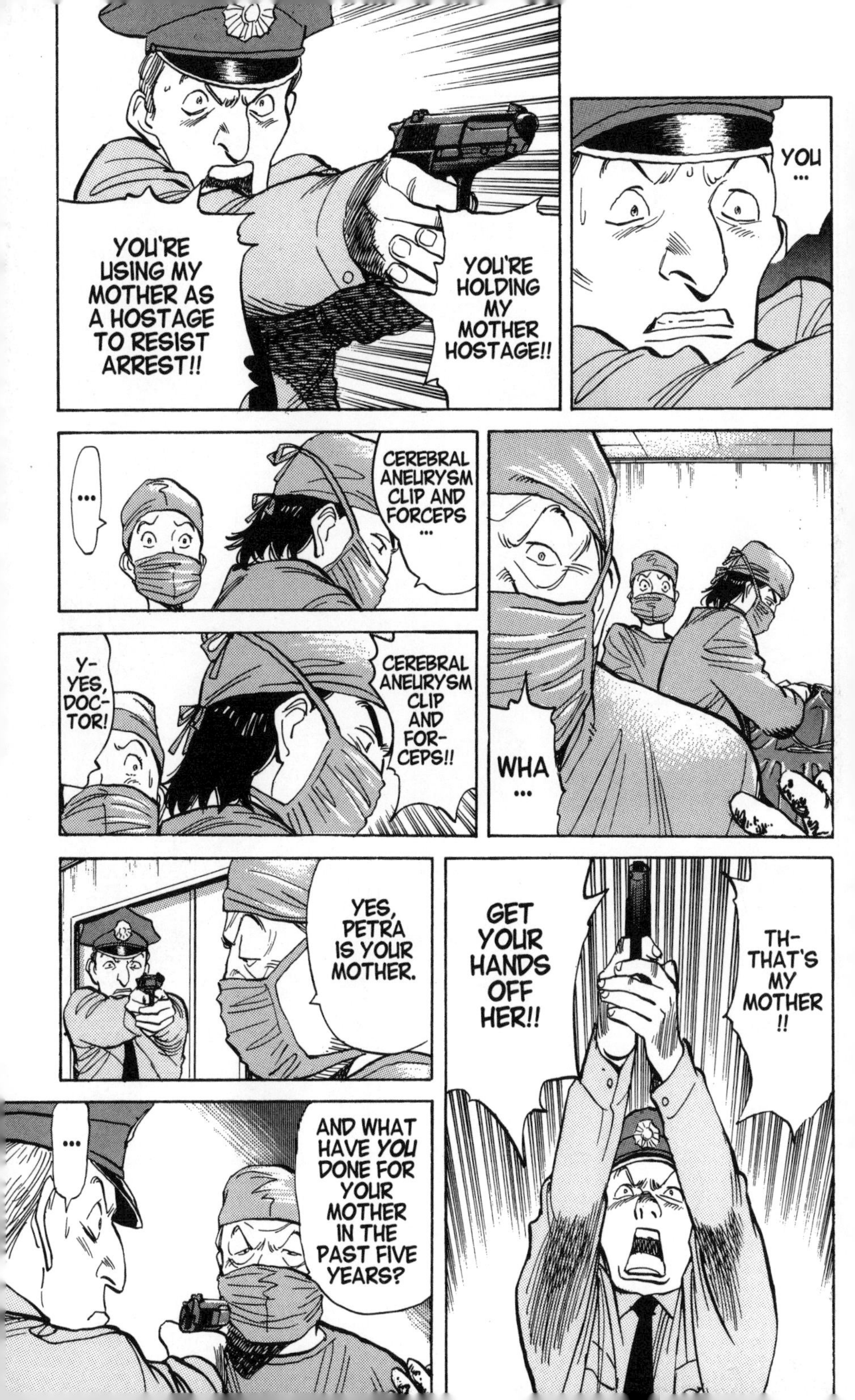
YOU ...
YOU'RE HOLDING MY MOTHER HOSTAGE!!
YOU'RE USING MY MOTHER AS A HOSTAGE TO RESIST ARREST!!
WHA ...
CEREBRAL ANEURYSM CLIP AND FORCEPS ...
...
CEREBRAL ANEURYSM CLIP AND FOR-CEPS!!
Y-YES, DOC-TOR!
TH-THAT'S MY MOTHER!!
GET YOUR HANDS OFF HER!!
YES, PETRA IS YOUR MOTHER.
AND WHAT HAVE *YOU* DONE FOR YOUR MOTHER IN THE PAST FIVE YEARS?
...

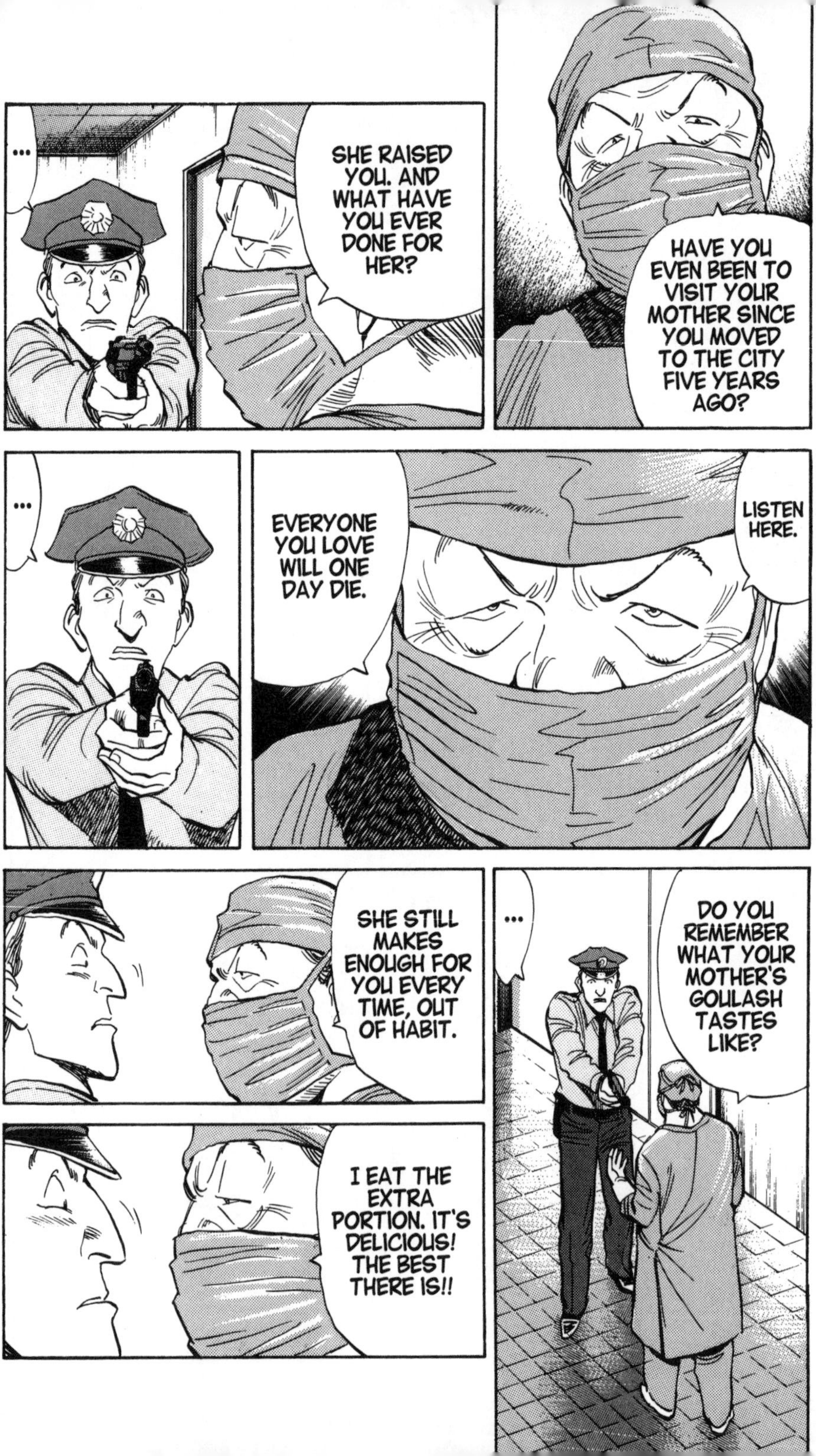
HAVE YOU EVEN BEEN TO VISIT YOUR MOTHER SINCE YOU MOVED TO THE CITY FIVE YEARS AGO?
SHE RAISED YOU. AND WHAT HAVE YOU EVER DONE FOR HER?
...
LISTEN HERE.
EVERYONE YOU LOVE WILL ONE DAY DIE.
...
DO YOU REMEMBER WHAT YOUR MOTHER'S GOULASH TASTES LIKE?
...
SHE STILL MAKES ENOUGH FOR YOU EVERY TIME, OUT OF HABIT.
I EAT THE EXTRA PORTION. IT'S DELICIOUS! THE BEST THERE IS!!

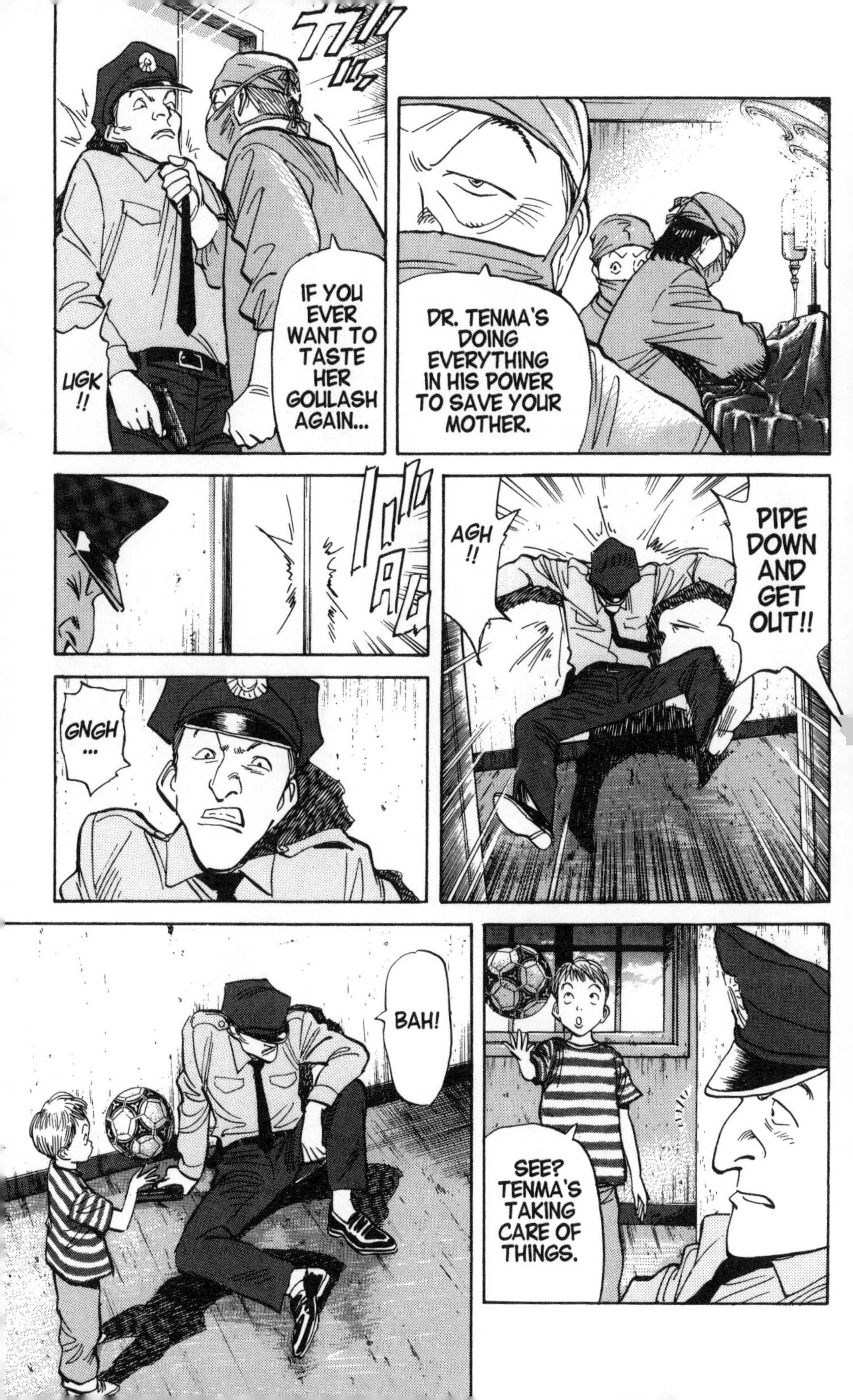
DR. TENMA'S DOING EVERYTHING IN HIS POWER TO SAVE YOUR MOTHER.
IF YOU EVER WANT TO TASTE HER GOULASH AGAIN...
UGK!!
PIPE DOWN AND GET OUT!!
AGH!!
GNGH...
SEE? TENMA'S TAKING CARE OF THINGS.
BAH!

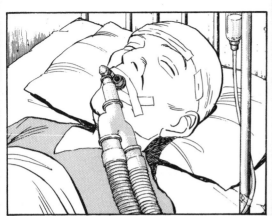

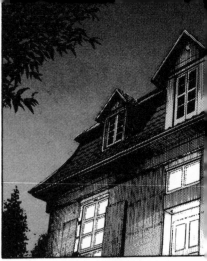

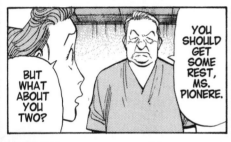

BLOOD PRESSURE, 140 OVER 86, HEART RATE 82.
HER VITAL SIGNS ARE GOOD.
YOU SHOULD GET SOME REST, MS. PIONERE.
BUT WHAT ABOUT YOU TWO?
I'M FINE. TAKE A BREAK. YOU DID GREAT.
WELL, ALL RIGHT THEN...
YOU TOO, DR. TENMA. GET SOME SLEEP.
NO, I'M FINE.
DON'T BE SILLY. YOU JUST WORKED THREE HOURS STRAIGHT ON A VERY DIFFICULT OPERATION!

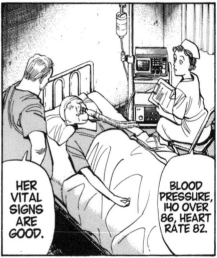

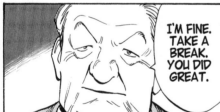

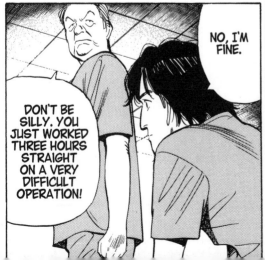

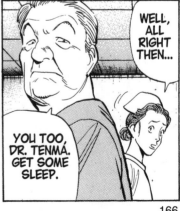

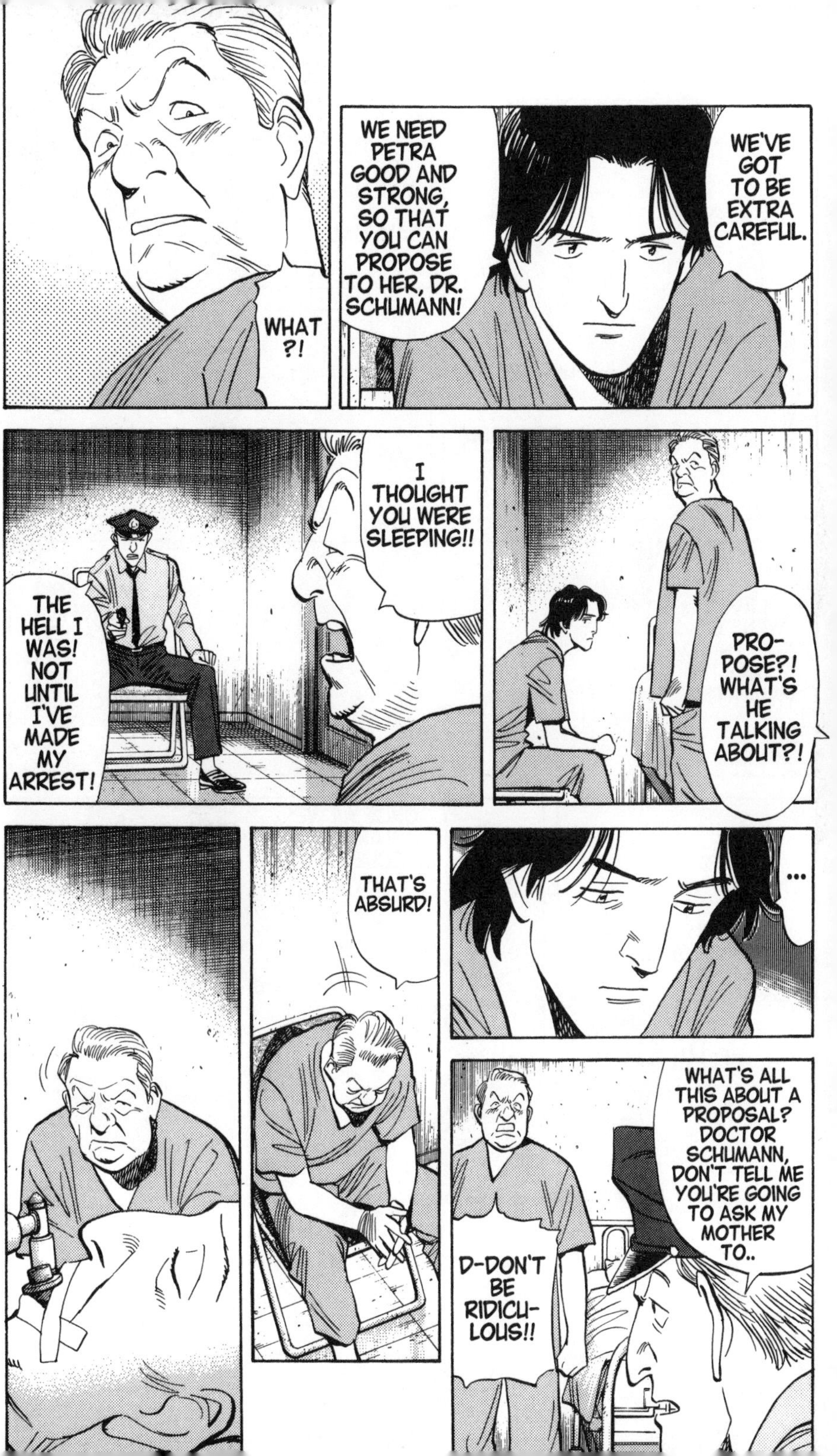
WE'VE GOT TO BE EXTRA CAREFUL.
WE NEED PETRA GOOD AND STRONG, SO THAT YOU CAN PROPOSE TO HER, DR. SCHUMANN!
WHAT?!
PRO-POSE?! WHAT'S HE TALKING ABOUT?!
I THOUGHT YOU WERE SLEEPING!!
THE HELL I WAS! NOT UNTIL I'VE MADE MY ARREST!
...
WHAT'S ALL THIS ABOUT A PROPOSAL? DOCTOR SCHUMANN, DON'T TELL ME YOU'RE GOING TO ASK MY MOTHER TO..
D-DON'T BE RIDICU-LOUS!!
THAT'S ABSURD!

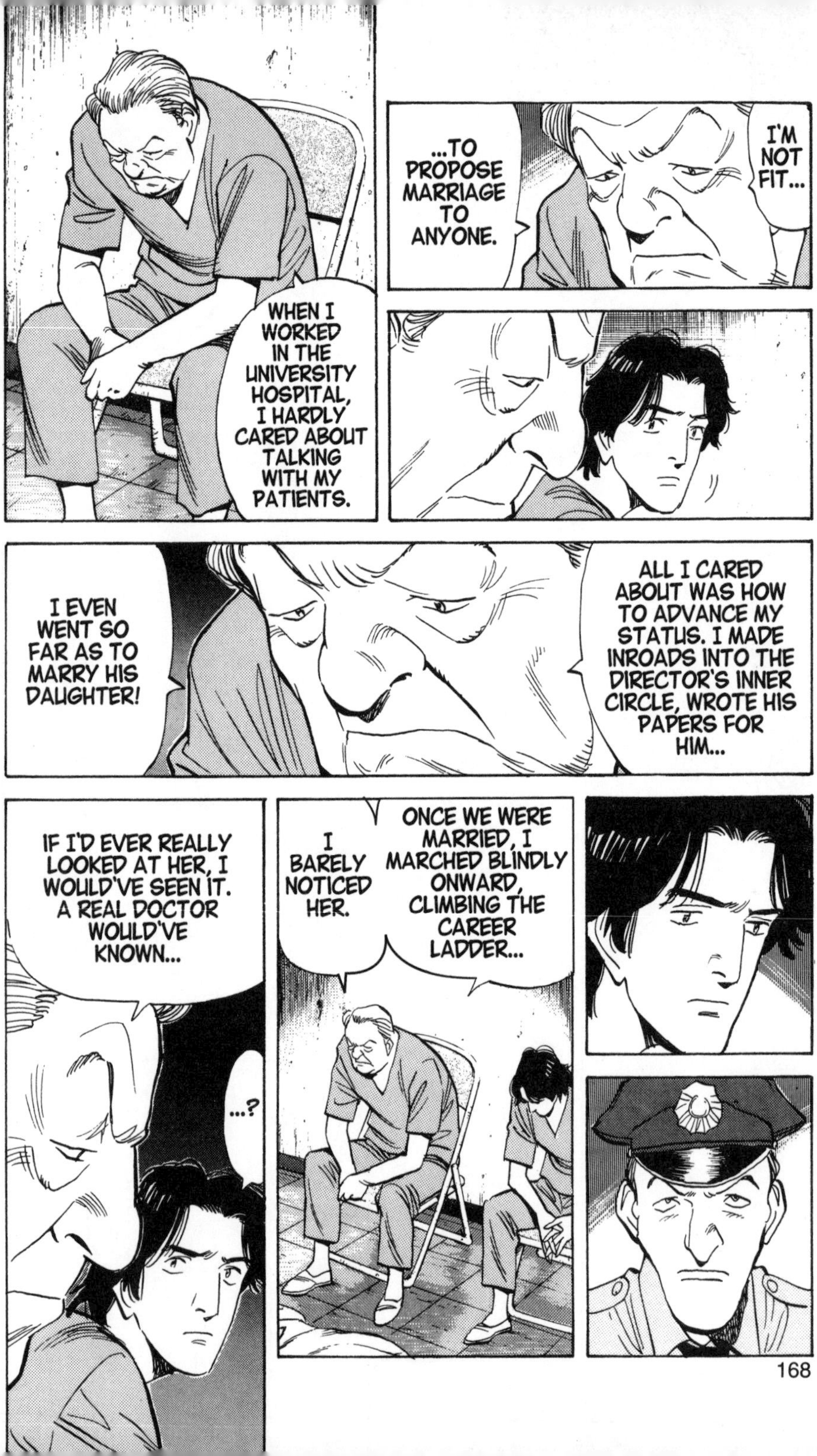
I'M NOT FIT...
...TO PROPOSE MARRIAGE TO ANYONE.
WHEN I WORKED IN THE UNIVERSITY HOSPITAL, I HARDLY CARED ABOUT TALKING WITH MY PATIENTS.
ALL I CARED ABOUT WAS HOW TO ADVANCE MY STATUS. I MADE INROADS INTO THE DIRECTOR'S INNER CIRCLE, WROTE HIS PAPERS FOR HIM...
I EVEN WENT SO FAR AS TO MARRY HIS DAUGHTER!
ONCE WE WERE MARRIED, I MARCHED BLINDLY ONWARD, CLIMBING THE CAREER LADDER...
I BARELY NOTICED HER.
IF I'D EVER REALLY LOOKED AT HER, I WOULD'VE SEEN IT. A REAL DOCTOR WOULD'VE KNOWN...
...?

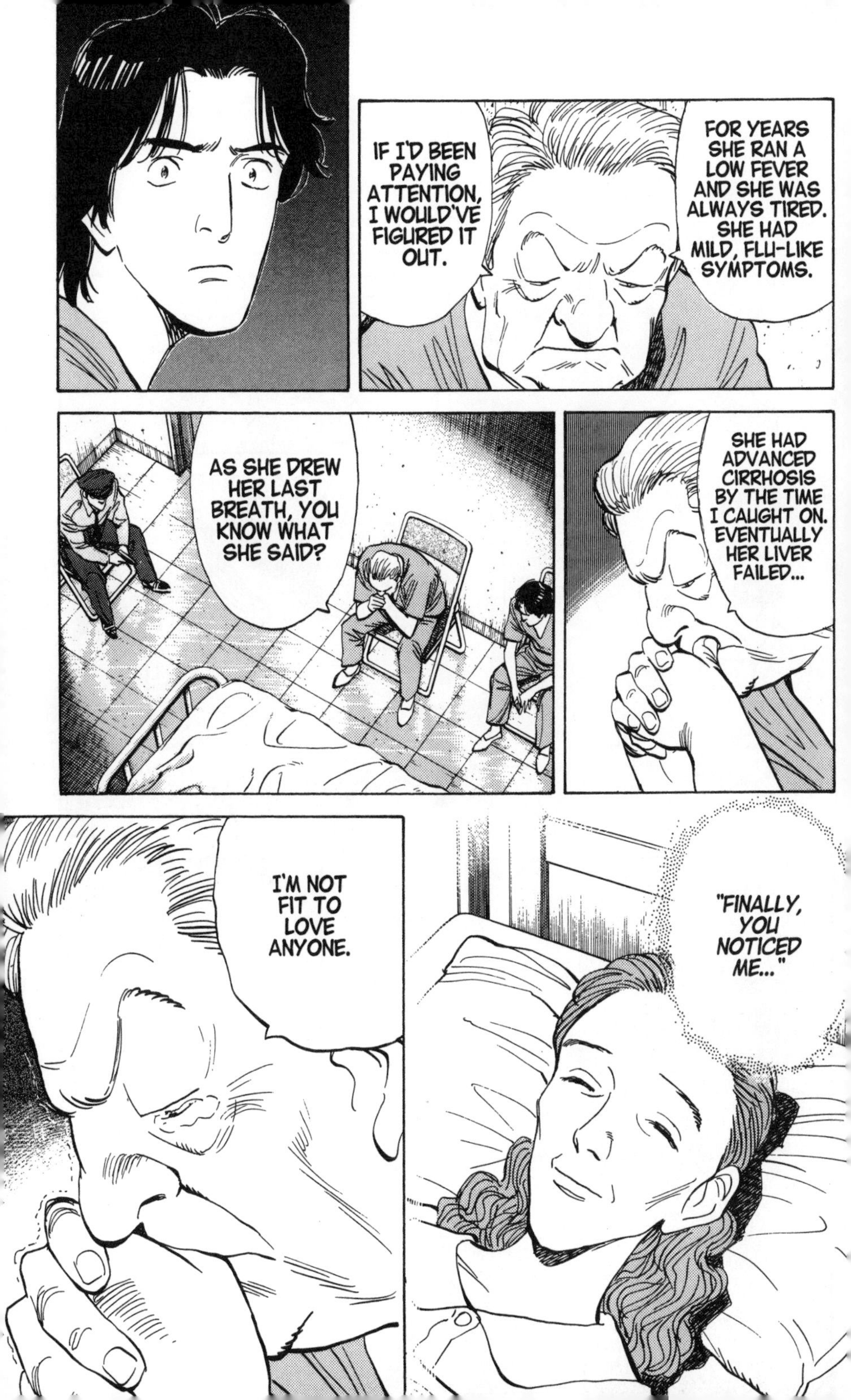
FOR YEARS SHE RAN A LOW FEVER AND SHE WAS ALWAYS TIRED. SHE HAD MILD, FLU-LIKE SYMPTOMS.
IF I'D BEEN PAYING ATTENTION, I WOULD'VE FIGURED IT OUT.
SHE HAD ADVANCED CIRRHOSIS BY THE TIME I CAUGHT ON. EVENTUALLY HER LIVER FAILED...
AS SHE DREW HER LAST BREATH, YOU KNOW WHAT SHE SAID?
"FINALLY, YOU NOTICED ME..."
I'M NOT FIT TO LOVE ANYONE.

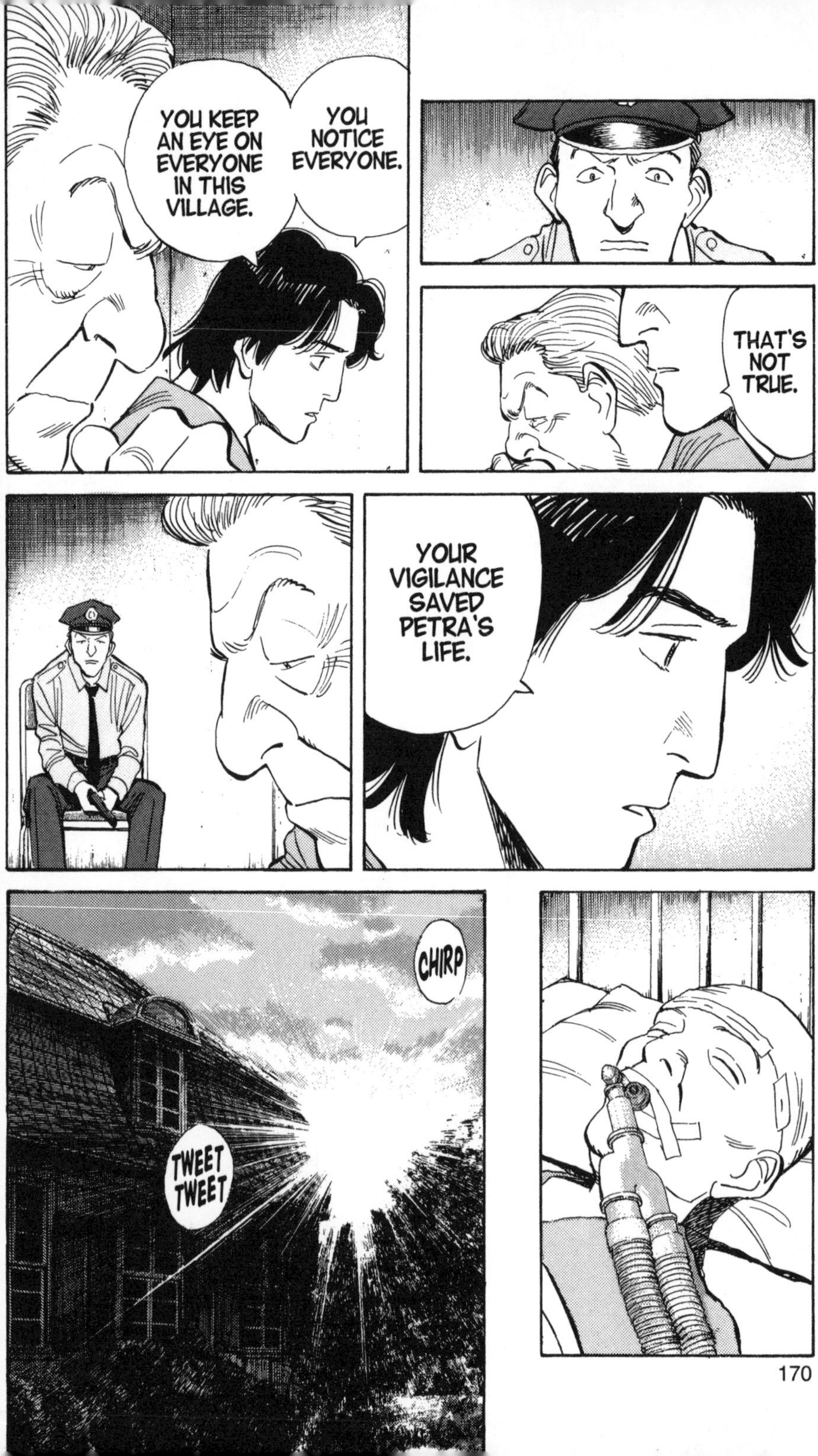
YOU NOTICE EVERYONE.
YOU KEEP AN EYE ON EVERYONE IN THIS VILLAGE.
THAT'S NOT TRUE.
YOUR VIGILANCE SAVED PETRA'S LIFE.
CHIRP
TWEET TWEET

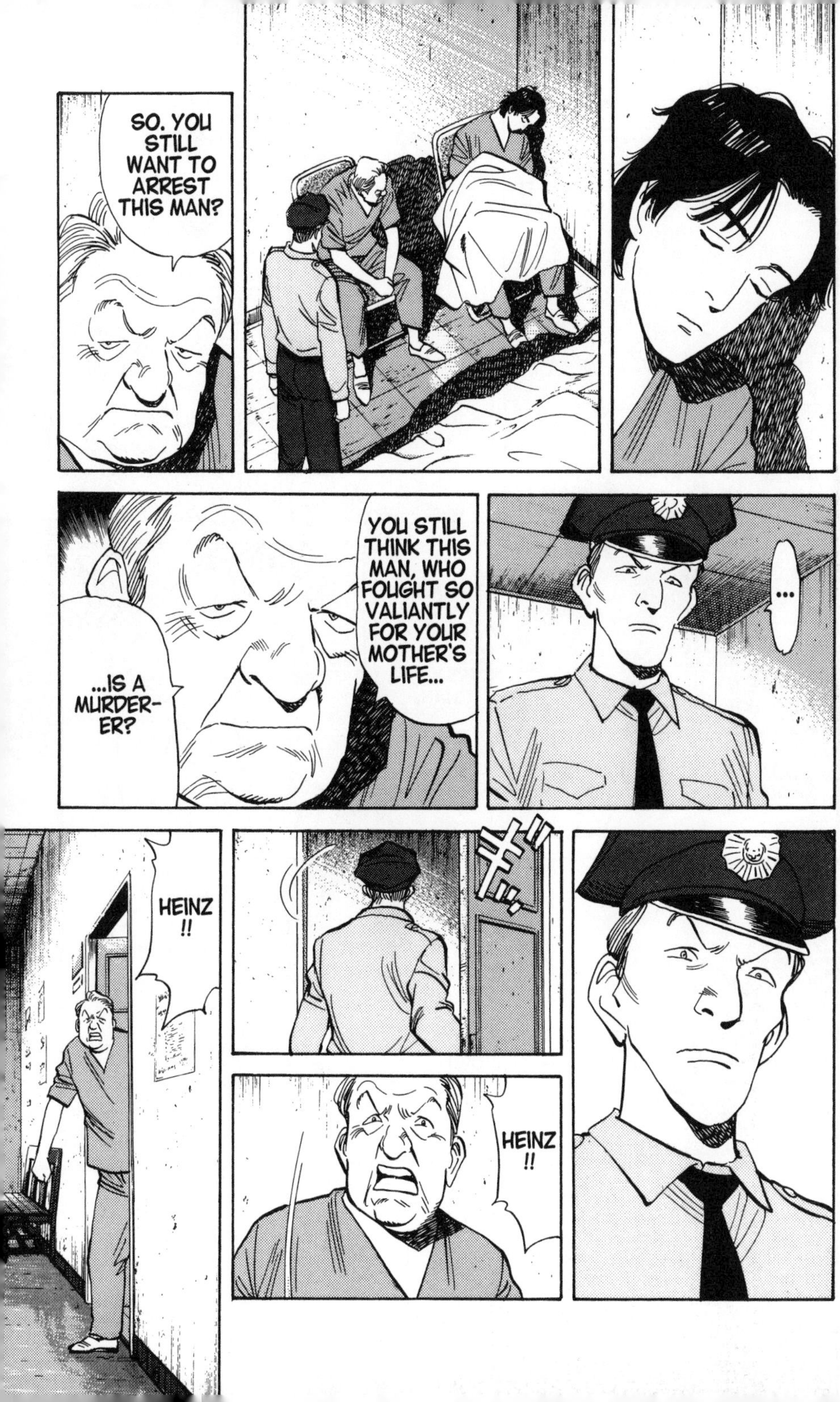
SO. YOU STILL WANT TO ARREST THIS MAN?
...
YOU STILL THINK THIS MAN, WHO FOUGHT SO VALIANTLY FOR YOUR MOTHER'S LIFE...
...IS A MURDERER?
HEINZ !!
HEINZ !!

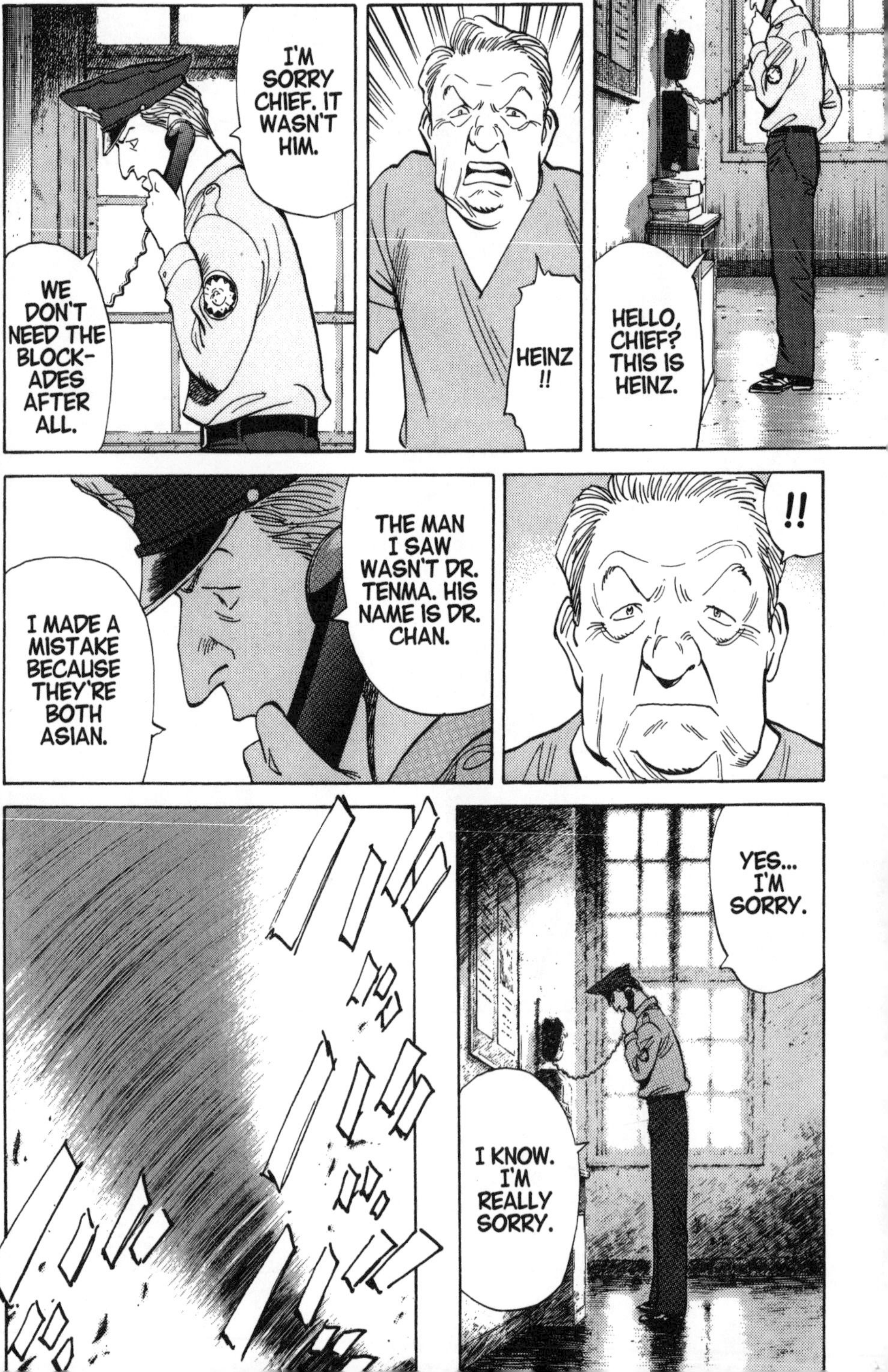
HELLO, CHIEF? THIS IS HEINZ.
HEINZ !!
I'M SORRY CHIEF. IT WASN'T HIM.
WE DON'T NEED THE BLOCKADES AFTER ALL.
!!
THE MAN I SAW WASN'T DR. TENMA. HIS NAME IS DR. CHAN.
I MADE A MISTAKE BECAUSE THEY'RE BOTH ASIAN.
YES... I'M SORRY.
I KNOW. I'M REALLY SORRY.

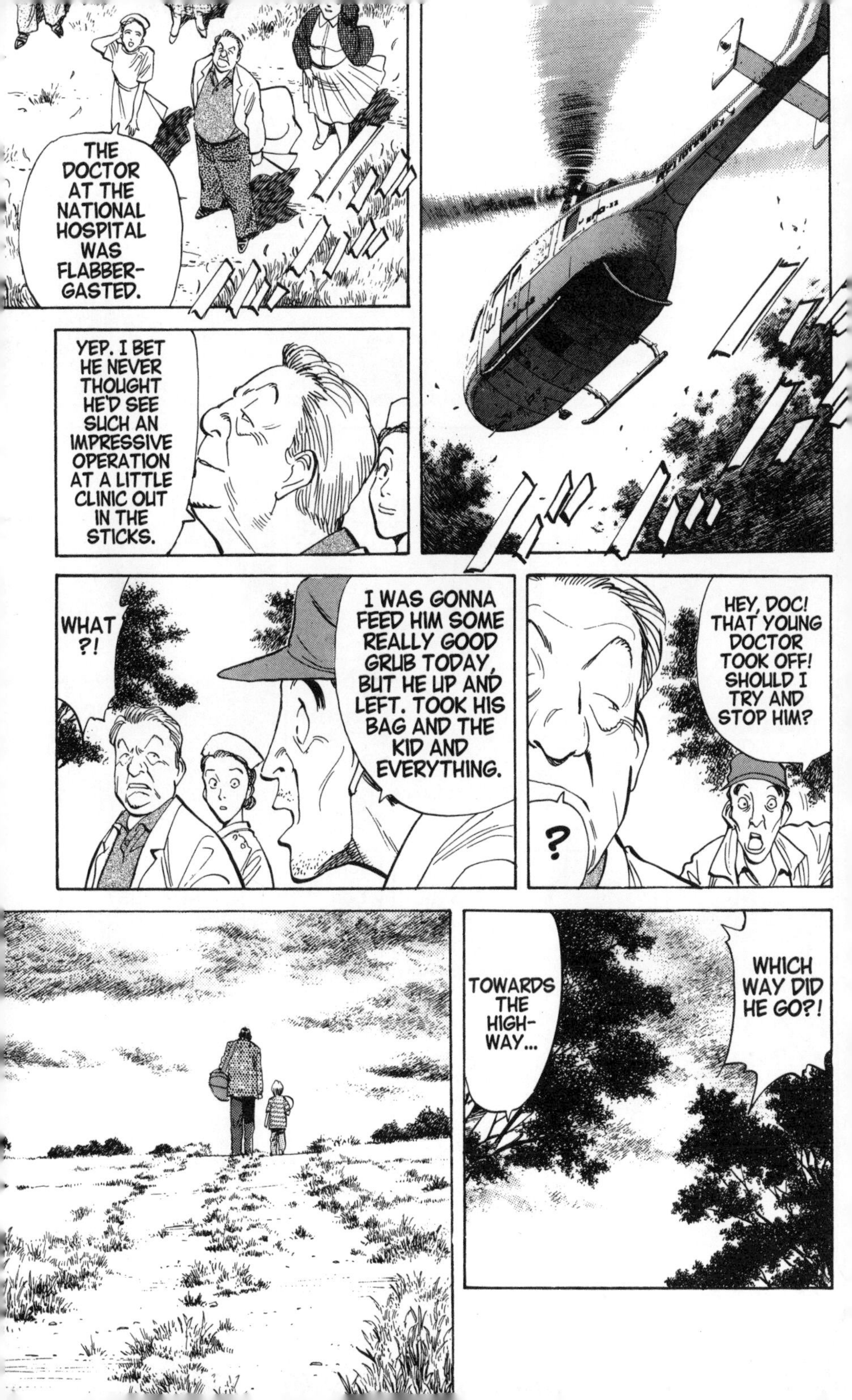
THE DOCTOR AT THE NATIONAL HOSPITAL WAS FLABBER-GASTED.
YEP. I BET HE NEVER THOUGHT HE'D SEE SUCH AN IMPRESSIVE OPERATION AT A LITTLE CLINIC OUT IN THE STICKS.
HEY, DOC! THAT YOUNG DOCTOR TOOK OFF! SHOULD I TRY AND STOP HIM?
?
I WAS GONNA FEED HIM SOME REALLY GOOD GRUB TODAY, BUT HE UP AND LEFT. TOOK HIS BAG AND THE KID AND EVERYTHING.
WHAT?!
WHICH WAY DID HE GO?!
TOWARDS THE HIGH-WAY...

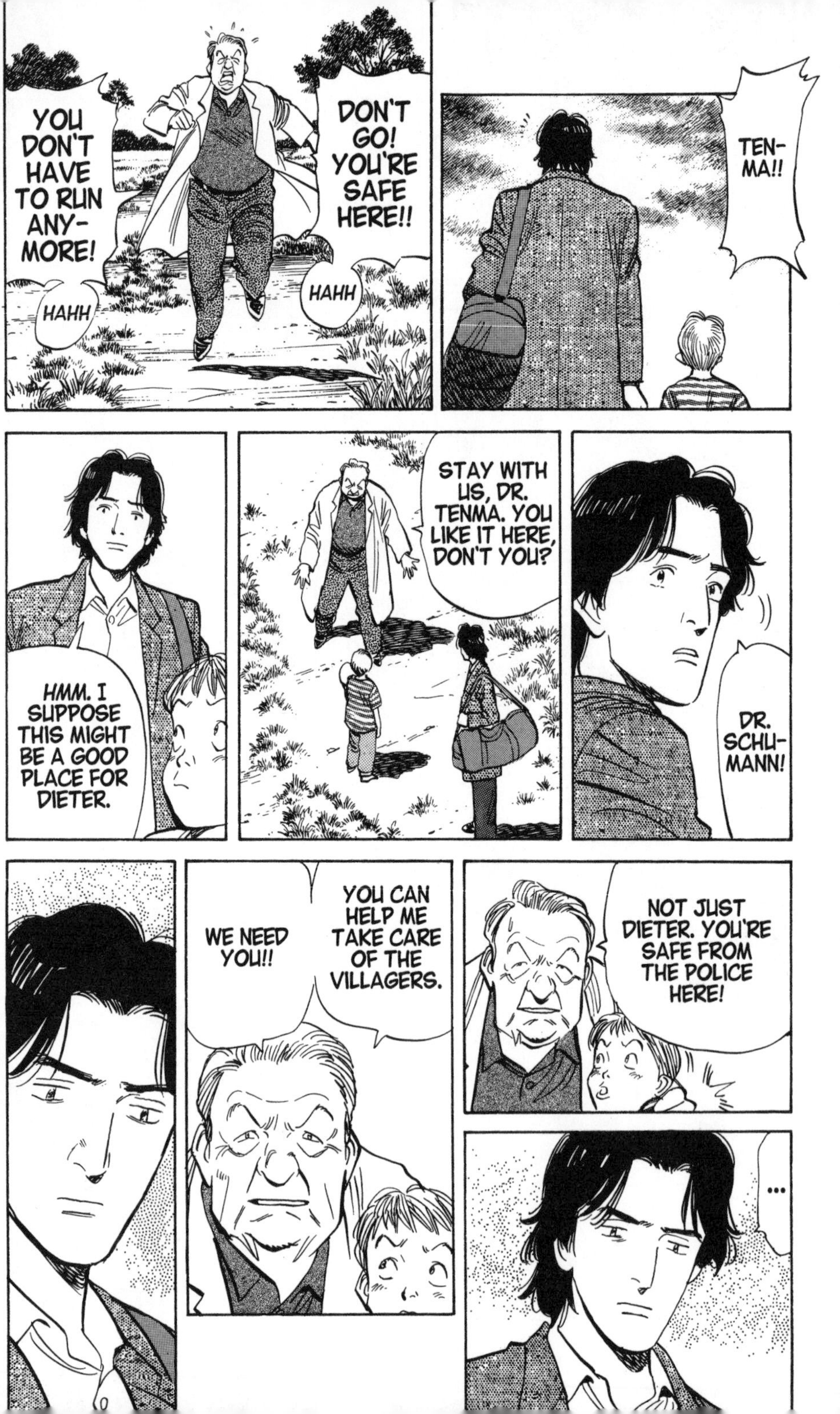
TEN-MA!!
DON'T GO! YOU'RE SAFE HERE!!
YOU DON'T HAVE TO RUN ANYMORE!
HAHH
HAHH
DR. SCHUMANN!
STAY WITH US, DR. TENMA. YOU LIKE IT HERE, DON'T YOU?
HMM. I SUPPOSE THIS MIGHT BE A GOOD PLACE FOR DIETER.
NOT JUST DIETER. YOU'RE SAFE FROM THE POLICE HERE!
...
YOU CAN HELP ME TAKE CARE OF THE VILLAGERS.
WE NEED YOU!!

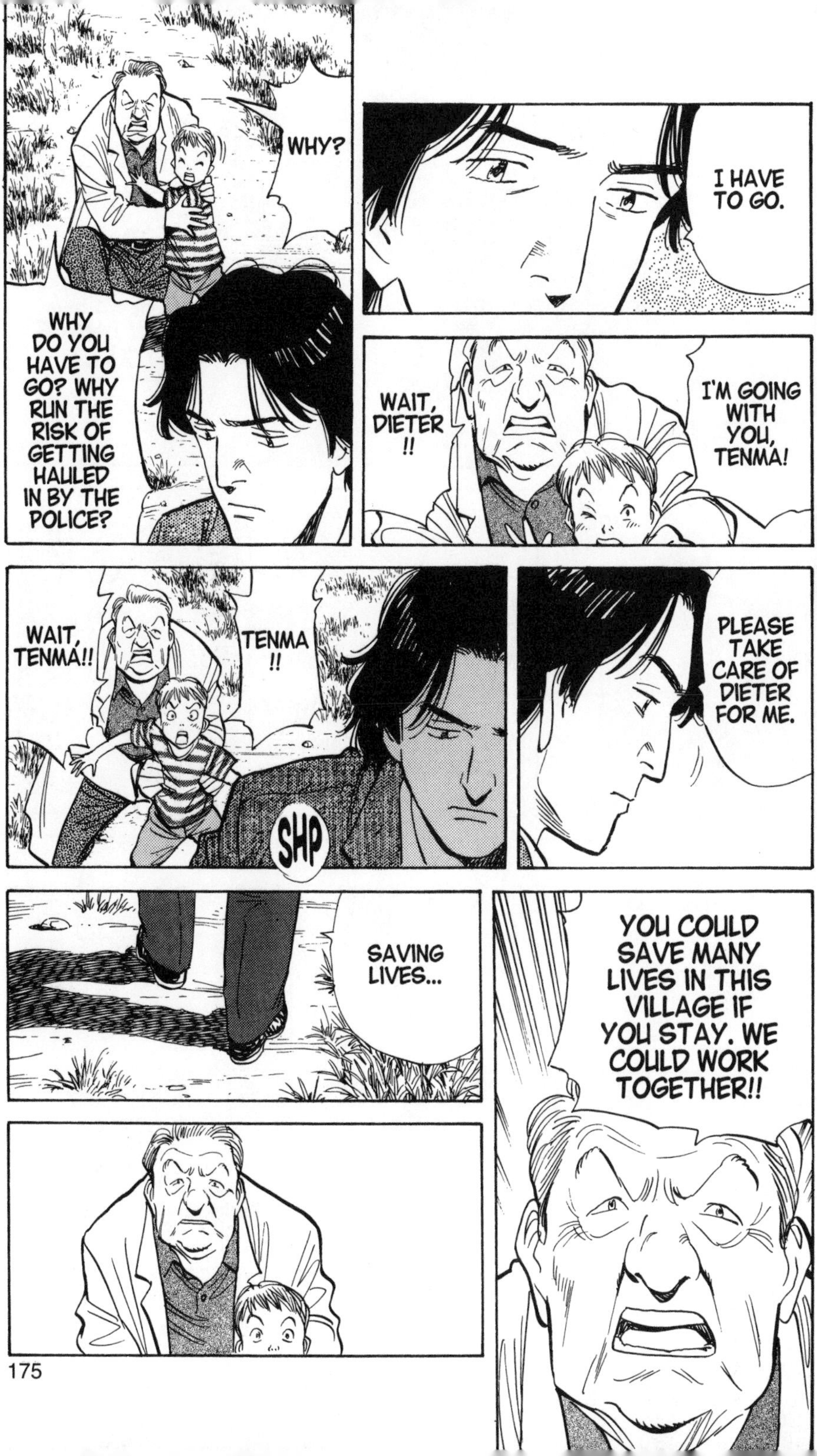
I HAVE TO GO.
I'M GOING WITH YOU, TENMA!
WAIT, DIETER!!
WHY?
WHY DO YOU HAVE TO GO? WHY RUN THE RISK OF GETTING HAULED IN BY THE POLICE?
PLEASE TAKE CARE OF DIETER FOR ME.
TENMA!!
WAIT, TENMA!!
SHP
YOU COULD SAVE MANY LIVES IN THIS VILLAGE IF YOU STAY. WE COULD WORK TOGETHER!!
SAVING LIVES...

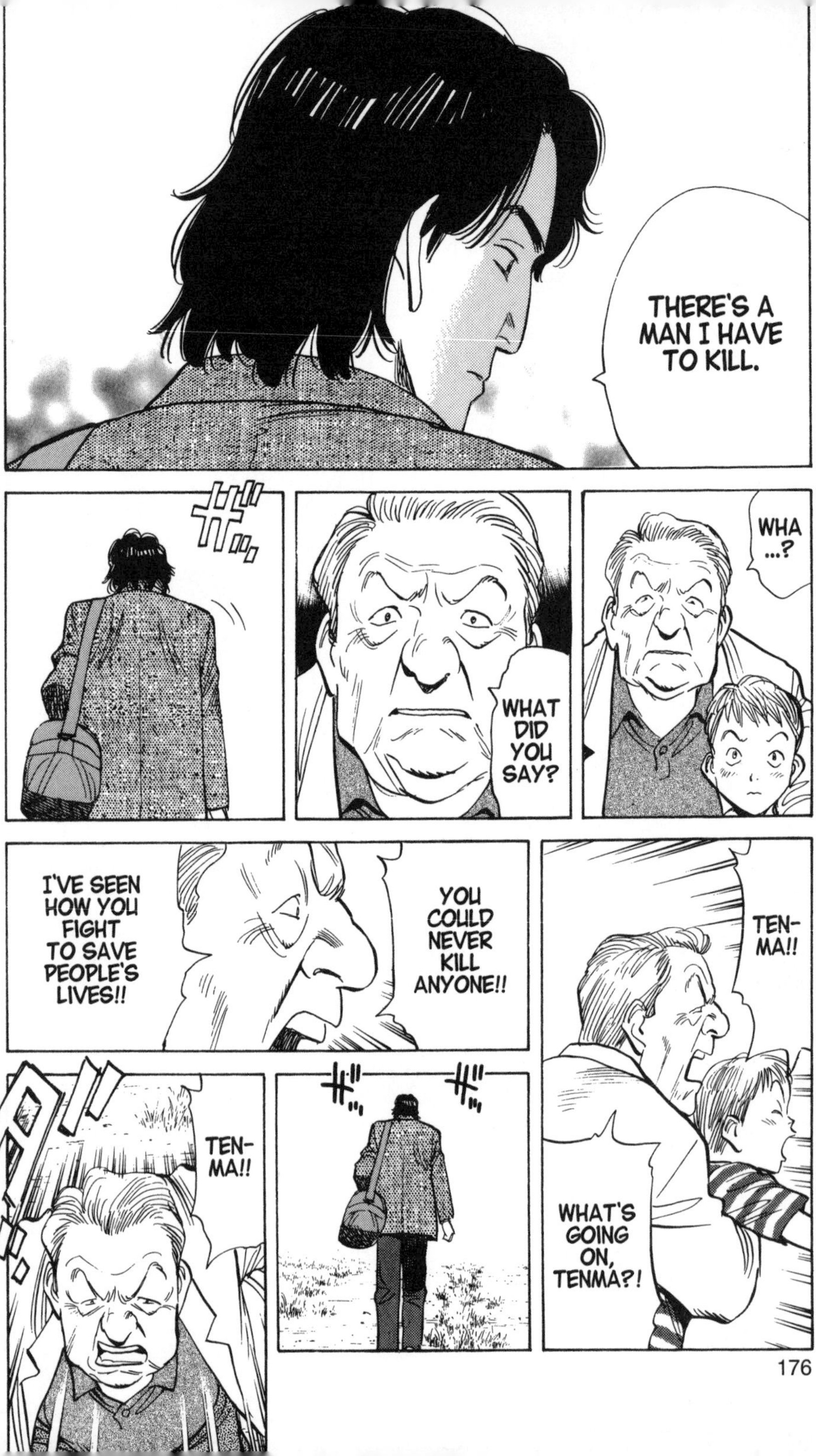
THERE'S A MAN I HAVE TO KILL.
WHA ...?
WHAT DID YOU SAY?
TEN-MA!!
WHAT'S GOING ON, TENMA?!
YOU COULD NEVER KILL ANYONE!!
I'VE SEEN HOW YOU FIGHT TO SAVE PEOPLE'S LIVES!!
TEN-MA!!

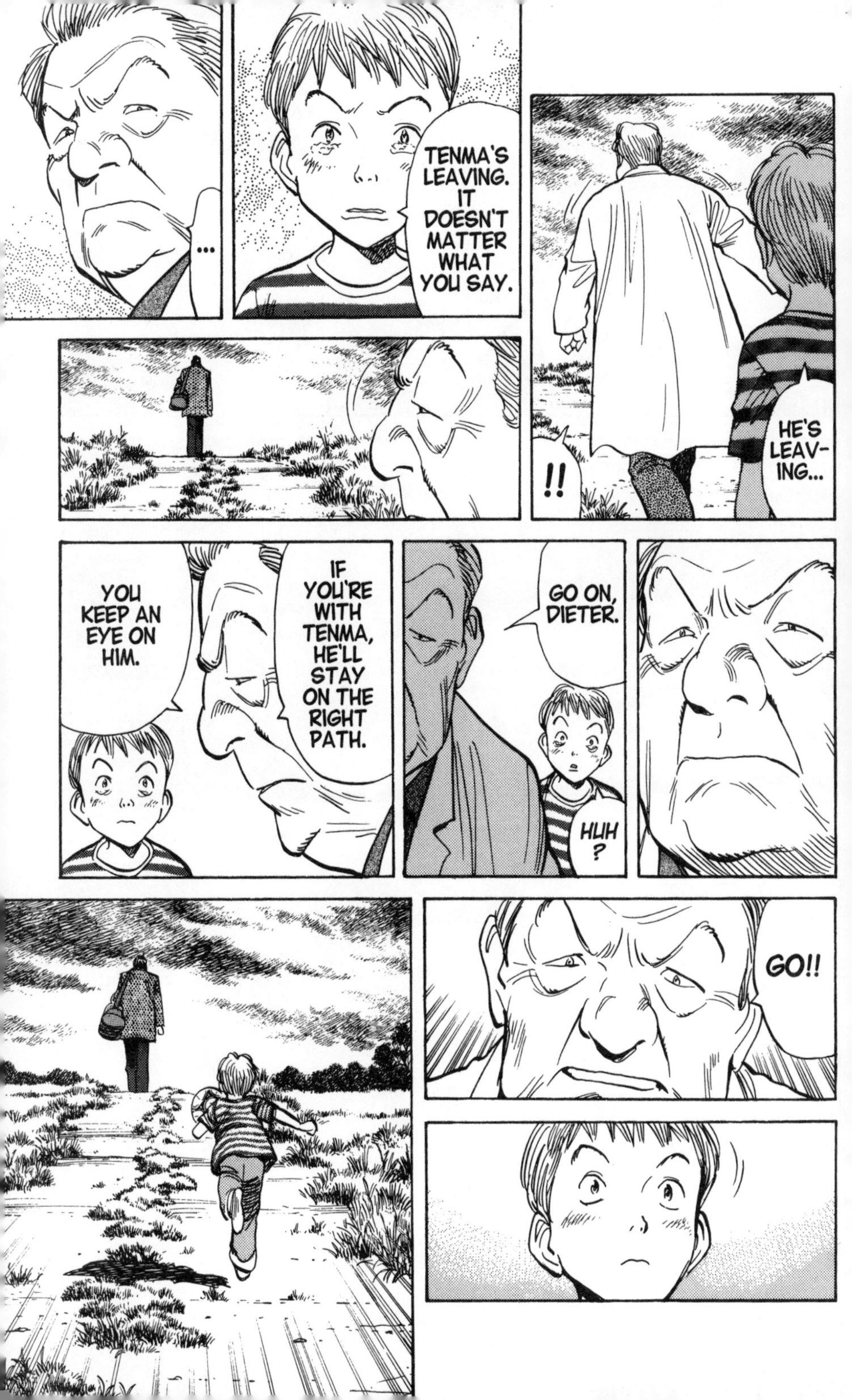
TENMA'S LEAVING. IT DOESN'T MATTER WHAT YOU SAY.
...
HE'S LEAV-ING...
!!
GO ON, DIETER.
HUH?
IF YOU'RE WITH TENMA, HE'LL STAY ON THE RIGHT PATH.
YOU KEEP AN EYE ON HIM.
GO!!

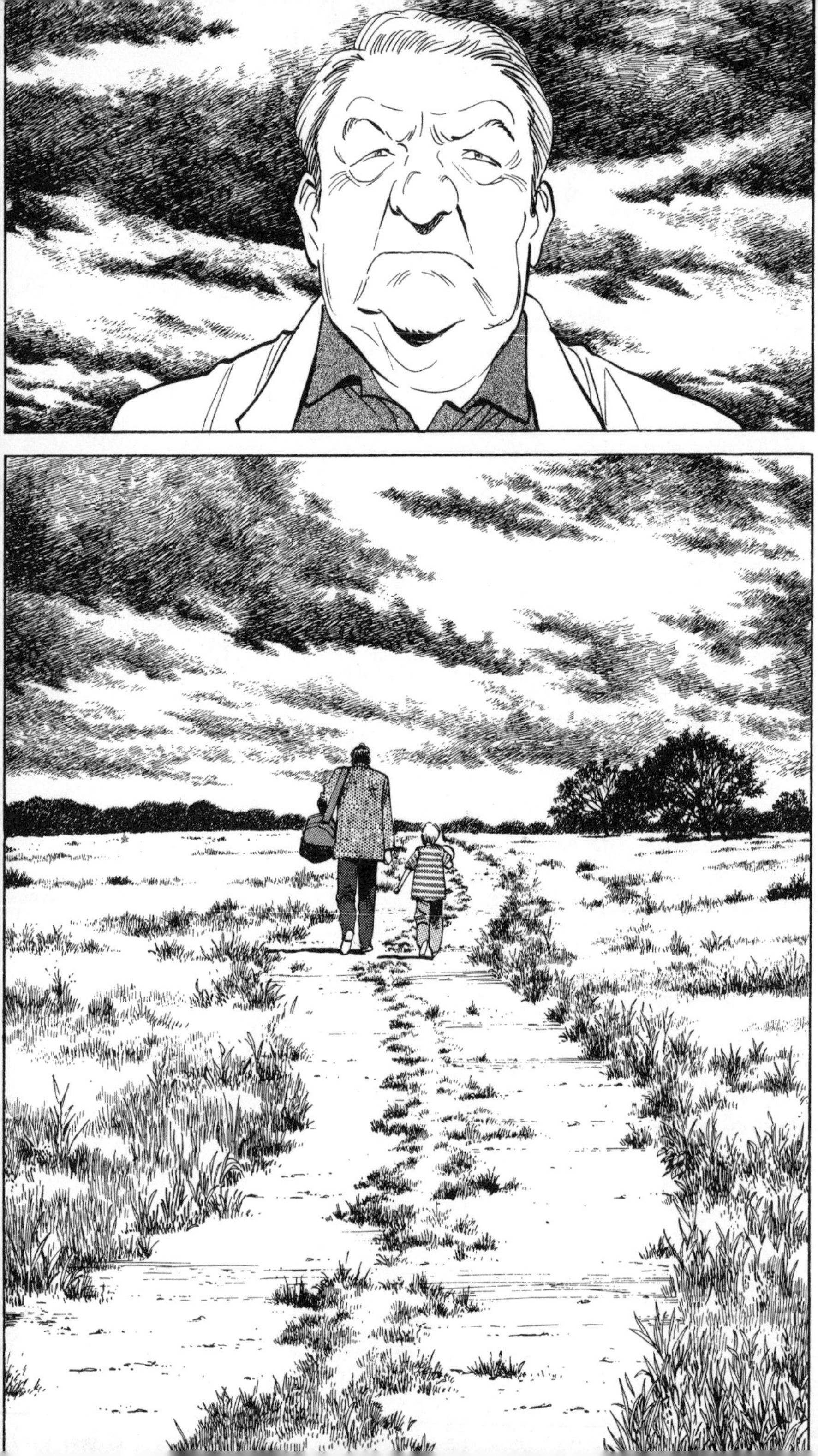

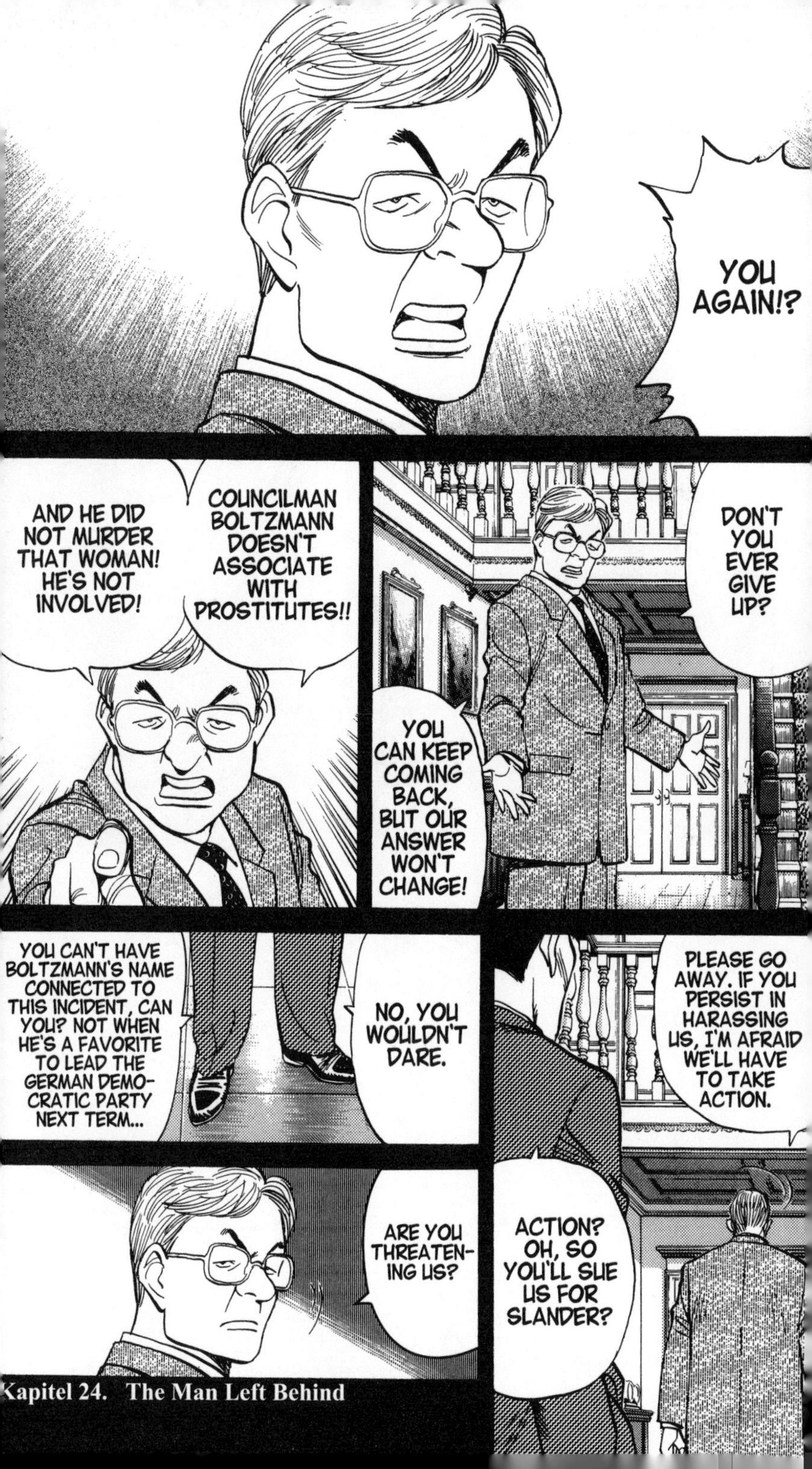
YOU AGAIN!?
DON'T YOU EVER GIVE UP?
YOU CAN KEEP COMING BACK, BUT OUR ANSWER WON'T CHANGE!
COUNCILMAN BOLTZMANN DOESN'T ASSOCIATE WITH PROSTITUTES!!
AND HE DID NOT MURDER THAT WOMAN! HE'S NOT INVOLVED!
PLEASE GO AWAY. IF YOU PERSIST IN HARASSING US, I'M AFRAID WE'LL HAVE TO TAKE ACTION.
ACTION? OH, SO YOU'LL SUE US FOR SLANDER?
NO, YOU WOULDN'T DARE.
YOU CAN'T HAVE BOLTZMANN'S NAME CONNECTED TO THIS INCIDENT, CAN YOU? NOT WHEN HE'S A FAVORITE TO LEAD THE GERMAN DEMO-CRATIC PARTY NEXT TERM...
ARE YOU THREATEN-ING US?

Kapitel 24. The Man Left Behind

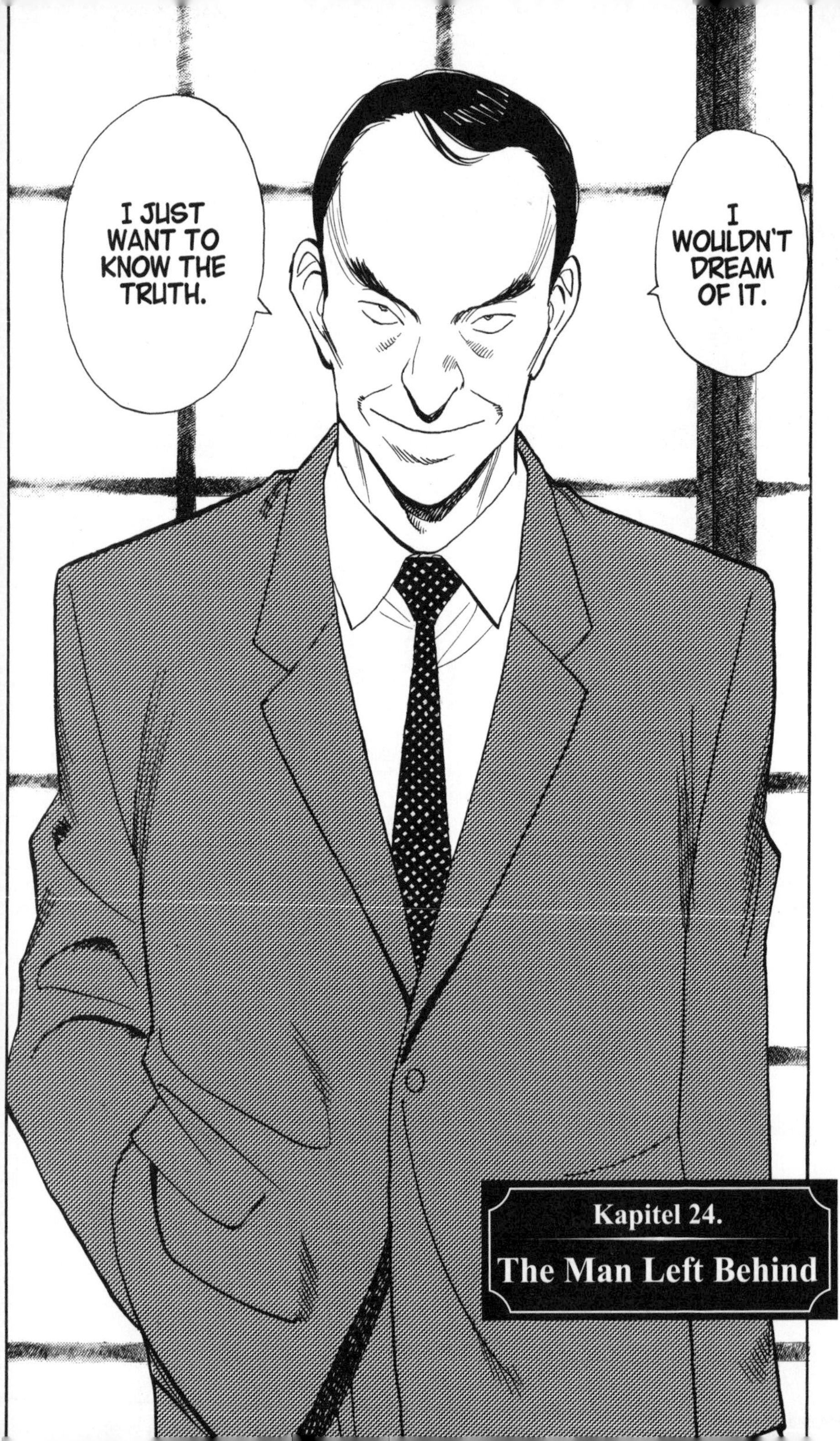
I WOULDN'T DREAM OF IT.
I JUST WANT TO KNOW THE TRUTH.
Kapitel 24.
The Man Left Behind

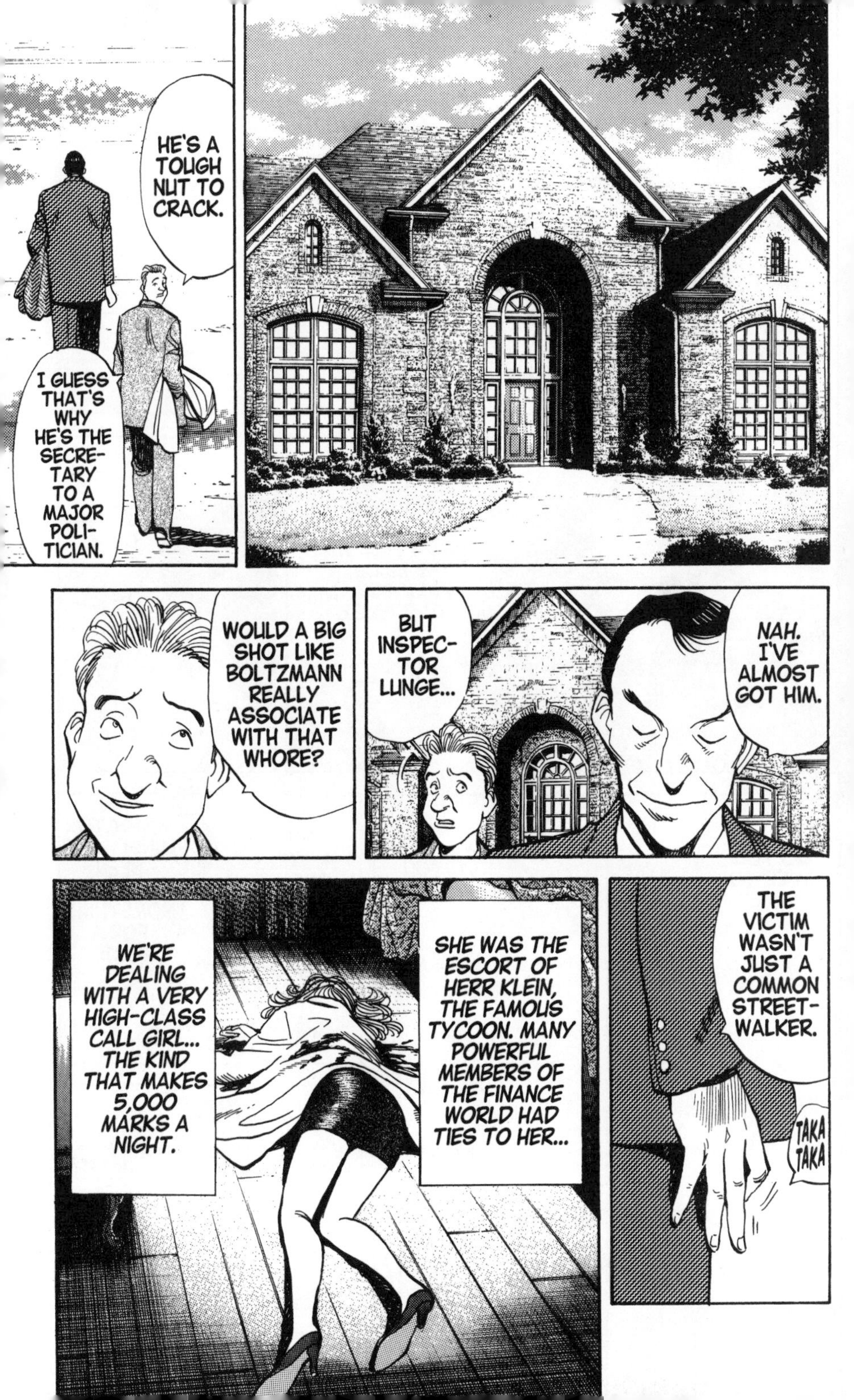
HE'S A TOUGH NUT TO CRACK.
I GUESS THAT'S WHY HE'S THE SECRETARY TO A MAJOR POLITICIAN.
NAH. I'VE ALMOST GOT HIM.
BUT INSPECTOR LUNGE...
WOULD A BIG SHOT LIKE BOLTZMANN REALLY ASSOCIATE WITH THAT WHORE?
THE VICTIM WASN'T JUST A COMMON STREET-WALKER.
TAKA TAKA
SHE WAS THE ESCORT OF HERR KLEIN, THE FAMOUS TYCOON. MANY POWERFUL MEMBERS OF THE FINANCE WORLD HAD TIES TO HER...
WE'RE DEALING WITH A VERY HIGH-CLASS CALL GIRL... THE KIND THAT MAKES 5,000 MARKS A NIGHT.

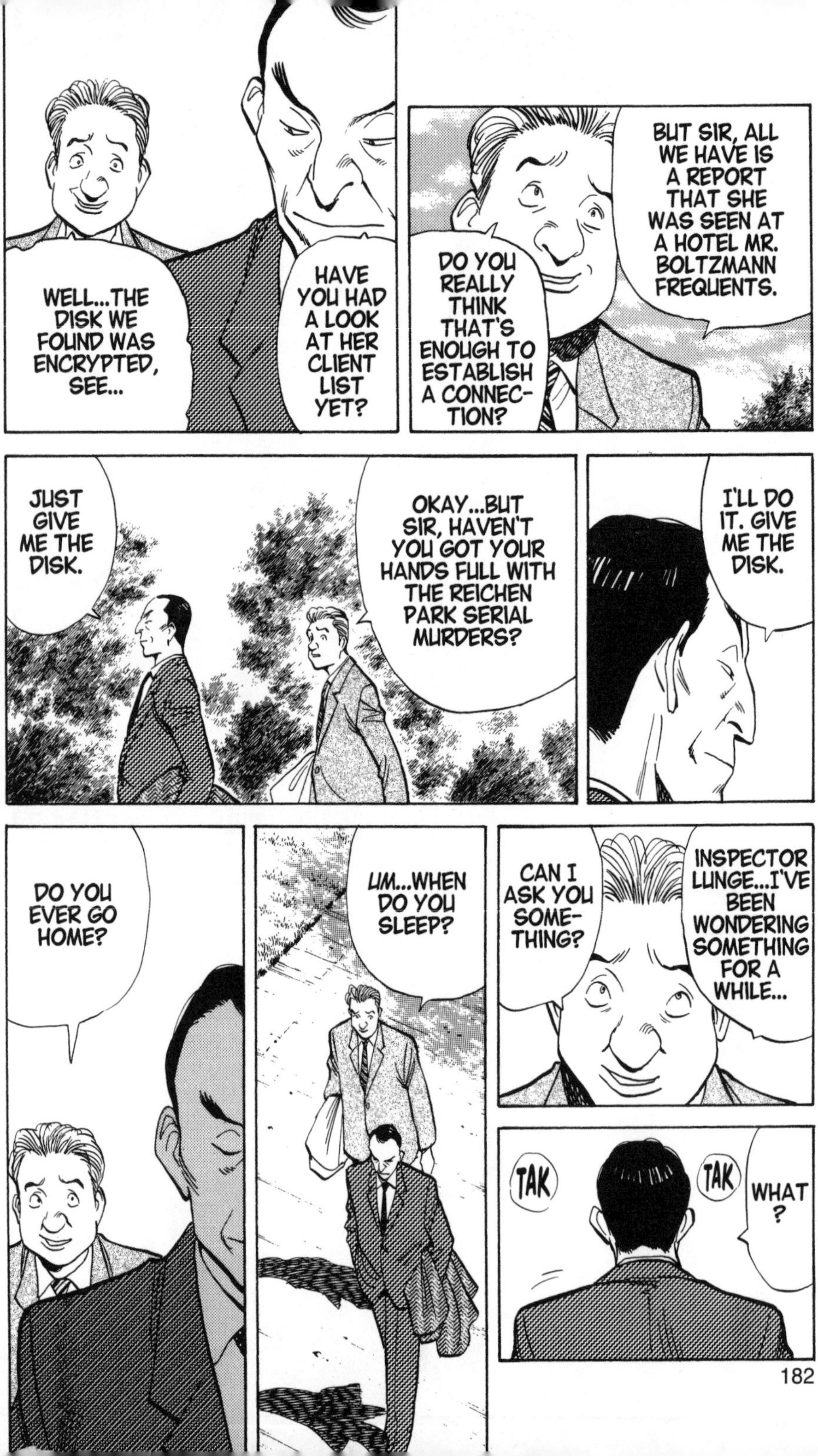
HAVE YOU HAD A LOOK AT HER CLIENT LIST YET?
WELL...THE DISK WE FOUND WAS ENCRYPTED, SEE...
BUT SIR, ALL WE HAVE IS A REPORT THAT SHE WAS SEEN AT A HOTEL MR. BOLTZMANN FREQUENTS.
DO YOU REALLY THINK THAT'S ENOUGH TO ESTABLISH A CONNECTION?
I'LL DO IT. GIVE ME THE DISK.
OKAY...BUT SIR, HAVEN'T YOU GOT YOUR HANDS FULL WITH THE REICHEN PARK SERIAL MURDERS?
JUST GIVE ME THE DISK.
INSPECTOR LUNGE...I'VE BEEN WONDERING SOMETHING FOR A WHILE...
CAN I ASK YOU SOMETHING?
TAK
WHAT?
TAK
UM...WHEN DO YOU SLEEP?
DO YOU EVER GO HOME?

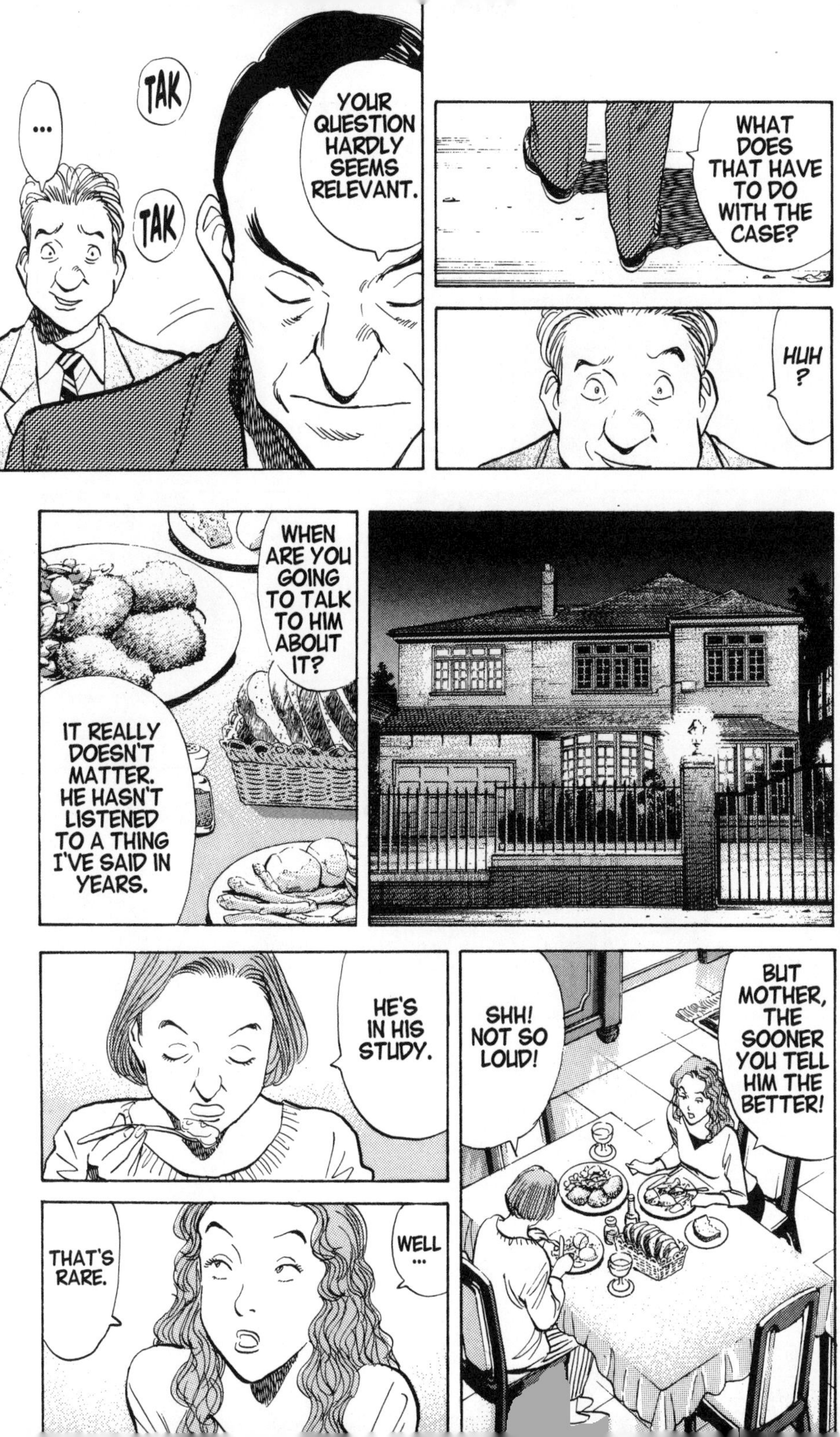
WHAT DOES THAT HAVE TO DO WITH THE CASE?
HUH?
YOUR QUESTION HARDLY SEEMS RELEVANT.
TAK
TAK
...
WHEN ARE YOU GOING TO TALK TO HIM ABOUT IT?
IT REALLY DOESN'T MATTER. HE HASN'T LISTENED TO A THING I'VE SAID IN YEARS.
BUT MOTHER, THE SOONER YOU TELL HIM THE BETTER!
SHH! NOT SO LOUD!
HE'S IN HIS STUDY.
WELL...
THAT'S RARE.

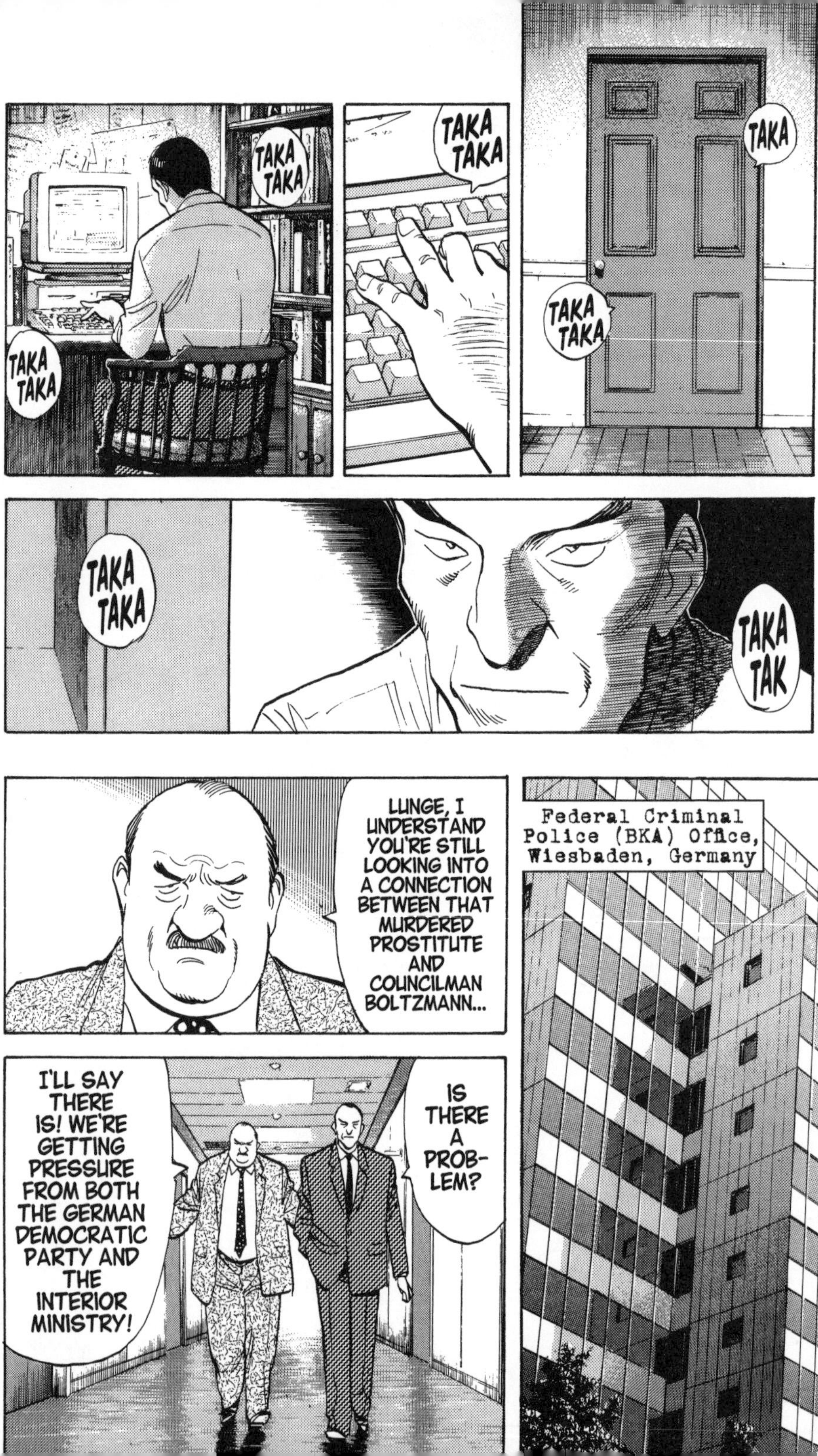
TAKA
TAKA TAKA
TAKA TAKA
TAKA TAKA
TAKA TAKA
TAKA TAK
TAKA TAKA
Federal Criminal Police (BKA) Office, Wiesbaden, Germany
LUNGE, I UNDERSTAND YOU'RE STILL LOOKING INTO A CONNECTION BETWEEN THAT MURDERED PROSTITUTE AND COUNCILMAN BOLTZMANN...
IS THERE A PROB-LEM?
I'LL SAY THERE IS! WE'RE GETTING PRESSURE FROM BOTH THE GERMAN DEMOCRATIC PARTY AND THE INTERIOR MINISTRY!

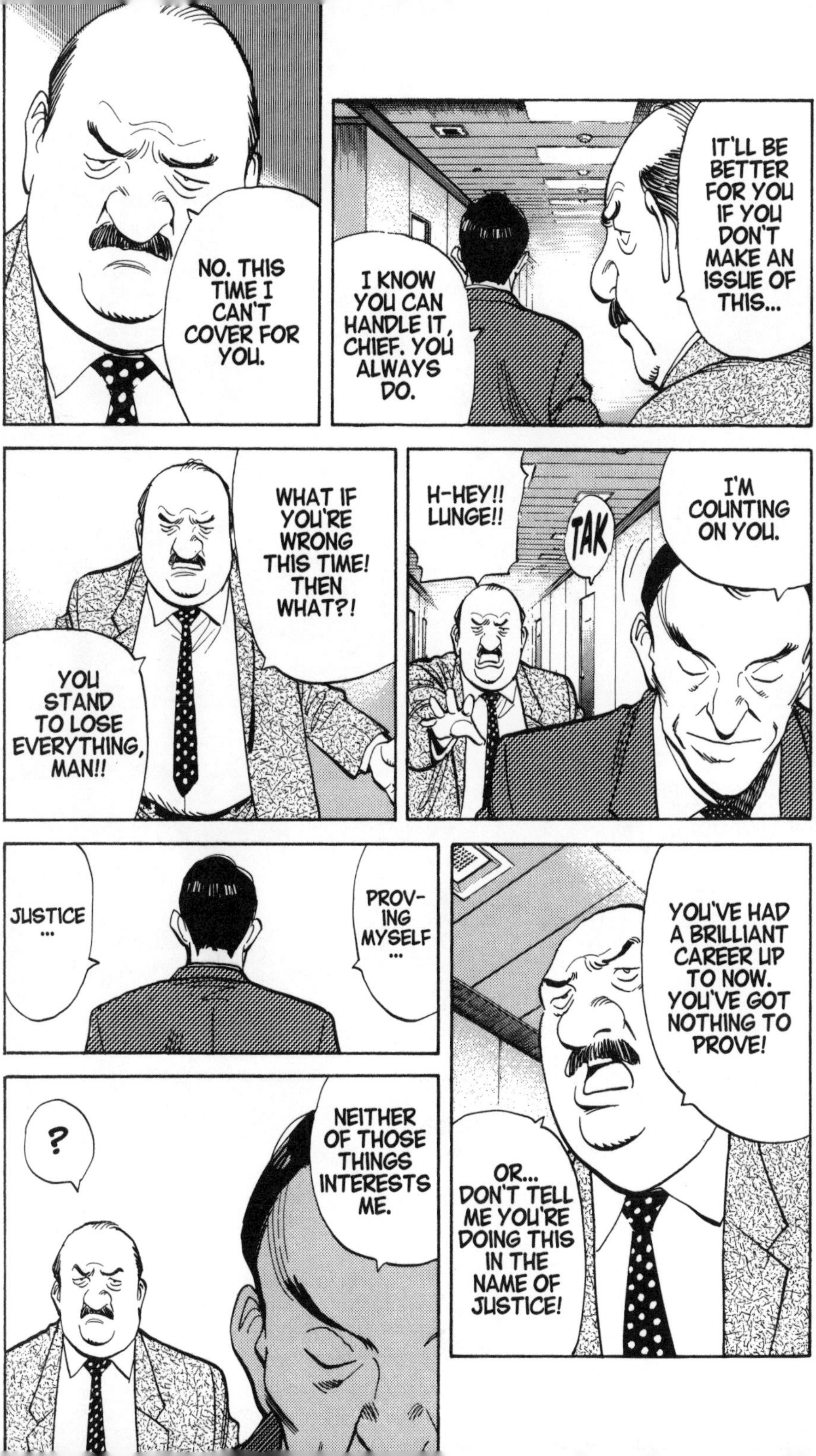
IT'LL BE BETTER FOR YOU IF YOU DON'T MAKE AN ISSUE OF THIS...
I KNOW YOU CAN HANDLE IT, CHIEF. YOU ALWAYS DO.
NO. THIS TIME I CAN'T COVER FOR YOU.
I'M COUNTING ON YOU.
TAK
H-HEY!! LUNGE!!
WHAT IF YOU'RE WRONG THIS TIME! THEN WHAT?!
YOU STAND TO LOSE EVERYTHING, MAN!!
YOU'VE HAD A BRILLIANT CAREER UP TO NOW. YOU'VE GOT NOTHING TO PROVE!
OR... DON'T TELL ME YOU'RE DOING THIS IN THE NAME OF JUSTICE!
PROV-ING MYSELF...
JUSTICE...
NEITHER OF THOSE THINGS INTERESTS ME.
?

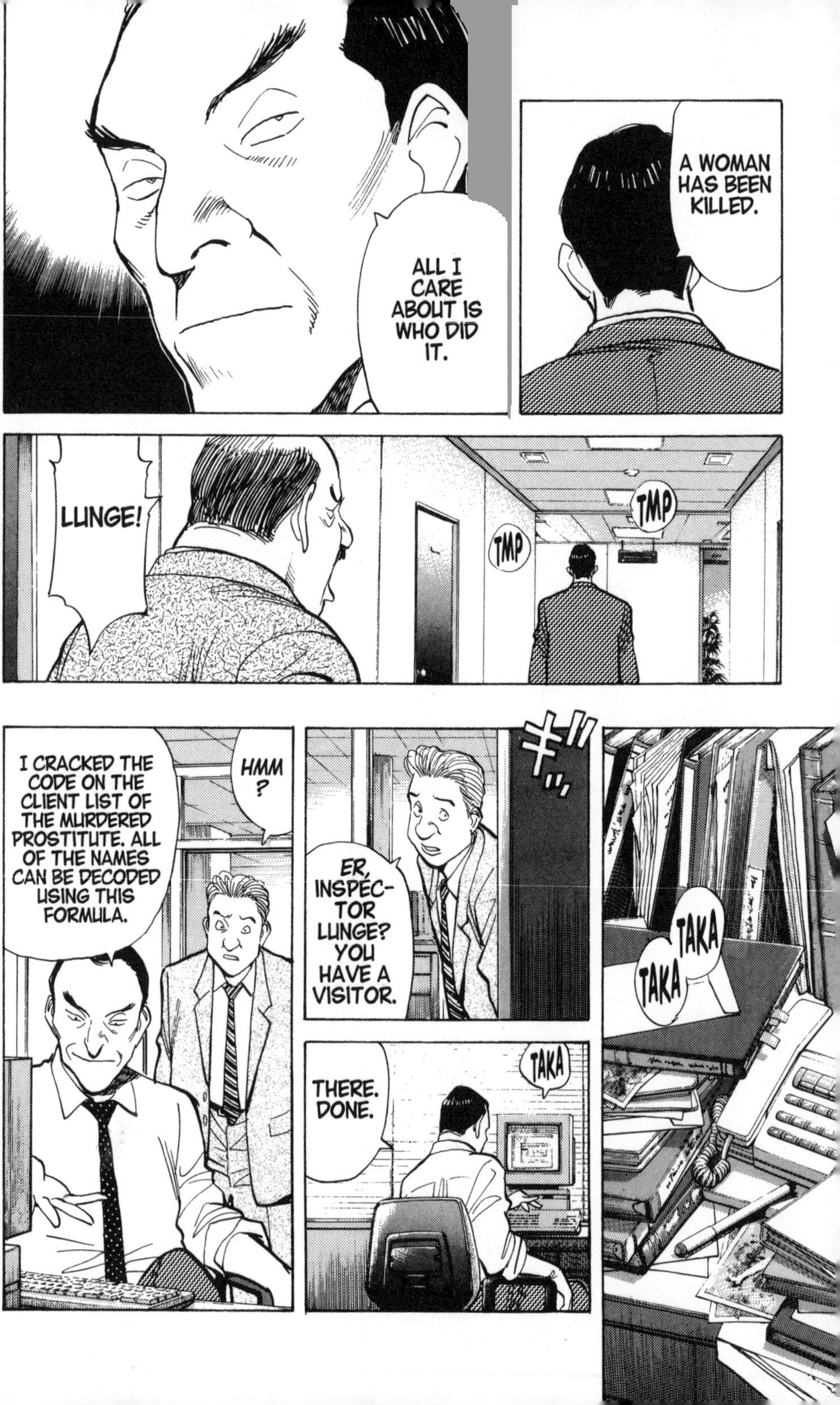
A WOMAN HAS BEEN KILLED.
ALL I CARE ABOUT IS WHO DID IT.
TMP
TMP
LUNGE!
TAKA
TAKA
ER, INSPECTOR LUNGE? YOU HAVE A VISITOR.
TAKA
THERE. DONE.
HMM?
I CRACKED THE CODE ON THE CLIENT LIST OF THE MURDERED PROSTITUTE. ALL OF THE NAMES CAN BE DECODED USING THIS FORMULA.

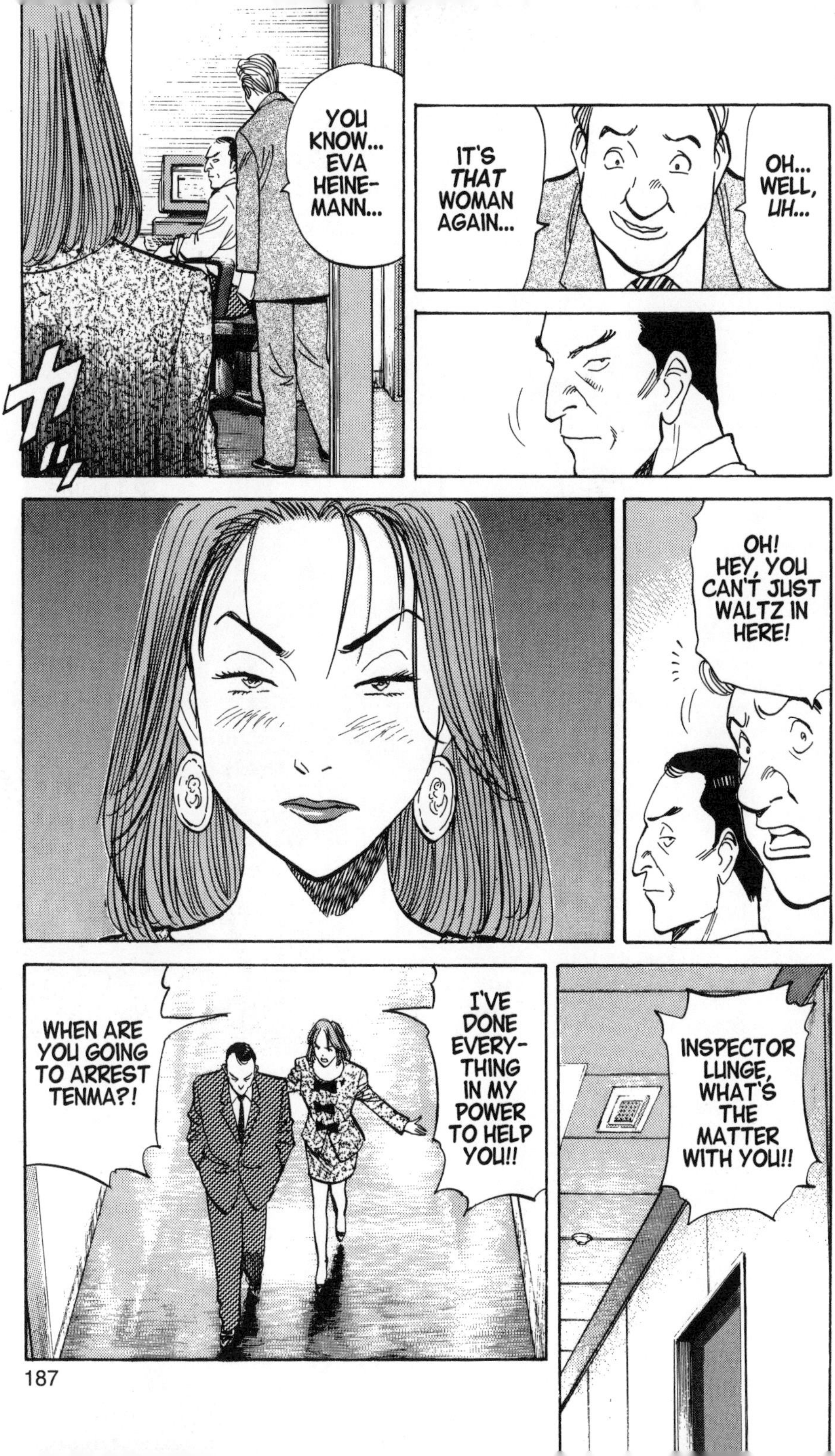
OH... WELL, UH...
IT'S *THAT* WOMAN AGAIN...
YOU KNOW... EVA HEINE-MANN...
ガッ
OH! HEY, YOU CAN'T JUST WALTZ IN HERE!
INSPECTOR LUNGE, WHAT'S THE MATTER WITH YOU!!
I'VE DONE EVERY-THING IN MY POWER TO HELP YOU!!
WHEN ARE YOU GOING TO ARREST TENMA?!

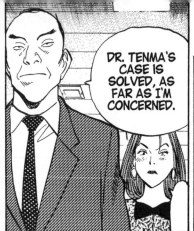

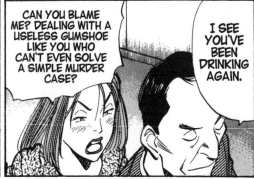

I SEE YOU'VE BEEN DRINKING AGAIN.
CAN YOU BLAME ME? DEALING WITH A USELESS GUMSHOE LIKE YOU WHO CAN'T EVEN SOLVE A SIMPLE MURDER CASE?
DR. TENMA'S CASE IS SOLVED, AS FAR AS I'M CONCERNED.
HE CLAIMS A MAN CALLED JOHAN IS RESPONSIBLE FOR ALL OF THE MIDDLE-AGE COUPLES WHO'VE BEEN MURDERED...AND FOR THE DEATHS AT THE HOSPITAL TEN YEARS AGO...
JOHAN IS ANOTHER IDENTITY WITHIN DR. TENMA.
IT'S THE ONLY LOGICAL EXPLANATION OF AN OTHERWISE ILLOGICAL CASE.
EVERY POLICE OFFICER IN GERMANY IS LOOKING FOR HIM. IT'S ONLY A MATTER OF TIME.
SO, ONCE YOU ISSUE YOUR WARRANT, YOUR WORK IS DONE, IS THAT IT?
OH, THERE ARE PLENTY OF THINGS I'D LIKE TO ASK DR. TENMA IF I COULD.
HE FASCINATES ME.
HOWEVER...
TAK

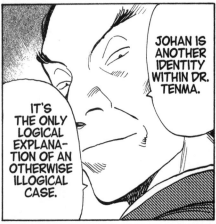

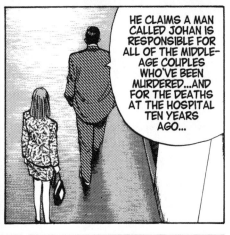

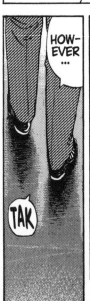

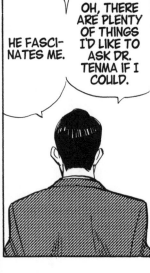

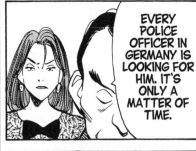

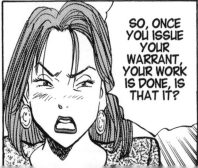

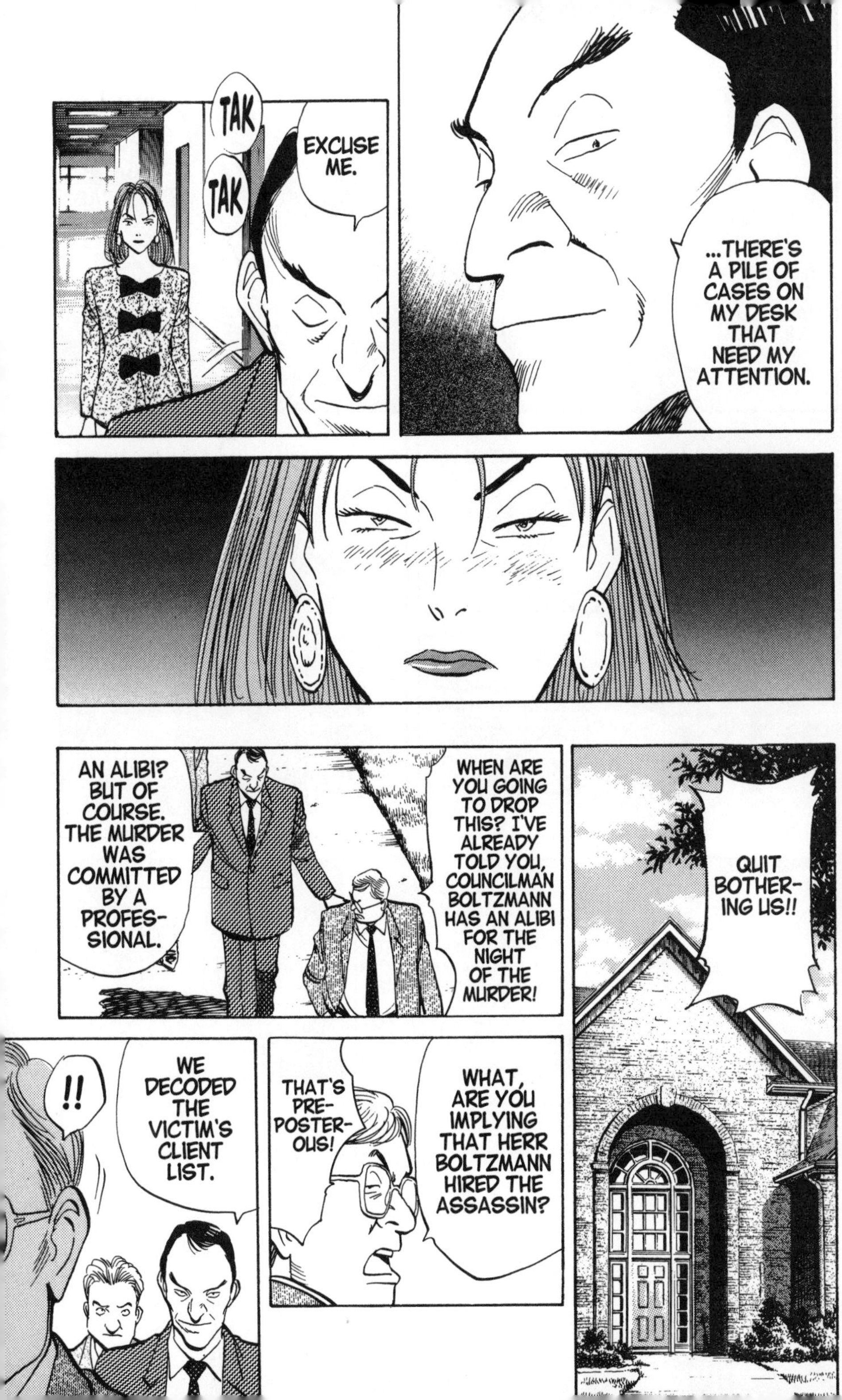
...THERE'S A PILE OF CASES ON MY DESK THAT NEED MY ATTENTION.
EXCUSE ME.
TAK
TAK
QUIT BOTHERING US!!
WHEN ARE YOU GOING TO DROP THIS? I'VE ALREADY TOLD YOU, COUNCILMAN BOLTZMANN HAS AN ALIBI FOR THE NIGHT OF THE MURDER!
AN ALIBI? BUT OF COURSE. THE MURDER WAS COMMITTED BY A PROFES-SIONAL.
WHAT, ARE YOU IMPLYING THAT HERR BOLTZMANN HIRED THE ASSASSIN?
THAT'S PRE-POSTER-OUS!
WE DECODED THE VICTIM'S CLIENT LIST.
!!

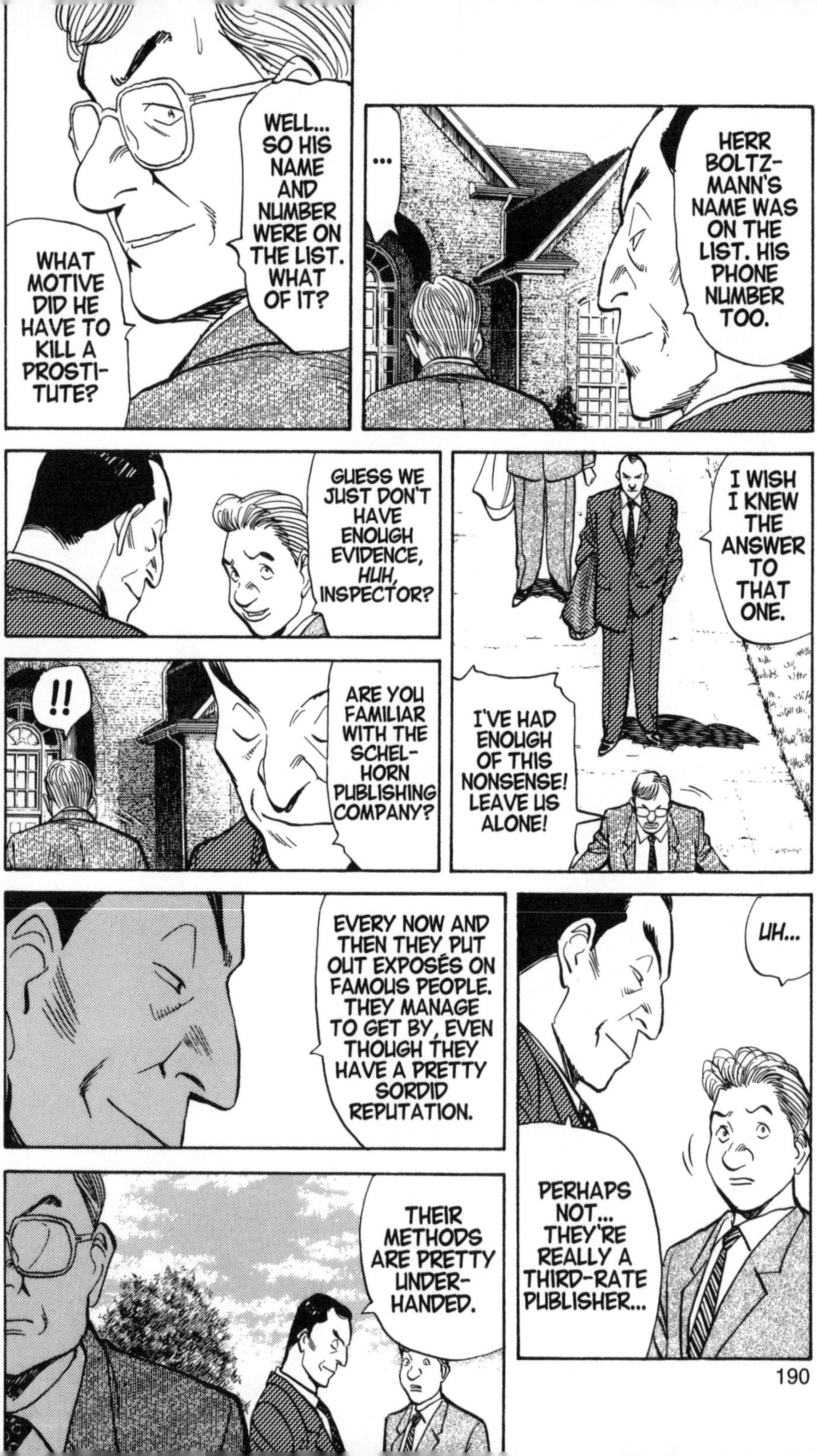
HERR BOLTZMANN'S NAME WAS ON THE LIST. HIS PHONE NUMBER TOO.
...
WELL... SO HIS NAME AND NUMBER WERE ON THE LIST. WHAT OF IT?
WHAT MOTIVE DID HE HAVE TO KILL A PROSTITUTE?
I WISH I KNEW THE ANSWER TO THAT ONE.
I'VE HAD ENOUGH OF THIS NONSENSE! LEAVE US ALONE!
GUESS WE JUST DON'T HAVE ENOUGH EVIDENCE, HUH, INSPECTOR?
ARE YOU FAMILIAR WITH THE SCHELHORN PUBLISHING COMPANY?
!!
UH...
PERHAPS NOT... THEY'RE REALLY A THIRD-RATE PUBLISHER...
EVERY NOW AND THEN THEY PUT OUT EXPOSÉS ON FAMOUS PEOPLE. THEY MANAGE TO GET BY, EVEN THOUGH THEY HAVE A PRETTY SORDID REPUTATION.
THEIR METHODS ARE PRETTY UNDERHANDED.

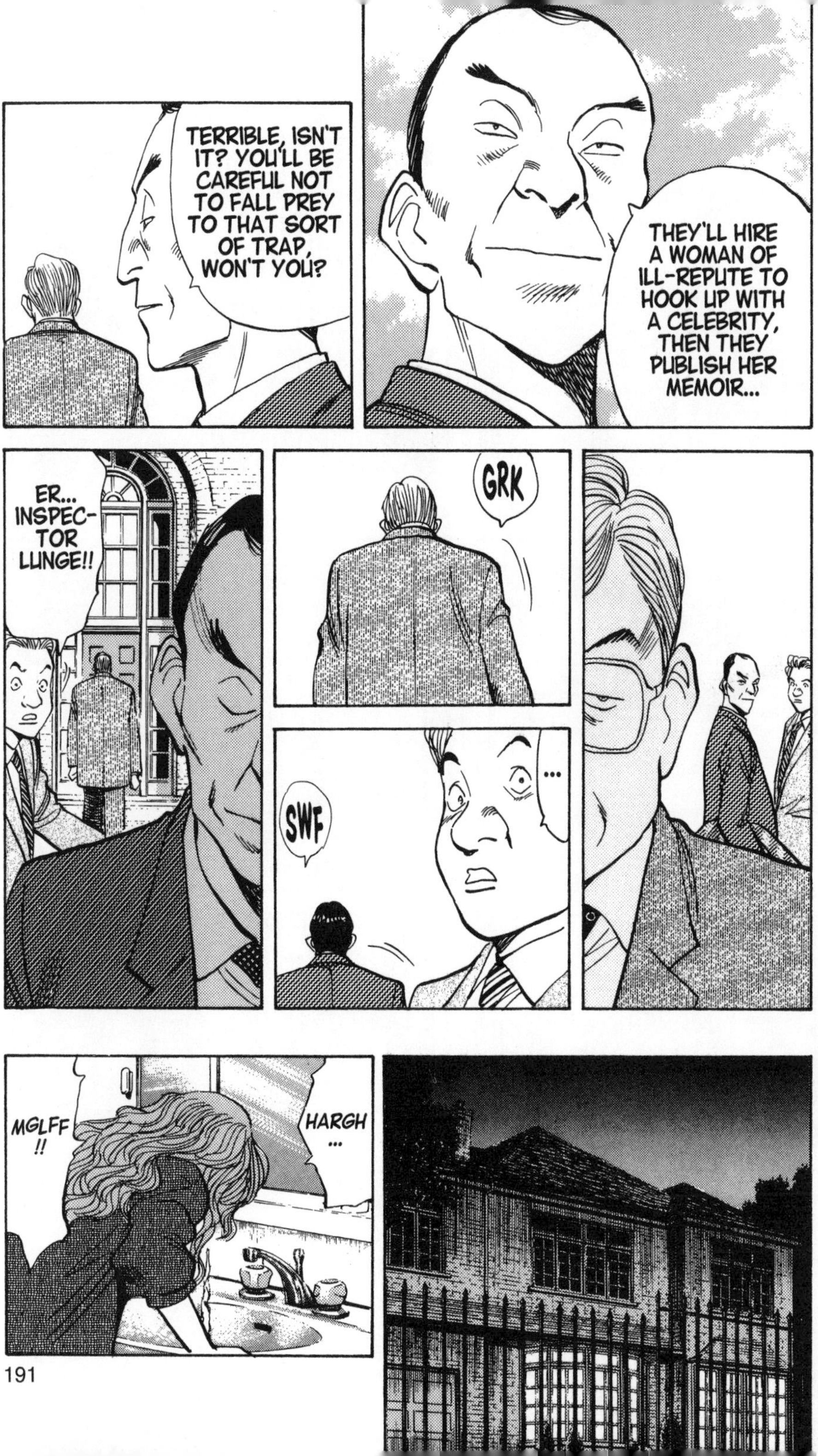
THEY'LL HIRE A WOMAN OF ILL-REPUTE TO HOOK UP WITH A CELEBRITY, THEN THEY PUBLISH HER MEMOIR...
TERRIBLE, ISN'T IT? YOU'LL BE CAREFUL NOT TO FALL PREY TO THAT SORT OF TRAP, WON'T YOU?
GRK
...
SWF
ER... INSPEC-TOR LUNGE!!
HARGH ...
MGLFF !!

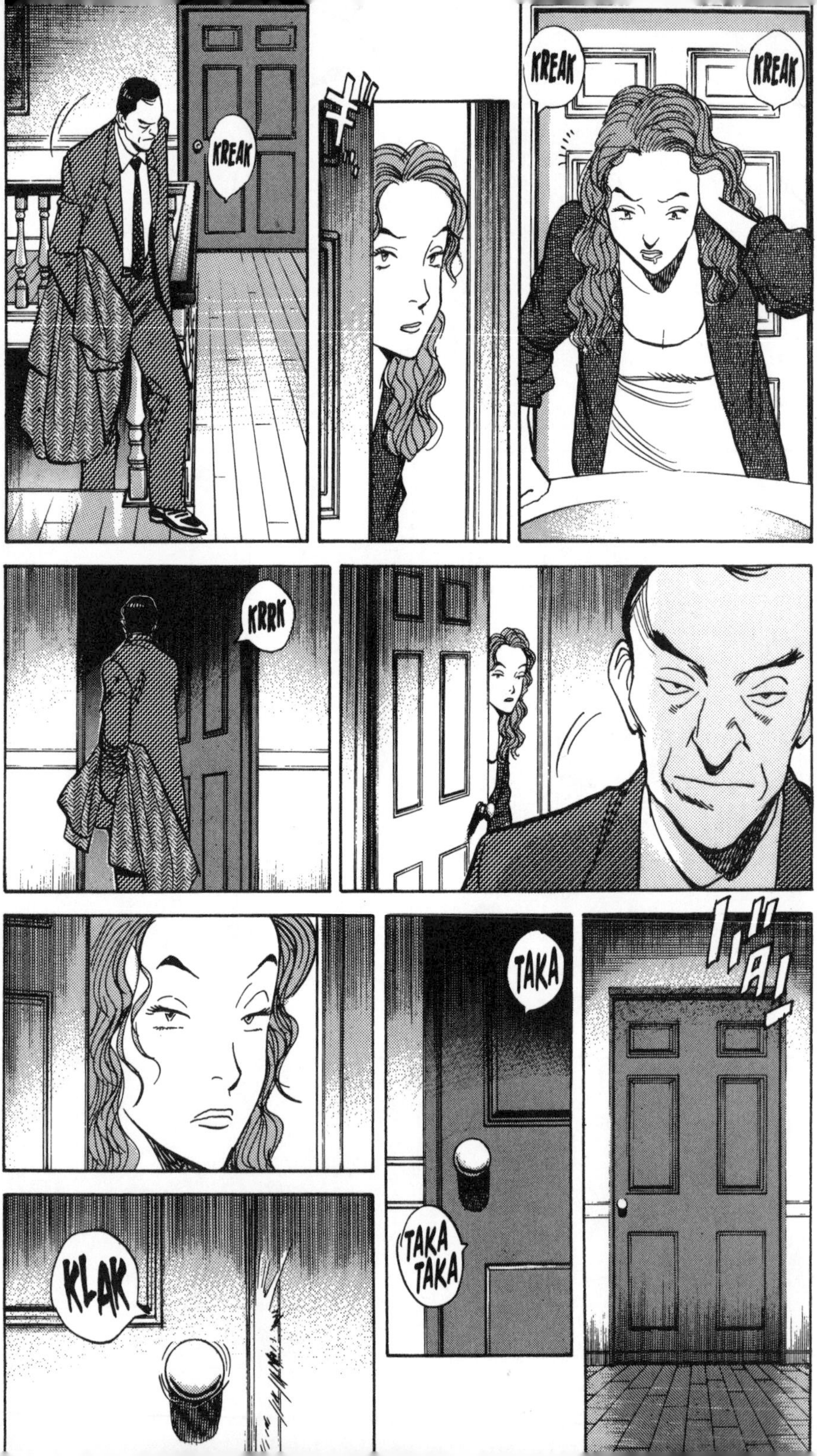
KREAK
KREAK
KREAK
KRRK
TAKA
TAKA TAKA
KLAK

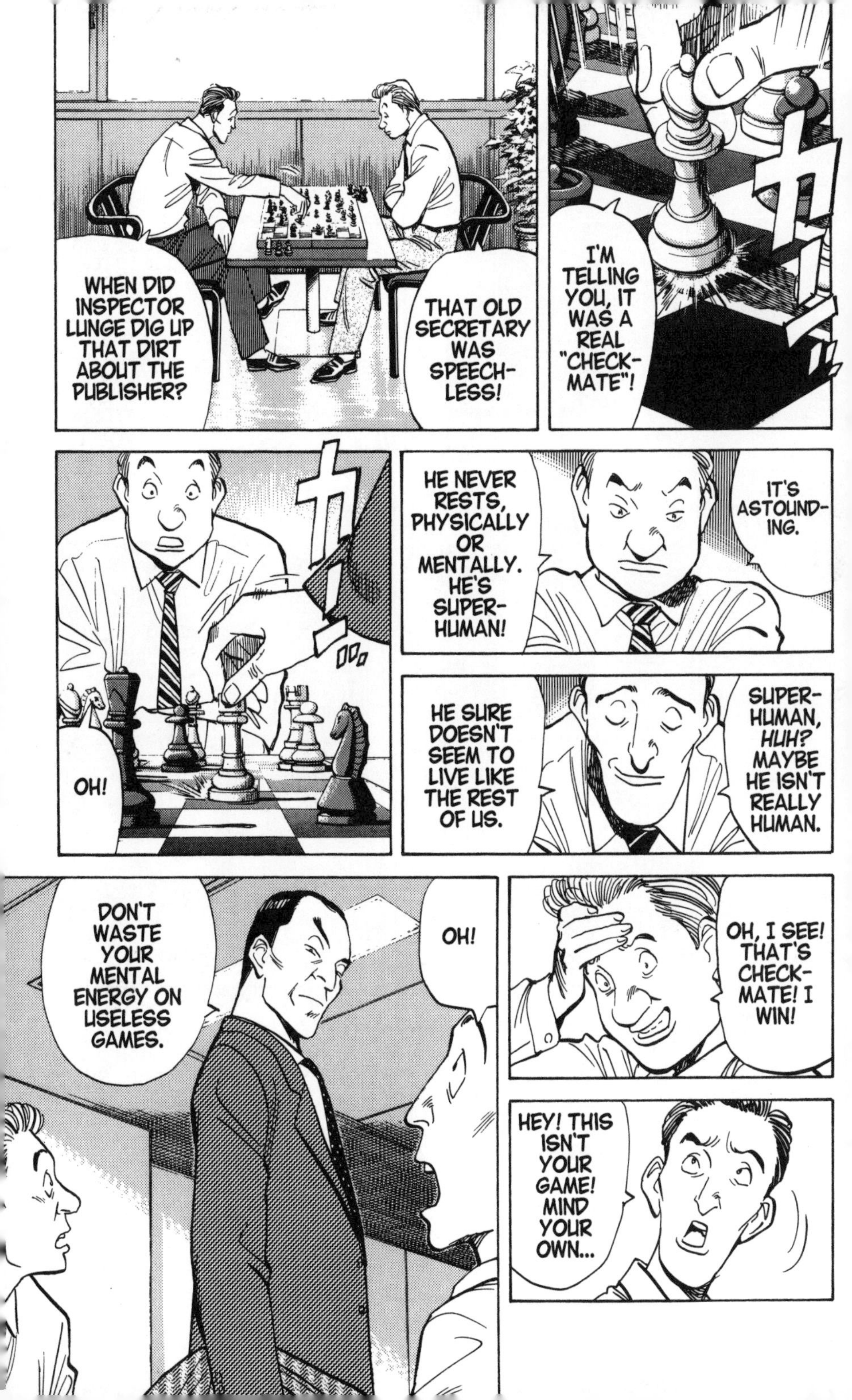
I'M TELLING YOU, IT WAS A REAL "CHECK-MATE"!
THAT OLD SECRETARY WAS SPEECH-LESS!
WHEN DID INSPECTOR LUNGE DIG UP THAT DIRT ABOUT THE PUBLISHER?
IT'S ASTOUND-ING.
HE NEVER RESTS, PHYSICALLY OR MENTALLY. HE'S SUPER-HUMAN!
SUPER-HUMAN, HUH? MAYBE HE ISN'T REALLY HUMAN.
HE SURE DOESN'T SEEM TO LIVE LIKE THE REST OF US.
OH!
OH, I SEE! THAT'S CHECK-MATE! I WIN!
HEY! THIS ISN'T YOUR GAME! MIND YOUR OWN...
OH!
DON'T WASTE YOUR MENTAL ENERGY ON USELESS GAMES.

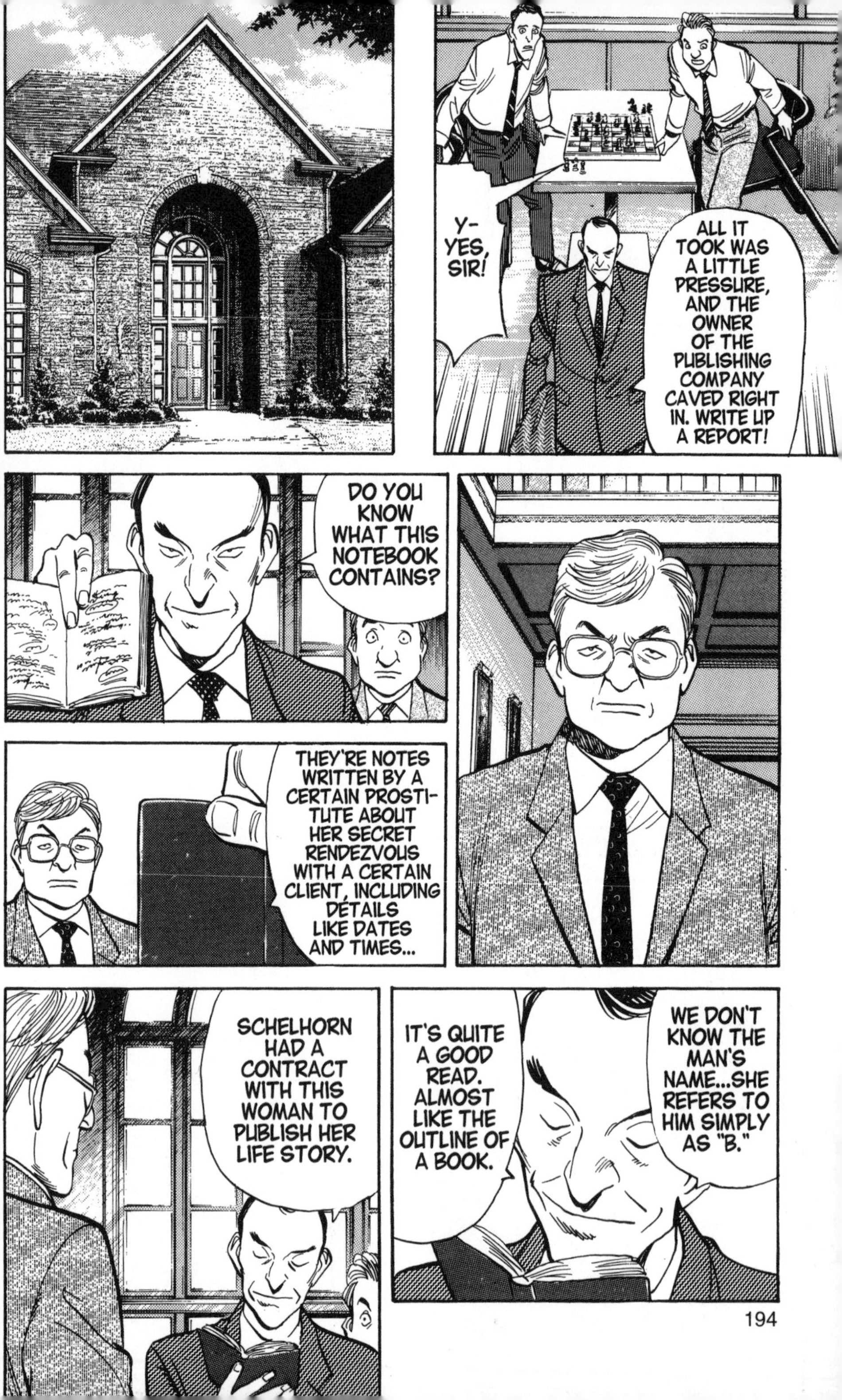
ALL IT TOOK WAS A LITTLE PRESSURE, AND THE OWNER OF THE PUBLISHING COMPANY CAVED RIGHT IN. WRITE UP A REPORT!
Y-YES, SIR!
DO YOU KNOW WHAT THIS NOTEBOOK CONTAINS?
THEY'RE NOTES WRITTEN BY A CERTAIN PROSTITUTE ABOUT HER SECRET RENDEZVOUS WITH A CERTAIN CLIENT, INCLUDING DETAILS LIKE DATES AND TIMES...
WE DON'T KNOW THE MAN'S NAME...SHE REFERS TO HIM SIMPLY AS "B."
IT'S QUITE A GOOD READ. ALMOST LIKE THE OUTLINE OF A BOOK.
SCHELHORN HAD A CONTRACT WITH THIS WOMAN TO PUBLISH HER LIFE STORY.

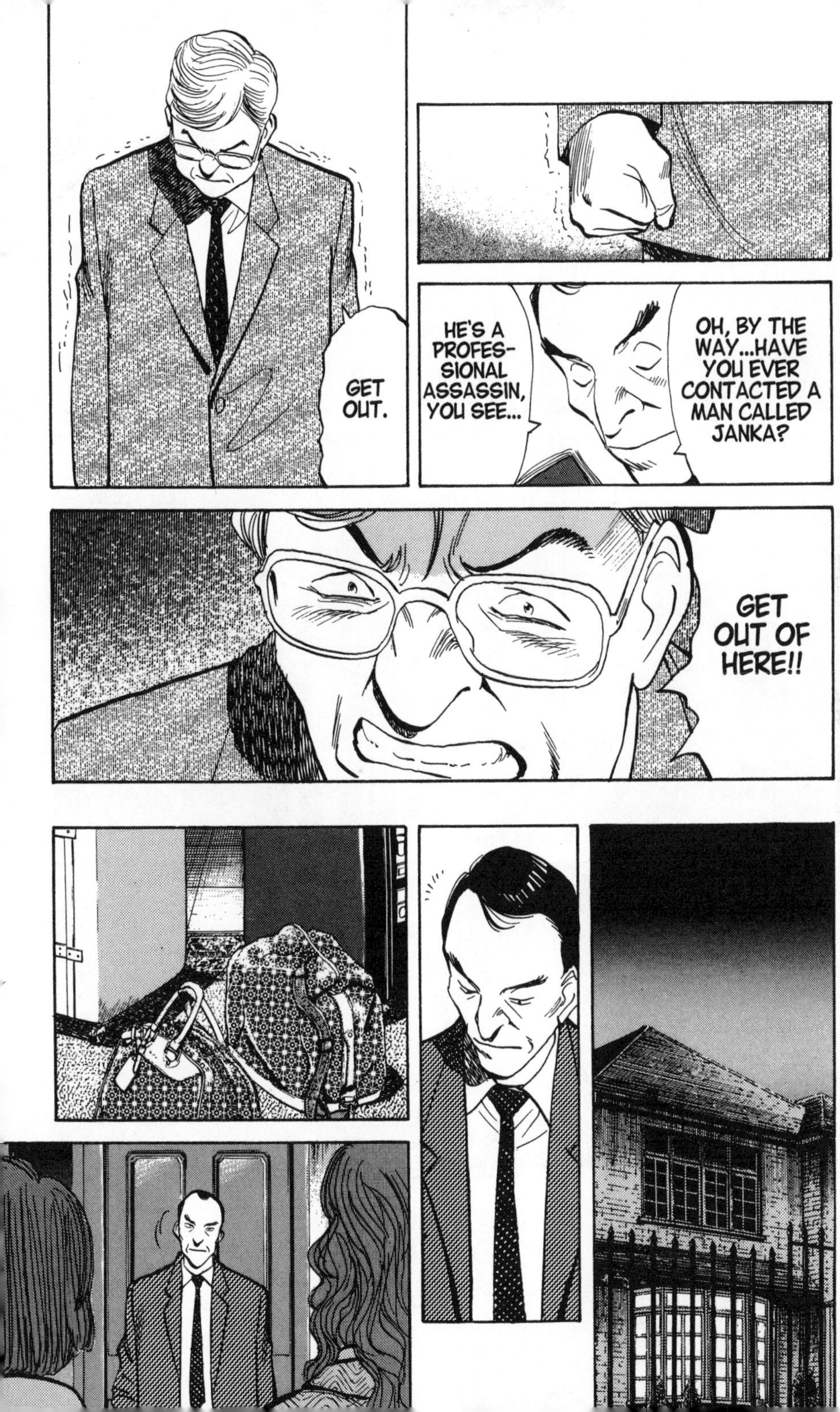
OH, BY THE WAY...HAVE YOU EVER CONTACTED A MAN CALLED JANKA?
HE'S A PROFES-SIONAL ASSASSIN, YOU SEE...
GET OUT.
GET OUT OF HERE!!

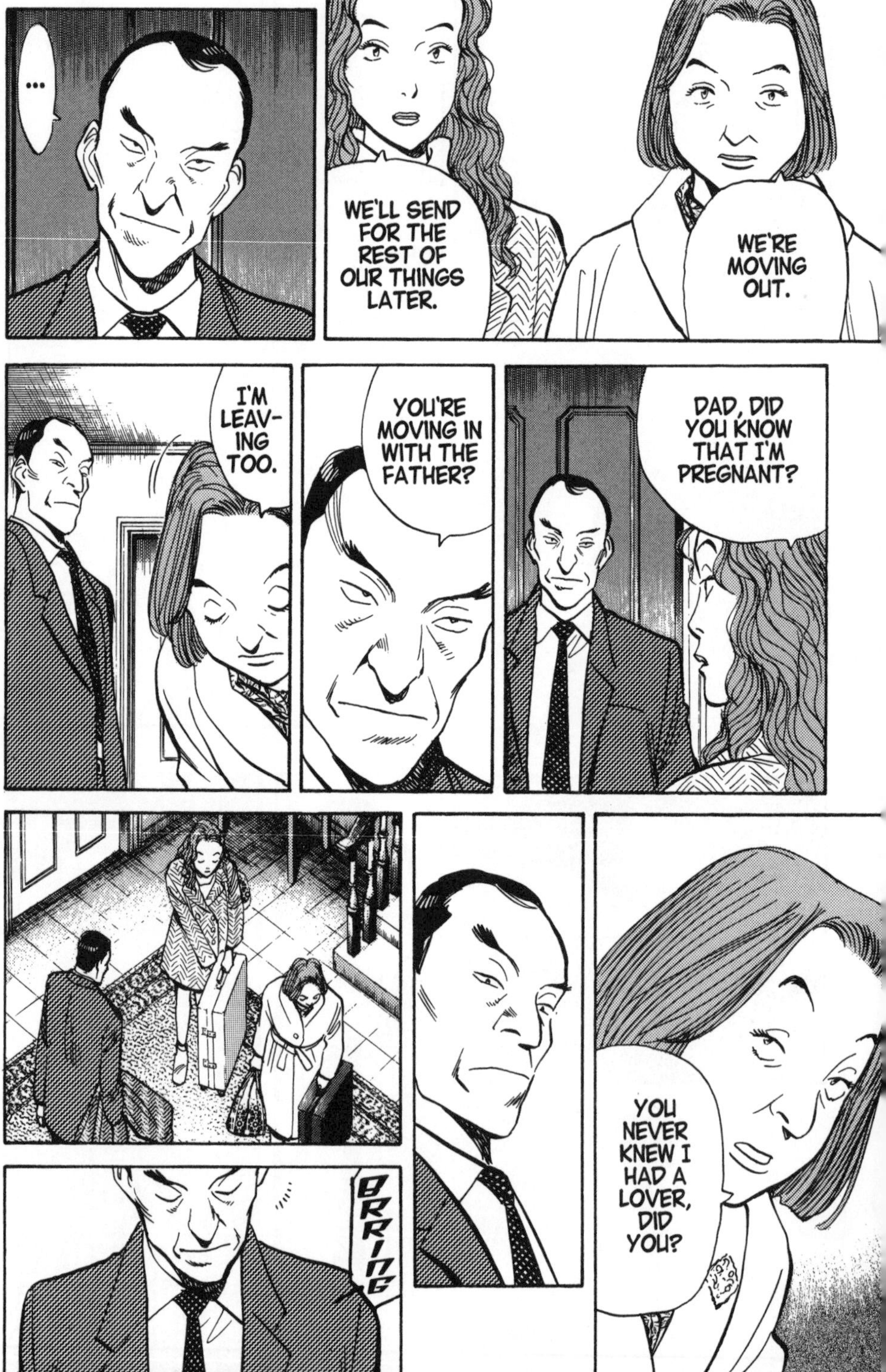
WE'RE MOVING OUT.
WE'LL SEND FOR THE REST OF OUR THINGS LATER.
...
DAD, DID YOU KNOW THAT I'M PREGNANT?
YOU'RE MOVING IN WITH THE FATHER?
I'M LEAV-ING TOO.
YOU NEVER KNEW I HAD A LOVER, DID YOU?
BRRING

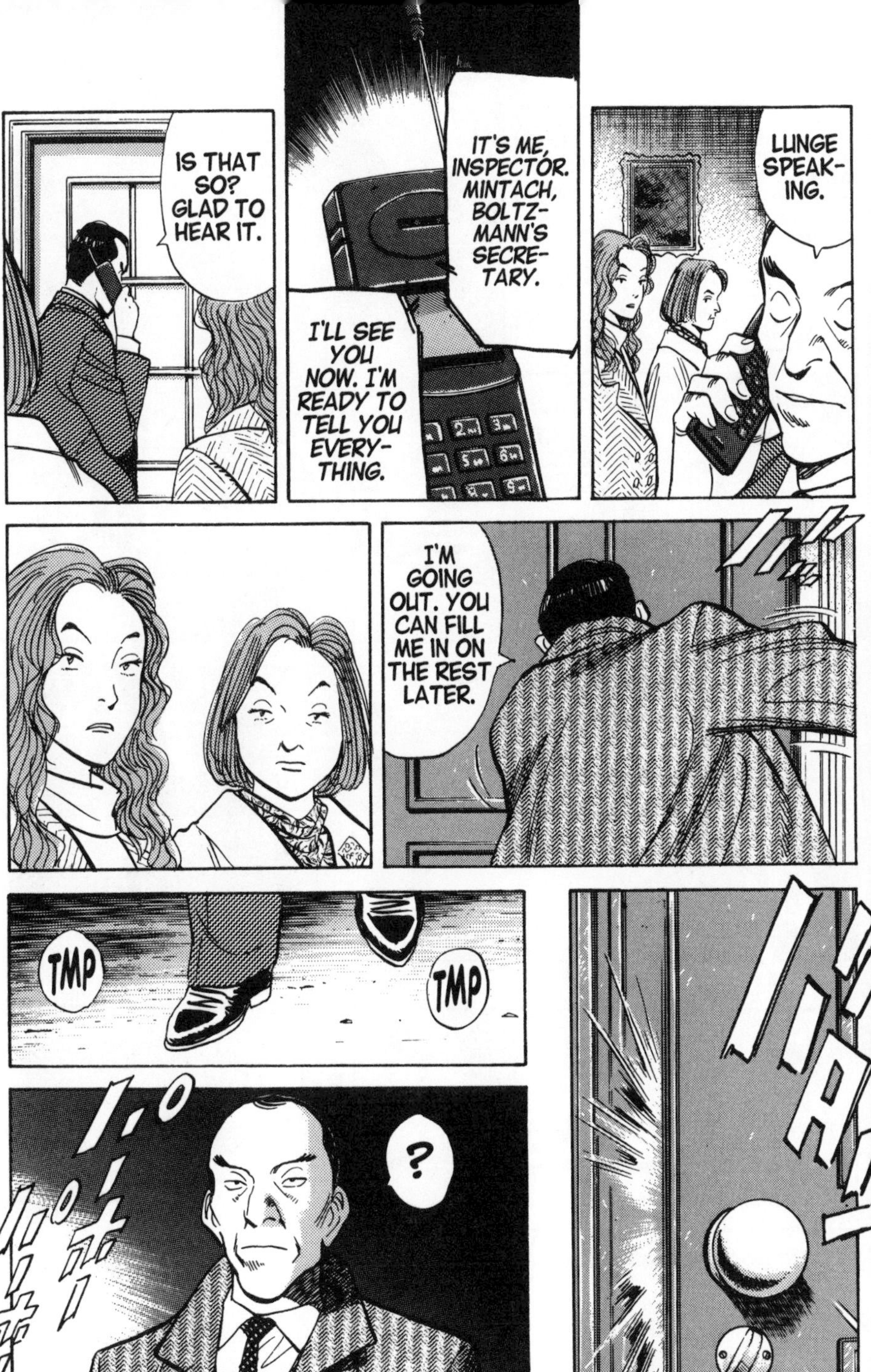
LUNGE SPEAKING.
IT'S ME, INSPECTOR. MINTACH, BOLTZMANN'S SECRETARY.
I'LL SEE YOU NOW. I'M READY TO TELL YOU EVERYTHING.
IS THAT SO? GLAD TO HEAR IT.
I'M GOING OUT. YOU CAN FILL ME IN ON THE REST LATER.
TMP
TMP
?

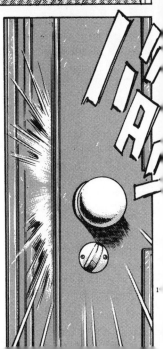

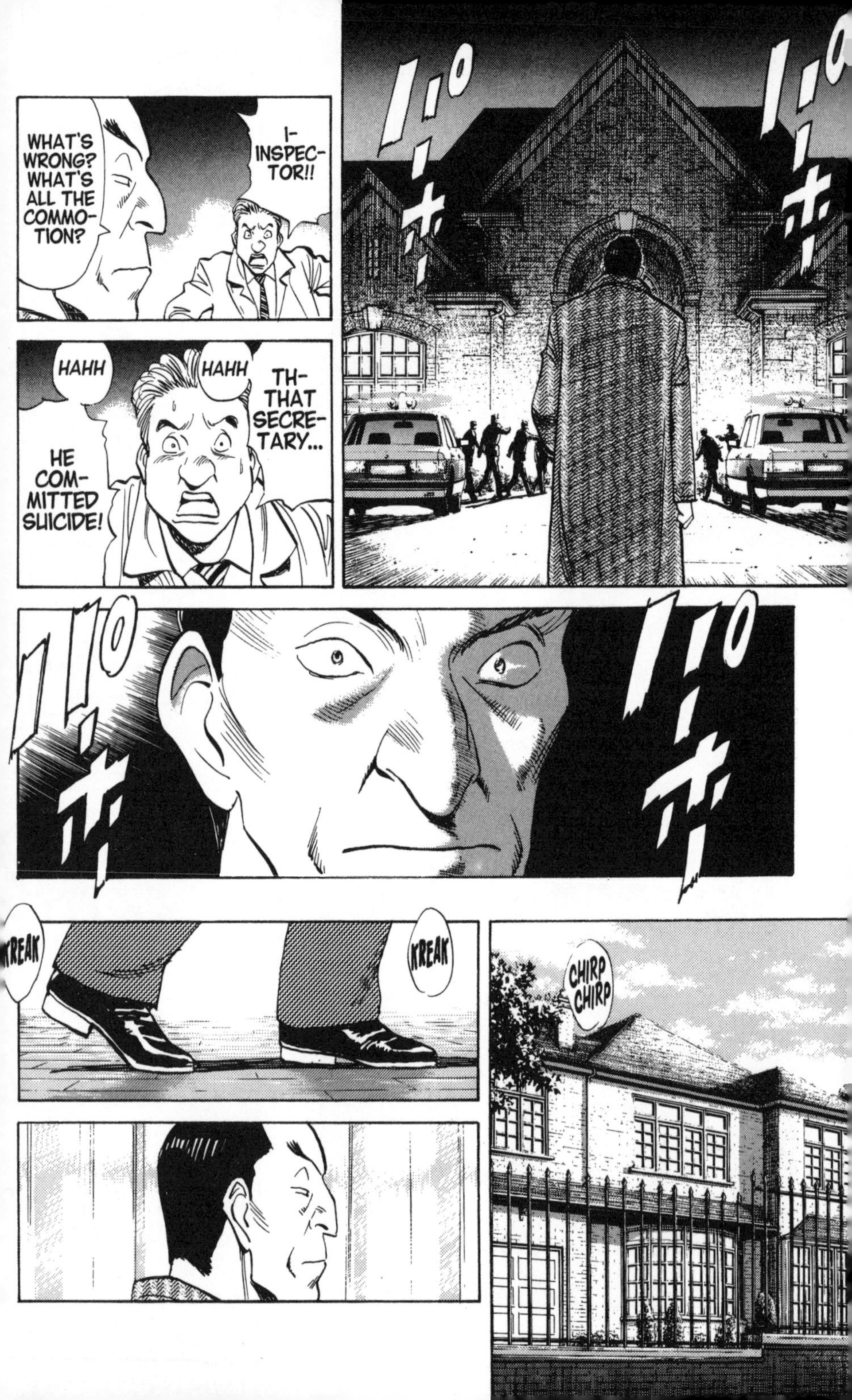
I-INSPECTOR!!
WHAT'S WRONG? WHAT'S ALL THE COMMOTION?
TH-THAT SECRETARY...
HAHH
HAHH
HE COMMITTED SUICIDE!
CHIRP CHIRP
KREAK
KREAK

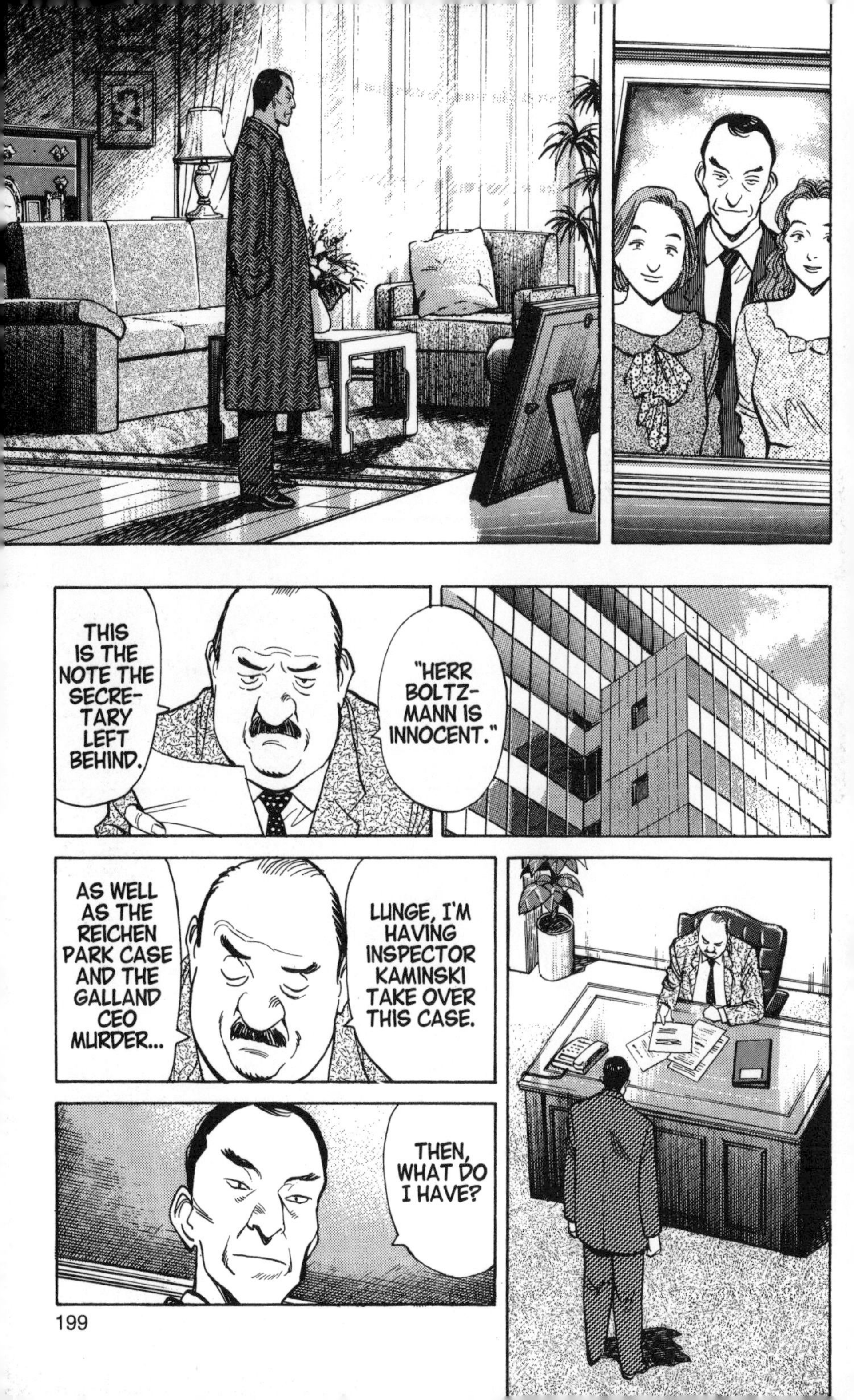
"HERR BOLTZMANN IS INNOCENT."
THIS IS THE NOTE THE SECRETARY LEFT BEHIND.
LUNGE, I'M HAVING INSPECTOR KAMINSKI TAKE OVER THIS CASE.
AS WELL AS THE REICHEN PARK CASE AND THE GALLAND CEO MURDER...
THEN, WHAT DO I HAVE?

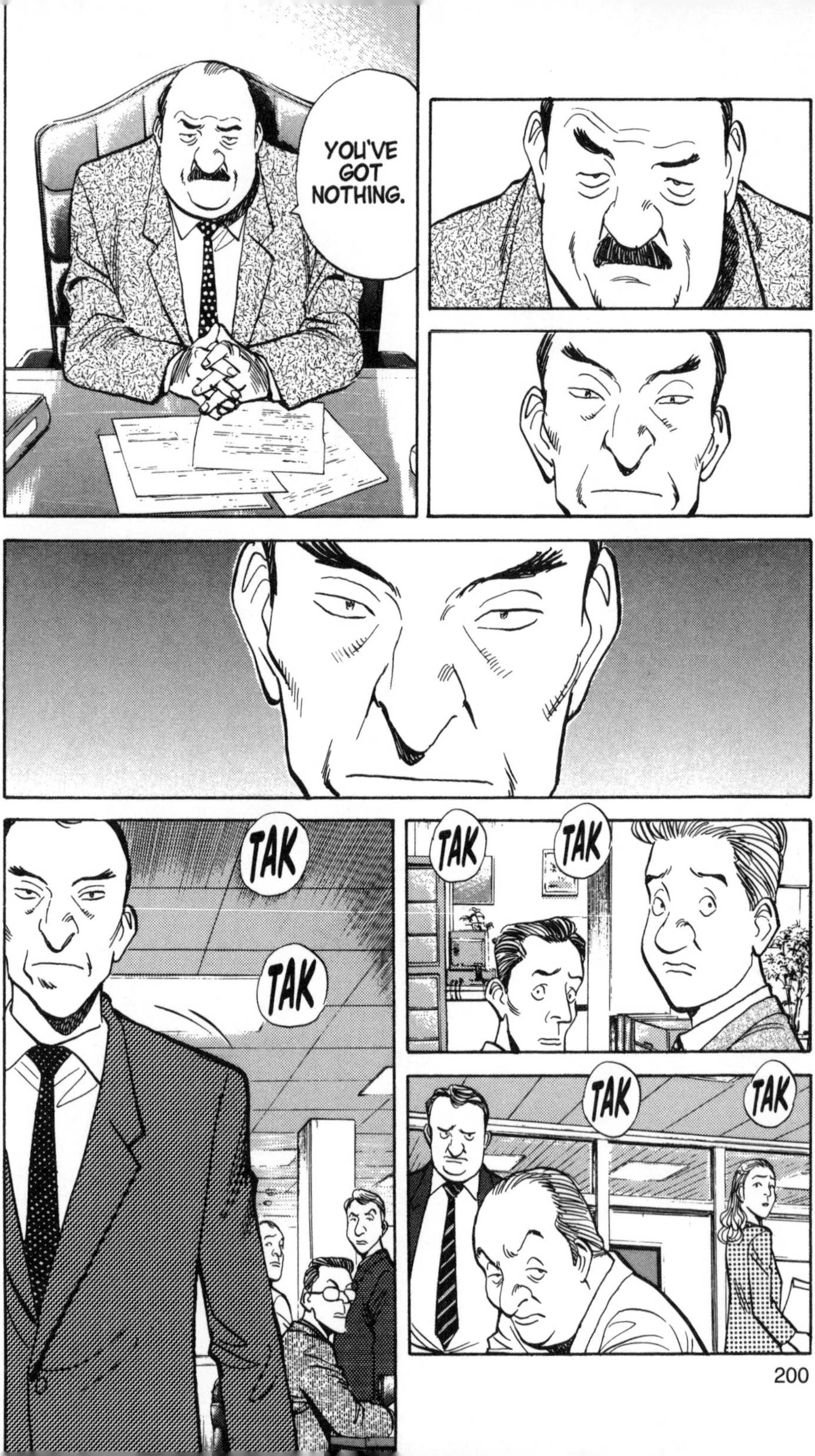
YOU'VE GOT NOTHING.
TAK
TAK
TAK
TAK
TAK
TAK

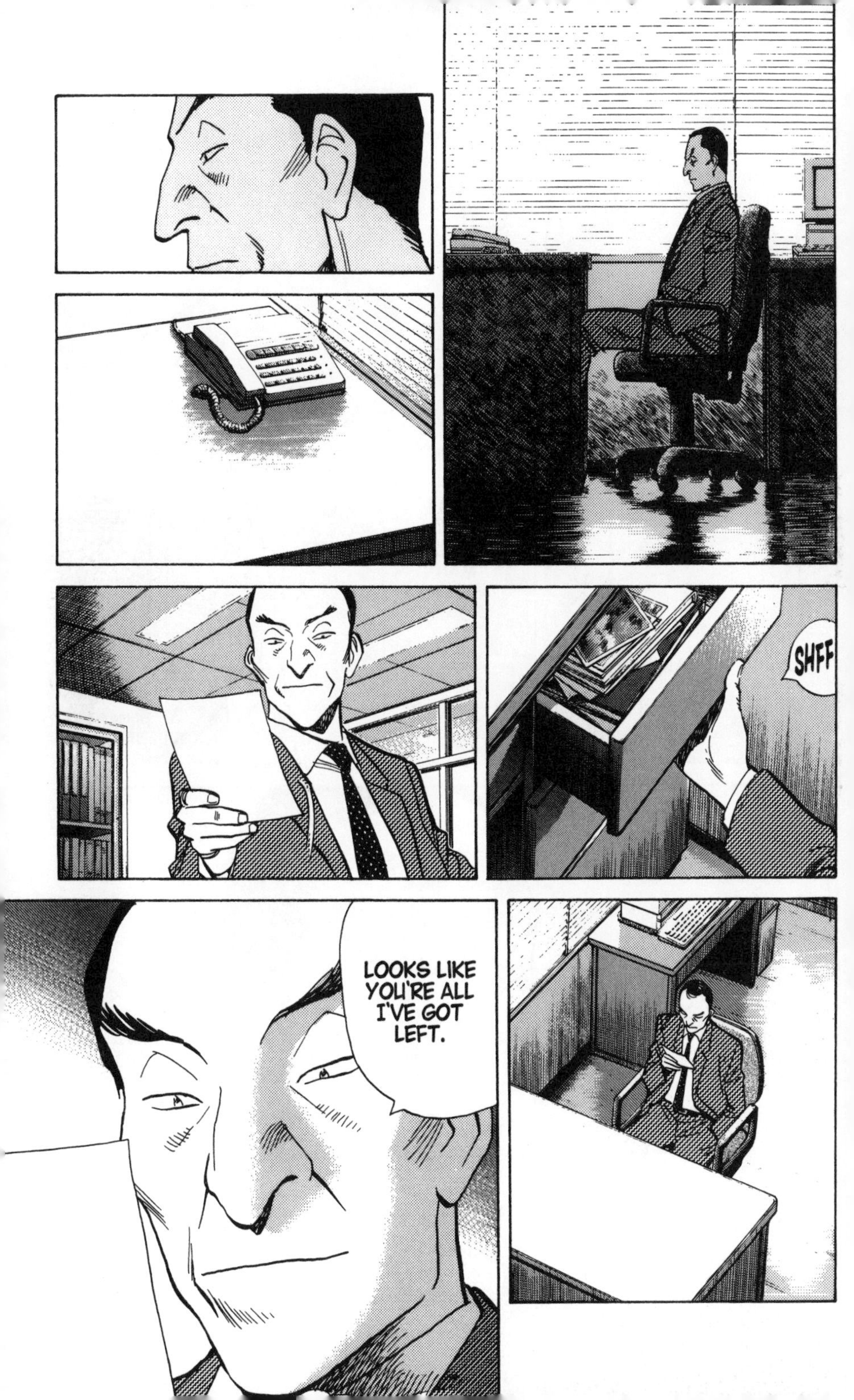
SHFF
LOOKS LIKE YOU'RE ALL I'VE GOT LEFT.

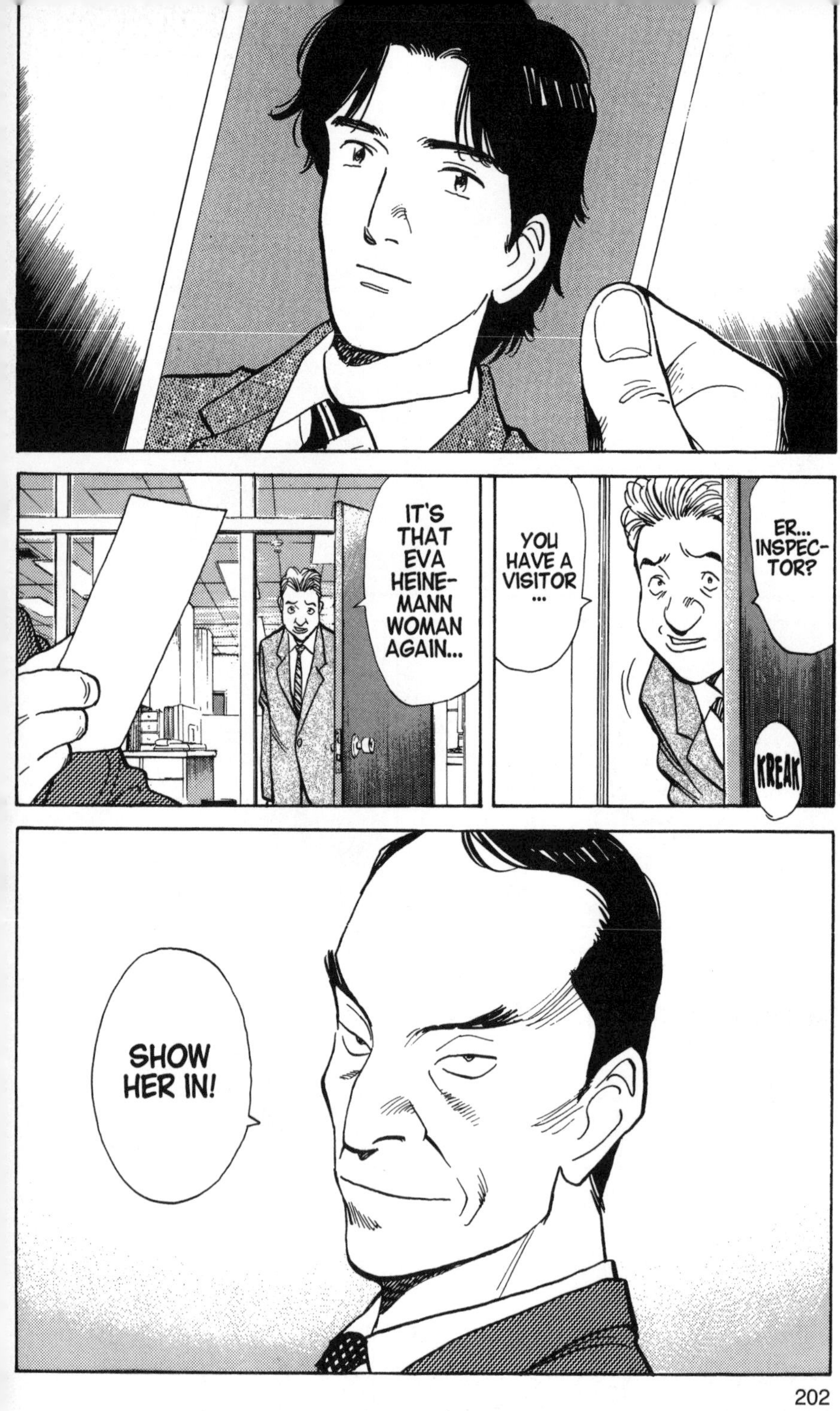
ER... INSPECTOR?
YOU HAVE A VISITOR ...
KREAK
IT'S THAT EVA HEINEMANN WOMAN AGAIN...
SHOW HER IN!

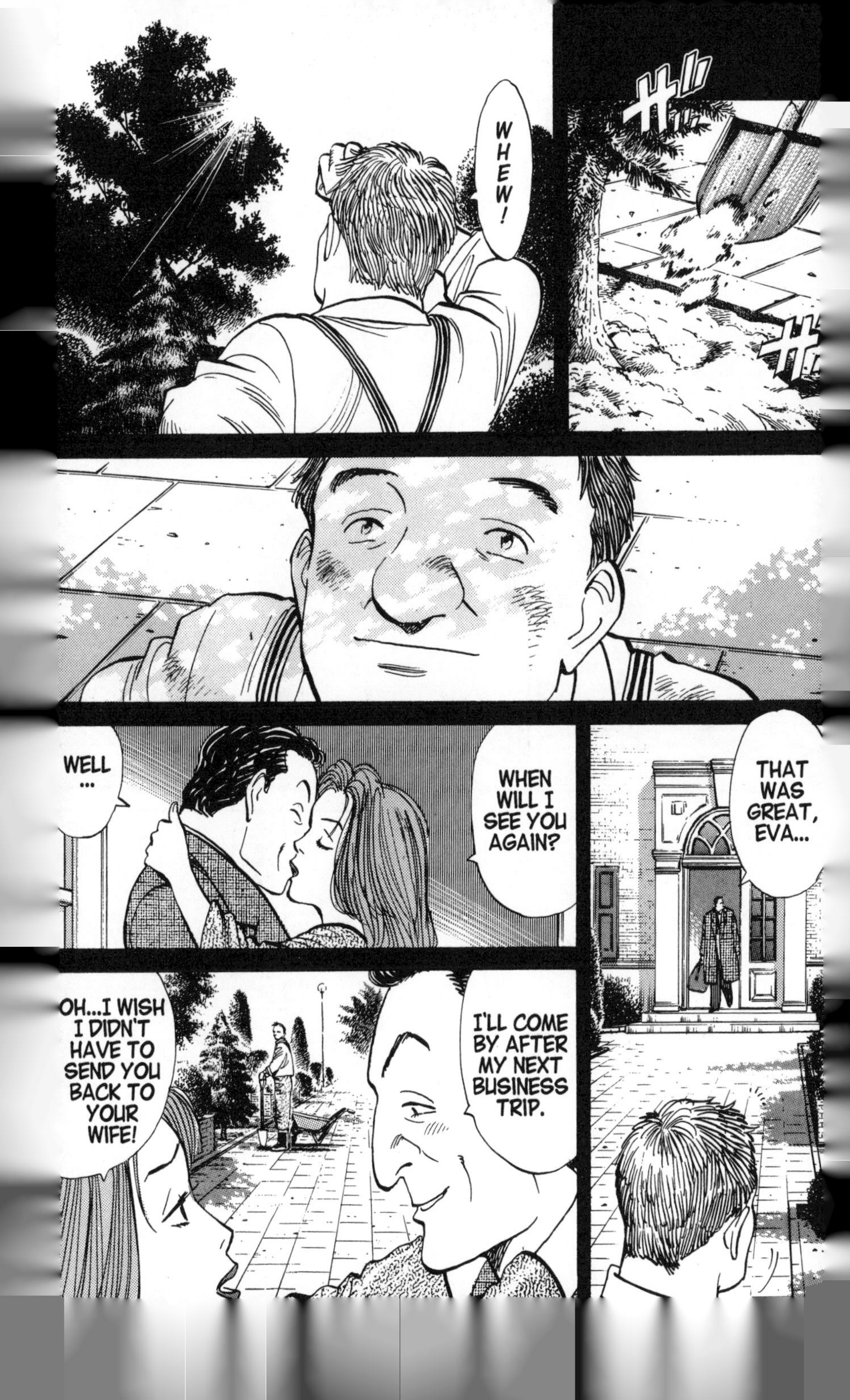
WHEW!
THAT WAS GREAT, EVA...
WHEN WILL I SEE YOU AGAIN?
WELL...
I'LL COME BY AFTER MY NEXT BUSINESS TRIP.
OH...I WISH I DIDN'T HAVE TO SEND YOU BACK TO YOUR WIFE!

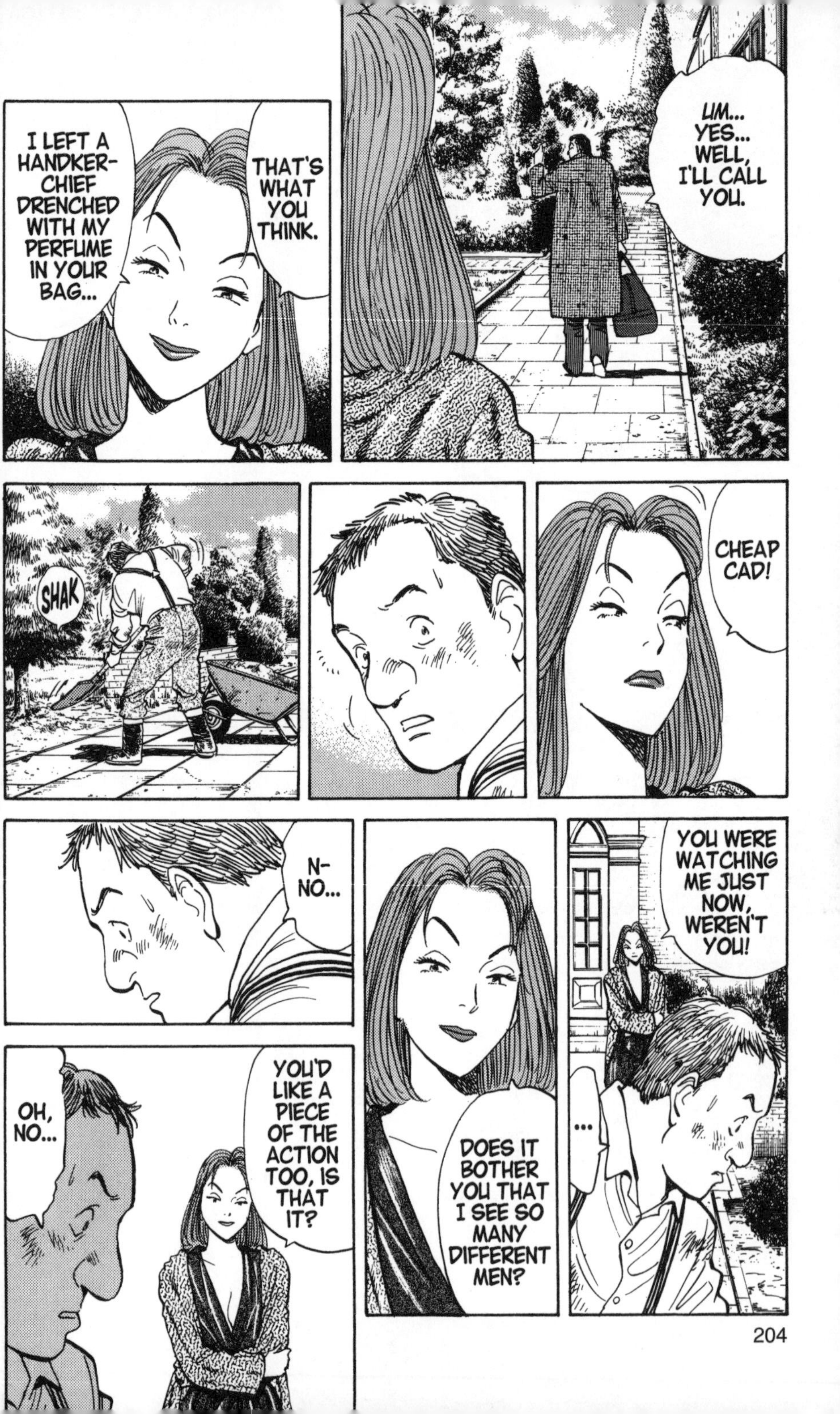
UM... YES... WELL, I'LL CALL YOU.
THAT'S WHAT YOU THINK.
I LEFT A HANDKER-CHIEF DRENCHED WITH MY PERFUME IN YOUR BAG...
CHEAP CAD!
SHAK
YOU WERE WATCHING ME JUST NOW, WEREN'T YOU!
...
DOES IT BOTHER YOU THAT I SEE SO MANY DIFFERENT MEN?
N-NO...
YOU'D LIKE A PIECE OF THE ACTION TOO, IS THAT IT?
OH, NO...

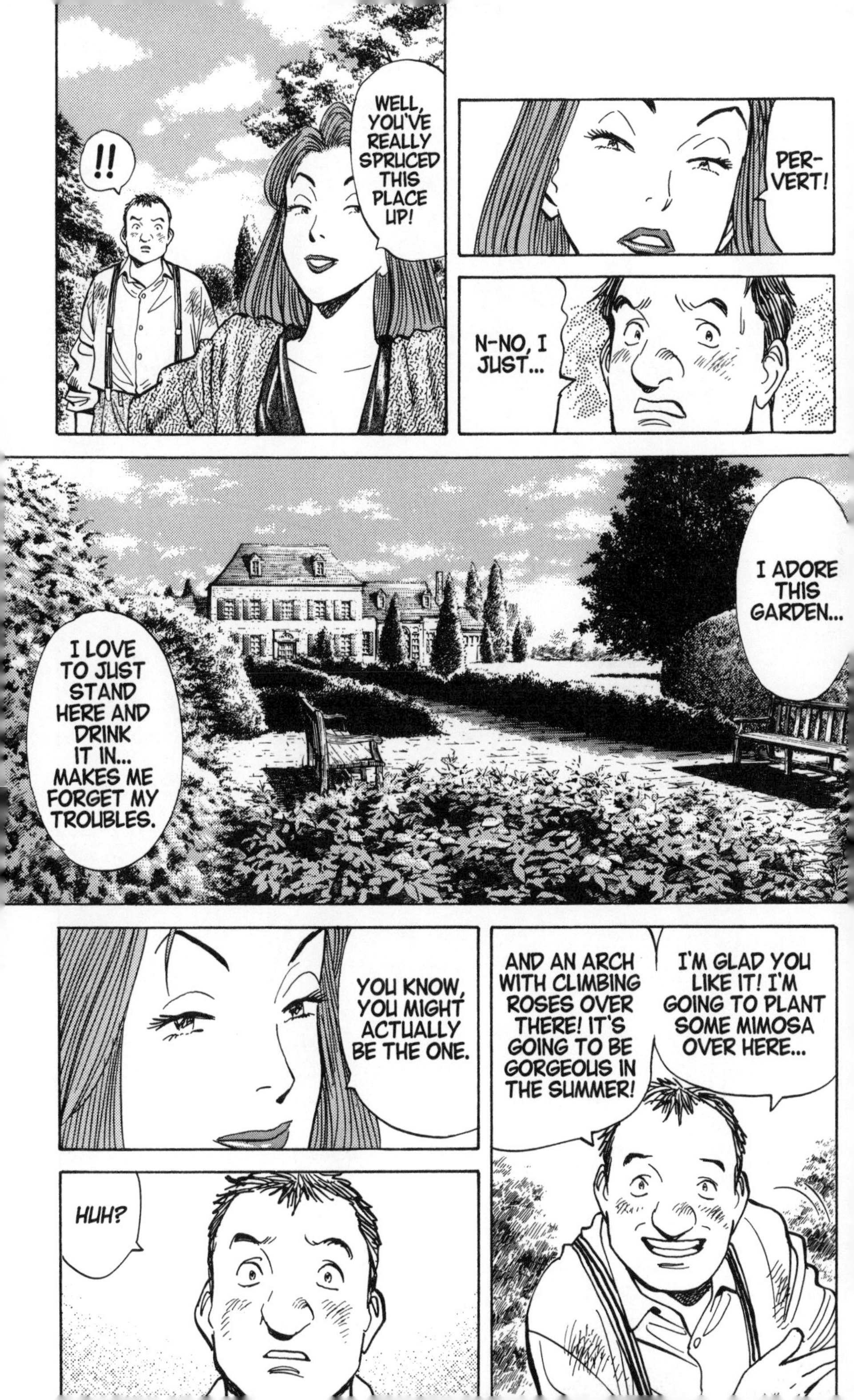
PER-VERT!
N-NO, I JUST...
WELL, YOU'VE REALLY SPRUCED THIS PLACE UP!
!!
I ADORE THIS GARDEN...
I LOVE TO JUST STAND HERE AND DRINK IT IN... MAKES ME FORGET MY TROUBLES.
I'M GLAD YOU LIKE IT! I'M GOING TO PLANT SOME MIMOSA OVER HERE...
AND AN ARCH WITH CLIMBING ROSES OVER THERE! IT'S GOING TO BE GORGEOUS IN THE SUMMER!
YOU KNOW, YOU MIGHT ACTUALLY BE THE ONE.
HUH?

Kapitel 25.
The Woman Left Behind

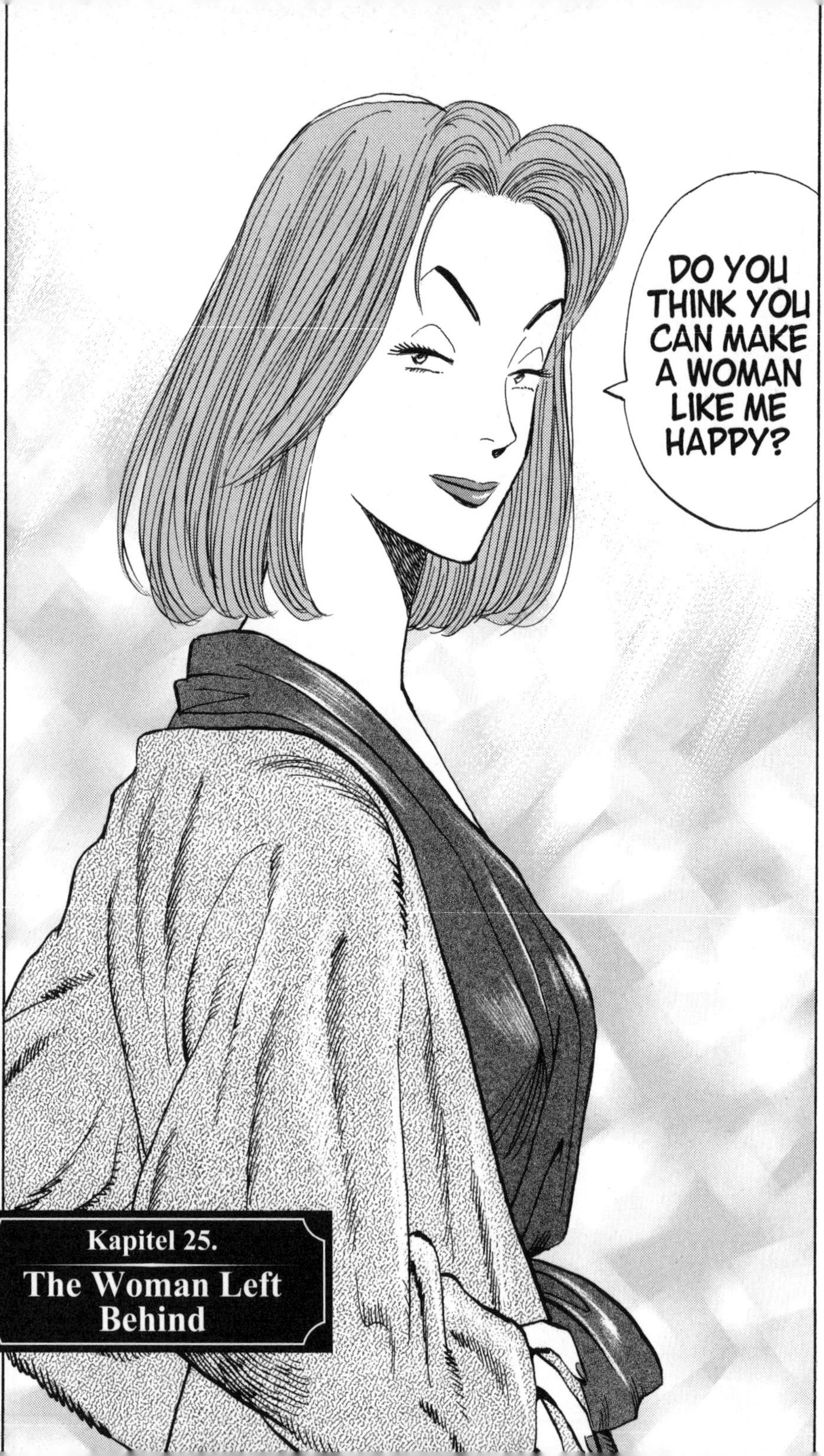
DO YOU THINK YOU CAN MAKE A WOMAN LIKE ME HAPPY?

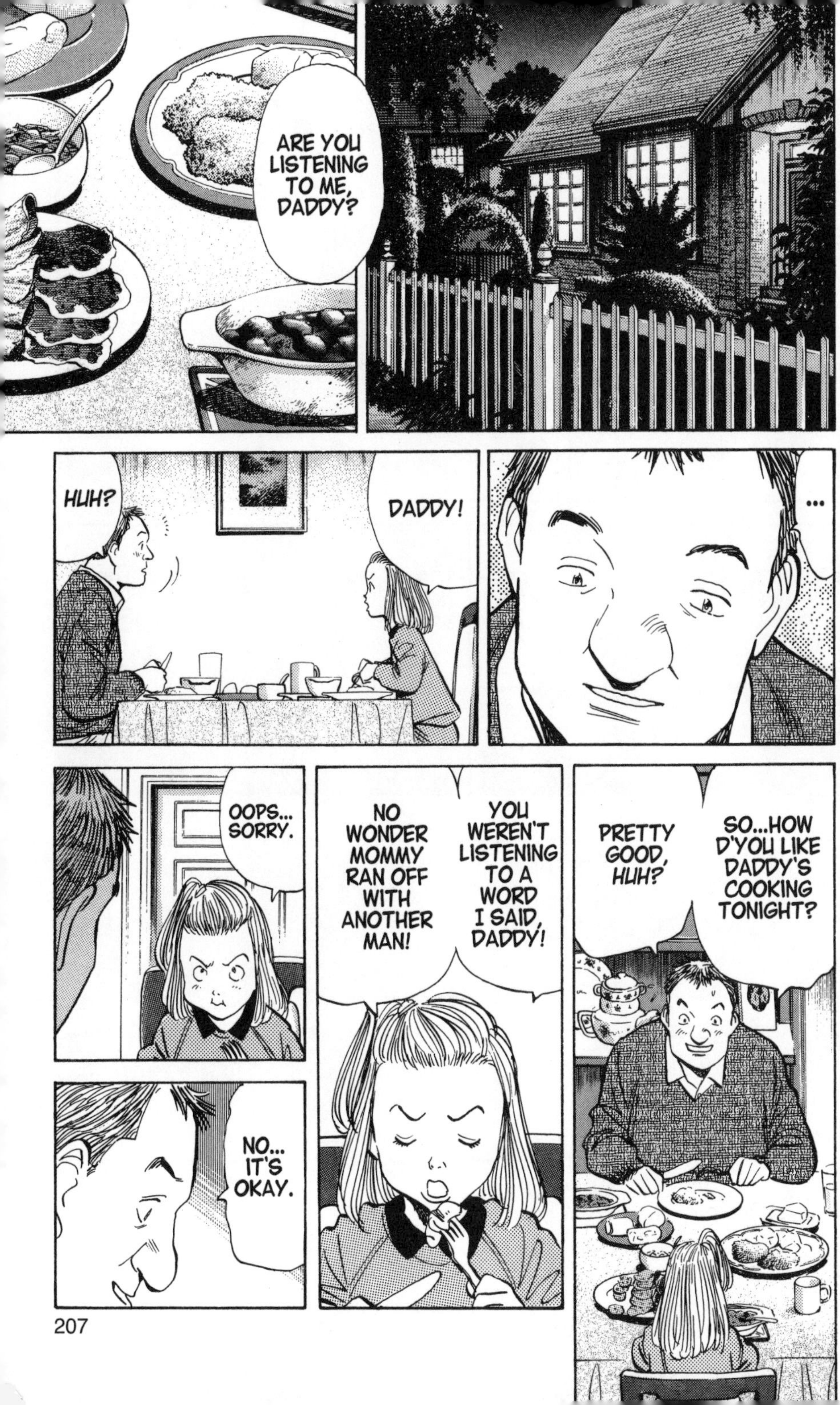
ARE YOU LISTENING TO ME, DADDY?
...
DADDY!
HUH?
SO...HOW D'YOU LIKE DADDY'S COOKING TONIGHT?
PRETTY GOOD, HUH?
YOU WEREN'T LISTENING TO A WORD I SAID, DADDY!
NO WONDER MOMMY RAN OFF WITH ANOTHER MAN!
OOPS... SORRY.
NO... IT'S OKAY.

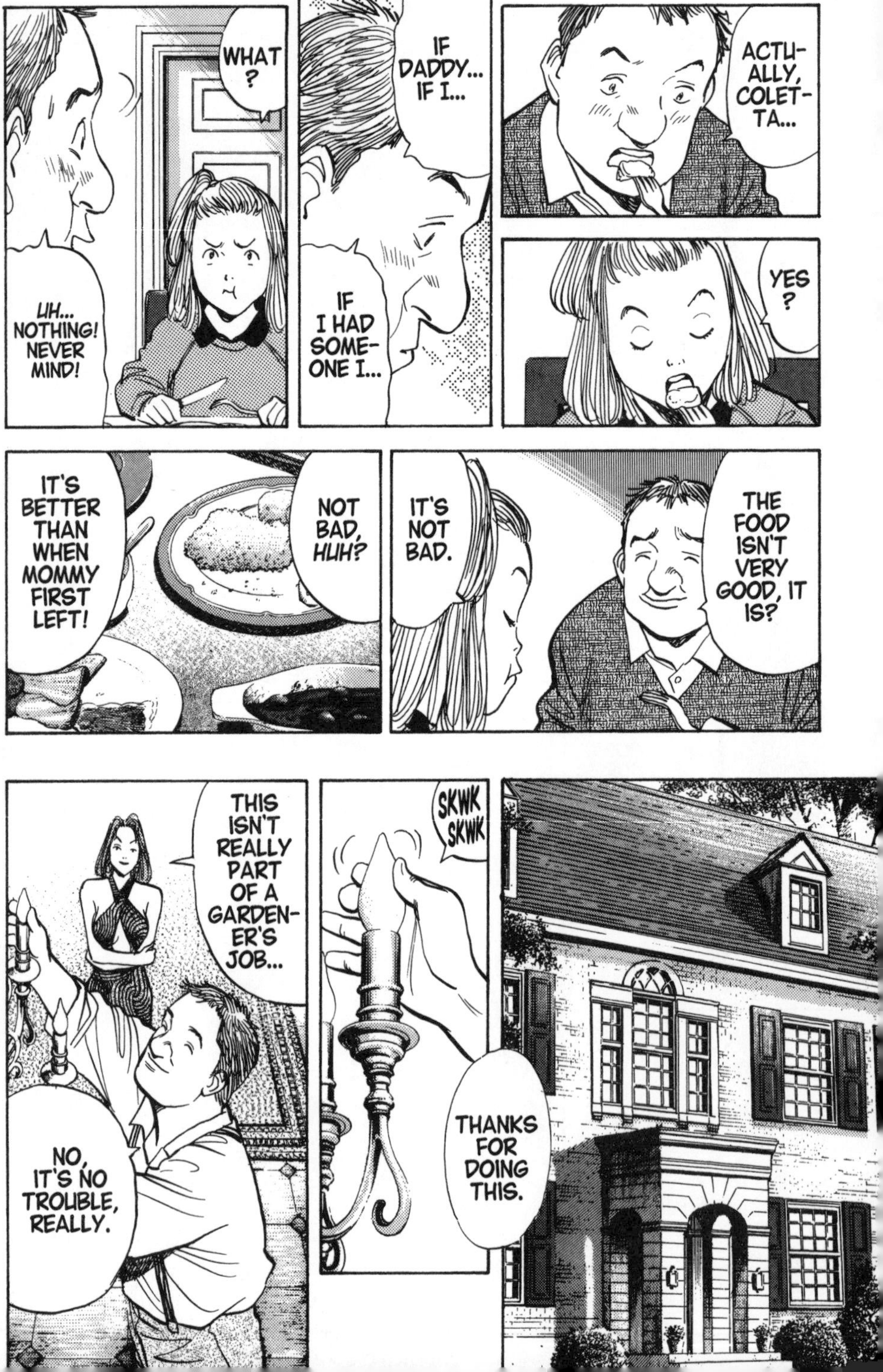
ACTU-ALLY, COLET-TA...
YES?
IF DADDY... IF I...
IF I HAD SOME-ONE I...
WHAT?
UH... NOTHING! NEVER MIND!
THE FOOD ISN'T VERY GOOD, IT IS?
IT'S NOT BAD.
NOT BAD, HUH?
IT'S BETTER THAN WHEN MOMMY FIRST LEFT!
SKWK SKWK
THANKS FOR DOING THIS.
THIS ISN'T REALLY PART OF A GARDEN-ER'S JOB...
NO, IT'S NO TROUBLE, REALLY.

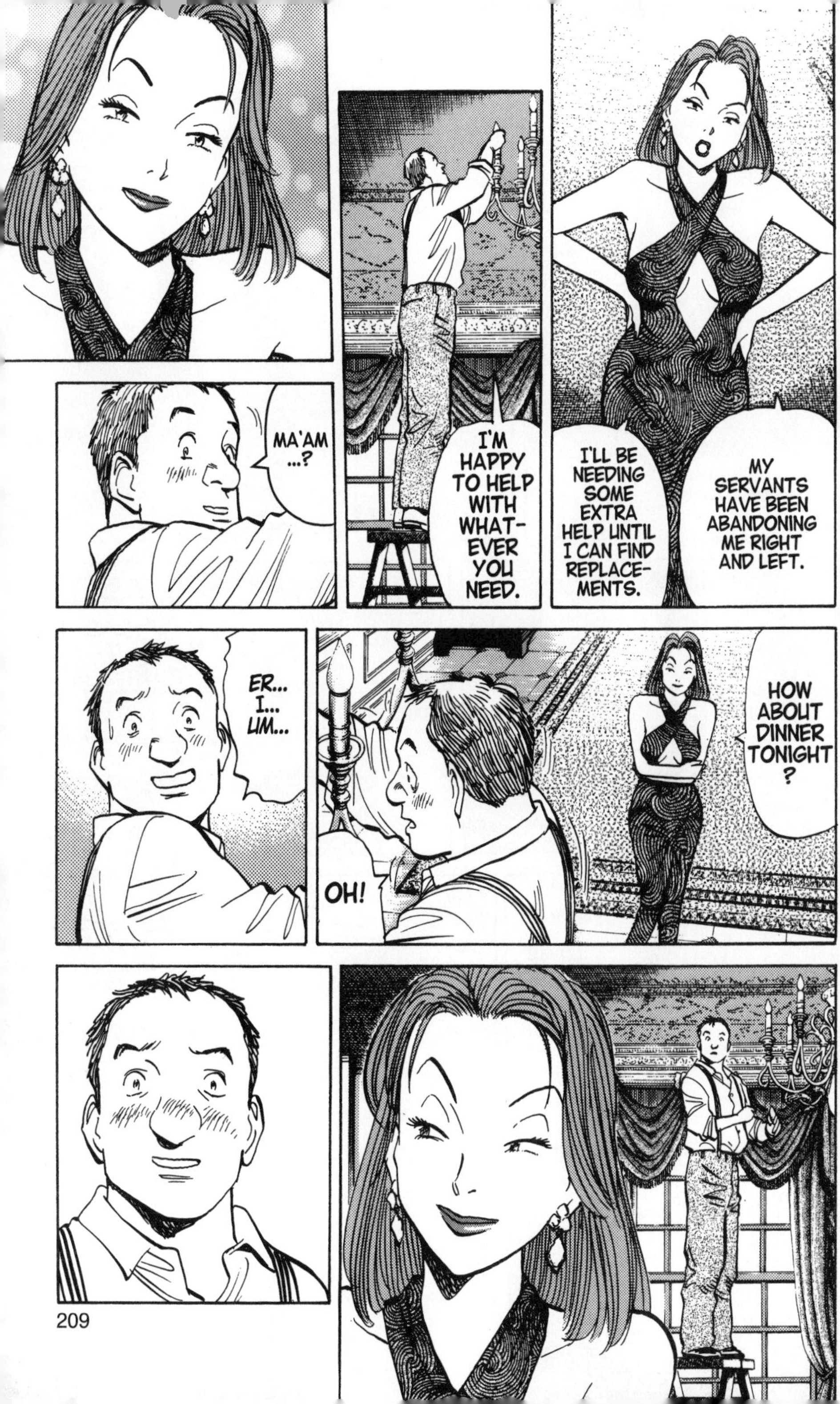
MY SERVANTS HAVE BEEN ABANDONING ME RIGHT AND LEFT.
I'LL BE NEEDING SOME EXTRA HELP UNTIL I CAN FIND REPLACEMENTS.
I'M HAPPY TO HELP WITH WHATEVER YOU NEED.
MA'AM ...?
HOW ABOUT DINNER TONIGHT?
OH!
ER... I... UM...

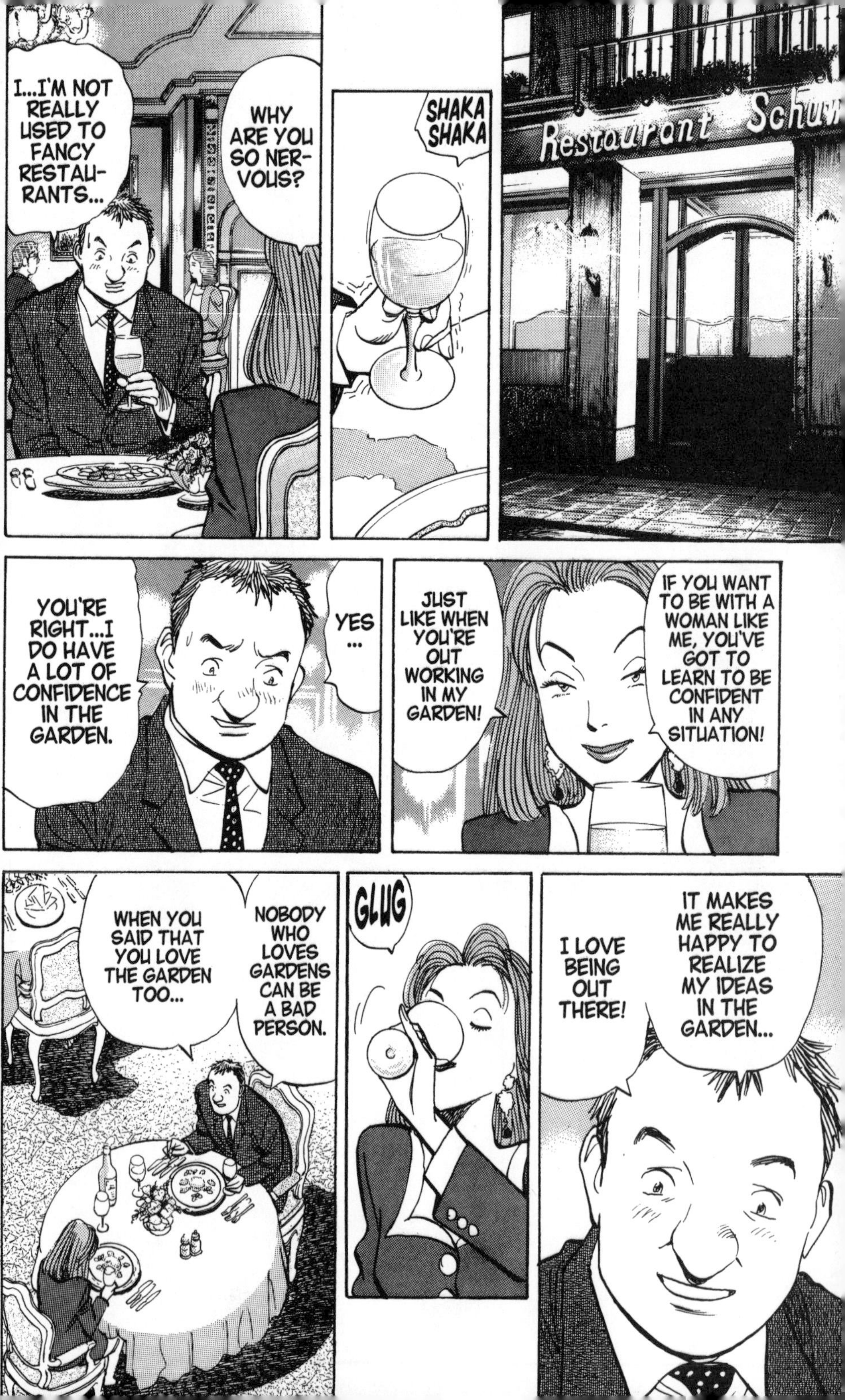
Restaurant
SHAKA SHAKA
WHY ARE YOU SO NER-VOUS?
I...I'M NOT REALLY USED TO FANCY RESTAU-RANTS...
IF YOU WANT TO BE WITH A WOMAN LIKE ME, YOU'VE GOT TO LEARN TO BE CONFIDENT IN ANY SITUATION!
JUST LIKE WHEN YOU'RE OUT WORKING IN MY GARDEN!
YES...
YOU'RE RIGHT...I DO HAVE A LOT OF CONFIDENCE IN THE GARDEN.
IT MAKES ME REALLY HAPPY TO REALIZE MY IDEAS IN THE GARDEN...
I LOVE BEING OUT THERE!
GLUG
NOBODY WHO LOVES GARDENS CAN BE A BAD PERSON.
WHEN YOU SAID THAT YOU LOVE THE GARDEN TOO...

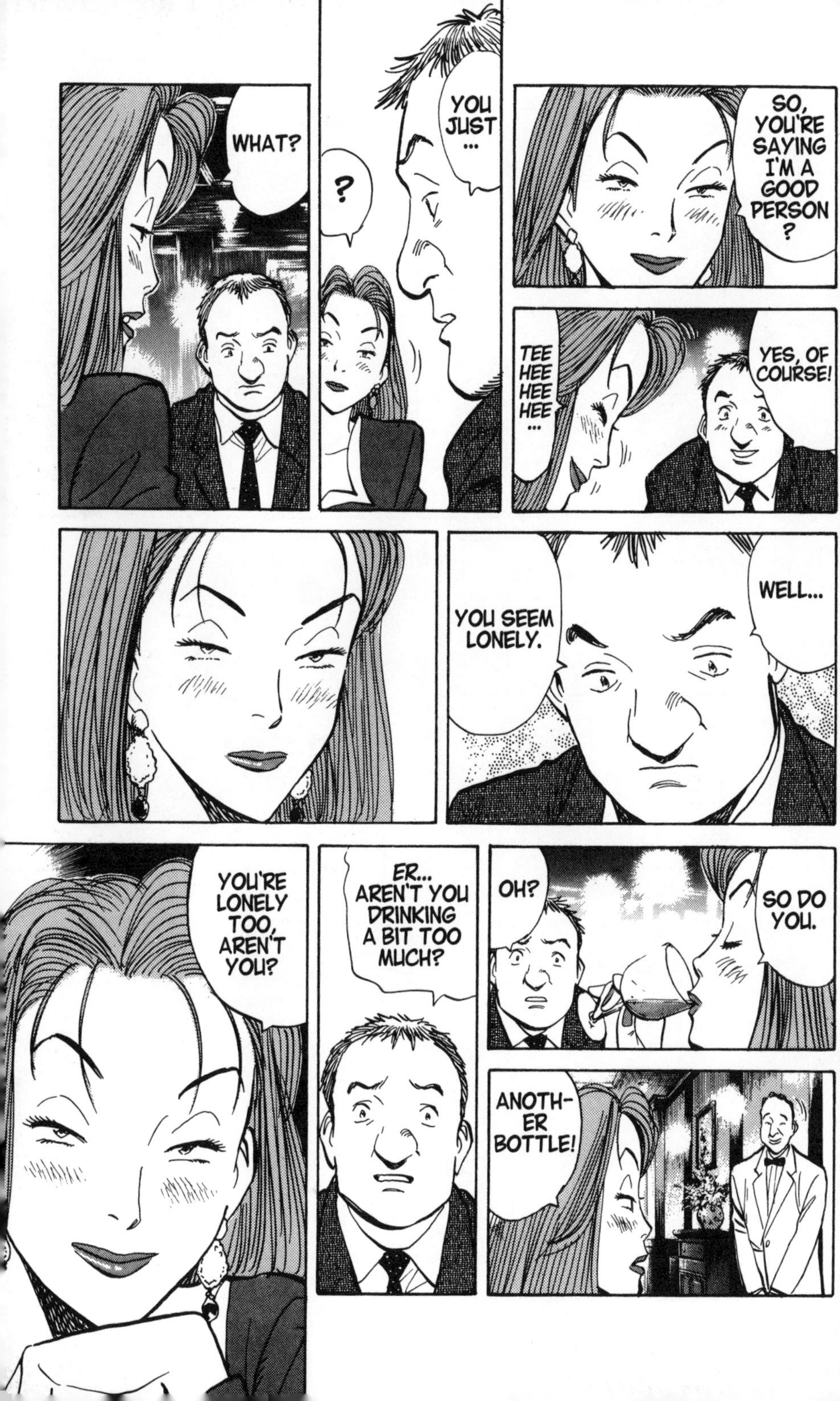
SO, YOU'RE SAYING I'M A GOOD PERSON?
YES, OF COURSE!
TEE HEE HEE HEE...
YOU JUST...
?
WHAT?
WELL...
YOU SEEM LONELY.
SO DO YOU.
OH?
ANOTH-ER BOTTLE!
ER... AREN'T YOU DRINKING A BIT TOO MUCH?
YOU'RE LONELY TOO, AREN'T YOU?

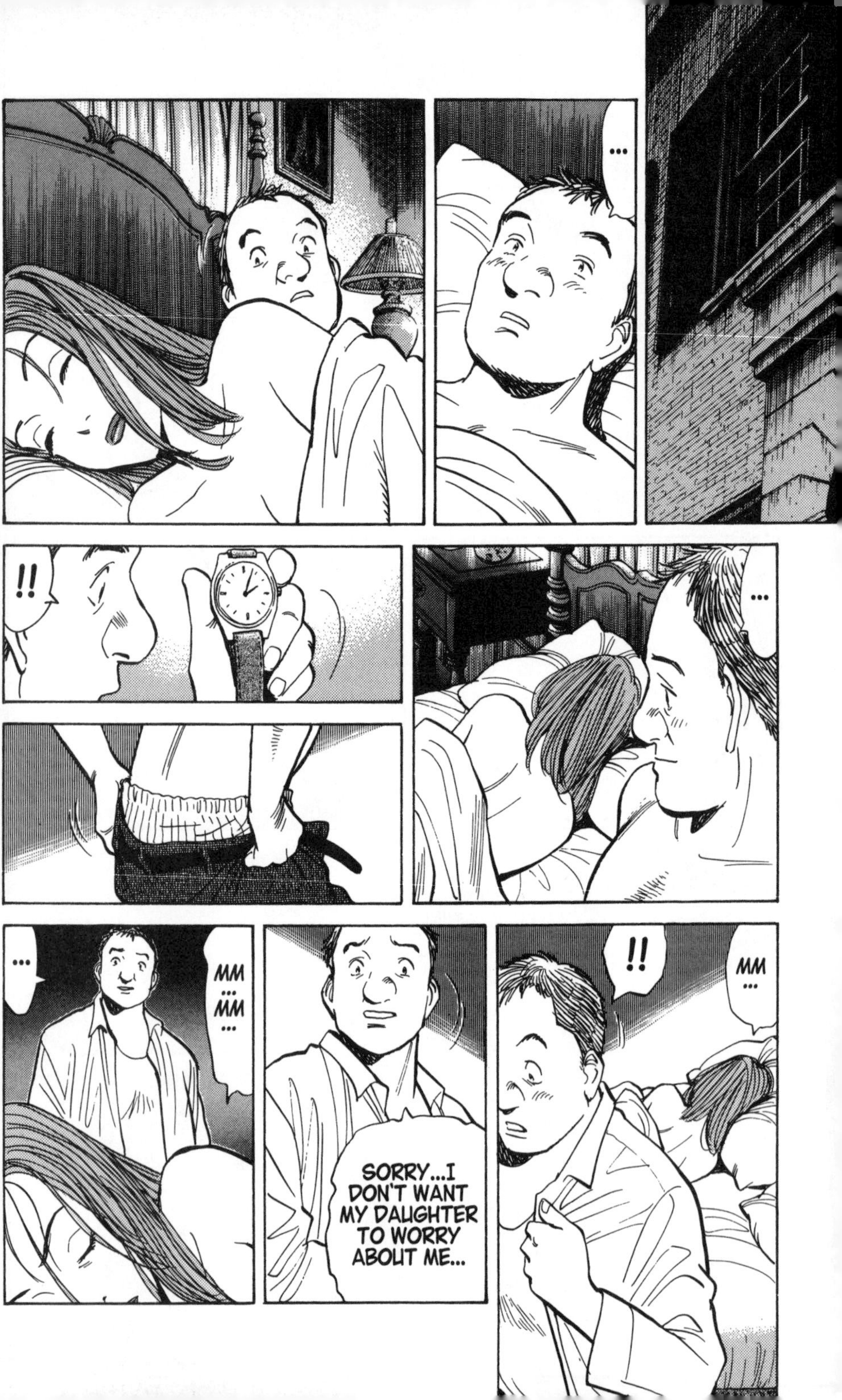
...
...
!!
MM ...
!!
SORRY...I DON'T WANT MY DAUGHTER TO WORRY ABOUT ME...
MM ... MM ...
...

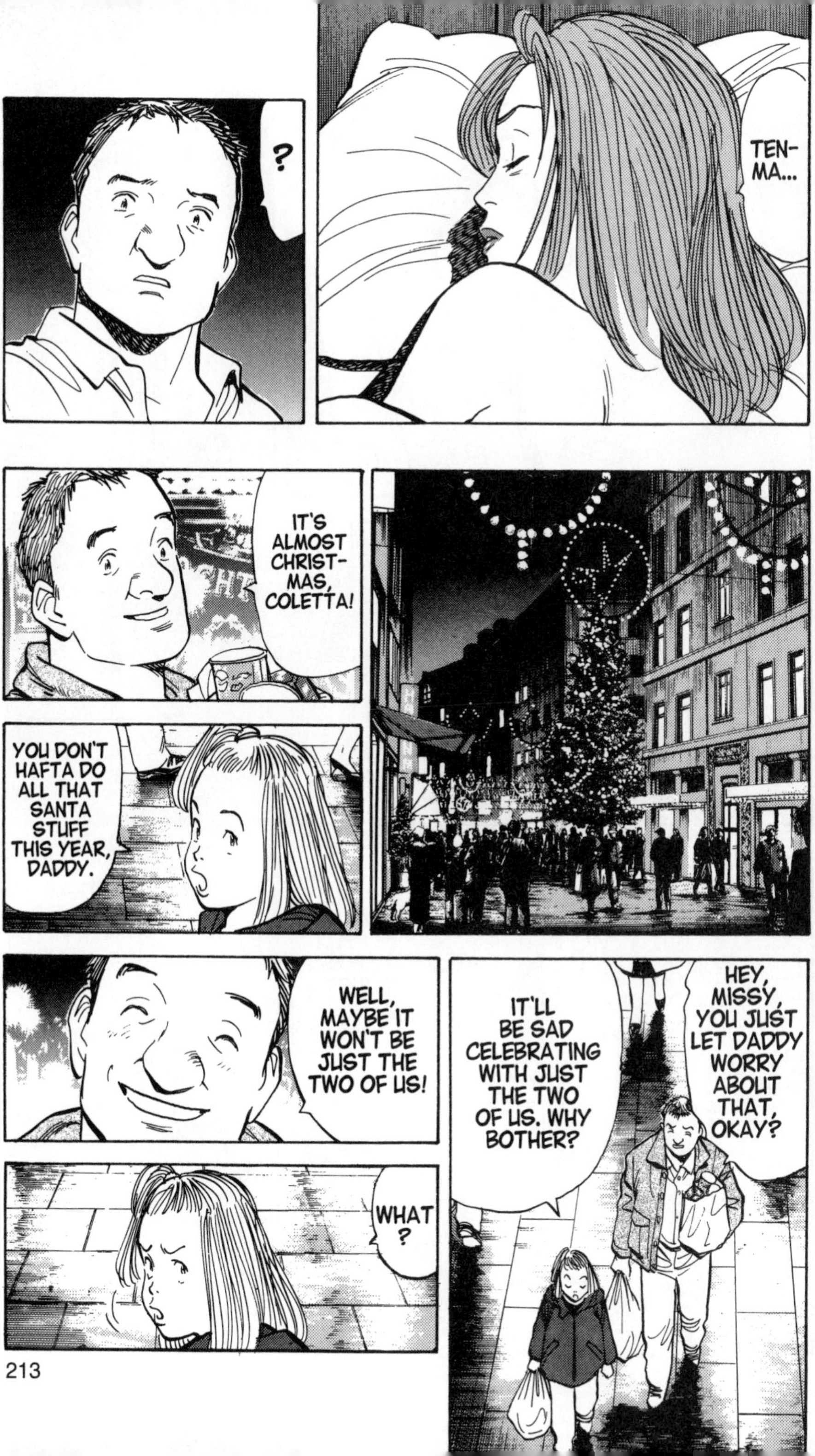
TEN-MA...
?
IT'S ALMOST CHRIST-MAS, COLETTA!
YOU DON'T HAFTA DO ALL THAT SANTA STUFF THIS YEAR, DADDY.
HEY, MISSY, YOU JUST LET DADDY WORRY ABOUT THAT, OKAY?
IT'LL BE SAD CELEBRATING WITH JUST THE TWO OF US. WHY BOTHER?
WELL, MAYBE IT WON'T BE JUST THE TWO OF US!
WHAT?

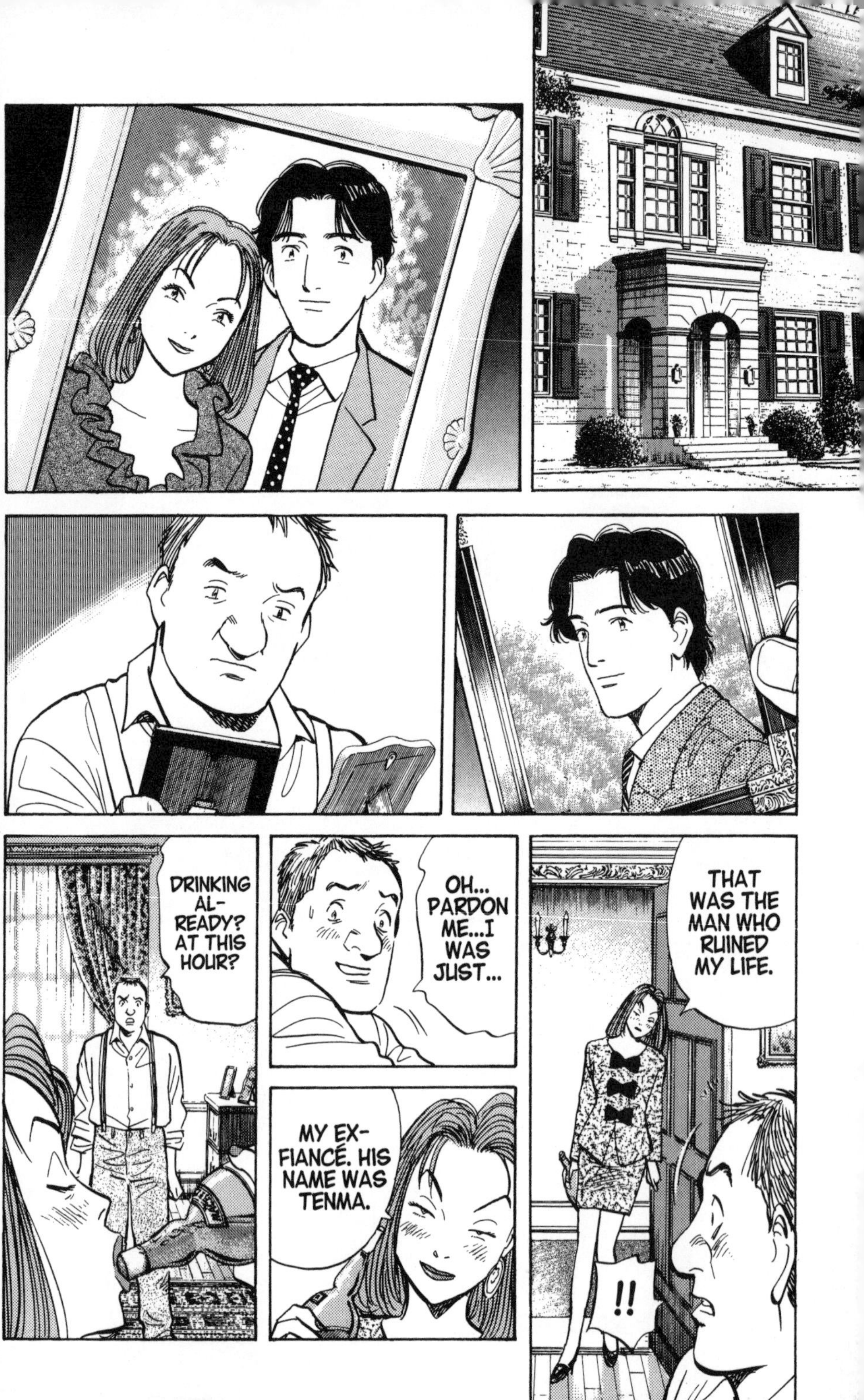
THAT WAS THE MAN WHO RUINED MY LIFE.
!!
OH... PARDON ME...I WAS JUST...
MY EX-FIANCÉ. HIS NAME WAS TENMA.
DRINKING AL-READY? AT THIS HOUR?

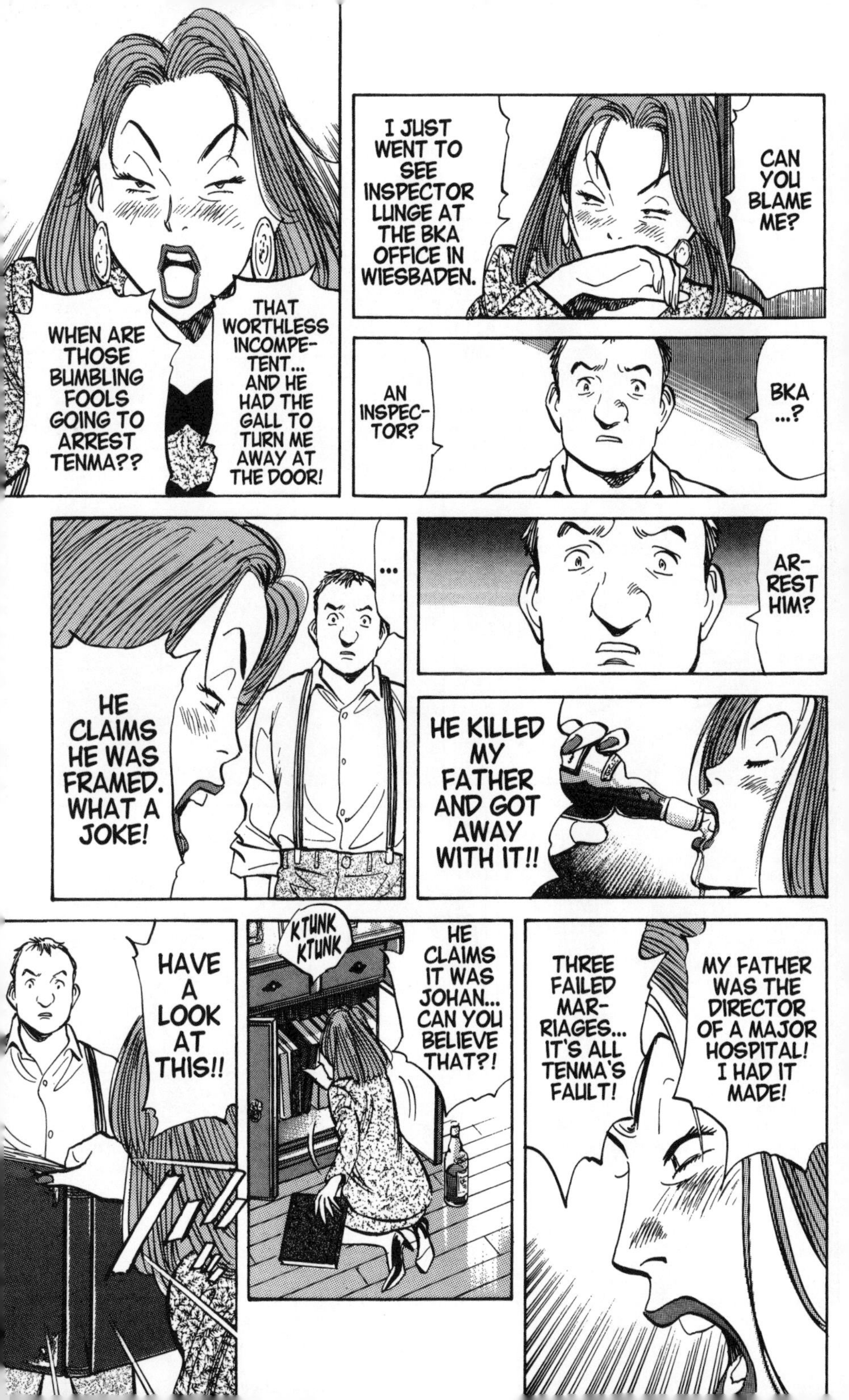
CAN YOU BLAME ME?
I JUST WENT TO SEE INSPECTOR LUNGE AT THE BKA OFFICE IN WIESBADEN.
BKA ...?
AN INSPEC-TOR?
THAT WORTHLESS INCOMPE-TENT... AND HE HAD THE GALL TO TURN ME AWAY AT THE DOOR!
WHEN ARE THOSE BUMBLING FOOLS GOING TO ARREST TENMA??
AR-REST HIM?
HE KILLED MY FATHER AND GOT AWAY WITH IT!!
...
HE CLAIMS HE WAS FRAMED. WHAT A JOKE!
MY FATHER WAS THE DIRECTOR OF A MAJOR HOSPITAL! I HAD IT MADE!
THREE FAILED MAR-RIAGES... IT'S ALL TENMA'S FAULT!
HE CLAIMS IT WAS JOHAN... CAN YOU BELIEVE THAT?!
KTUNK KTUNK
HAVE A LOOK AT THIS!!

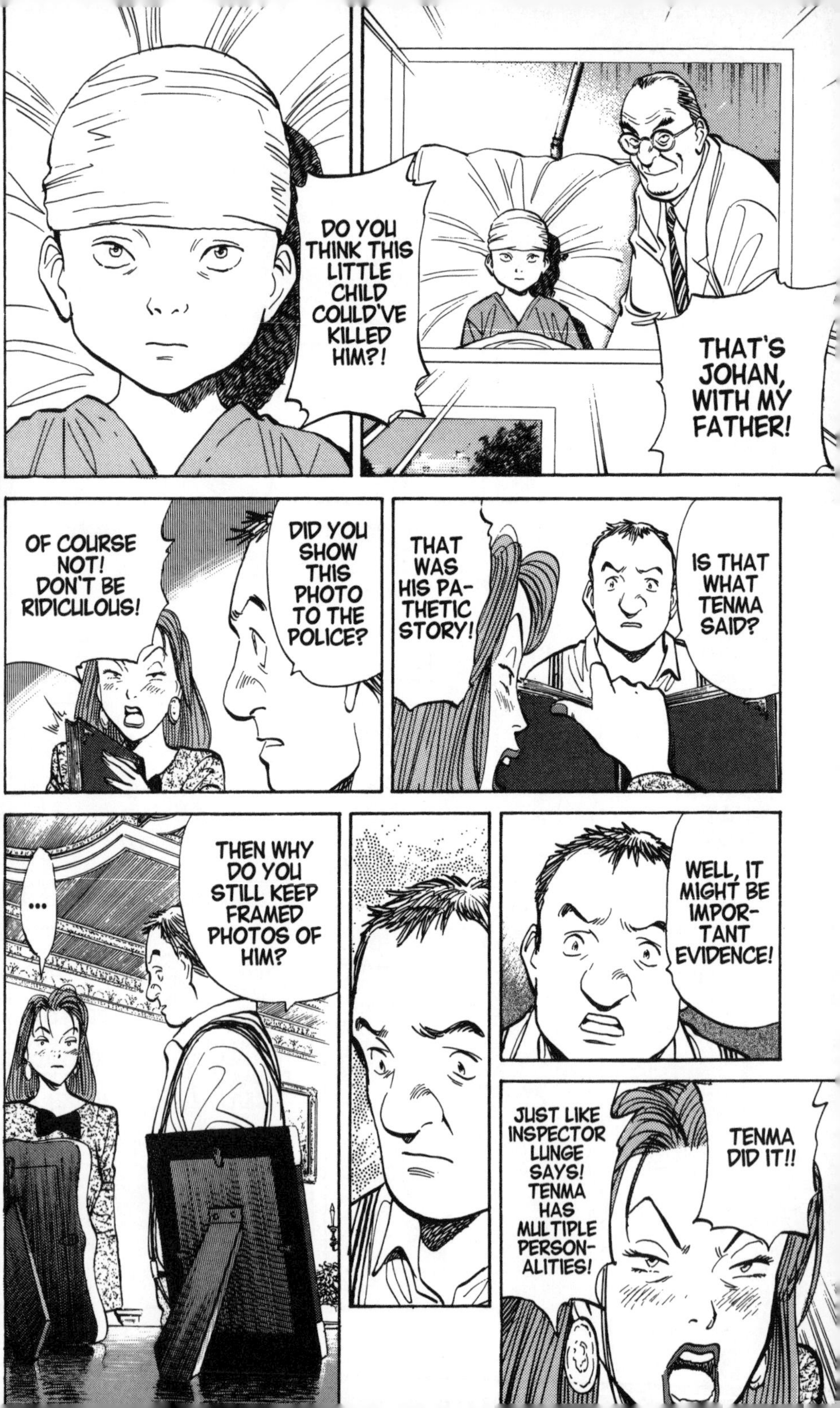
THAT'S JOHAN, WITH MY FATHER!
DO YOU THINK THIS LITTLE CHILD COULD'VE KILLED HIM?!
IS THAT WHAT TENMA SAID?
THAT WAS HIS PATHETIC STORY!
DID YOU SHOW THIS PHOTO TO THE POLICE?
OF COURSE NOT! DON'T BE RIDICULOUS!
WELL, IT MIGHT BE IMPORTANT EVIDENCE!
TENMA DID IT!!
JUST LIKE INSPECTOR LUNGE SAYS! TENMA HAS MULTIPLE PERSONALITIES!
THEN WHY DO YOU STILL KEEP FRAMED PHOTOS OF HIM?
...

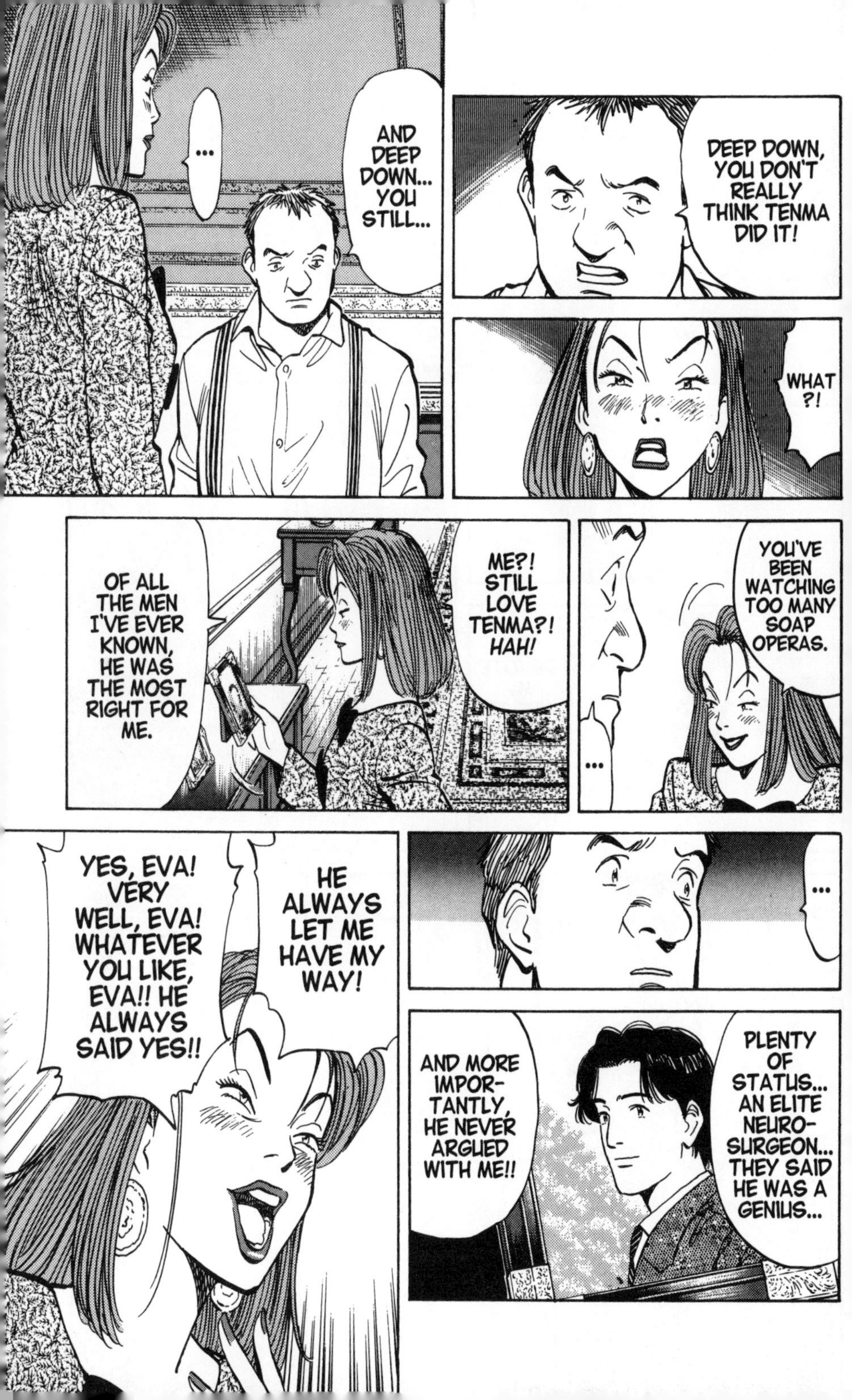
DEEP DOWN, YOU DON'T REALLY THINK TENMA DID IT!
WHAT?!
AND DEEP DOWN... YOU STILL...
...
YOU'VE BEEN WATCHING TOO MANY SOAP OPERAS.
...
ME?! STILL LOVE TENMA?! HAH!
OF ALL THE MEN I'VE EVER KNOWN, HE WAS THE MOST RIGHT FOR ME.
...
PLENTY OF STATUS... AN ELITE NEUROSURGEON... THEY SAID HE WAS A GENIUS...
AND MORE IMPORTANTLY, HE NEVER ARGUED WITH ME!!
HE ALWAYS LET ME HAVE MY WAY!
YES, EVA! VERY WELL, EVA! WHATEVER YOU LIKE, EVA!! HE ALWAYS SAID YES!!

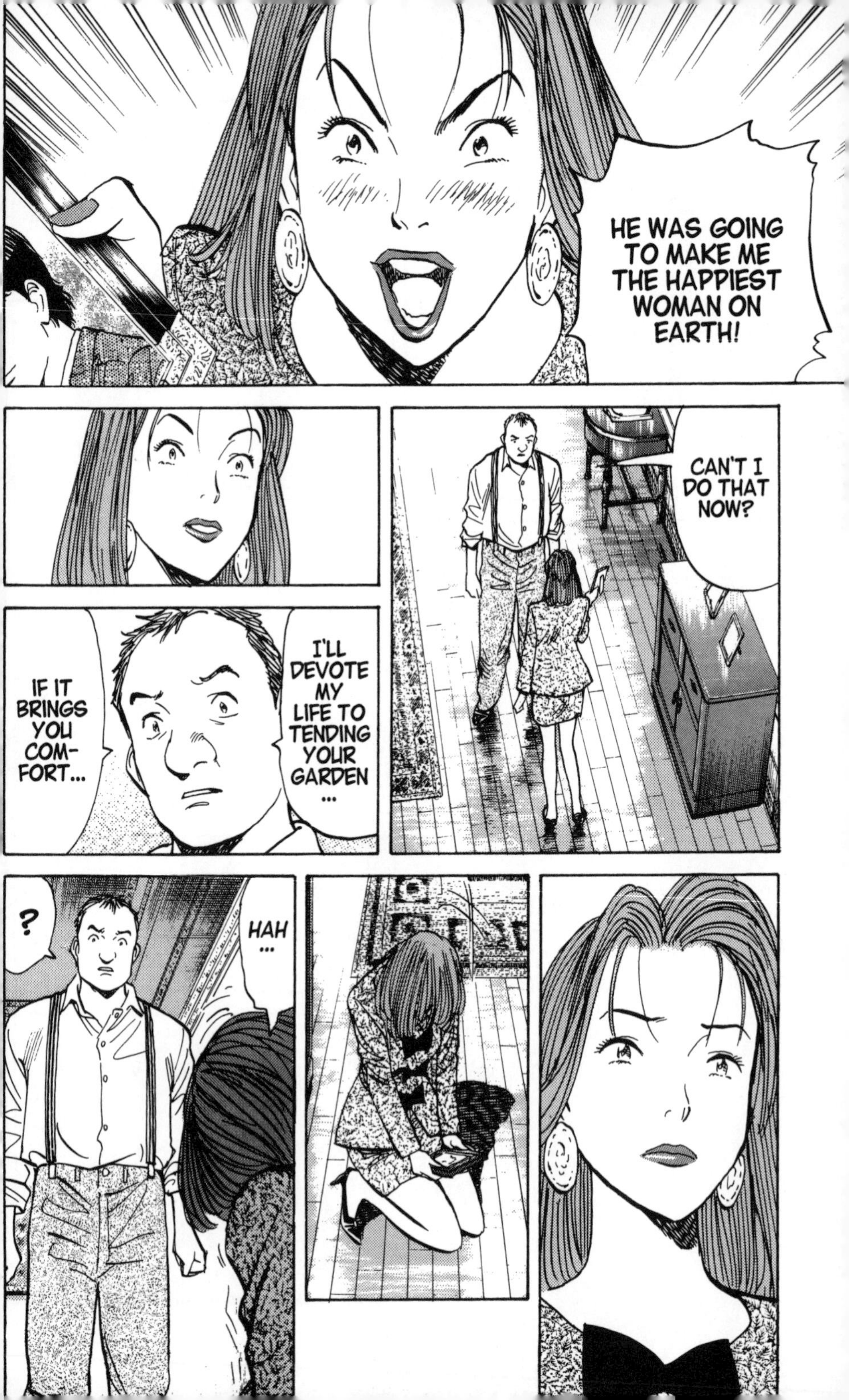
HE WAS GOING TO MAKE ME THE HAPPIEST WOMAN ON EARTH!
CAN'T I DO THAT NOW?
I'LL DEVOTE MY LIFE TO TENDING YOUR GARDEN ...
IF IT BRINGS YOU COM-FORT...
HAH ...
?

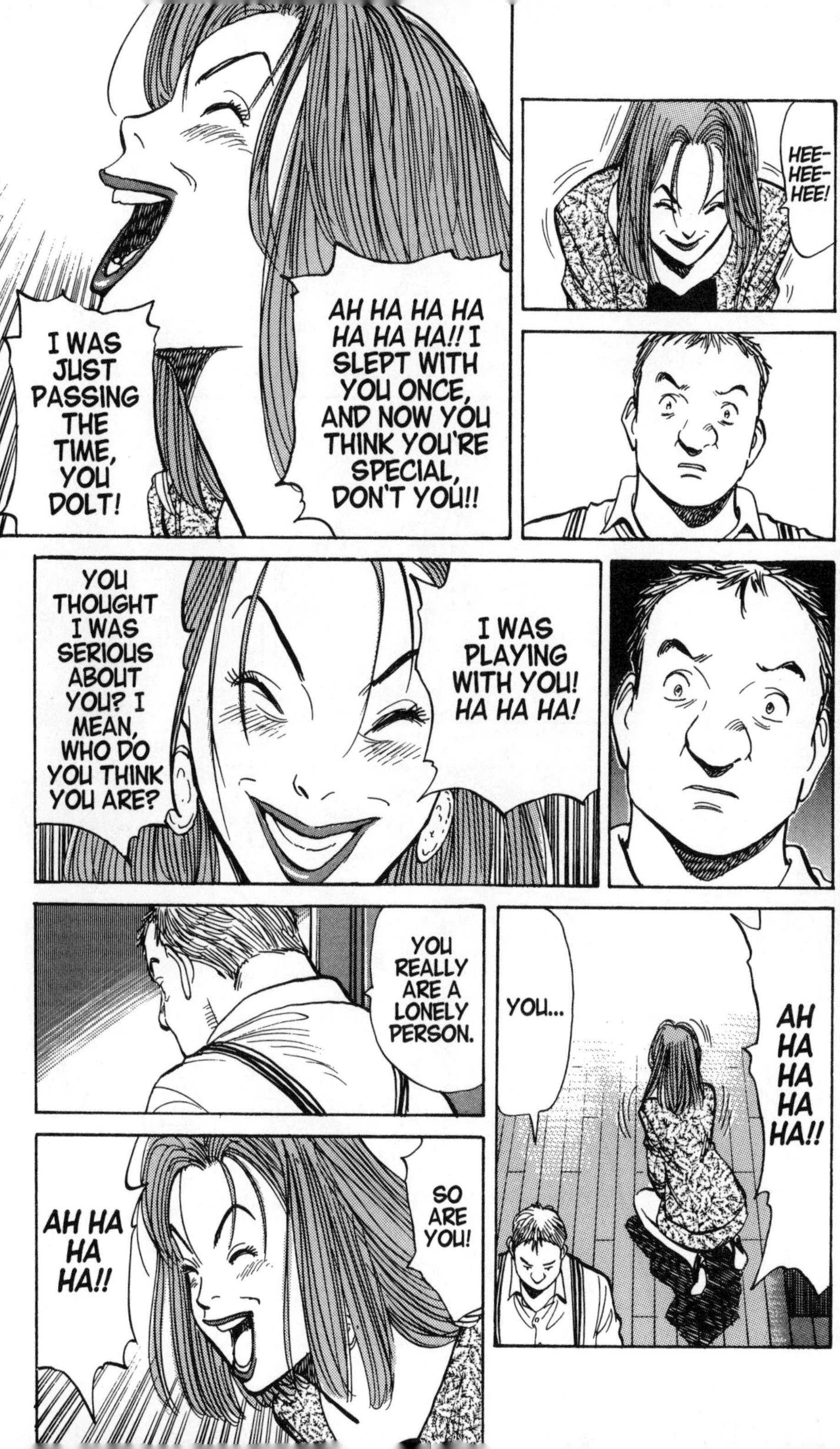
HEE-HEE-HEE!
AH HA HA HA HA HA HA!! I SLEPT WITH YOU ONCE, AND NOW YOU THINK YOU'RE SPECIAL, DON'T YOU!!
I WAS JUST PASSING THE TIME, YOU DOLT!
I WAS PLAYING WITH YOU! HA HA HA!
YOU THOUGHT I WAS SERIOUS ABOUT YOU? I MEAN, WHO DO YOU THINK YOU ARE?
AH HA HA HA HA!!
YOU...
YOU REALLY ARE A LONELY PERSON.
SO ARE YOU!
AH HA HA HA!!

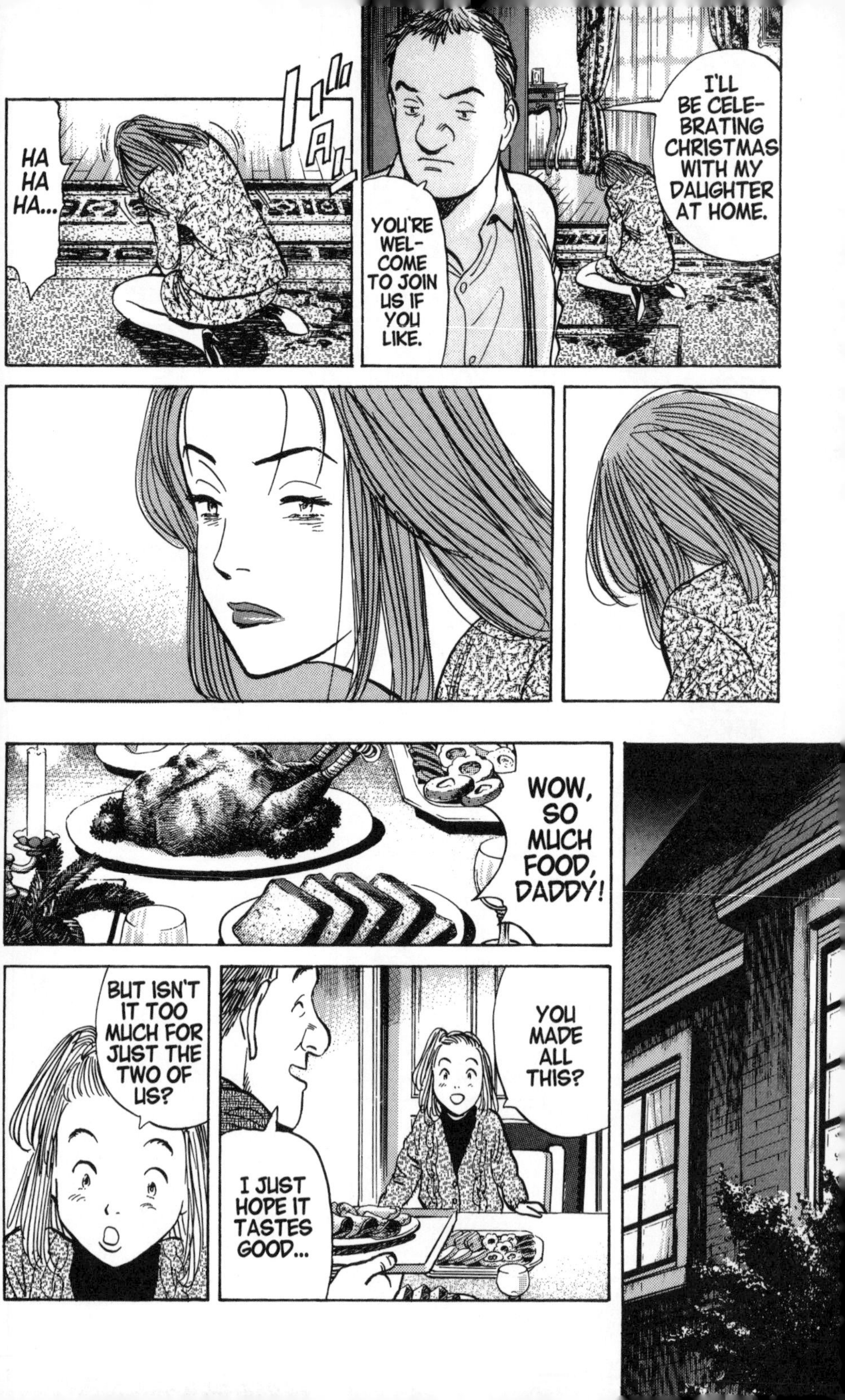
I'LL BE CELEBRATING CHRISTMAS WITH MY DAUGHTER AT HOME.
YOU'RE WELCOME TO JOIN US IF YOU LIKE.
HA HA HA...
WOW, SO MUCH FOOD, DADDY!
YOU MADE ALL THIS?
I JUST HOPE IT TASTES GOOD...
BUT ISN'T IT TOO MUCH FOR JUST THE TWO OF US?

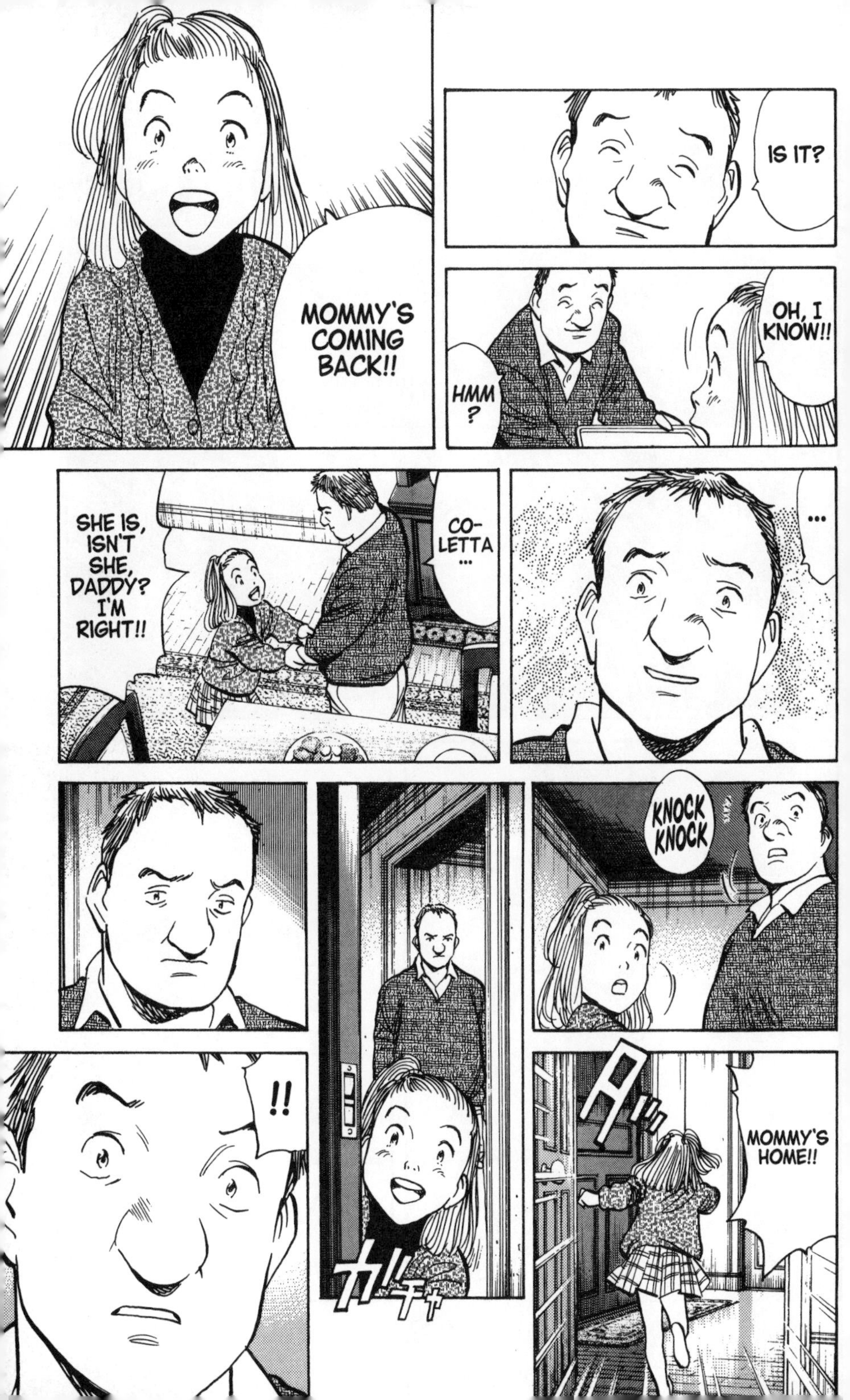

IS IT?
OH, I KNOW!!
HMM?
MOMMY'S COMING BACK!!
...
CO-LETTA...
SHE IS, ISN'T SHE, DADDY? I'M RIGHT!!
KNOCK KNOCK
ダッ
MOMMY'S HOME!!
ガチャ
!!

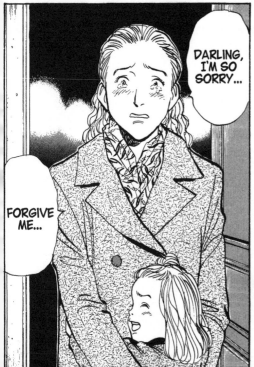

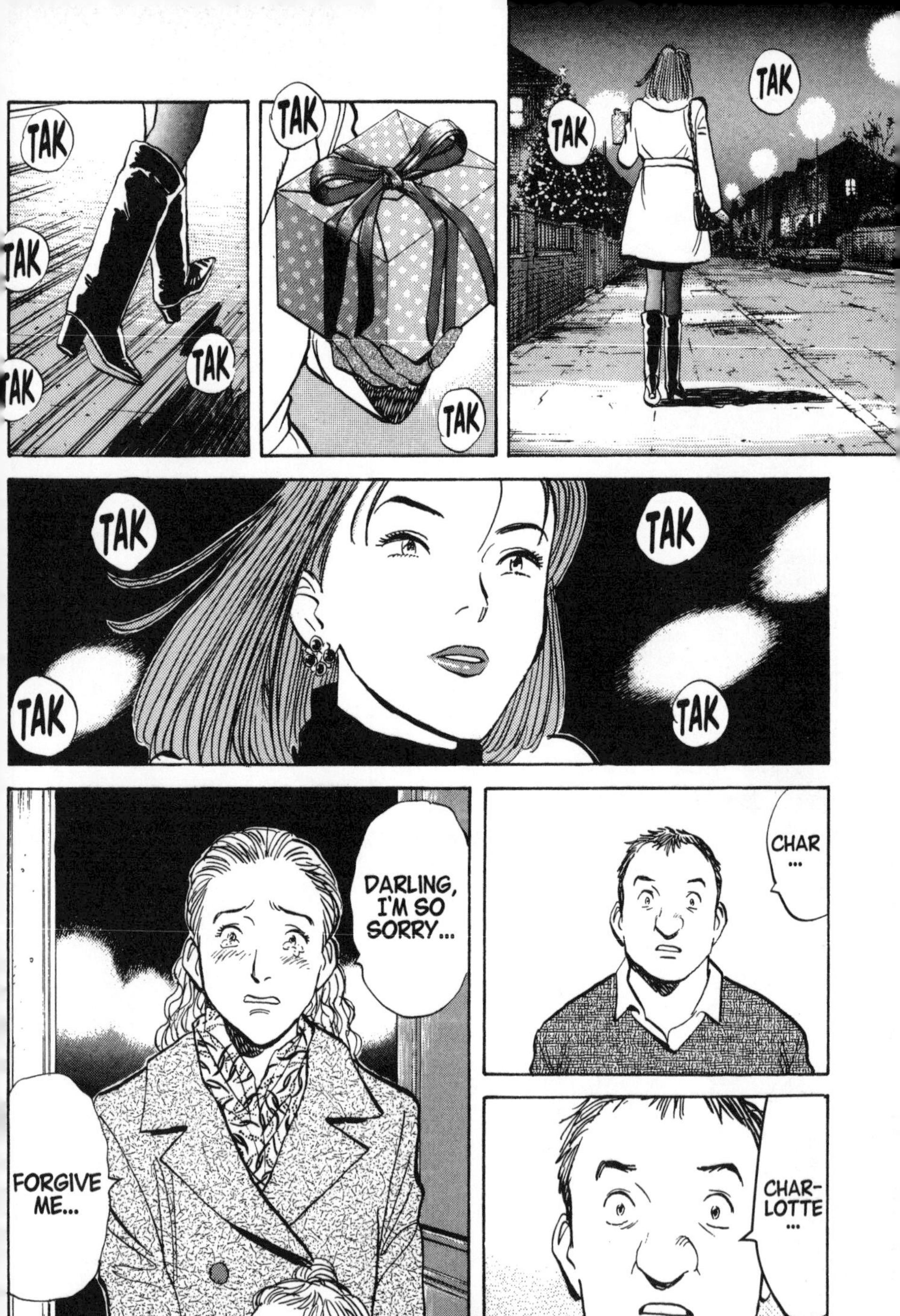
TAK
TAK
TAK
TAK
TAK
TAK
TAK
TAK
TAK
TAK
TAK
TAK
CHAR...
CHAR-LOTTE...
DARLING, I'M SO SORRY...
FORGIVE ME...

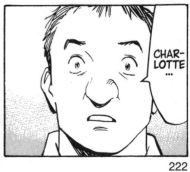

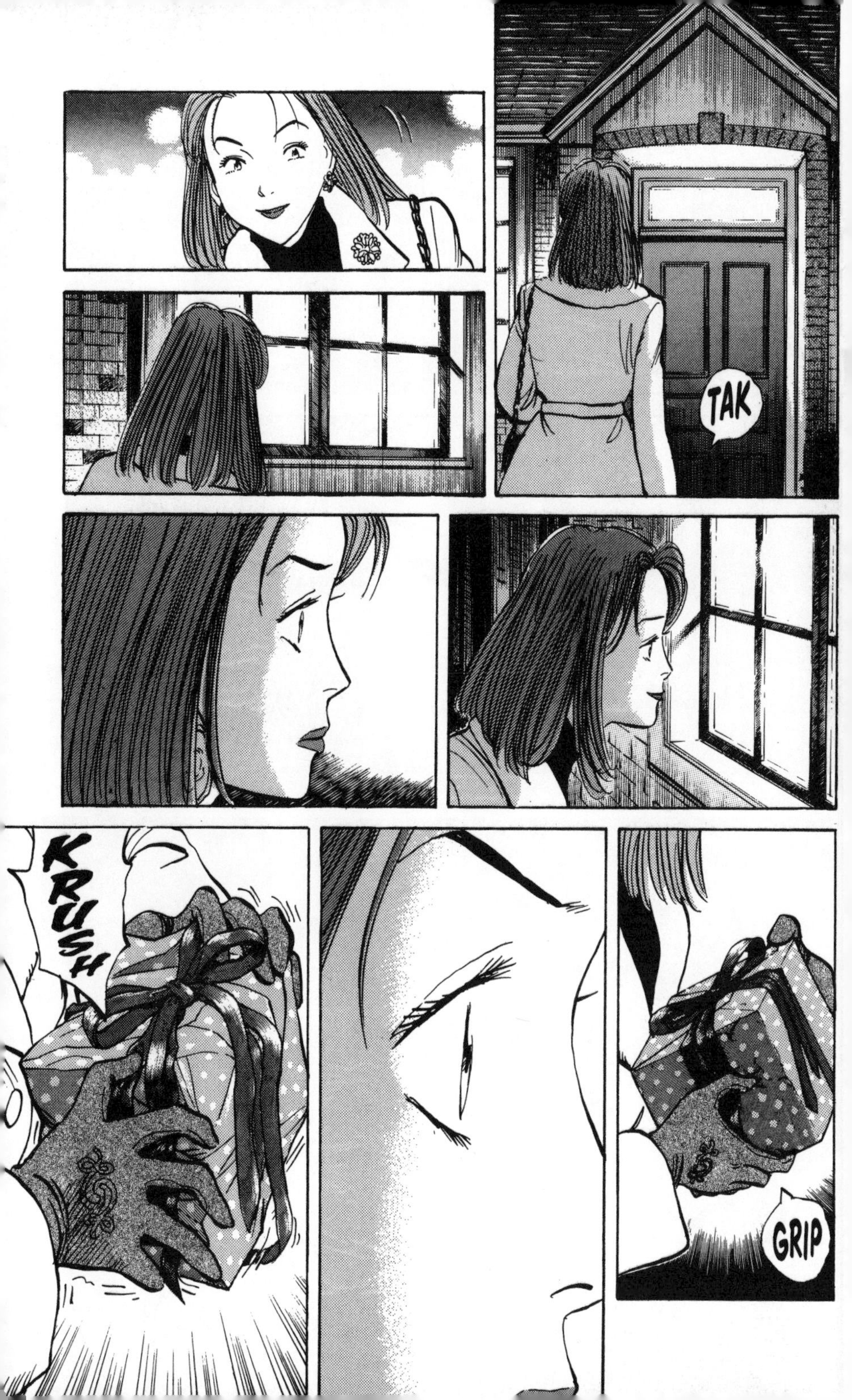
TAK
GRIP
KRUSH

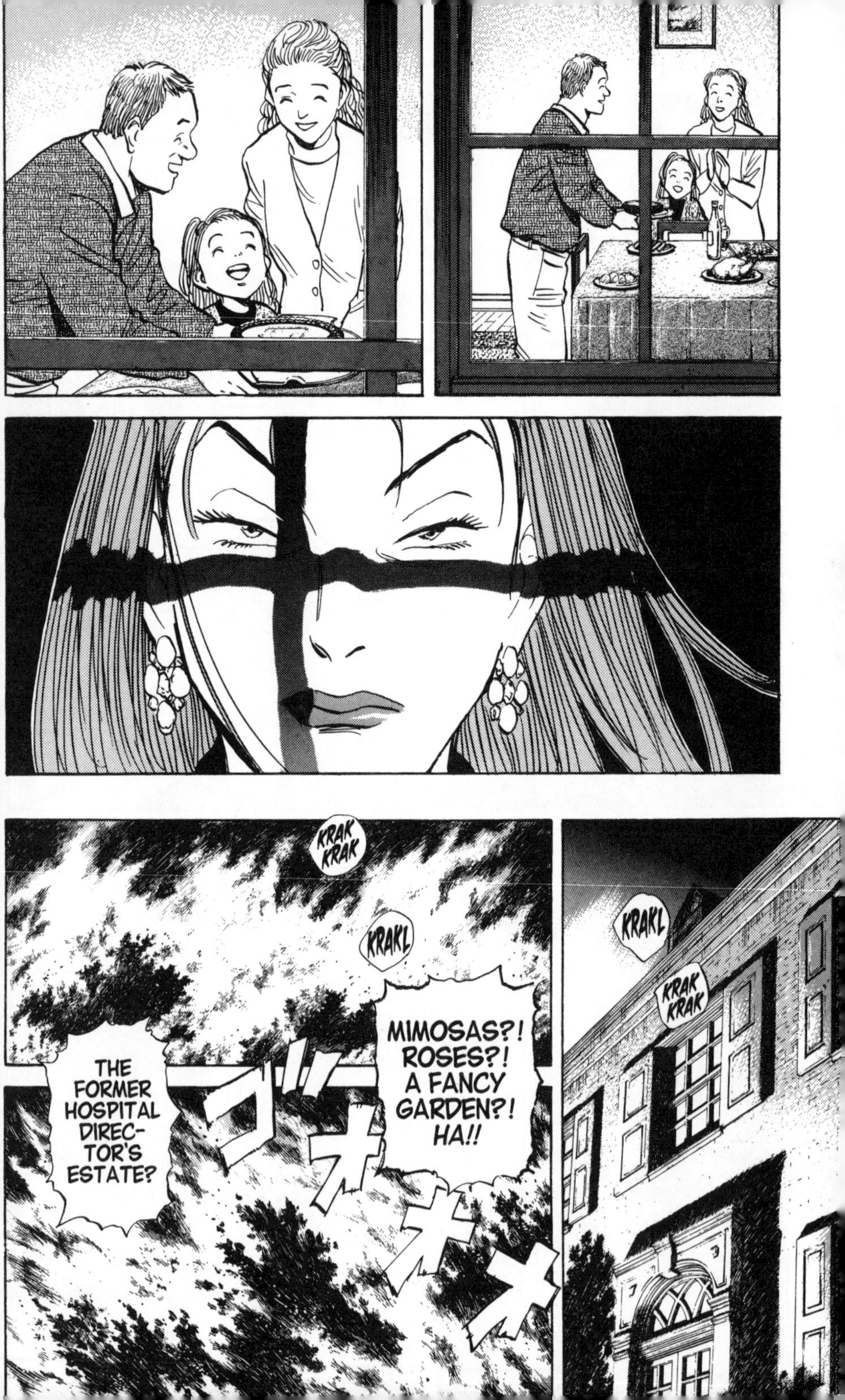
KRAKL
KRAK KRAK
KRAK KRAK
KRAKL
MIMOSAS?! ROSES?! A FANCY GARDEN?! HA!!
THE FORMER HOSPITAL DIREC-TOR'S ESTATE?

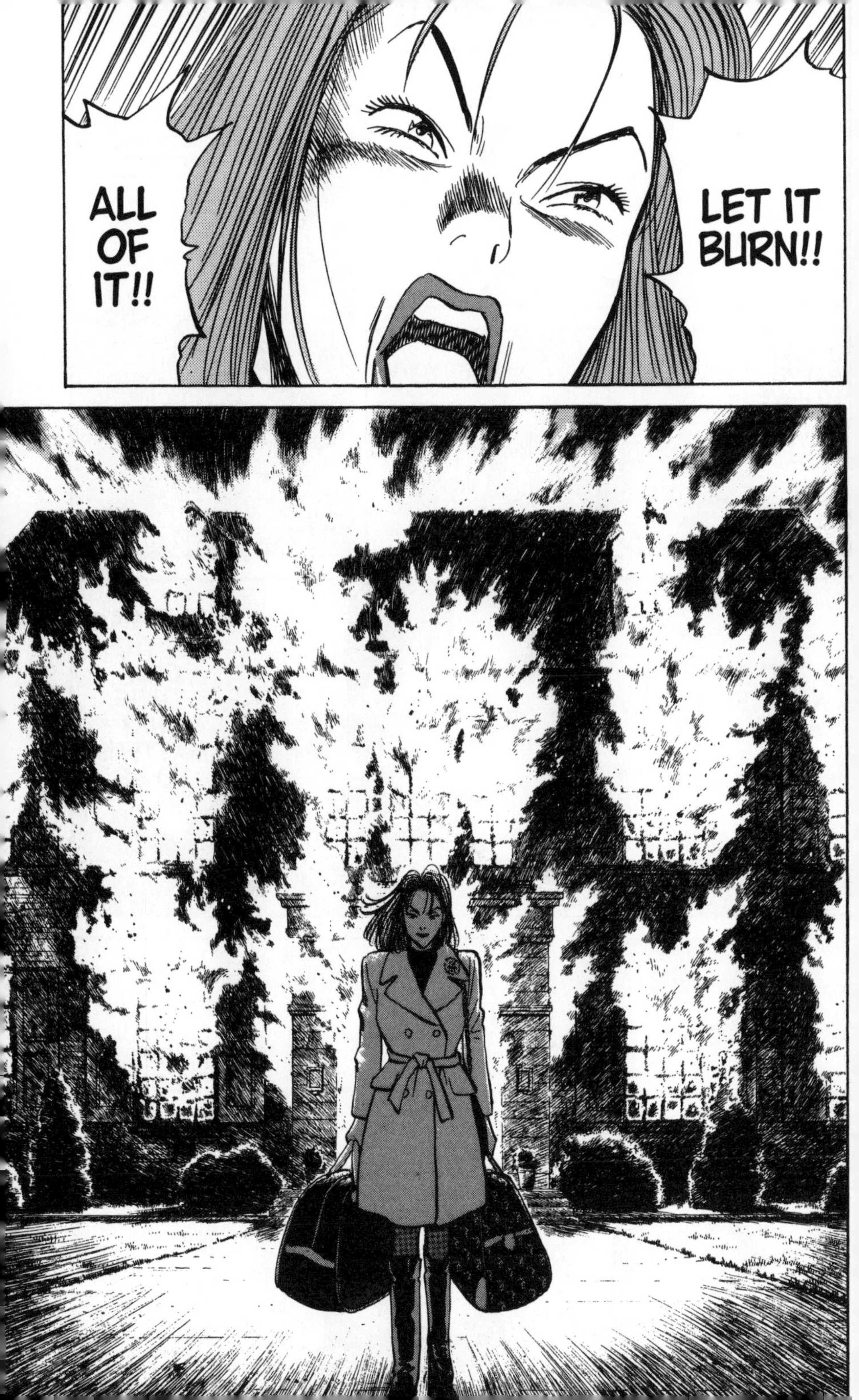
LET IT BURN!!
ALL OF IT!!

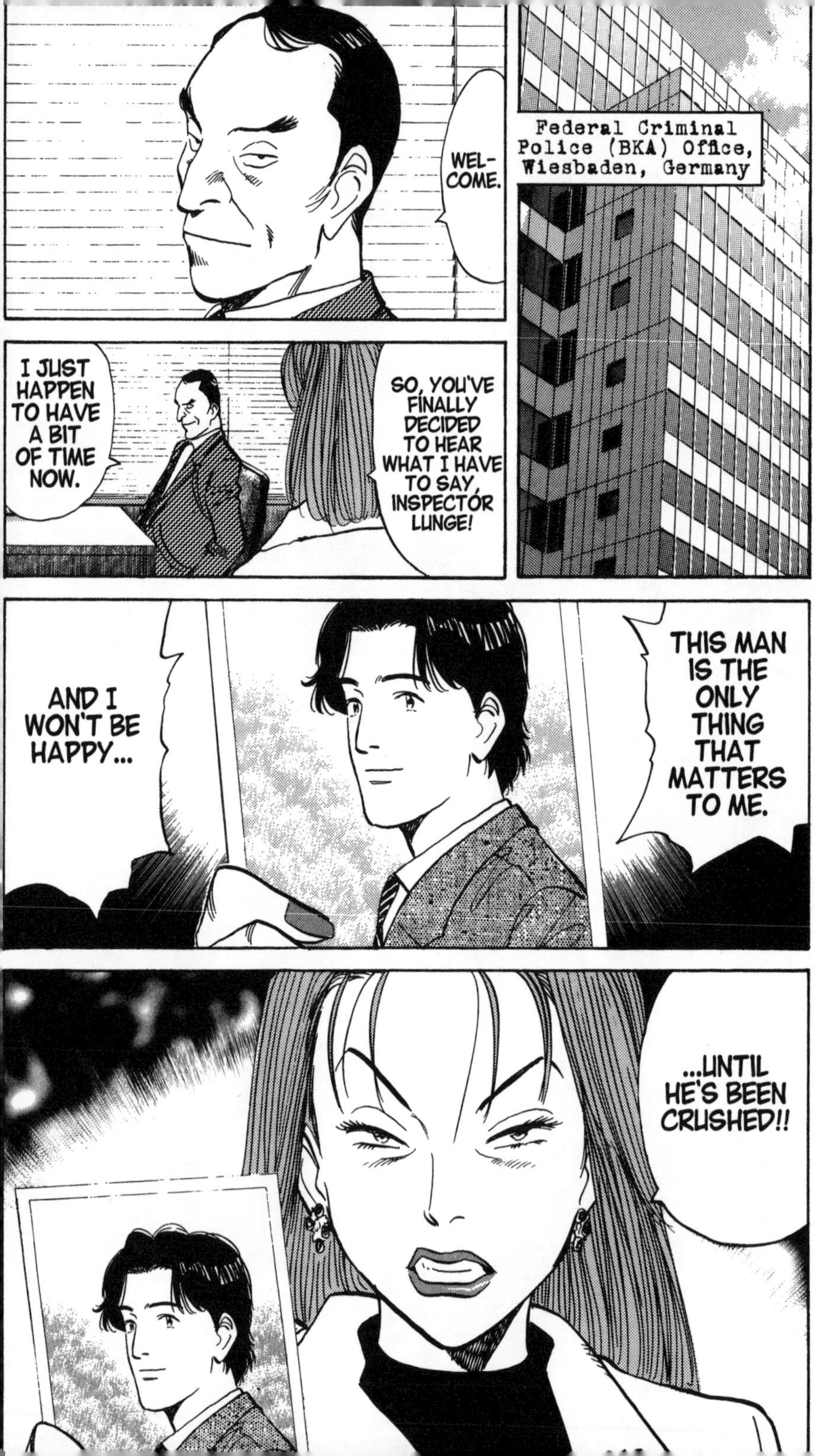
Federal Criminal Police (BKA) Office, Wiesbaden, Germany
WEL-COME.
SO, YOU'VE FINALLY DECIDED TO HEAR WHAT I HAVE TO SAY, INSPECTOR LUNGE!
I JUST HAPPEN TO HAVE A BIT OF TIME NOW.
THIS MAN IS THE ONLY THING THAT MATTERS TO ME.
AND I WON'T BE HAPPY...
...UNTIL HE'S BEEN CRUSHED!!

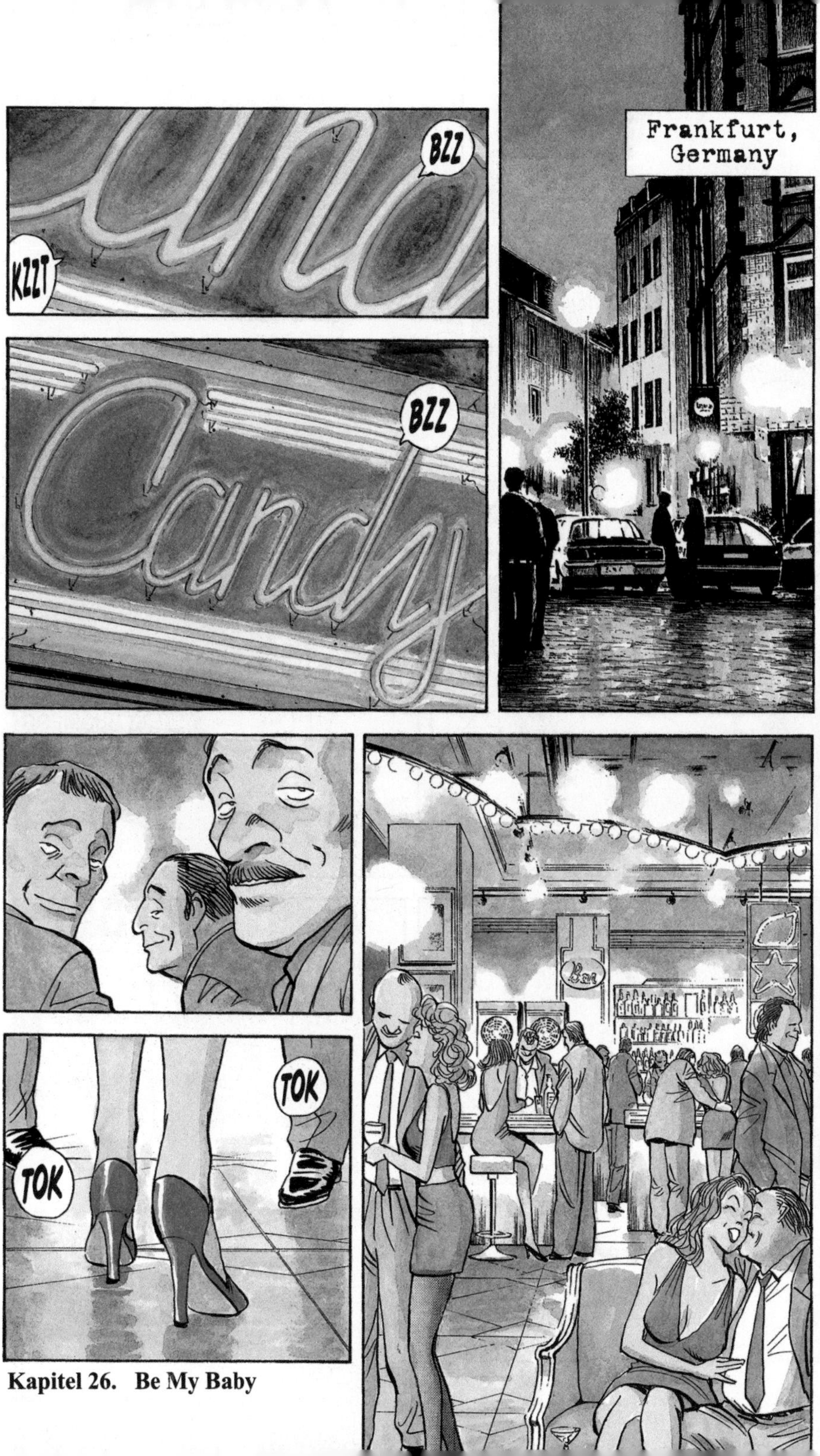
Frankfurt, Germany
BZZ
KZZT
BZZ
Bar
TOK
TOK

Kapitel 26. Be My Baby

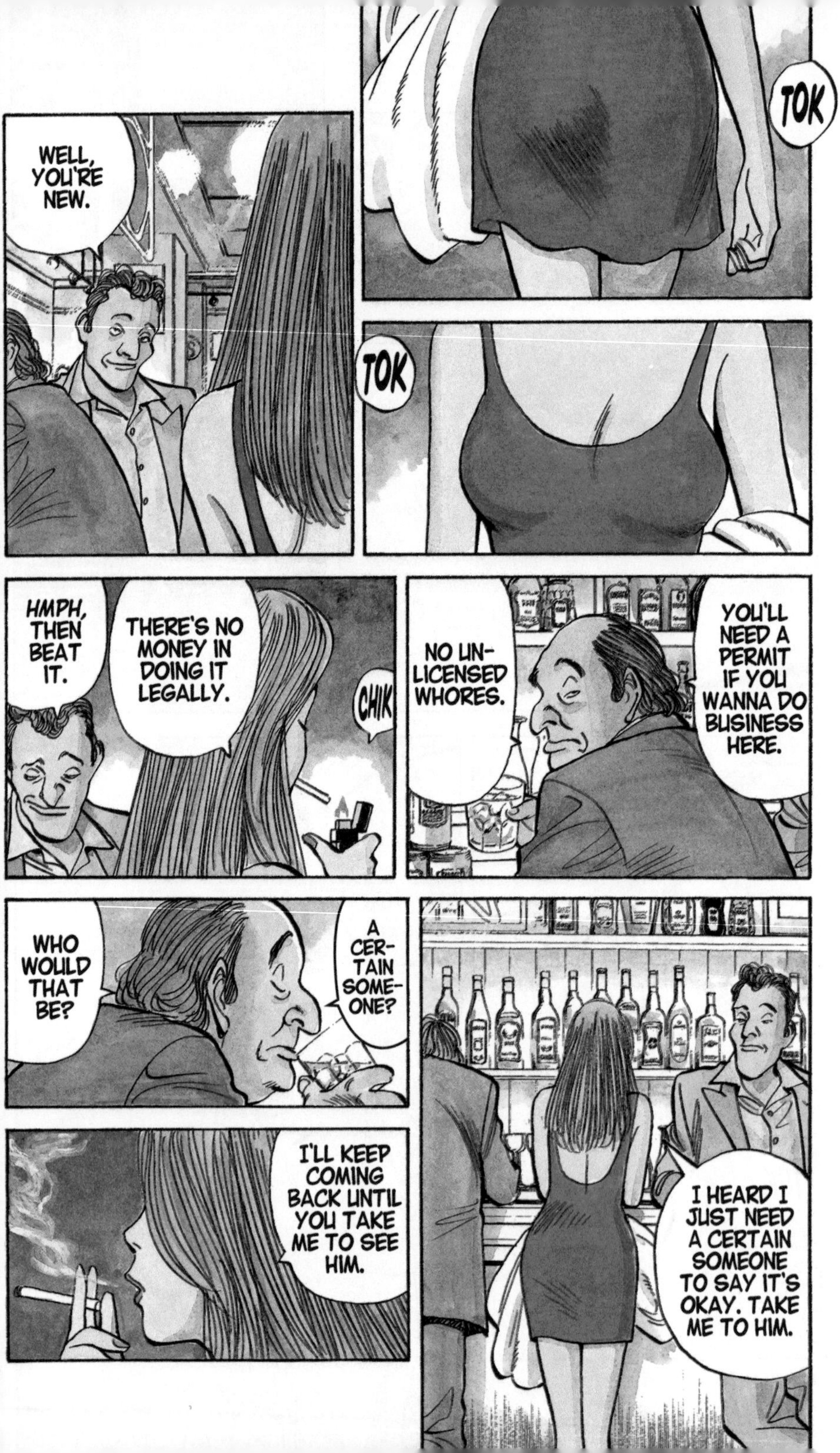
TOK
TOK
WELL, YOU'RE NEW.
YOU'LL NEED A PERMIT IF YOU WANNA DO BUSINESS HERE.
NO UNLICENSED WHORES.
CHIK
THERE'S NO MONEY IN DOING IT LEGALLY.
HMPH, THEN BEAT IT.
I HEARD I JUST NEED A CERTAIN SOMEONE TO SAY IT'S OKAY. TAKE ME TO HIM.
A CERTAIN SOMEONE?
WHO WOULD THAT BE?
I'LL KEEP COMING BACK UNTIL YOU TAKE ME TO SEE HIM.

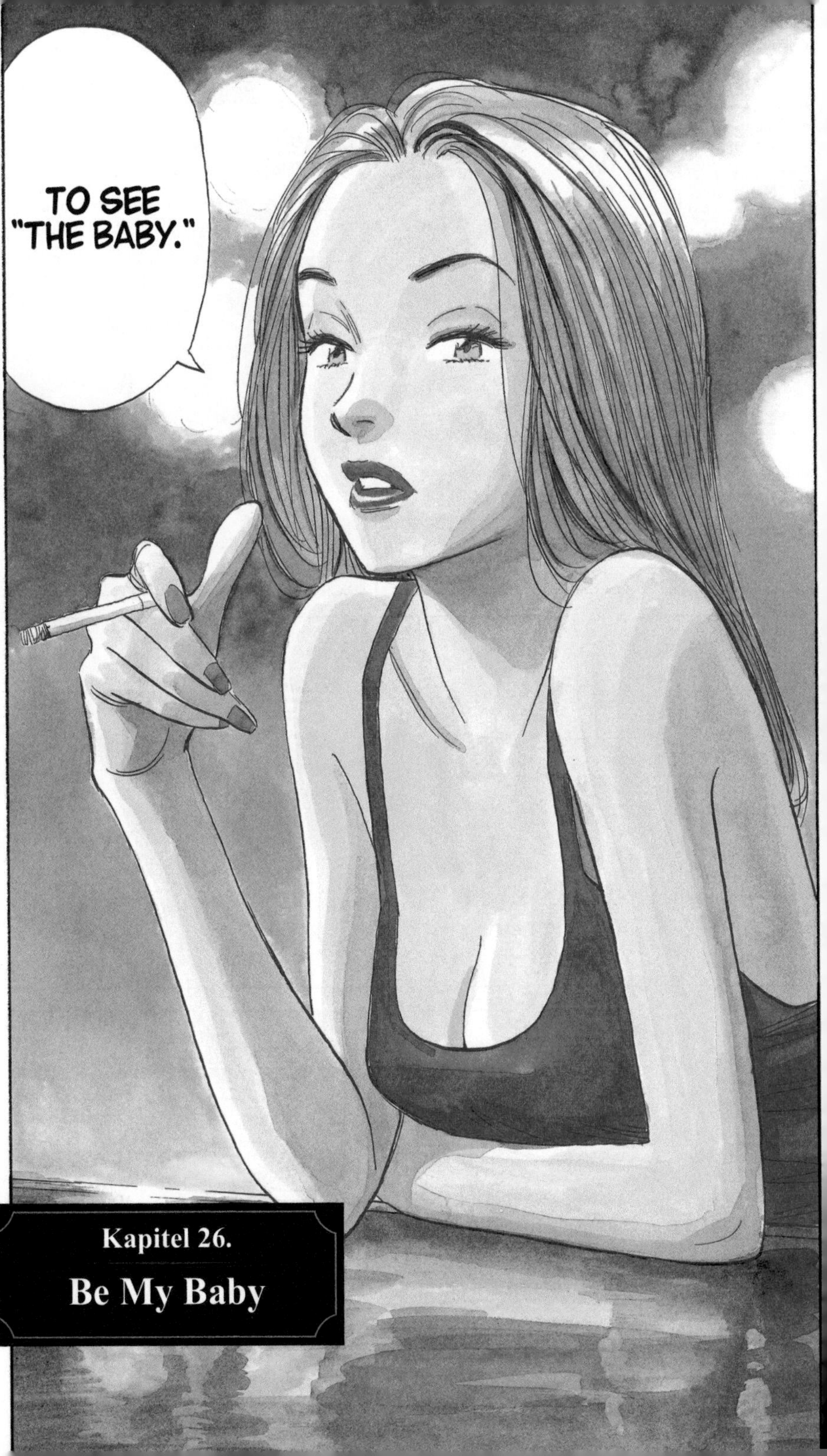
TO SEE "THE BABY."
Kapitel 26.
Be My Baby

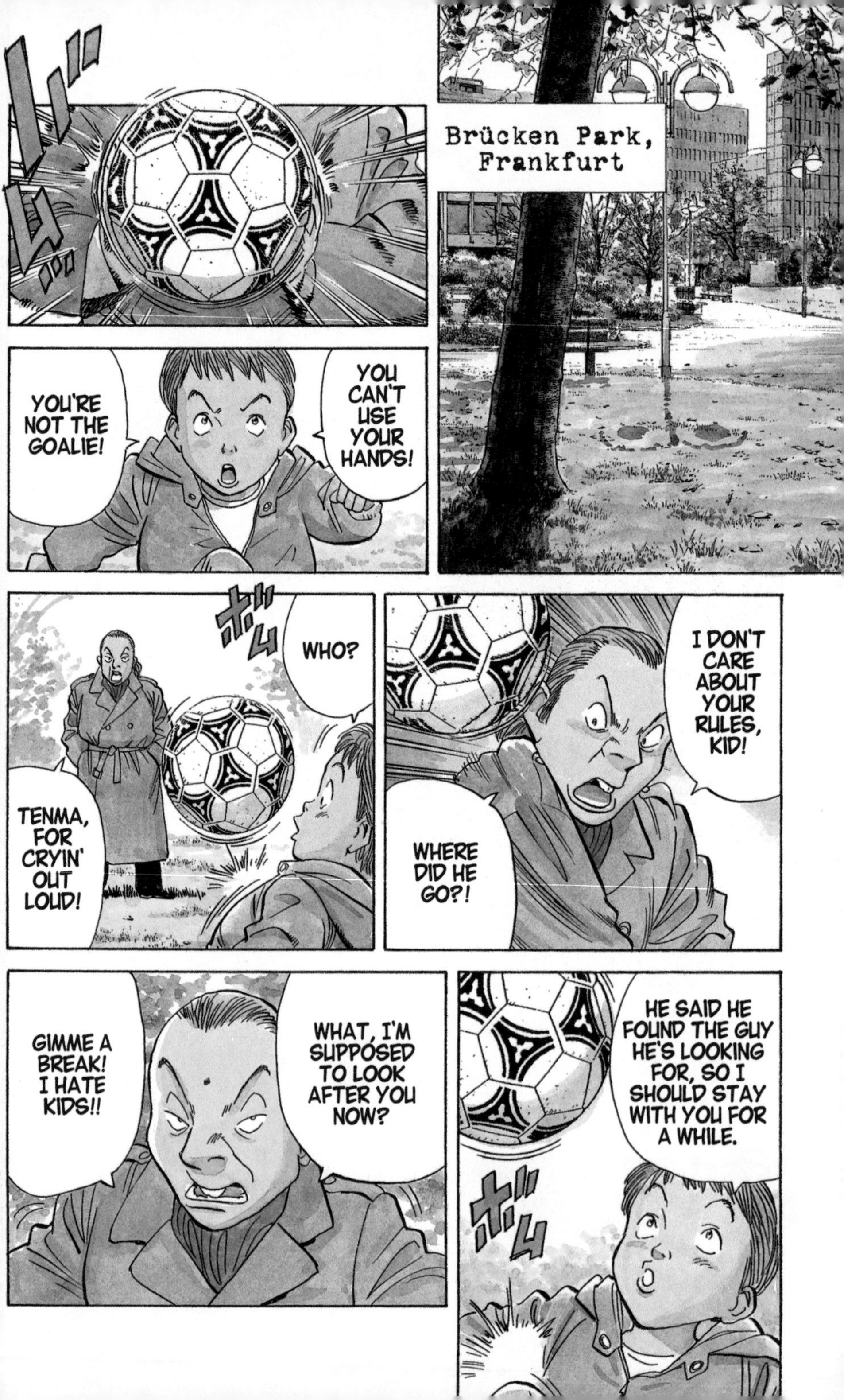
Brücken Park, Frankfurt
YOU CAN'T USE YOUR HANDS!
YOU'RE NOT THE GOALIE!
I DON'T CARE ABOUT YOUR RULES, KID!
WHERE DID HE GO?!
WHO?
TENMA, FOR CRYIN' OUT LOUD!
HE SAID HE FOUND THE GUY HE'S LOOKING FOR, SO I SHOULD STAY WITH YOU FOR A WHILE.
WHAT, I'M SUPPOSED TO LOOK AFTER YOU NOW?
GIMME A BREAK! I HATE KIDS!!

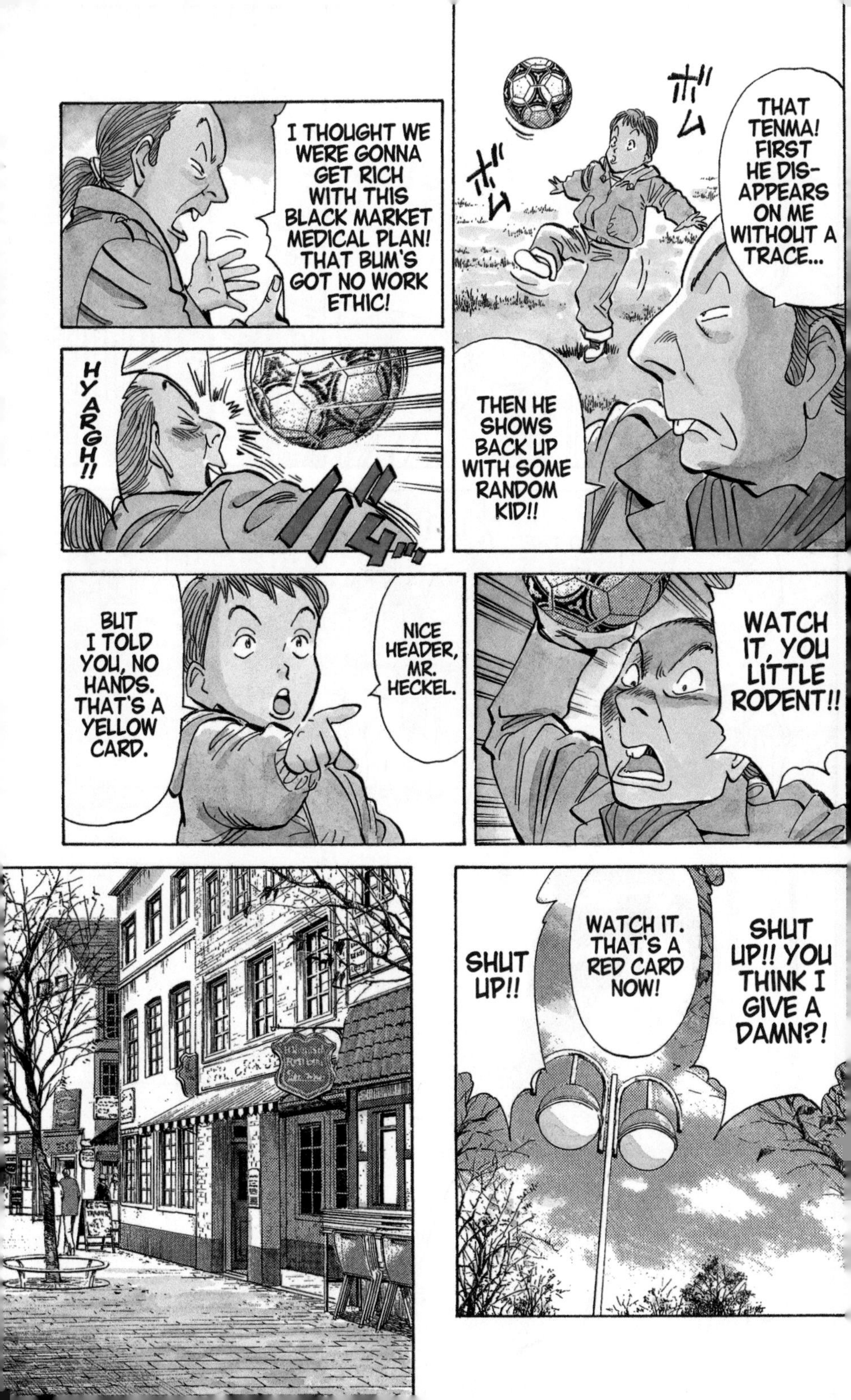
ボム
ボム
THAT TENMA! FIRST HE DIS-APPEARS ON ME WITHOUT A TRACE...
THEN HE SHOWS BACK UP WITH SOME RANDOM KID!!
I THOUGHT WE WERE GONNA GET RICH WITH THIS BLACK MARKET MEDICAL PLAN! THAT BUM'S GOT NO WORK ETHIC!
HYARGH!!
バム
WATCH IT, YOU LITTLE RODENT!!
NICE HEADER, MR. HECKEL.
BUT I TOLD YOU, NO HANDS. THAT'S A YELLOW CARD.
SHUT UP!! YOU THINK I GIVE A DAMN?!
WATCH IT. THAT'S A RED CARD NOW!
SHUT UP!!

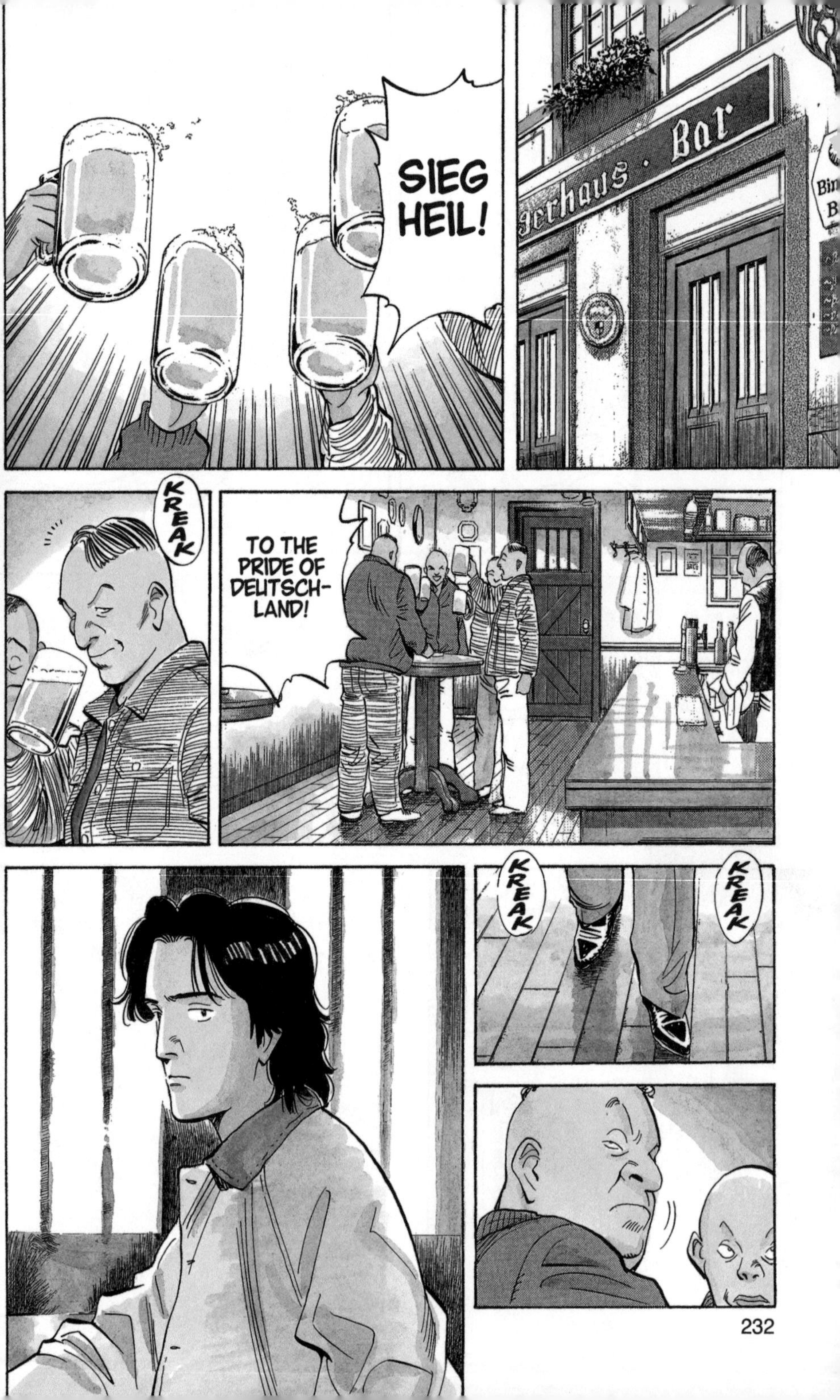
Bar
SIEG HEIL!
TO THE PRIDE OF DEUTSCHLAND!
KREAK
KREAK
KREAK

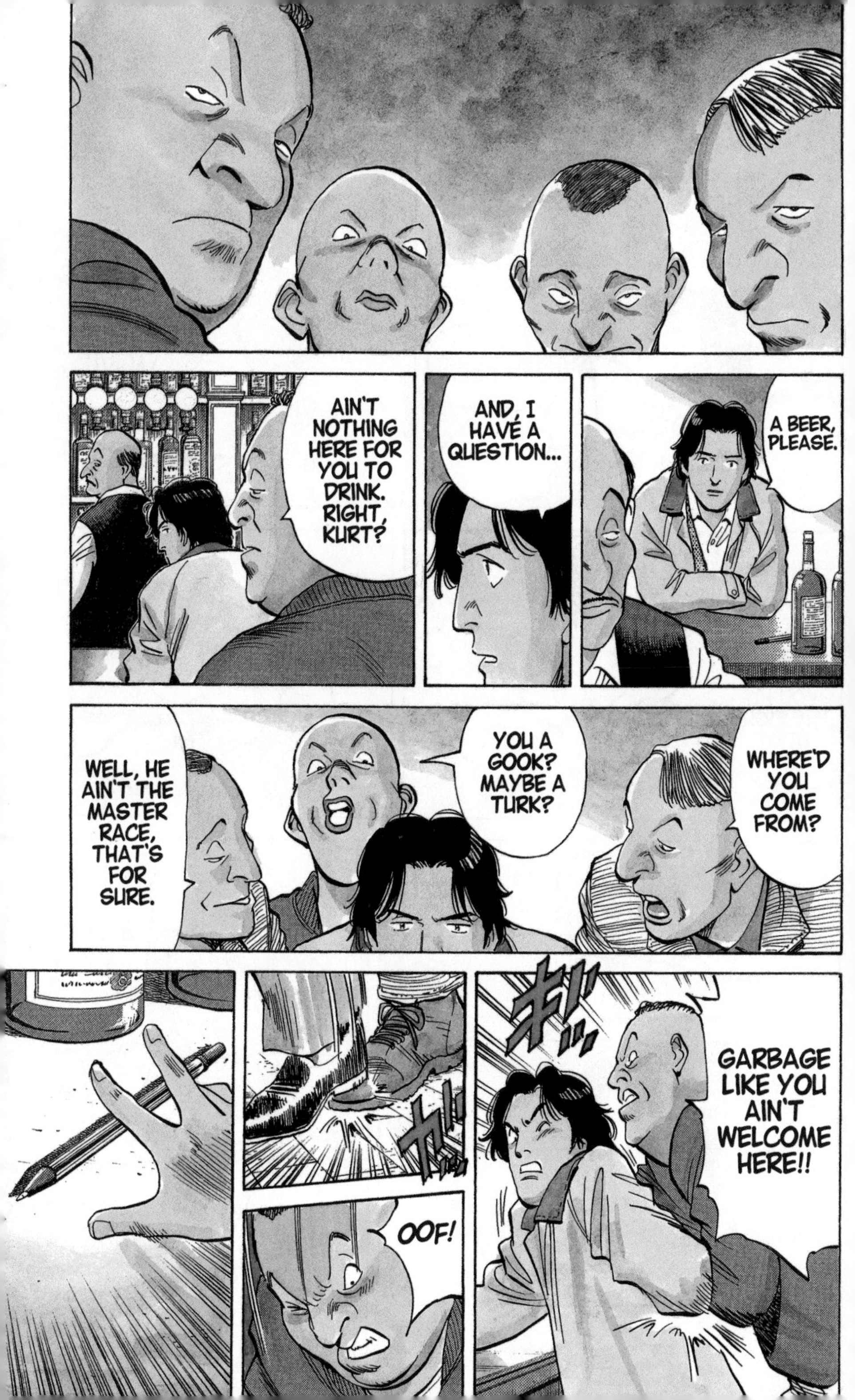
A BEER, PLEASE.
AND, I HAVE A QUESTION...
AIN'T NOTHING HERE FOR YOU TO DRINK. RIGHT, KURT?
WHERE'D YOU COME FROM?
YOU A GOOK? MAYBE A TURK?
WELL, HE AIN'T THE MASTER RACE, THAT'S FOR SURE.
GARBAGE LIKE YOU AIN'T WELCOME HERE!!
OOF!

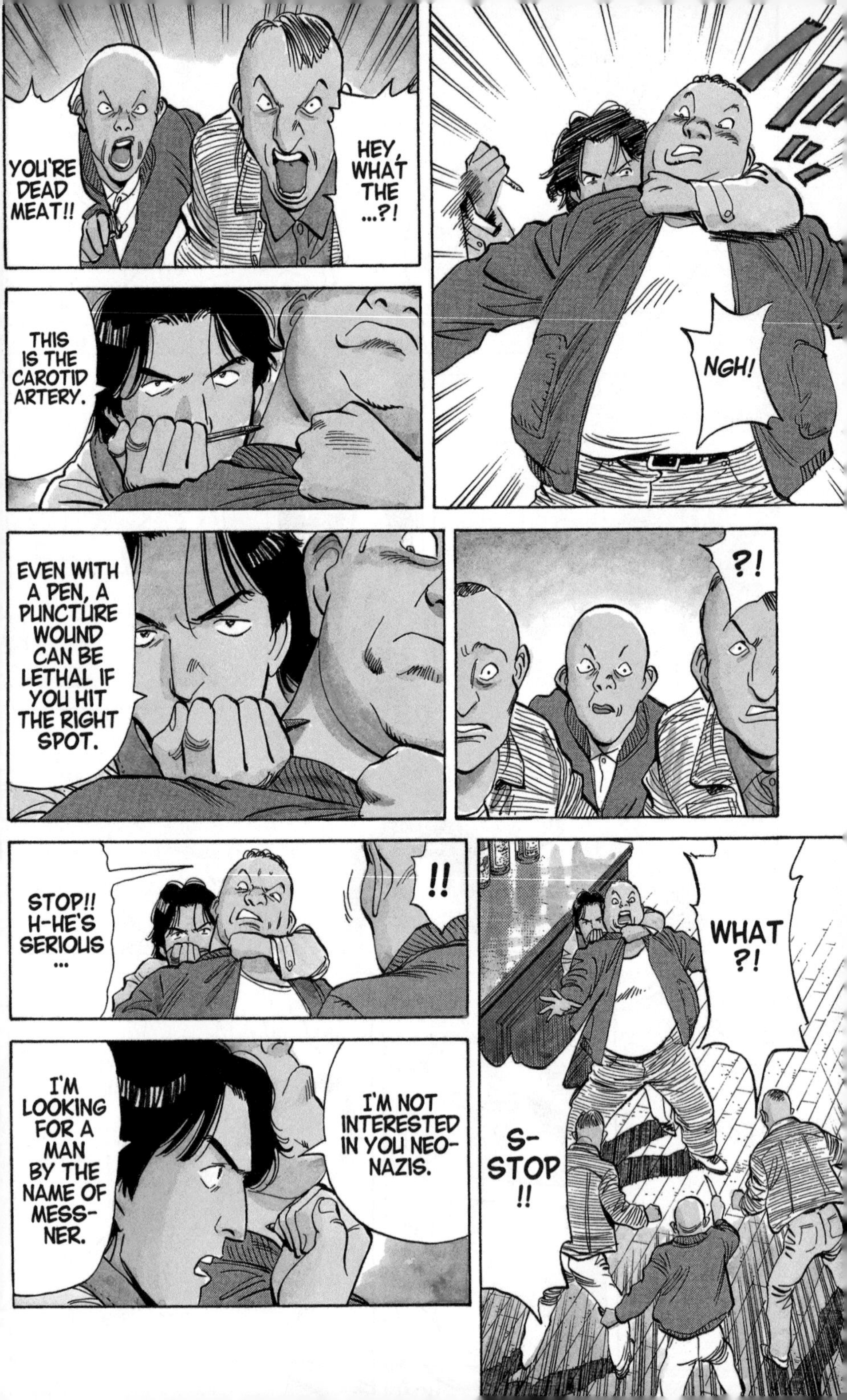
NGH!
HEY, WHAT THE ...?!
YOU'RE DEAD MEAT!!
THIS IS THE CAROTID ARTERY.
?!
EVEN WITH A PEN, A PUNCTURE WOUND CAN BE LETHAL IF YOU HIT THE RIGHT SPOT.
WHAT?!
S-STOP!!
!!
STOP!! H-HE'S SERIOUS...
I'M NOT INTERESTED IN YOU NEO-NAZIS.
I'M LOOKING FOR A MAN BY THE NAME OF MESSNER.

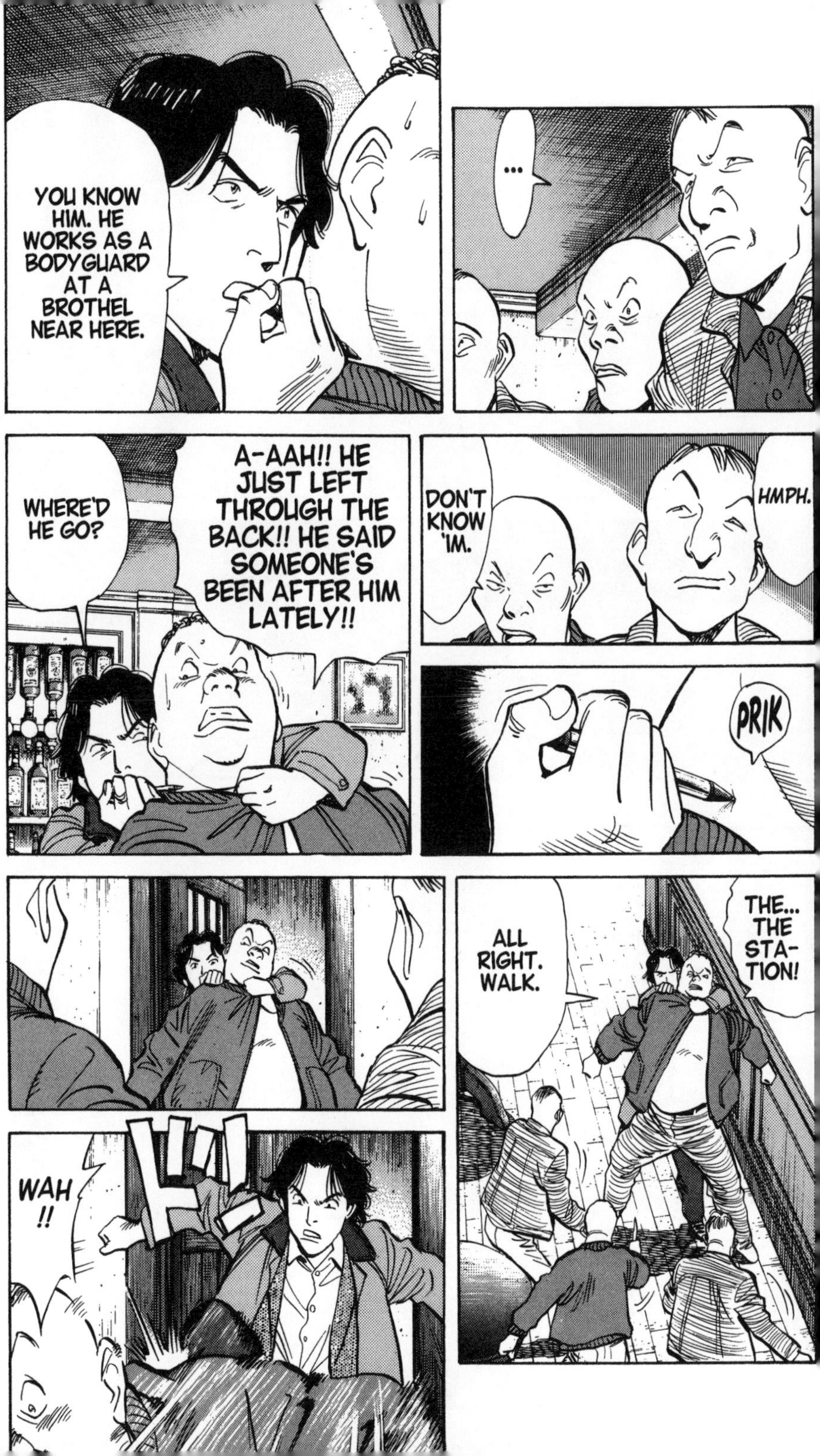
...
YOU KNOW HIM. HE WORKS AS A BODYGUARD AT A BROTHEL NEAR HERE.
HMPH.
DON'T KNOW 'IM.
PRIK
A-AAH!! HE JUST LEFT THROUGH THE BACK!! HE SAID SOMEONE'S BEEN AFTER HIM LATELY!!
WHERE'D HE GO?
THE... THE STA-TION!
ALL RIGHT. WALK.
WAH !!

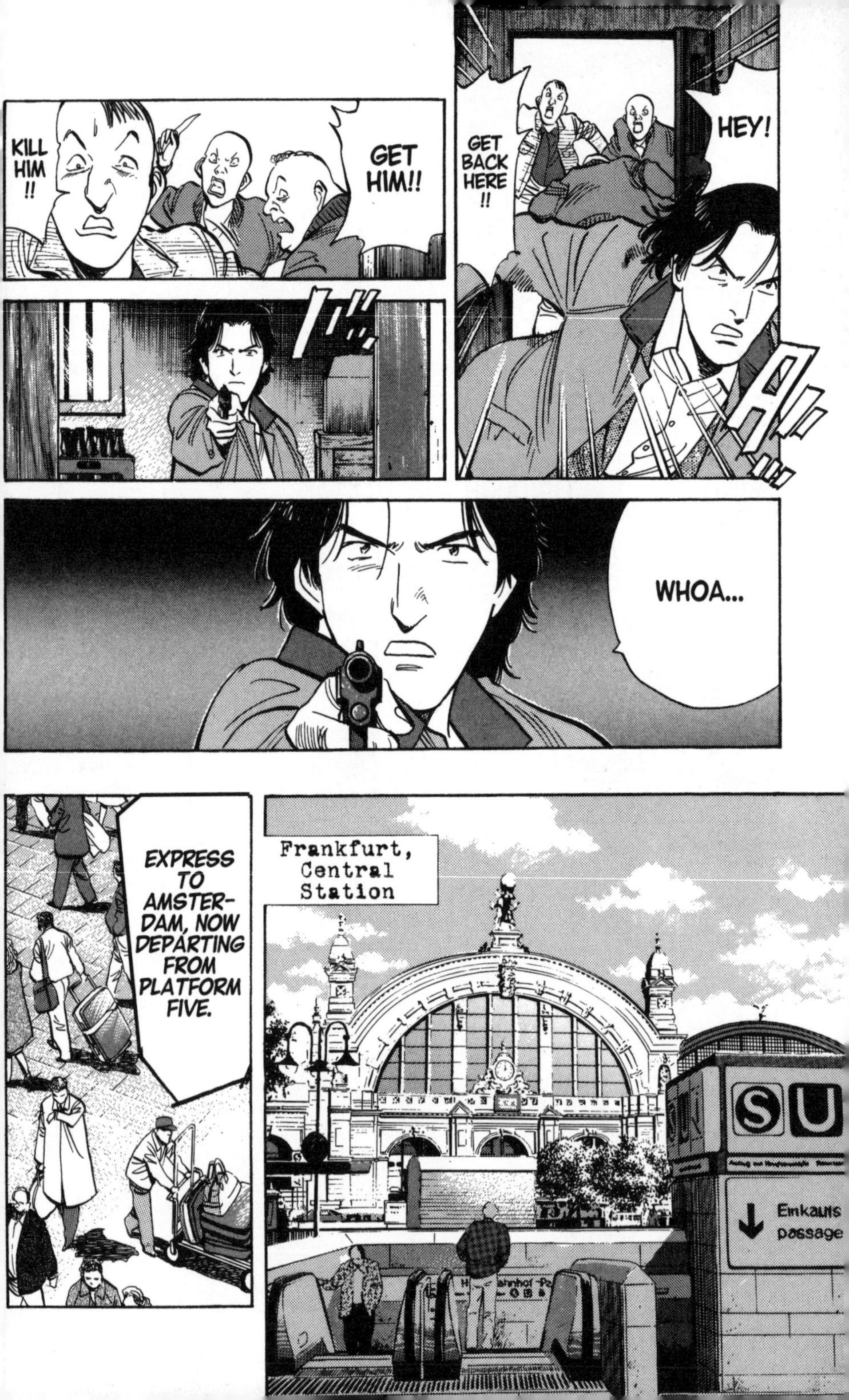
HEY!
GET BACK HERE !!
GET HIM!!
KILL HIM !!
WHOA...
Frankfurt, Central Station
S U
Einkaufs passage
EXPRESS TO AMSTER-DAM, NOW DEPARTING FROM PLATFORM FIVE.

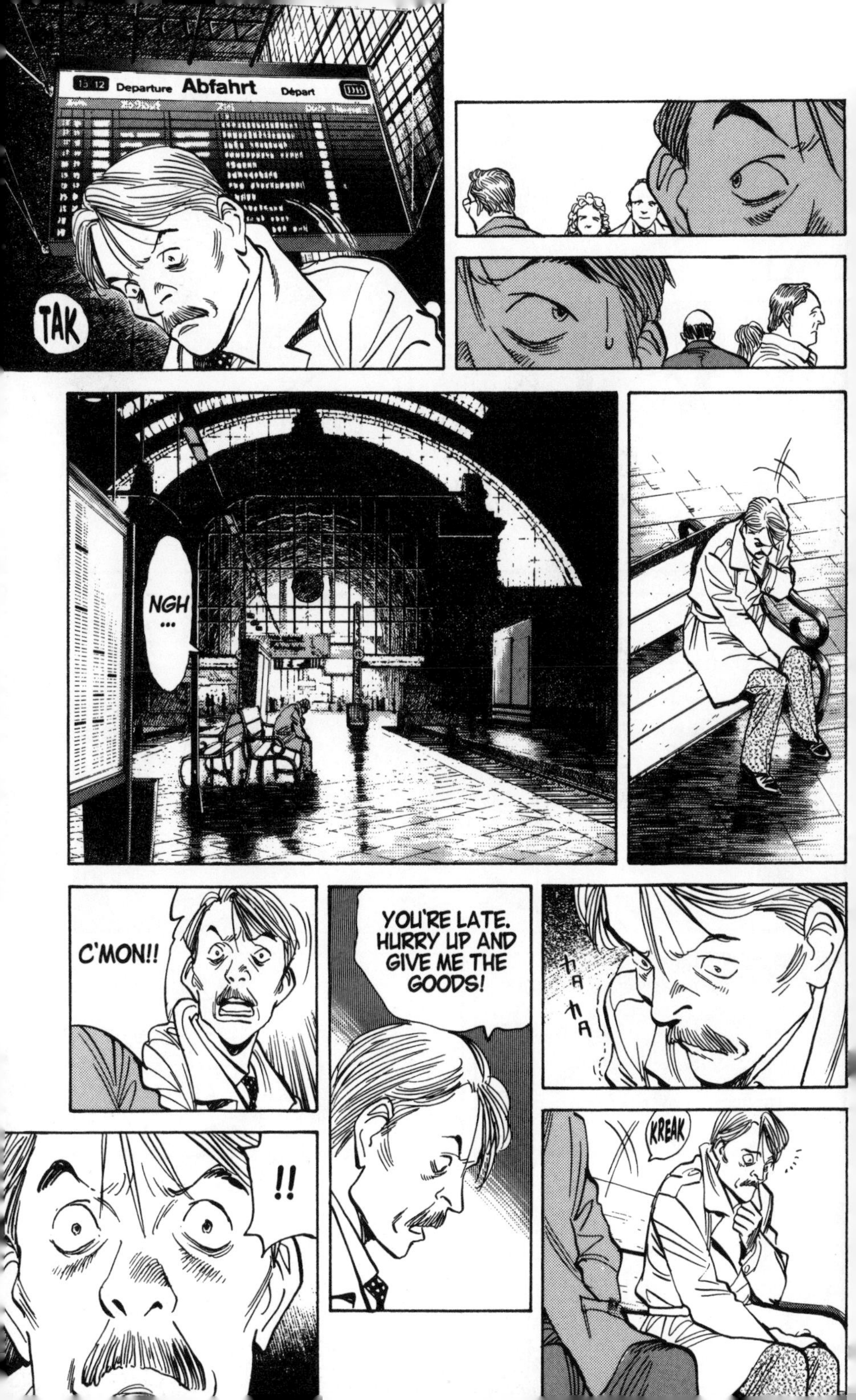
Departure Abfahrt Départ
TAK
NGH ...
KREAK
YOU'RE LATE. HURRY UP AND GIVE ME THE GOODS!
C'MON!!
!!

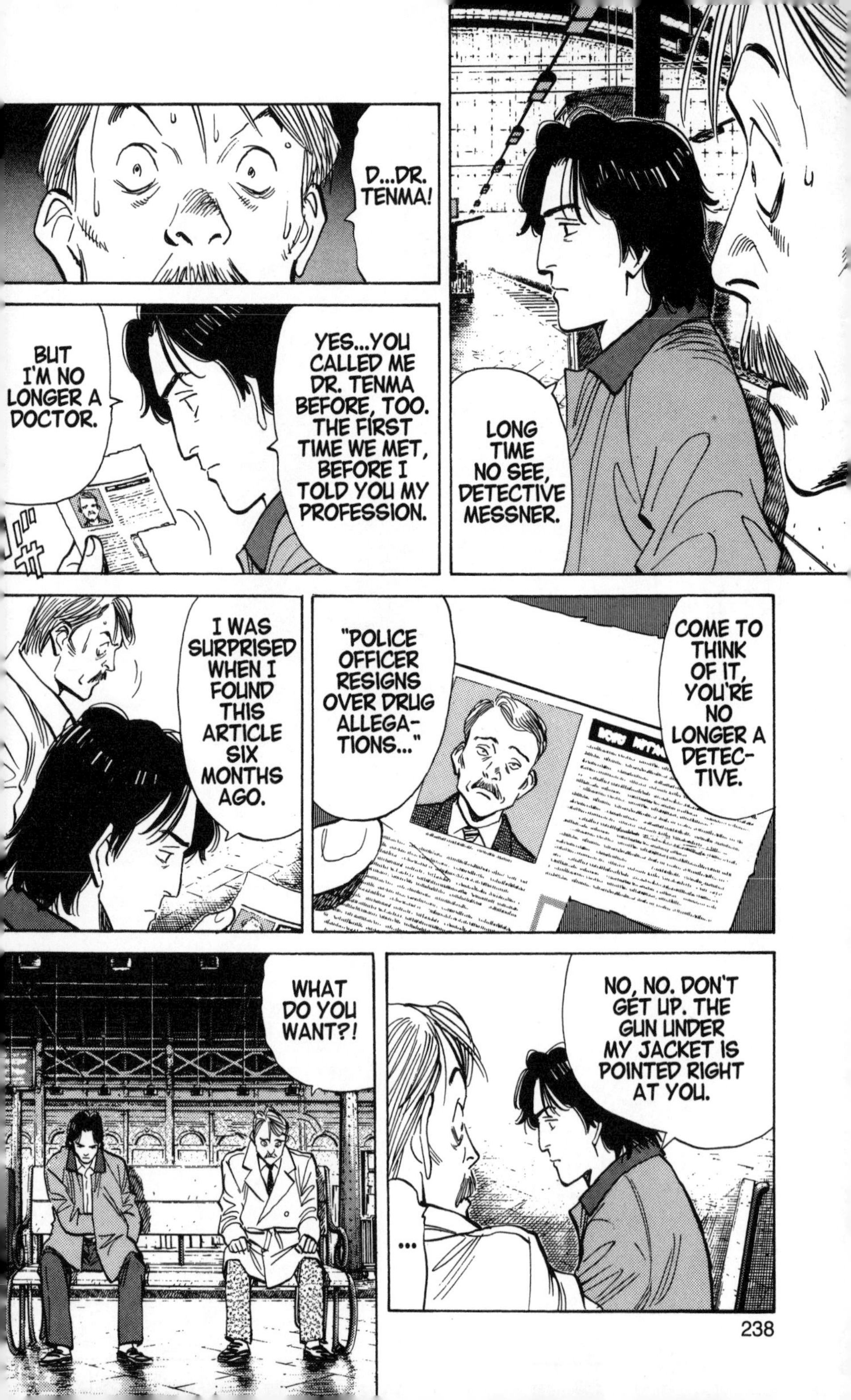
LONG TIME NO SEE, DETECTIVE MESSNER.
D...DR. TENMA!
YES...YOU CALLED ME DR. TENMA BEFORE, TOO. THE FIRST TIME WE MET, BEFORE I TOLD YOU MY PROFESSION.
BUT I'M NO LONGER A DOCTOR.
COME TO THINK OF IT, YOU'RE NO LONGER A DETEC-TIVE.
"POLICE OFFICER RESIGNS OVER DRUG ALLEGA-TIONS..."
I WAS SURPRISED WHEN I FOUND THIS ARTICLE SIX MONTHS AGO.
NO, NO. DON'T GET UP. THE GUN UNDER MY JACKET IS POINTED RIGHT AT YOU.
...
WHAT DO YOU WANT?!

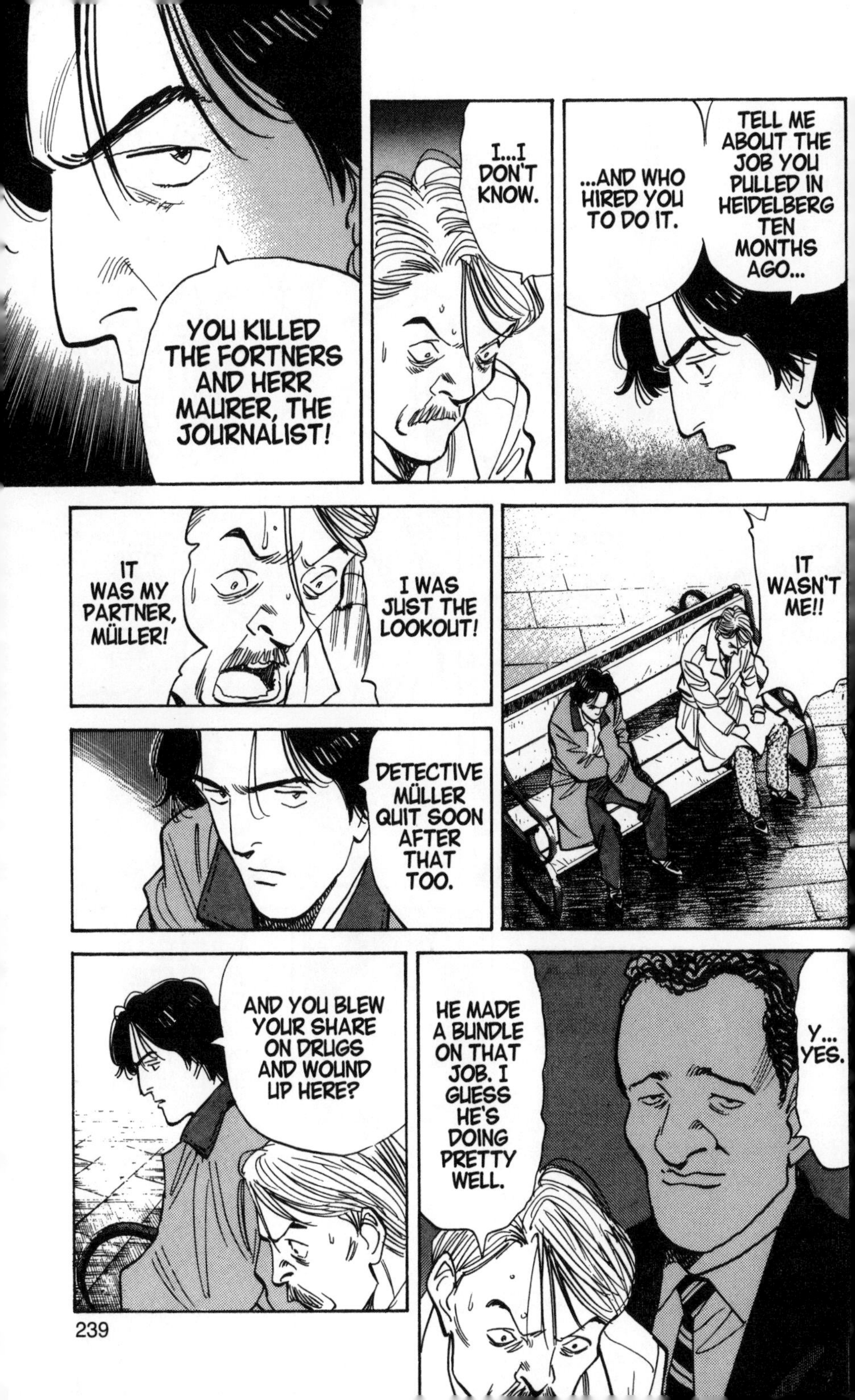
TELL ME ABOUT THE JOB YOU PULLED IN HEIDELBERG TEN MONTHS AGO...
...AND WHO HIRED YOU TO DO IT.
I...I DON'T KNOW.
YOU KILLED THE FORTNERS AND HERR MAURER, THE JOURNALIST!
IT WASN'T ME!!
IT WAS MY PARTNER, MÜLLER!
I WAS JUST THE LOOKOUT!
DETECTIVE MÜLLER QUIT SOON AFTER THAT TOO.
Y... YES.
HE MADE A BUNDLE ON THAT JOB. I GUESS HE'S DOING PRETTY WELL.
AND YOU BLEW YOUR SHARE ON DRUGS AND WOUND UP HERE?

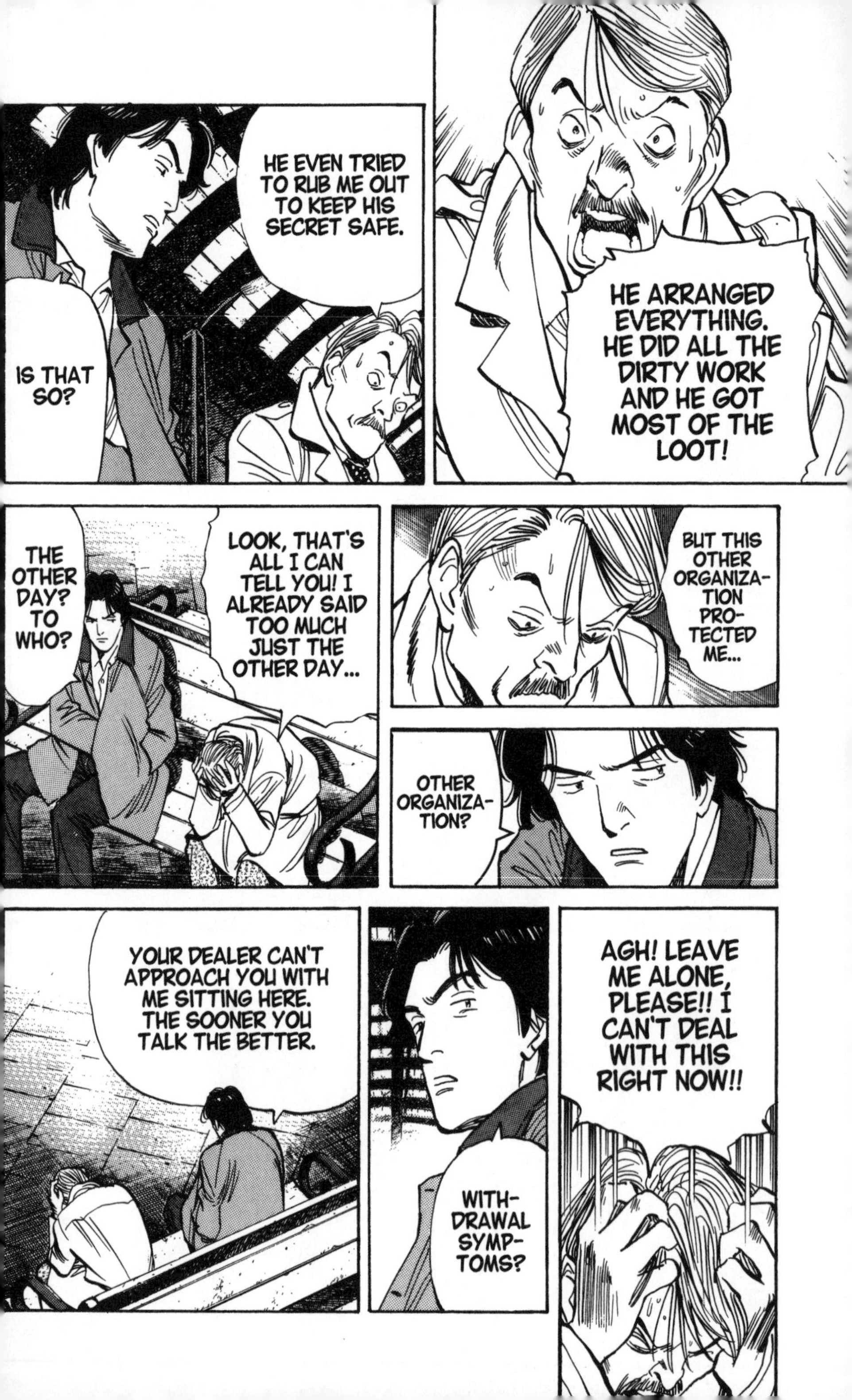
HE ARRANGED EVERYTHING. HE DID ALL THE DIRTY WORK AND HE GOT MOST OF THE LOOT!
HE EVEN TRIED TO RUB ME OUT TO KEEP HIS SECRET SAFE.
IS THAT SO?
BUT THIS OTHER ORGANIZA-TION PRO-TECTED ME...
OTHER ORGANIZA-TION?
LOOK, THAT'S ALL I CAN TELL YOU! I ALREADY SAID TOO MUCH JUST THE OTHER DAY...
THE OTHER DAY? TO WHO?
AGH! LEAVE ME ALONE, PLEASE!! I CAN'T DEAL WITH THIS RIGHT NOW!!
WITH-DRAWAL SYMP-TOMS?
YOUR DEALER CAN'T APPROACH YOU WITH ME SITTING HERE. THE SOONER YOU TALK THE BETTER.

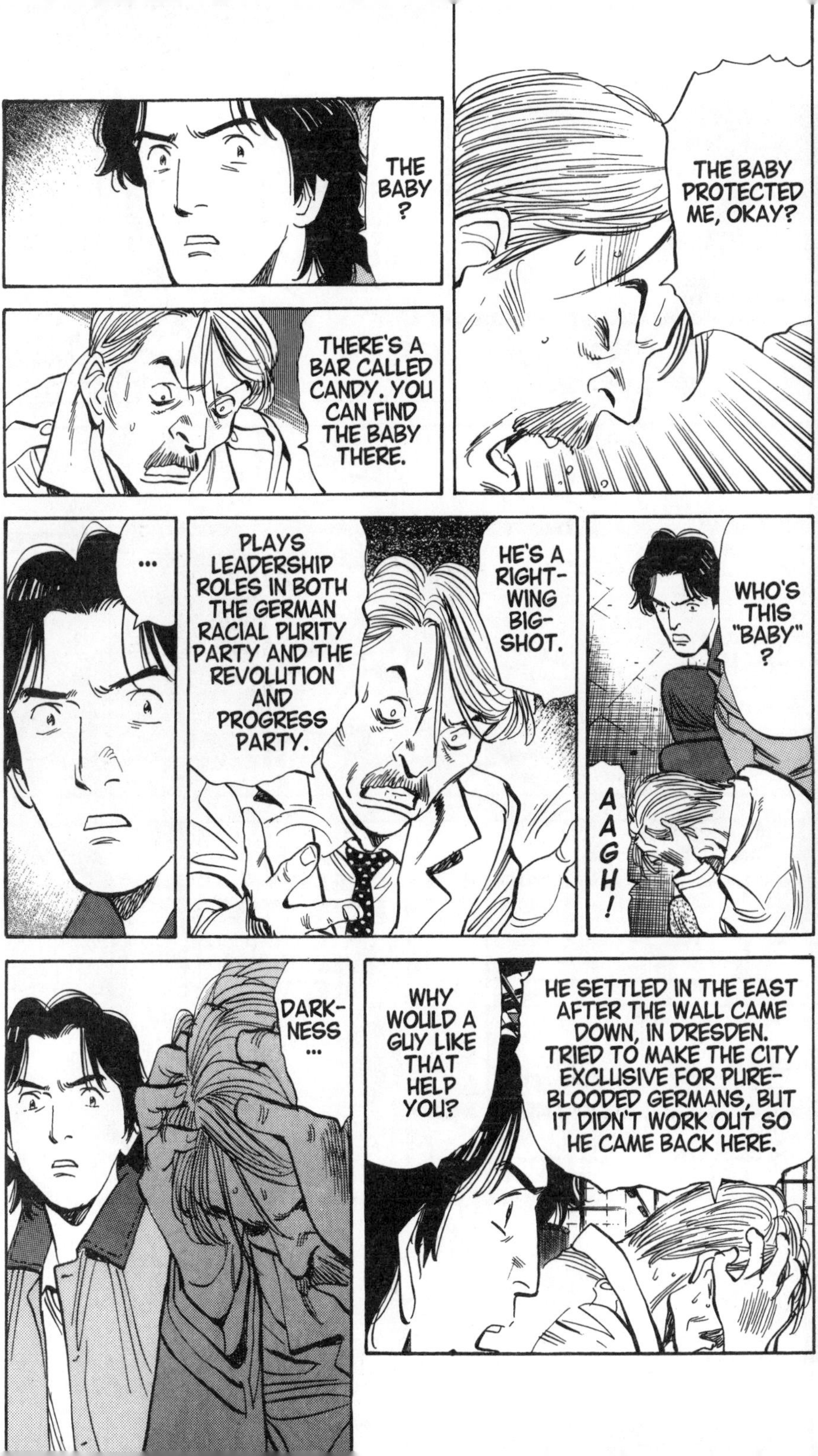
THE BABY PROTECTED ME, OKAY?
THE BABY?
THERE'S A BAR CALLED CANDY. YOU CAN FIND THE BABY THERE.
WHO'S THIS "BABY"?
AAGH!
HE'S A RIGHT-WING BIG-SHOT.
PLAYS LEADERSHIP ROLES IN BOTH THE GERMAN RACIAL PURITY PARTY AND THE REVOLUTION AND PROGRESS PARTY.
...
HE SETTLED IN THE EAST AFTER THE WALL CAME DOWN, IN DRESDEN. TRIED TO MAKE THE CITY EXCLUSIVE FOR PURE-BLOODED GERMANS, BUT IT DIDN'T WORK OUT SO HE CAME BACK HERE.
WHY WOULD A GUY LIKE THAT HELP YOU?
DARKNESS...

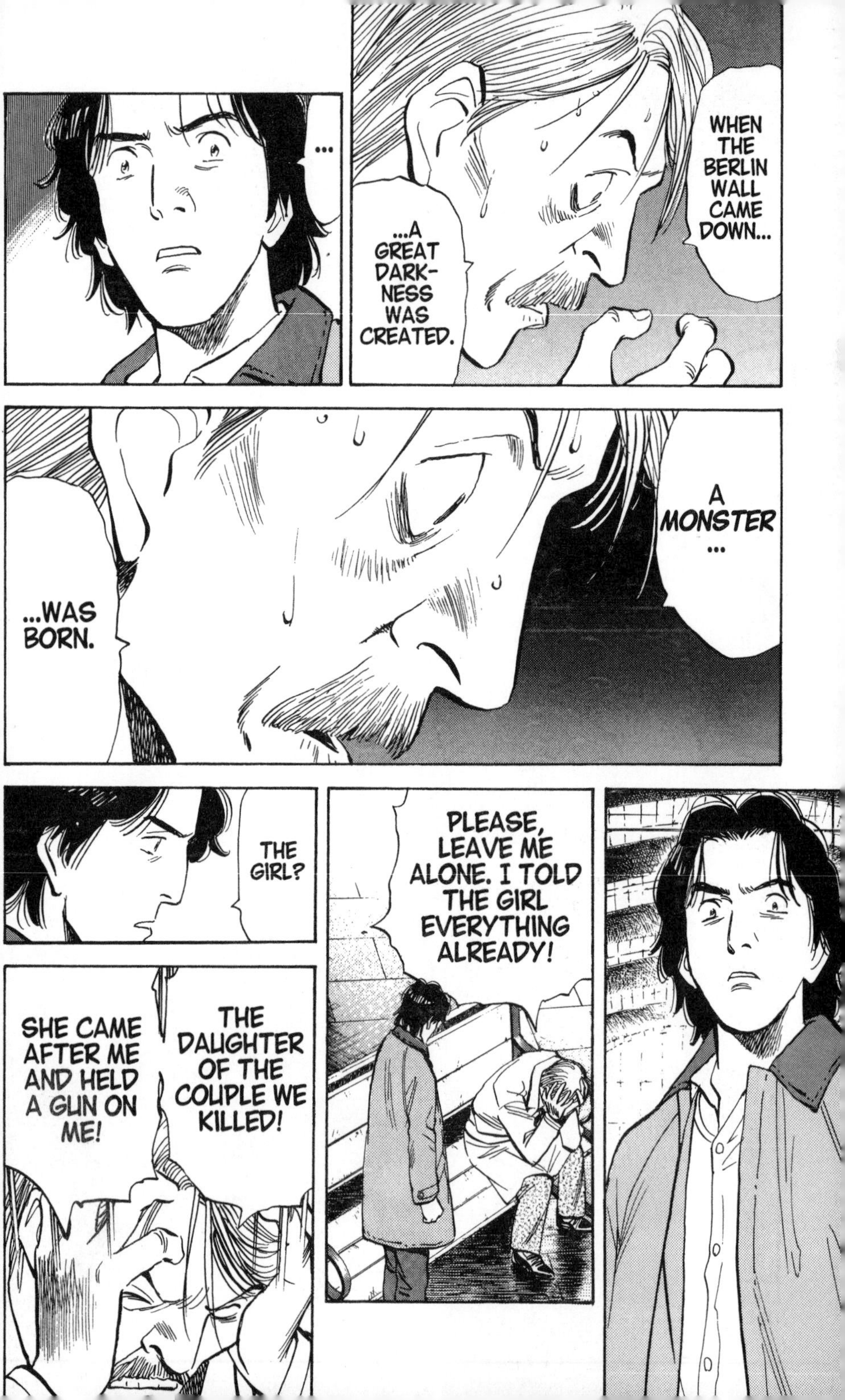
WHEN THE BERLIN WALL CAME DOWN...
...A GREAT DARKNESS WAS CREATED.
...
A MONSTER ...
...WAS BORN.
PLEASE, LEAVE ME ALONE. I TOLD THE GIRL EVERYTHING ALREADY!
THE GIRL?
THE DAUGHTER OF THE COUPLE WE KILLED!
SHE CAME AFTER ME AND HELD A GUN ON ME!

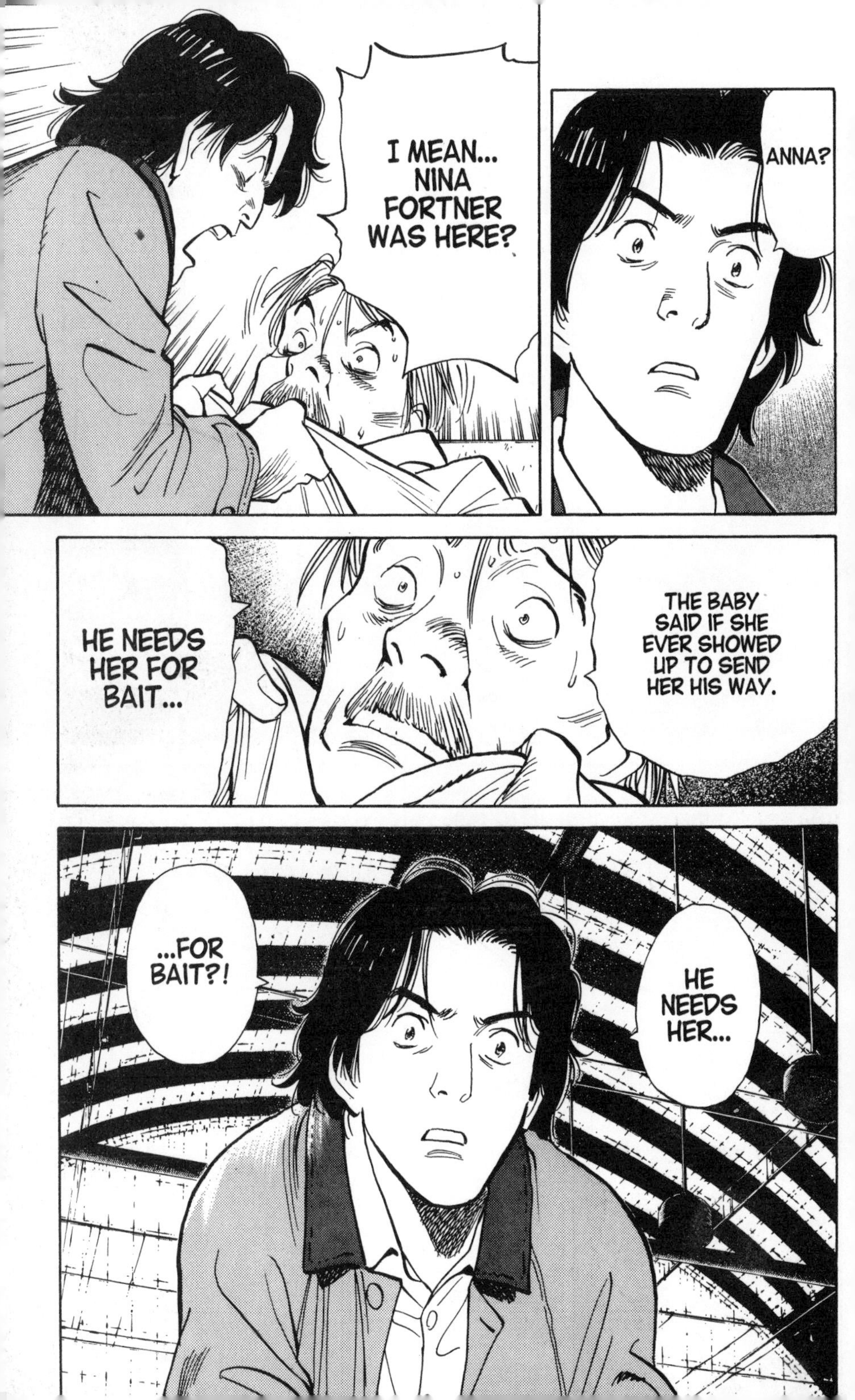
ANNA?
I MEAN... NINA FORTNER WAS HERE?
THE BABY SAID IF SHE EVER SHOWED UP TO SEND HER HIS WAY.
HE NEEDS HER FOR BAIT...
HE NEEDS HER...
...FOR BAIT?!

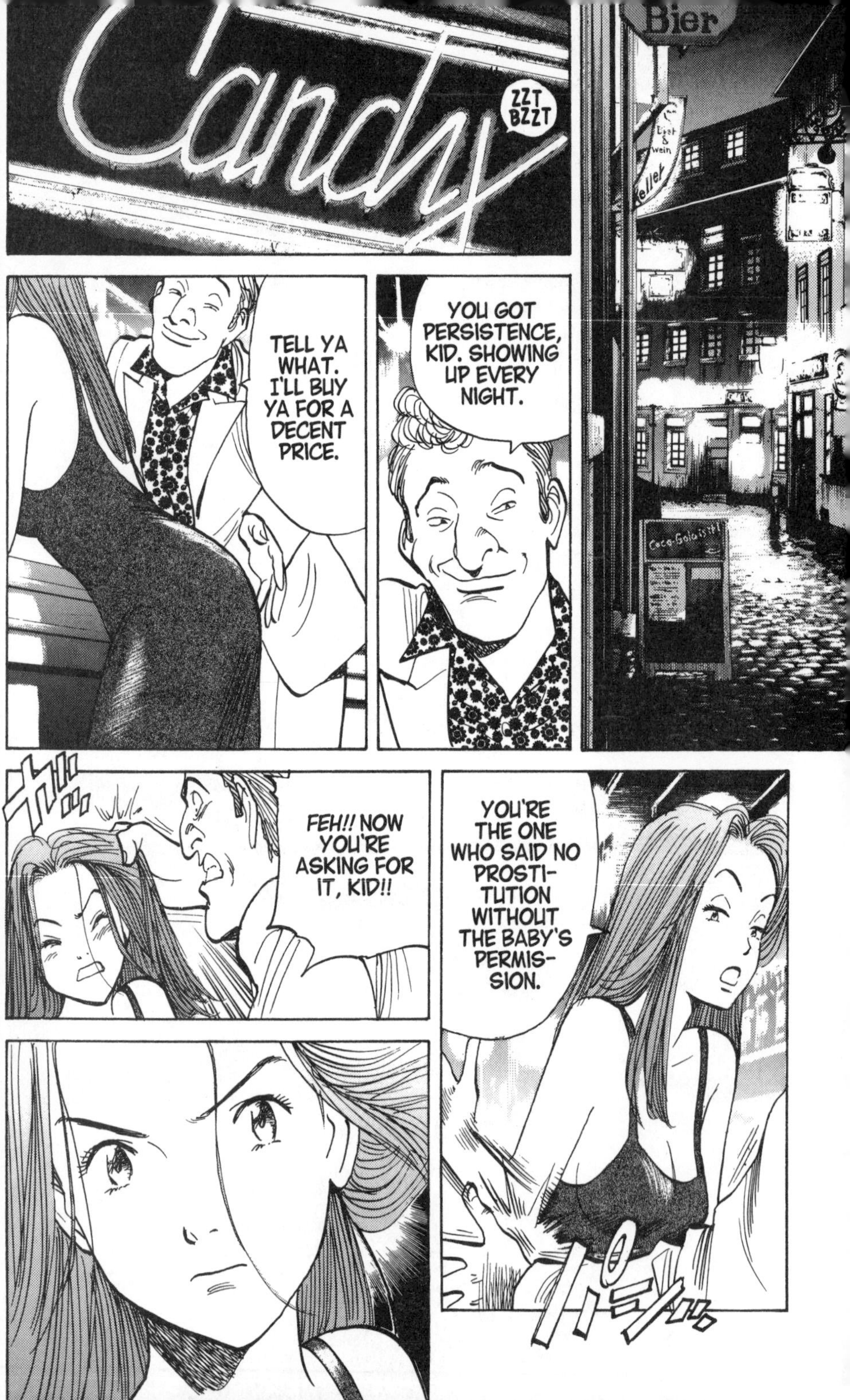
Bier
Candy
ZZT BZZT
YOU GOT PERSISTENCE, KID. SHOWING UP EVERY NIGHT.
TELL YA WHAT. I'LL BUY YA FOR A DECENT PRICE.
YOU'RE THE ONE WHO SAID NO PROSTI- TUTION WITHOUT THE BABY'S PERMIS- SION.
FEH!! NOW YOU'RE ASKING FOR IT, KID!!

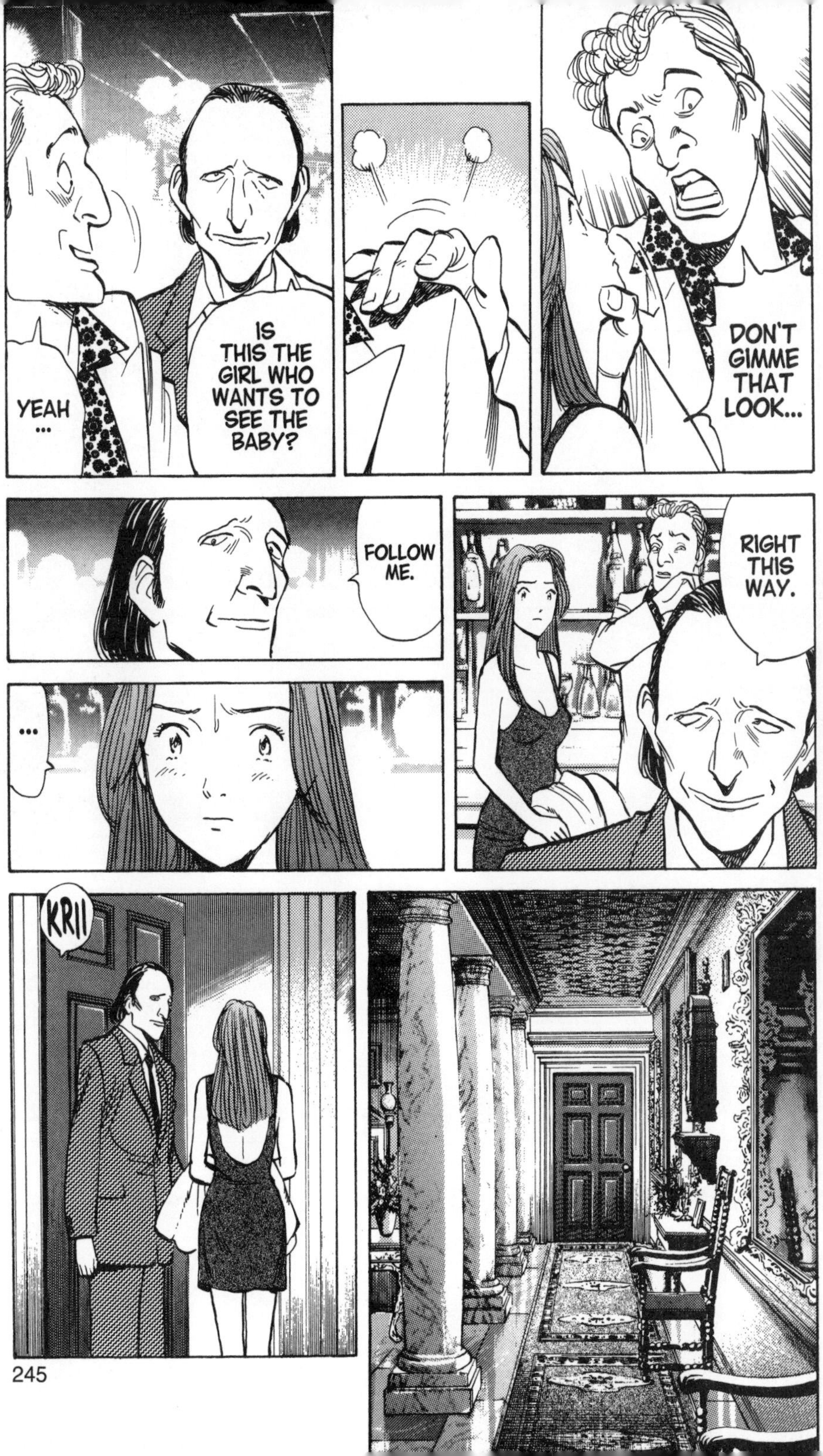
DON'T GIMME THAT LOOK...
IS THIS THE GIRL WHO WANTS TO SEE THE BABY?
YEAH ...
RIGHT THIS WAY.
FOLLOW ME.
...
KRII

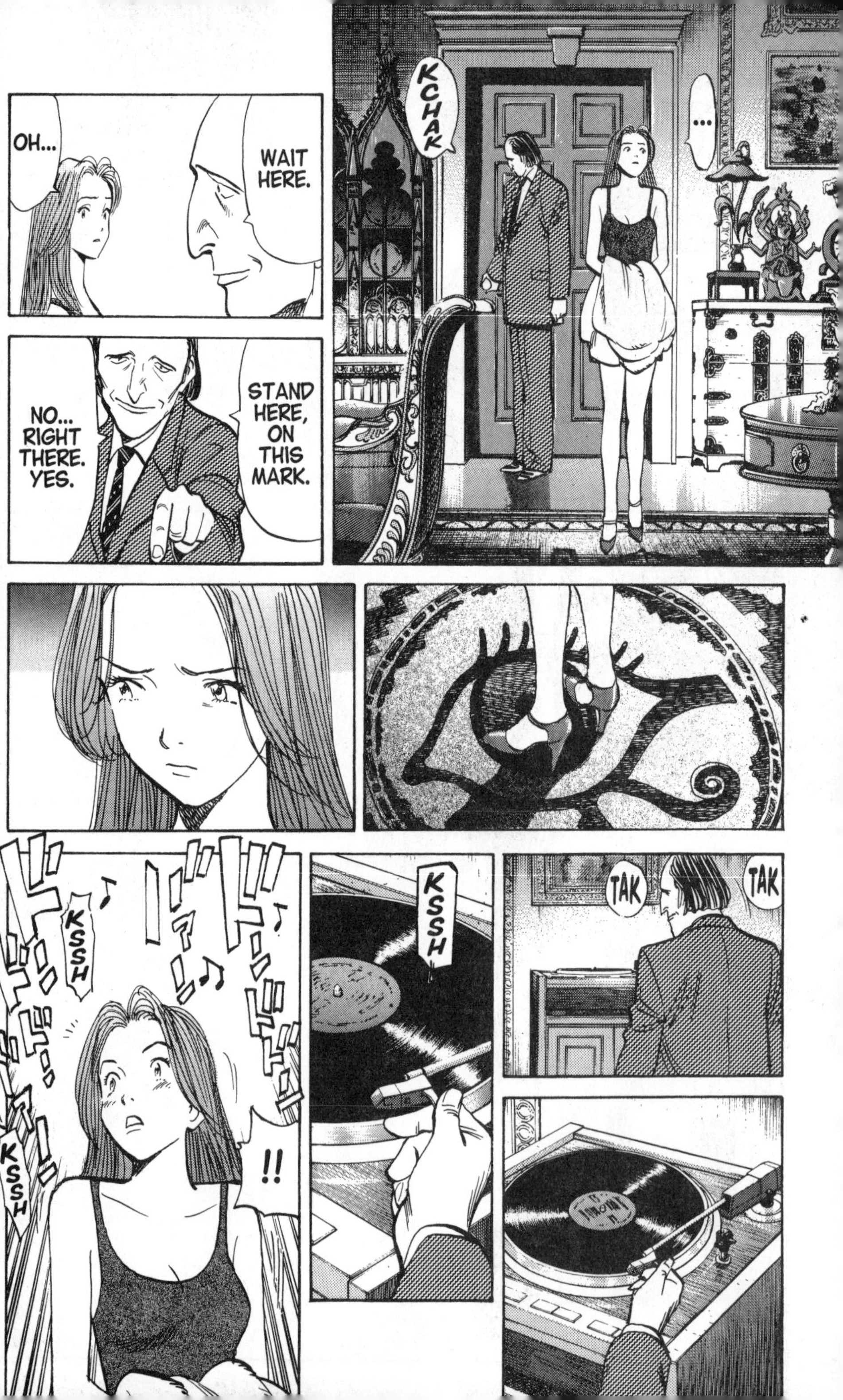
KCHAK
...
WAIT HERE.
OH...
STAND HERE, ON THIS MARK.
NO... RIGHT THERE. YES.
TAK
TAK
KSSH
KSSH
!!
KSSH

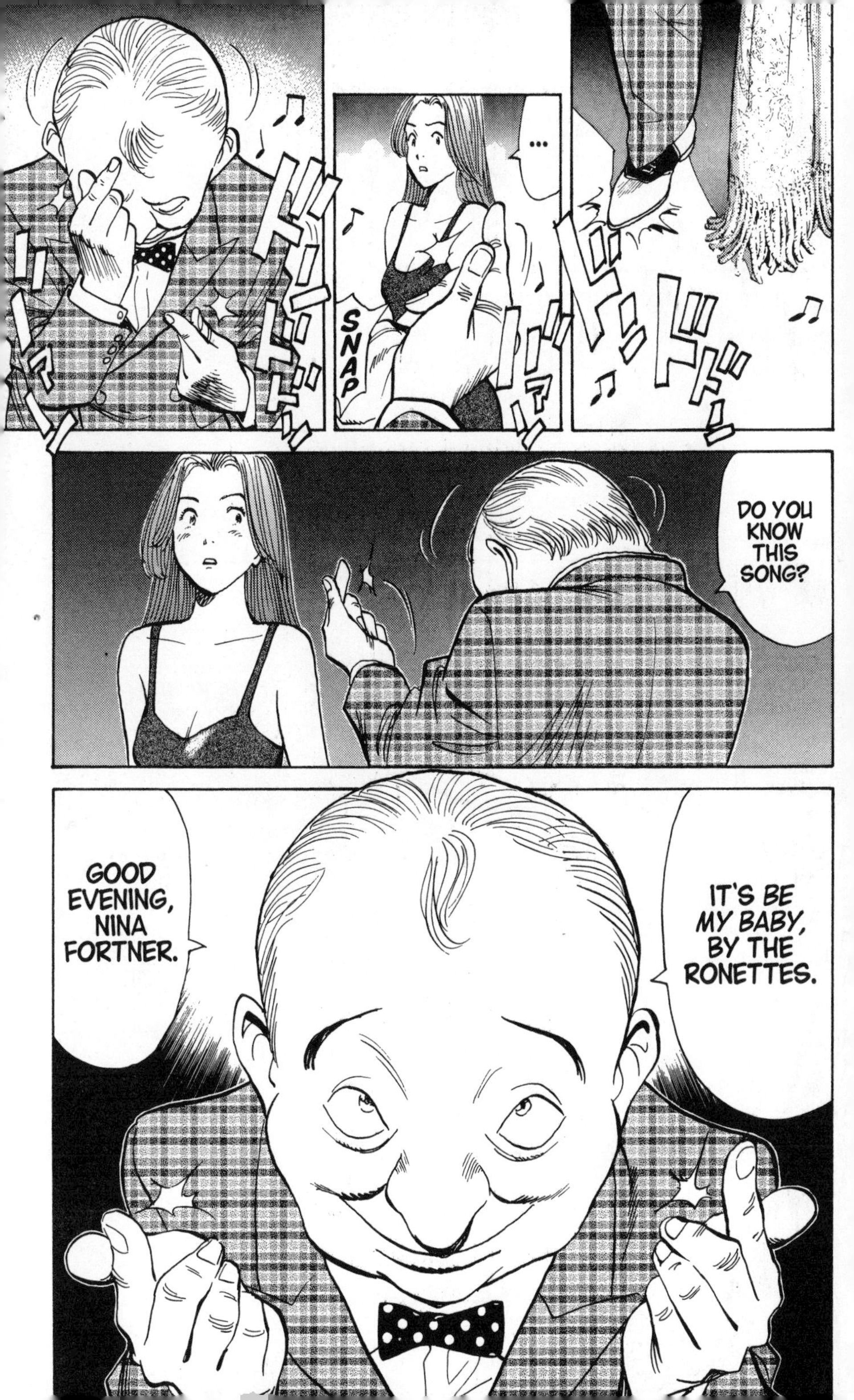
...
SNAP
DO YOU KNOW THIS SONG?
IT'S BE MY BABY, BY THE RONETTES.
GOOD EVENING, NINA FORTNER.

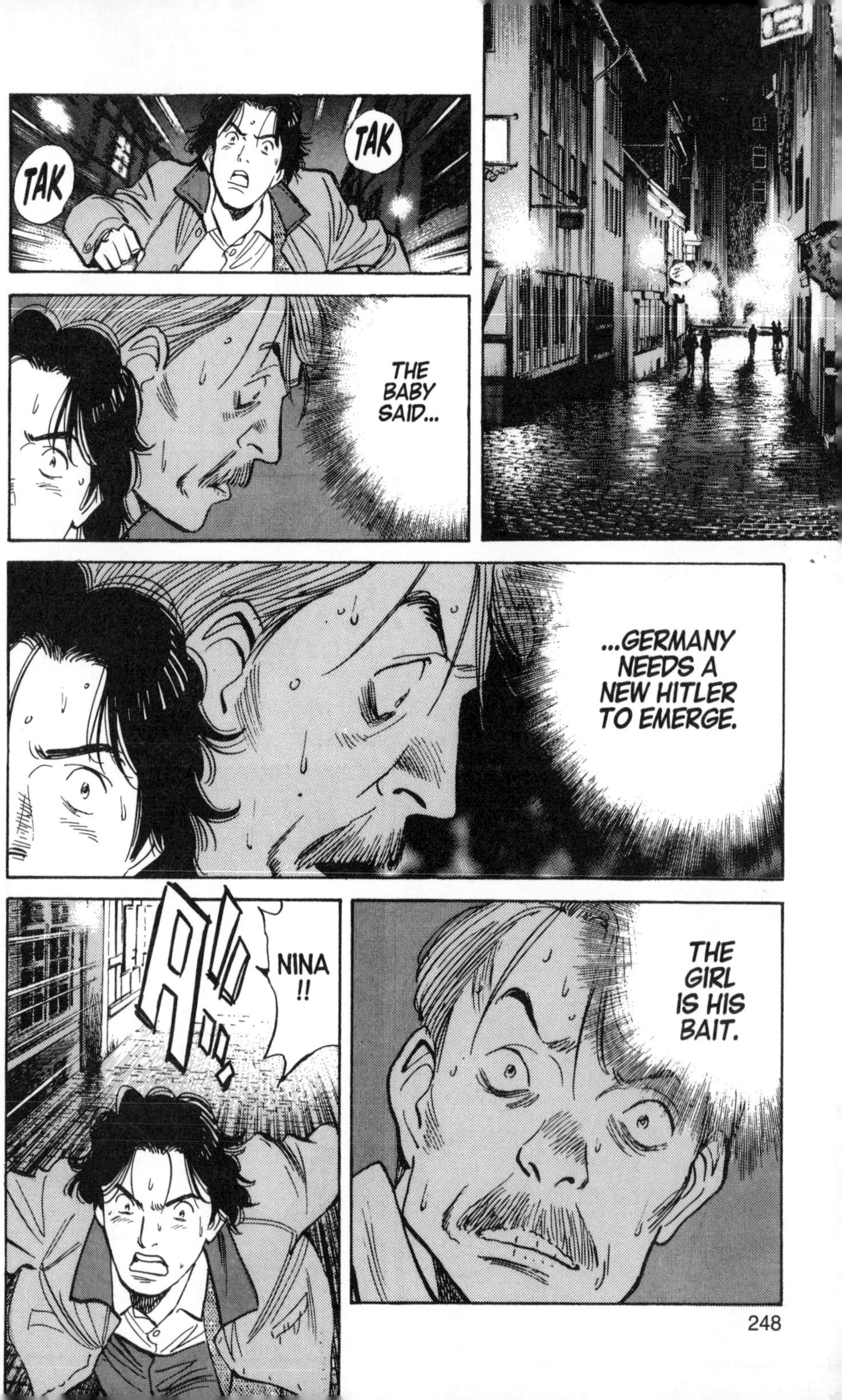
TAK
TAK
THE BABY SAID...
...GERMANY NEEDS A NEW HITLER TO EMERGE.
THE GIRL IS HIS BAIT.
NINA !!

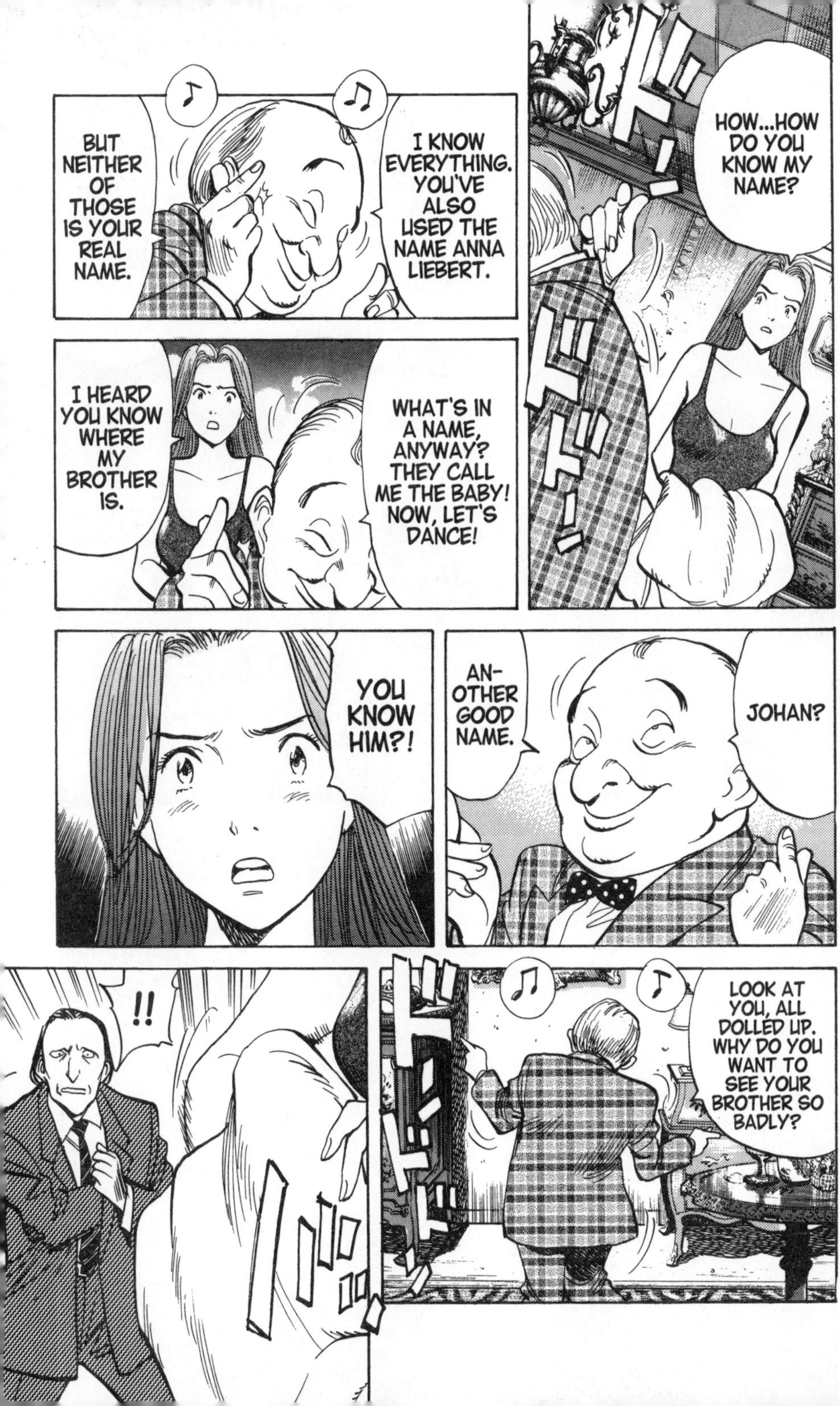
HOW...HOW DO YOU KNOW MY NAME?
I KNOW EVERYTHING. YOU'VE ALSO USED THE NAME ANNA LIEBERT.
BUT NEITHER OF THOSE IS YOUR REAL NAME.
WHAT'S IN A NAME, ANYWAY? THEY CALL ME THE BABY! NOW, LET'S DANCE!
I HEARD YOU KNOW WHERE MY BROTHER IS.
JOHAN?
AN-OTHER GOOD NAME.
YOU KNOW HIM?!
LOOK AT YOU, ALL DOLLED UP. WHY DO YOU WANT TO SEE YOUR BROTHER SO BADLY?
!!

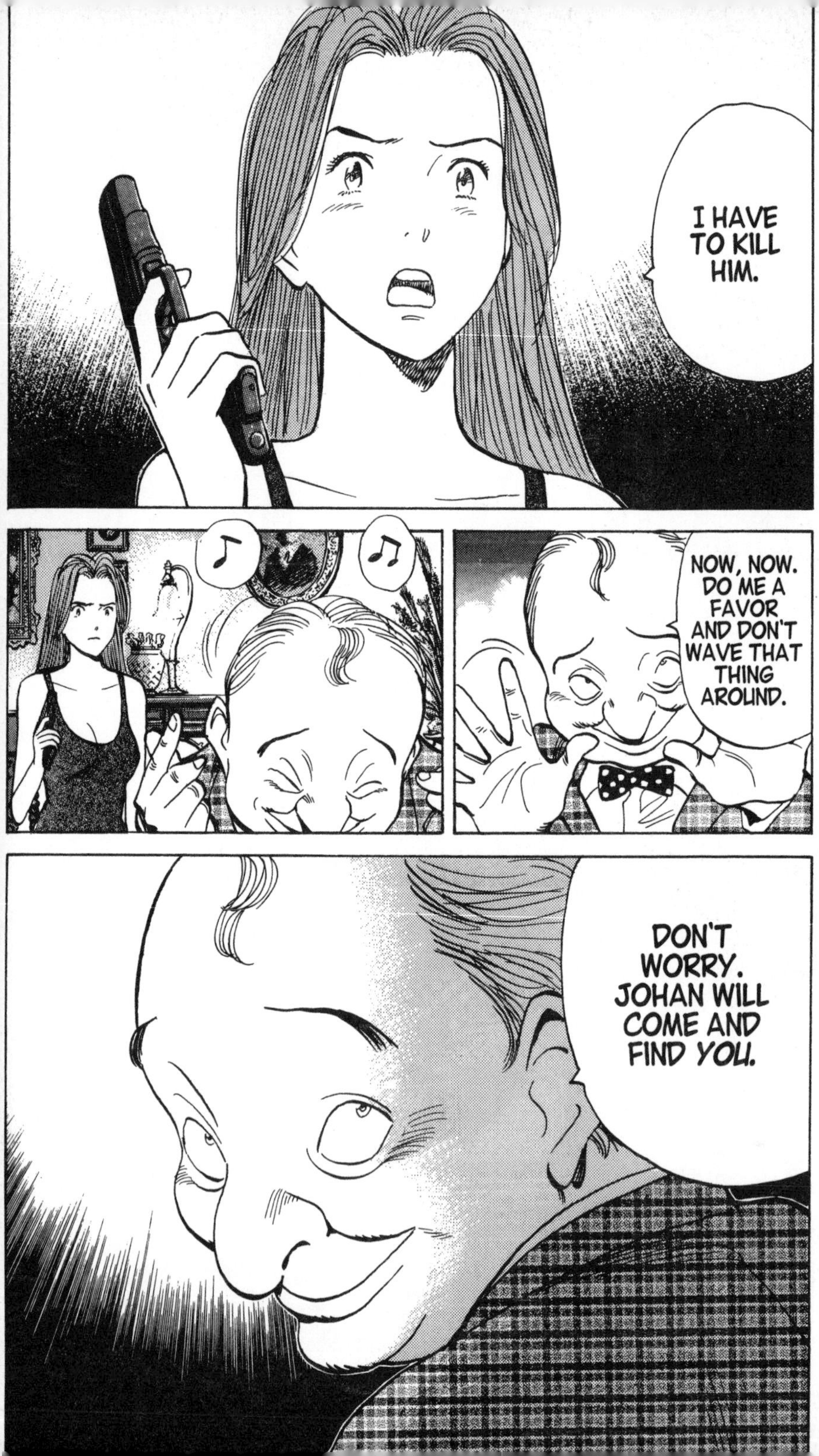
I HAVE TO KILL HIM.
NOW, NOW. DO ME A FAVOR AND DON'T WAVE THAT THING AROUND.
♪
♫
DON'T WORRY. JOHAN WILL COME AND FIND YOU.

Kapitel 27. Professor Gedrich

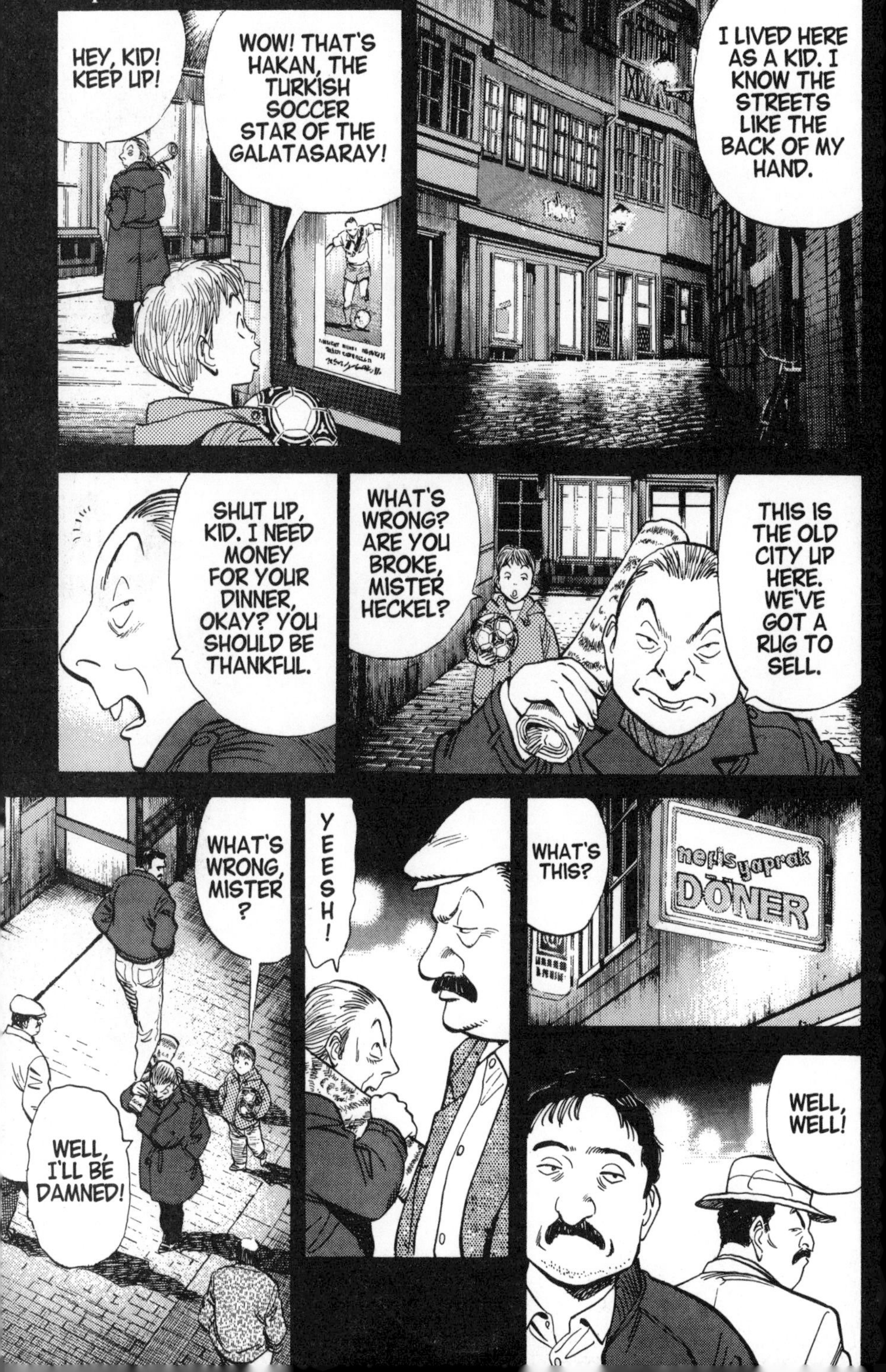
I LIVED HERE AS A KID. I KNOW THE STREETS LIKE THE BACK OF MY HAND.
WOW! THAT'S HAKAN, THE TURKISH SOCCER STAR OF THE GALATASARAY!
HEY, KID! KEEP UP!
THIS IS THE OLD CITY UP HERE. WE'VE GOT A RUG TO SELL.
WHAT'S WRONG? ARE YOU BROKE, MISTER HECKEL?
SHUT UP, KID. I NEED MONEY FOR YOUR DINNER, OKAY? YOU SHOULD BE THANKFUL.
WHAT'S THIS?
DÖNER
WELL, WELL!
YEESH!
WHAT'S WRONG, MISTER?
WELL, I'LL BE DAMNED!

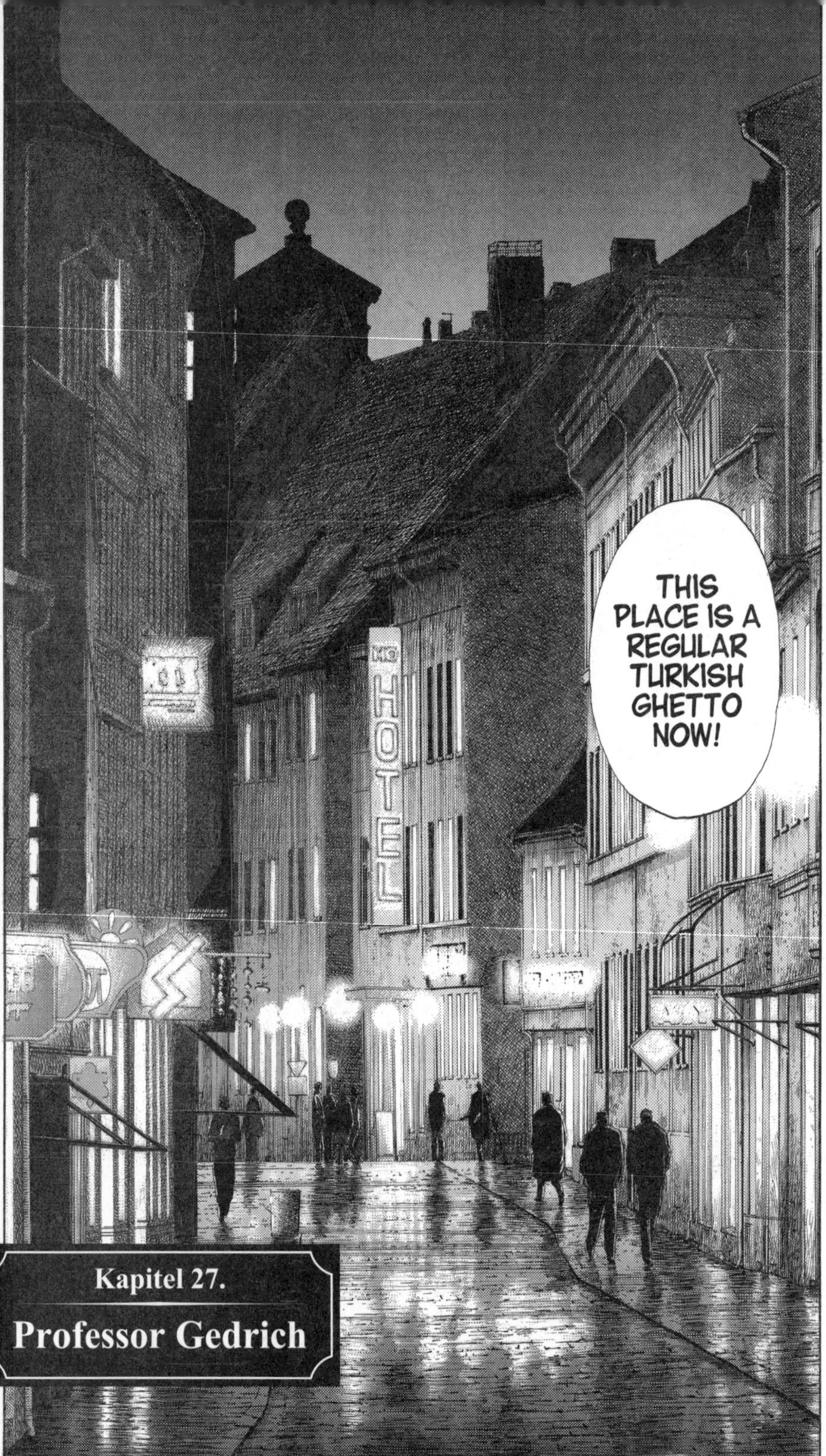
THIS PLACE IS A REGULAR TURKISH GHETTO NOW!
HOTEL

Kapitel 27.
Professor Gedrich

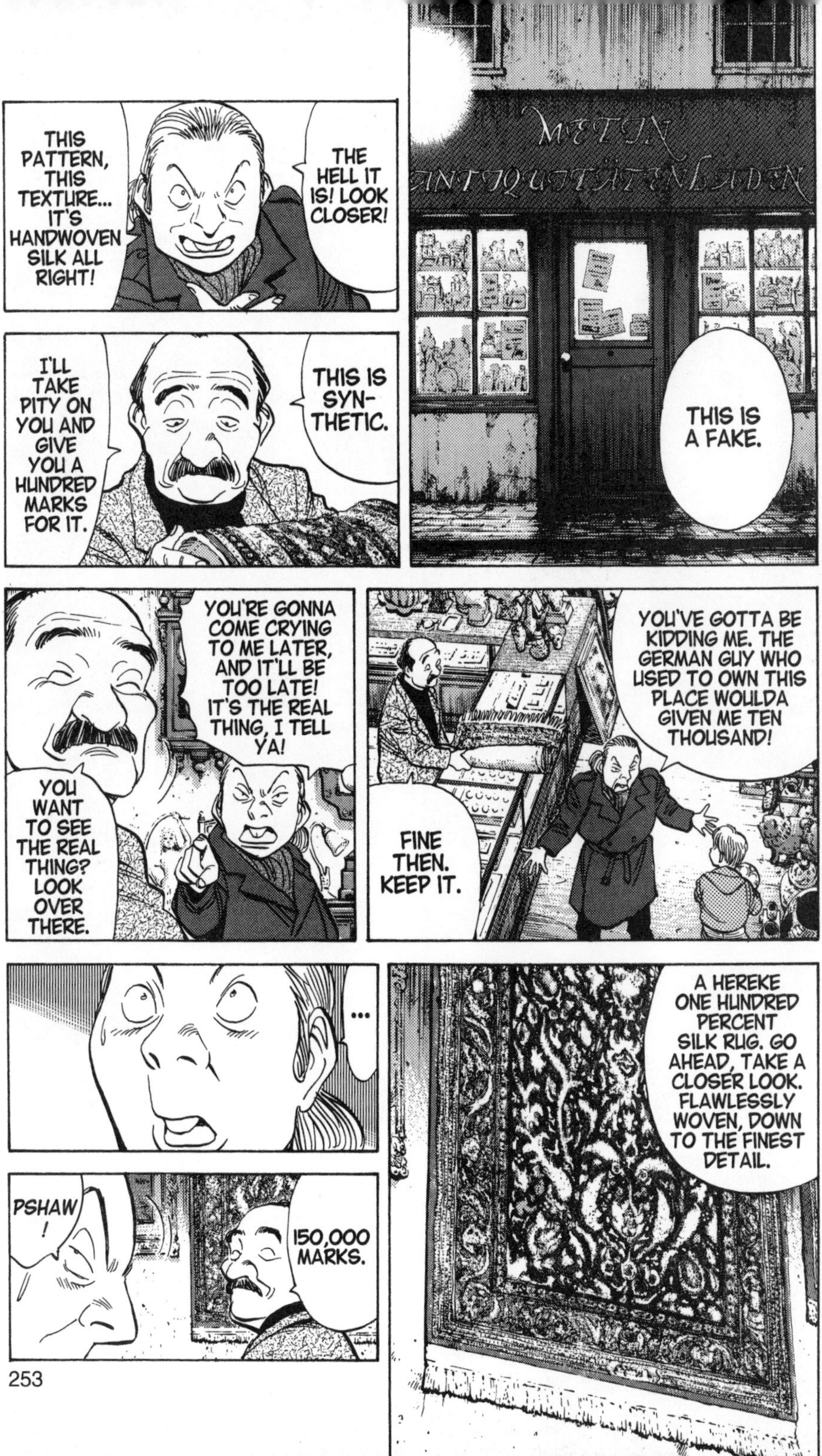
THIS IS A FAKE.
THE HELL IT IS! LOOK CLOSER!
THIS PATTERN, THIS TEXTURE... IT'S HANDWOVEN SILK ALL RIGHT!
THIS IS SYNTHETIC.
I'LL TAKE PITY ON YOU AND GIVE YOU A HUNDRED MARKS FOR IT.
YOU'VE GOTTA BE KIDDING ME. THE GERMAN GUY WHO USED TO OWN THIS PLACE WOULDA GIVEN ME TEN THOUSAND!
FINE THEN. KEEP IT.
YOU'RE GONNA COME CRYING TO ME LATER, AND IT'LL BE TOO LATE! IT'S THE REAL THING, I TELL YA!
YOU WANT TO SEE THE REAL THING? LOOK OVER THERE.
A HEREKE ONE HUNDRED PERCENT SILK RUG. GO AHEAD, TAKE A CLOSER LOOK. FLAWLESSLY WOVEN, DOWN TO THE FINEST DETAIL.
...
150,000 MARKS.
PSHAW!

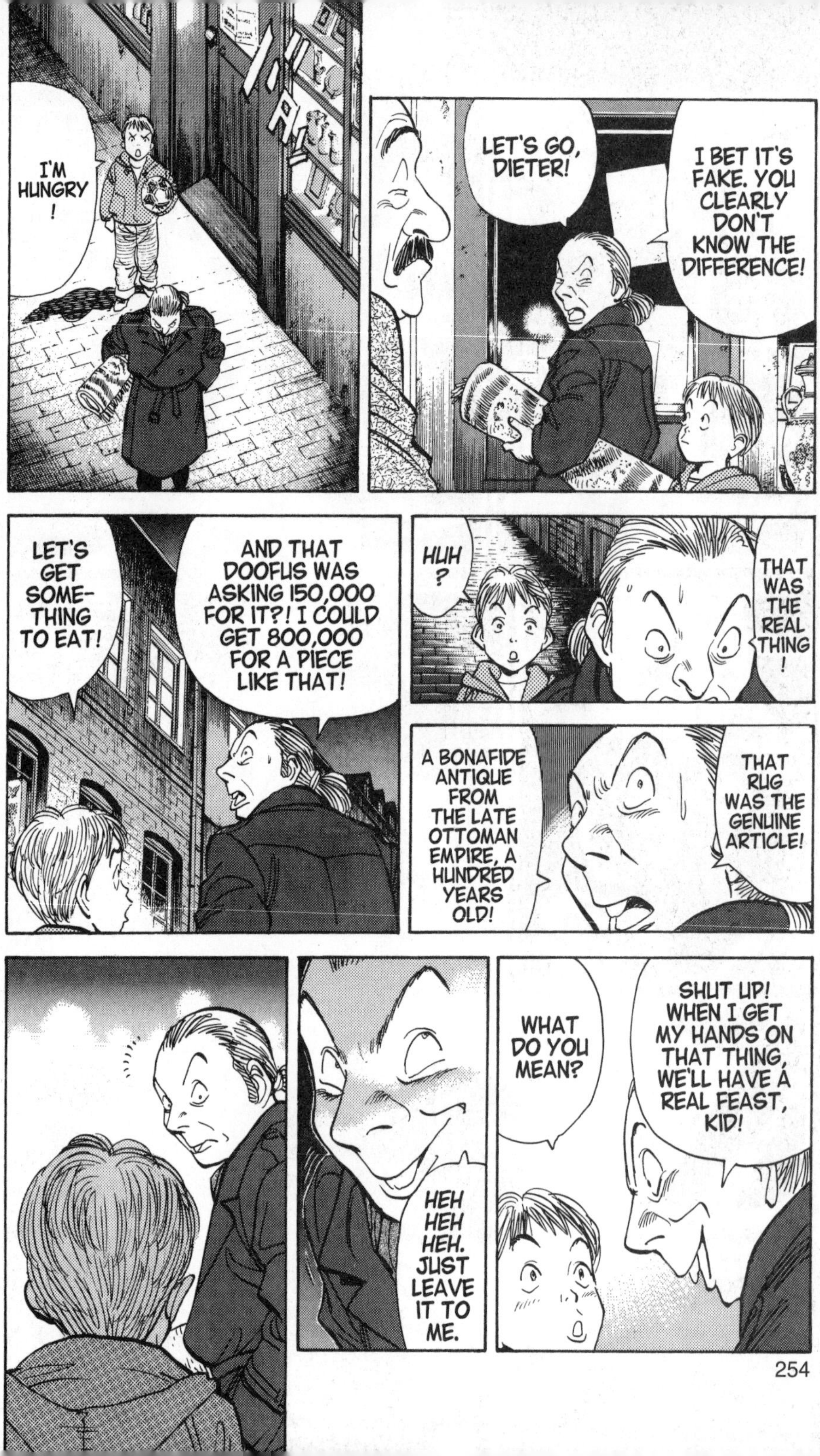
I BET IT'S FAKE. YOU CLEARLY DON'T KNOW THE DIFFERENCE!
LET'S GO, DIETER!
I'M HUNGRY!
THAT WAS THE REAL THING!
HUH?
THAT RUG WAS THE GENUINE ARTICLE!
A BONAFIDE ANTIQUE FROM THE LATE OTTOMAN EMPIRE, A HUNDRED YEARS OLD!
AND THAT DOOFUS WAS ASKING 150,000 FOR IT?! I COULD GET 800,000 FOR A PIECE LIKE THAT!
LET'S GET SOME-THING TO EAT!
SHUT UP! WHEN I GET MY HANDS ON THAT THING, WE'LL HAVE A REAL FEAST, KID!
WHAT DO YOU MEAN?
HEH HEH HEH. JUST LEAVE IT TO ME.

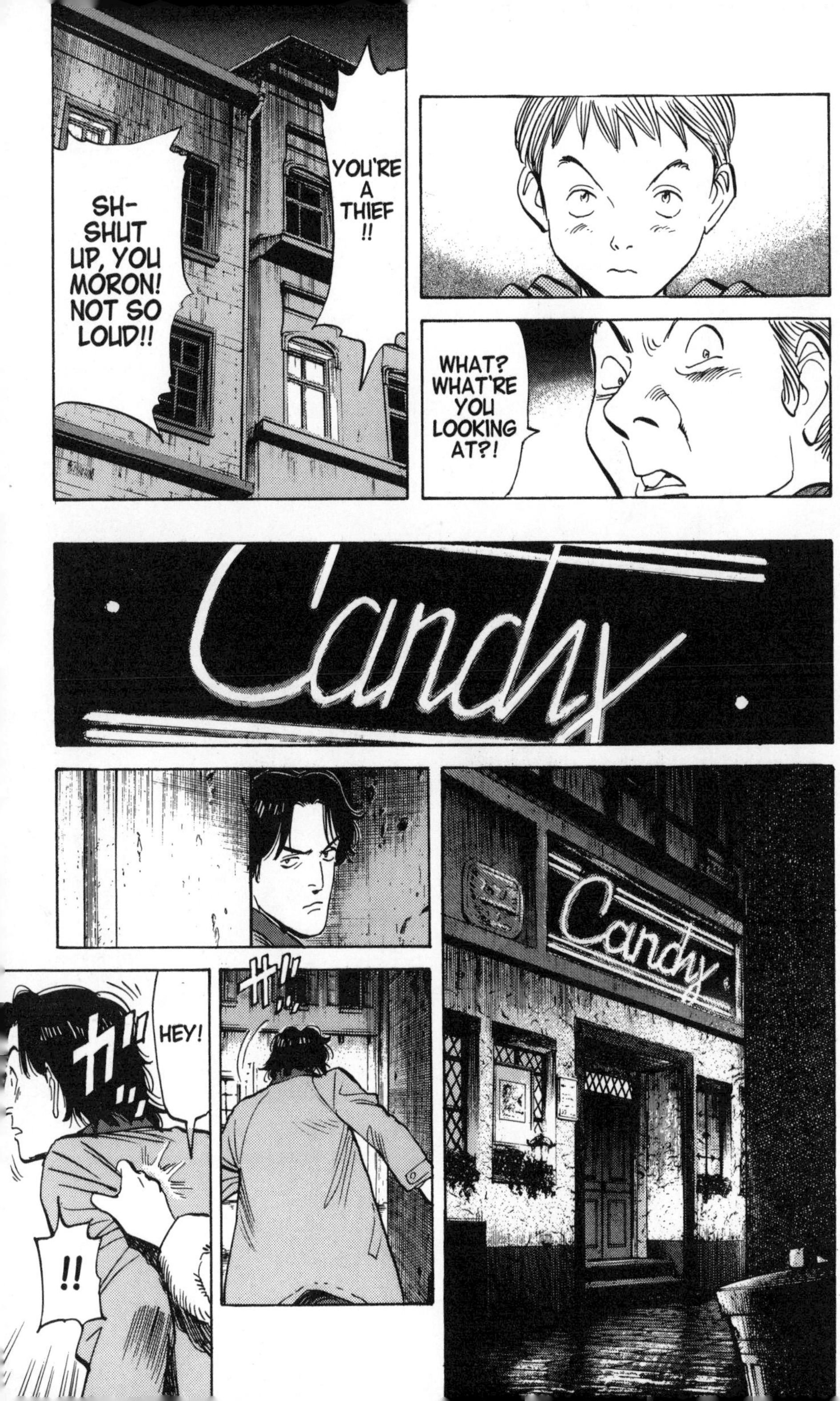
WHAT? WHAT'RE YOU LOOKING AT?!
YOU'RE A THIEF!!
SH-SHUT UP, YOU MORON! NOT SO LOUD!!
Candy
Candy
HEY!
!!

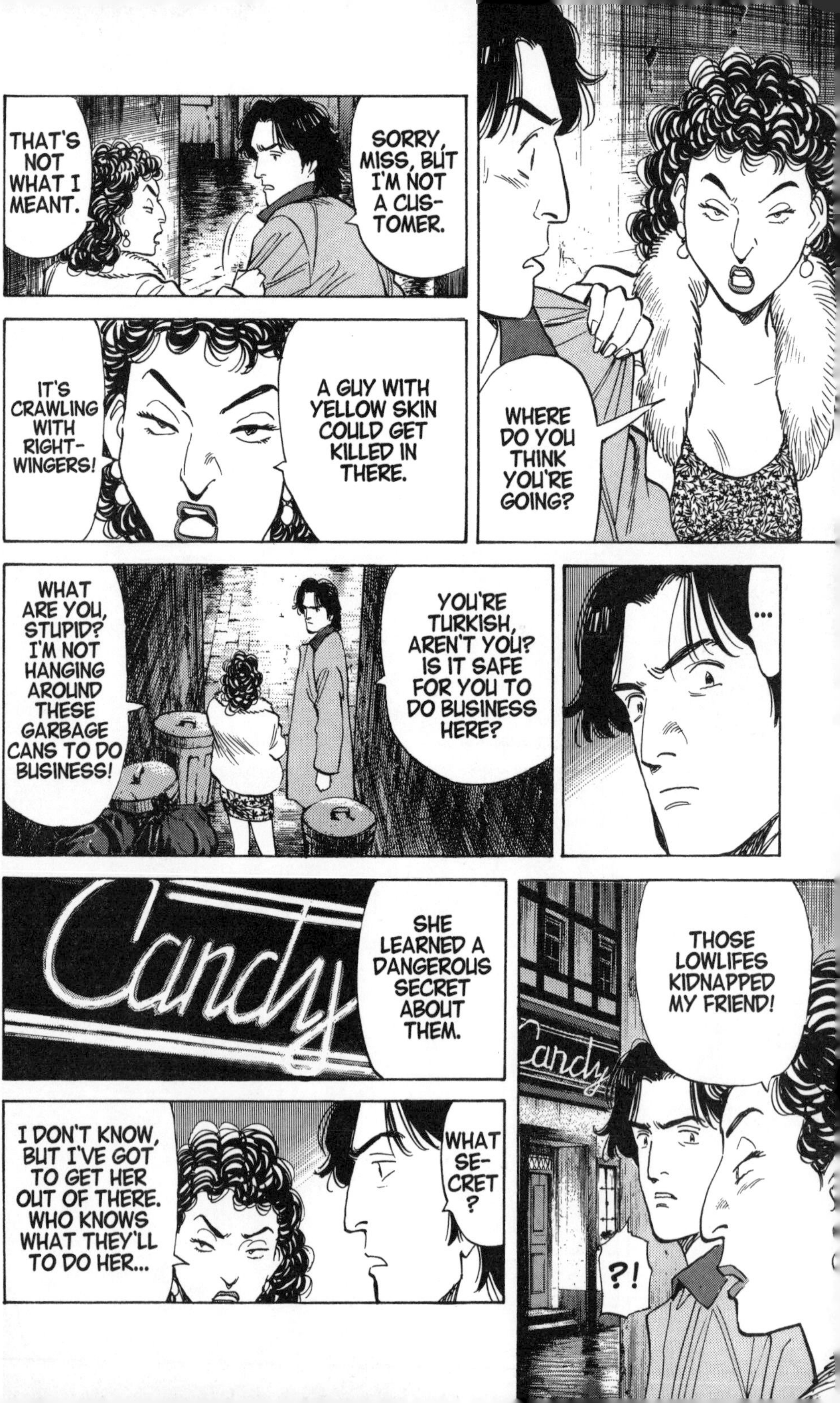
WHERE DO YOU THINK YOU'RE GOING?
SORRY, MISS, BUT I'M NOT A CUS-TOMER.
THAT'S NOT WHAT I MEANT.
A GUY WITH YELLOW SKIN COULD GET KILLED IN THERE.
IT'S CRAWLING WITH RIGHT-WINGERS!
...
YOU'RE TURKISH, AREN'T YOU? IS IT SAFE FOR YOU TO DO BUSINESS HERE?
WHAT ARE YOU, STUPID? I'M NOT HANGING AROUND THESE GARBAGE CANS TO DO BUSINESS!
THOSE LOWLIFES KIDNAPPED MY FRIEND!
Candy
?!
Candy
SHE LEARNED A DANGEROUS SECRET ABOUT THEM.
WHAT SE-CRET?
I DON'T KNOW, BUT I'VE GOT TO GET HER OUT OF THERE. WHO KNOWS WHAT THEY'LL TO DO HER...

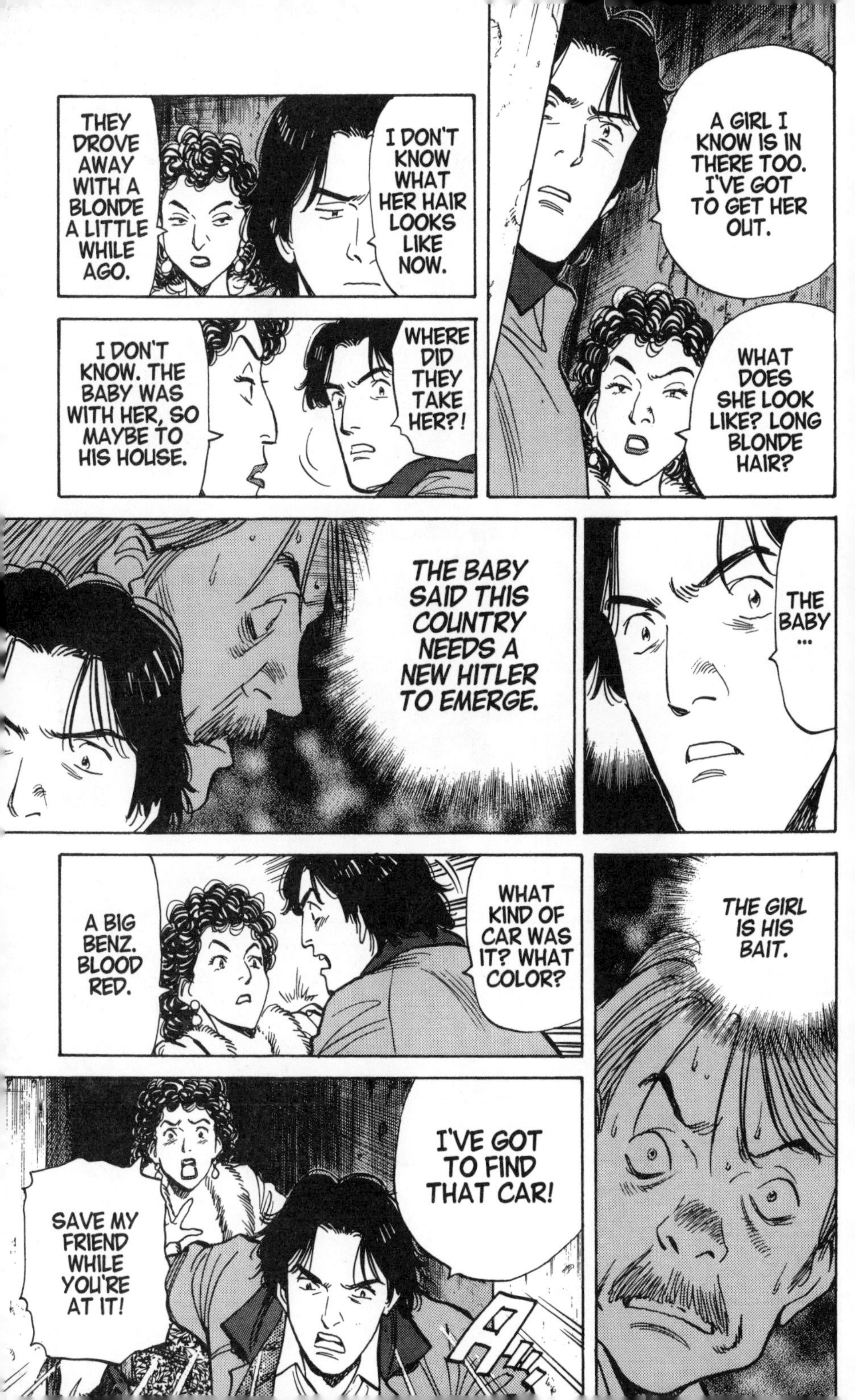
A GIRL I KNOW IS IN THERE TOO. I'VE GOT TO GET HER OUT.
WHAT DOES SHE LOOK LIKE? LONG BLONDE HAIR?
I DON'T KNOW WHAT HER HAIR LOOKS LIKE NOW.
THEY DROVE AWAY WITH A BLONDE A LITTLE WHILE AGO.
WHERE DID THEY TAKE HER?!
I DON'T KNOW. THE BABY WAS WITH HER, SO MAYBE TO HIS HOUSE.
THE BABY...
THE BABY SAID THIS COUNTRY NEEDS A NEW HITLER TO EMERGE.
THE GIRL IS HIS BAIT.
WHAT KIND OF CAR WAS IT? WHAT COLOR?
A BIG BENZ. BLOOD RED.
I'VE GOT TO FIND THAT CAR!
SAVE MY FRIEND WHILE YOU'RE AT IT!

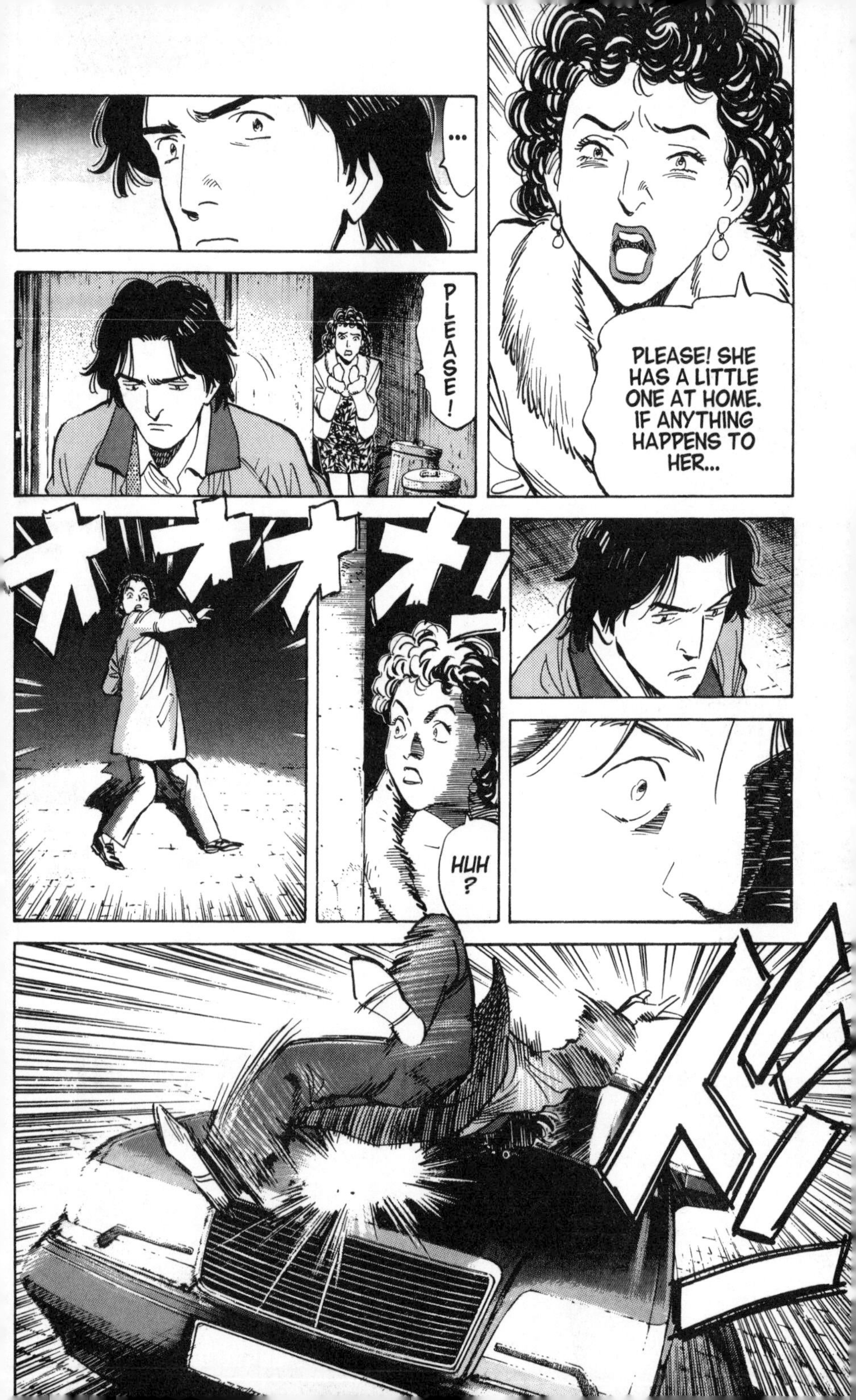
PLEASE! SHE HAS A LITTLE ONE AT HOME. IF ANYTHING HAPPENS TO HER...
...
PLEASE!
HUH?

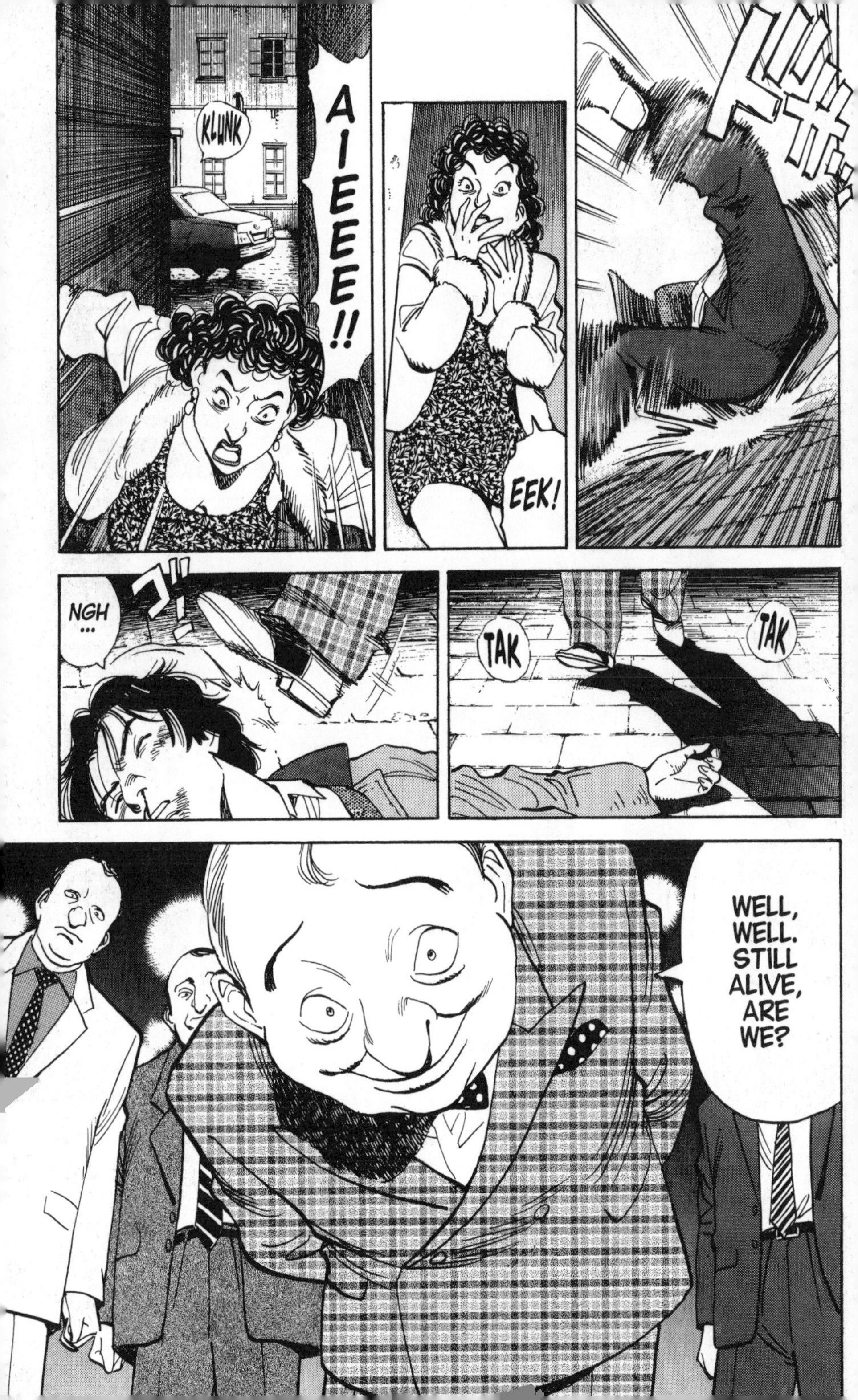
EEK!
AIEEEE!!
KLUNK
TAK
TAK
NGH ...
WELL, WELL. STILL ALIVE, ARE WE?

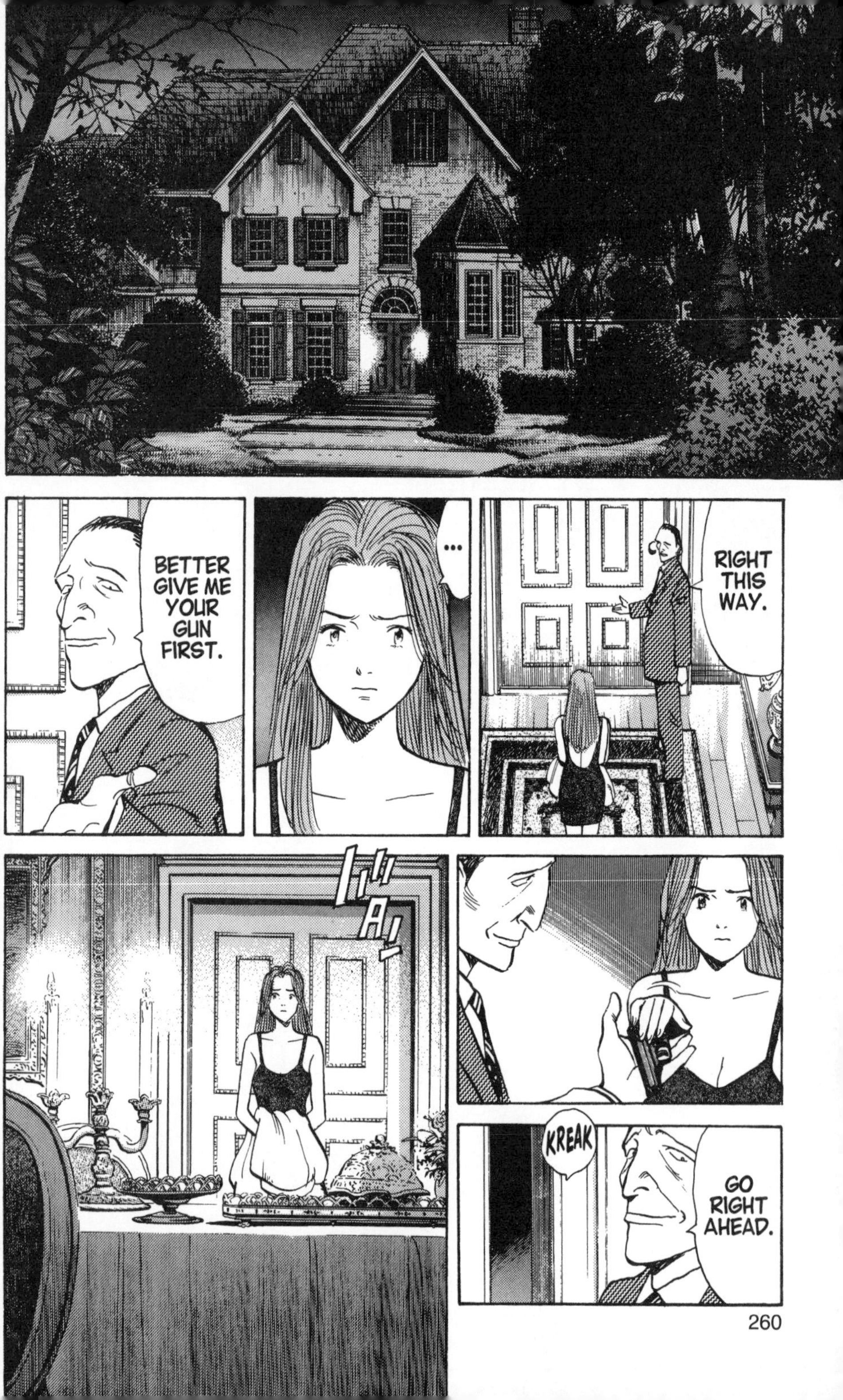
RIGHT THIS WAY.
...
BETTER GIVE ME YOUR GUN FIRST.
KREAK
GO RIGHT AHEAD.
HA...

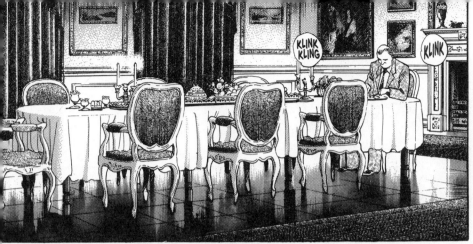

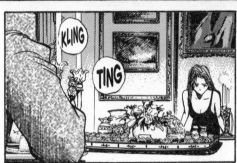

KLINK
KLINK KLING
TAKE ANY SEAT YOU LIKE.
KLINK
KLINK
KLING
TING
SO, YOU'RE THE GIRL THE BABY BROUGHT IN?
LET'S SEE YOUR FACE.
AREN'T YOU A BEAUTY!
NOT THAT I'D EXPECT ANY LESS OF JOHAN'S TWIN.

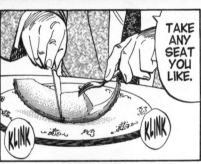

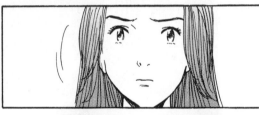

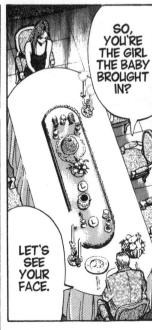

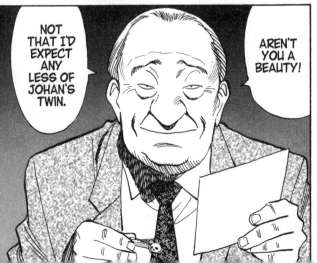

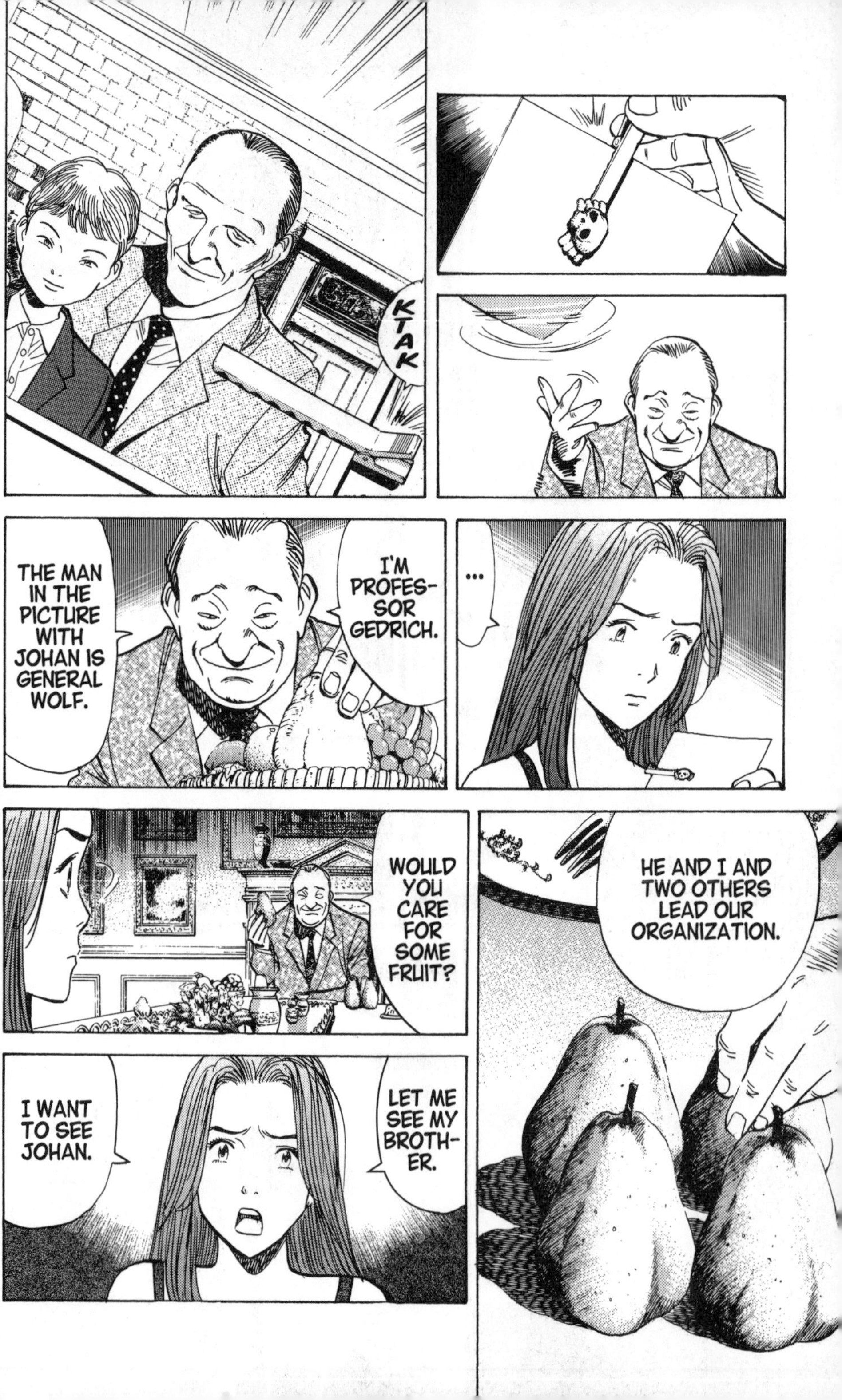
KTAK
...
I'M PROFESSOR GEDRICH.
THE MAN IN THE PICTURE WITH JOHAN IS GENERAL WOLF.
HE AND I AND TWO OTHERS LEAD OUR ORGANIZATION.
WOULD YOU CARE FOR SOME FRUIT?
LET ME SEE MY BROTHER.
I WANT TO SEE JOHAN.

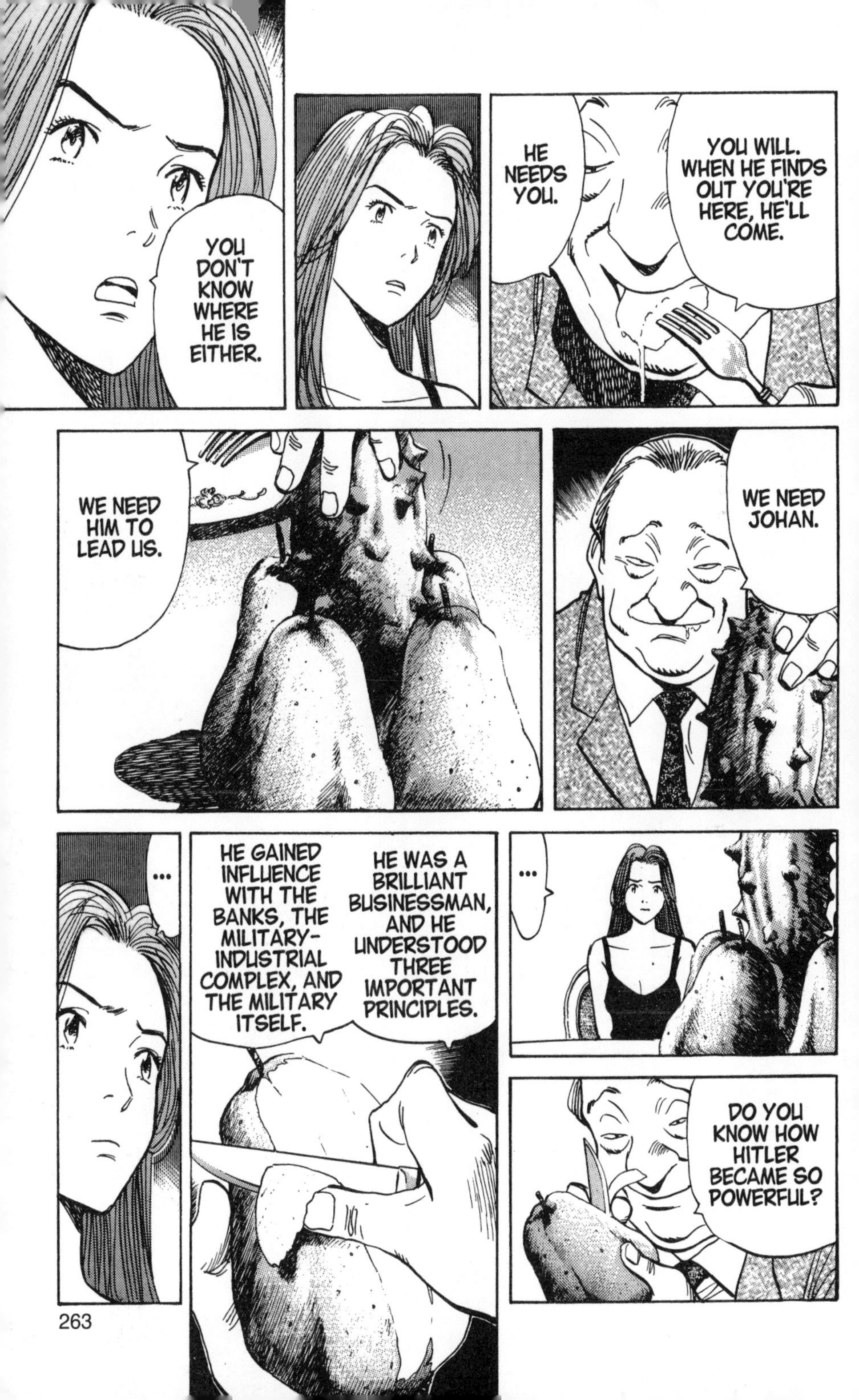
YOU WILL. WHEN HE FINDS OUT YOU'RE HERE, HE'LL COME.
HE NEEDS YOU.
YOU DON'T KNOW WHERE HE IS EITHER.
WE NEED JOHAN.
WE NEED HIM TO LEAD US.
...
DO YOU KNOW HOW HITLER BECAME SO POWERFUL?
HE WAS A BRILLIANT BUSINESSMAN, AND HE UNDERSTOOD THREE IMPORTANT PRINCIPLES.
HE GAINED INFLUENCE WITH THE BANKS, THE MILITARY-INDUSTRIAL COMPLEX, AND THE MILITARY ITSELF.
...

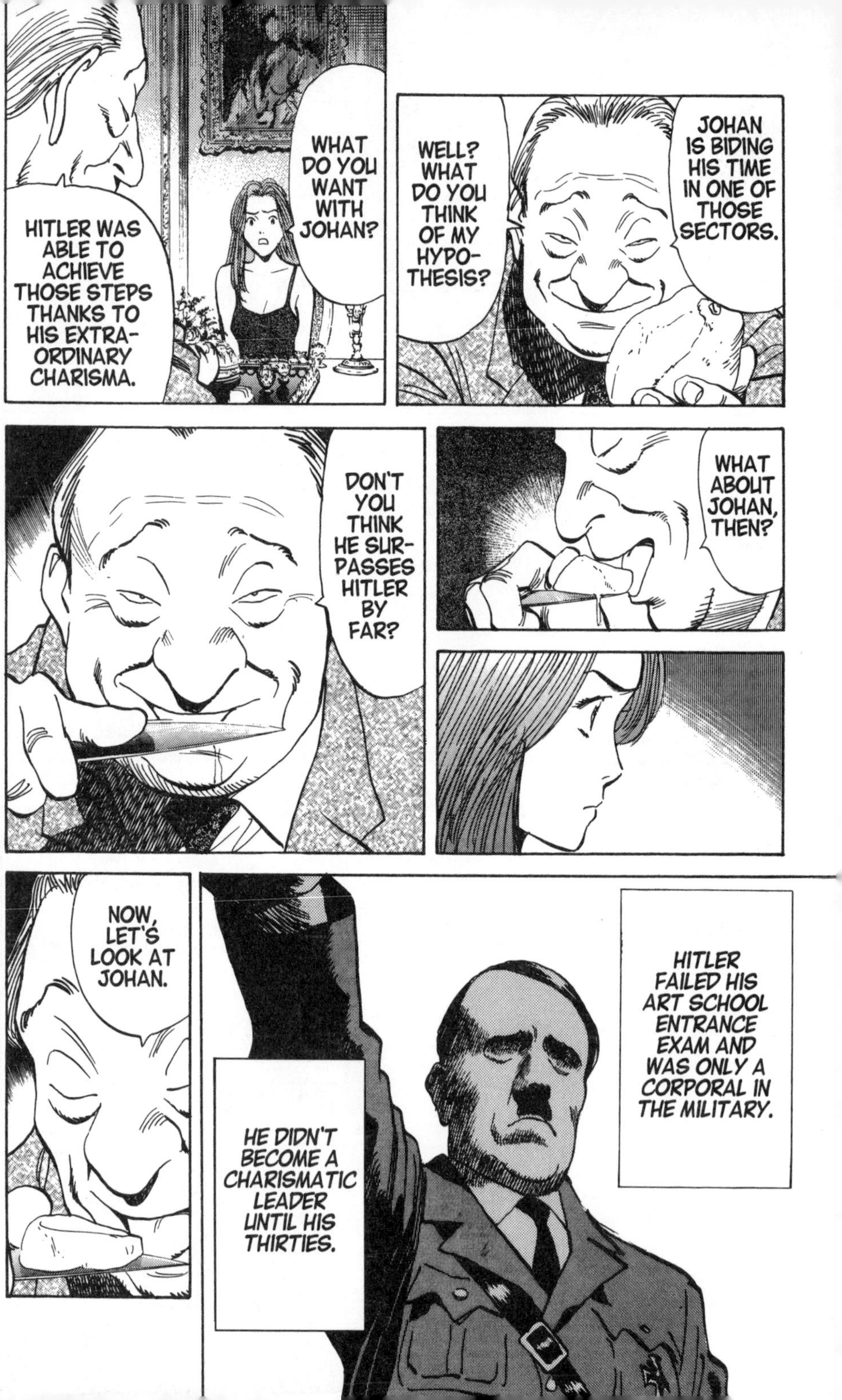
JOHAN IS BIDING HIS TIME IN ONE OF THOSE SECTORS.
WELL? WHAT DO YOU THINK OF MY HYPOTHESIS?
WHAT DO YOU WANT WITH JOHAN?
HITLER WAS ABLE TO ACHIEVE THOSE STEPS THANKS TO HIS EXTRAORDINARY CHARISMA.
WHAT ABOUT JOHAN, THEN?
DON'T YOU THINK HE SURPASSES HITLER BY FAR?
HITLER FAILED HIS ART SCHOOL ENTRANCE EXAM AND WAS ONLY A CORPORAL IN THE MILITARY.
HE DIDN'T BECOME A CHARISMATIC LEADER UNTIL HIS THIRTIES.
NOW, LET'S LOOK AT JOHAN.

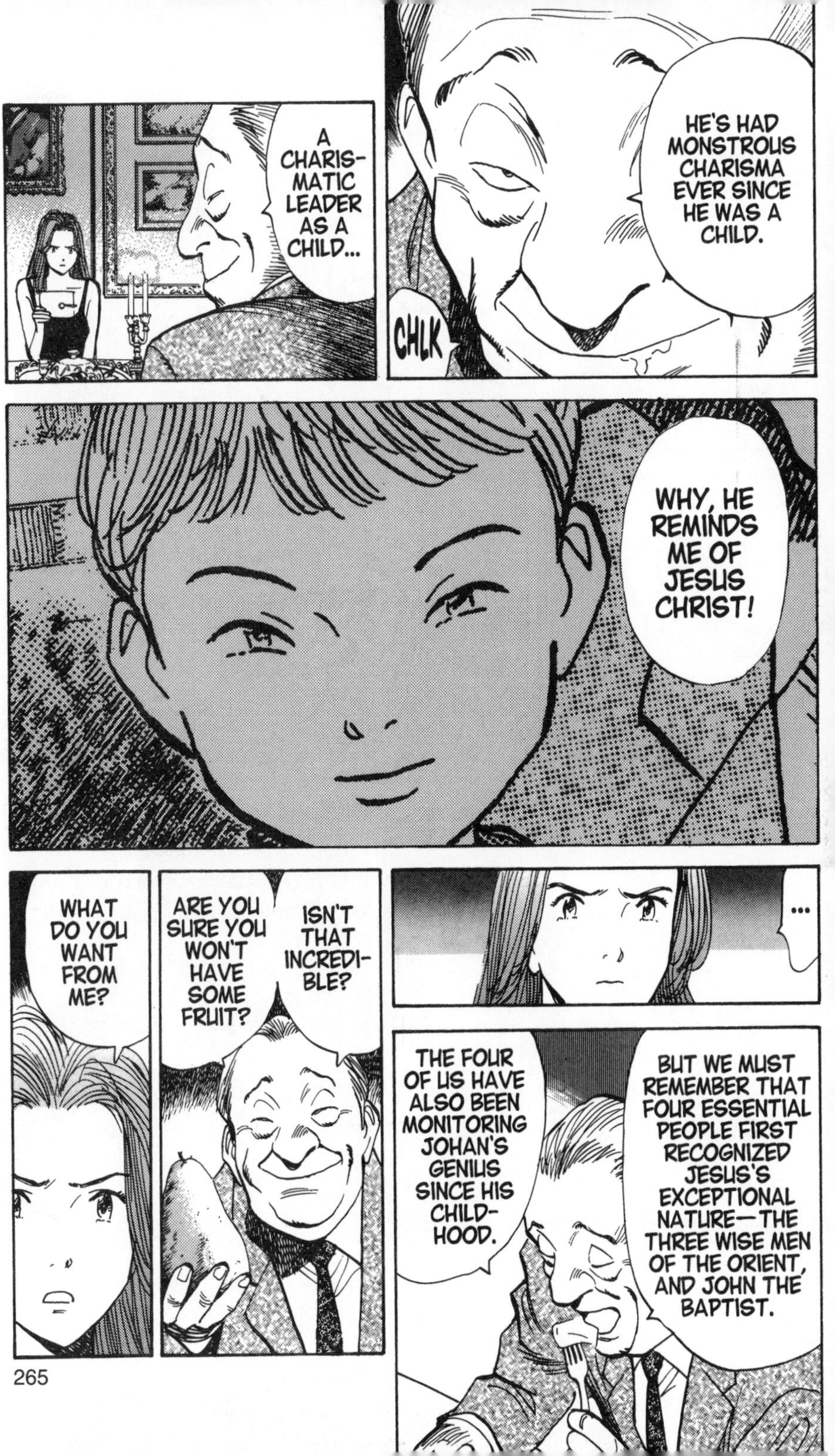
HE'S HAD MONSTROUS CHARISMA EVER SINCE HE WAS A CHILD.
CHLK
A CHARIS-MATIC LEADER AS A CHILD...
WHY, HE REMINDS ME OF JESUS CHRIST!
...
BUT WE MUST REMEMBER THAT FOUR ESSENTIAL PEOPLE FIRST RECOGNIZED JESUS'S EXCEPTIONAL NATURE—THE THREE WISE MEN OF THE ORIENT, AND JOHN THE BAPTIST.
THE FOUR OF US HAVE ALSO BEEN MONITORING JOHAN'S GENIUS SINCE HIS CHILD-HOOD.
ISN'T THAT INCREDI-BLE?
ARE YOU SURE YOU WON'T HAVE SOME FRUIT?
WHAT DO YOU WANT FROM ME?

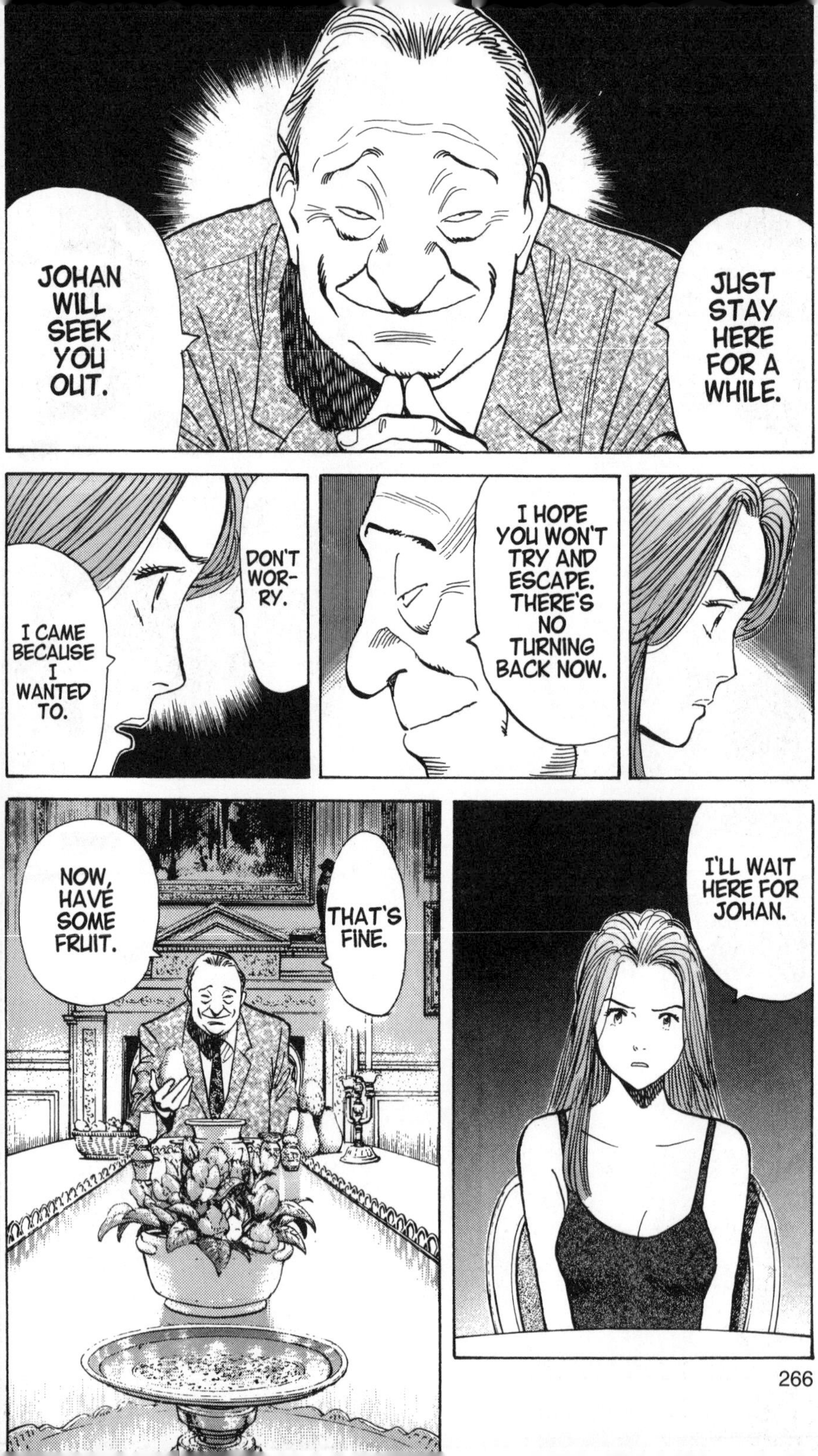
JUST STAY HERE FOR A WHILE.
JOHAN WILL SEEK YOU OUT.
I HOPE YOU WON'T TRY AND ESCAPE. THERE'S NO TURNING BACK NOW.
DON'T WORRY.
I CAME BECAUSE I WANTED TO.
I'LL WAIT HERE FOR JOHAN.
THAT'S FINE.
NOW, HAVE SOME FRUIT.

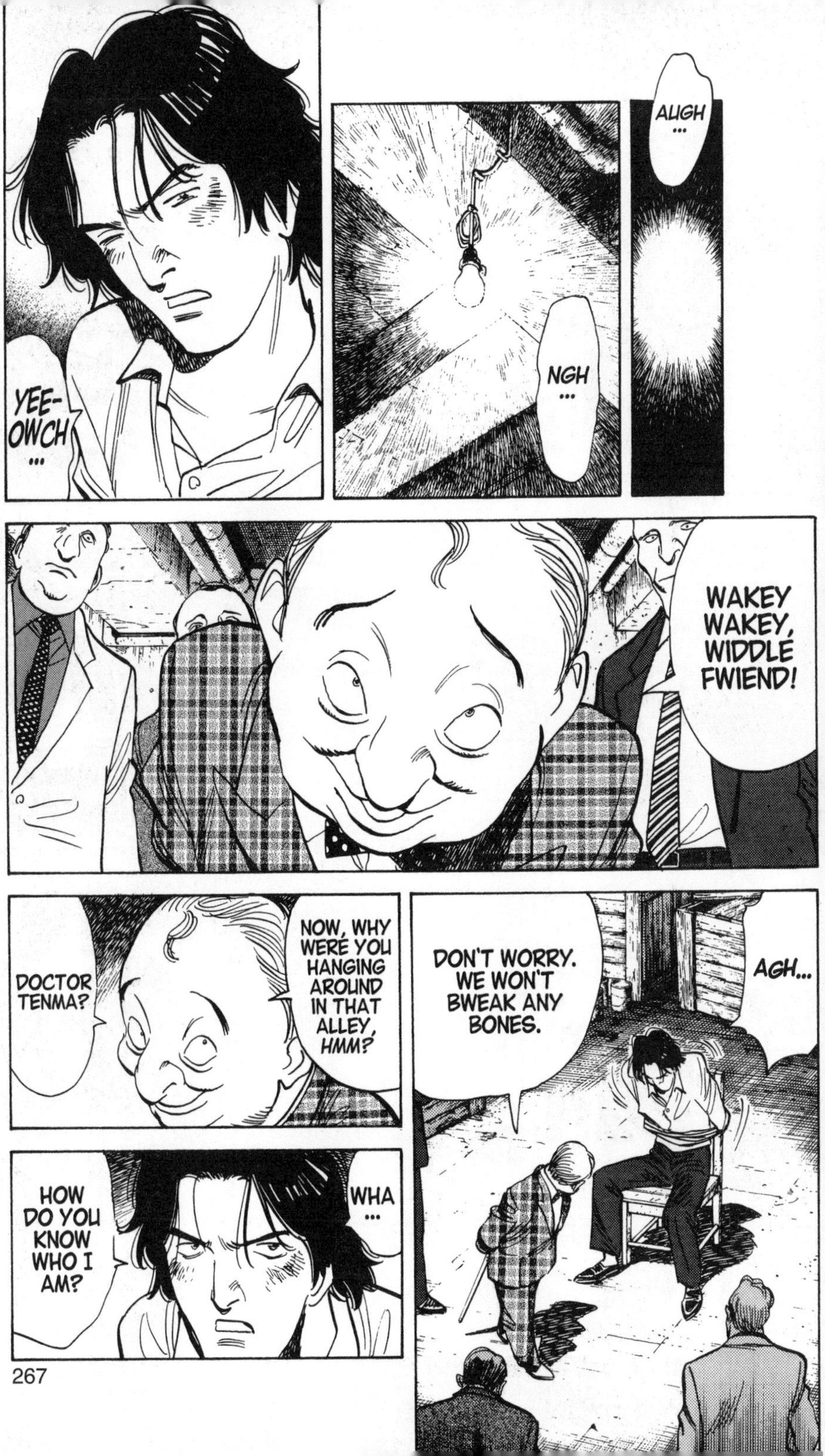
AUGH ...
NGH ...
YEE-OWCH ...
WAKEY WAKEY, WIDDLE FWIEND!
AGH...
DON'T WORRY. WE WON'T BWEAK ANY BONES.
NOW, WHY WERE YOU HANGING AROUND IN THAT ALLEY, HMM?
DOCTOR TENMA?
WHA ...
HOW DO YOU KNOW WHO I AM?

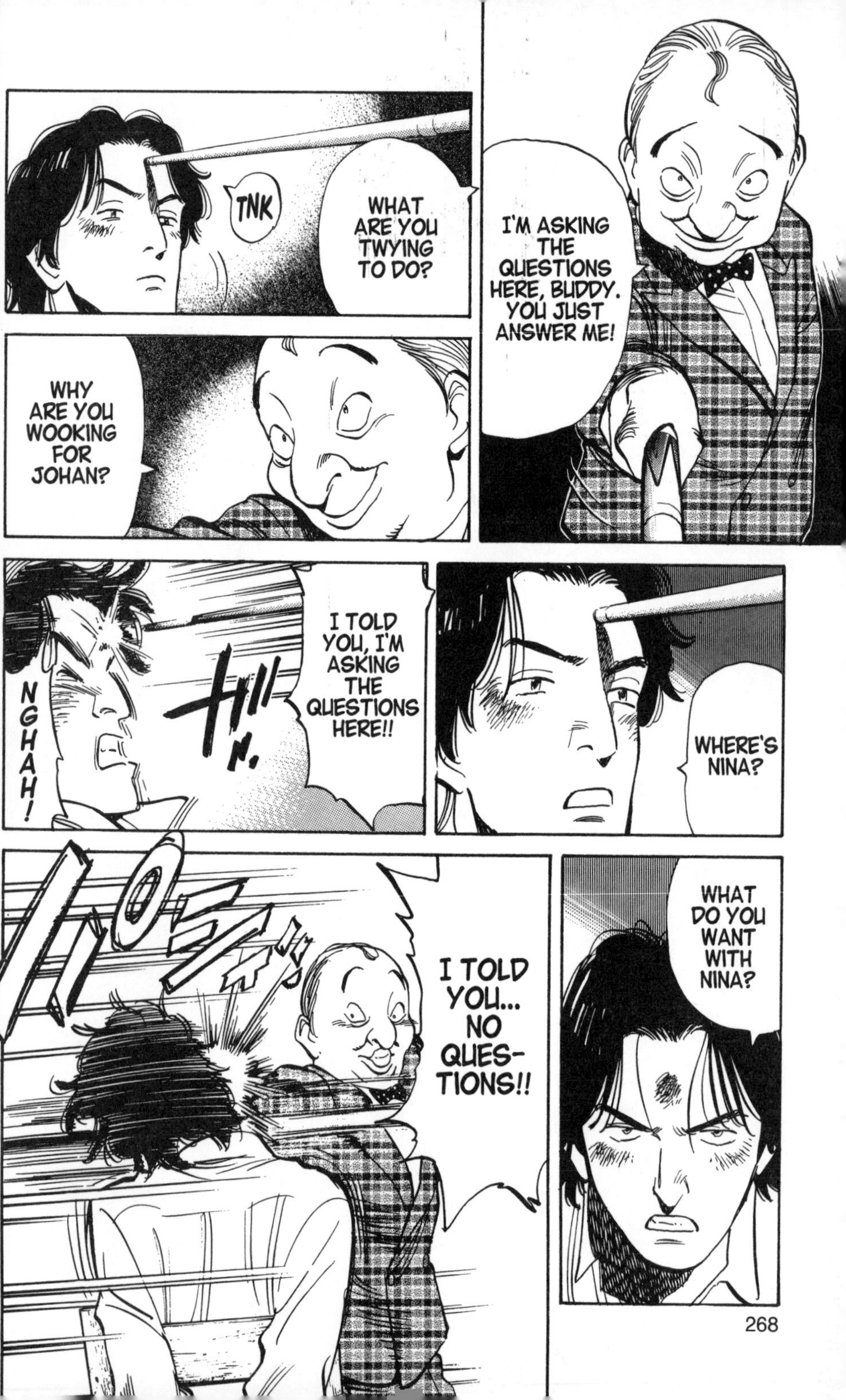
I'M ASKING THE QUESTIONS HERE, BUDDY. YOU JUST ANSWER ME!
TNK
WHAT ARE YOU TWYING TO DO?
WHY ARE YOU WOOKING FOR JOHAN?
WHERE'S NINA?
I TOLD YOU, I'M ASKING THE QUESTIONS HERE!!
NGHAH!
WHAT DO YOU WANT WITH NINA?
I TOLD YOU... NO QUES-TIONS!!

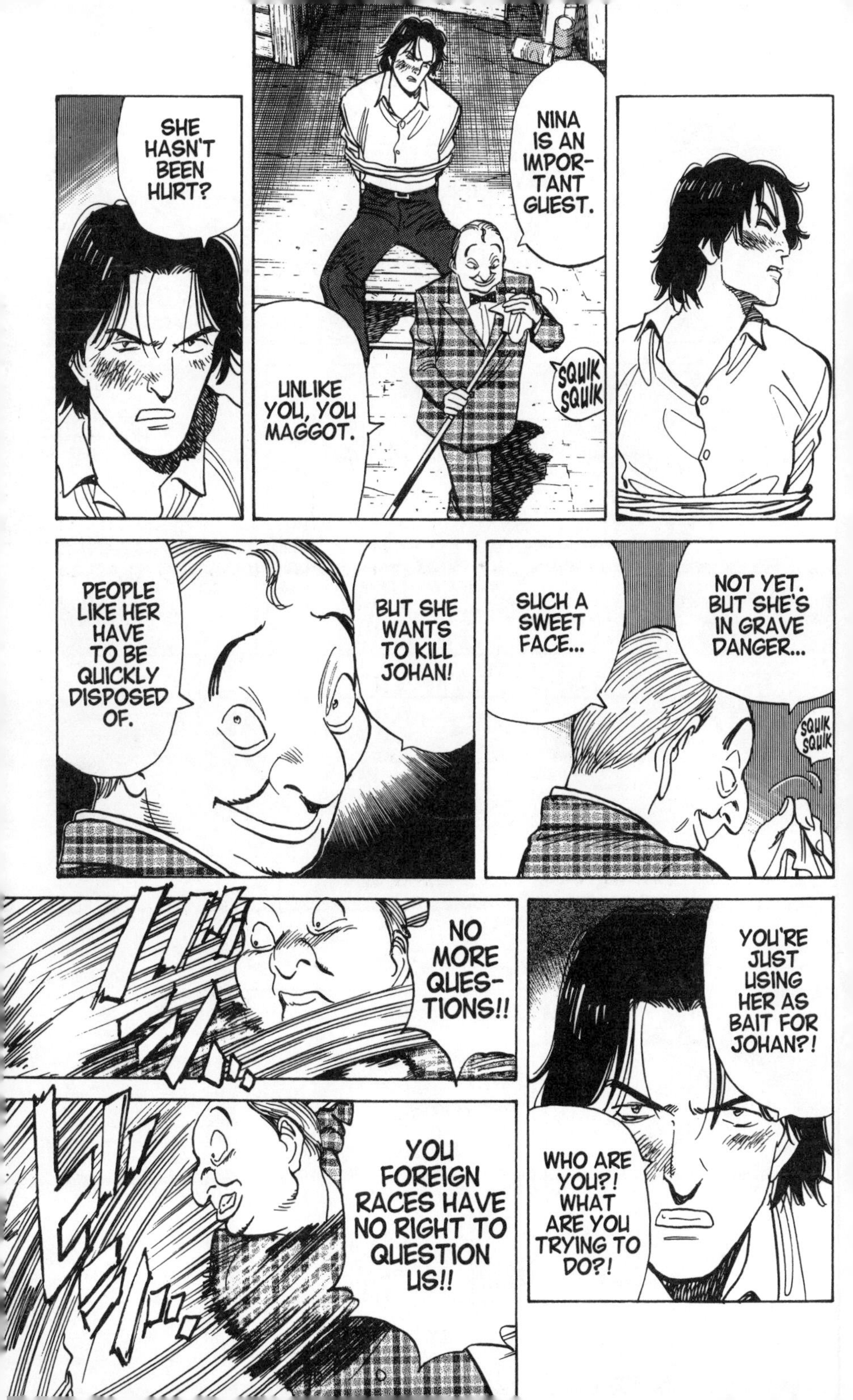
NINA IS AN IMPORTANT GUEST.
SQUIK SQUIK
UNLIKE YOU, YOU MAGGOT.
SHE HASN'T BEEN HURT?
NOT YET. BUT SHE'S IN GRAVE DANGER...
SQUIK SQUIK
SUCH A SWEET FACE...
BUT SHE WANTS TO KILL JOHAN!
PEOPLE LIKE HER HAVE TO BE QUICKLY DISPOSED OF.
YOU'RE JUST USING HER AS BAIT FOR JOHAN?!
WHO ARE YOU?! WHAT ARE YOU TRYING TO DO?!
NO MORE QUESTIONS!!
YOU FOREIGN RACES HAVE NO RIGHT TO QUESTION US!!

THAT KIND OF DISWESPECTFUL ATTITUDE IS WHAT GETS NEIGHBORHOODS TORCHED!

WE'LL LIGHT UP THE NIGHT SKY TONIGHT!

SKWIK SKWIK

THAT'S RIGHT...

NEIGHBOR-HOODS... TORCHED ?

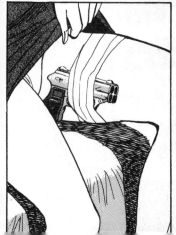

...JOHAN WILL COME.

IF I STAY HERE...

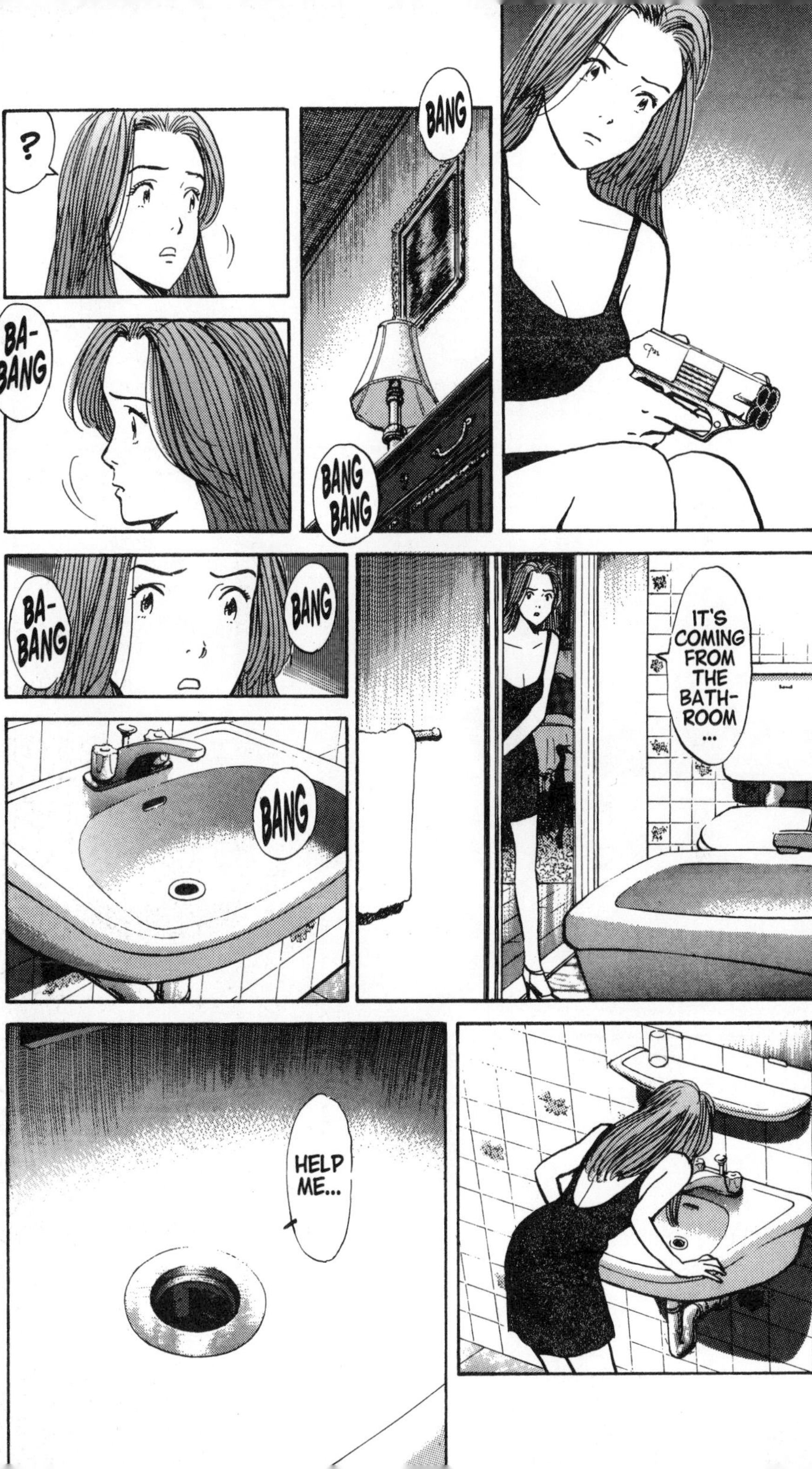
BANG
BANG BANG
?
BA-BANG
IT'S COMING FROM THE BATHROOM...
BANG
BA-BANG
BANG
HELP ME...

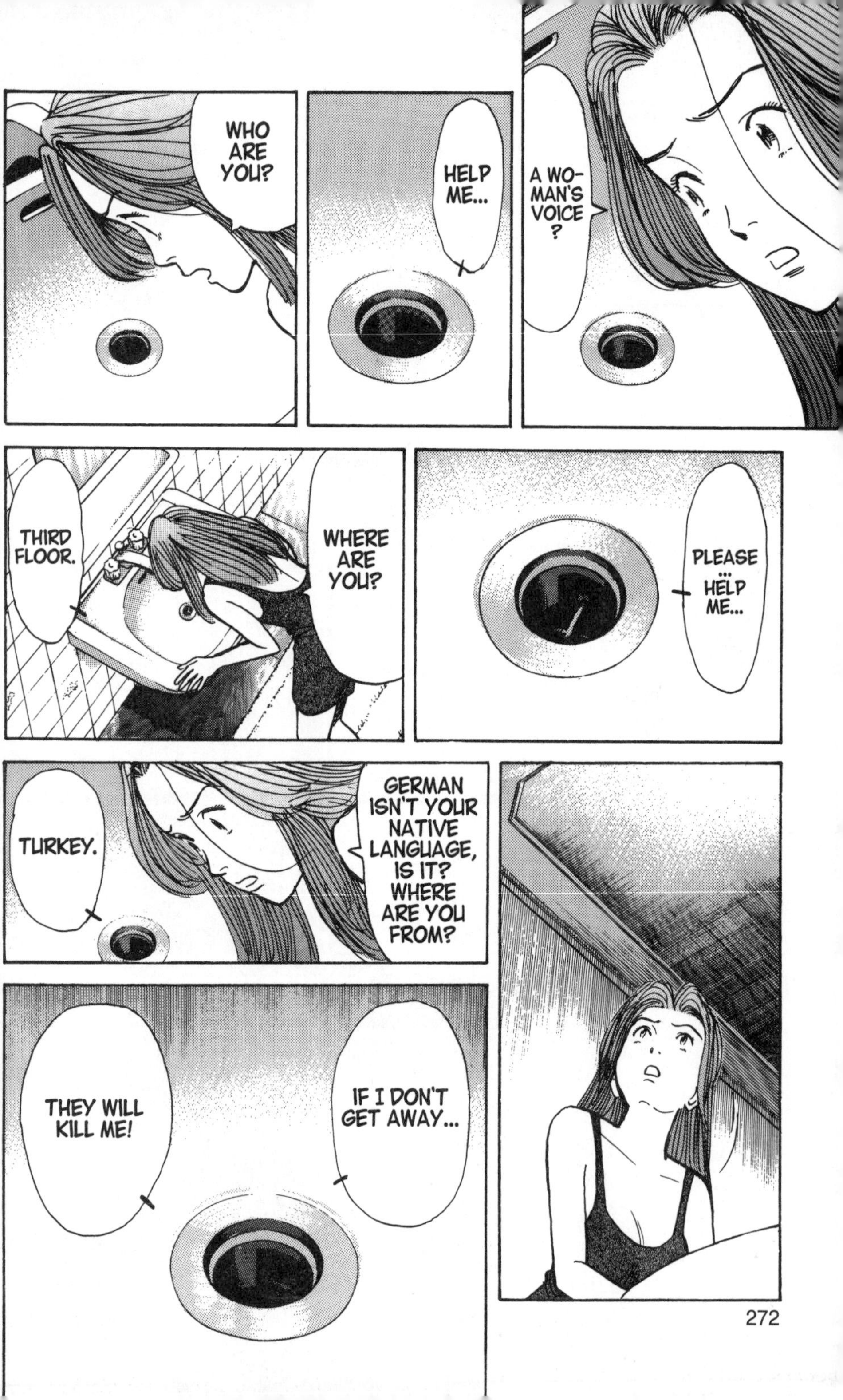
A WO-MAN'S VOICE?
HELP ME...
WHO ARE YOU?
PLEASE... HELP ME...
WHERE ARE YOU?
THIRD FLOOR.
GERMAN ISN'T YOUR NATIVE LANGUAGE, IS IT? WHERE ARE YOU FROM?
TURKEY.
IF I DON'T GET AWAY...
THEY WILL KILL ME!

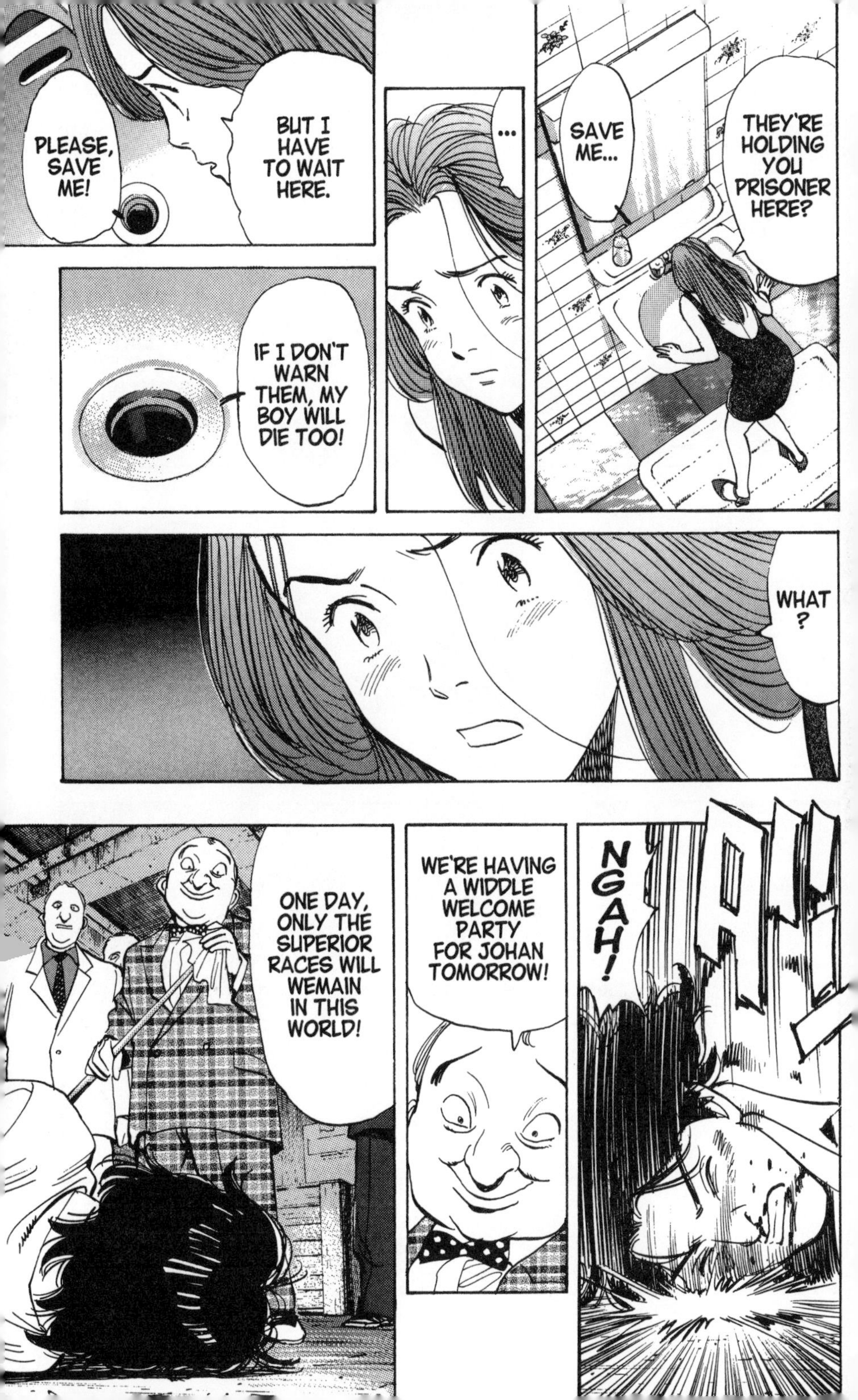
THEY'RE HOLDING YOU PRISONER HERE?
SAVE ME...
...
BUT I HAVE TO WAIT HERE.
PLEASE, SAVE ME!
IF I DON'T WARN THEM, MY BOY WILL DIE TOO!
WHAT?
NGAH!
WE'RE HAVING A WIDDLE WELCOME PARTY FOR JOHAN TOMORROW!
ONE DAY, ONLY THE SUPERIOR RACES WILL WEMAIN IN THIS WORLD!

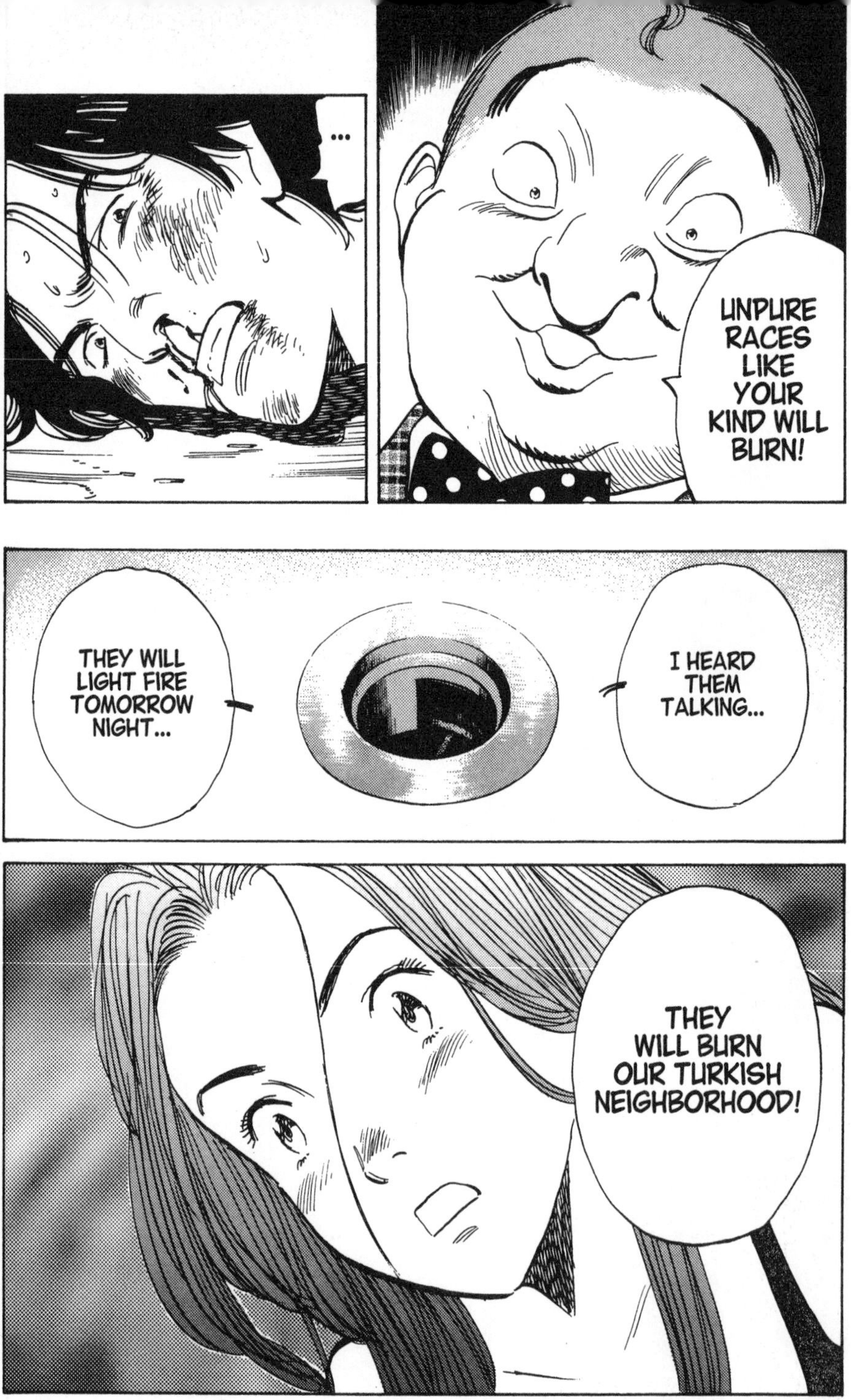
UNPURE RACES LIKE YOUR KIND WILL BURN!
...
I HEARD THEM TALKING...
THEY WILL LIGHT FIRE TOMORROW NIGHT...
THEY WILL BURN OUR TURKISH NEIGHBORHOOD!

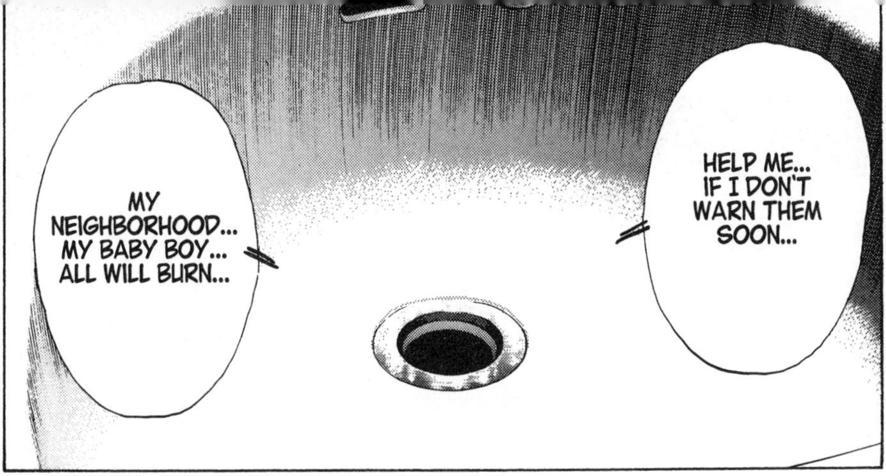
HELP ME... IF I DON'T WARN THEM SOON...
MY NEIGHBORHOOD... MY BABY BOY... ALL WILL BURN...

Kapitel 28.

Ayşe's Friend

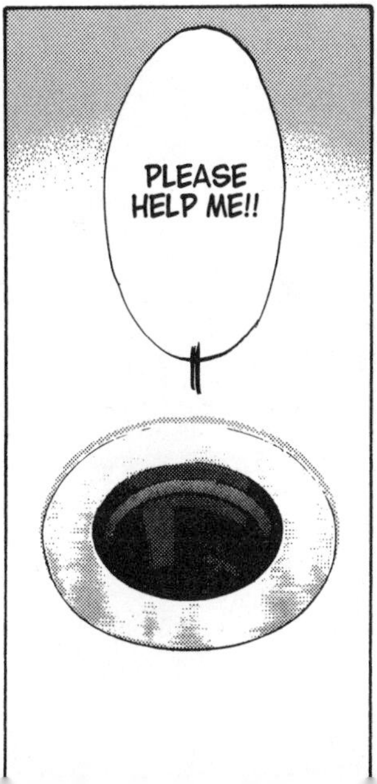
PLEASE HELP ME!!

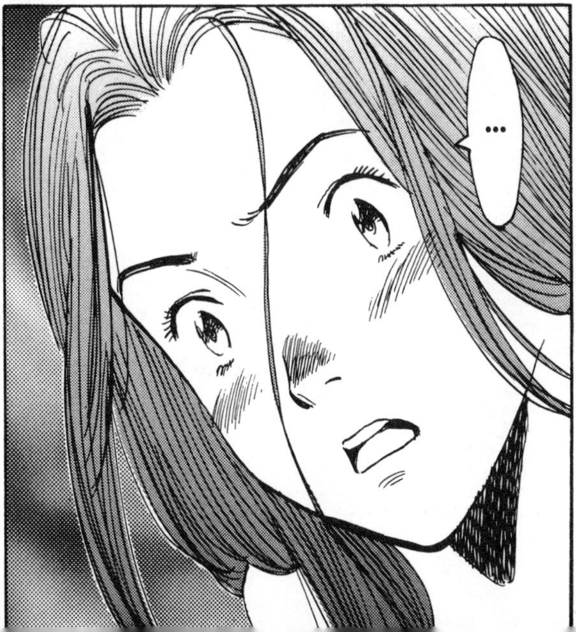
...

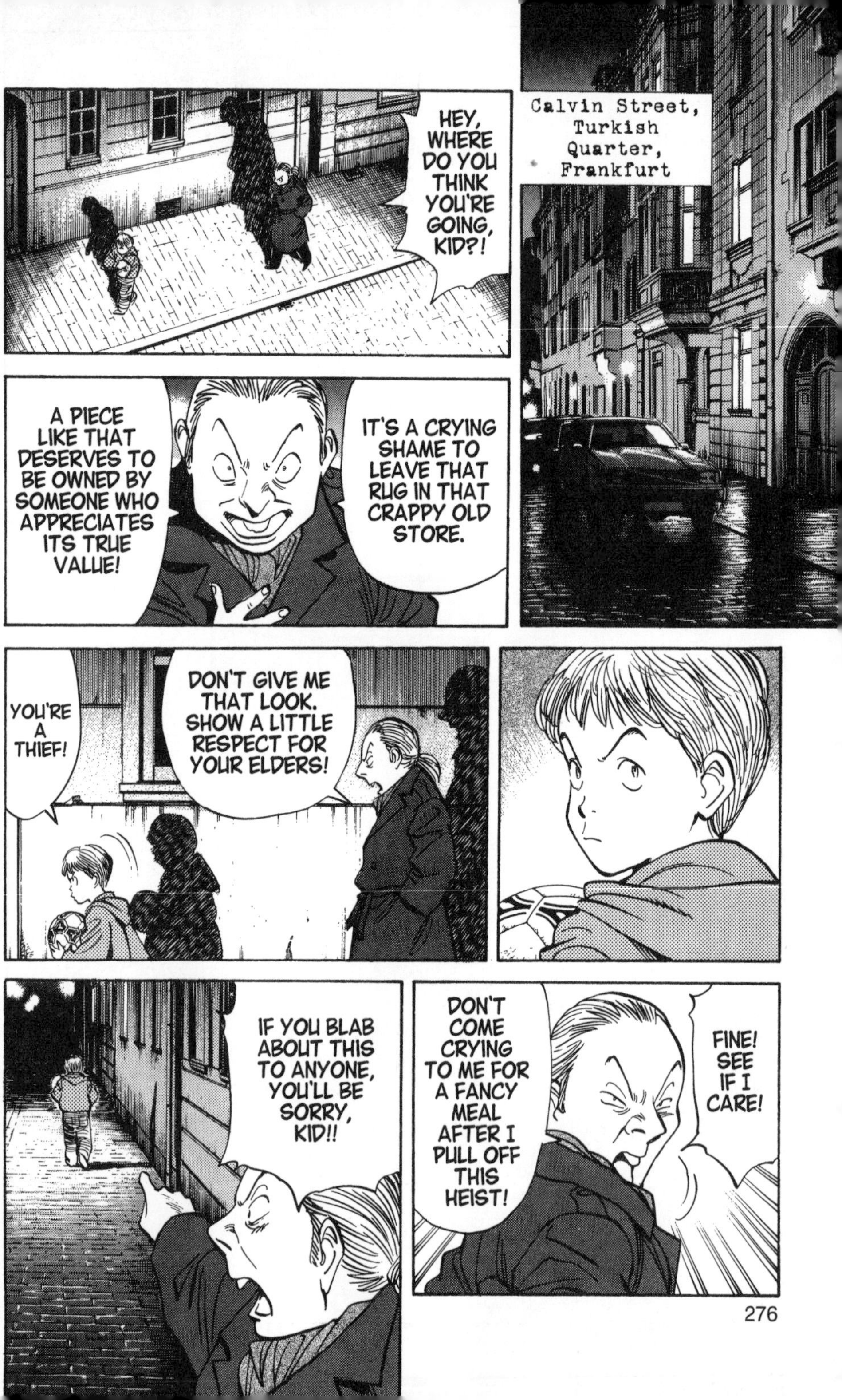
Calvin Street, Turkish Quarter, Frankfurt
HEY, WHERE DO YOU THINK YOU'RE GOING, KID?!
IT'S A CRYING SHAME TO LEAVE THAT RUG IN THAT CRAPPY OLD STORE.
A PIECE LIKE THAT DESERVES TO BE OWNED BY SOMEONE WHO APPRECIATES ITS TRUE VALUE!
DON'T GIVE ME THAT LOOK. SHOW A LITTLE RESPECT FOR YOUR ELDERS!
YOU'RE A THIEF!
FINE! SEE IF I CARE!
DON'T COME CRYING TO ME FOR A FANCY MEAL AFTER I PULL OFF THIS HEIST!
IF YOU BLAB ABOUT THIS TO ANYONE, YOU'LL BE SORRY, KID!!

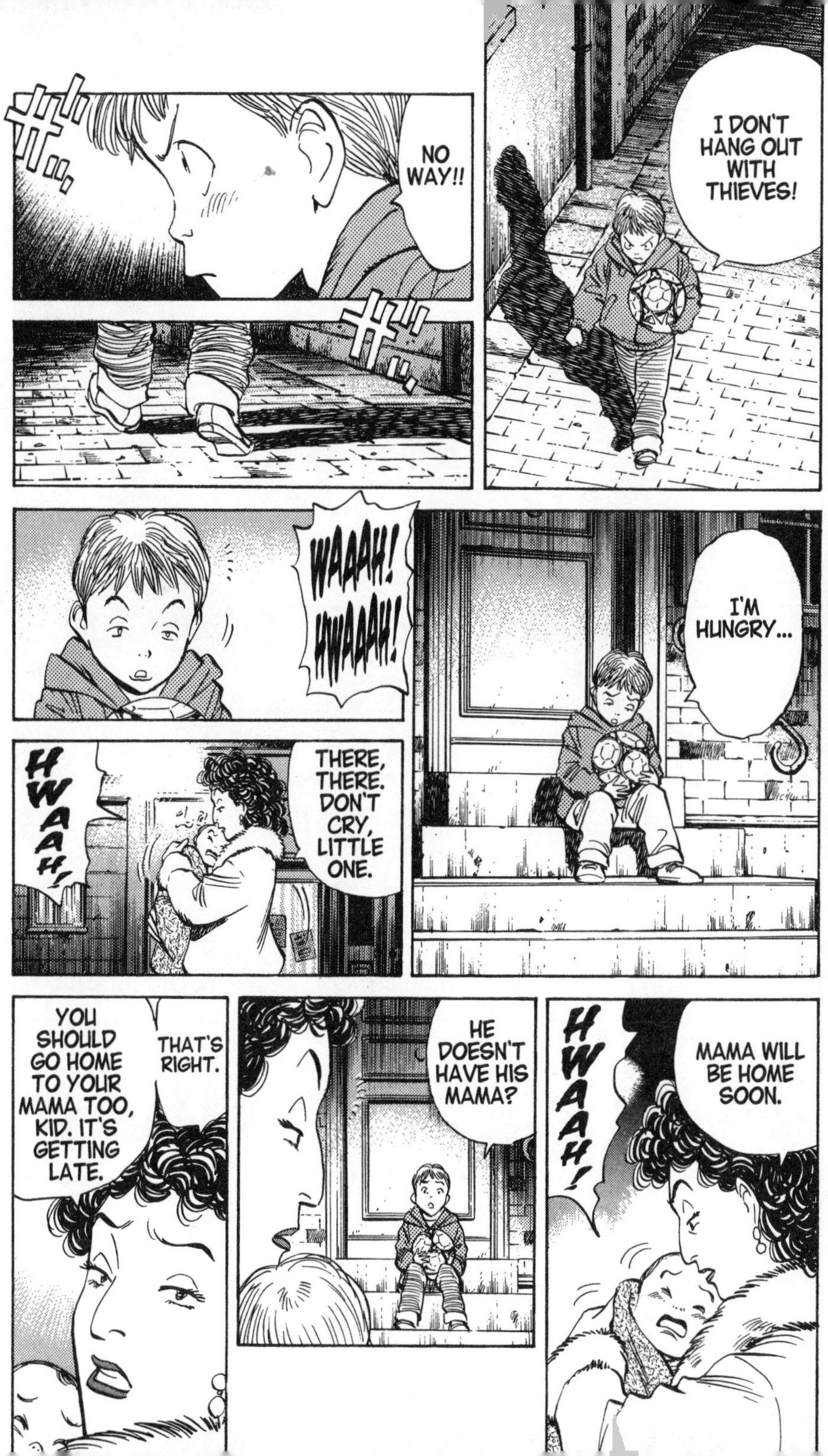
I DON'T HANG OUT WITH THIEVES!
NO WAY!!
I'M HUNGRY...
WAAAH! HWAAAH!
HWAAH!
THERE, THERE. DON'T CRY, LITTLE ONE.
HWAAH!
MAMA WILL BE HOME SOON.
HE DOESN'T HAVE HIS MAMA?
THAT'S RIGHT.
YOU SHOULD GO HOME TO YOUR MAMA TOO, KID. IT'S GETTING LATE.

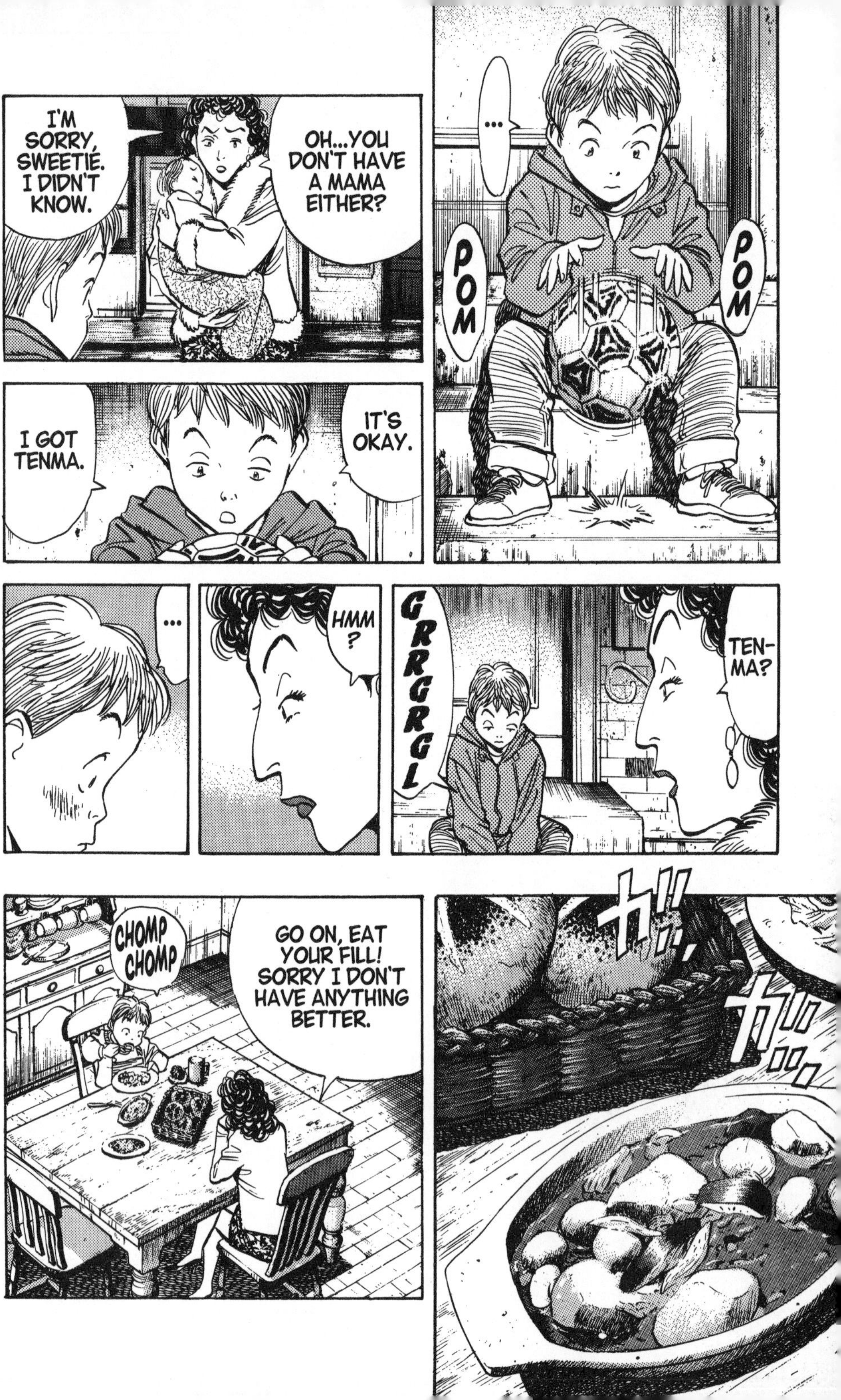
...
POM
POM
OH...YOU DON'T HAVE A MAMA EITHER?
I'M SORRY, SWEETIE. I DIDN'T KNOW.
IT'S OKAY.
I GOT TENMA.
TEN-MA?
GRRGRGL
HMM?
...
カ!!
カッ
GO ON, EAT YOUR FILL! SORRY I DON'T HAVE ANYTHING BETTER.
CHOMP CHOMP

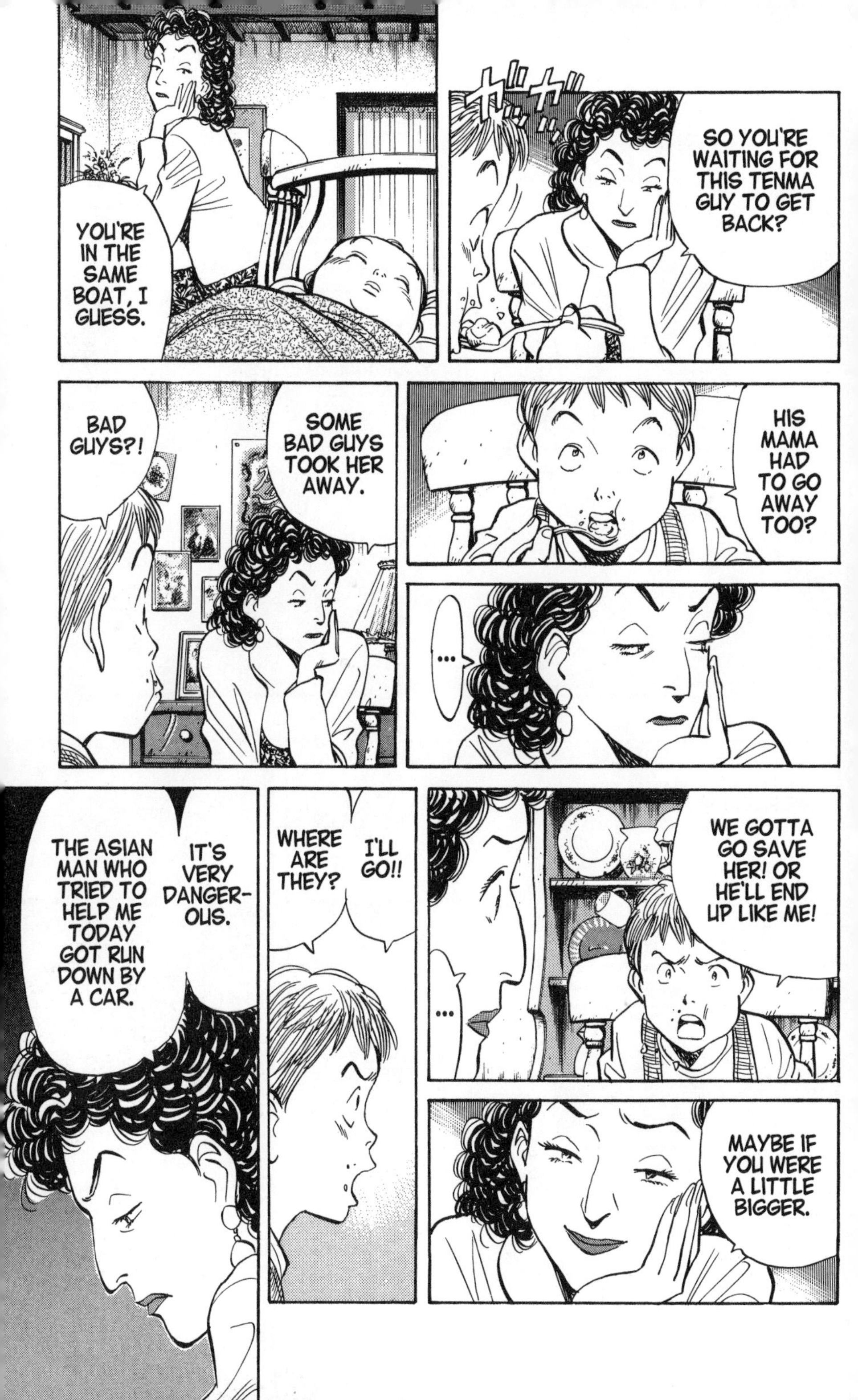
ガツガツ
SO YOU'RE WAITING FOR THIS TENMA GUY TO GET BACK?
YOU'RE IN THE SAME BOAT, I GUESS.
HIS MAMA HAD TO GO AWAY TOO?
...
SOME BAD GUYS TOOK HER AWAY.
BAD GUYS?!
WE GOTTA GO SAVE HER! OR HE'LL END UP LIKE ME!
...
MAYBE IF YOU WERE A LITTLE BIGGER.
I'LL GO!!
WHERE ARE THEY?
IT'S VERY DANGER-OUS.
THE ASIAN MAN WHO TRIED TO HELP ME TODAY GOT RUN DOWN BY A CAR.

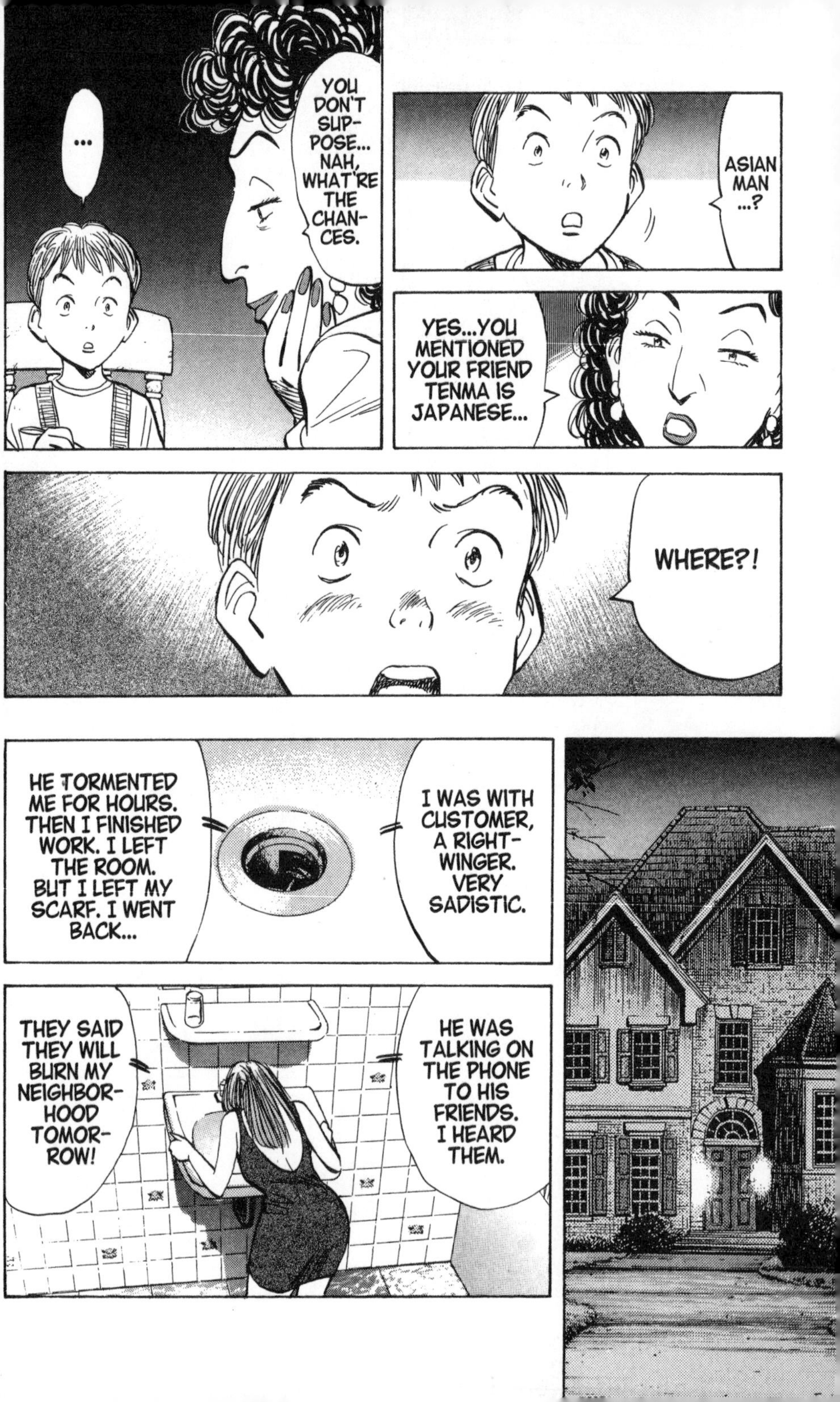
ASIAN MAN ...?
YES...YOU MENTIONED YOUR FRIEND TENMA IS JAPANESE...
YOU DON'T SUP-POSE... NAH, WHAT'RE THE CHAN-CES.
...
WHERE?!
I WAS WITH CUSTOMER, A RIGHT-WINGER. VERY SADISTIC.
HE TORMENTED ME FOR HOURS. THEN I FINISHED WORK. I LEFT THE ROOM. BUT I LEFT MY SCARF. I WENT BACK...
HE WAS TALKING ON THE PHONE TO HIS FRIENDS. I HEARD THEM.
THEY SAID THEY WILL BURN MY NEIGHBOR-HOOD TOMOR-ROW!

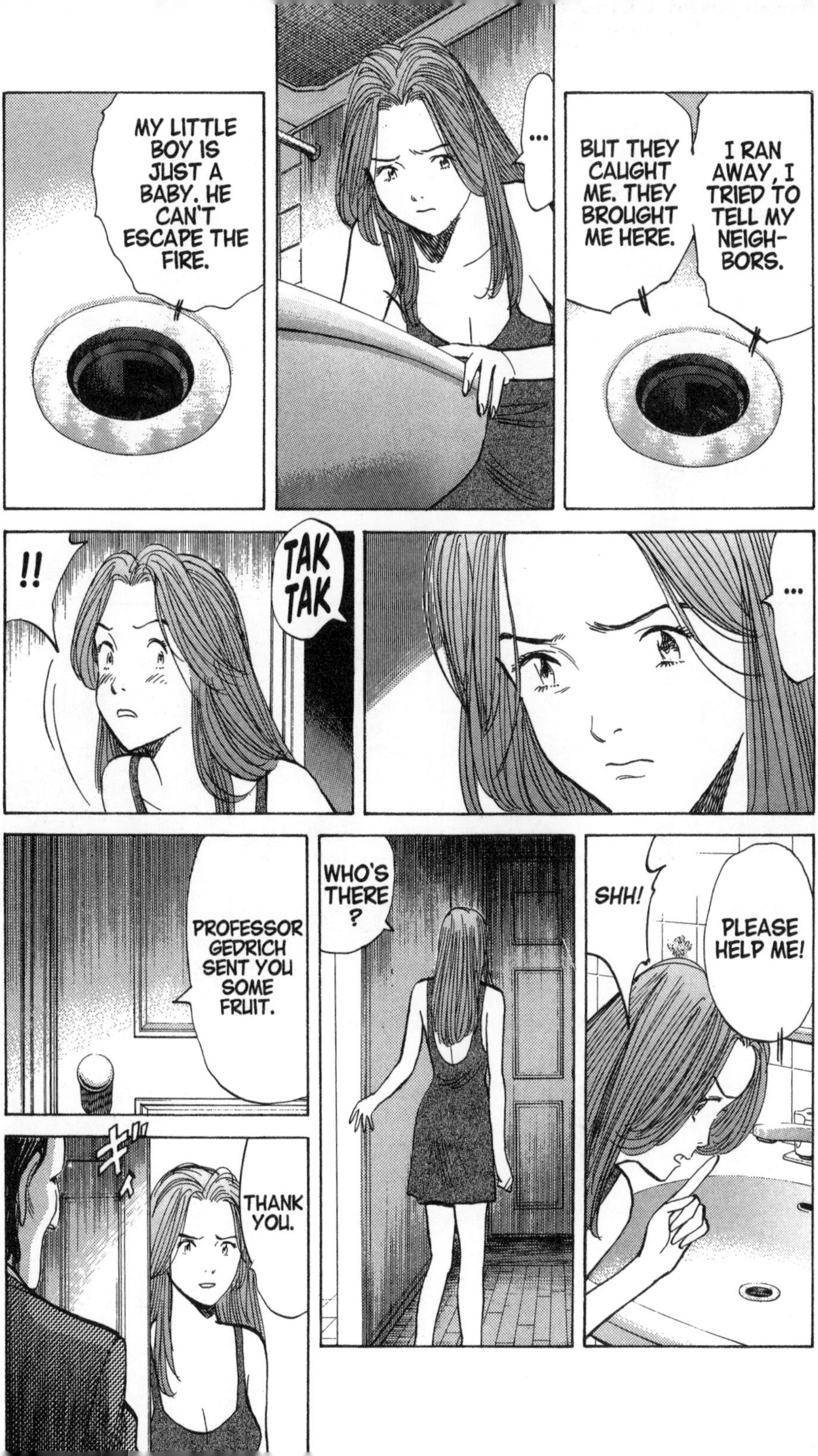
I RAN AWAY, I TRIED TO TELL MY NEIGHBORS.
BUT THEY CAUGHT ME. THEY BROUGHT ME HERE.
...
MY LITTLE BOY IS JUST A BABY. HE CAN'T ESCAPE THE FIRE.
...
TAK TAK
!!
PLEASE HELP ME!
SHH!
WHO'S THERE?
PROFESSOR GEDRICH SENT YOU SOME FRUIT.
ギィ
THANK YOU.

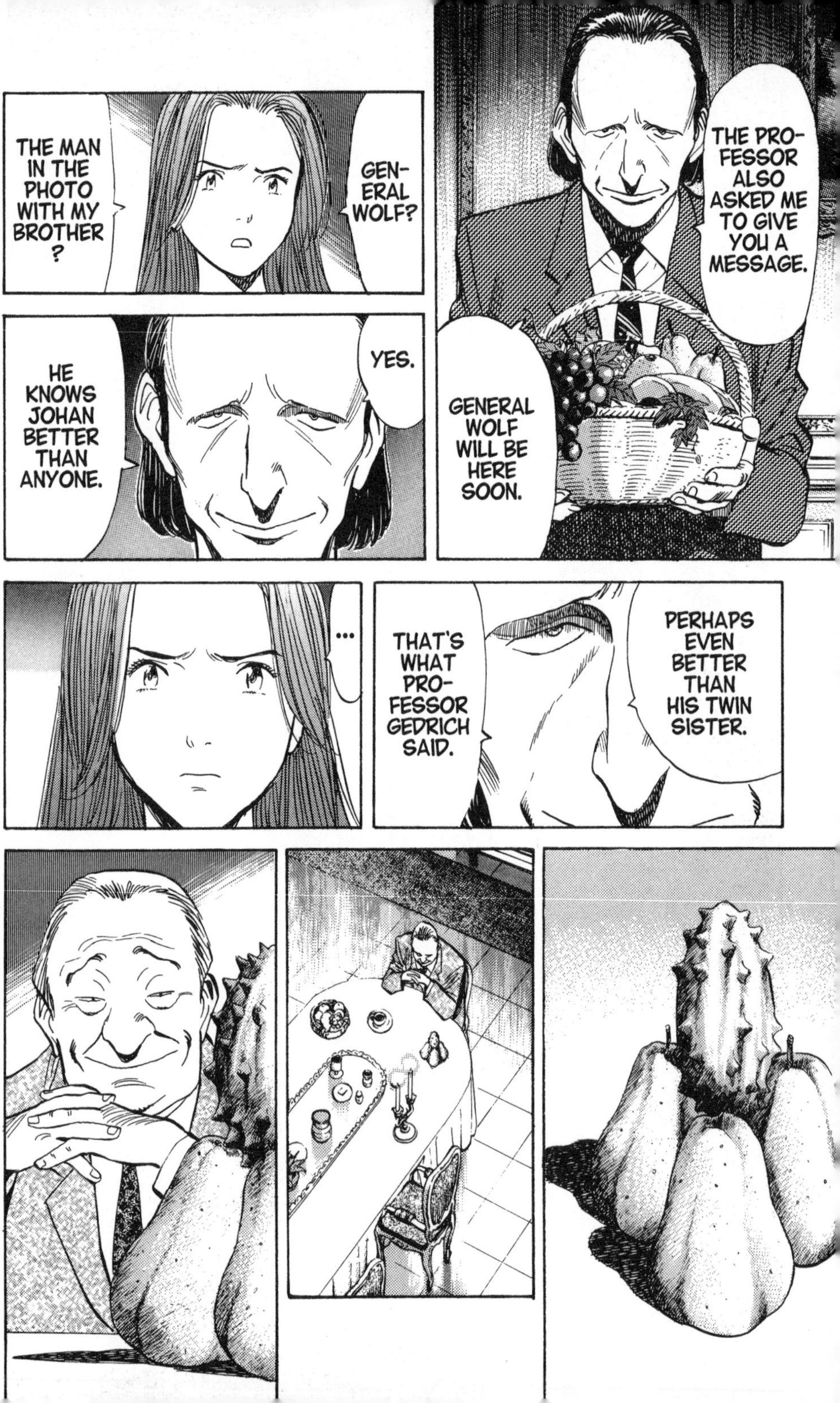
THE PRO-FESSOR ALSO ASKED ME TO GIVE YOU A MESSAGE.
GENERAL WOLF WILL BE HERE SOON.
GEN-ERAL WOLF?
THE MAN IN THE PHOTO WITH MY BROTHER?
YES.
HE KNOWS JOHAN BETTER THAN ANYONE.
PERHAPS EVEN BETTER THAN HIS TWIN SISTER.
THAT'S WHAT PRO-FESSOR GEDRICH SAID.
...

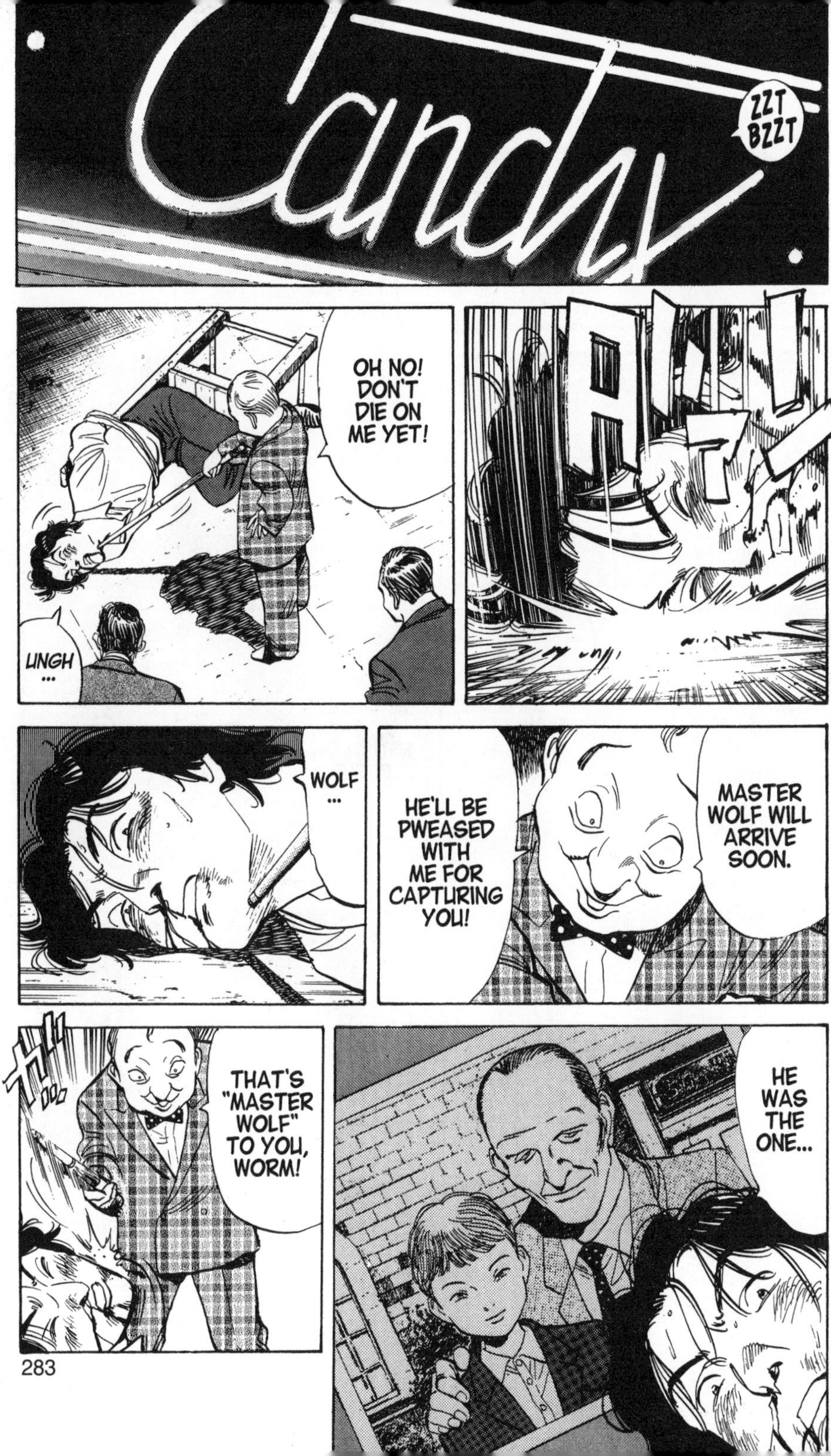
Candy
ZZT BZZT
OH NO! DON'T DIE ON ME YET!
UNGH ...
MASTER WOLF WILL ARRIVE SOON.
HE'LL BE PWEASED WITH ME FOR CAPTURING YOU!
WOLF ...
HE WAS THE ONE...
THAT'S "MASTER WOLF" TO YOU, WORM!

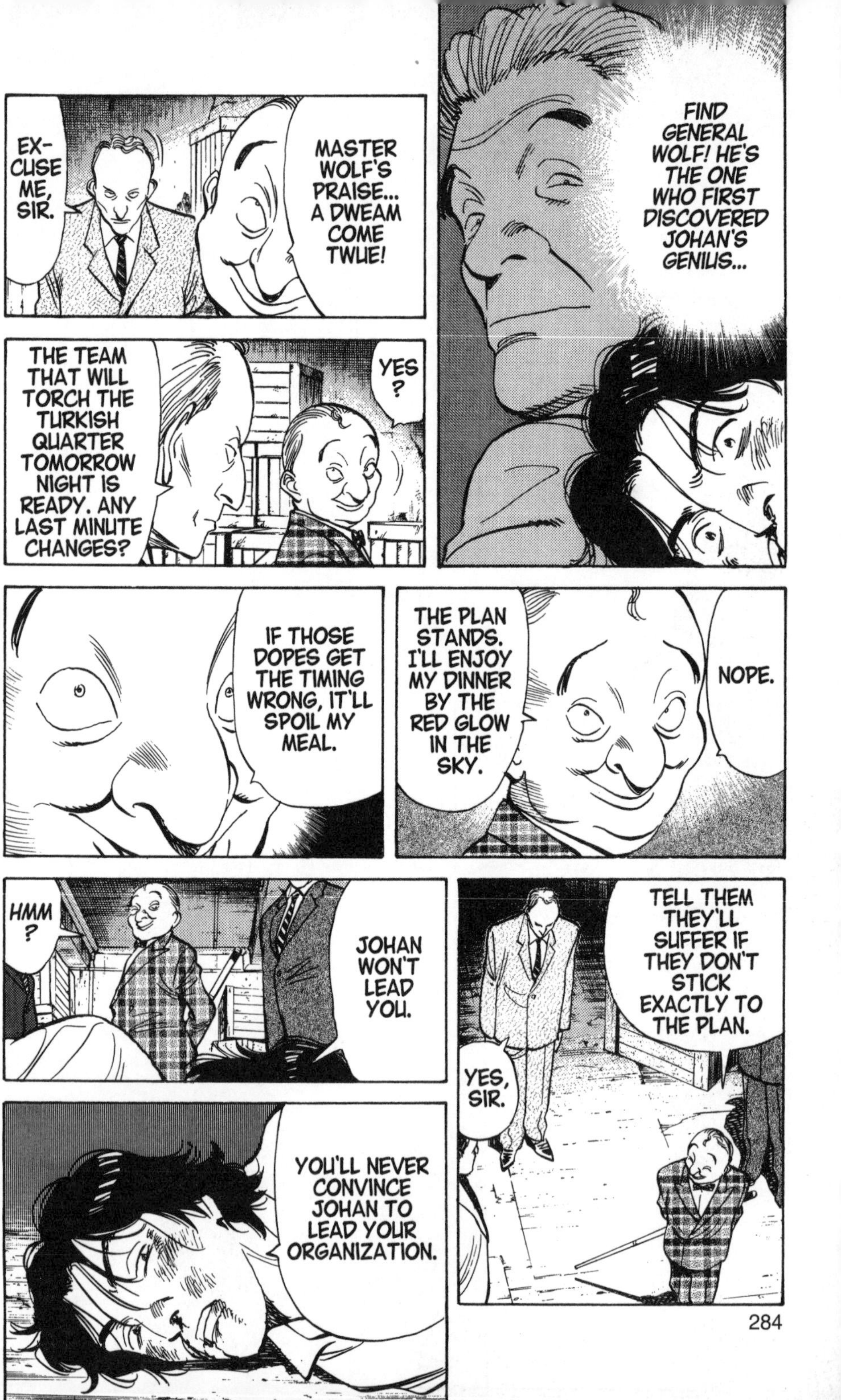
FIND GENERAL WOLF! HE'S THE ONE WHO FIRST DISCOVERED JOHAN'S GENIUS...
MASTER WOLF'S PRAISE... A DWEAM COME TWUE!
EX-CUSE ME, SIR.
YES?
THE TEAM THAT WILL TORCH THE TURKISH QUARTER TOMORROW NIGHT IS READY. ANY LAST MINUTE CHANGES?
NOPE.
THE PLAN STANDS. I'LL ENJOY MY DINNER BY THE RED GLOW IN THE SKY.
IF THOSE DOPES GET THE TIMING WRONG, IT'LL SPOIL MY MEAL.
TELL THEM THEY'LL SUFFER IF THEY DON'T STICK EXACTLY TO THE PLAN.
YES, SIR.
JOHAN WON'T LEAD YOU.
HMM?
YOU'LL NEVER CONVINCE JOHAN TO LEAD YOUR ORGANIZATION.

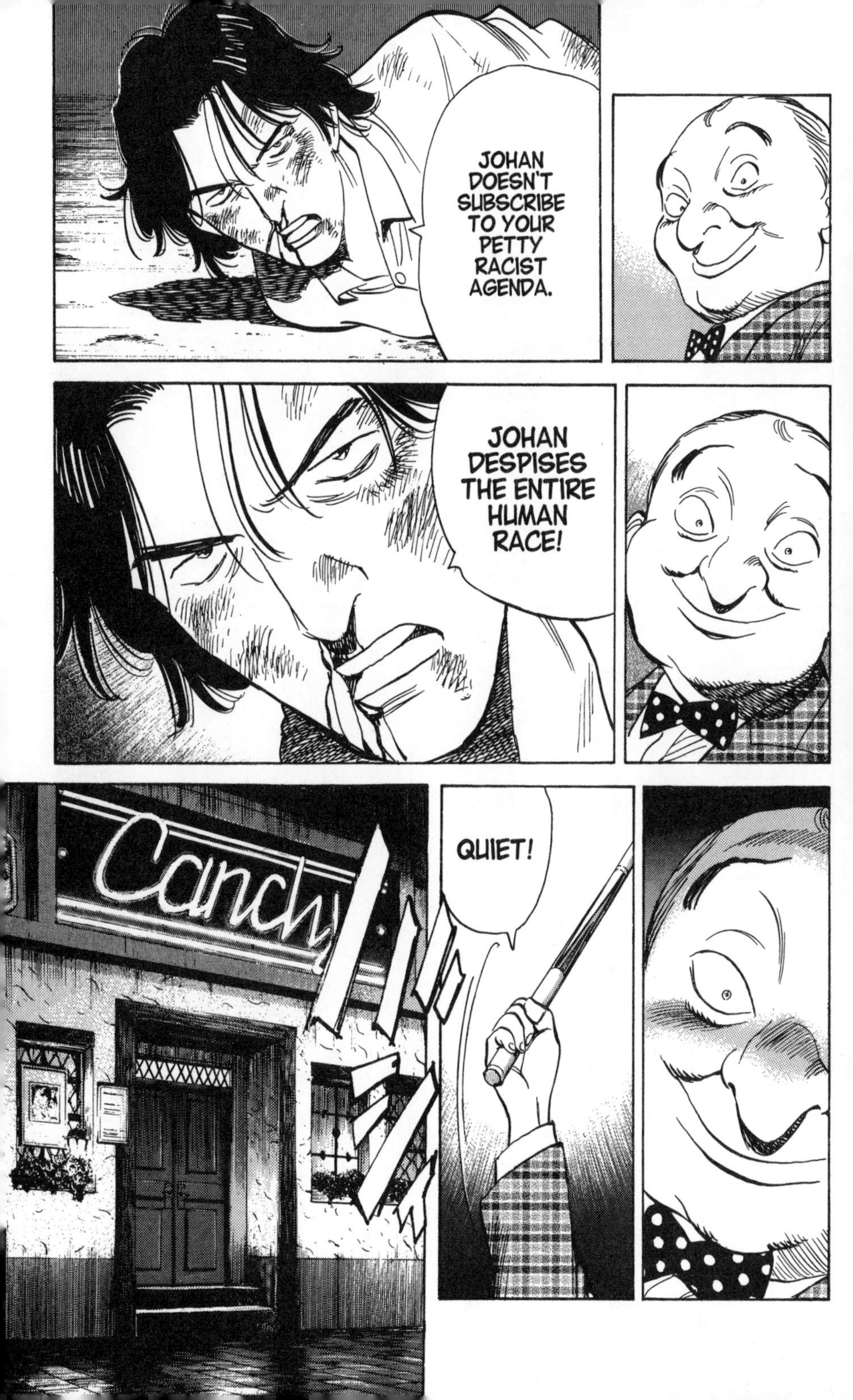

JOHAN DOESN'T SUBSCRIBE TO YOUR PETTY RACIST AGENDA.
JOHAN DESPISES THE ENTIRE HUMAN RACE!
QUIET!
Candy

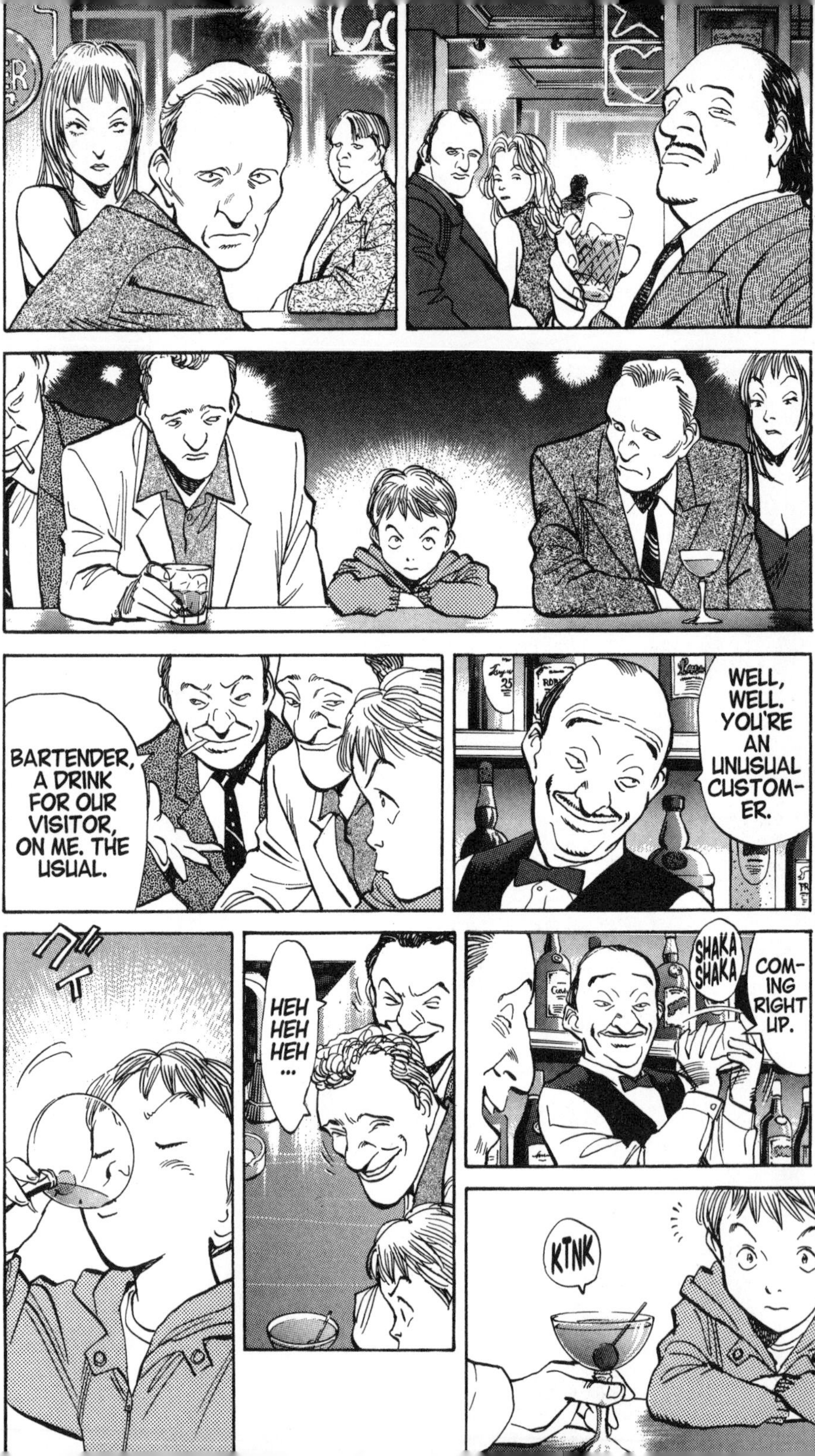

WELL, WELL. YOU'RE AN UNUSUAL CUSTOMER.
BARTENDER, A DRINK FOR OUR VISITOR, ON ME. THE USUAL.
COMING RIGHT UP.
SHAKA SHAKA
HEH HEH HEH...
KINK

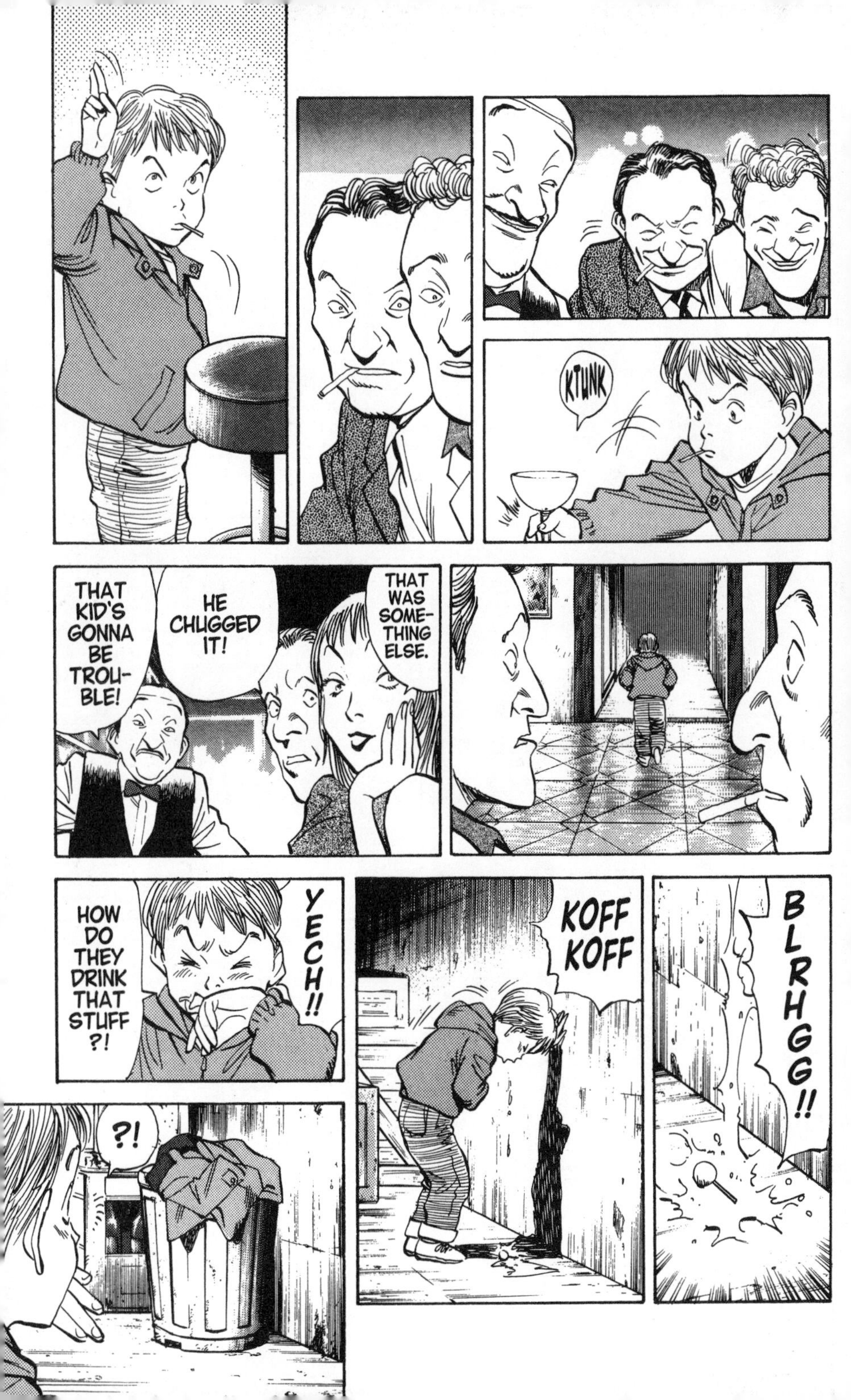
KTUNK
THAT WAS SOME-THING ELSE.
HE CHUGGED IT!
THAT KID'S GONNA BE TROU-BLE!
BLRHGG!!
KOFF KOFF
YECH!!
HOW DO THEY DRINK THAT STUFF?!
?!

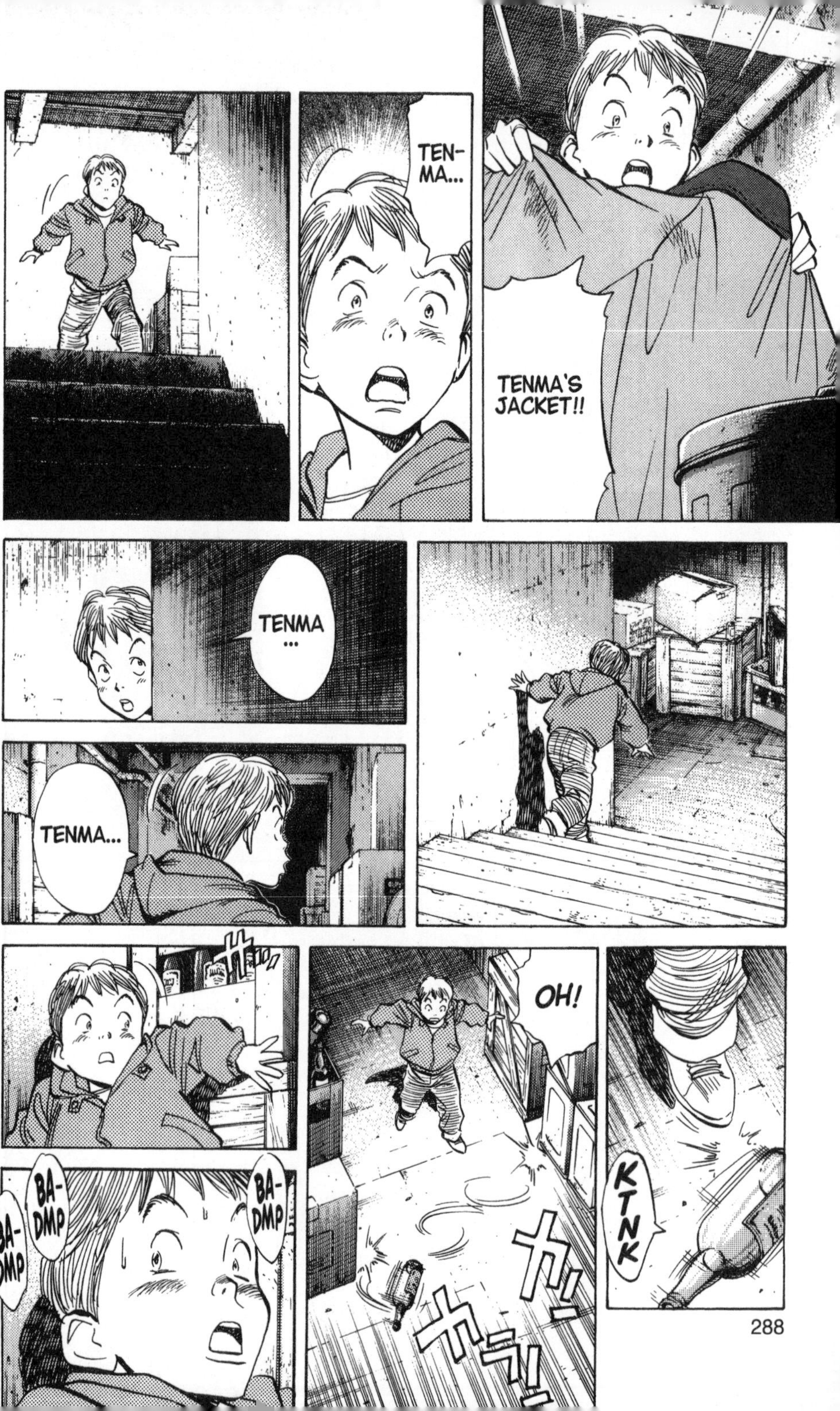
TENMA'S JACKET!!
TEN-MA...
TENMA ...
TENMA...
KTNK
OH!
BA-DMP
BA-DMP
BA-DMP

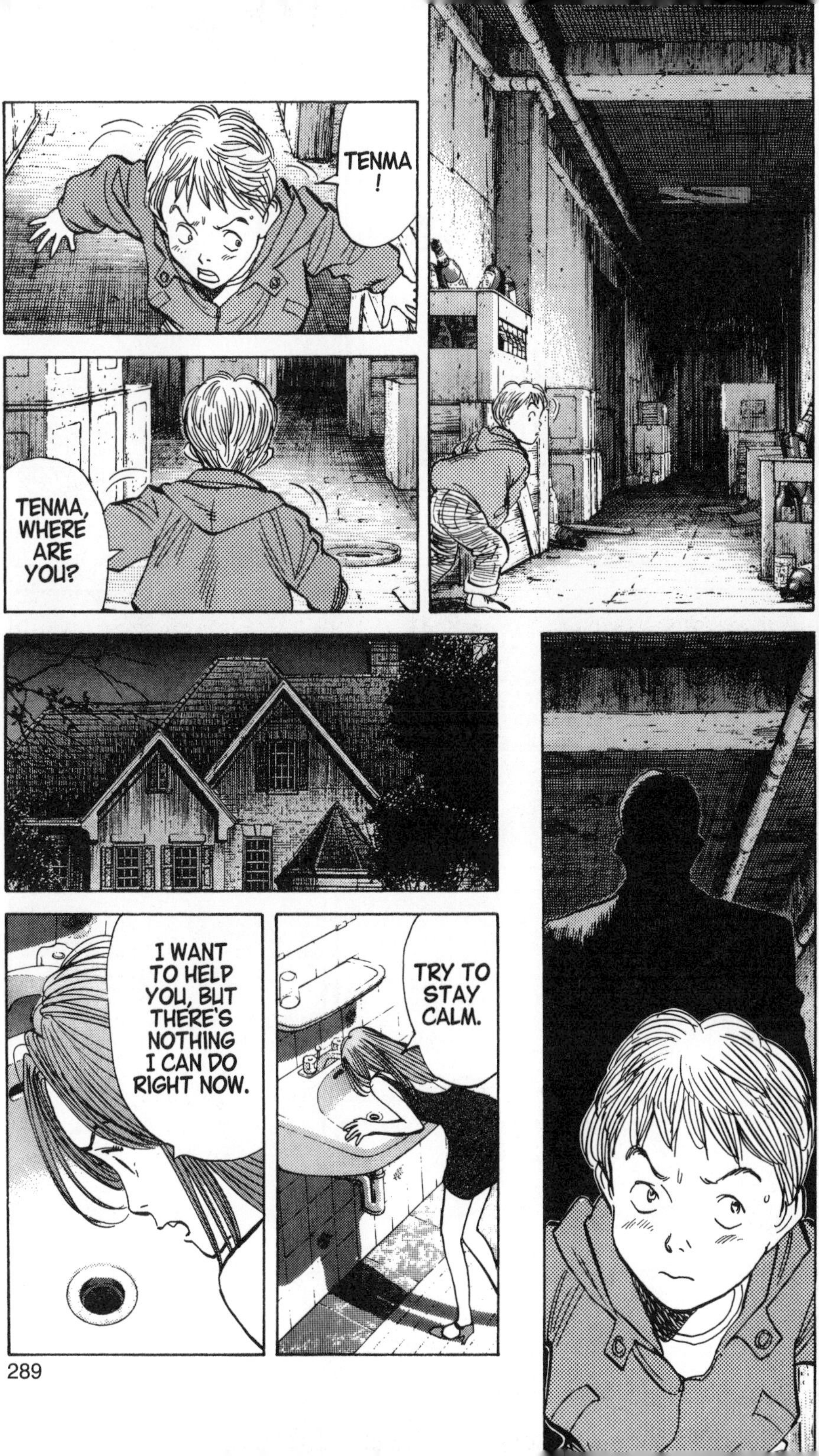
TENMA!
TENMA, WHERE ARE YOU?
TRY TO STAY CALM.
I WANT TO HELP YOU, BUT THERE'S NOTHING I CAN DO RIGHT NOW.

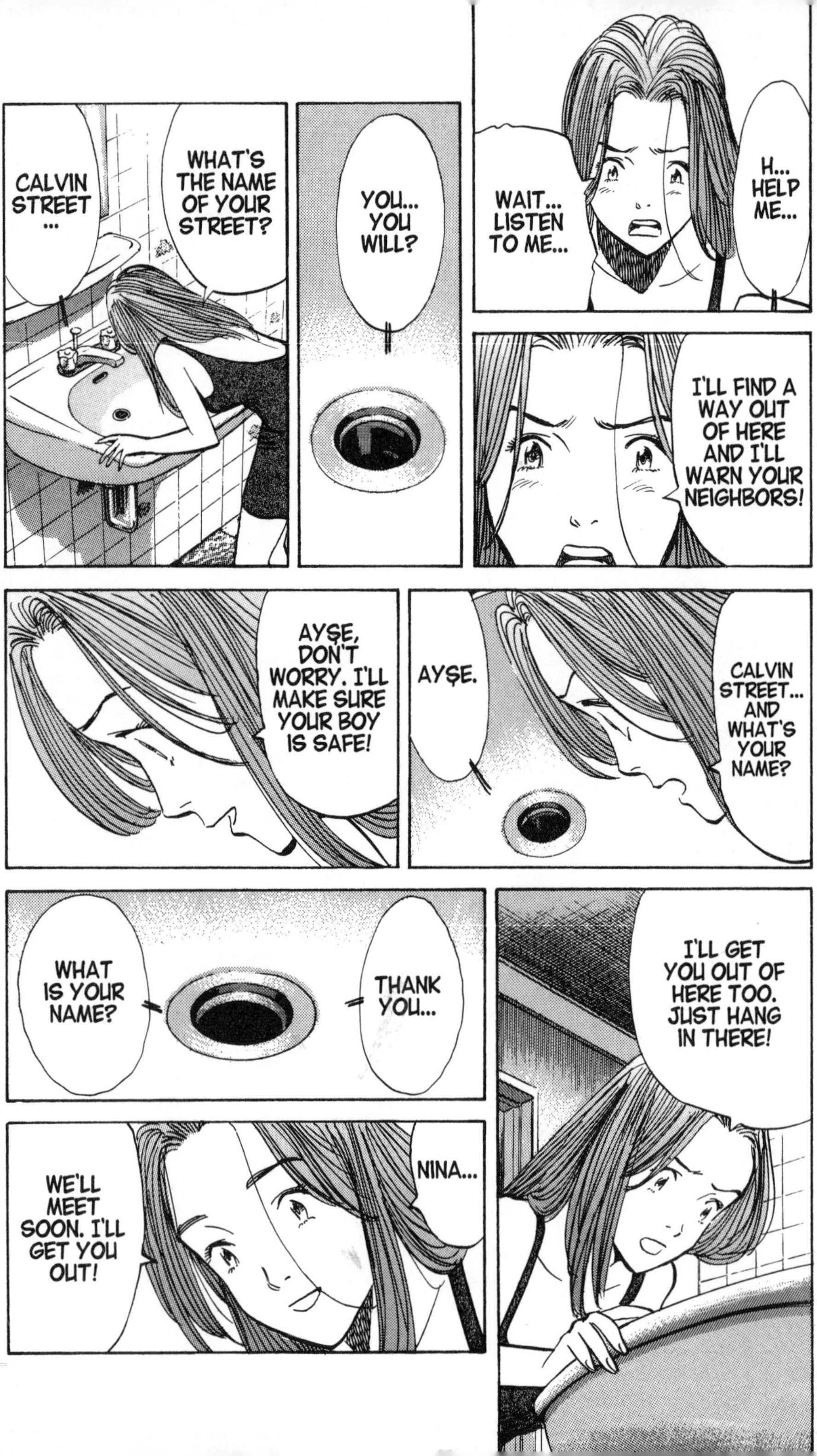

H... HELP ME...
WAIT... LISTEN TO ME...
I'LL FIND A WAY OUT OF HERE AND I'LL WARN YOUR NEIGHBORS!
YOU... YOU WILL?
WHAT'S THE NAME OF YOUR STREET?
CALVIN STREET ...
CALVIN STREET... AND WHAT'S YOUR NAME?
AYŞE.
AYŞE, DON'T WORRY. I'LL MAKE SURE YOUR BOY IS SAFE!
I'LL GET YOU OUT OF HERE TOO. JUST HANG IN THERE!
THANK YOU...
WHAT IS YOUR NAME?
NINA...
WE'LL MEET SOON. I'LL GET YOU OUT!

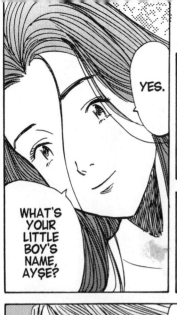

NINA ...
MANY BAD THINGS HAPPEN TO ME SINCE I COME TO GERMANY. YOU ARE THE FIRST GOOD PERSON I MEET...
WE ARE FRIENDS.
YES.
WHAT'S YOUR LITTLE BOY'S NAME, AYŞE?
AYŞE ?
AYŞE ?
WHAM

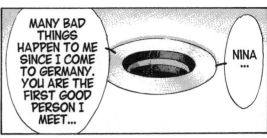

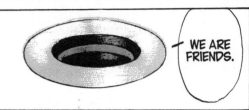

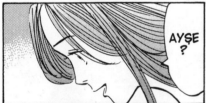

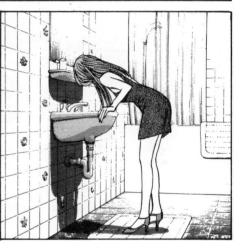

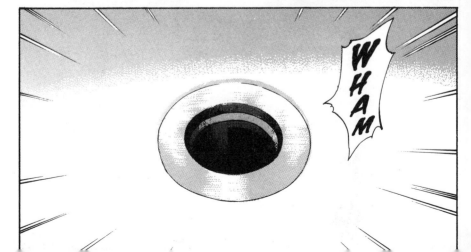

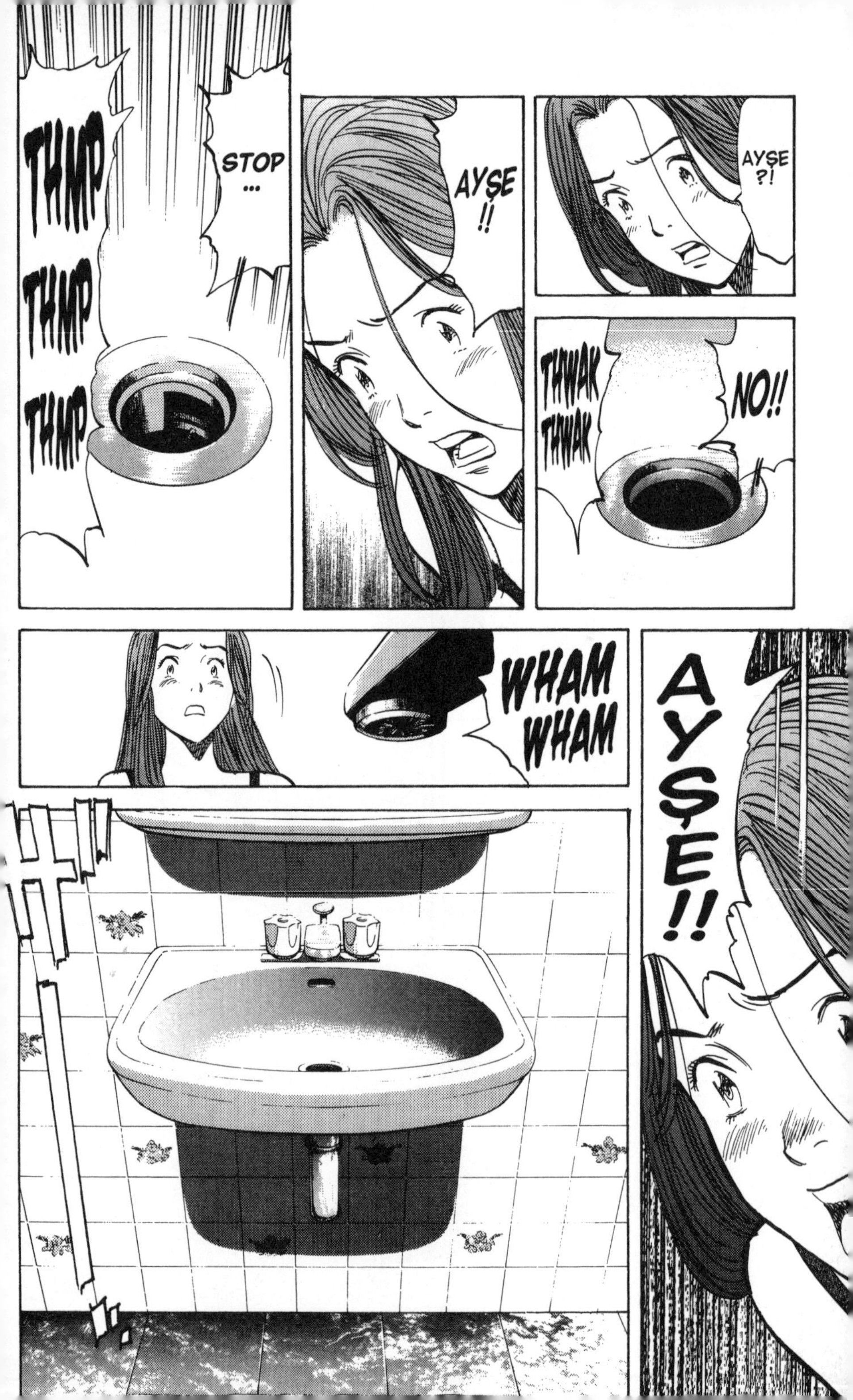
AYŞE ?!
NO!!
THWAK THWAK
AYŞE !!
STOP ...
THMP THMP THMP
AYŞE!!
WHAM WHAM

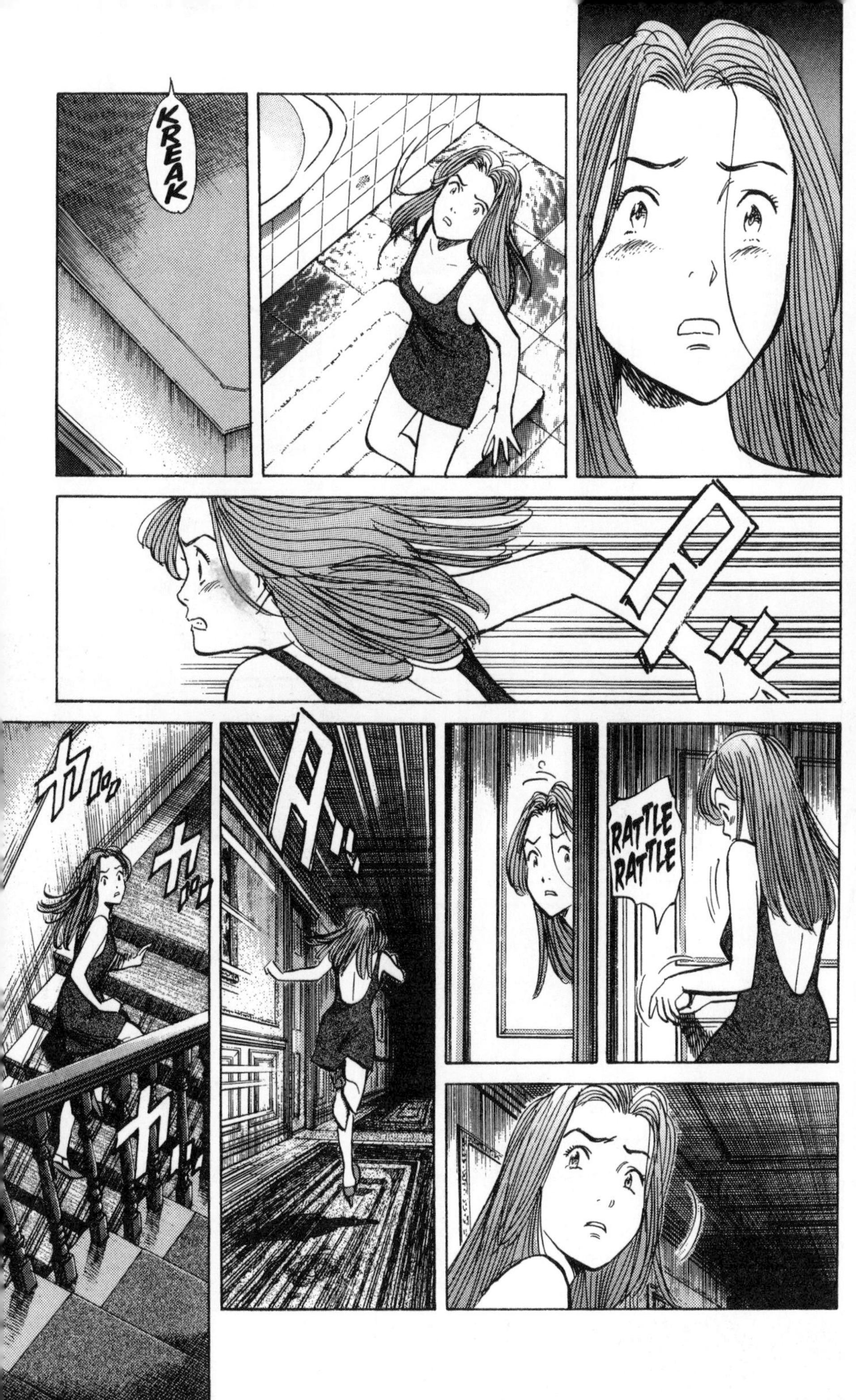
KREAK
RATTLE RATTLE

RATTLE

KREAK

!!

KREAK

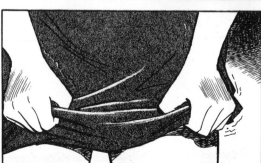

294

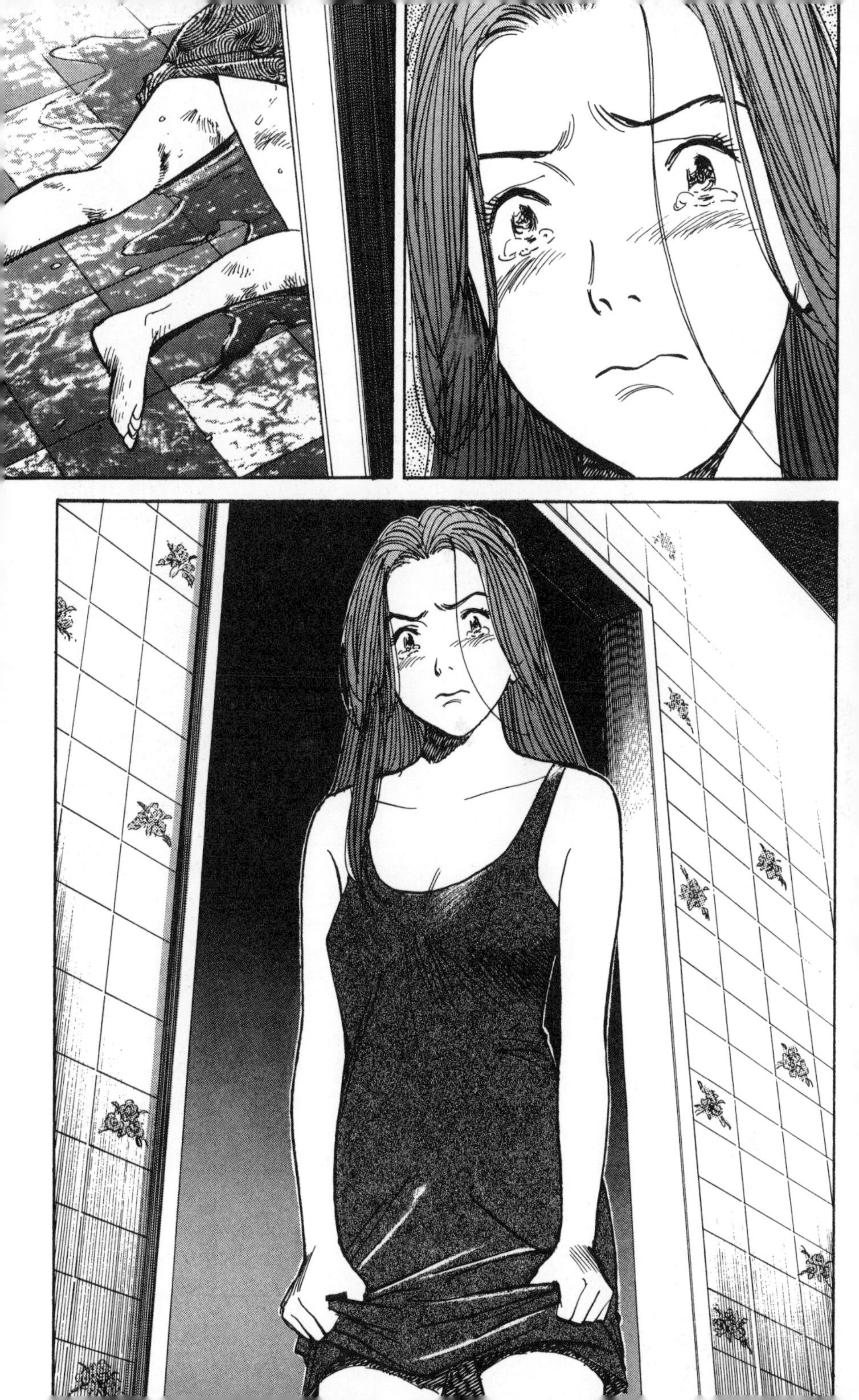

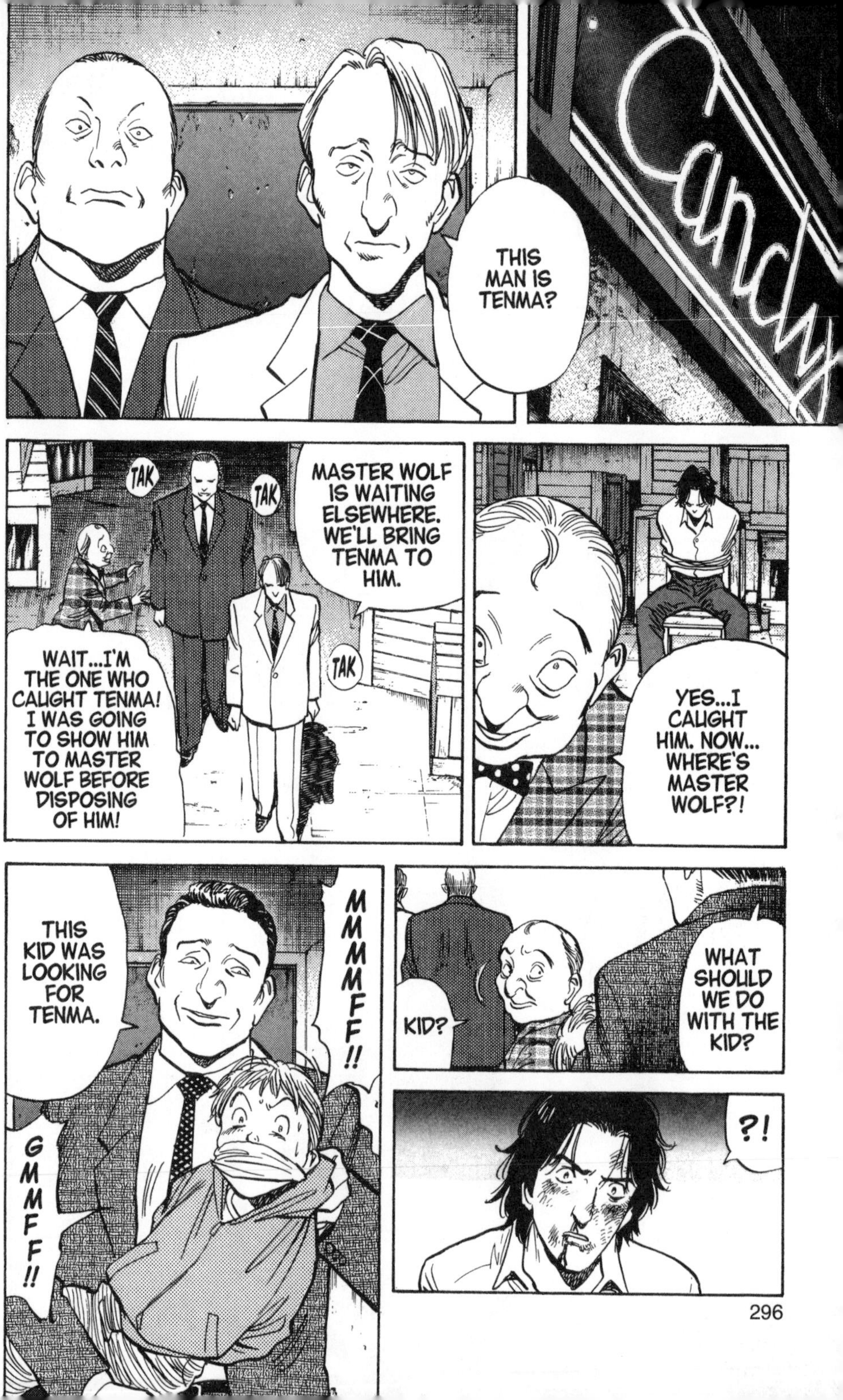
THIS MAN IS TENMA?
YES...I CAUGHT HIM. NOW... WHERE'S MASTER WOLF?!
MASTER WOLF IS WAITING ELSEWHERE. WE'LL BRING TENMA TO HIM.
TAK
TAK
TAK
WAIT...I'M THE ONE WHO CAUGHT TENMA! I WAS GOING TO SHOW HIM TO MASTER WOLF BEFORE DISPOSING OF HIM!
WHAT SHOULD WE DO WITH THE KID?
KID?
?!
MMMMFF!!
THIS KID WAS LOOKING FOR TENMA.
GMMFF!!

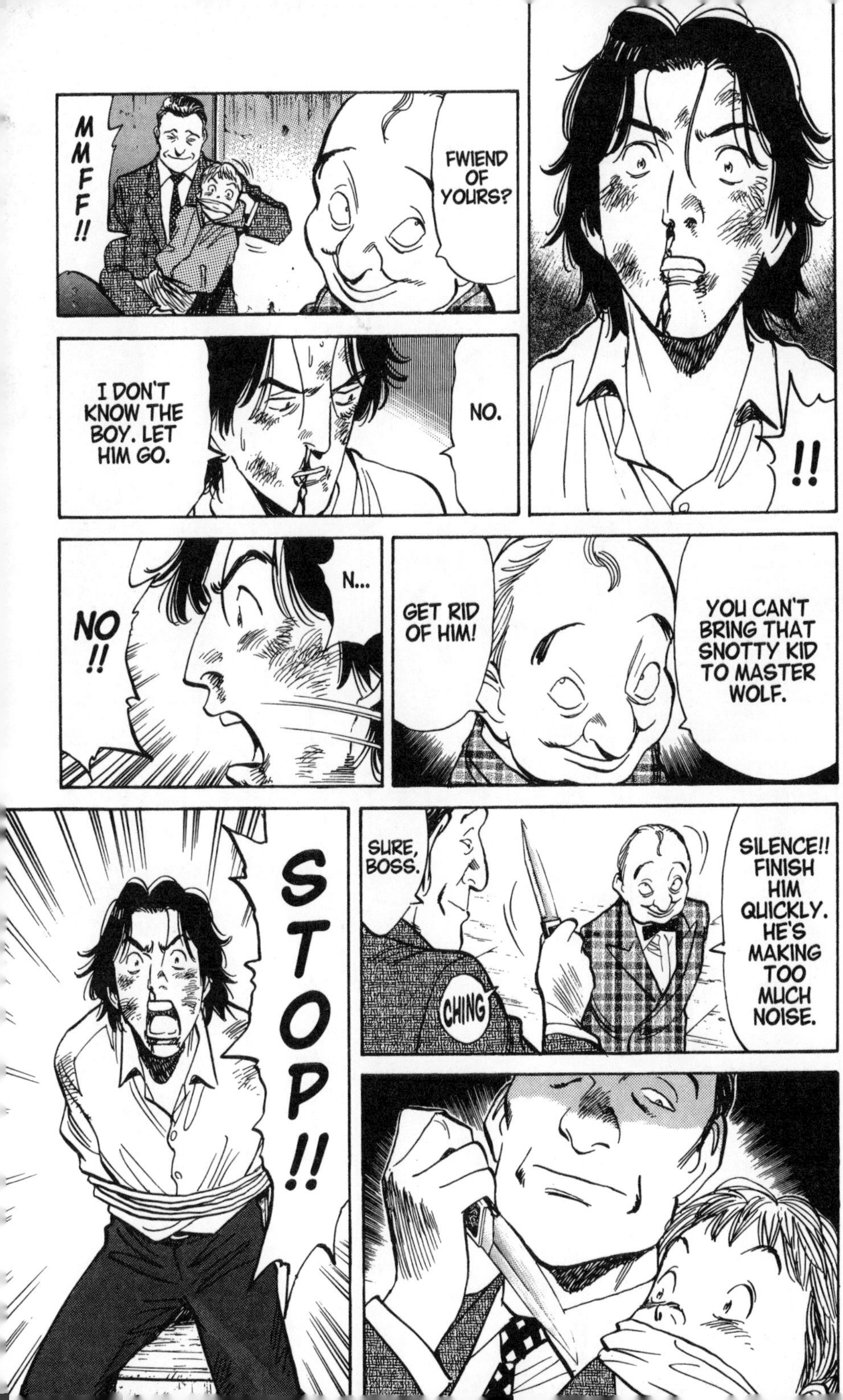
!!
FWIEND OF YOURS?
MMFF!!
NO.
I DON'T KNOW THE BOY. LET HIM GO.
YOU CAN'T BRING THAT SNOTTY KID TO MASTER WOLF.
GET RID OF HIM!
N...
NO!!
SILENCE!! FINISH HIM QUICKLY. HE'S MAKING TOO MUCH NOISE.
SURE, BOSS.
CHING
STOP!!

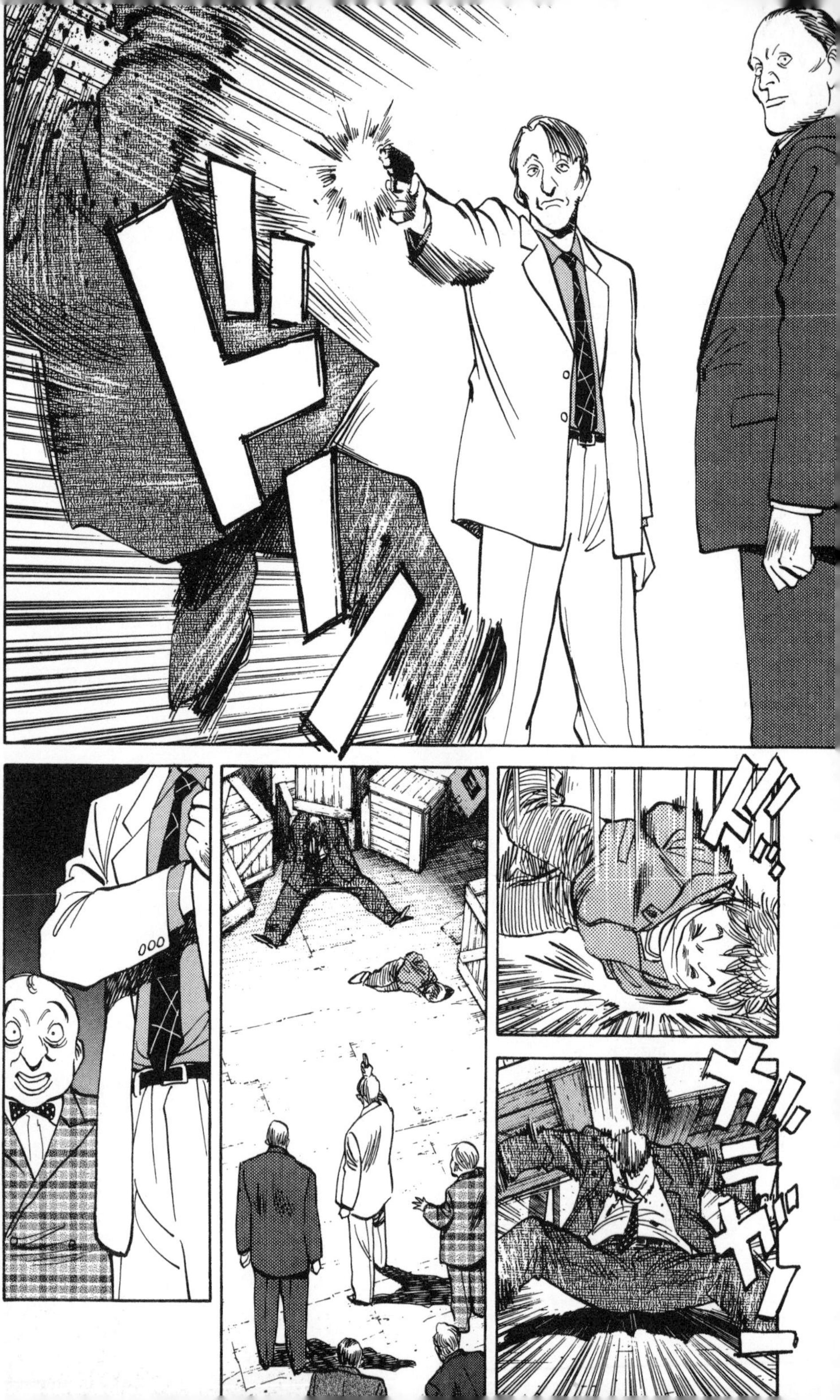
ドン

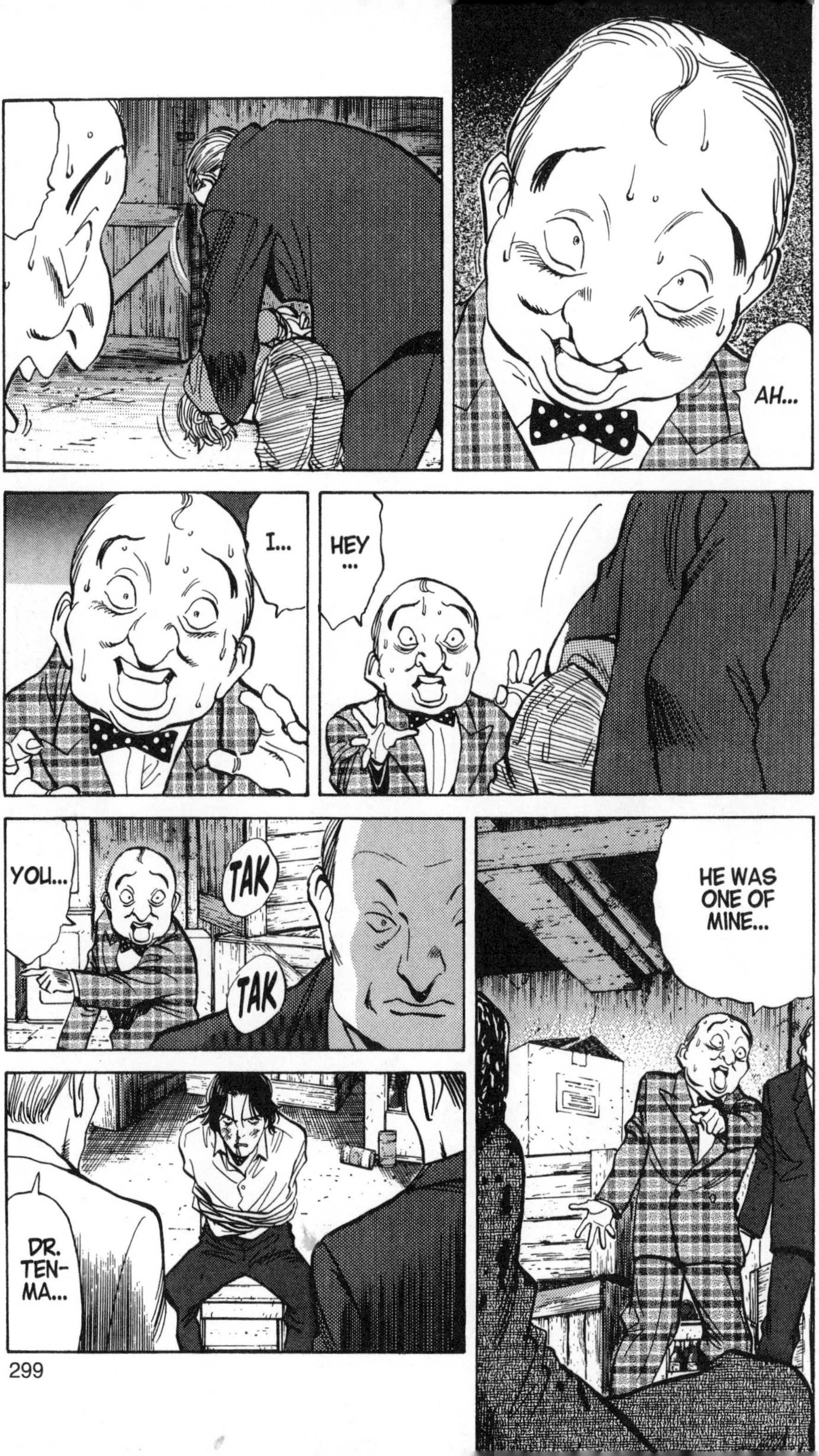
AH...
HEY ...
I...
HE WAS ONE OF MINE...
YOU...
TAK
TAK
DR. TEN-MA...

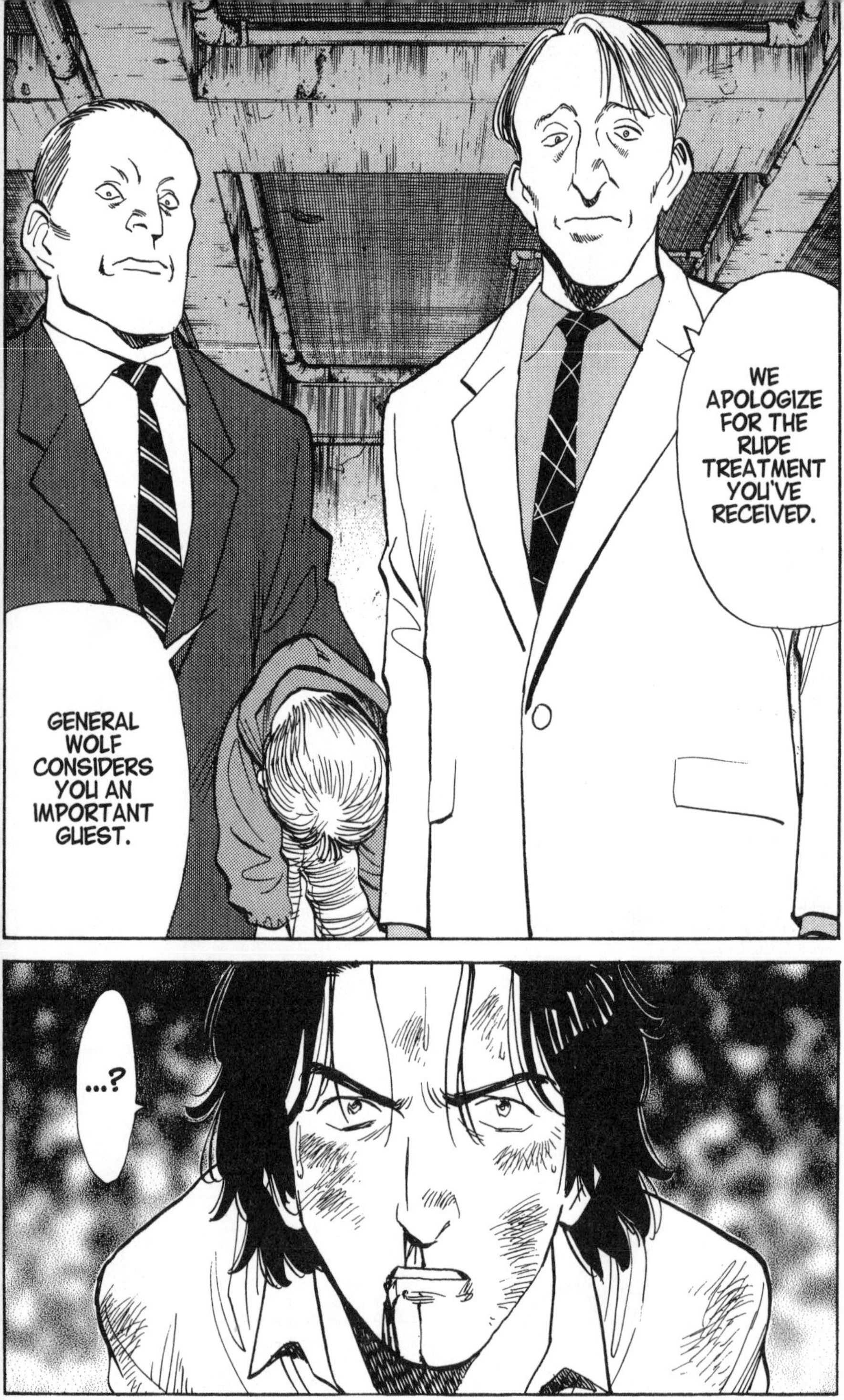
WE APOLOGIZE FOR THE RUDE TREATMENT YOU'VE RECEIVED.
GENERAL WOLF CONSIDERS YOU AN IMPORTANT GUEST.
...?

Kapitel 29. Wolf's Confession

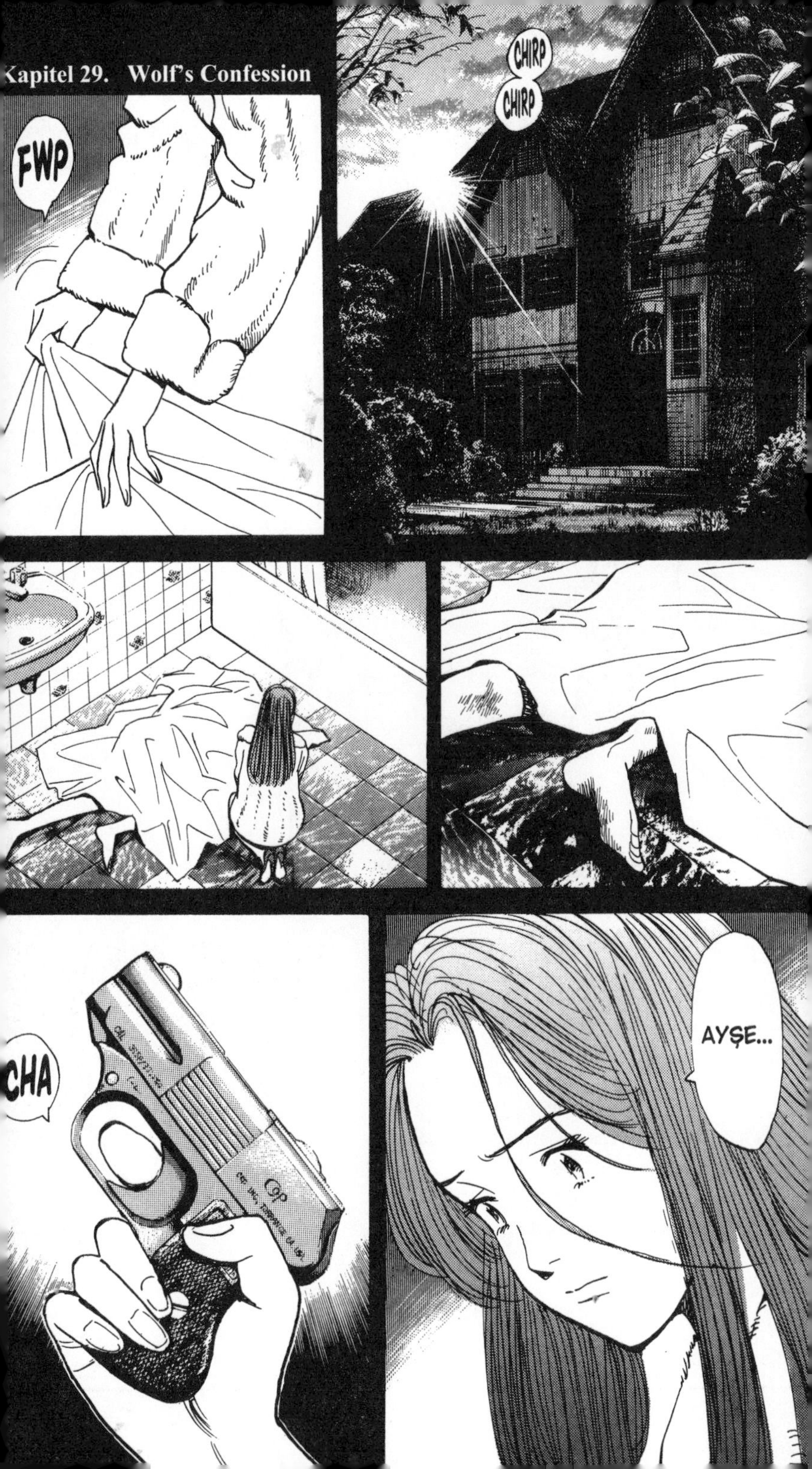
CHIRP
CHIRP
FWP
AYŞE...
CHA

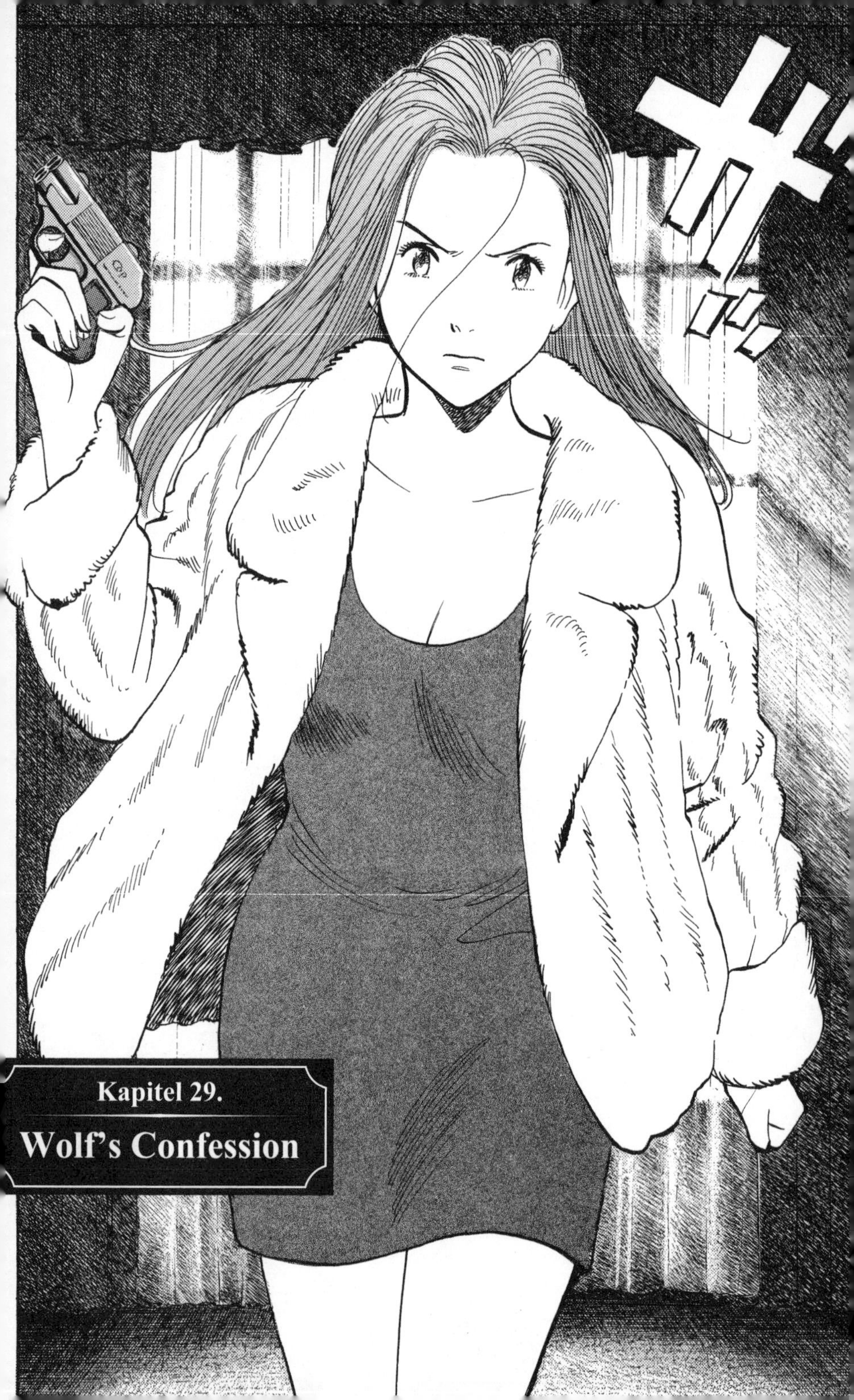
ザッ
Kapitel 29.
Wolf's Confession

IF I DON'T WARN THEM SOON...MY NEIGHBOR-HOOD...

MY BABY BOY... ALL WILL BURN...

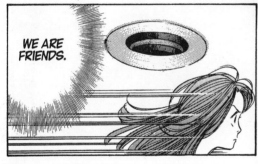

WE ARE FRIENDS.

WHA ...?

WE ARE FRIENDS !!

YES, AYŞE.

TAK

...

WHAT'S GOING ON? WH...

...!!

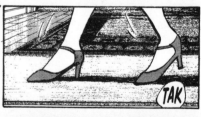
TAK

TAK

TAK

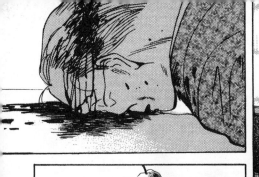

HAHH

HAHH

PROFES-
SOR
GEDRICH!

HAHH

HAHH

HAHH

HAHH

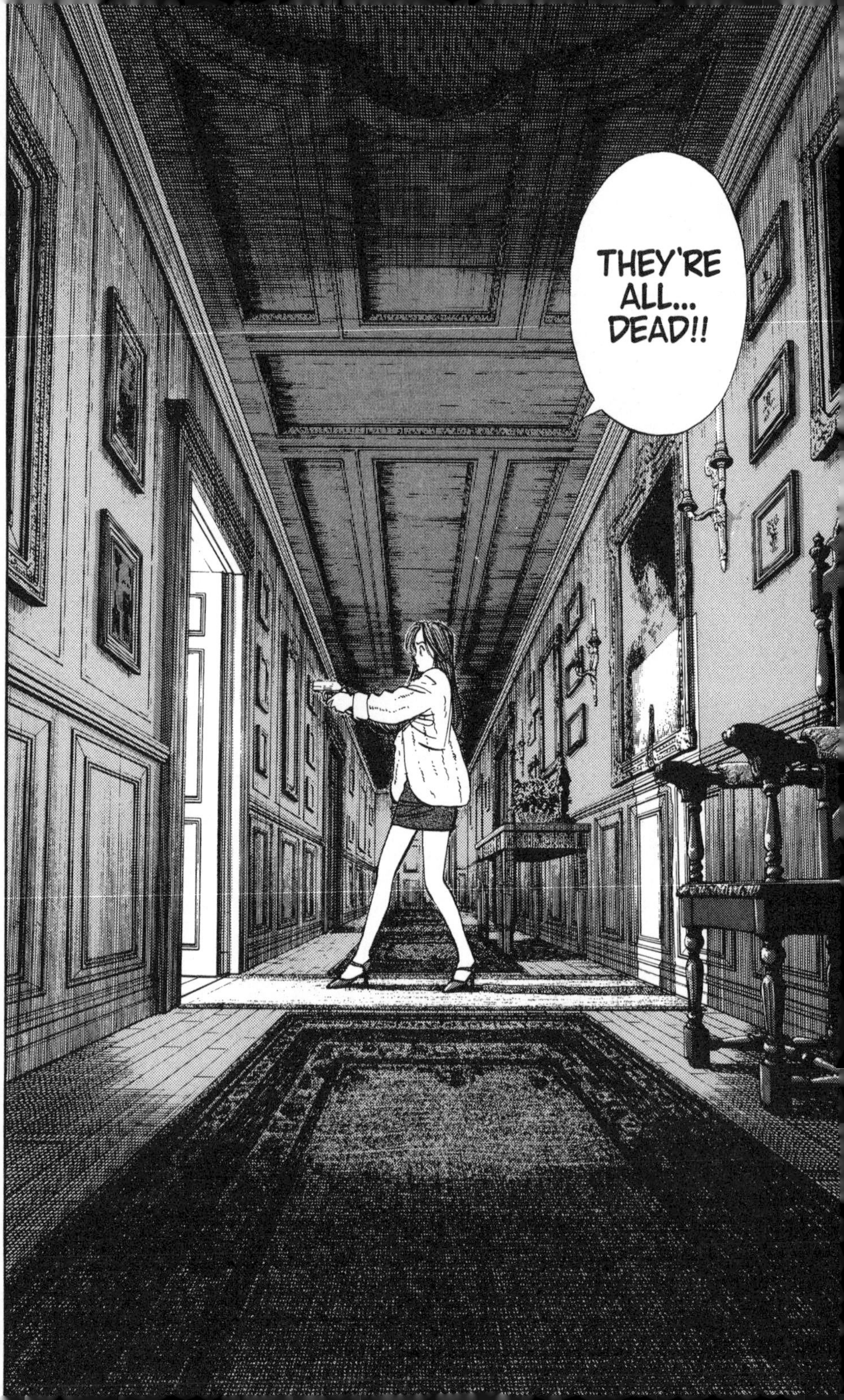
THEY'RE ALL... DEAD!!

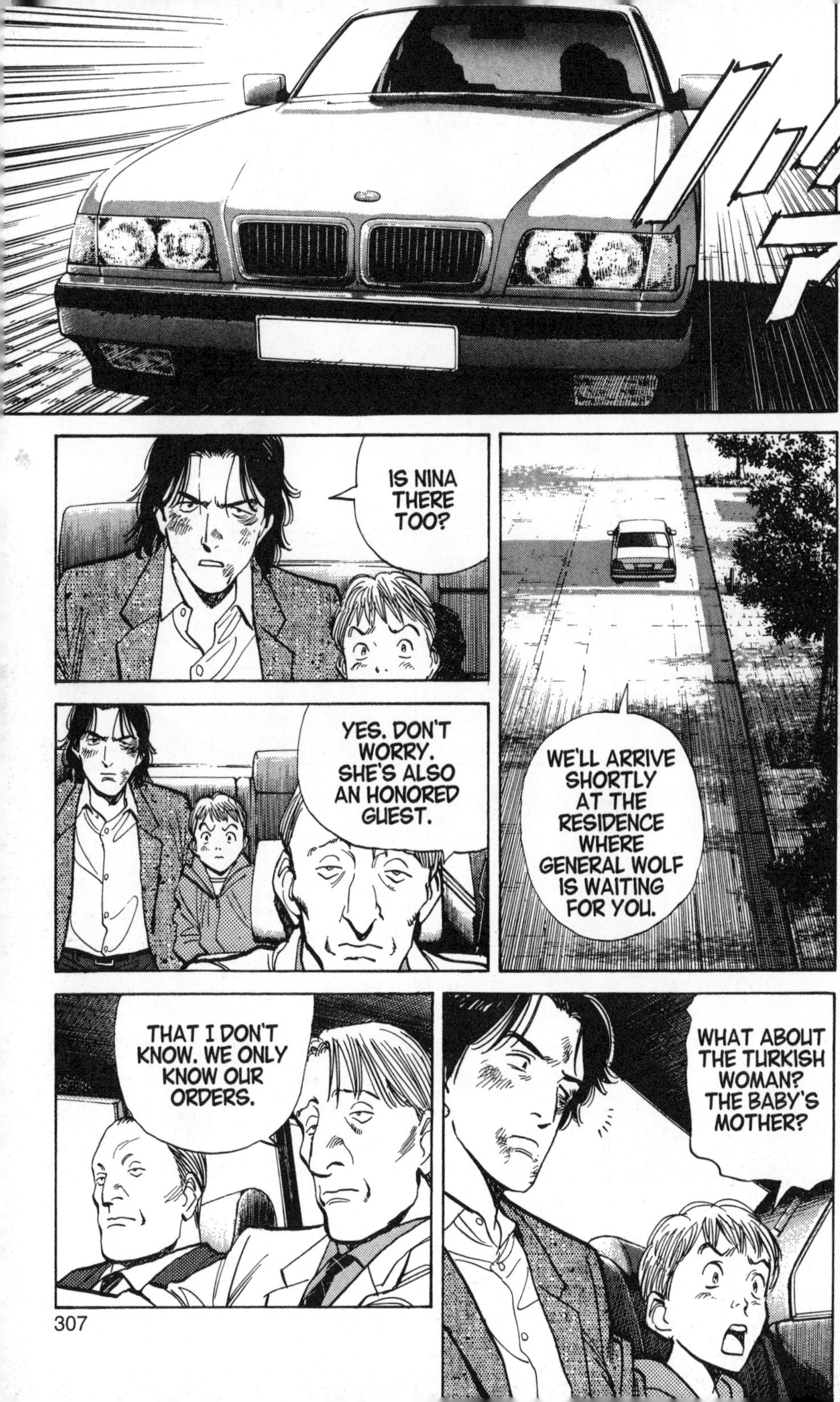
WE'LL ARRIVE SHORTLY AT THE RESIDENCE WHERE GENERAL WOLF IS WAITING FOR YOU.
IS NINA THERE TOO?
YES. DON'T WORRY. SHE'S ALSO AN HONORED GUEST.
WHAT ABOUT THE TURKISH WOMAN? THE BABY'S MOTHER?
THAT I DON'T KNOW. WE ONLY KNOW OUR ORDERS.

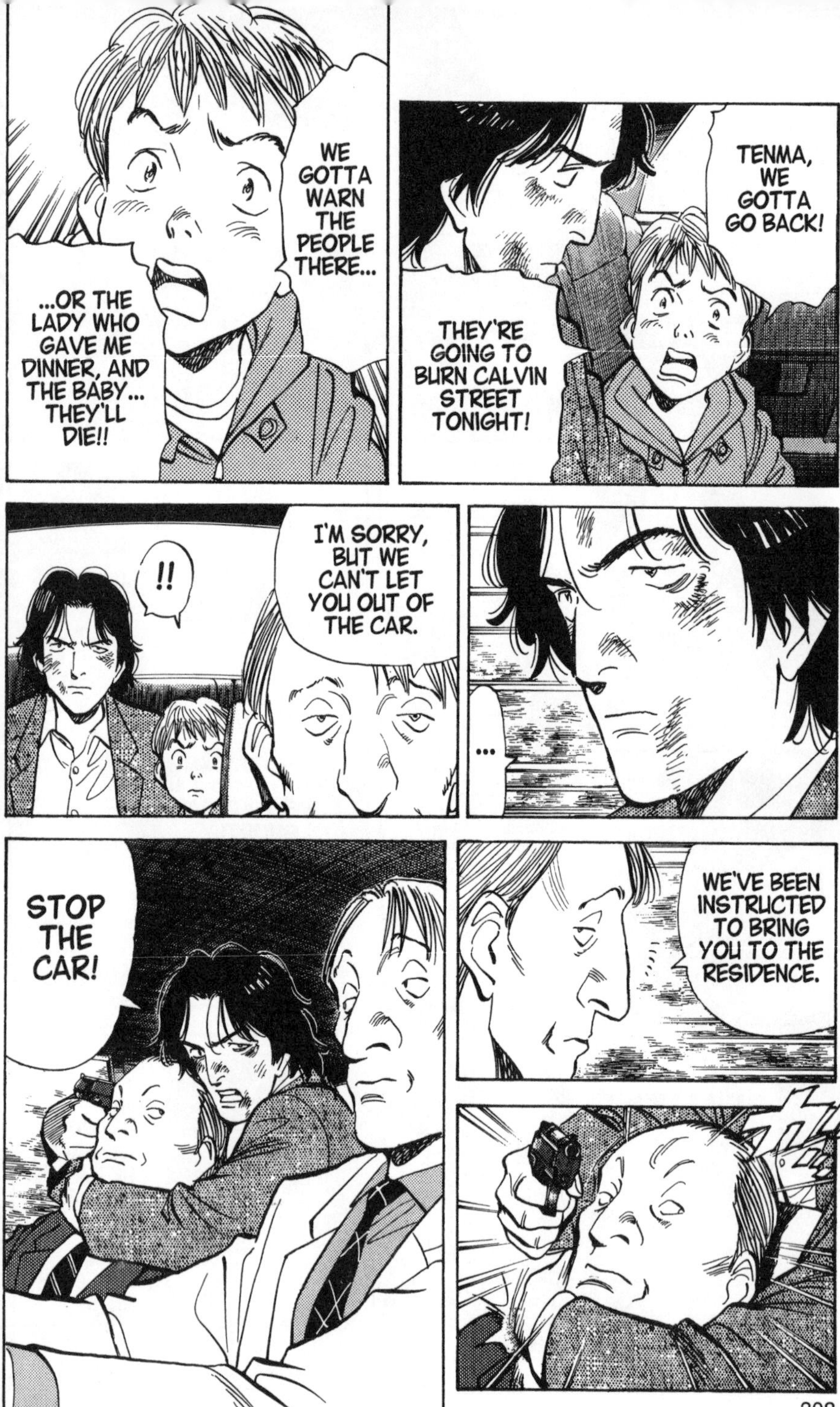
TENMA, WE GOTTA GO BACK!
THEY'RE GOING TO BURN CALVIN STREET TONIGHT!
WE GOTTA WARN THE PEOPLE THERE...
...OR THE LADY WHO GAVE ME DINNER, AND THE BABY... THEY'LL DIE!!
...
I'M SORRY, BUT WE CAN'T LET YOU OUT OF THE CAR.
!!
WE'VE BEEN INSTRUCTED TO BRING YOU TO THE RESIDENCE.
STOP THE CAR!

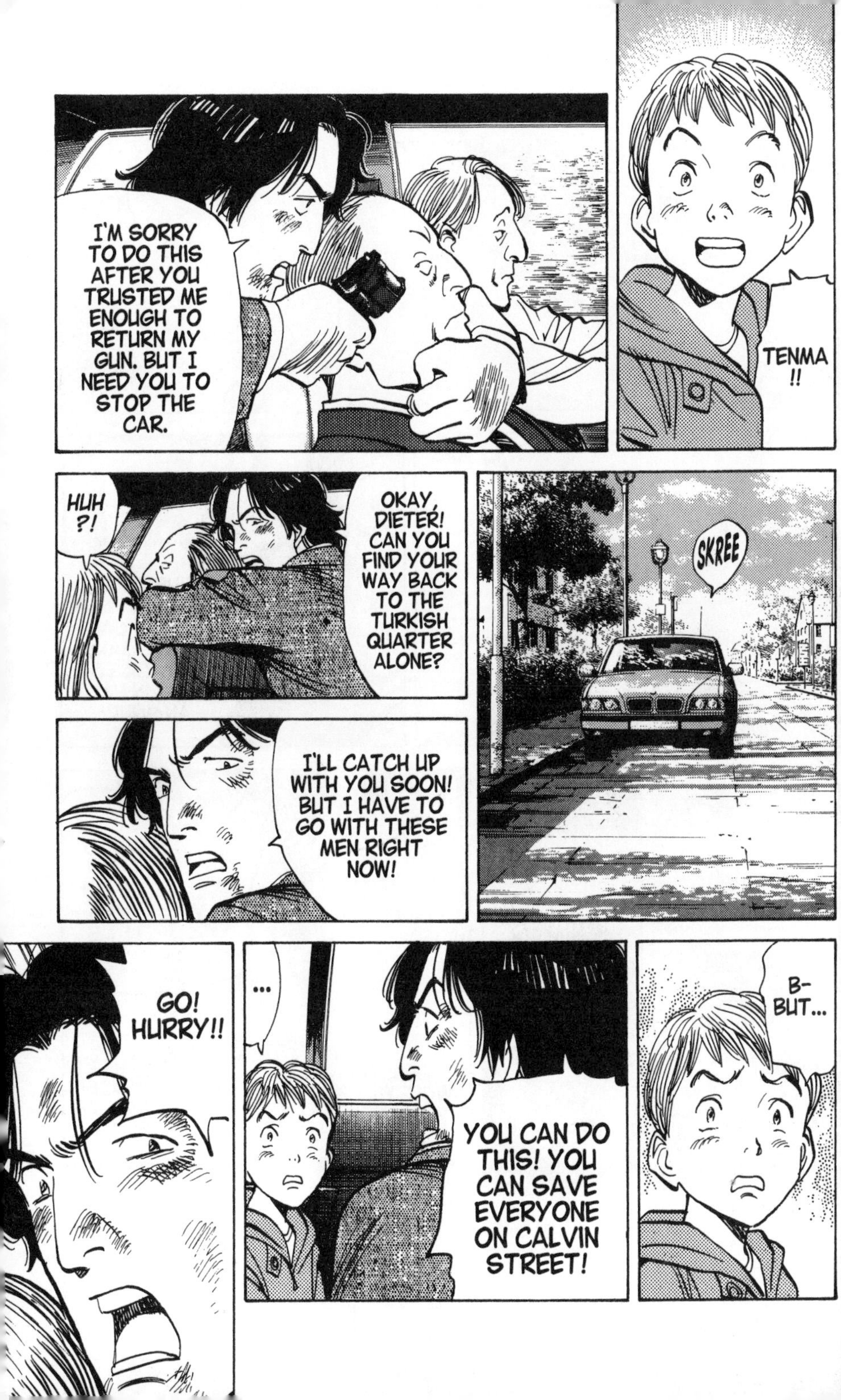
TENMA !!
I'M SORRY TO DO THIS AFTER YOU TRUSTED ME ENOUGH TO RETURN MY GUN. BUT I NEED YOU TO STOP THE CAR.
SKREE
OKAY, DIETER! CAN YOU FIND YOUR WAY BACK TO THE TURKISH QUARTER ALONE?
HUH ?!
I'LL CATCH UP WITH YOU SOON! BUT I HAVE TO GO WITH THESE MEN RIGHT NOW!
B- BUT...
...
YOU CAN DO THIS! YOU CAN SAVE EVERYONE ON CALVIN STREET!
GO! HURRY!!

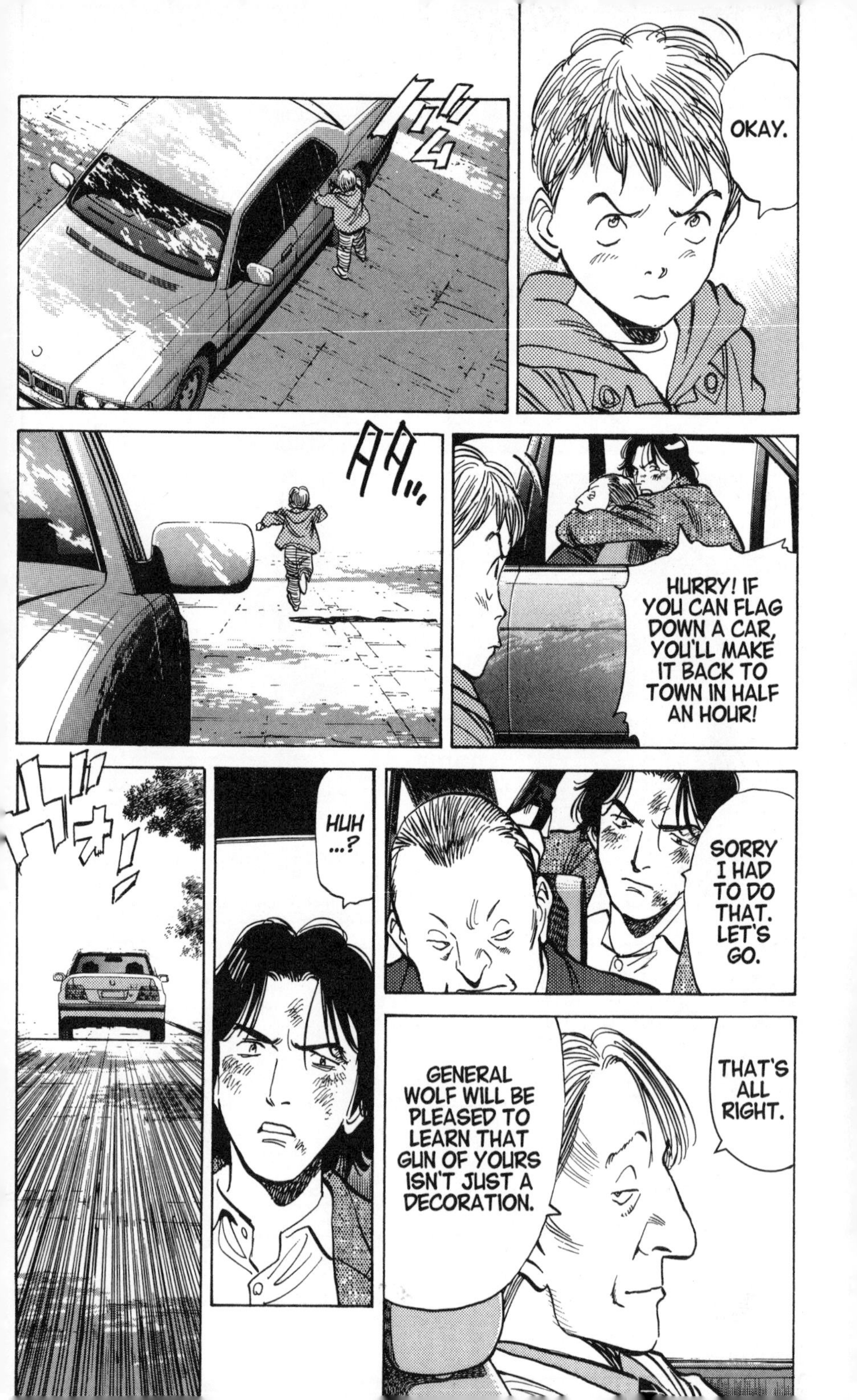
OKAY.
HURRY! IF YOU CAN FLAG DOWN A CAR, YOU'LL MAKE IT BACK TO TOWN IN HALF AN HOUR!
SORRY I HAD TO DO THAT. LET'S GO.
THAT'S ALL RIGHT.
GENERAL WOLF WILL BE PLEASED TO LEARN THAT GUN OF YOURS ISN'T JUST A DECORATION.
HUH ...?

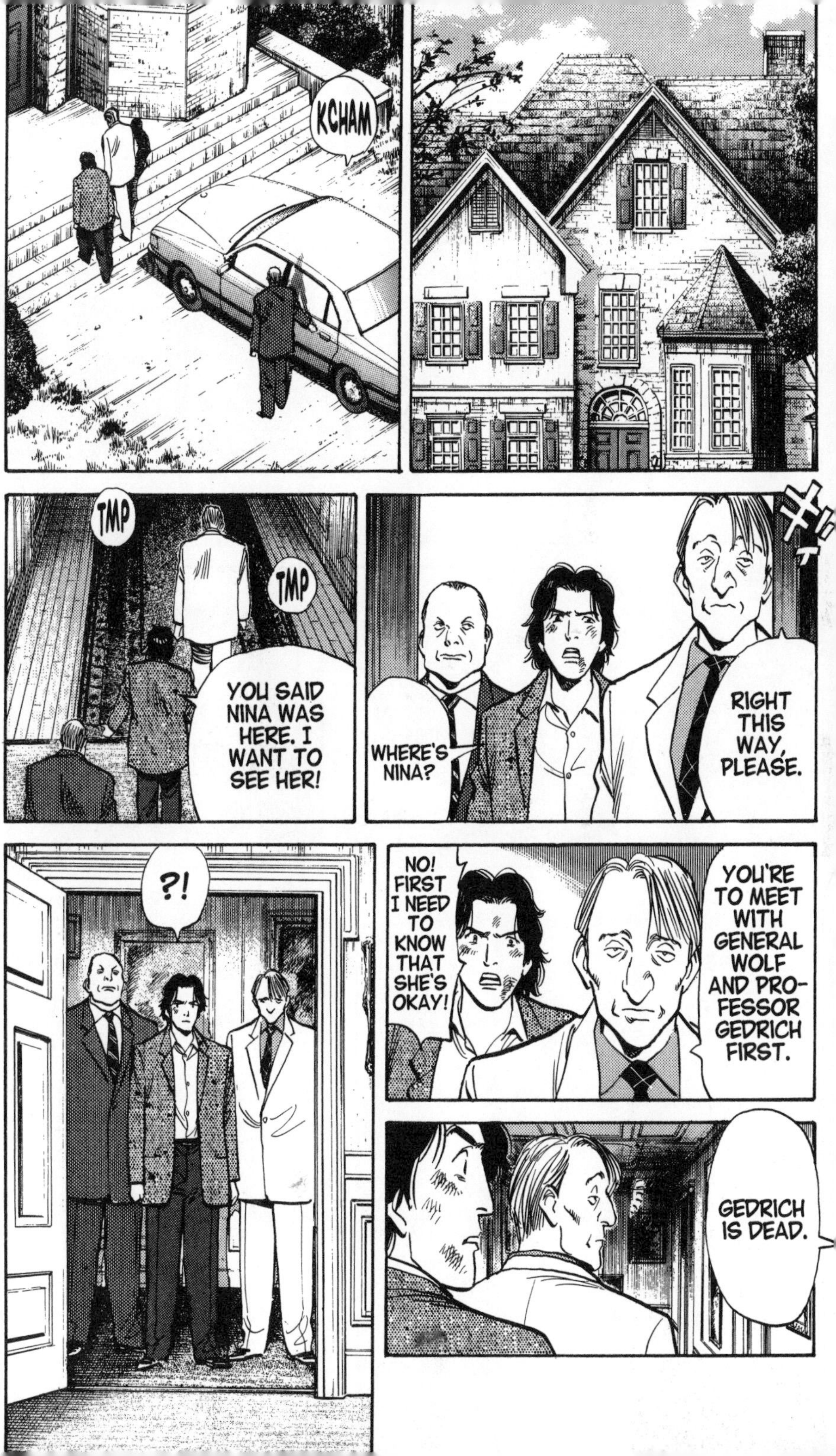
KCHAM
RIGHT THIS WAY, PLEASE.
WHERE'S NINA?
TMP
TMP
YOU SAID NINA WAS HERE. I WANT TO SEE HER!
YOU'RE TO MEET WITH GENERAL WOLF AND PROFESSOR GEDRICH FIRST.
NO! FIRST I NEED TO KNOW THAT SHE'S OKAY!
GEDRICH IS DEAD.
?!

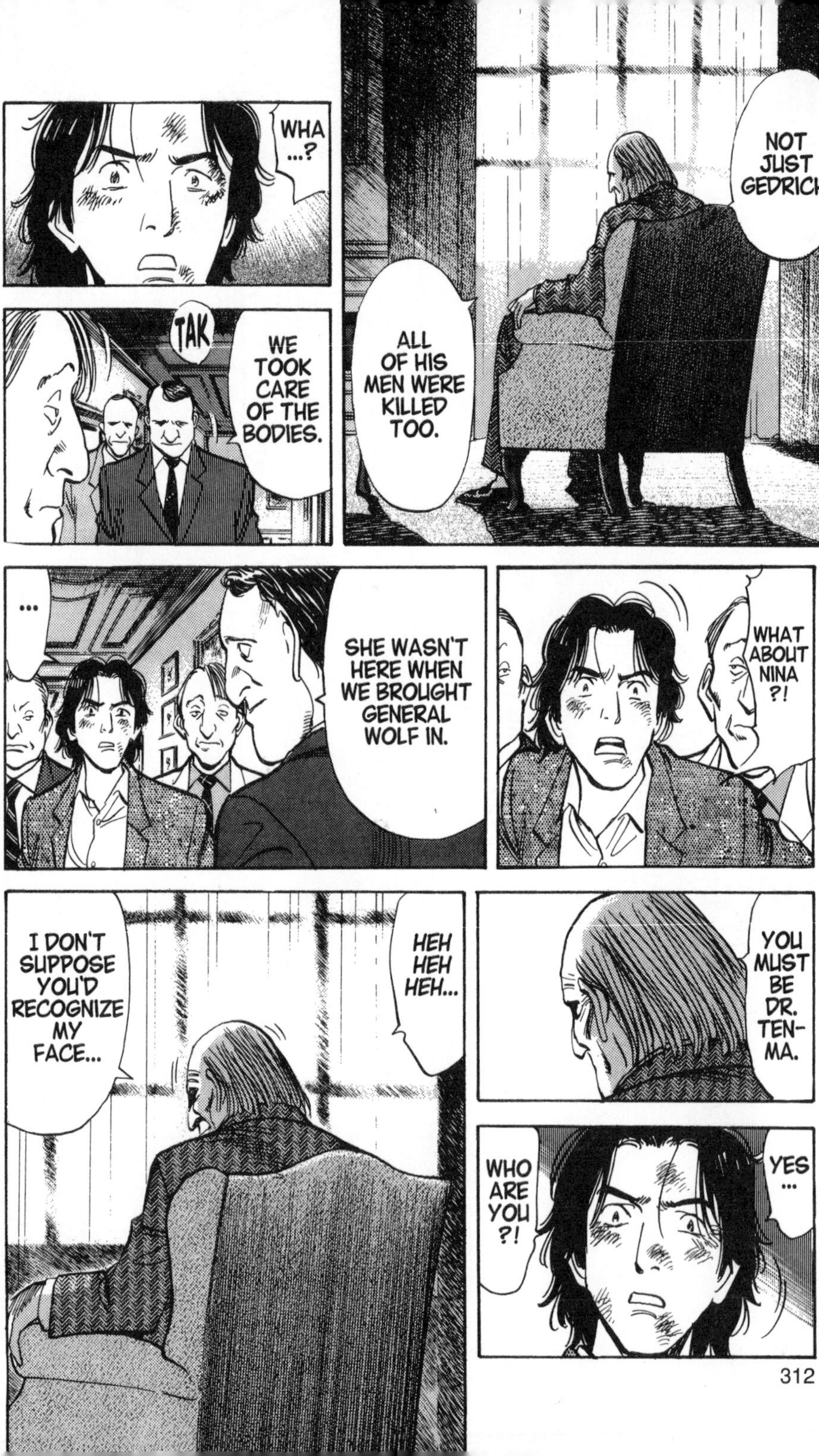
NOT JUST GEDRICH.
ALL OF HIS MEN WERE KILLED TOO.
WHA ...?
TAK
WE TOOK CARE OF THE BODIES.
WHAT ABOUT NINA ?!
SHE WASN'T HERE WHEN WE BROUGHT GENERAL WOLF IN.
...
YOU MUST BE DR. TEN-MA.
YES ...
WHO ARE YOU ?!
HEH HEH HEH...
I DON'T SUPPOSE YOU'D RECOGNIZE MY FACE...

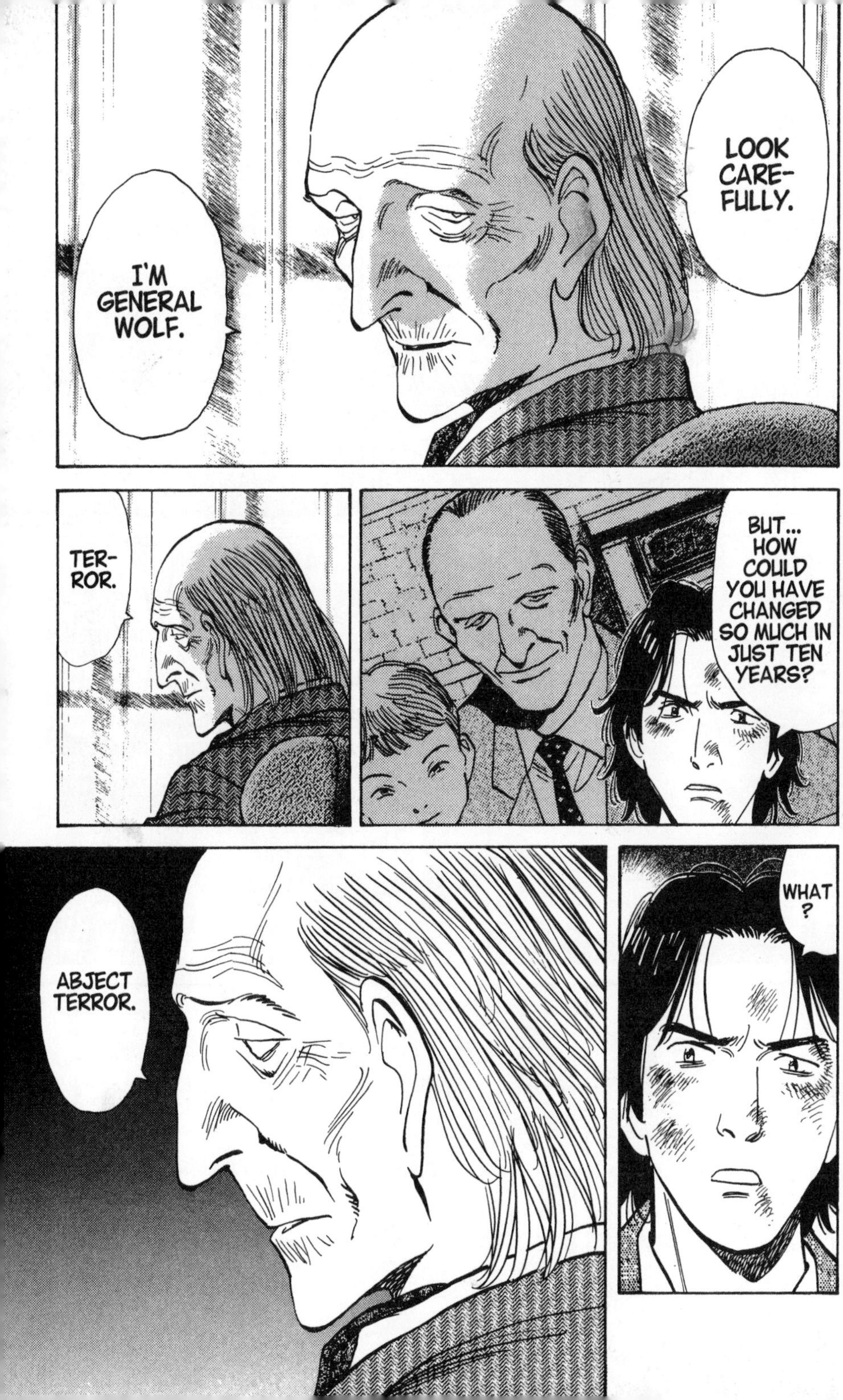
LOOK CARE-FULLY.
I'M GENERAL WOLF.
BUT... HOW COULD YOU HAVE CHANGED SO MUCH IN JUST TEN YEARS?
TER-ROR.
WHAT?
ABJECT TERROR.

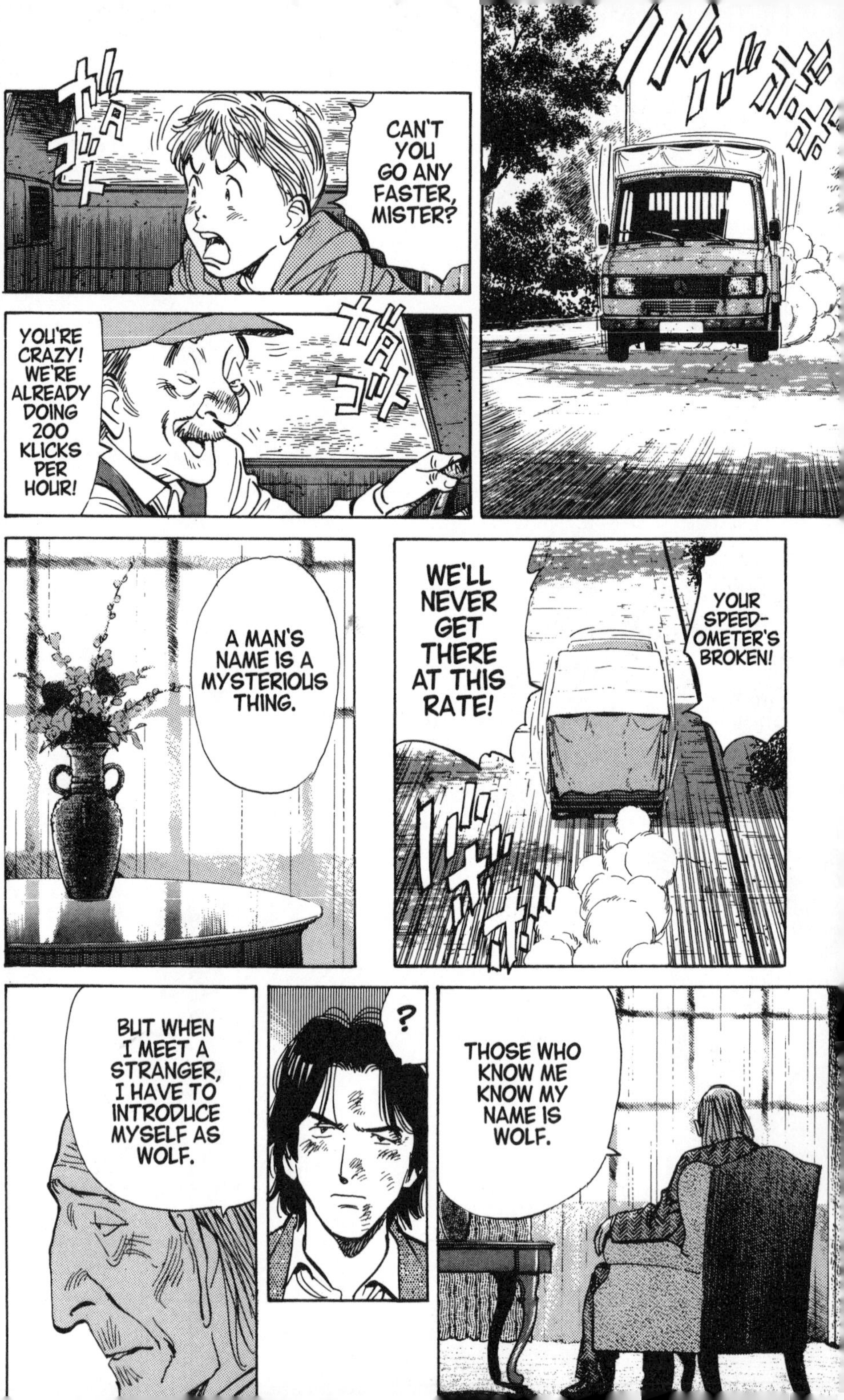

CAN'T YOU GO ANY FASTER, MISTER?
ガタゴト
ガタゴト
YOU'RE CRAZY! WE'RE ALREADY DOING 200 KLICKS PER HOUR!
YOUR SPEED-OMETER'S BROKEN!
WE'LL NEVER GET THERE AT THIS RATE!
A MAN'S NAME IS A MYSTERIOUS THING.
THOSE WHO KNOW ME KNOW MY NAME IS WOLF.
?
BUT WHEN I MEET A STRANGER, I HAVE TO INTRODUCE MYSELF AS WOLF.

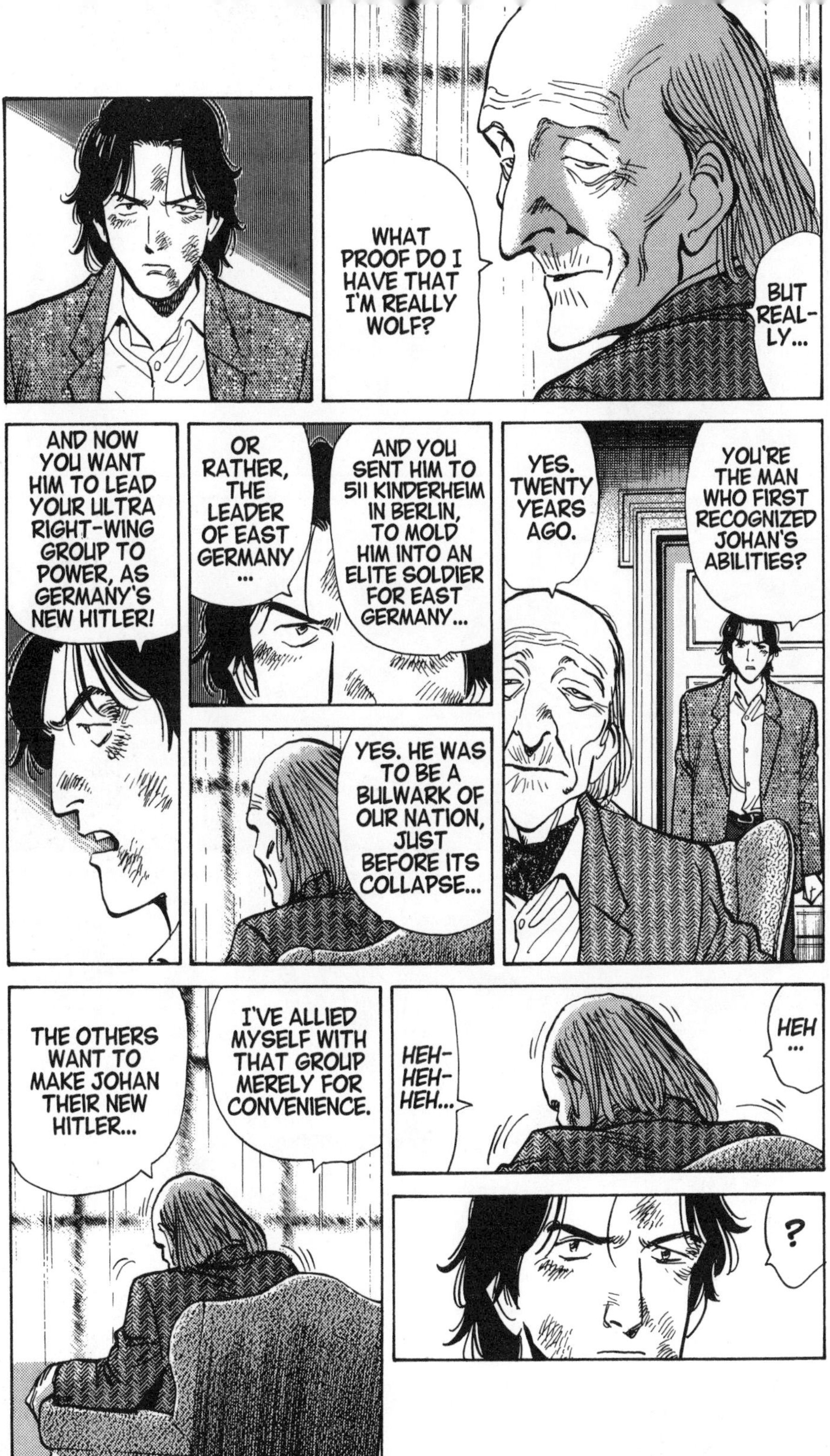
BUT REALLY...
WHAT PROOF DO I HAVE THAT I'M REALLY WOLF?
YOU'RE THE MAN WHO FIRST RECOGNIZED JOHAN'S ABILITIES?
YES. TWENTY YEARS AGO.
AND YOU SENT HIM TO 511 KINDERHEIM IN BERLIN, TO MOLD HIM INTO AN ELITE SOLDIER FOR EAST GERMANY...
OR RATHER, THE LEADER OF EAST GERMANY...
YES. HE WAS TO BE A BULWARK OF OUR NATION, JUST BEFORE ITS COLLAPSE...
AND NOW YOU WANT HIM TO LEAD YOUR ULTRA RIGHT-WING GROUP TO POWER, AS GERMANY'S NEW HITLER!
HEH...
HEH-HEH-HEH...
?
I'VE ALLIED MYSELF WITH THAT GROUP MERELY FOR CONVENIENCE.
THE OTHERS WANT TO MAKE JOHAN THEIR NEW HITLER...

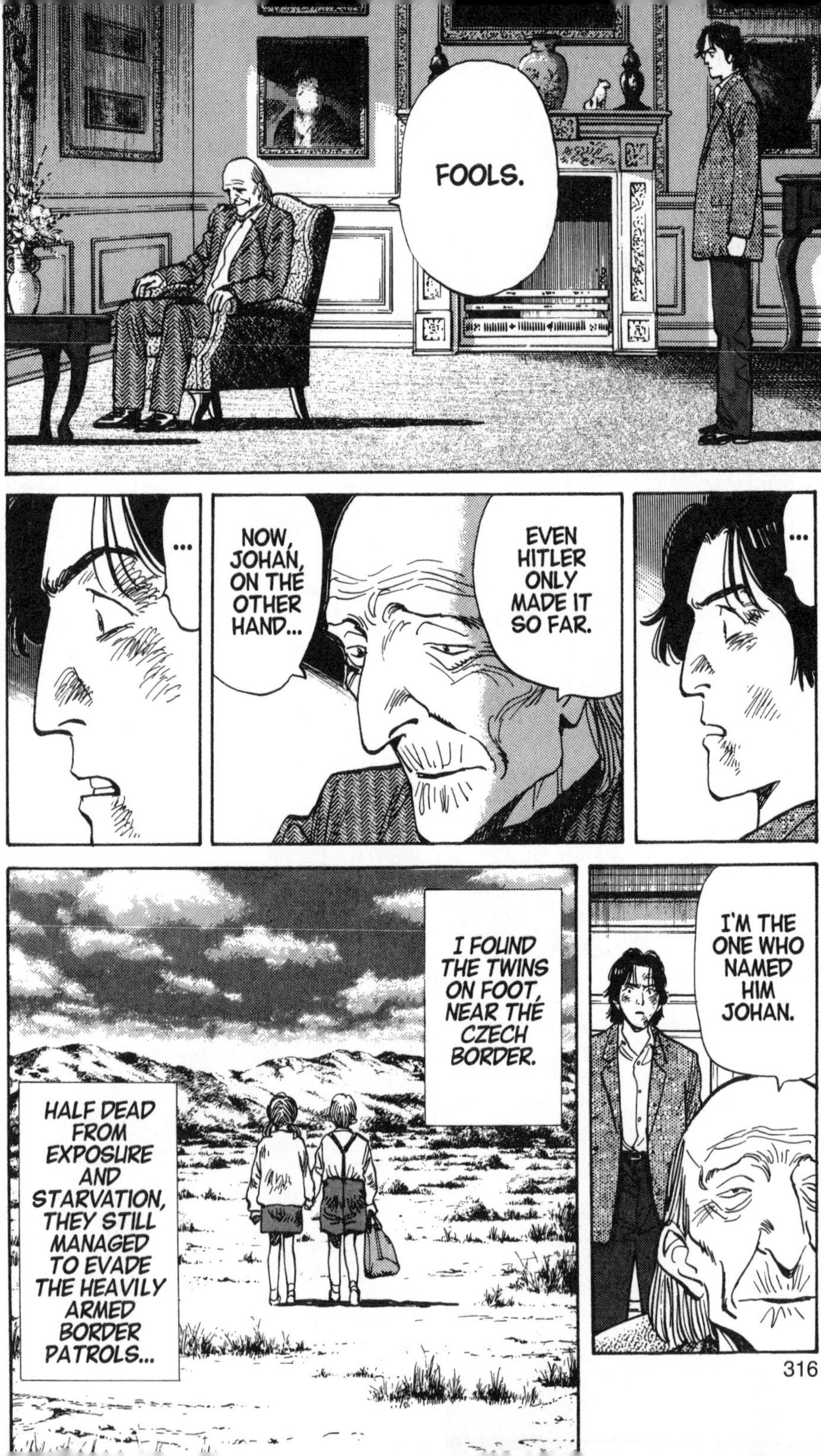
FOOLS.
...
EVEN HITLER ONLY MADE IT SO FAR.
NOW, JOHAN, ON THE OTHER HAND...
...
I'M THE ONE WHO NAMED HIM JOHAN.
I FOUND THE TWINS ON FOOT, NEAR THE CZECH BORDER.
HALF DEAD FROM EXPOSURE AND STARVATION, THEY STILL MANAGED TO EVADE THE HEAVILY ARMED BORDER PATROLS...

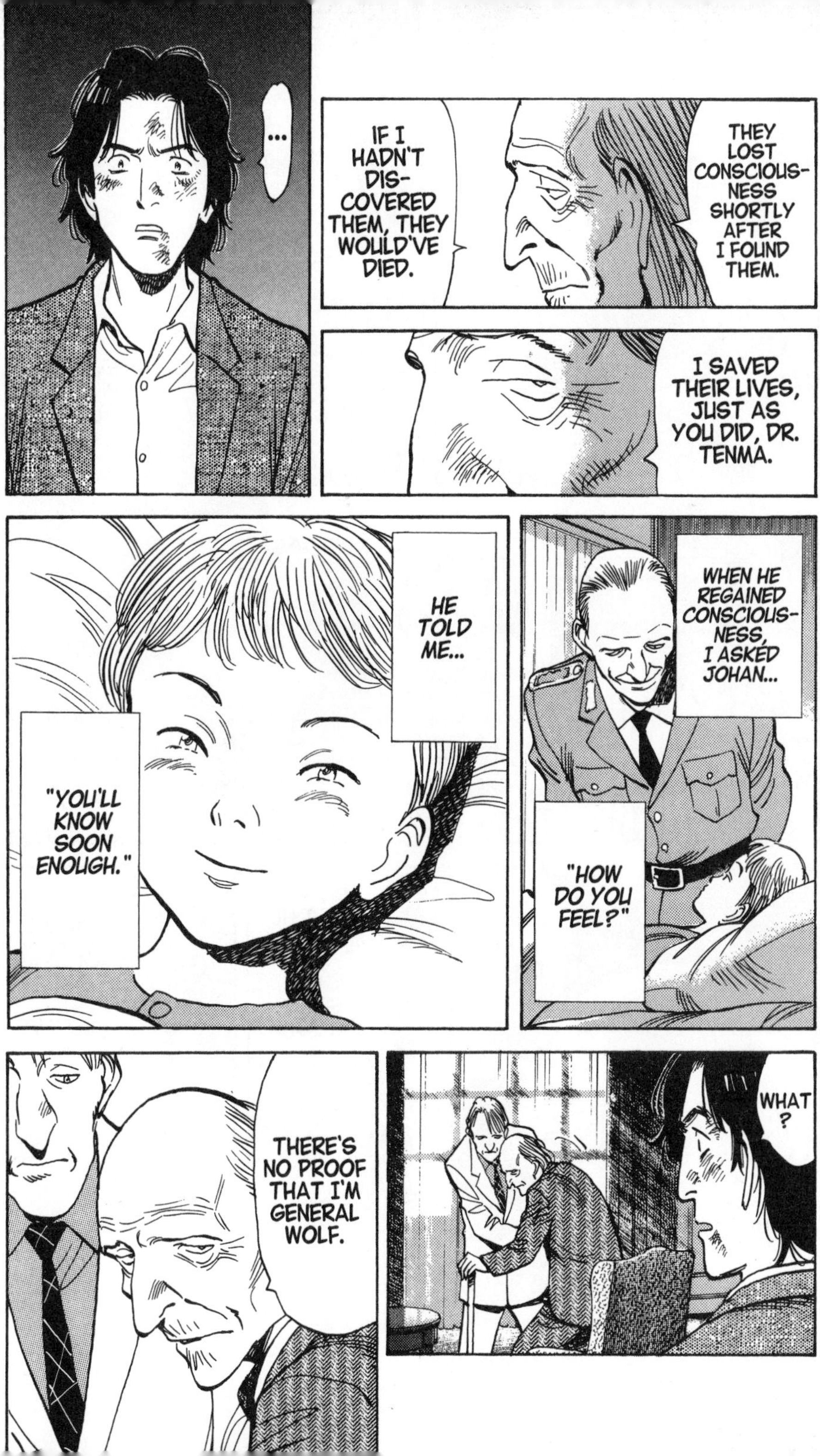
THEY LOST CONSCIOUSNESS SHORTLY AFTER I FOUND THEM.
IF I HADN'T DISCOVERED THEM, THEY WOULD'VE DIED.
I SAVED THEIR LIVES, JUST AS YOU DID, DR. TENMA.
...
WHEN HE REGAINED CONSCIOUSNESS, I ASKED JOHAN...
"HOW DO YOU FEEL?"
HE TOLD ME...
"YOU'LL KNOW SOON ENOUGH."
WHAT?
THERE'S NO PROOF THAT I'M GENERAL WOLF.

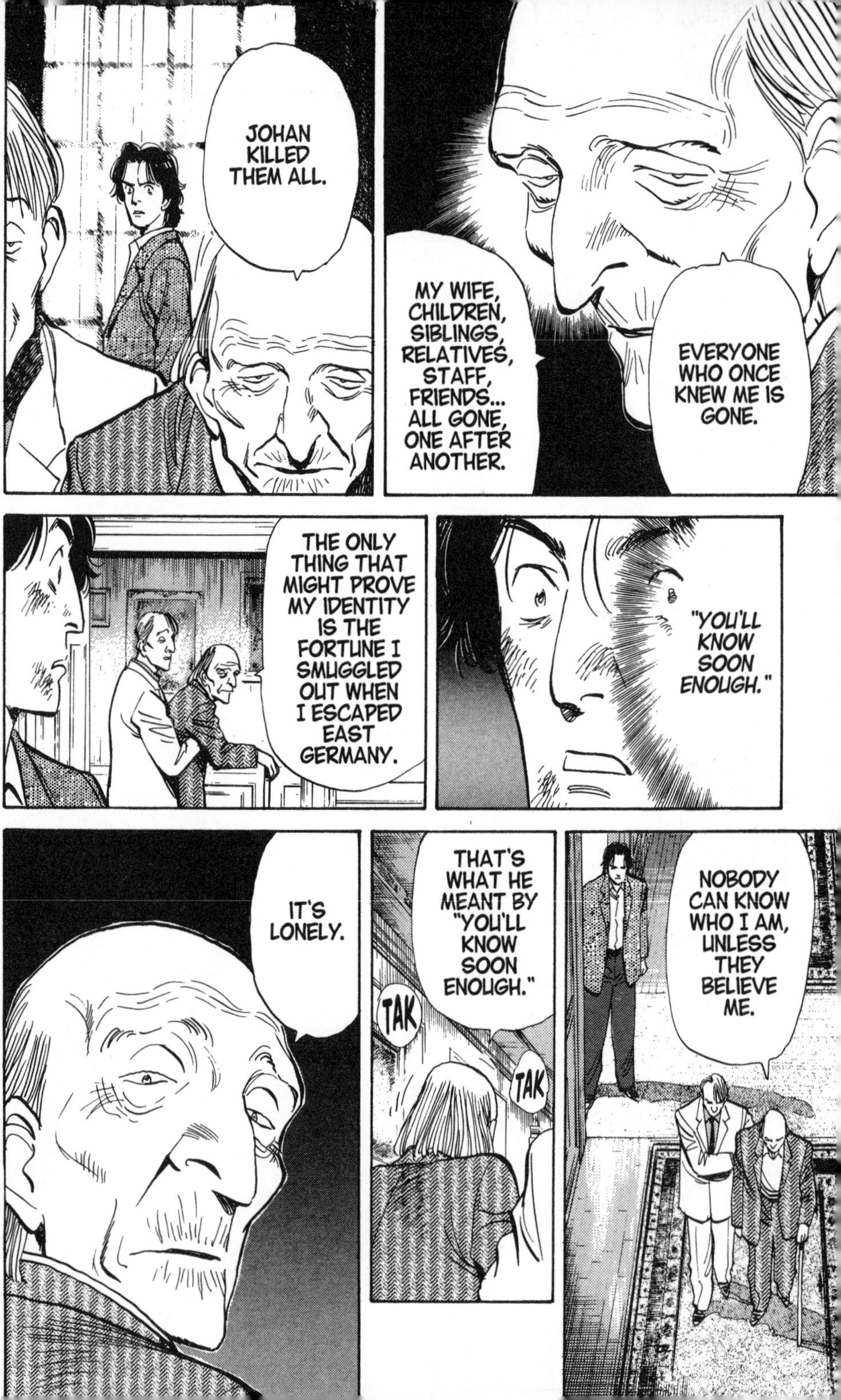
EVERYONE WHO ONCE KNEW ME IS GONE.
MY WIFE, CHILDREN, SIBLINGS, RELATIVES, STAFF, FRIENDS... ALL GONE, ONE AFTER ANOTHER.
JOHAN KILLED THEM ALL.
"YOU'LL KNOW SOON ENOUGH."
THE ONLY THING THAT MIGHT PROVE MY IDENTITY IS THE FORTUNE I SMUGGLED OUT WHEN I ESCAPED EAST GERMANY.
NOBODY CAN KNOW WHO I AM, UNLESS THEY BELIEVE ME.
THAT'S WHAT HE MEANT BY "YOU'LL KNOW SOON ENOUGH."
TAK
TAK
IT'S LONELY.

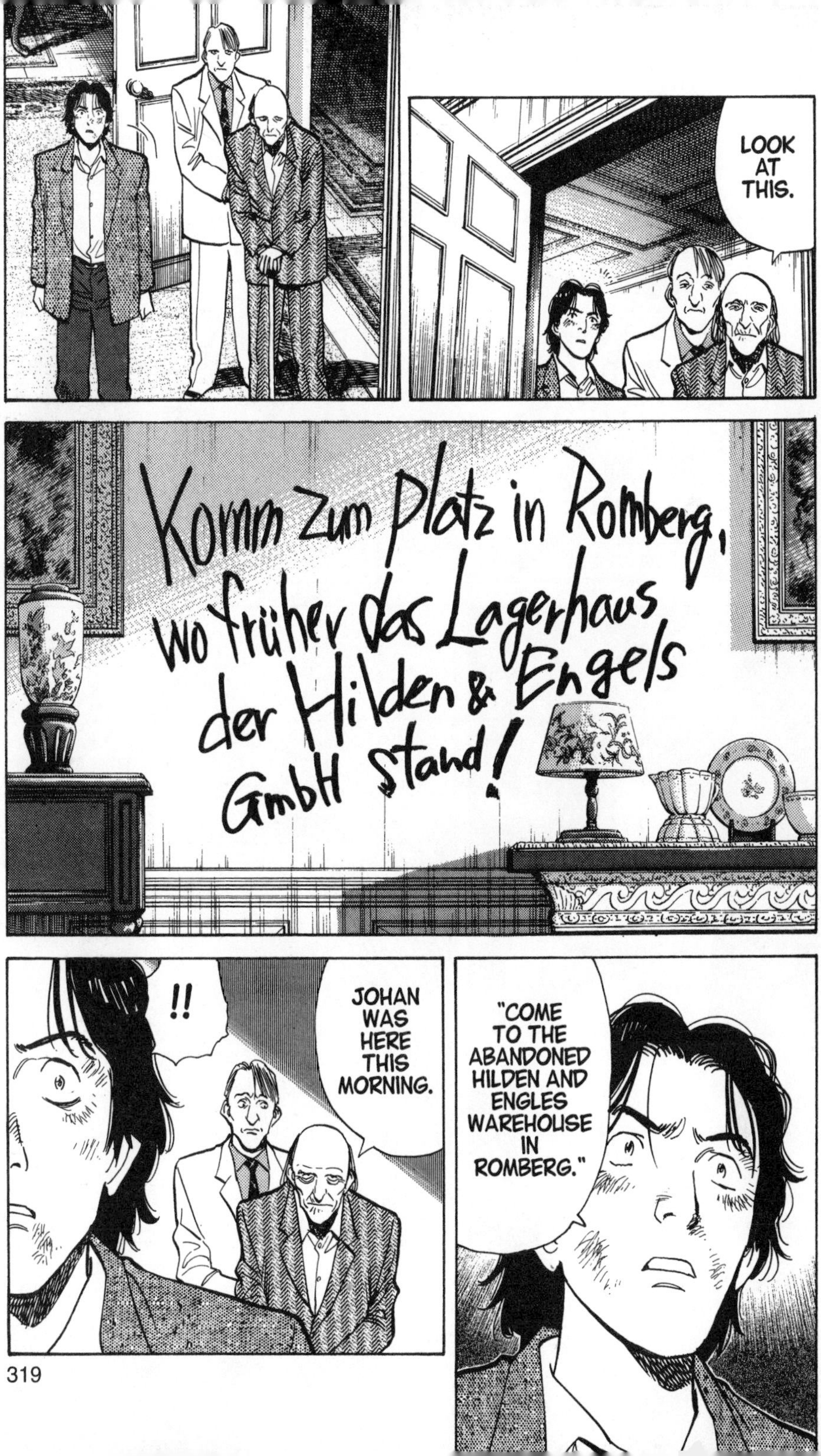
LOOK AT THIS.
Komm zum Platz in Romberg, wo früher das Lagerhaus der Hilden & Engels GmbH stand!
"COME TO THE ABANDONED HILDEN AND ENGLES WAREHOUSE IN ROMBERG."
JOHAN WAS HERE THIS MORNING.
!!

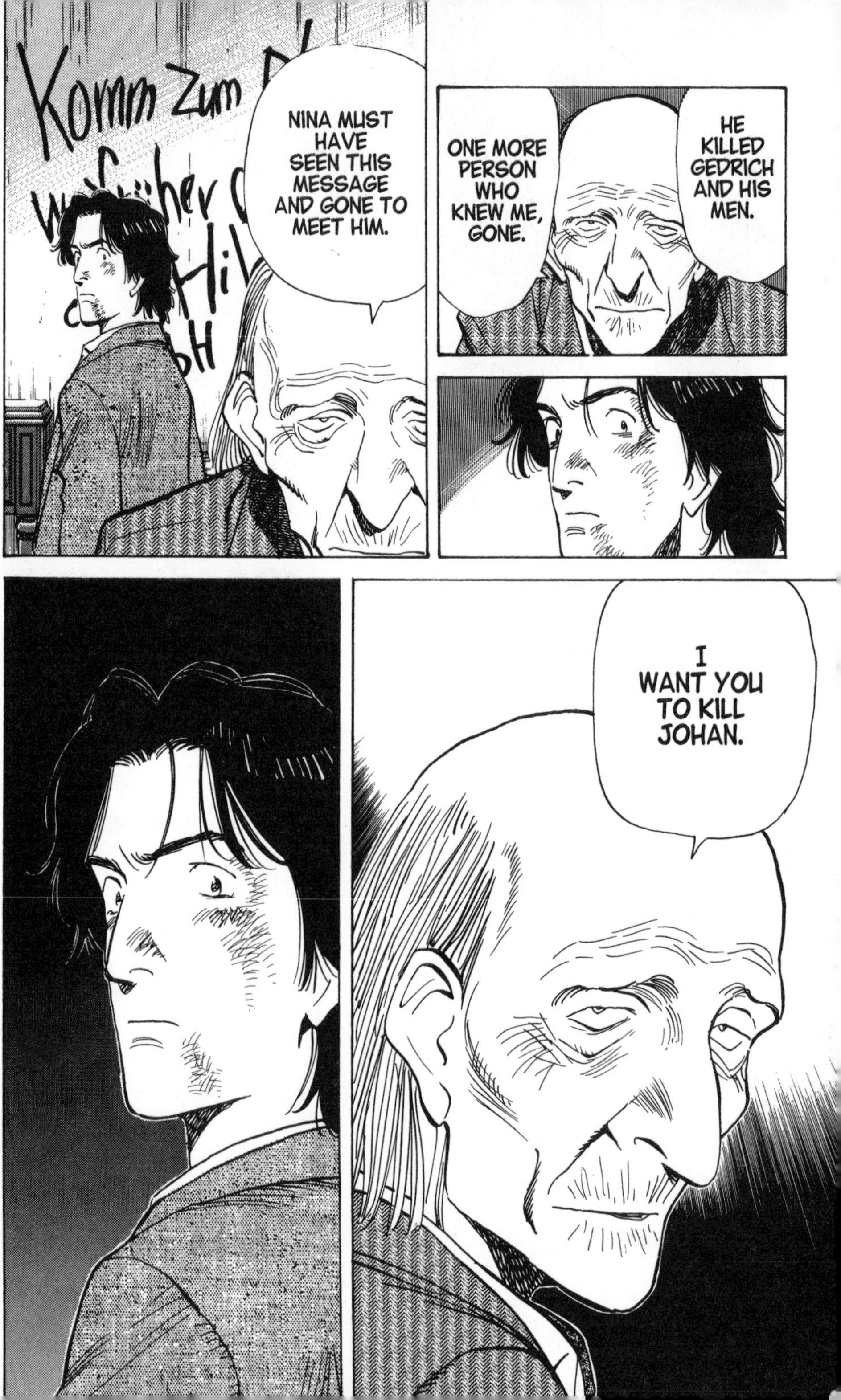
HE KILLED GEDRICH AND HIS MEN.
ONE MORE PERSON WHO KNEW ME, GONE.
Komm zum
NINA MUST HAVE SEEN THIS MESSAGE AND GONE TO MEET HIM.
I WANT YOU TO KILL JOHAN.

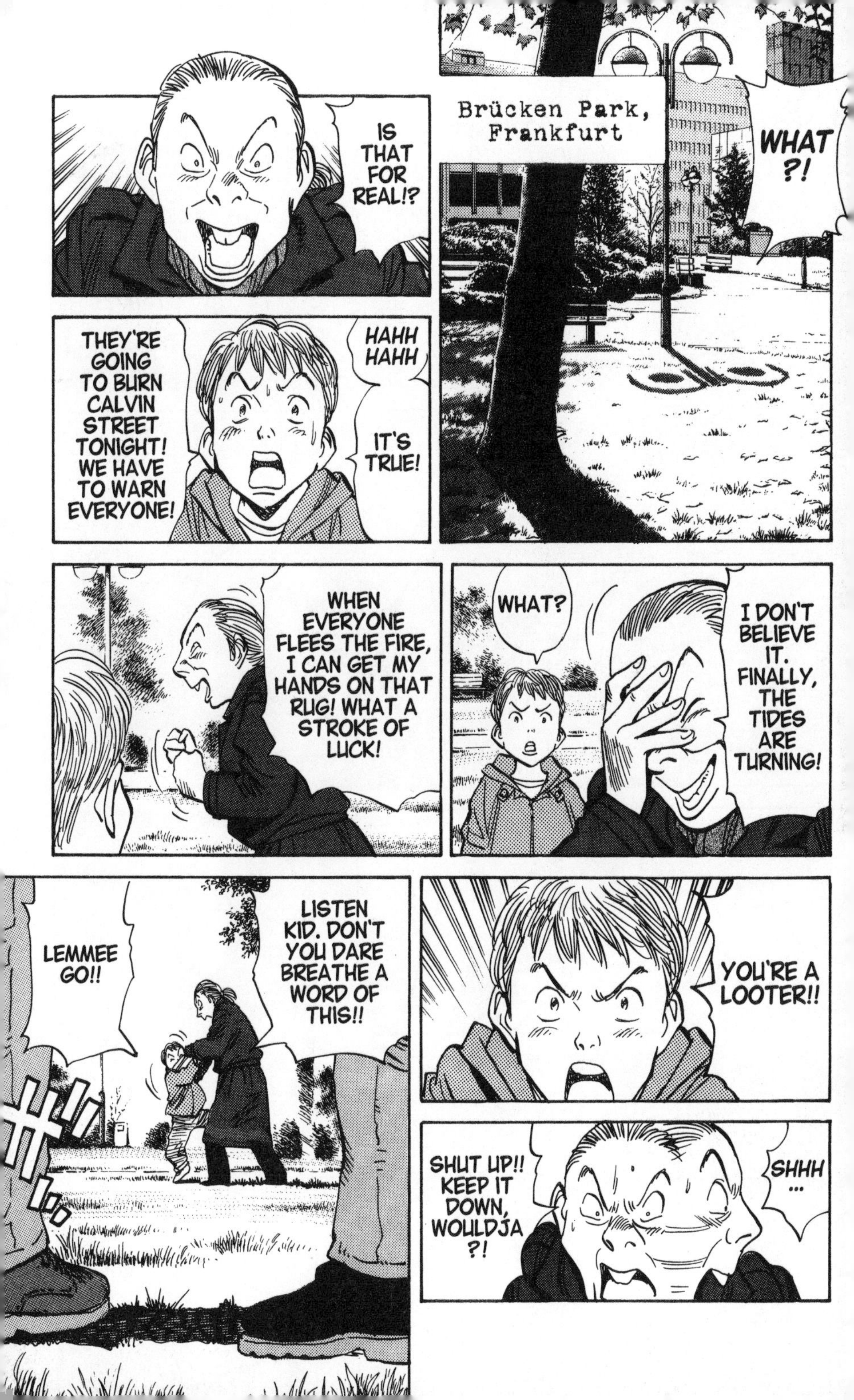
Brücken Park, Frankfurt
WHAT?!
IS THAT FOR REAL!?
HAHH HAHH
IT'S TRUE!
THEY'RE GOING TO BURN CALVIN STREET TONIGHT! WE HAVE TO WARN EVERYONE!
I DON'T BELIEVE IT. FINALLY, THE TIDES ARE TURNING!
WHAT?
WHEN EVERYONE FLEES THE FIRE, I CAN GET MY HANDS ON THAT RUG! WHAT A STROKE OF LUCK!
YOU'RE A LOOTER!!
SHHH...
SHUT UP!! KEEP IT DOWN, WOULDJA?!
LISTEN KID. DON'T YOU DARE BREATHE A WORD OF THIS!!
LEMMEE GO!!

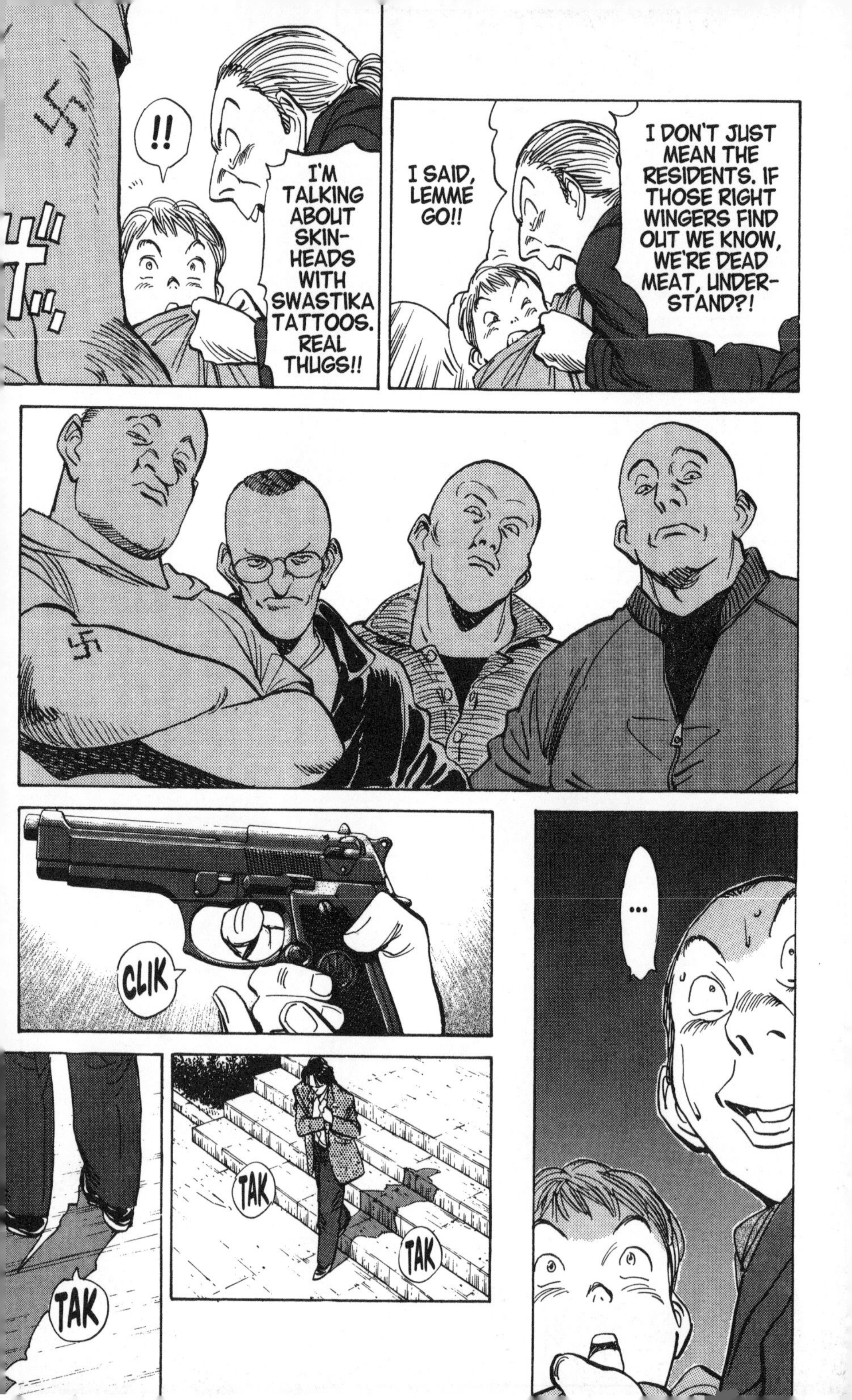

I DON'T JUST MEAN THE RESIDENTS. IF THOSE RIGHT WINGERS FIND OUT WE KNOW, WE'RE DEAD MEAT, UNDERSTAND?!
I SAID, LEMME GO!!
I'M TALKING ABOUT SKINHEADS WITH SWASTIKA TATTOOS. REAL THUGS!!
!!
...
CLIK
TAK
TAK
TAK

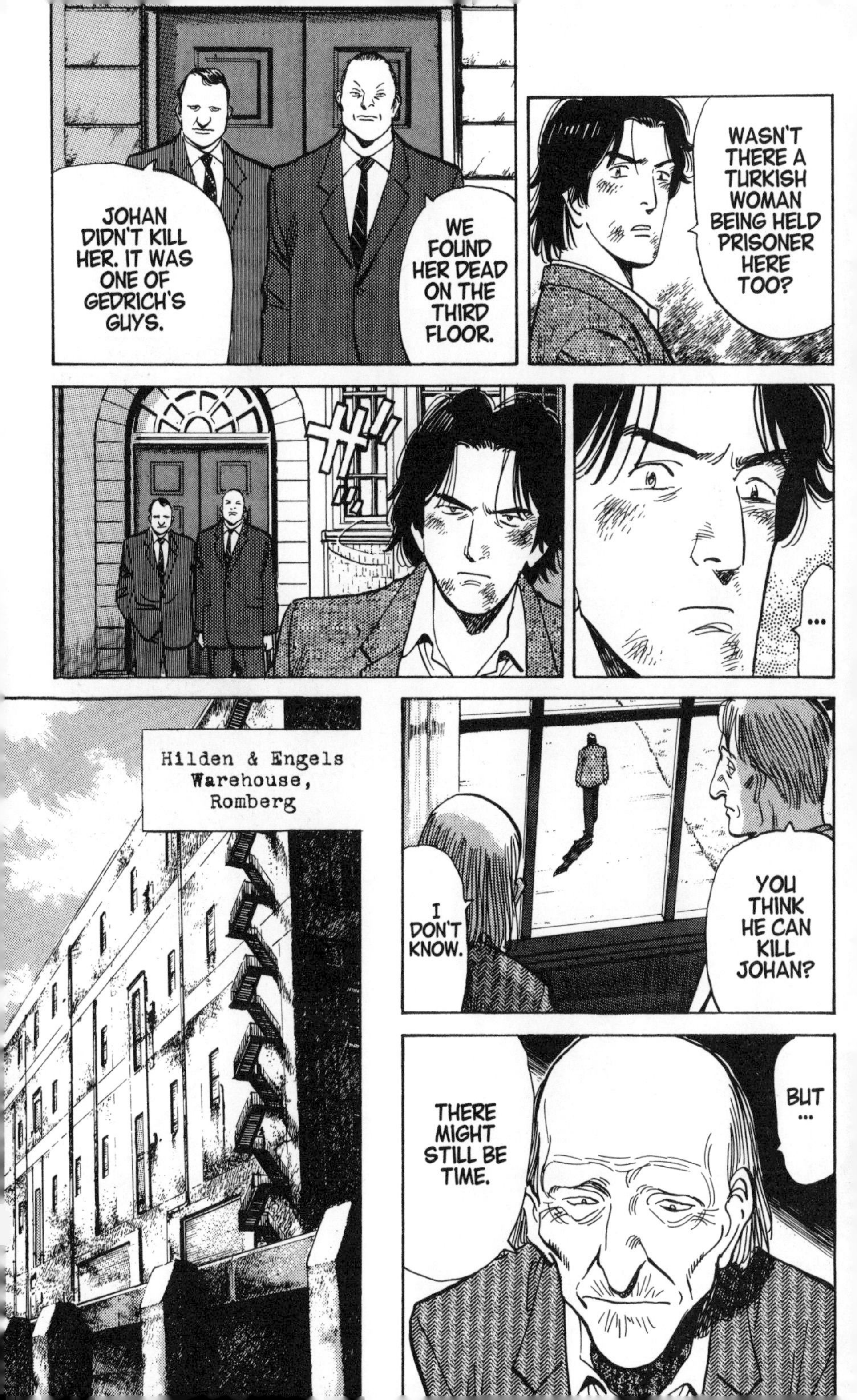
WASN'T THERE A TURKISH WOMAN BEING HELD PRISONER HERE TOO?
WE FOUND HER DEAD ON THE THIRD FLOOR.
JOHAN DIDN'T KILL HER. IT WAS ONE OF GEDRICH'S GUYS.
...
YOU THINK HE CAN KILL JOHAN?
I DON'T KNOW.
BUT ...
THERE MIGHT STILL BE TIME.
Hilden & Engels Warehouse, Romberg

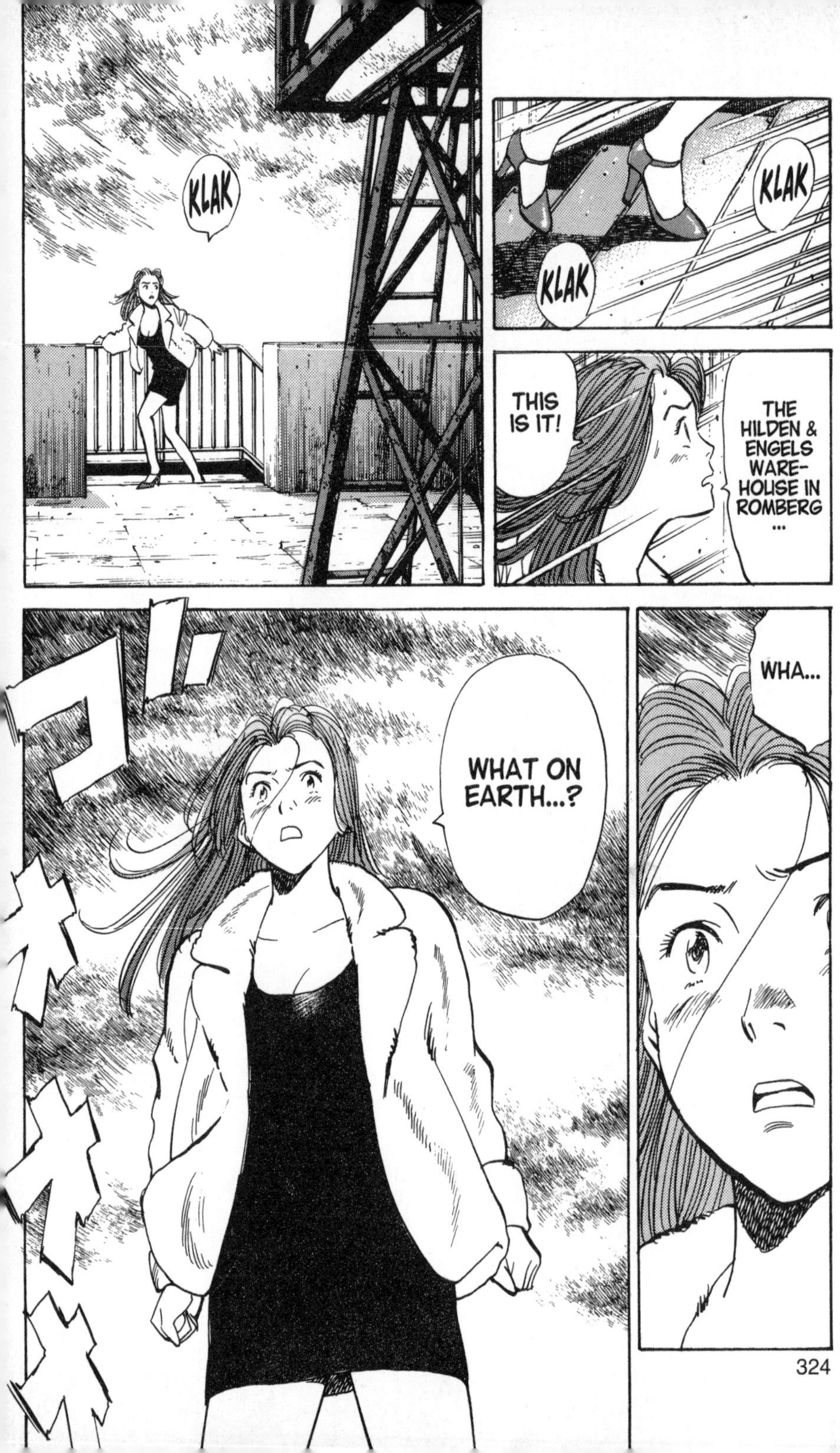
KLAK
KLAK
THE HILDEN & ENGELS WARE-HOUSE IN ROMBERG...
THIS IS IT!
KLAK
WHA...
WHAT ON EARTH...?

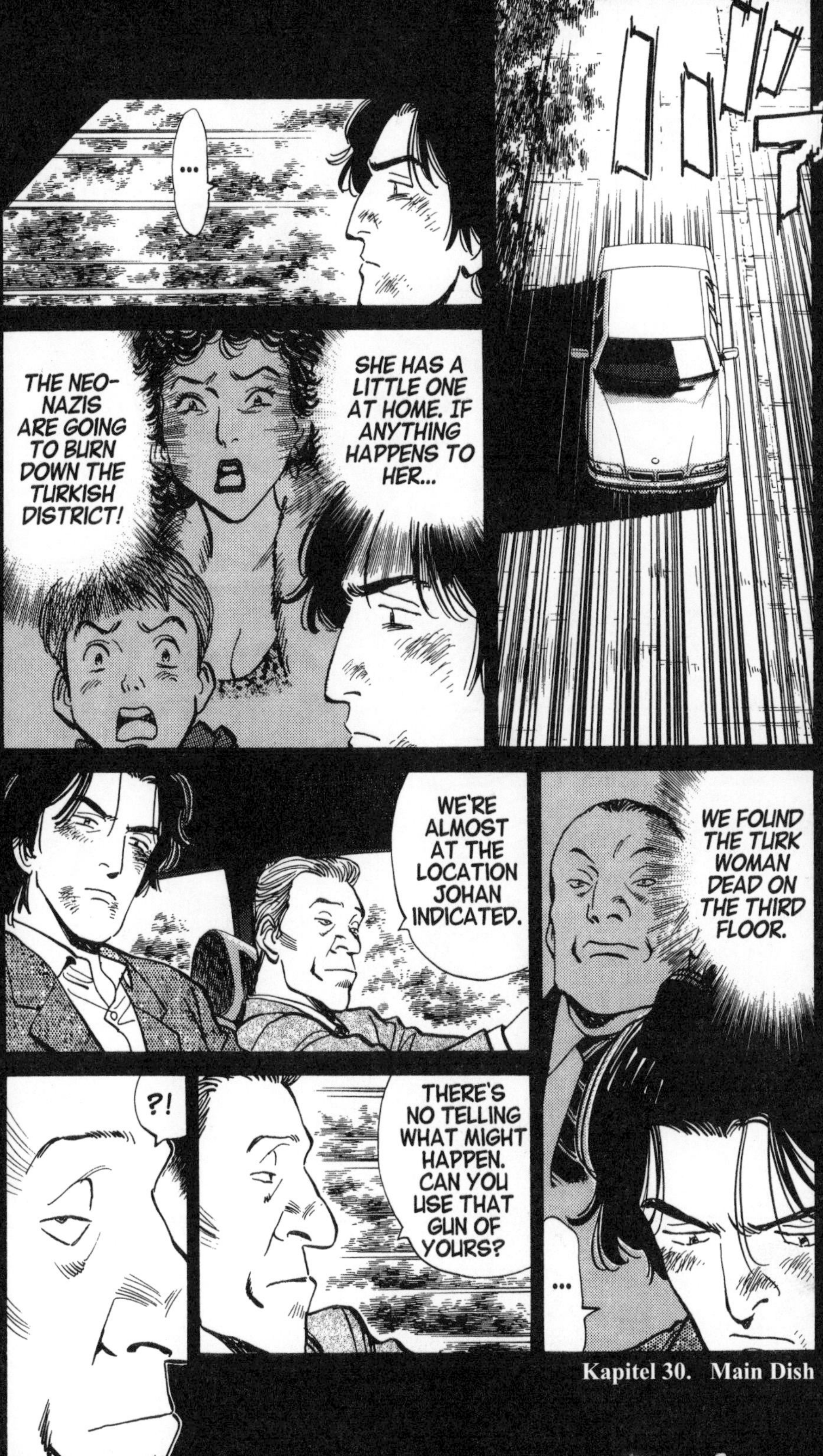
...
SHE HAS A LITTLE ONE AT HOME. IF ANYTHING HAPPENS TO HER...
THE NEO-NAZIS ARE GOING TO BURN DOWN THE TURKISH DISTRICT!
WE FOUND THE TURK WOMAN DEAD ON THE THIRD FLOOR.
...
WE'RE ALMOST AT THE LOCATION JOHAN INDICATED.
THERE'S NO TELLING WHAT MIGHT HAPPEN. CAN YOU USE THAT GUN OF YOURS?
?!

Kapitel 30. Main Dish

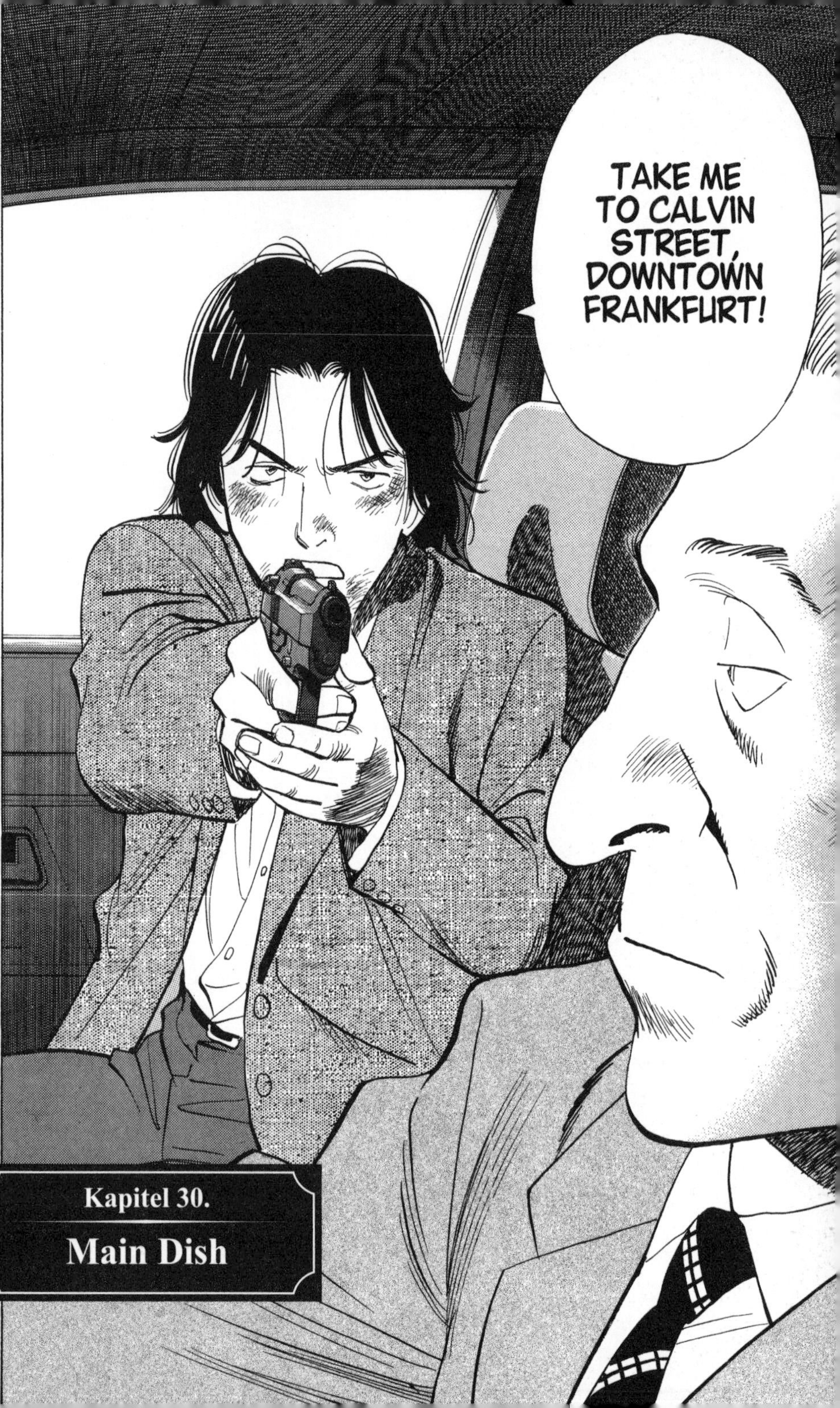
TAKE ME TO CALVIN STREET, DOWNTOWN FRANKFURT!
Kapitel 30.
Main Dish

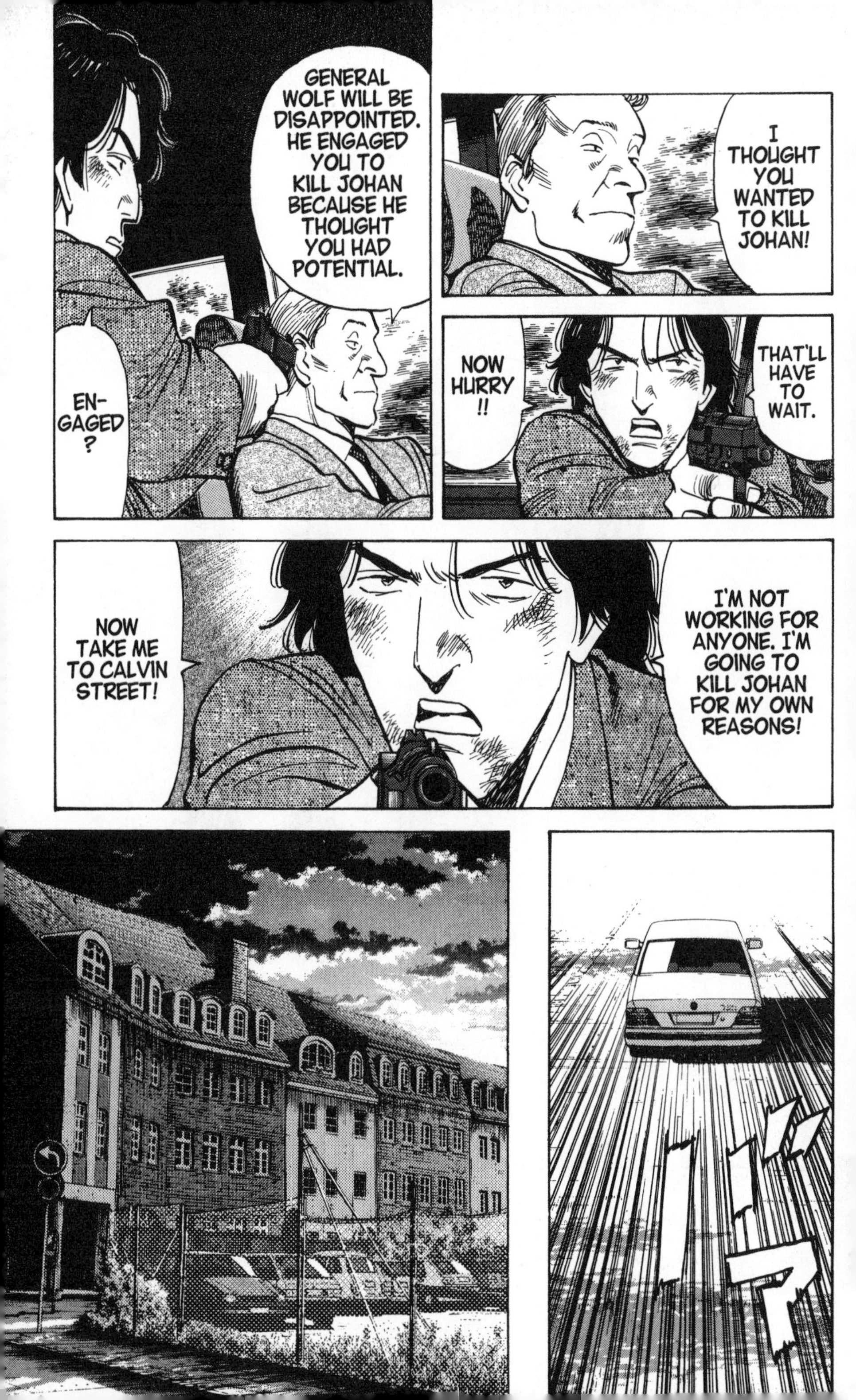
I THOUGHT YOU WANTED TO KILL JOHAN!
THAT'LL HAVE TO WAIT.
NOW HURRY!!
GENERAL WOLF WILL BE DISAPPOINTED. HE ENGAGED YOU TO KILL JOHAN BECAUSE HE THOUGHT YOU HAD POTENTIAL.
EN-GAGED?
I'M NOT WORKING FOR ANYONE. I'M GOING TO KILL JOHAN FOR MY OWN REASONS!
NOW TAKE ME TO CALVIN STREET!

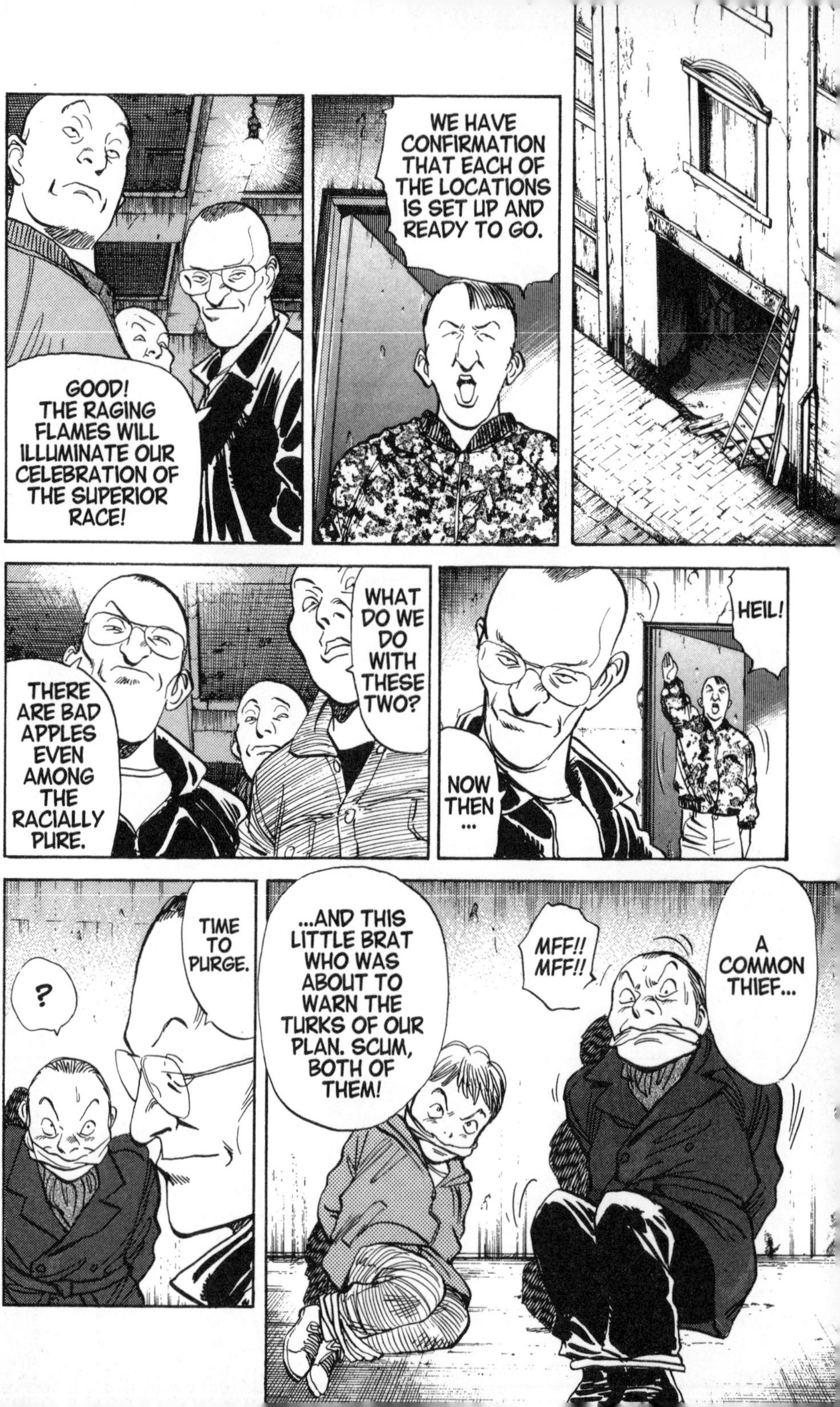
WE HAVE CONFIRMATION THAT EACH OF THE LOCATIONS IS SET UP AND READY TO GO.
GOOD! THE RAGING FLAMES WILL ILLUMINATE OUR CELEBRATION OF THE SUPERIOR RACE!
HEIL!
NOW THEN ...
WHAT DO WE DO WITH THESE TWO?
THERE ARE BAD APPLES EVEN AMONG THE RACIALLY PURE.
A COMMON THIEF...
MFF!! MFF!!
...AND THIS LITTLE BRAT WHO WAS ABOUT TO WARN THE TURKS OF OUR PLAN. SCUM, BOTH OF THEM!
TIME TO PURGE.
?

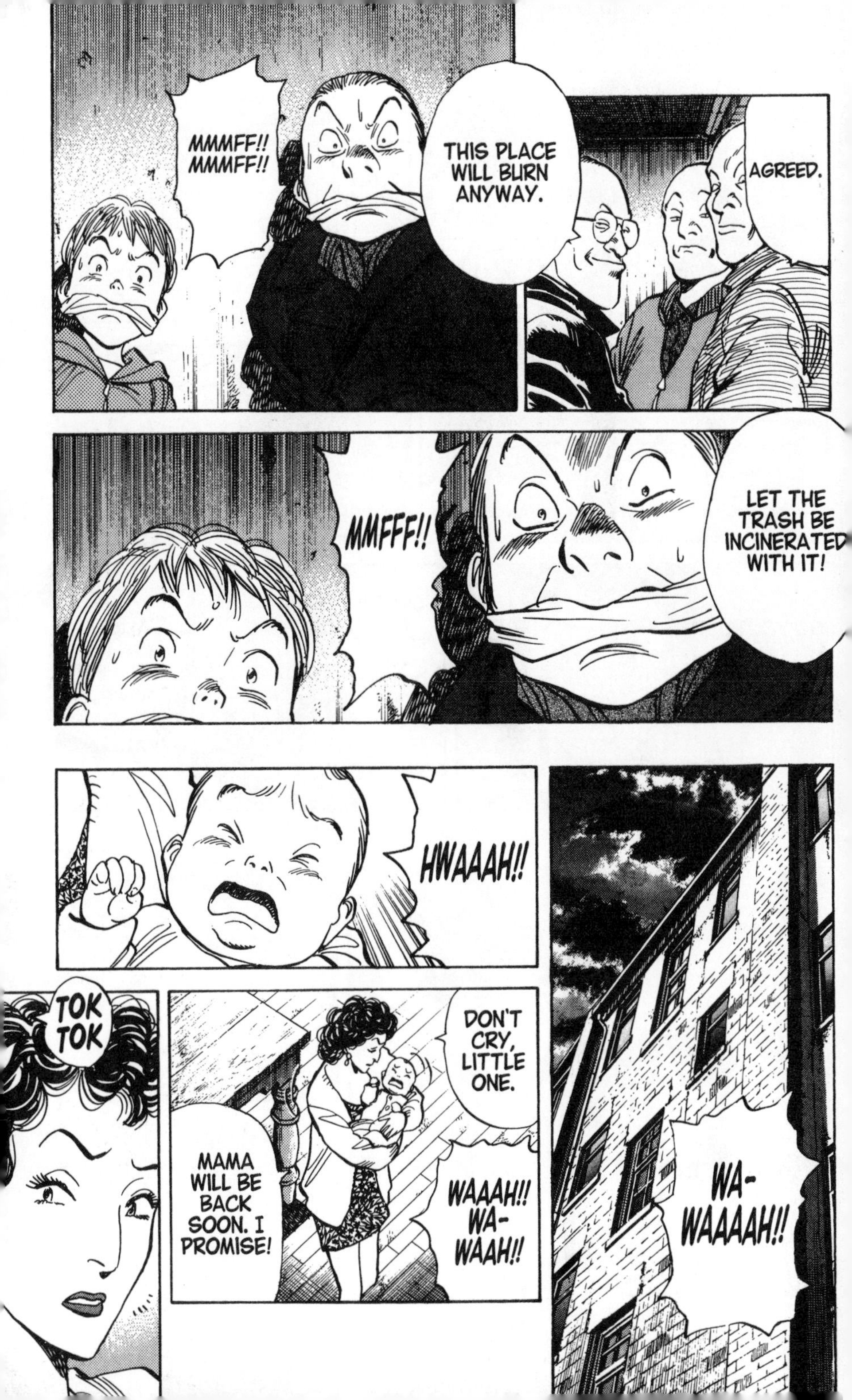
THIS PLACE WILL BURN ANYWAY.
AGREED.
MMMFF!! MMMFF!!
LET THE TRASH BE INCINERATED WITH IT!
MMFFF!!
WA-WAAAAH!!
HWAAAH!!
DON'T CRY, LITTLE ONE.
WAAAH!! WA-WAAH!!
MAMA WILL BE BACK SOON. I PROMISE!
TOK TOK

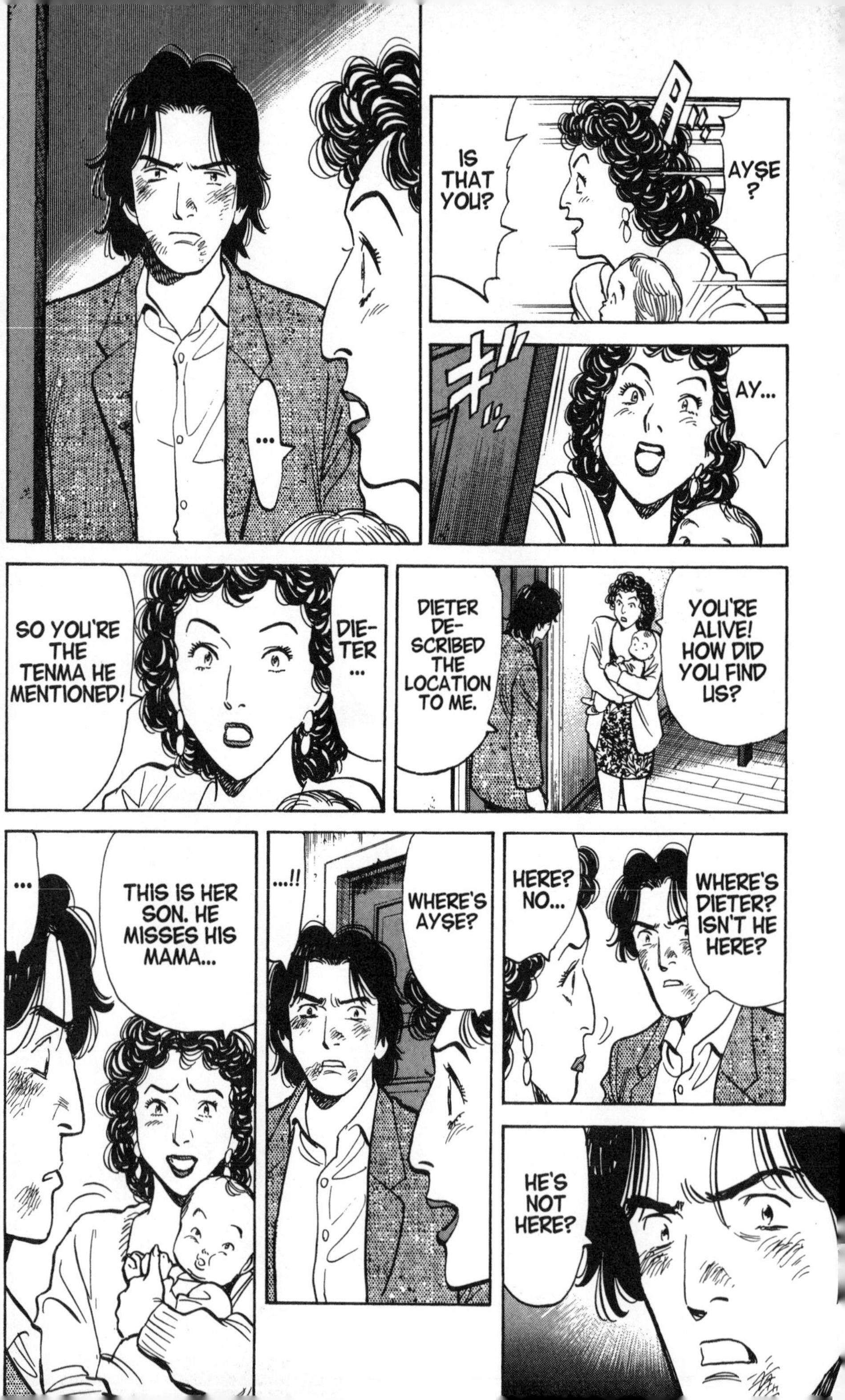
AYŞE ?
IS THAT YOU?
AY...
...
YOU'RE ALIVE! HOW DID YOU FIND US?
DIETER DE-SCRIBED THE LOCATION TO ME.
DIE-TER...
SO YOU'RE THE TENMA HE MENTIONED!
WHERE'S DIETER? ISN'T HE HERE?
HERE? NO...
HE'S NOT HERE?
WHERE'S AYŞE?
...!!
THIS IS HER SON. HE MISSES HIS MAMA...
...

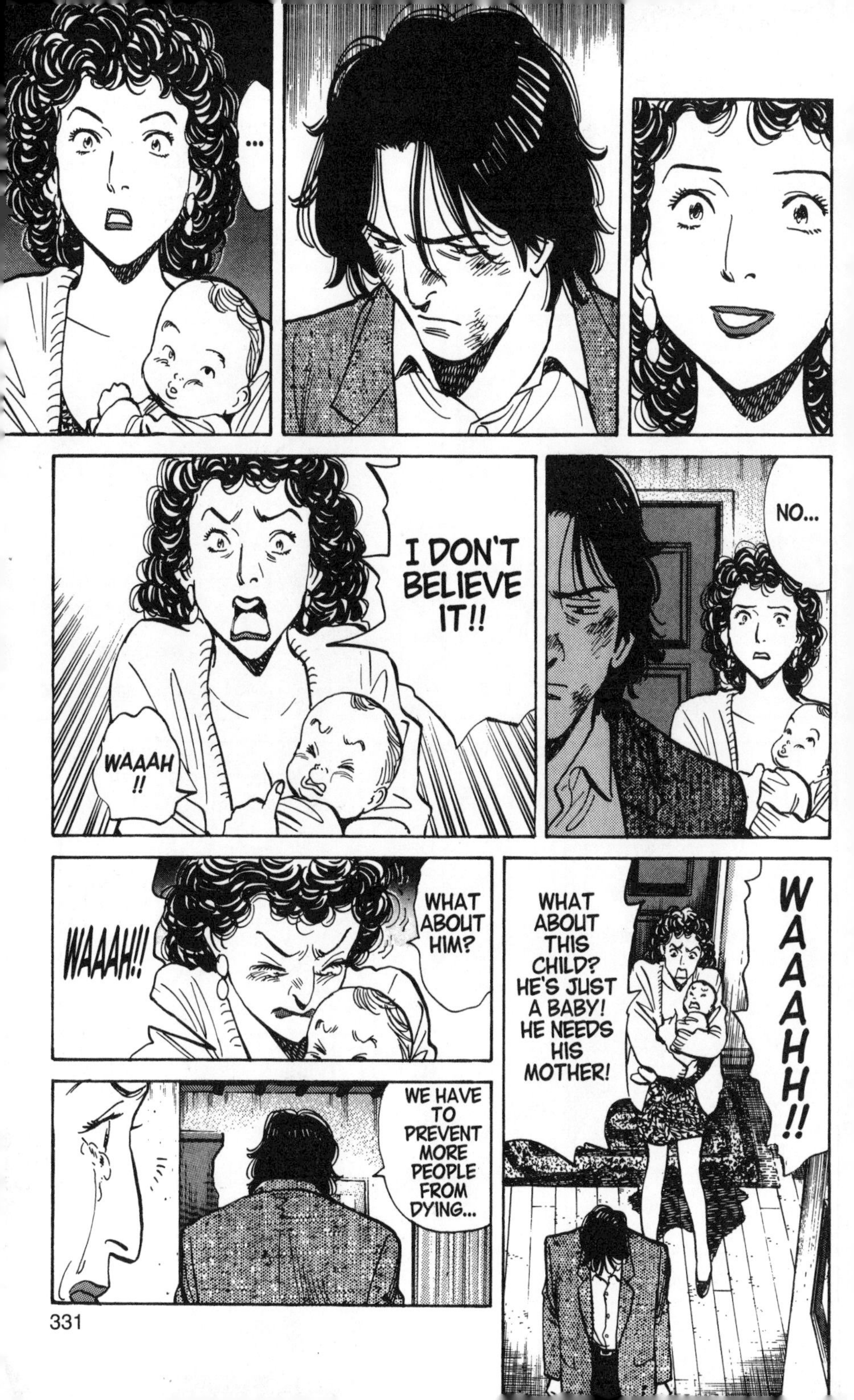
...
NO...
I DON'T BELIEVE IT!!
WAAAH !!
WAAAHH!!
WHAT ABOUT THIS CHILD? HE'S JUST A BABY! HE NEEDS HIS MOTHER!
WHAT ABOUT HIM?
WAAAH!!
WE HAVE TO PREVENT MORE PEOPLE FROM DYING...

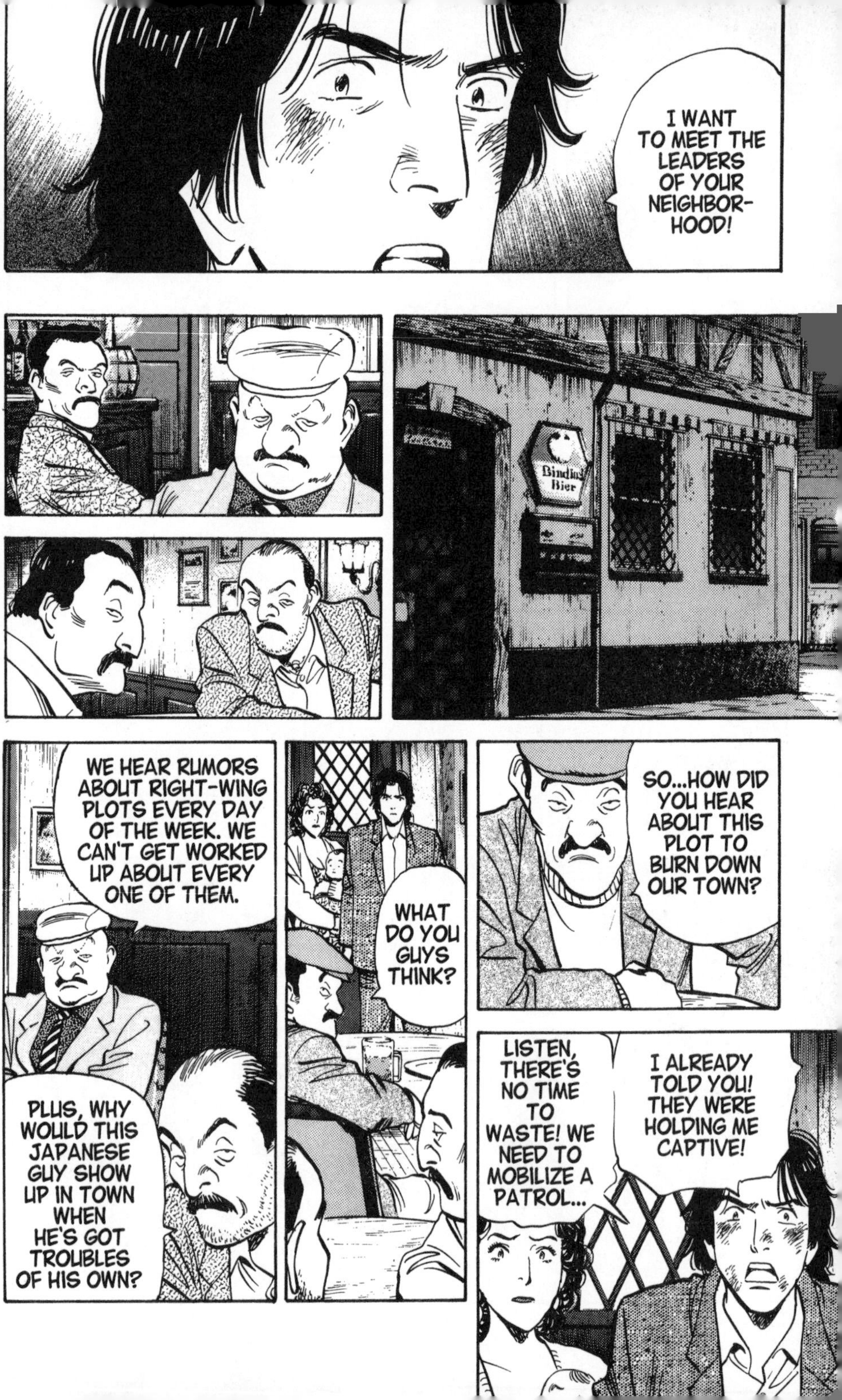
I WANT TO MEET THE LEADERS OF YOUR NEIGHBOR-HOOD!
Bier
SO...HOW DID YOU HEAR ABOUT THIS PLOT TO BURN DOWN OUR TOWN?
I ALREADY TOLD YOU! THEY WERE HOLDING ME CAPTIVE!
LISTEN, THERE'S NO TIME TO WASTE! WE NEED TO MOBILIZE A PATROL...
WHAT DO YOU GUYS THINK?
WE HEAR RUMORS ABOUT RIGHT-WING PLOTS EVERY DAY OF THE WEEK. WE CAN'T GET WORKED UP ABOUT EVERY ONE OF THEM.
PLUS, WHY WOULD THIS JAPANESE GUY SHOW UP IN TOWN WHEN HE'S GOT TROUBLES OF HIS OWN?

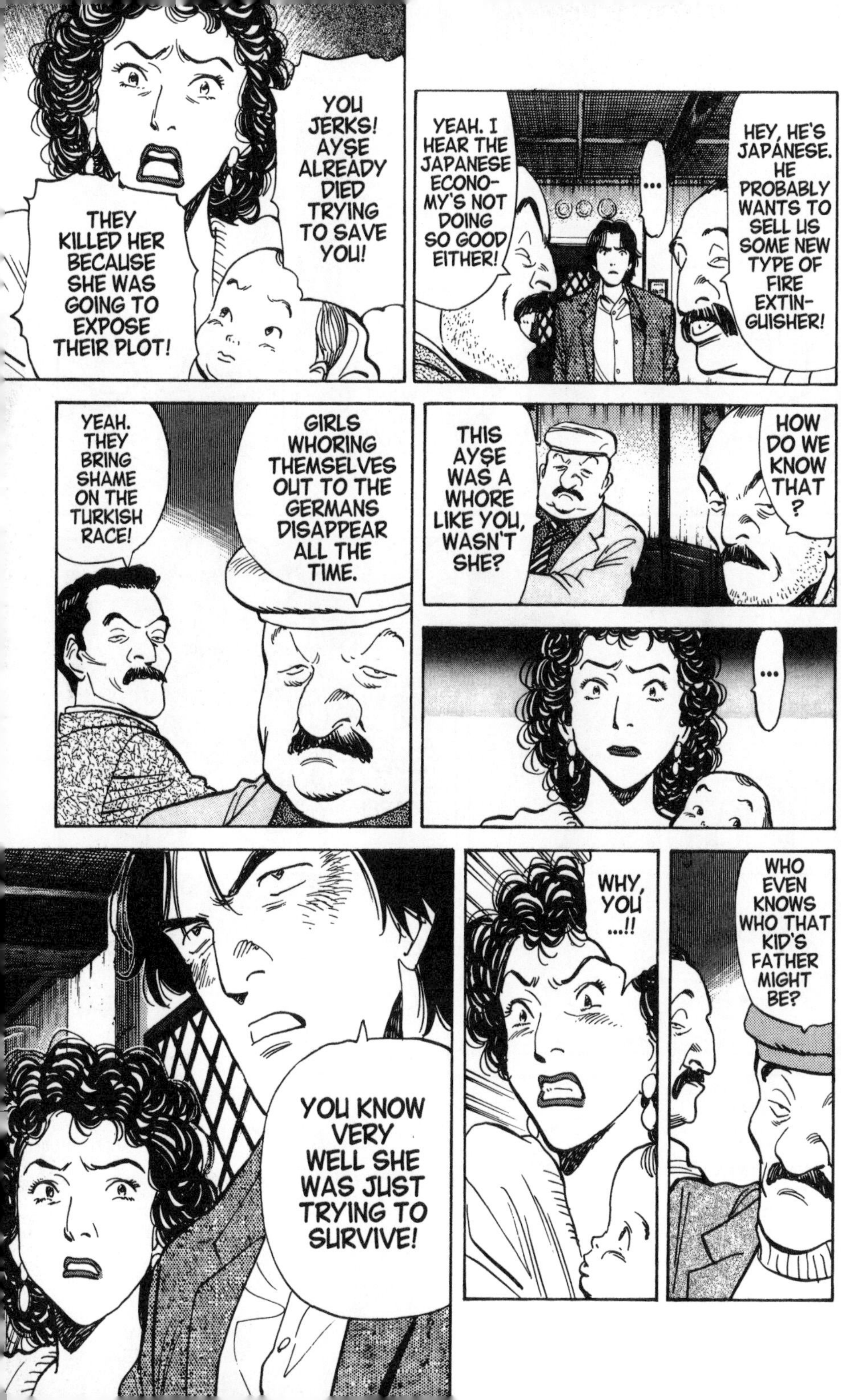
HEY, HE'S JAPANESE. HE PROBABLY WANTS TO SELL US SOME NEW TYPE OF FIRE EXTINGUISHER!
...
YEAH. I HEAR THE JAPANESE ECONOMY'S NOT DOING SO GOOD EITHER!
YOU JERKS! AYŞE ALREADY DIED TRYING TO SAVE YOU!
THEY KILLED HER BECAUSE SHE WAS GOING TO EXPOSE THEIR PLOT!
HOW DO WE KNOW THAT?
THIS AYŞE WAS A WHORE LIKE YOU, WASN'T SHE?
...
GIRLS WHORING THEMSELVES OUT TO THE GERMANS DISAPPEAR ALL THE TIME.
YEAH. THEY BRING SHAME ON THE TURKISH RACE!
WHO EVEN KNOWS WHO THAT KID'S FATHER MIGHT BE?
WHY, YOU ...!!
YOU KNOW VERY WELL SHE WAS JUST TRYING TO SURVIVE!

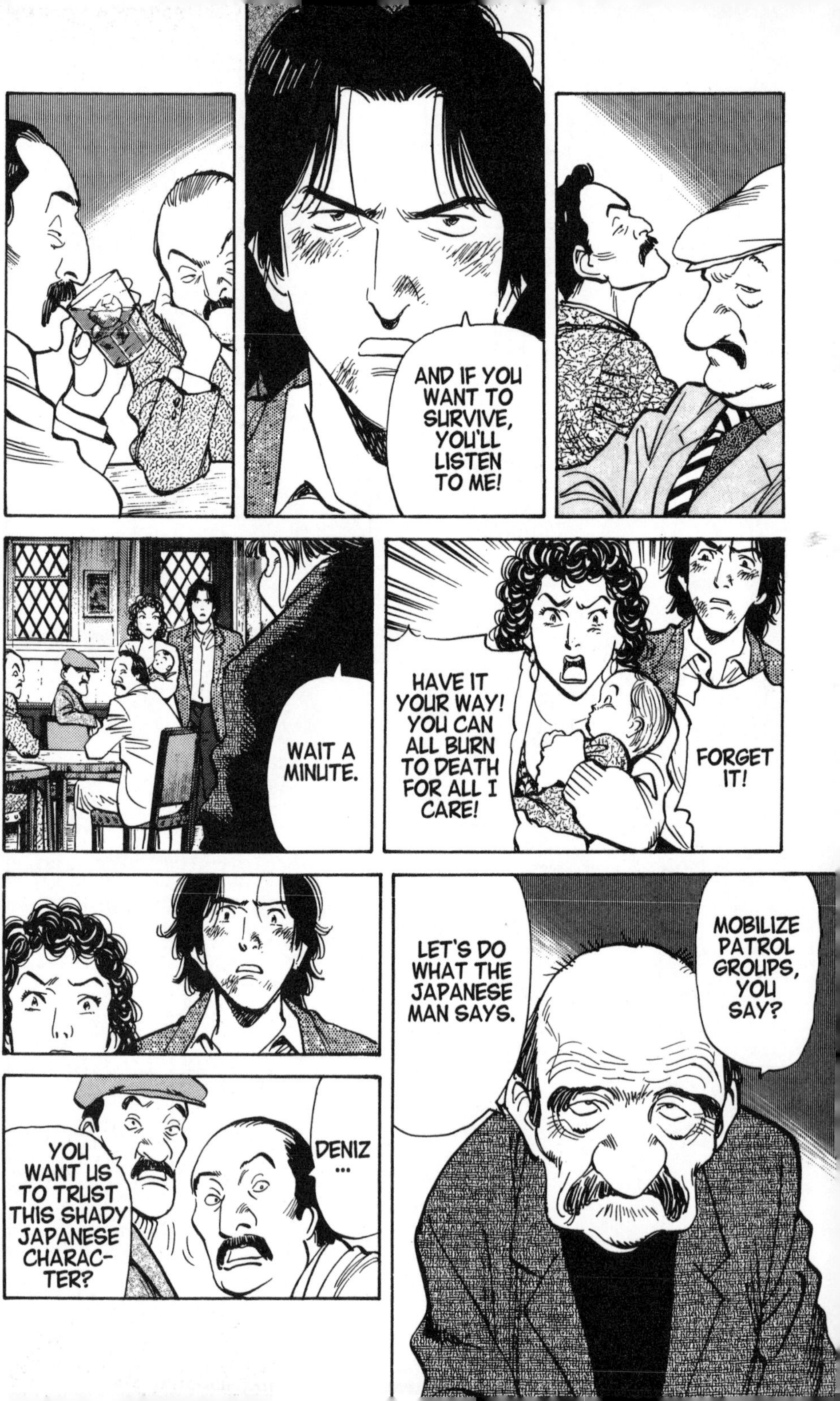
AND IF YOU WANT TO SURVIVE, YOU'LL LISTEN TO ME!
FORGET IT!
HAVE IT YOUR WAY! YOU CAN ALL BURN TO DEATH FOR ALL I CARE!
WAIT A MINUTE.
MOBILIZE PATROL GROUPS, YOU SAY?
LET'S DO WHAT THE JAPANESE MAN SAYS.
DENIZ ...
YOU WANT US TO TRUST THIS SHADY JAPANESE CHARAC-TER?

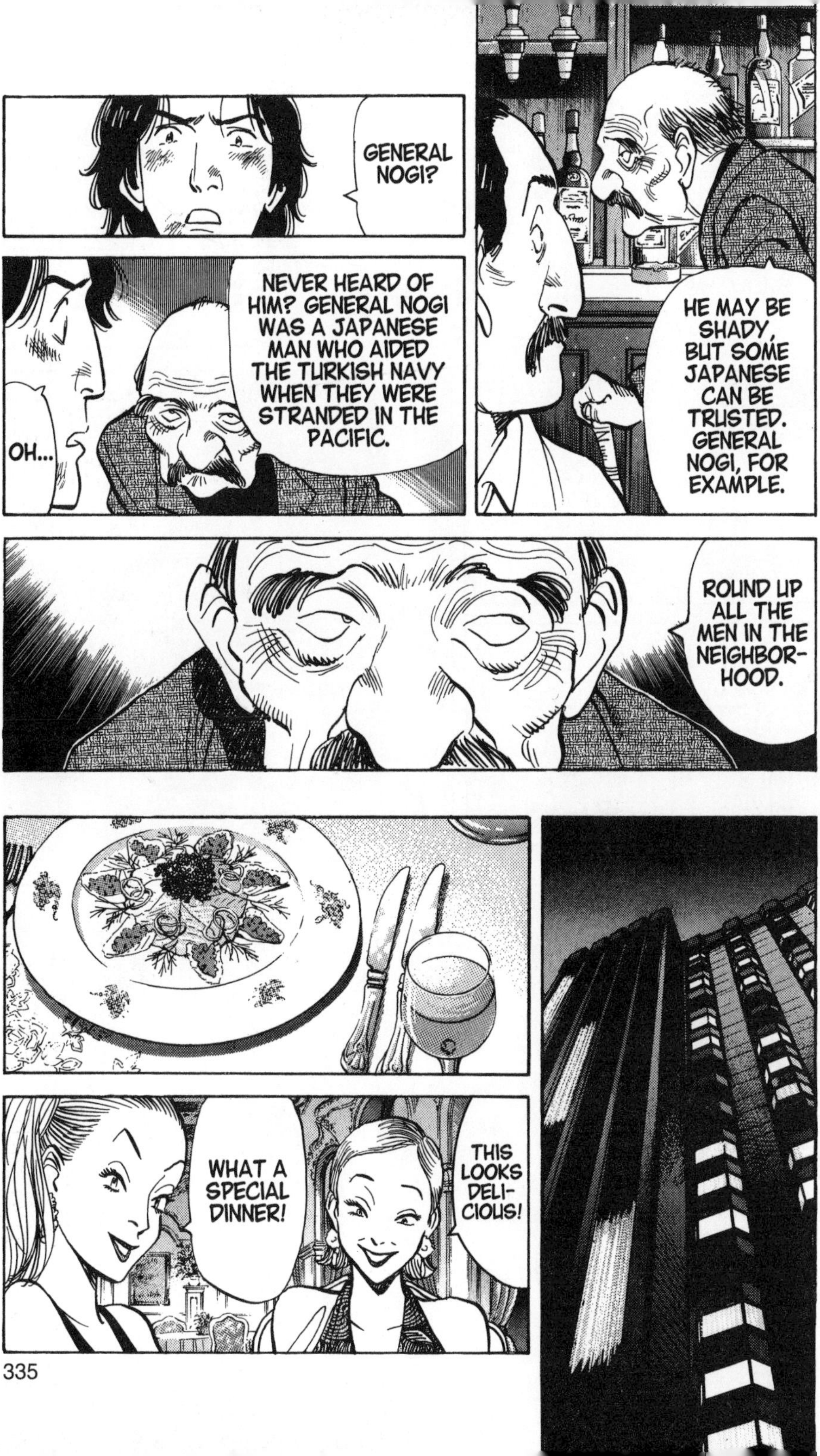
HE MAY BE SHADY, BUT SOME JAPANESE CAN BE TRUSTED. GENERAL NOGI, FOR EXAMPLE.
GENERAL NOGI?
NEVER HEARD OF HIM? GENERAL NOGI WAS A JAPANESE MAN WHO AIDED THE TURKISH NAVY WHEN THEY WERE STRANDED IN THE PACIFIC.
OH...
ROUND UP ALL THE MEN IN THE NEIGHBOR-HOOD.
THIS LOOKS DELI-CIOUS!
WHAT A SPECIAL DINNER!

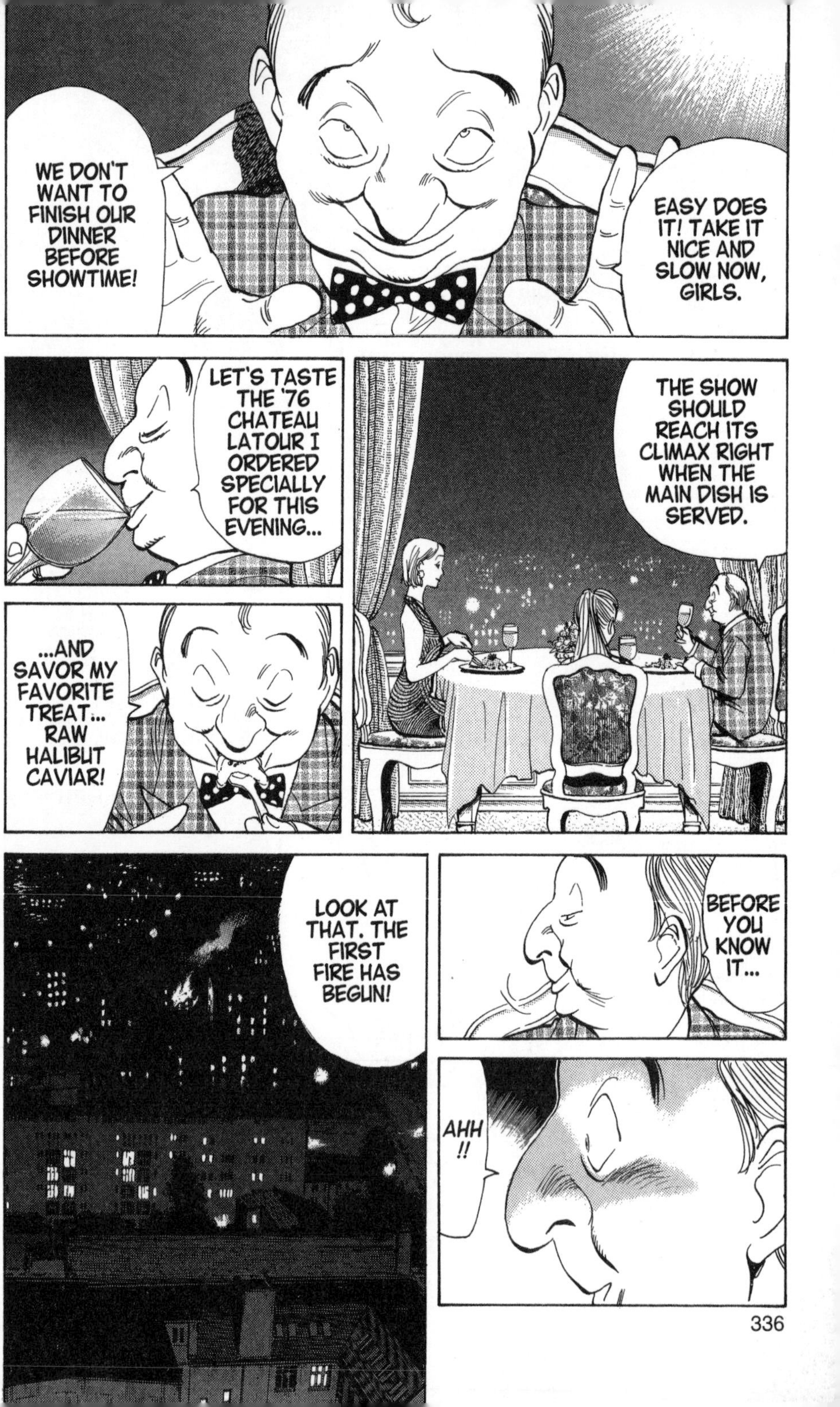
EASY DOES IT! TAKE IT NICE AND SLOW NOW, GIRLS.
WE DON'T WANT TO FINISH OUR DINNER BEFORE SHOWTIME!
THE SHOW SHOULD REACH ITS CLIMAX RIGHT WHEN THE MAIN DISH IS SERVED.
LET'S TASTE THE '76 CHATEAU LATOUR I ORDERED SPECIALLY FOR THIS EVENING...
...AND SAVOR MY FAVORITE TREAT... RAW HALIBUT CAVIAR!
BEFORE YOU KNOW IT...
AHH !!
LOOK AT THAT. THE FIRST FIRE HAS BEGUN!

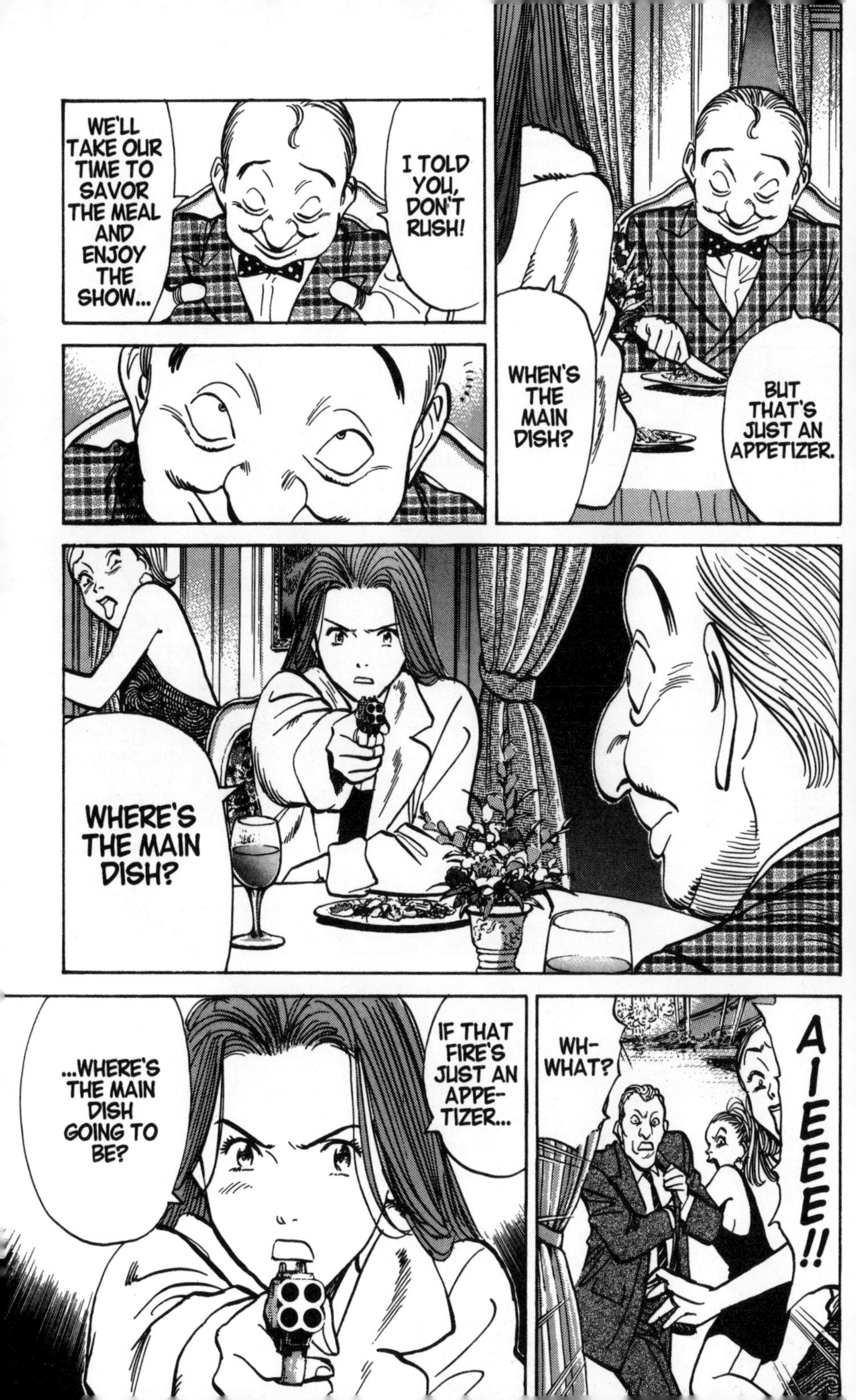
BUT THAT'S JUST AN APPETIZER.
WHEN'S THE MAIN DISH?
I TOLD YOU, DON'T RUSH!
WE'LL TAKE OUR TIME TO SAVOR THE MEAL AND ENJOY THE SHOW...
WHERE'S THE MAIN DISH?
AIEEE!!
WH-WHAT?
IF THAT FIRE'S JUST AN APPE-TIZER...
...WHERE'S THE MAIN DISH GOING TO BE?

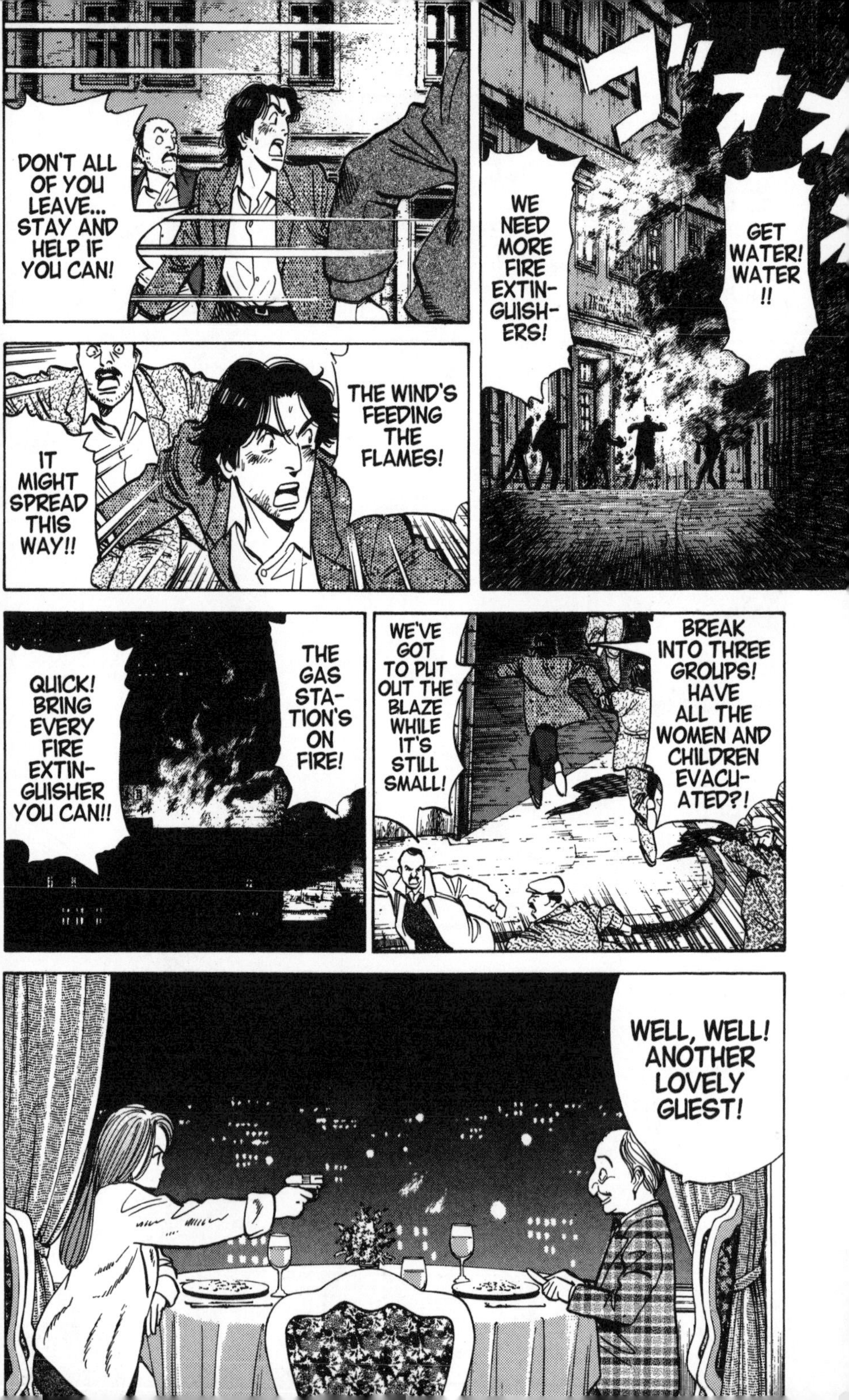
GET WATER! WATER !!
WE NEED MORE FIRE EXTINGUISHERS!
DON'T ALL OF YOU LEAVE... STAY AND HELP IF YOU CAN!
THE WIND'S FEEDING THE FLAMES!
IT MIGHT SPREAD THIS WAY!!
BREAK INTO THREE GROUPS! HAVE ALL THE WOMEN AND CHILDREN EVACUATED?!
WE'VE GOT TO PUT OUT THE BLAZE WHILE IT'S STILL SMALL!
THE GAS STATION'S ON FIRE!
QUICK! BRING EVERY FIRE EXTINGUISHER YOU CAN!!
WELL, WELL! ANOTHER LOVELY GUEST!

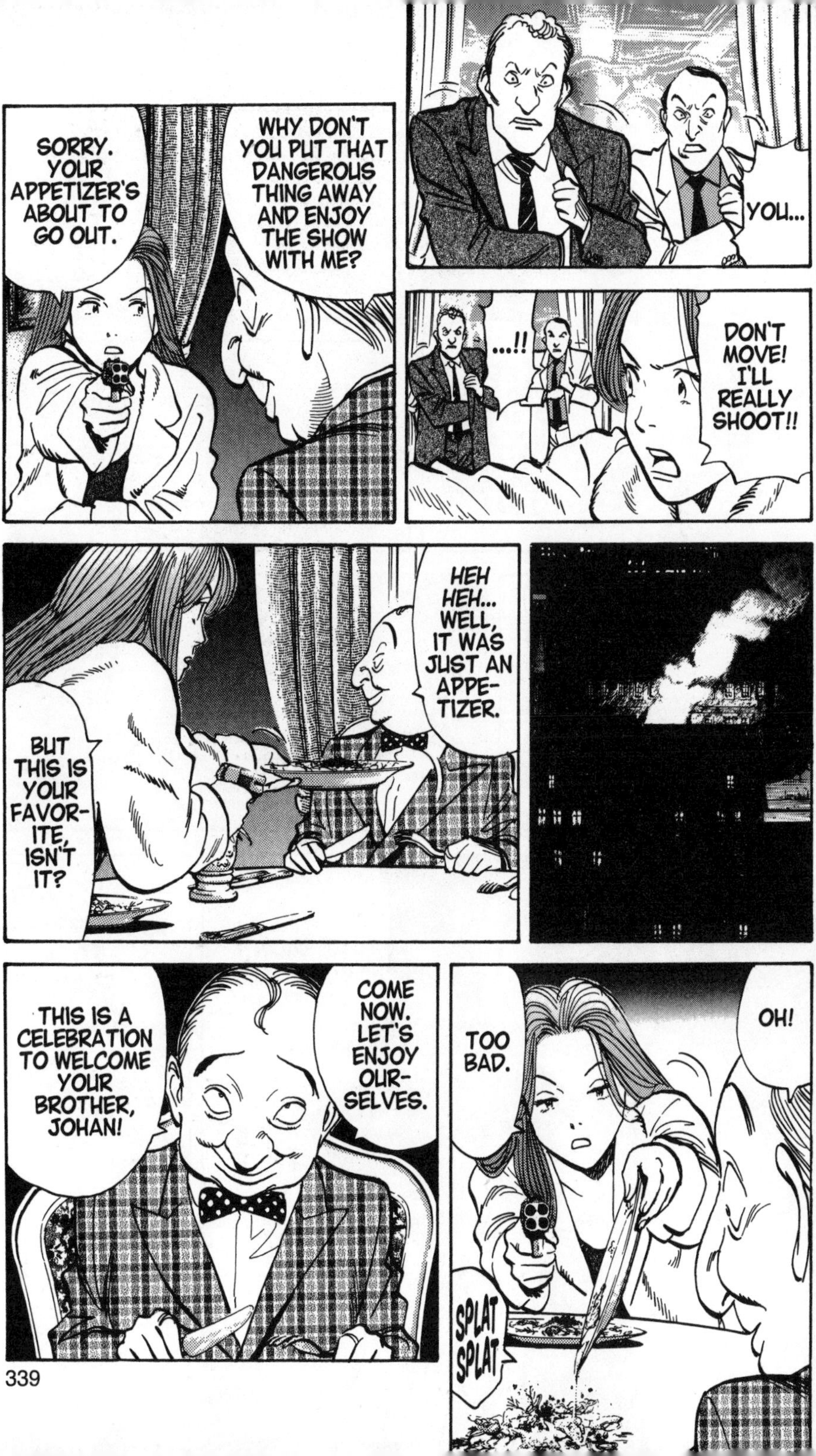
YOU...
DON'T MOVE! I'LL REALLY SHOOT!!
...!!
WHY DON'T YOU PUT THAT DANGEROUS THING AWAY AND ENJOY THE SHOW WITH ME?
SORRY. YOUR APPETIZER'S ABOUT TO GO OUT.
HEH HEH... WELL, IT WAS JUST AN APPE-TIZER.
BUT THIS IS YOUR FAVOR-ITE, ISN'T IT?
OH!
TOO BAD.
SPLAT SPLAT
COME NOW. LET'S ENJOY OUR-SELVES.
THIS IS A CELEBRATION TO WELCOME YOUR BROTHER, JOHAN!

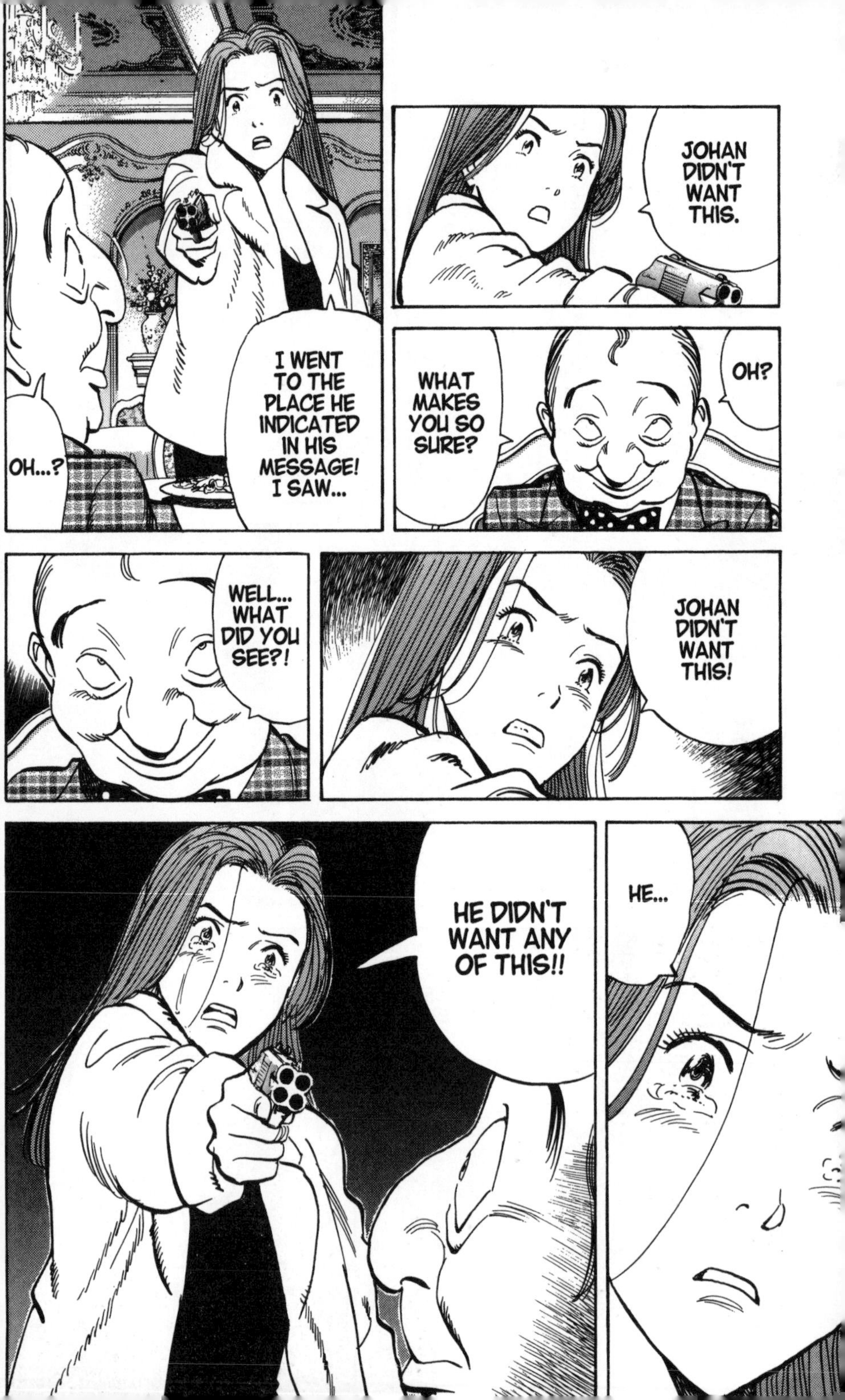
JOHAN DIDN'T WANT THIS.
OH?
WHAT MAKES YOU SO SURE?
I WENT TO THE PLACE HE INDICATED IN HIS MESSAGE! I SAW...
OH...?
JOHAN DIDN'T WANT THIS!
WELL... WHAT DID YOU SEE?!
HE...
HE DIDN'T WANT ANY OF THIS!!

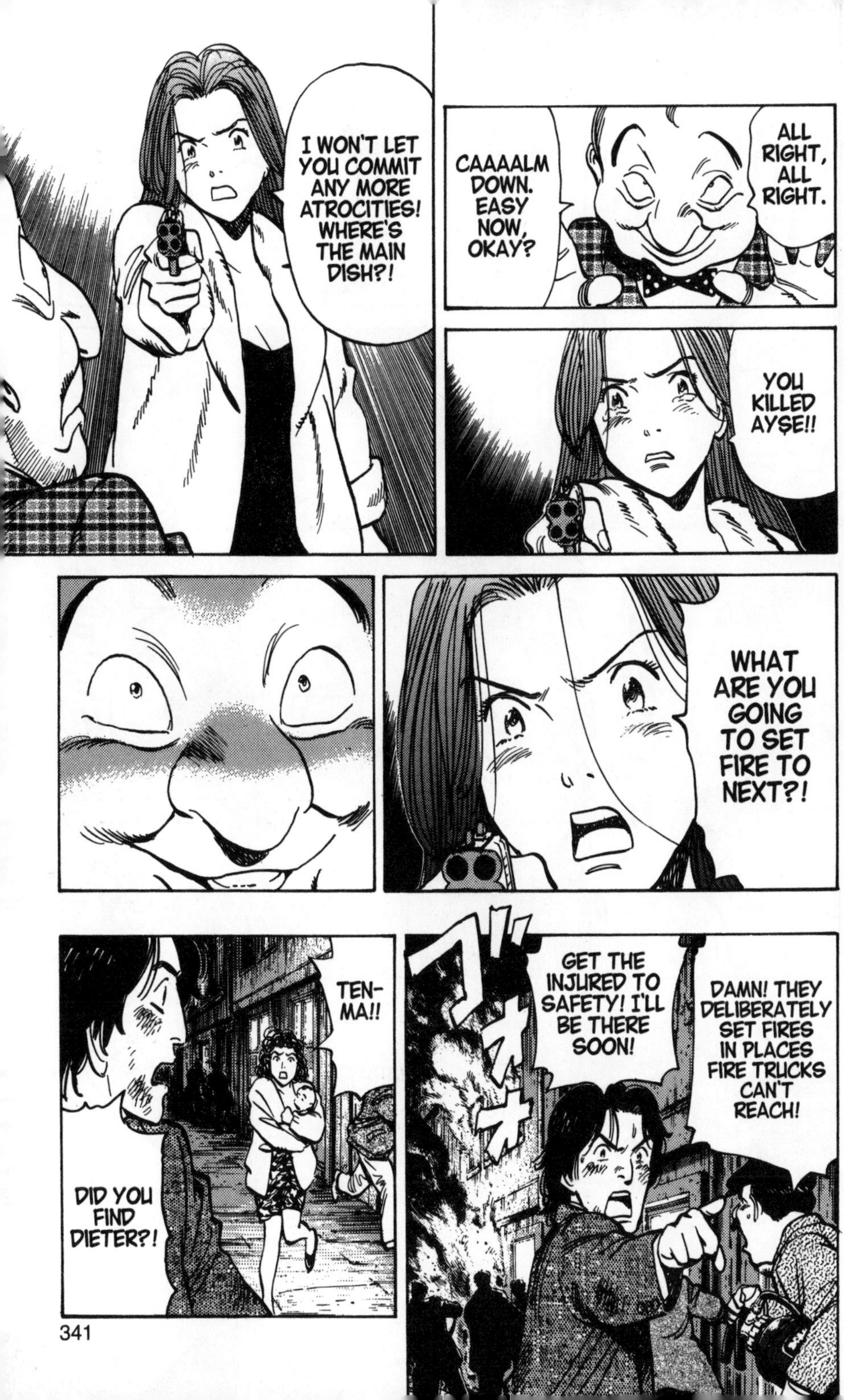
ALL RIGHT, ALL RIGHT.
CAAAALM DOWN. EASY NOW, OKAY?
YOU KILLED AYŞE!!
I WON'T LET YOU COMMIT ANY MORE ATROCITIES! WHERE'S THE MAIN DISH?!
WHAT ARE YOU GOING TO SET FIRE TO NEXT?!
DAMN! THEY DELIBERATELY SET FIRES IN PLACES FIRE TRUCKS CAN'T REACH!
GET THE INJURED TO SAFETY! I'LL BE THERE SOON!
TEN-MA!!
DID YOU FIND DIETER?!

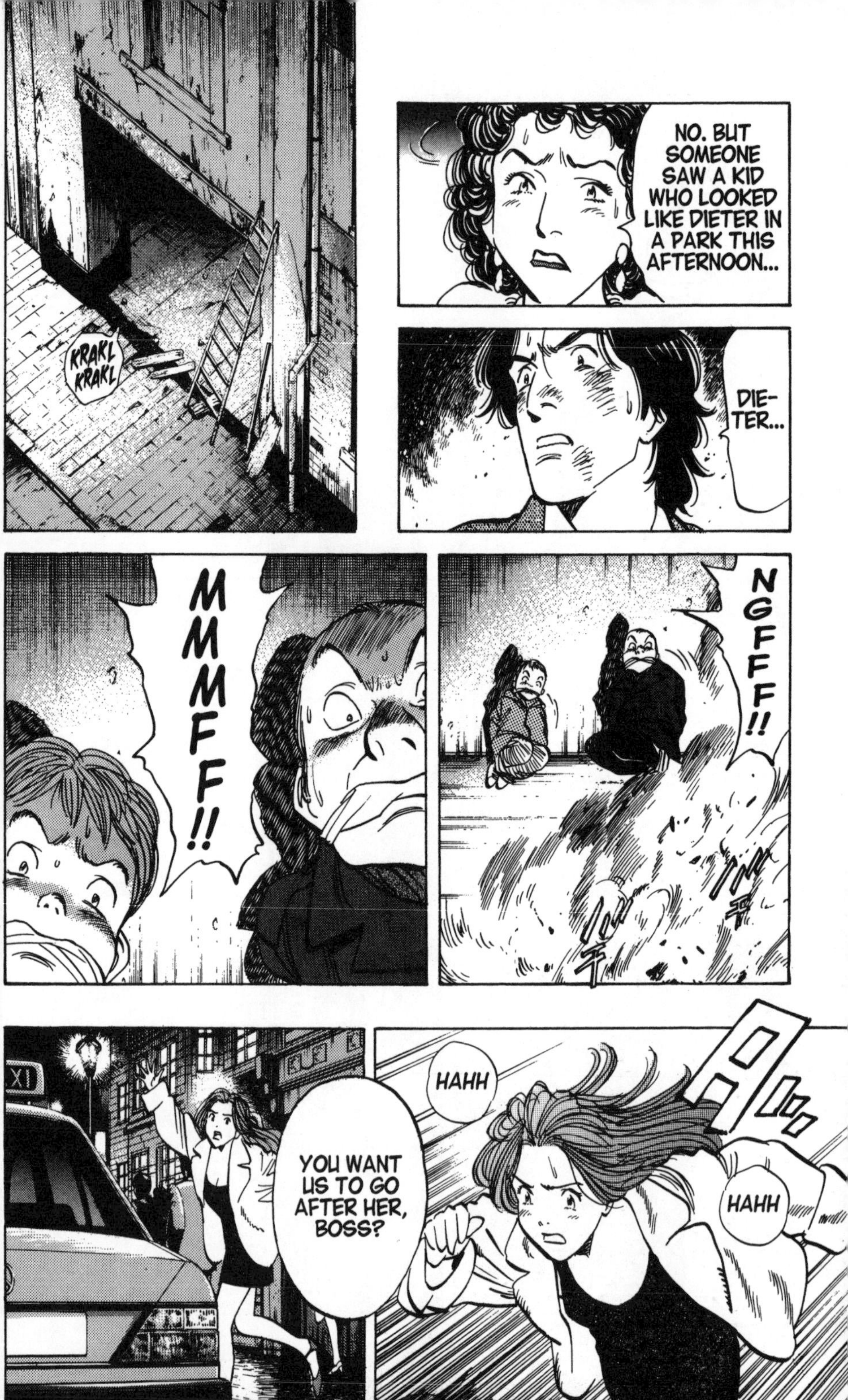
NO. BUT SOMEONE SAW A KID WHO LOOKED LIKE DIETER IN A PARK THIS AFTERNOON...
DIE-TER...
KRAKL KRAKL
NGFFFF!!
MMMFF!!
HAHH
HAHH
YOU WANT US TO GO AFTER HER, BOSS?

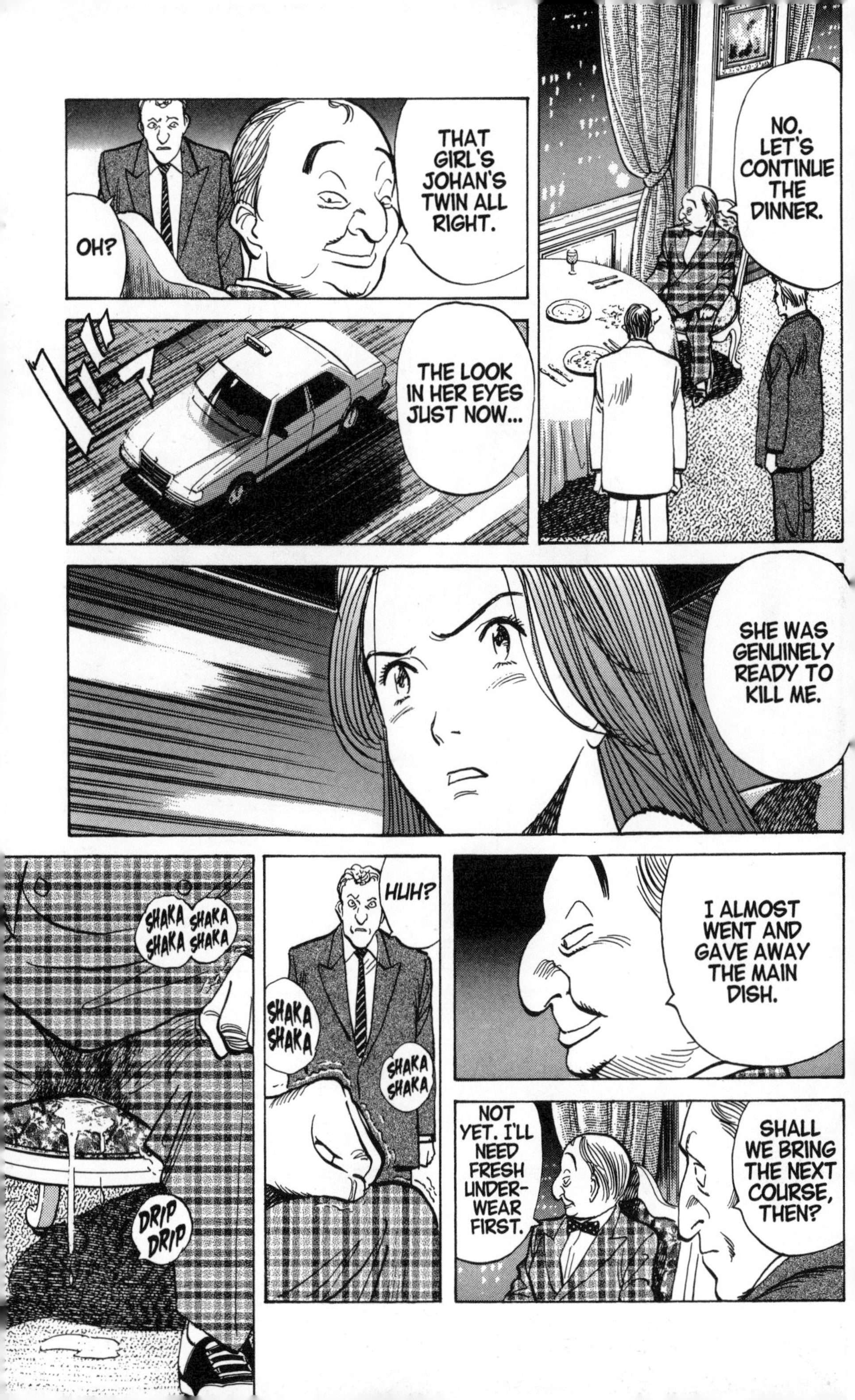
NO. LET'S CONTINUE THE DINNER.
THAT GIRL'S JOHAN'S TWIN ALL RIGHT.
OH?
THE LOOK IN HER EYES JUST NOW...
SHE WAS GENUINELY READY TO KILL ME.
I ALMOST WENT AND GAVE AWAY THE MAIN DISH.
SHALL WE BRING THE NEXT COURSE, THEN?
NOT YET. I'LL NEED FRESH UNDER-WEAR FIRST.
HUH?
SHAKA SHAKA
SHAKA SHAKA
SHAKA SHAKA
SHAKA SHAKA
DRIP DRIP

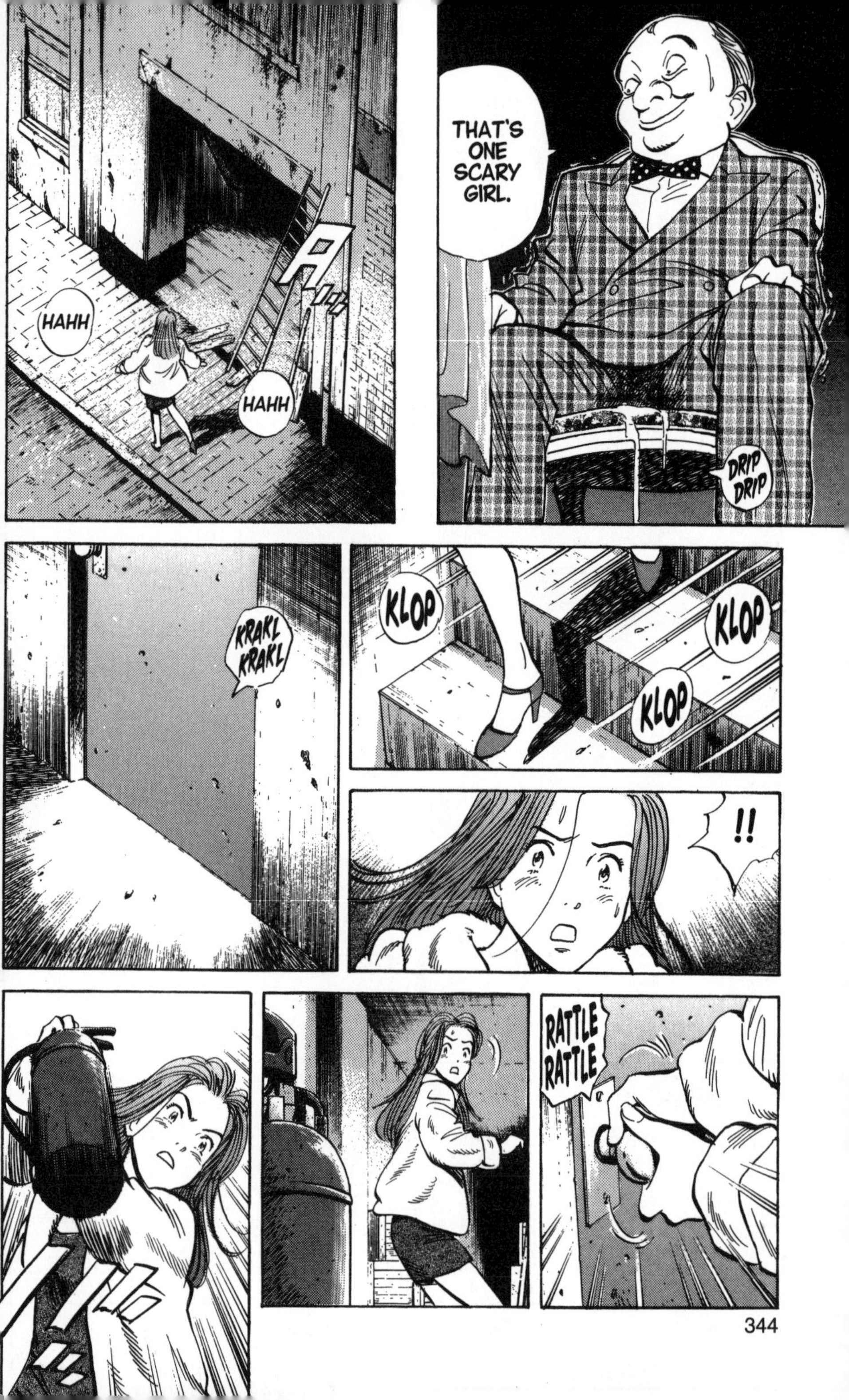
THAT'S ONE SCARY GIRL.
DRIP DRIP
HAHH
HAHH
KLOP
KLOP
KLOP
!!
KRAKL KRAKL
RATTLE RATTLE

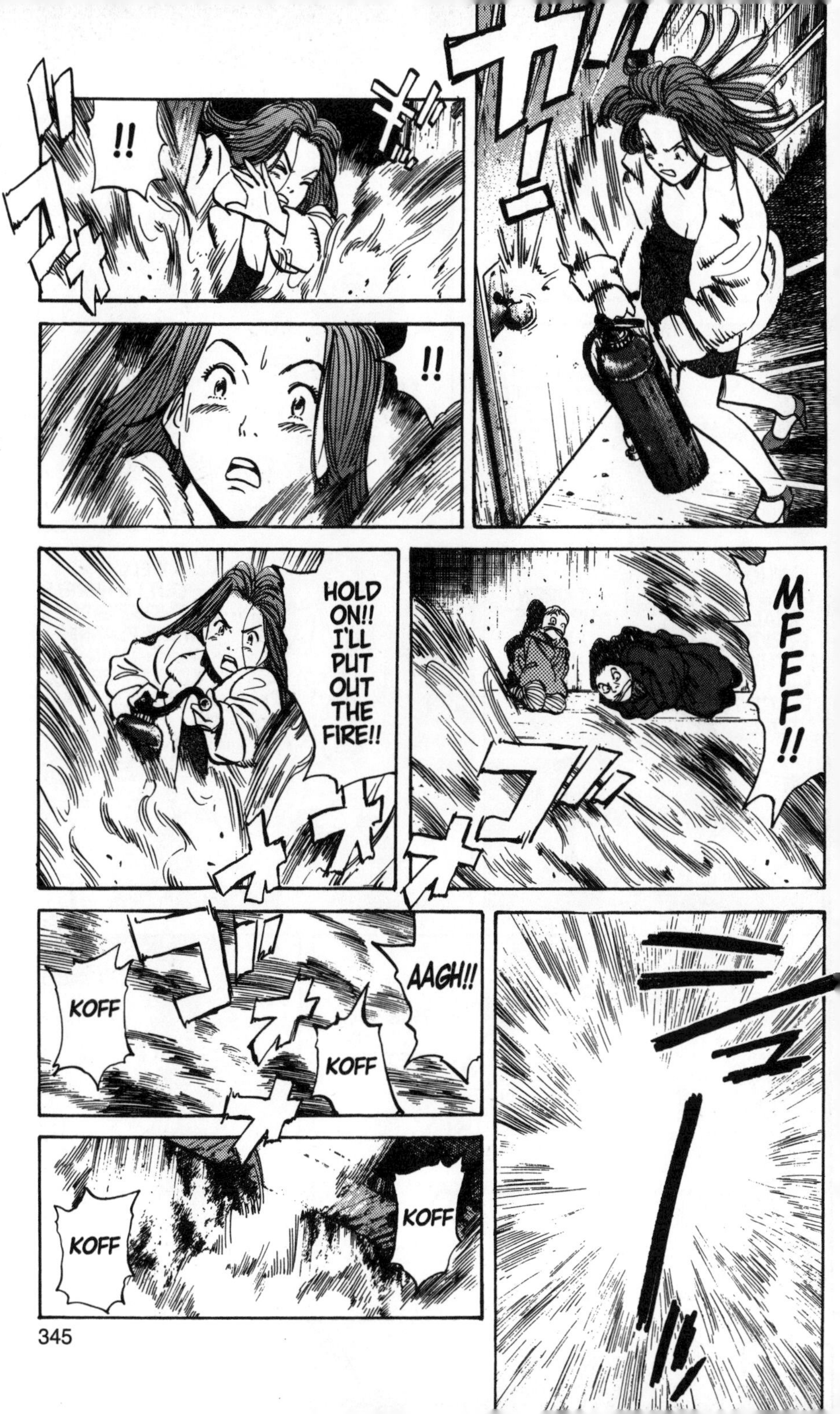
!!
!!
MFFFF!!
HOLD ON!! I'LL PUT OUT THE FIRE!!
AAGH!!
KOFF
KOFF
KOFF
KOFF

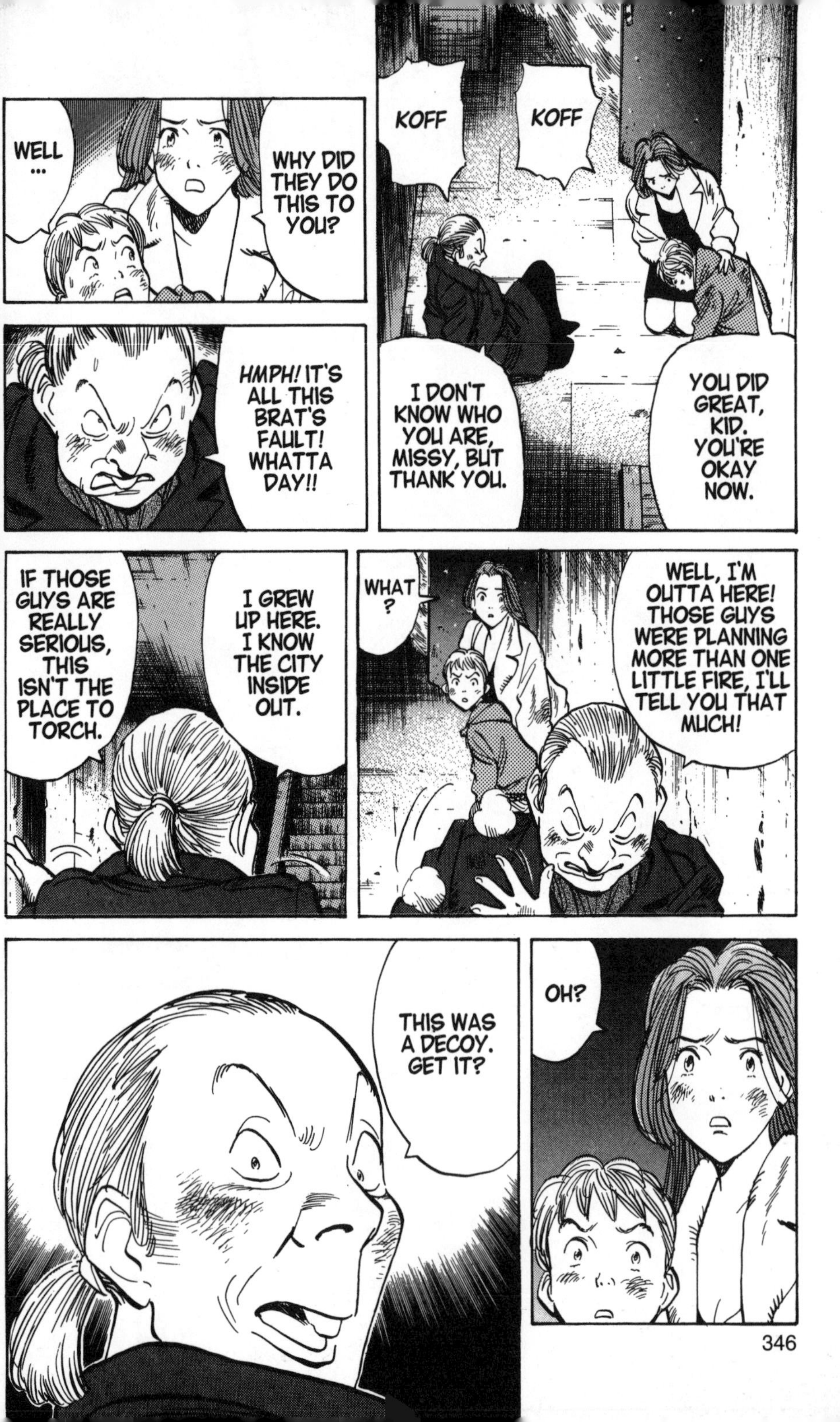
KOFF
KOFF
YOU DID GREAT, KID. YOU'RE OKAY NOW.
I DON'T KNOW WHO YOU ARE, MISSY, BUT THANK YOU.
WHY DID THEY DO THIS TO YOU?
WELL ...
HMPH! IT'S ALL THIS BRAT'S FAULT! WHATTA DAY!!
WELL, I'M OUTTA HERE! THOSE GUYS WERE PLANNING MORE THAN ONE LITTLE FIRE, I'LL TELL YOU THAT MUCH!
WHAT ?
I GREW UP HERE. I KNOW THE CITY INSIDE OUT.
IF THOSE GUYS ARE REALLY SERIOUS, THIS ISN'T THE PLACE TO TORCH.
OH?
THIS WAS A DECOY. GET IT?

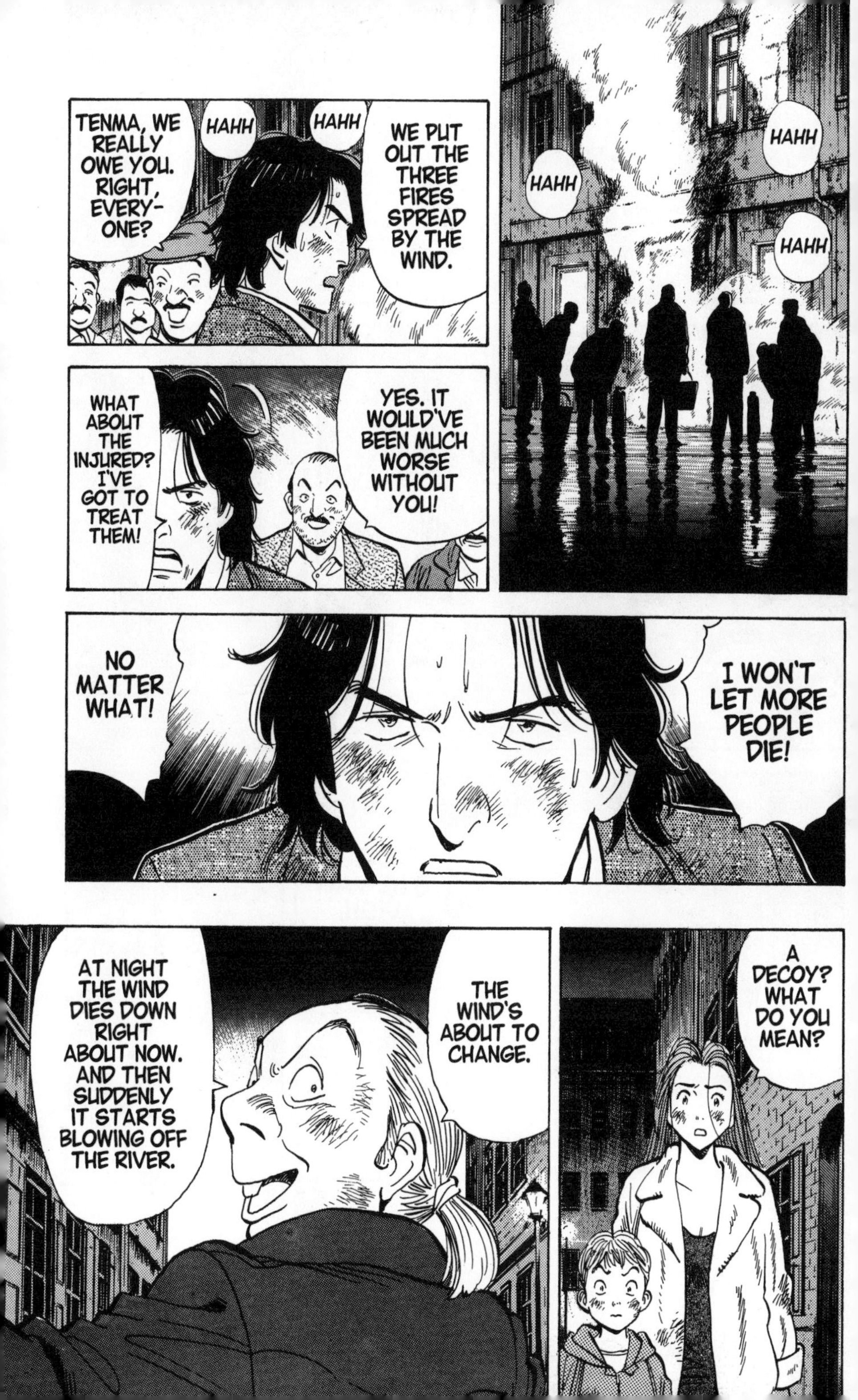
HAHH
HAHH
HAHH
HAHH
HAHH
WE PUT OUT THE THREE FIRES SPREAD BY THE WIND.
TENMA, WE REALLY OWE YOU. RIGHT, EVERY-ONE?
YES. IT WOULD'VE BEEN MUCH WORSE WITHOUT YOU!
WHAT ABOUT THE INJURED? I'VE GOT TO TREAT THEM!
I WON'T LET MORE PEOPLE DIE!
NO MATTER WHAT!
A DECOY? WHAT DO YOU MEAN?
THE WIND'S ABOUT TO CHANGE.
AT NIGHT THE WIND DIES DOWN RIGHT ABOUT NOW. AND THEN SUDDENLY IT STARTS BLOWING OFF THE RIVER.

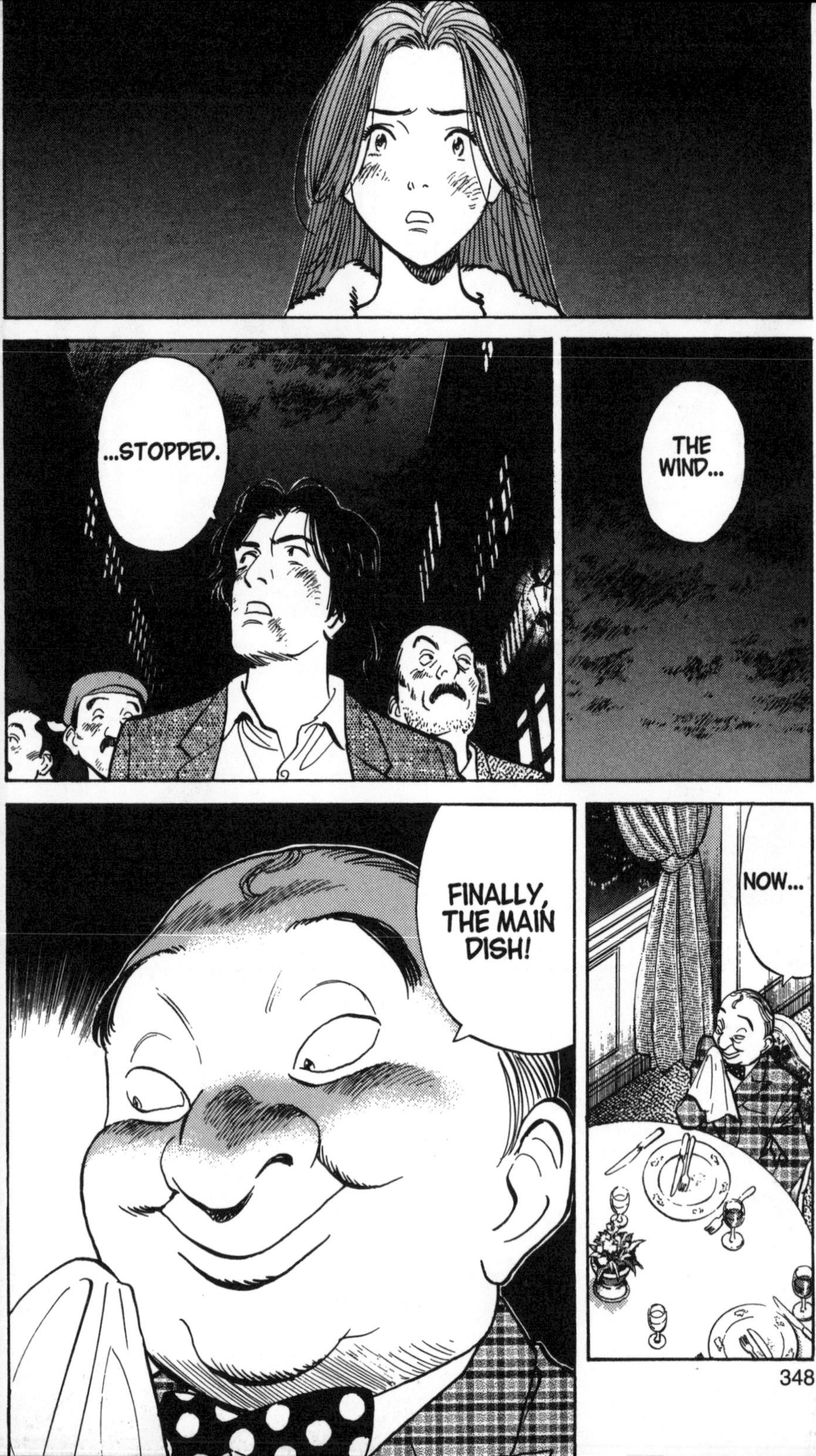
THE WIND...
...STOPPED.
NOW...
FINALLY, THE MAIN DISH!

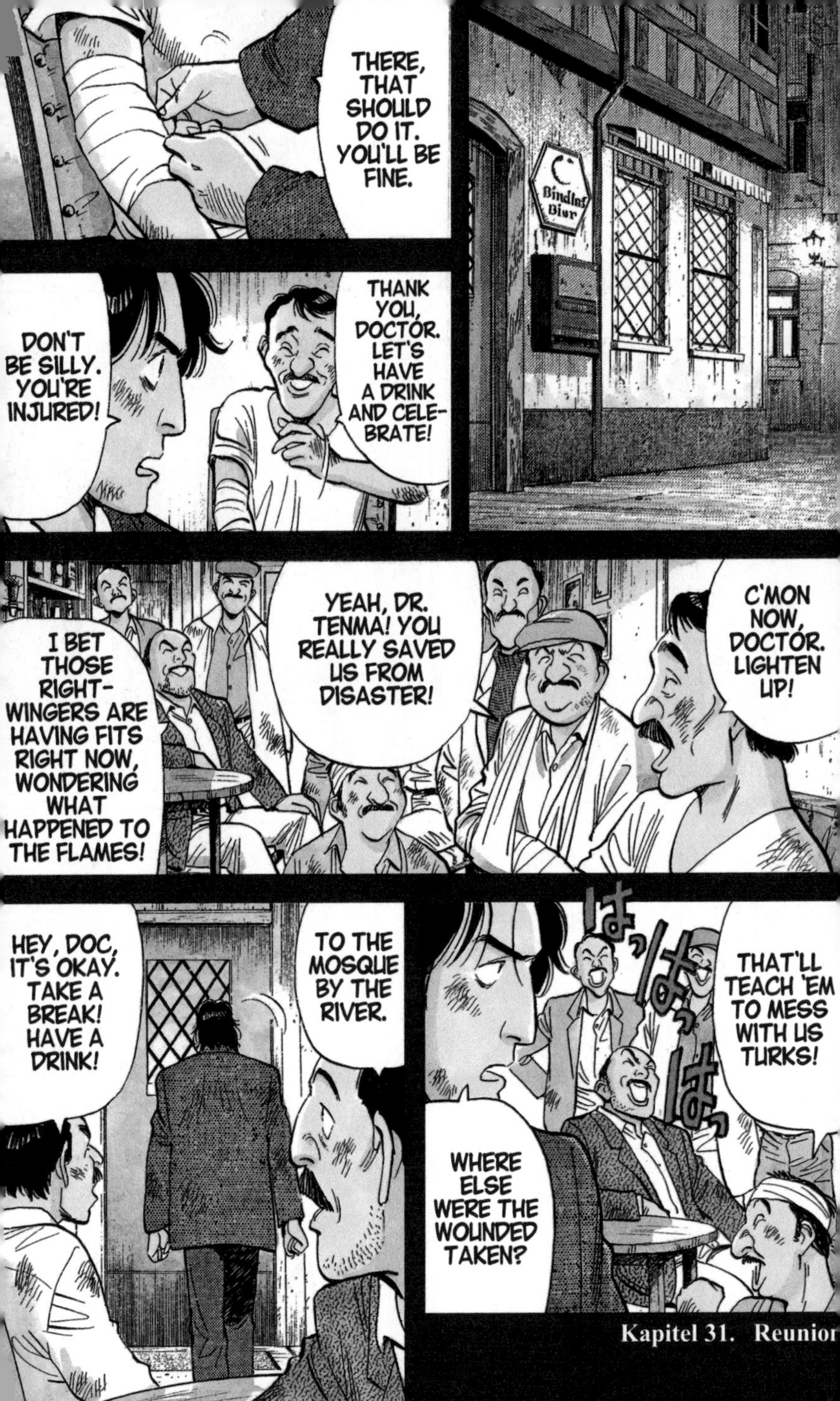
Binding Bier
THERE, THAT SHOULD DO IT. YOU'LL BE FINE.
THANK YOU, DOCTOR. LET'S HAVE A DRINK AND CELEBRATE!
DON'T BE SILLY. YOU'RE INJURED!
C'MON NOW, DOCTOR. LIGHTEN UP!
YEAH, DR. TENMA! YOU REALLY SAVED US FROM DISASTER!
I BET THOSE RIGHT-WINGERS ARE HAVING FITS RIGHT NOW, WONDERING WHAT HAPPENED TO THE FLAMES!
はっはっはっ
THAT'LL TEACH 'EM TO MESS WITH US TURKS!
WHERE ELSE WERE THE WOUNDED TAKEN?
TO THE MOSQUE BY THE RIVER.
HEY, DOC, IT'S OKAY. TAKE A BREAK! HAVE A DRINK!

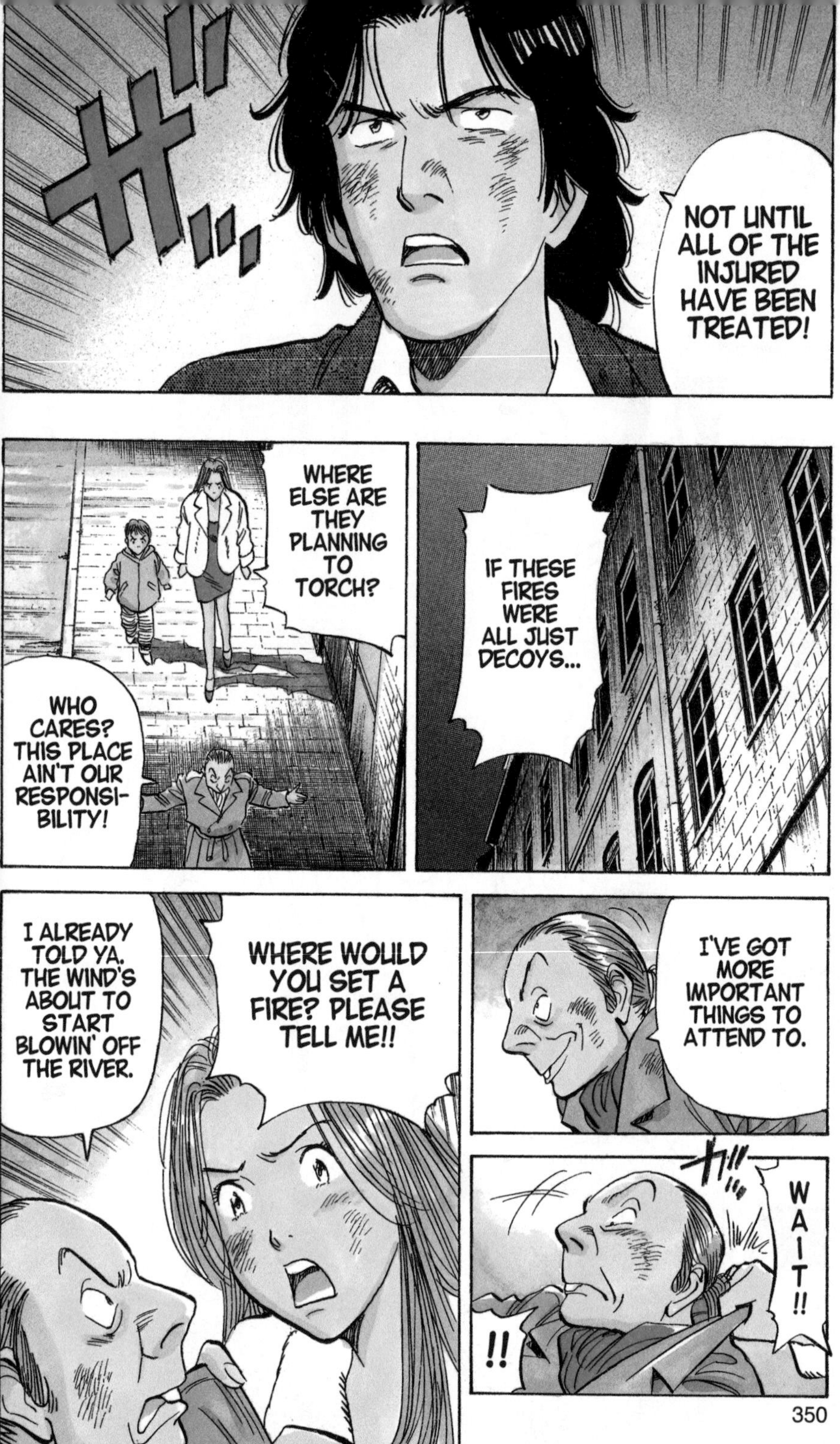
ザッ
NOT UNTIL ALL OF THE INJURED HAVE BEEN TREATED!
IF THESE FIRES WERE ALL JUST DECOYS...
WHERE ELSE ARE THEY PLANNING TO TORCH?
WHO CARES? THIS PLACE AIN'T OUR RESPONSIBILITY!
I'VE GOT MORE IMPORTANT THINGS TO ATTEND TO.
ガッ
WAIT!!
!!
WHERE WOULD YOU SET A FIRE? PLEASE TELL ME!!
I ALREADY TOLD YA. THE WIND'S ABOUT TO START BLOWIN' OFF THE RIVER.

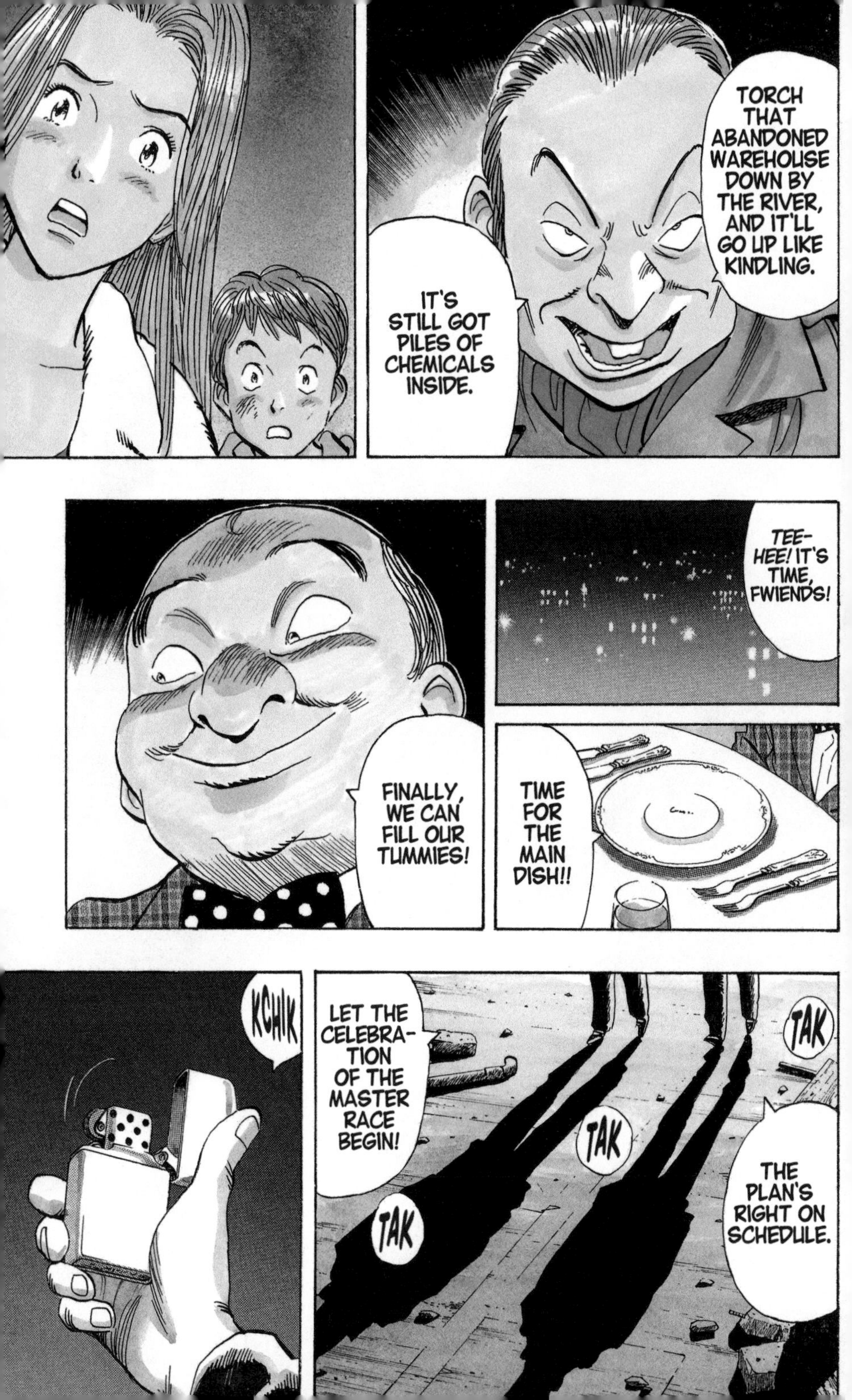
TORCH THAT ABANDONED WAREHOUSE DOWN BY THE RIVER, AND IT'LL GO UP LIKE KINDLING.
IT'S STILL GOT PILES OF CHEMICALS INSIDE.
TEE-HEE! IT'S TIME, FWIENDS!
TIME FOR THE MAIN DISH!!
FINALLY, WE CAN FILL OUR TUMMIES!
TAK
LET THE CELEBRATION OF THE MASTER RACE BEGIN!
THE PLAN'S RIGHT ON SCHEDULE.
TAK
TAK
KCHIK

Kapitel 31.
Reunion

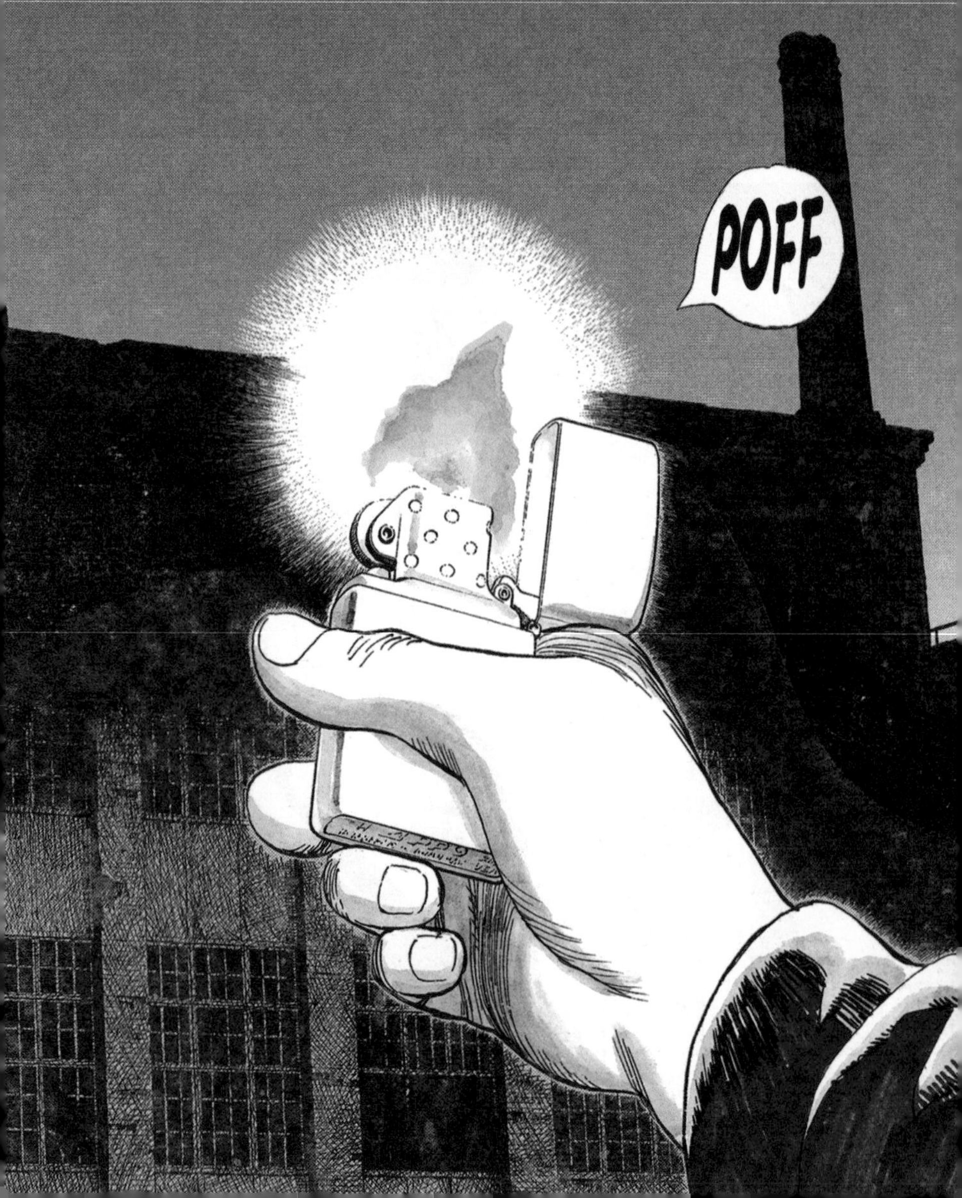
POFF

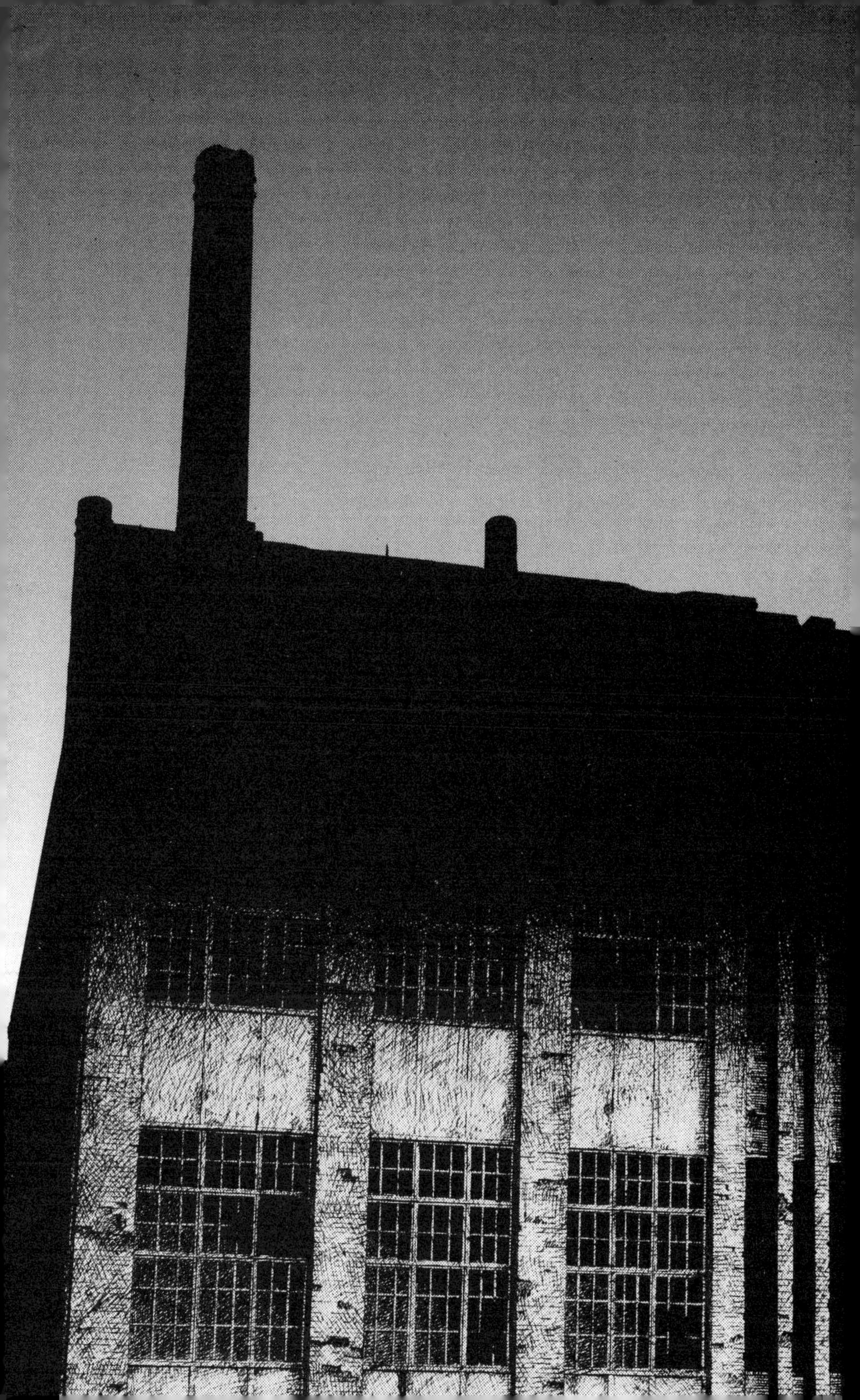

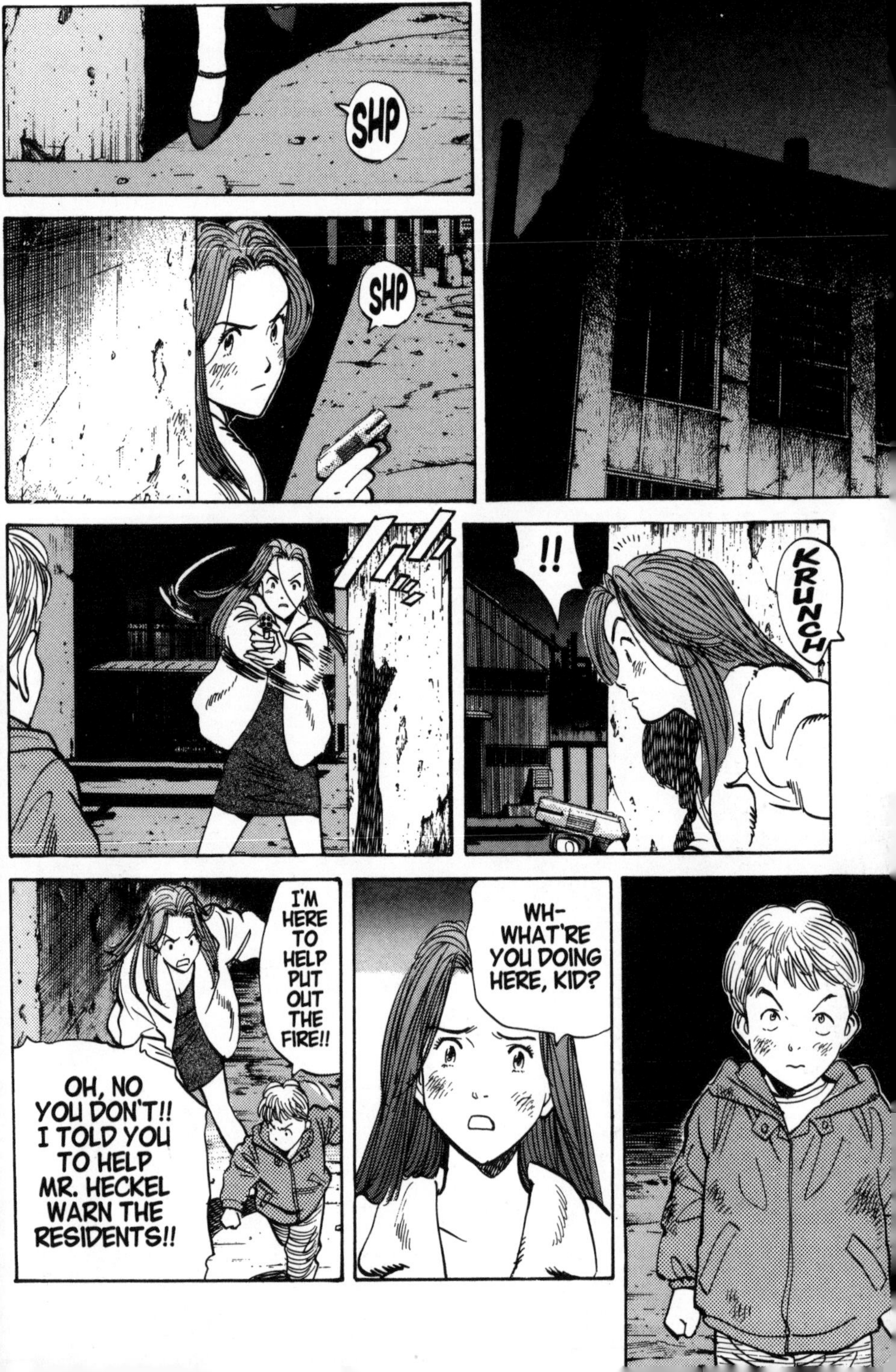
SHP
SHP
!!
KRUNCH
WH-WHAT'RE YOU DOING HERE, KID?
I'M HERE TO HELP PUT OUT THE FIRE!!
OH, NO YOU DON'T!! I TOLD YOU TO HELP MR. HECKEL WARN THE RESIDENTS!!

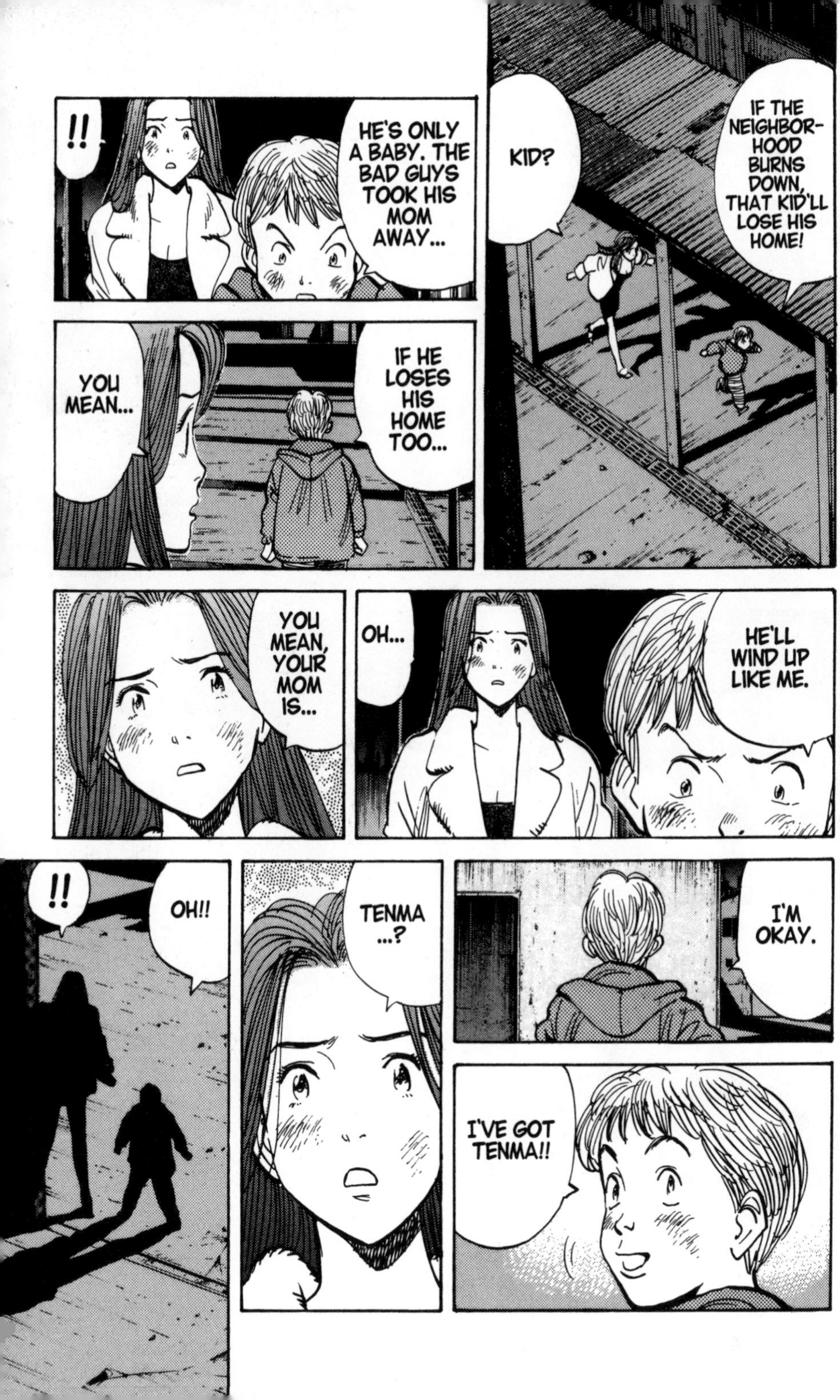
IF THE NEIGHBOR-HOOD BURNS DOWN, THAT KID'LL LOSE HIS HOME!
KID?
HE'S ONLY A BABY. THE BAD GUYS TOOK HIS MOM AWAY...
!!
IF HE LOSES HIS HOME TOO...
YOU MEAN...
HE'LL WIND UP LIKE ME.
OH...
YOU MEAN, YOUR MOM IS...
I'M OKAY.
I'VE GOT TENMA!!
TENMA ...?
OH!!
!!

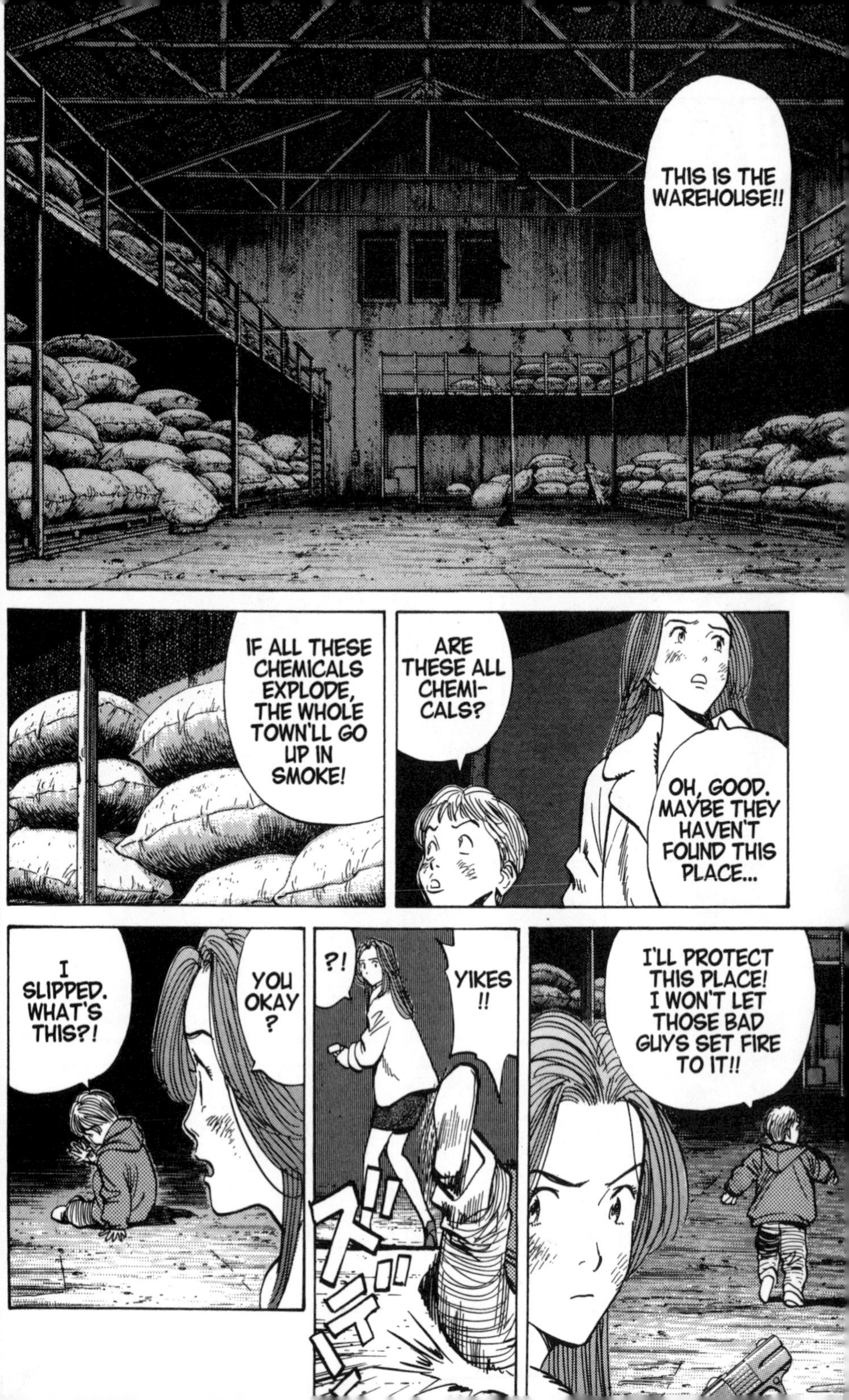
THIS IS THE WAREHOUSE!!
ARE THESE ALL CHEMI-CALS?
OH, GOOD. MAYBE THEY HAVEN'T FOUND THIS PLACE...
IF ALL THESE CHEMICALS EXPLODE, THE WHOLE TOWN'LL GO UP IN SMOKE!
I'LL PROTECT THIS PLACE! I WON'T LET THOSE BAD GUYS SET FIRE TO IT!!
YIKES !!
?!
YOU OKAY ?
I SLIPPED. WHAT'S THIS?!

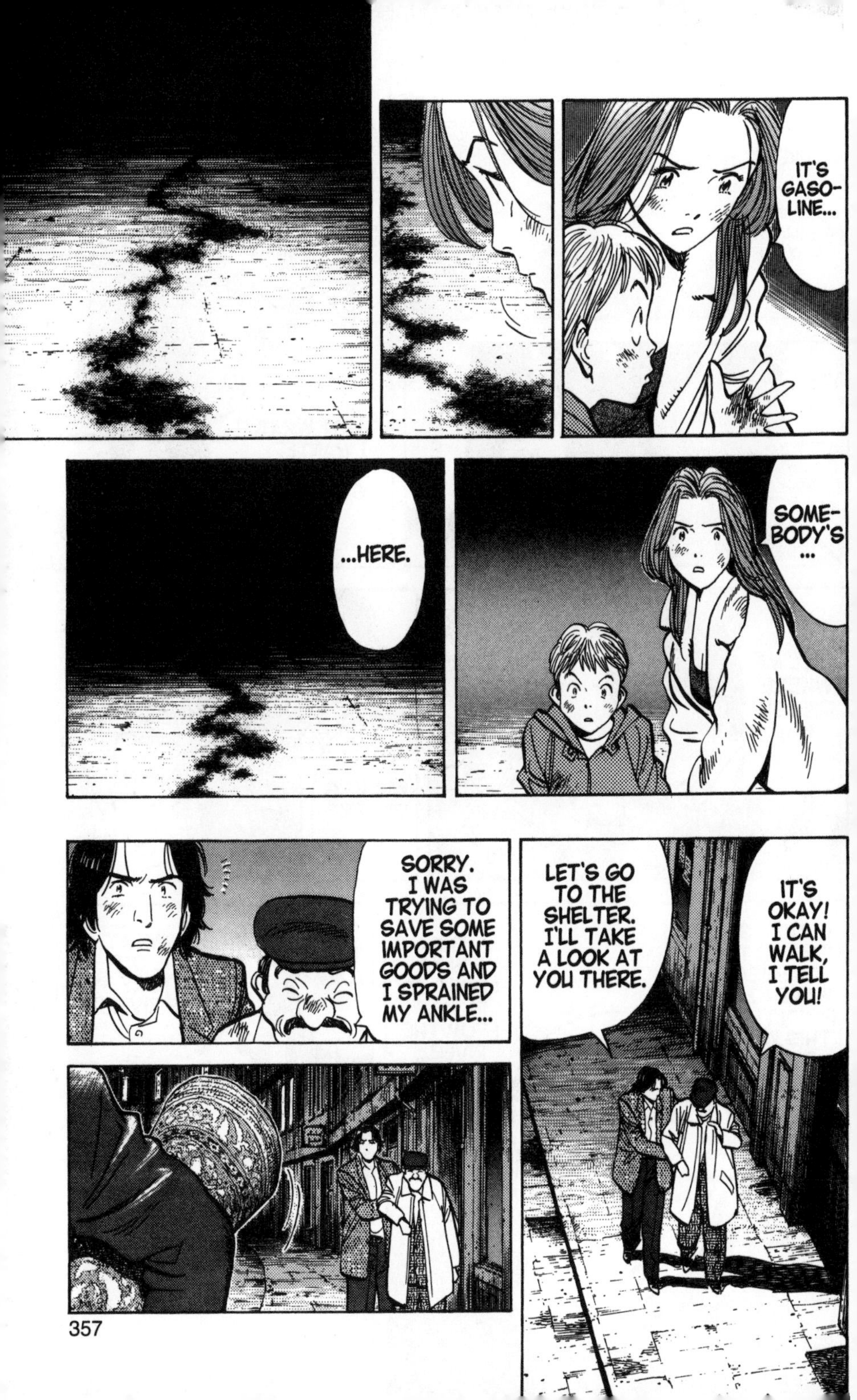
IT'S GASO-LINE...
SOME-BODY'S ...
...HERE.
IT'S OKAY! I CAN WALK, I TELL YOU!
LET'S GO TO THE SHELTER. I'LL TAKE A LOOK AT YOU THERE.
SORRY. I WAS TRYING TO SAVE SOME IMPORTANT GOODS AND I SPRAINED MY ANKLE...

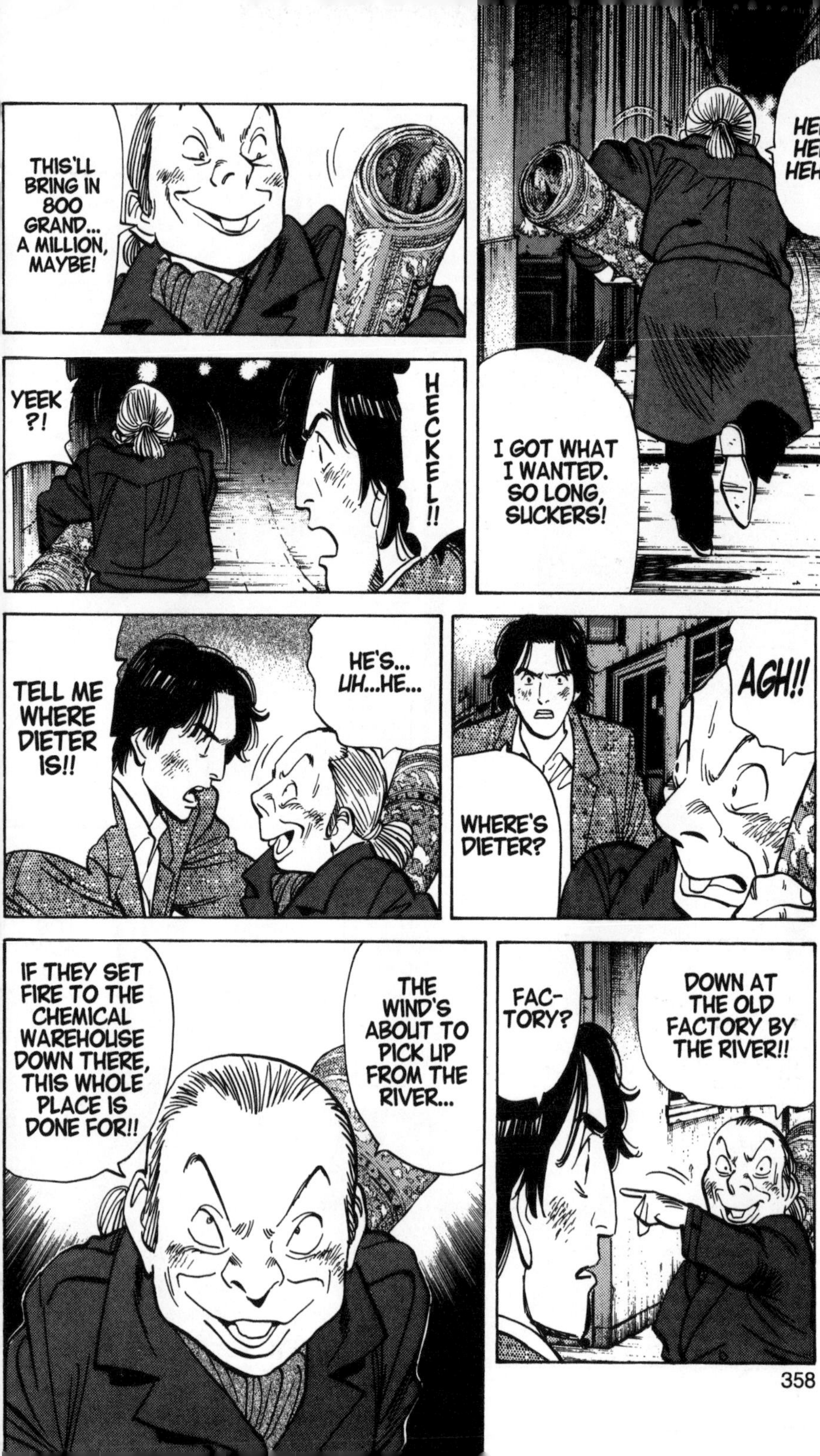
HEH HEH HEH...
I GOT WHAT I WANTED. SO LONG, SUCKERS!
THIS'LL BRING IN 800 GRAND... A MILLION, MAYBE!
HECKEL!!
YEEK ?!
AGH!!
WHERE'S DIETER?
HE'S... UH...HE...
TELL ME WHERE DIETER IS!!
DOWN AT THE OLD FACTORY BY THE RIVER!!
FAC-TORY?
THE WIND'S ABOUT TO PICK UP FROM THE RIVER...
IF THEY SET FIRE TO THE CHEMICAL WAREHOUSE DOWN THERE, THIS WHOLE PLACE IS DONE FOR!!

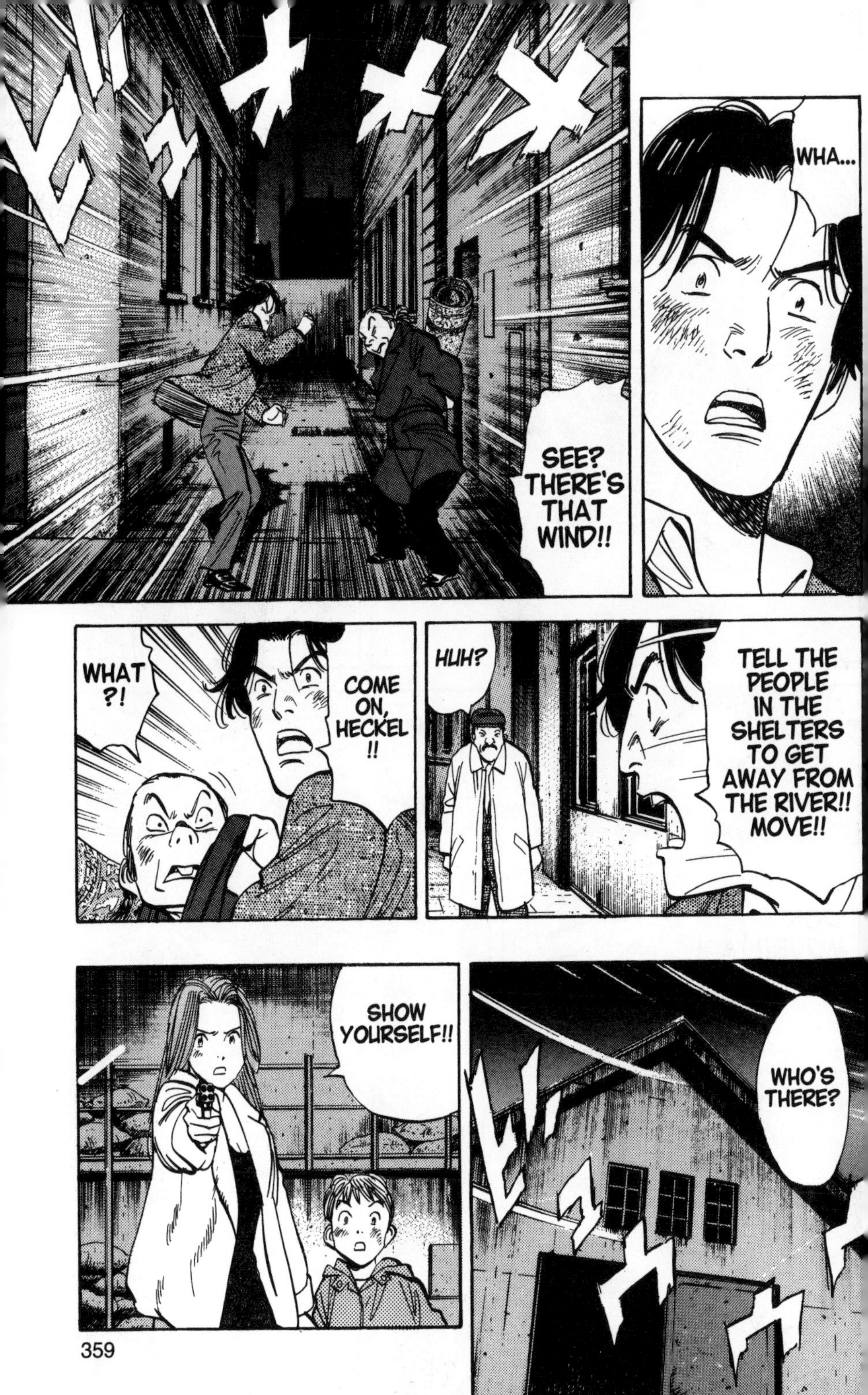
WHA...
SEE? THERE'S THAT WIND!!
TELL THE PEOPLE IN THE SHELTERS TO GET AWAY FROM THE RIVER!! MOVE!!
HUH?
COME ON, HECKEL!!
WHAT?!
WHO'S THERE?
SHOW YOURSELF!!

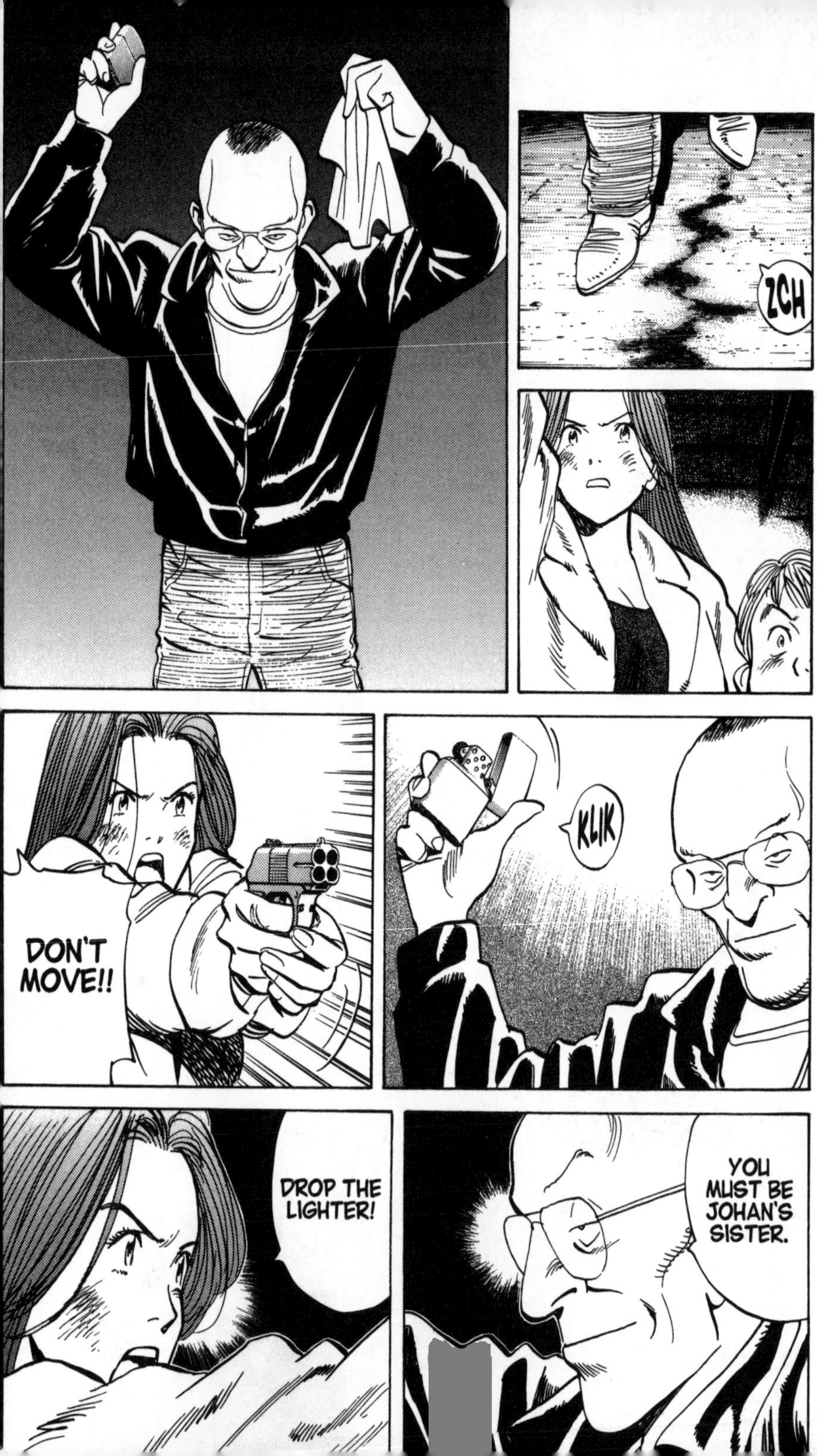
ZCH
KLIK
DON'T MOVE!!
YOU MUST BE JOHAN'S SISTER.
DROP THE LIGHTER!

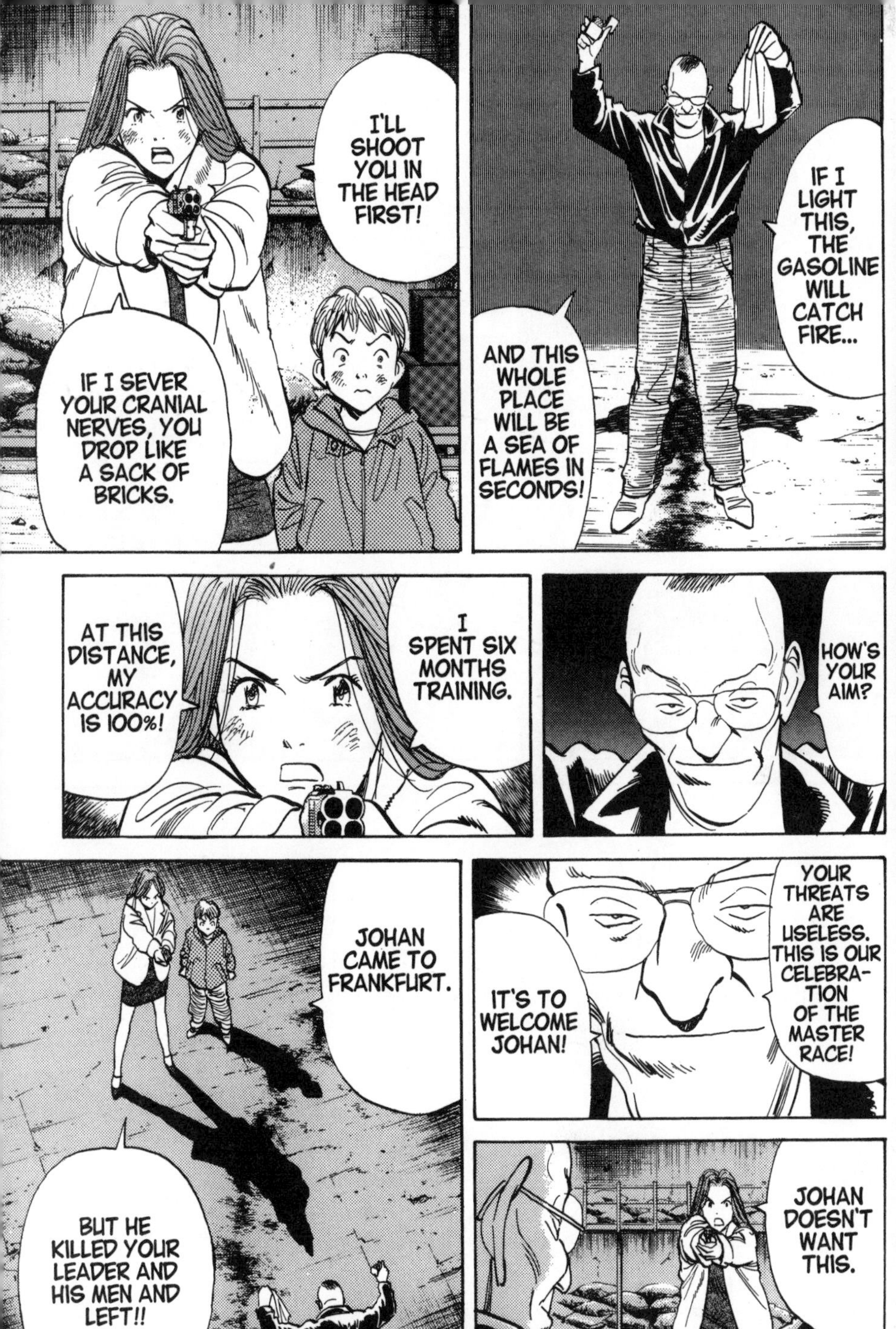
IF I LIGHT THIS, THE GASOLINE WILL CATCH FIRE...
AND THIS WHOLE PLACE WILL BE A SEA OF FLAMES IN SECONDS!
I'LL SHOOT YOU IN THE HEAD FIRST!
IF I SEVER YOUR CRANIAL NERVES, YOU DROP LIKE A SACK OF BRICKS.
HOW'S YOUR AIM?
I SPENT SIX MONTHS TRAINING.
AT THIS DISTANCE, MY ACCURACY IS 100%!
YOUR THREATS ARE USELESS. THIS IS OUR CELEBRATION OF THE MASTER RACE!
IT'S TO WELCOME JOHAN!
JOHAN DOESN'T WANT THIS.
JOHAN CAME TO FRANKFURT.
BUT HE KILLED YOUR LEADER AND HIS MEN AND LEFT!!

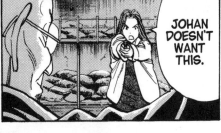

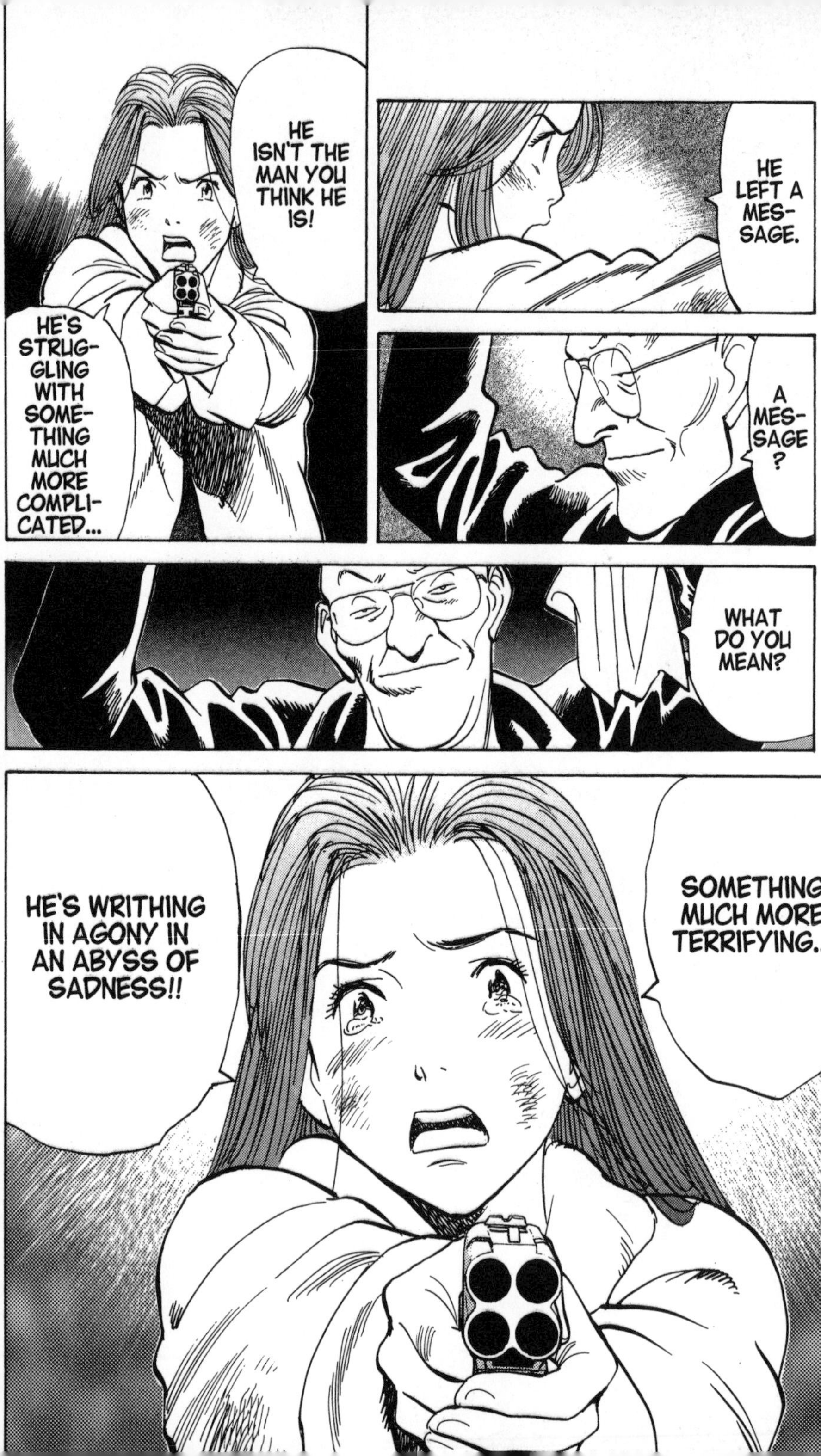
HE LEFT A MES- SAGE.
A MES- SAGE?
HE ISN'T THE MAN YOU THINK HE IS!
HE'S STRUG- GLING WITH SOME- THING MUCH MORE COMPLI- CATED...
WHAT DO YOU MEAN?
SOMETHING MUCH MORE TERRIFYING...
HE'S WRITHING IN AGONY IN AN ABYSS OF SADNESS!!

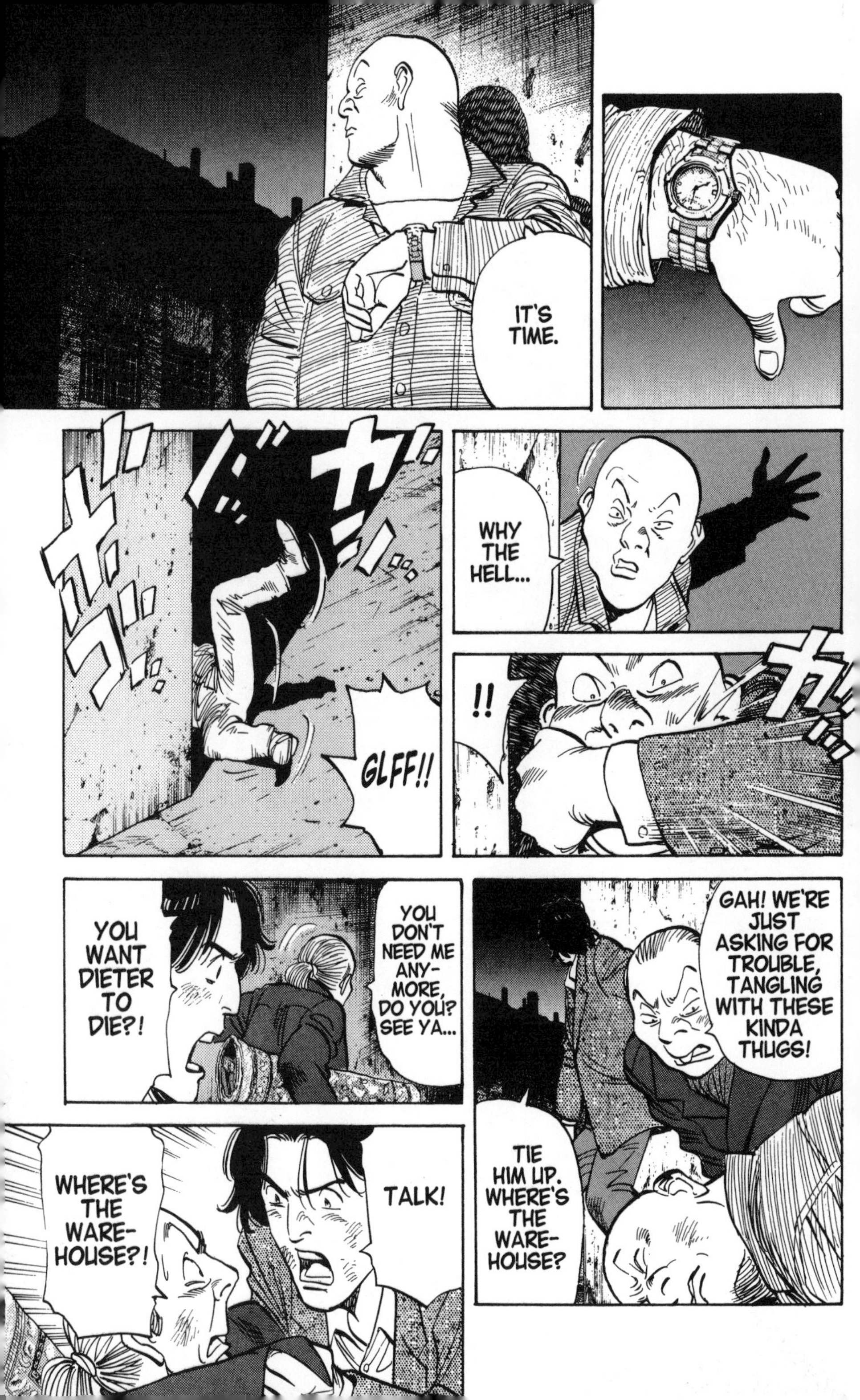
IT'S TIME.
WHY THE HELL...
!!
GLFF!!
GAH! WE'RE JUST ASKING FOR TROUBLE, TANGLING WITH THESE KINDA THUGS!
TIE HIM UP. WHERE'S THE WARE-HOUSE?
YOU DON'T NEED ME ANY-MORE, DO YOU? SEE YA...
YOU WANT DIETER TO DIE?!
TALK!
WHERE'S THE WARE-HOUSE?!

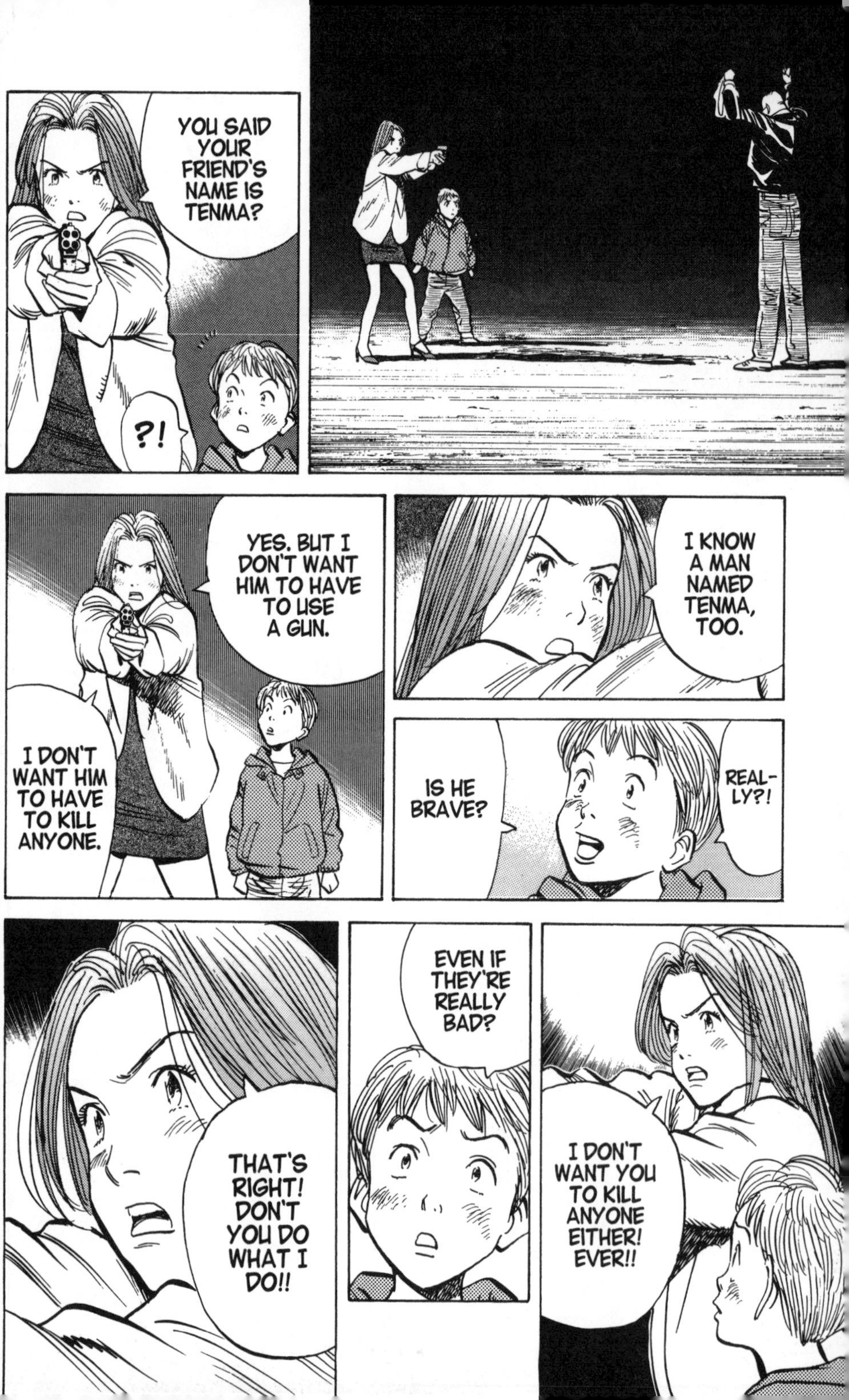
YOU SAID YOUR FRIEND'S NAME IS TENMA?
?!
I KNOW A MAN NAMED TENMA, TOO.
REAL-LY?!
IS HE BRAVE?
YES. BUT I DON'T WANT HIM TO HAVE TO USE A GUN.
I DON'T WANT HIM TO HAVE TO KILL ANYONE.
I DON'T WANT YOU TO KILL ANYONE EITHER! EVER!!
EVEN IF THEY'RE REALLY BAD?
THAT'S RIGHT! DON'T YOU DO WHAT I DO!!

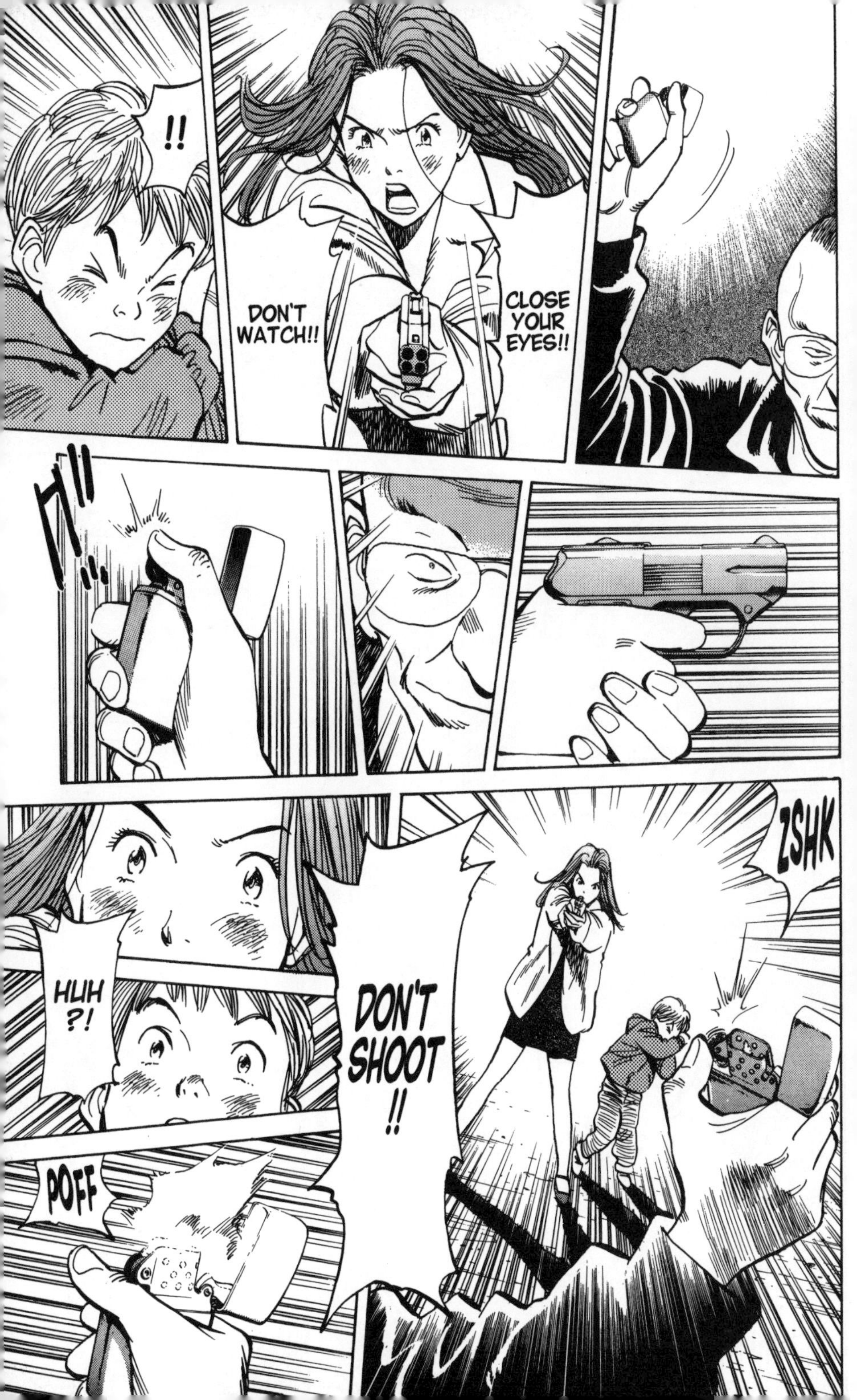
CLOSE YOUR EYES!!
DON'T WATCH!!
!!
ZSHK
DON'T SHOOT !!
HUH ?!
POFF

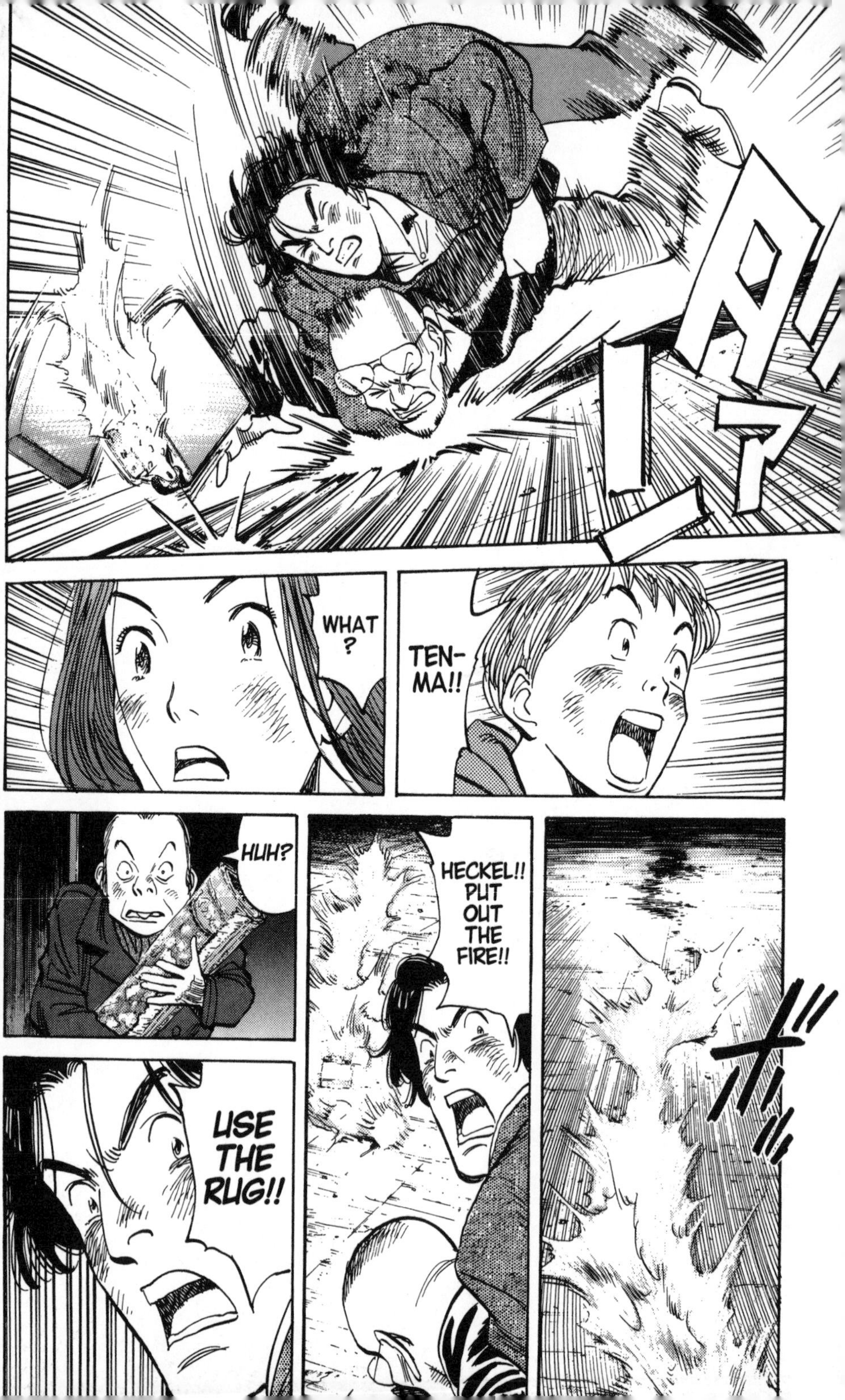
TEN-MA!!
WHAT ?
HECKEL!! PUT OUT THE FIRE!!
HUH?
USE THE RUG!!

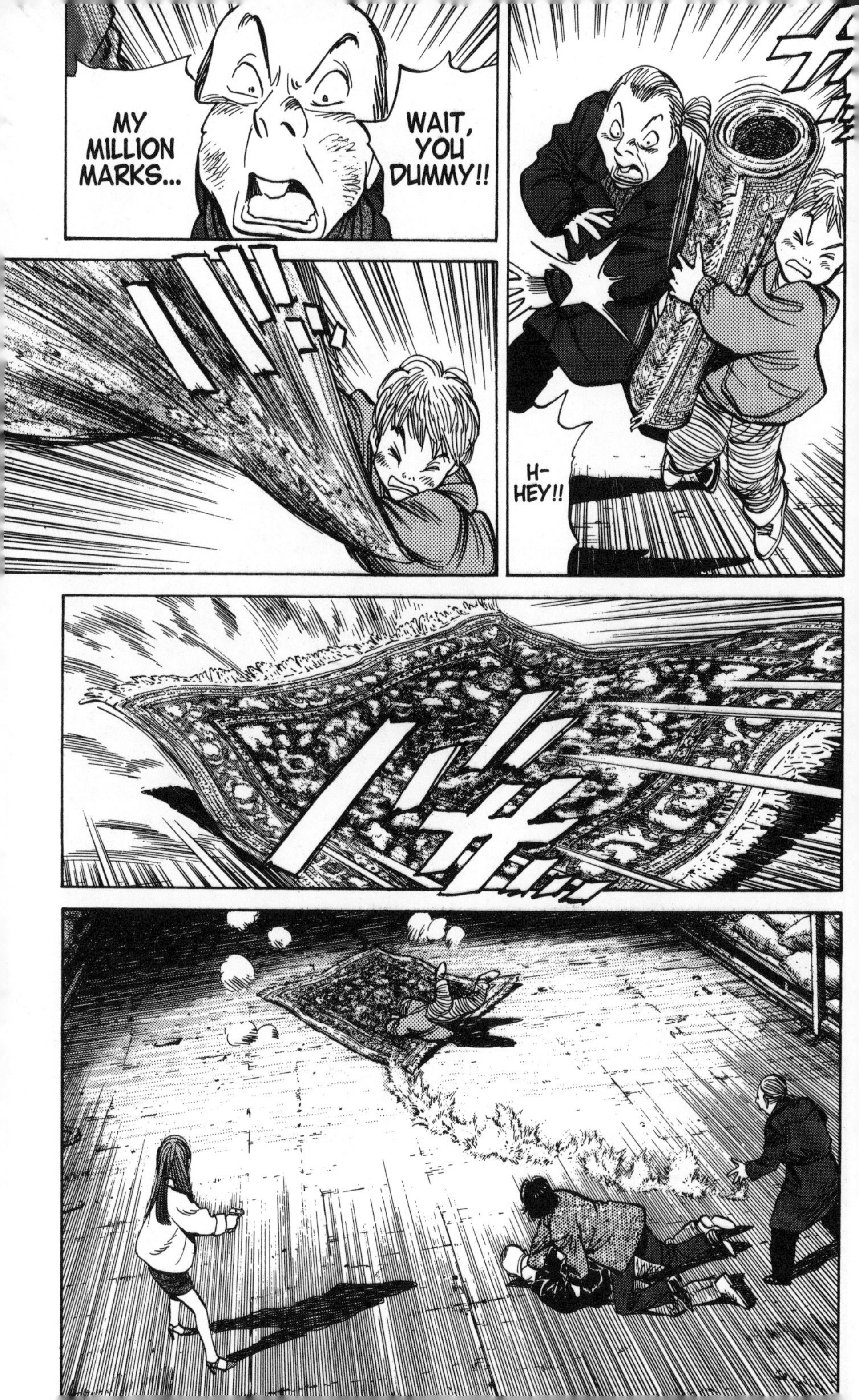
WAIT, YOU DUMMY!!
MY MILLION MARKS...
H-HEY!!

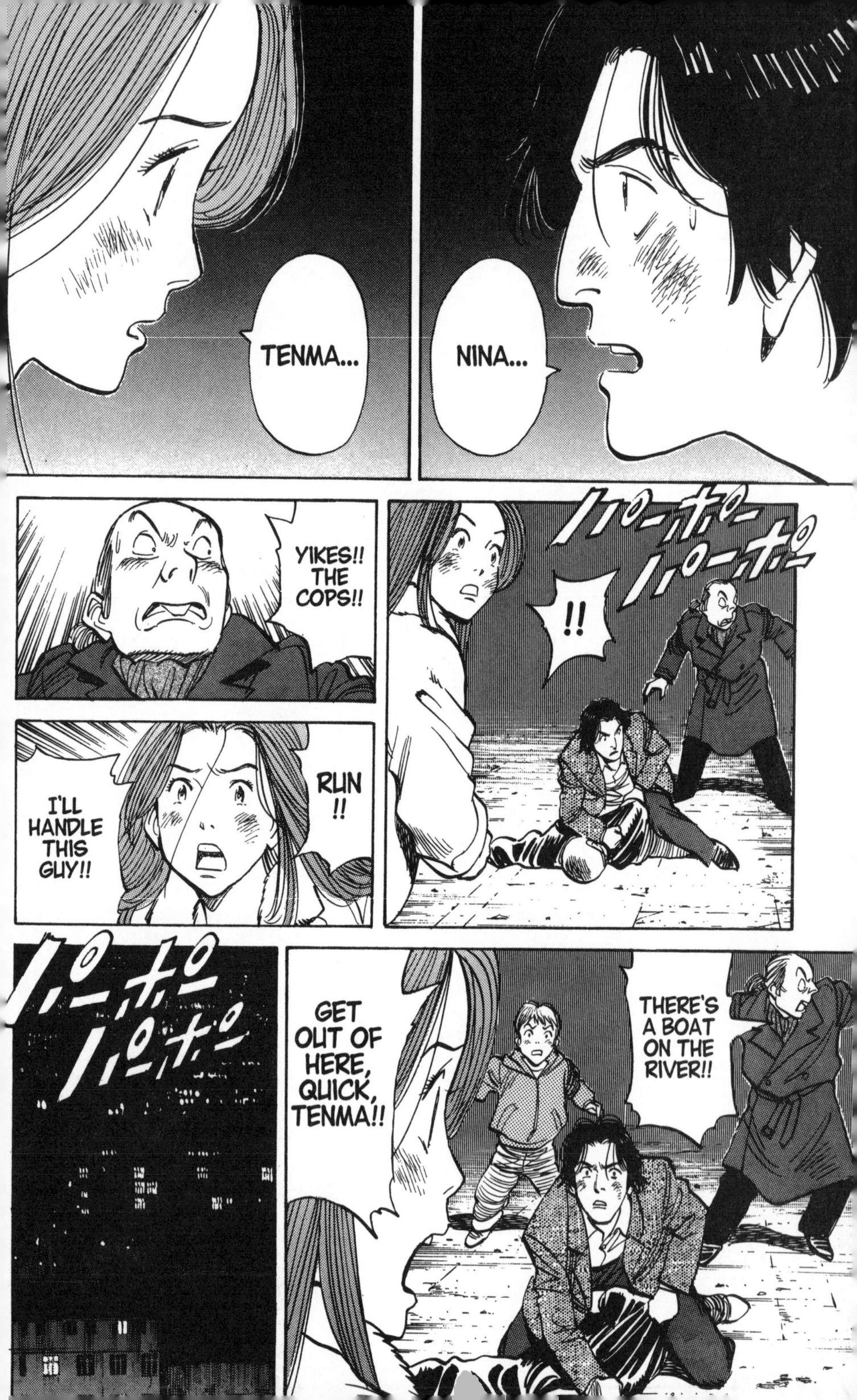
NINA...
TENMA...
パーポーパーポー
!!
YIKES!! THE COPS!!
RUN!!
I'LL HANDLE THIS GUY!!
THERE'S A BOAT ON THE RIVER!!
GET OUT OF HERE, QUICK, TENMA!!
パーポーパーポー

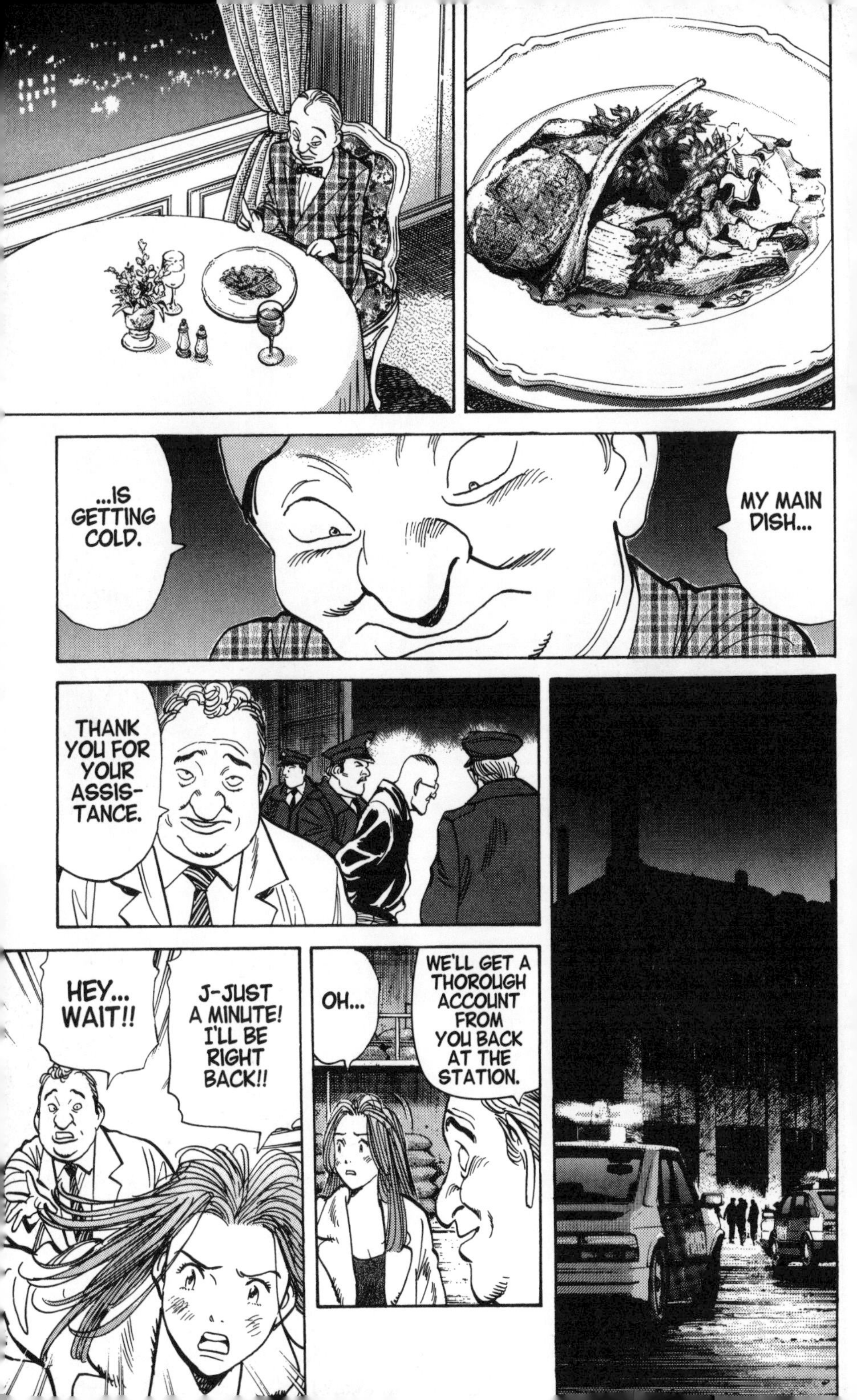
MY MAIN DISH...
...IS GETTING COLD.
THANK YOU FOR YOUR ASSIS- TANCE.
WE'LL GET A THOROUGH ACCOUNT FROM YOU BACK AT THE STATION.
OH...
J-JUST A MINUTE! I'LL BE RIGHT BACK!!
HEY... WAIT!!

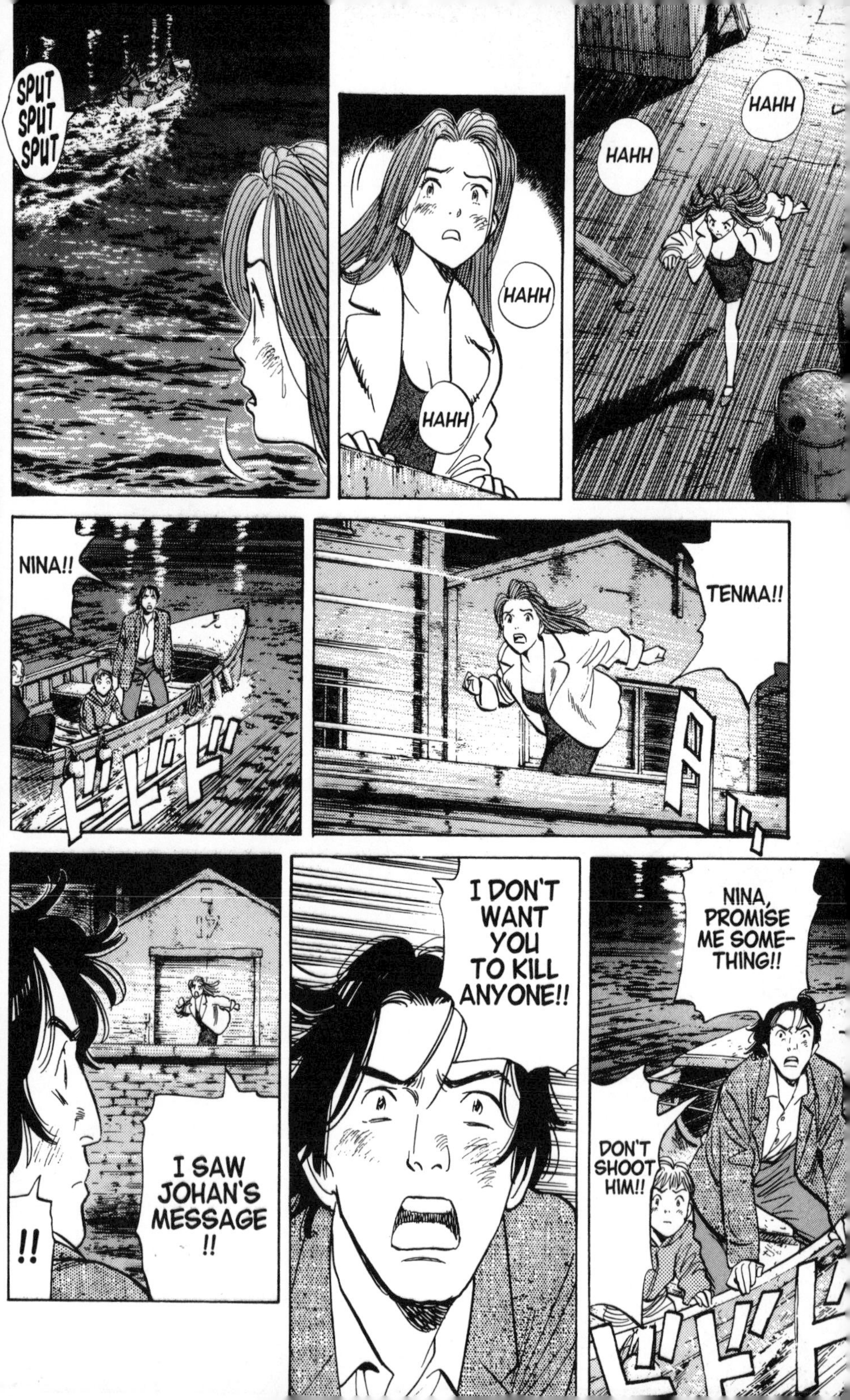
HAHH
HAHH
HAHH
HAHH
SPUT SPUT SPUT
TENMA!!
NINA!!
NINA, PROMISE ME SOMETHING!!
DON'T SHOOT HIM!!
I DON'T WANT YOU TO KILL ANYONE!!
I SAW JOHAN'S MESSAGE!!
!!

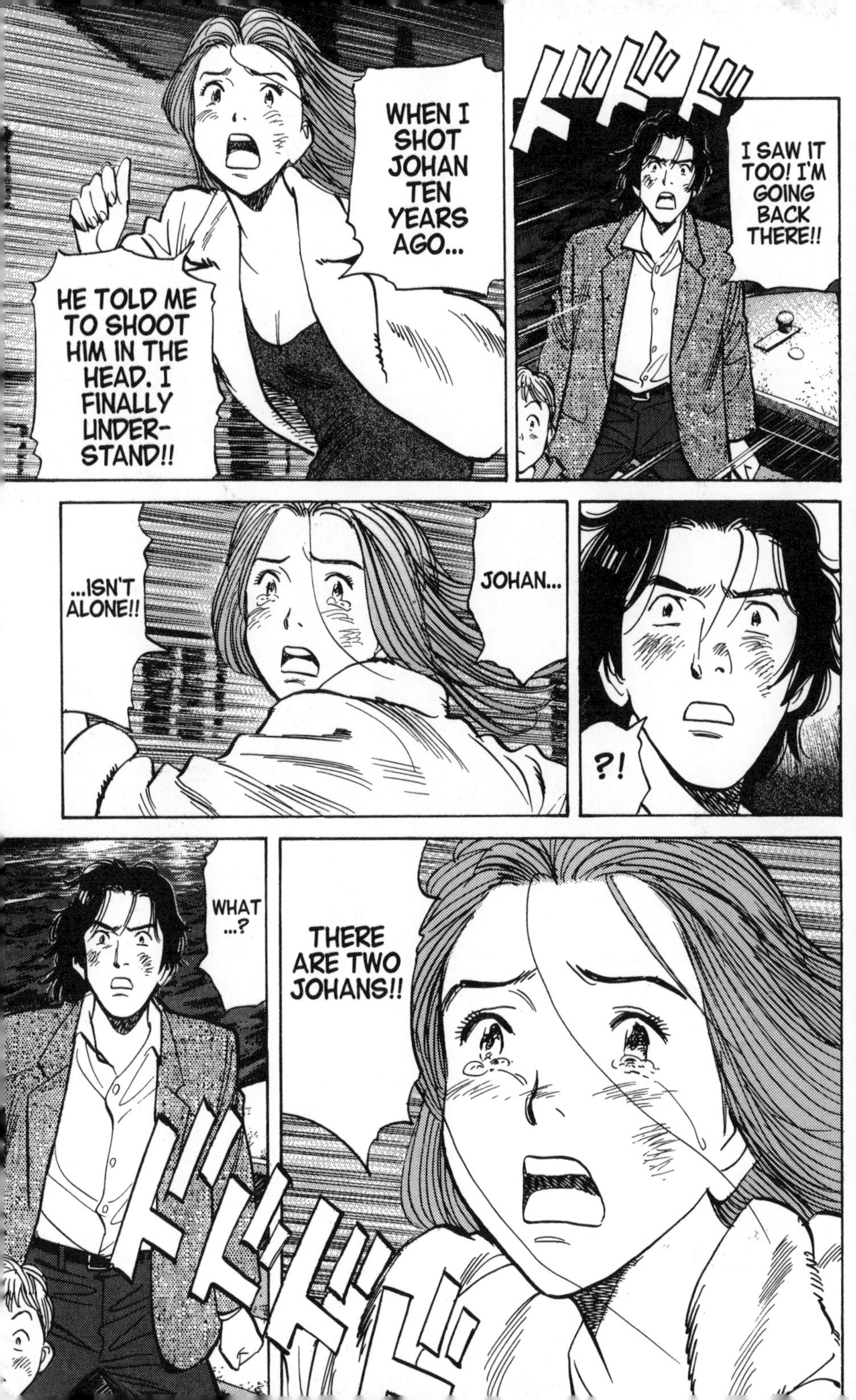
I SAW IT TOO! I'M GOING BACK THERE!!
WHEN I SHOT JOHAN TEN YEARS AGO...
HE TOLD ME TO SHOOT HIM IN THE HEAD. I FINALLY UNDER-STAND!!
?!
JOHAN...
...ISN'T ALONE!!
THERE ARE TWO JOHANS!!
WHAT ...?

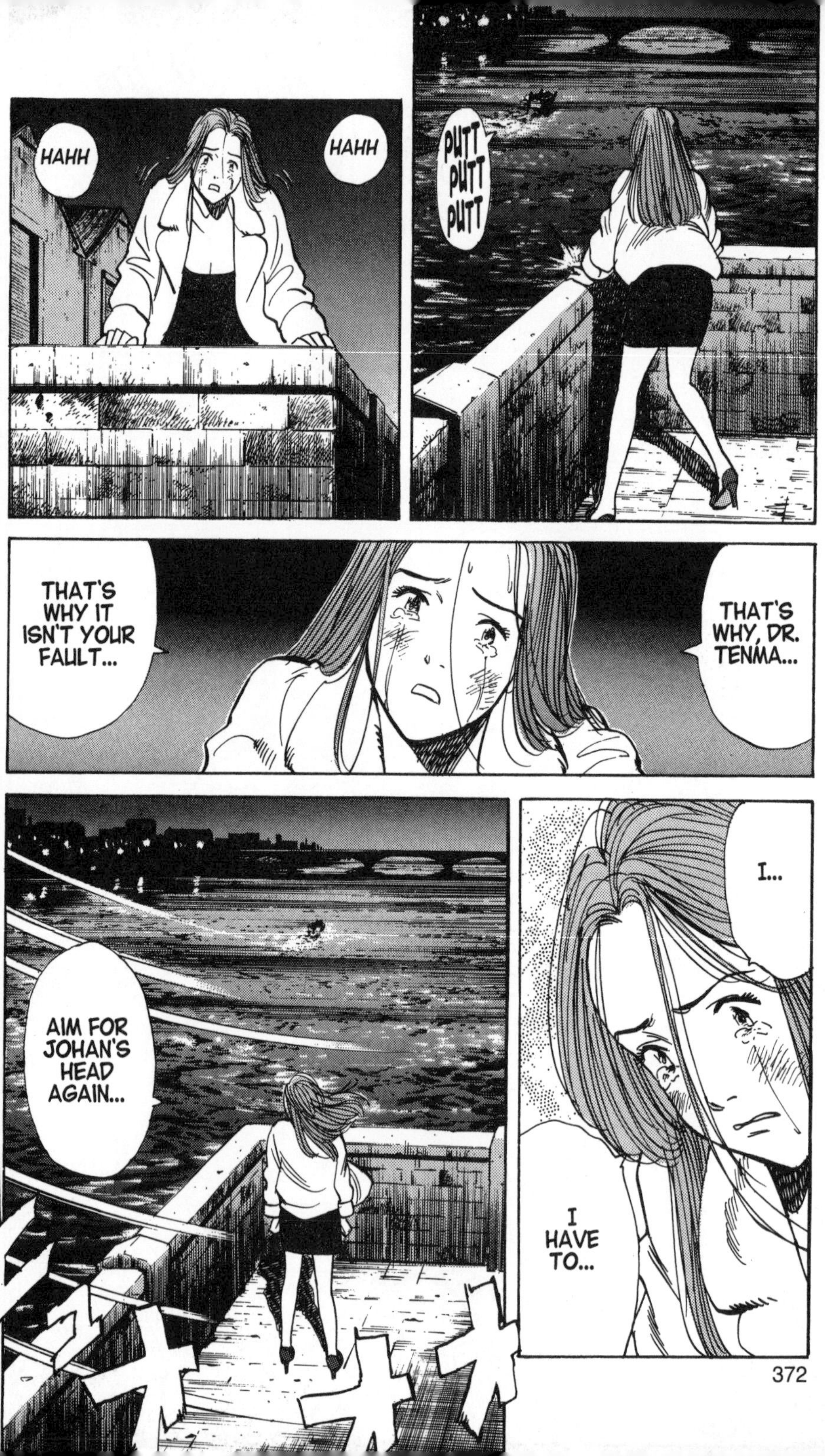
PUTT PUTT PUTT
HAHH
HAHH
THAT'S WHY, DR. TENMA...
THAT'S WHY IT ISN'T YOUR FAULT...
I...
I HAVE TO...
AIM FOR JOHAN'S HEAD AGAIN...

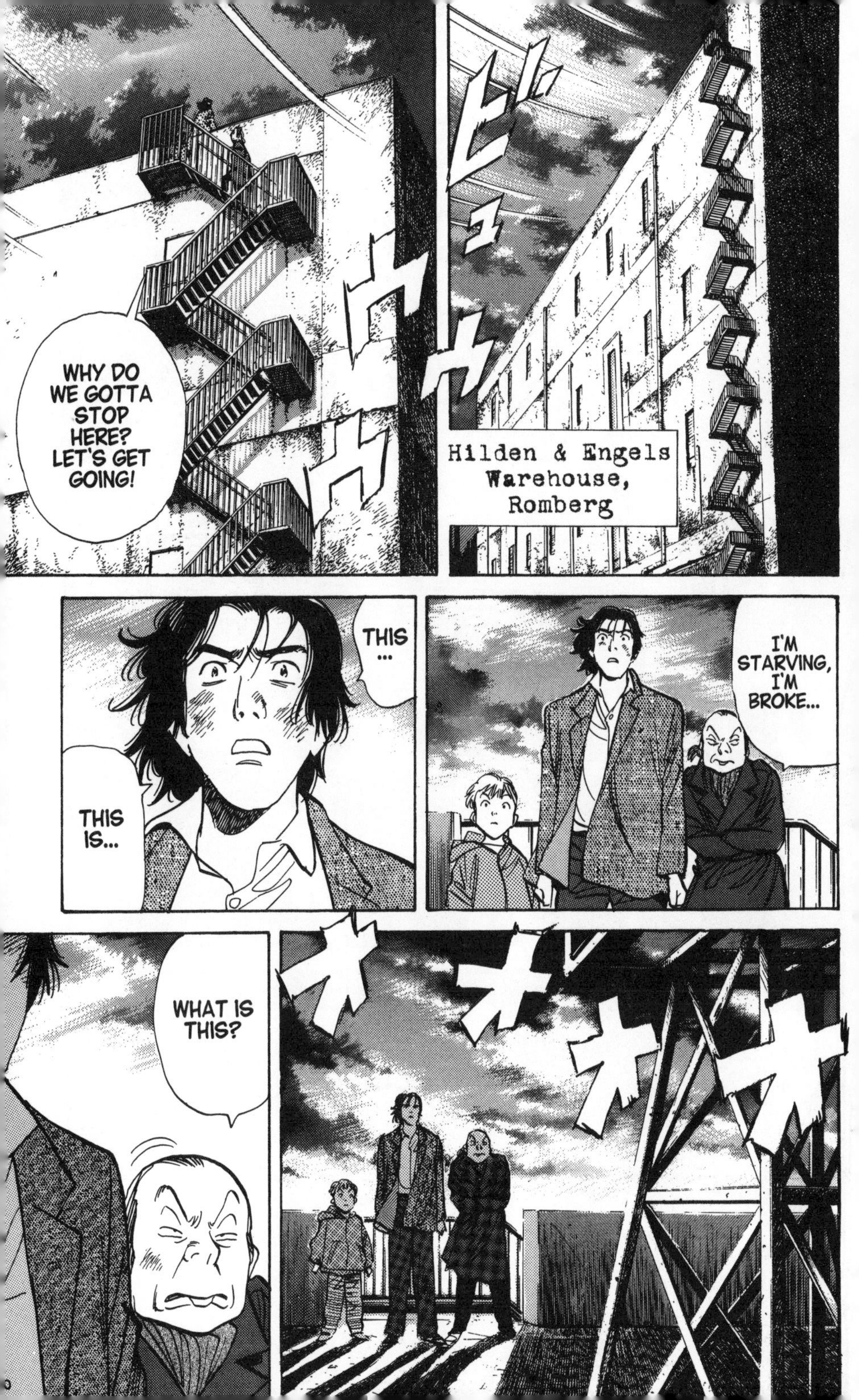
Hilden & Engels Warehouse, Romberg
WHY DO WE GOTTA STOP HERE? LET'S GET GOING!
I'M STARVING, I'M BROKE...
THIS ...
THIS IS...
WHAT IS THIS?

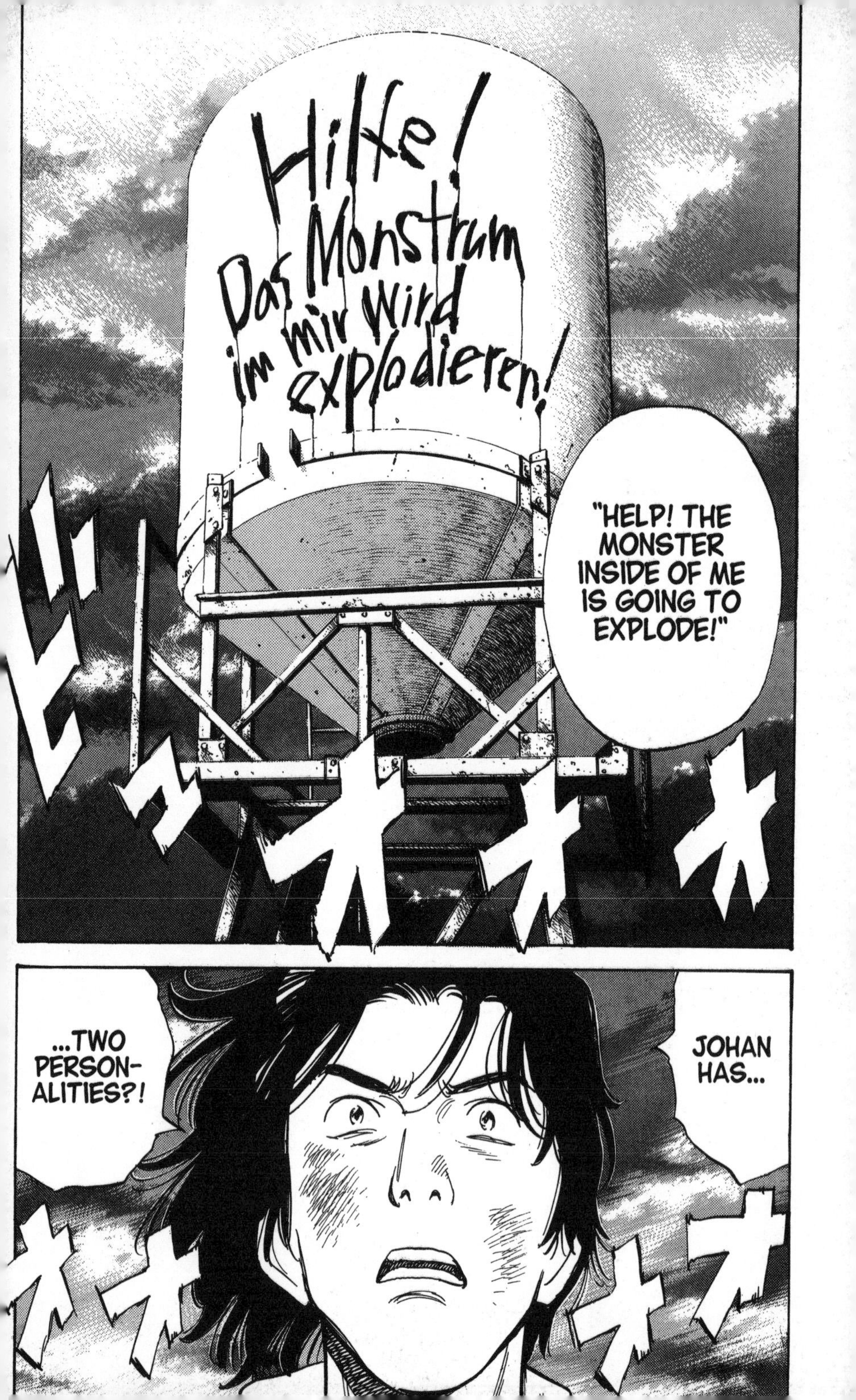
Hilfe! Das Monstrum im mir wird explodieren!
"HELP! THE MONSTER INSIDE OF ME IS GOING TO EXPLODE!"
JOHAN HAS...
...TWO PERSON-ALITIES?!

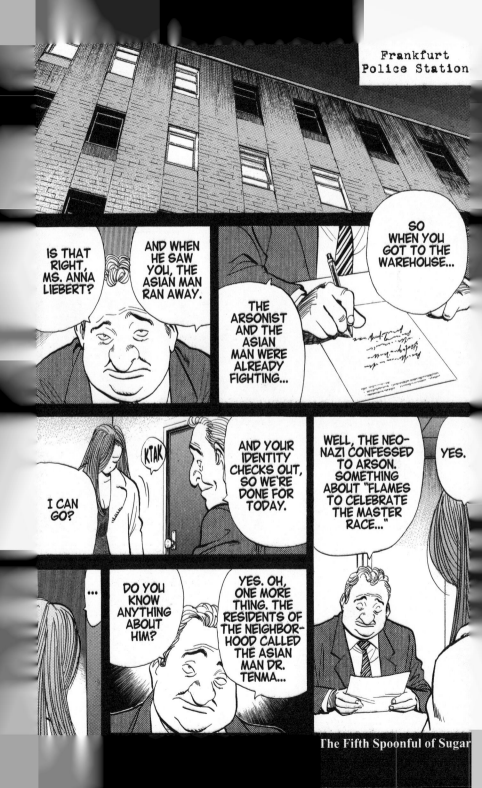

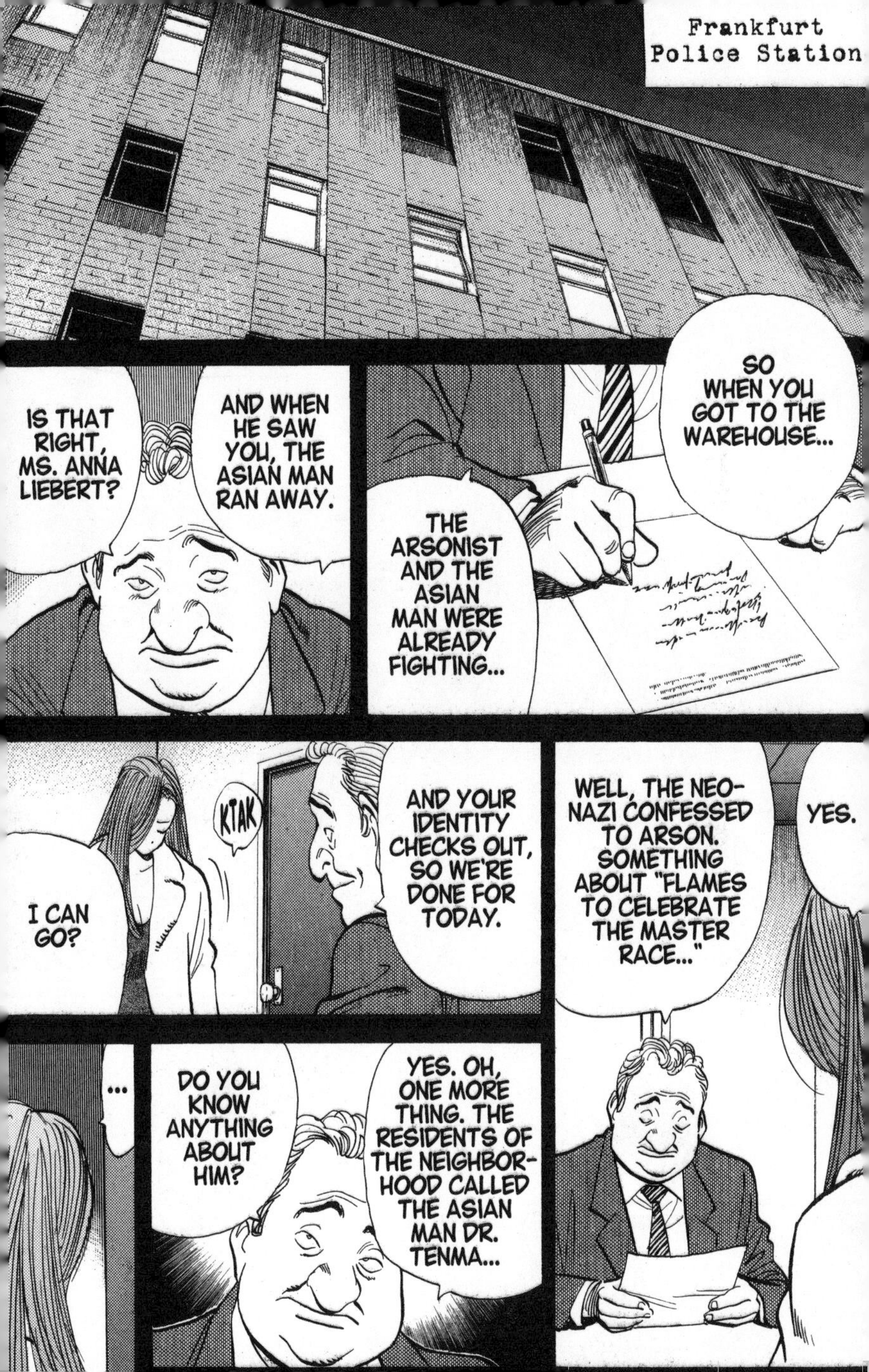
Frankfurt Police Station
SO WHEN YOU GOT TO THE WAREHOUSE...
THE ARSONIST AND THE ASIAN MAN WERE ALREADY FIGHTING...
AND WHEN HE SAW YOU, THE ASIAN MAN RAN AWAY.
IS THAT RIGHT, MS. ANNA LIEBERT?
YES.
WELL, THE NEO-NAZI CONFESSED TO ARSON. SOMETHING ABOUT "FLAMES TO CELEBRATE THE MASTER RACE..."
AND YOUR IDENTITY CHECKS OUT, SO WE'RE DONE FOR TODAY.
KTAK
I CAN GO?
YES. OH, ONE MORE THING. THE RESIDENTS OF THE NEIGHBOR-HOOD CALLED THE ASIAN MAN DR. TENMA...
DO YOU KNOW ANYTHING ABOUT HIM?
...

The Fifth Spoonful of Sugar

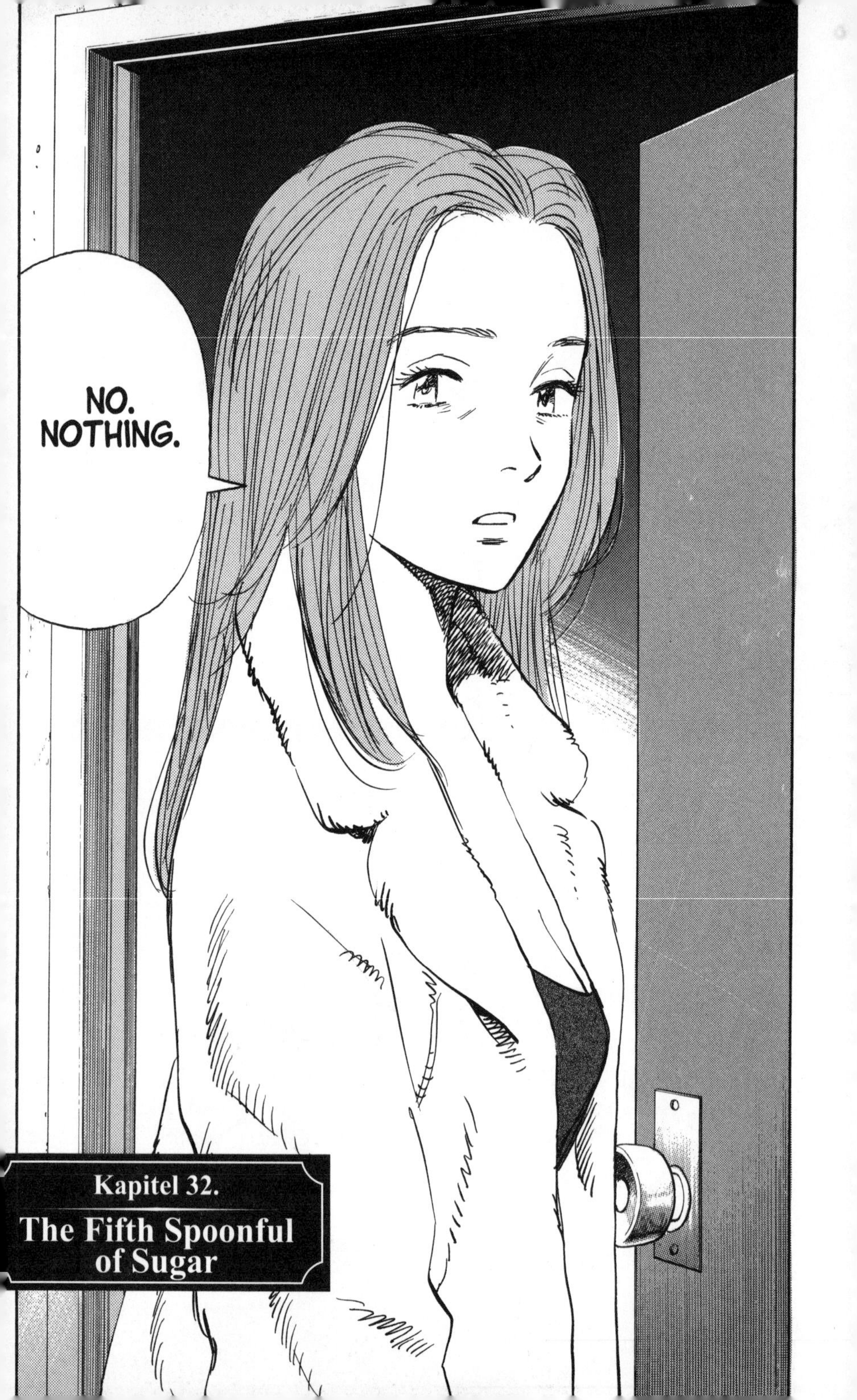
NO. NOTHING.

Kapitel 32.
The Fifth Spoonful of Sugar

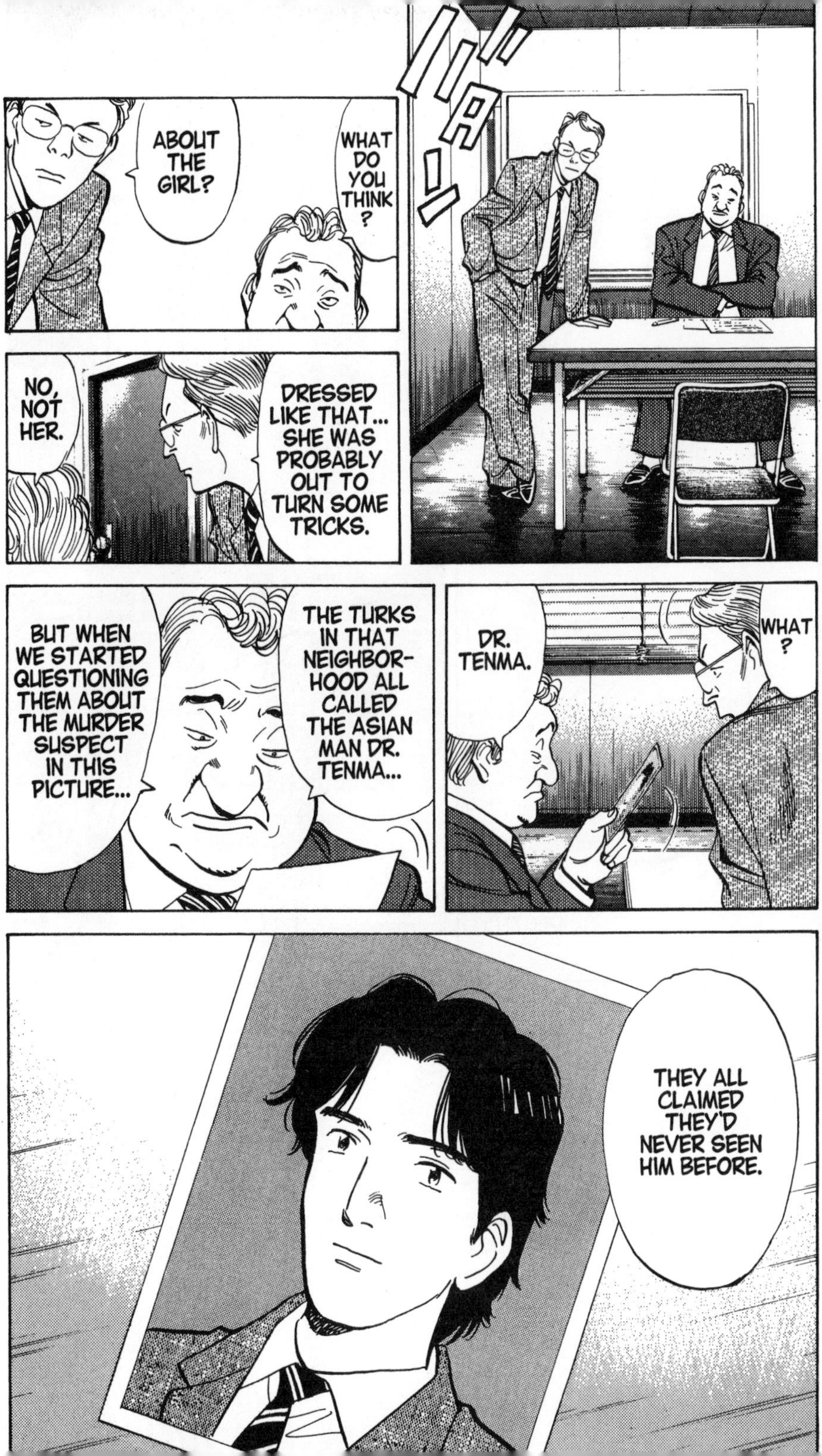
WHAT DO YOU THINK?
ABOUT THE GIRL?
DRESSED LIKE THAT... SHE WAS PROBABLY OUT TO TURN SOME TRICKS.
NO, NOT HER.
WHAT?
DR. TENMA.
THE TURKS IN THAT NEIGHBOR-HOOD ALL CALLED THE ASIAN MAN DR. TENMA...
BUT WHEN WE STARTED QUESTIONING THEM ABOUT THE MURDER SUSPECT IN THIS PICTURE...
THEY ALL CLAIMED THEY'D NEVER SEEN HIM BEFORE.

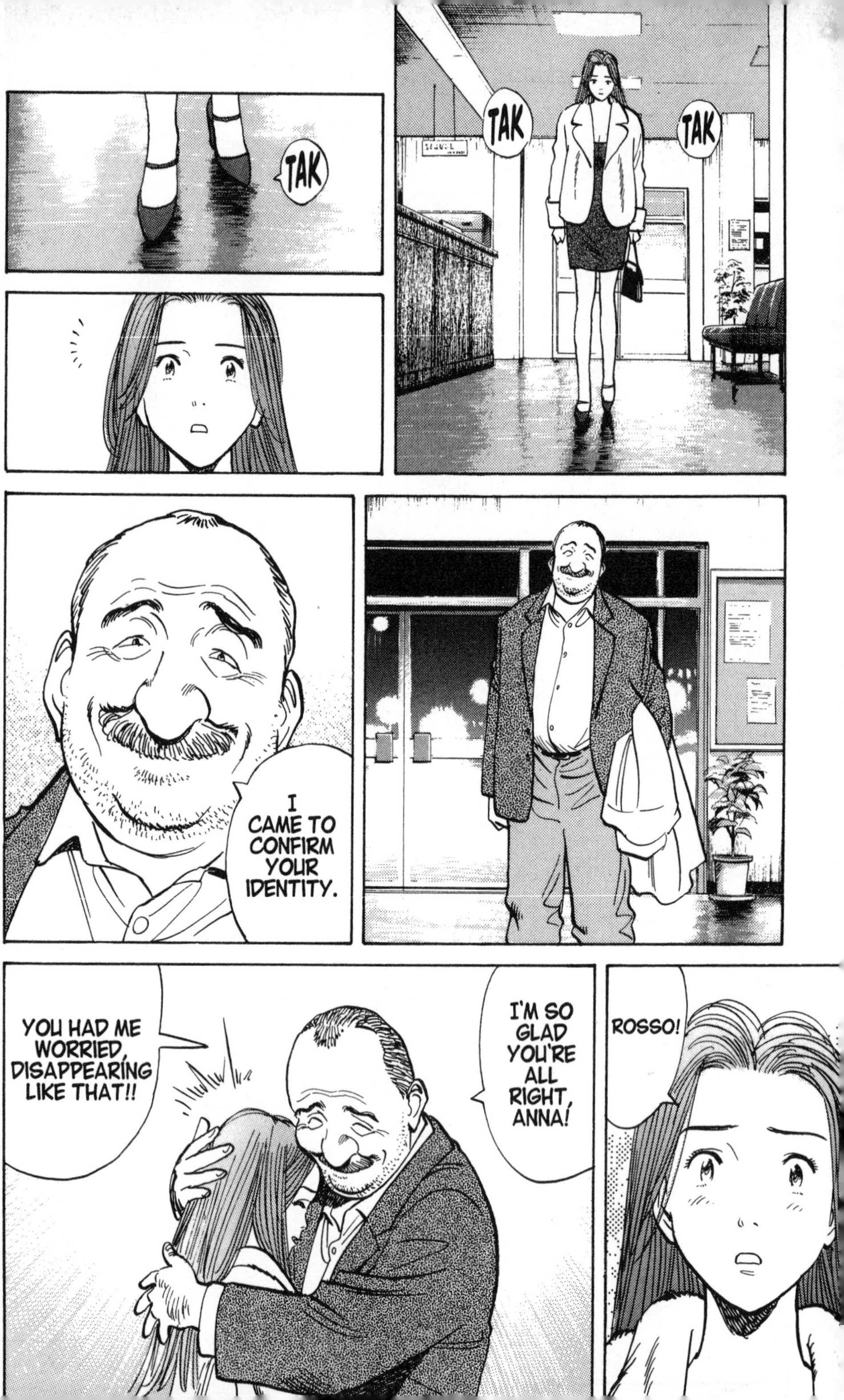
TAK
TAK
TAK
I CAME TO CONFIRM YOUR IDENTITY.
ROSSO!
I'M SO GLAD YOU'RE ALL RIGHT, ANNA!
YOU HAD ME WORRIED, DISAPPEARING LIKE THAT!!

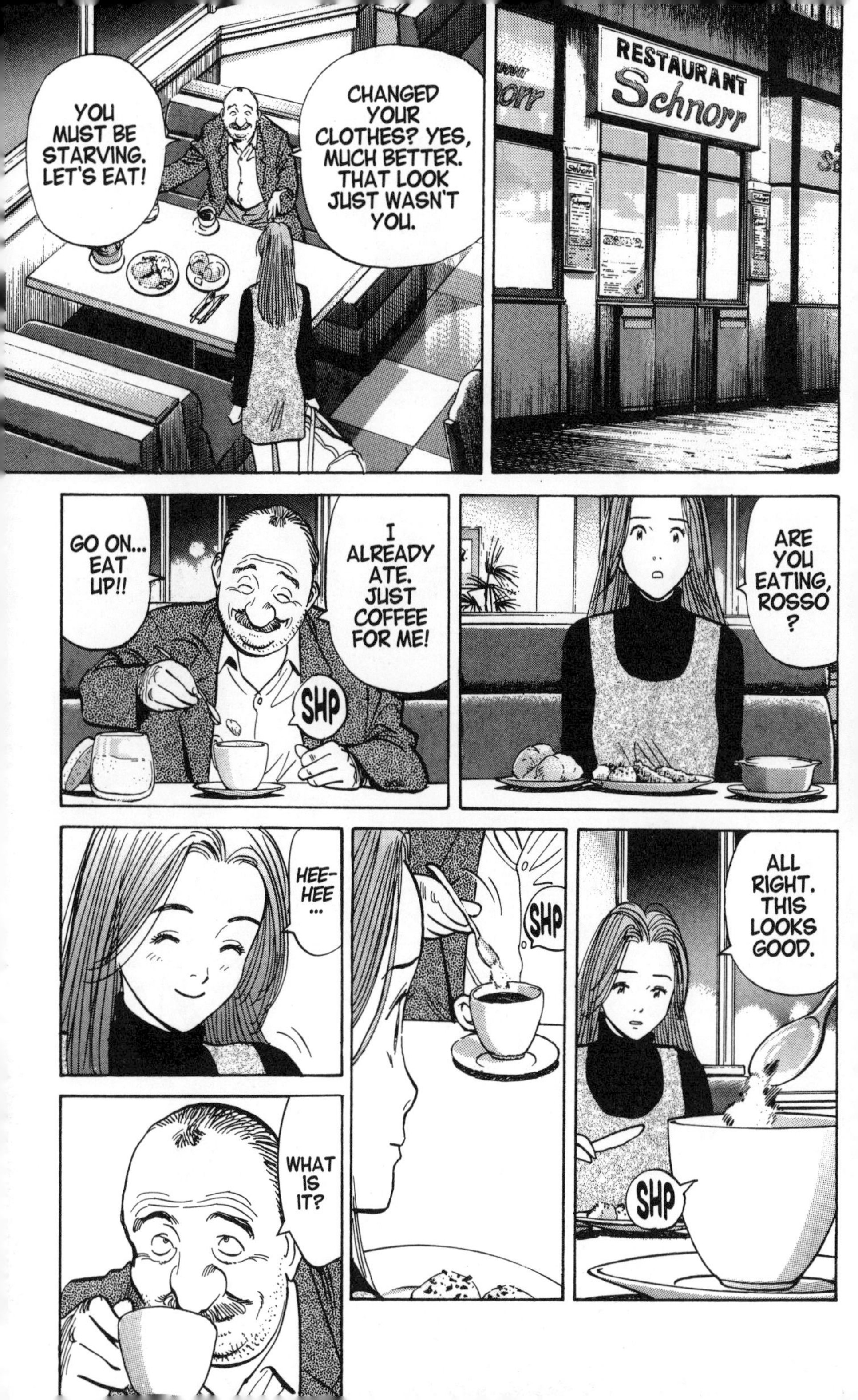
RESTAURANT Schnorr
CHANGED YOUR CLOTHES? YES, MUCH BETTER. THAT LOOK JUST WASN'T YOU.
YOU MUST BE STARVING. LET'S EAT!
ARE YOU EATING, ROSSO?
I ALREADY ATE. JUST COFFEE FOR ME!
GO ON... EAT UP!!
SHP
ALL RIGHT. THIS LOOKS GOOD.
SHP
SHP
HEE-HEE...
WHAT IS IT?

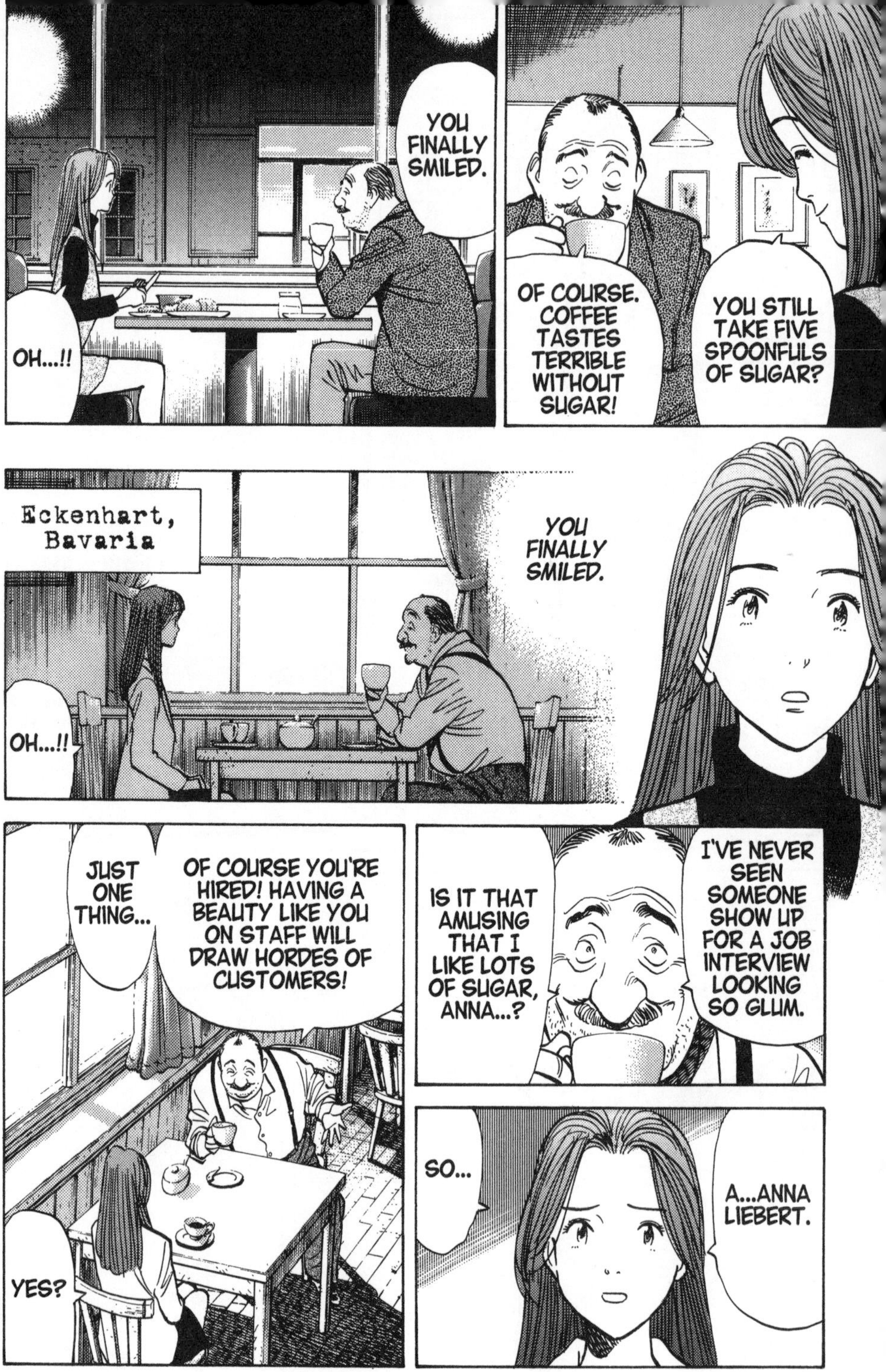
YOU STILL TAKE FIVE SPOONFULS OF SUGAR?
OF COURSE. COFFEE TASTES TERRIBLE WITHOUT SUGAR!
YOU FINALLY SMILED.
OH...!!
Eckenhart, Bavaria
YOU FINALLY SMILED.
OH...!!
I'VE NEVER SEEN SOMEONE SHOW UP FOR A JOB INTERVIEW LOOKING SO GLUM.
IS IT THAT AMUSING THAT I LIKE LOTS OF SUGAR, ANNA...?
A...ANNA LIEBERT.
SO...
OF COURSE YOU'RE HIRED! HAVING A BEAUTY LIKE YOU ON STAFF WILL DRAW HORDES OF CUSTOMERS!
JUST ONE THING...
YES?

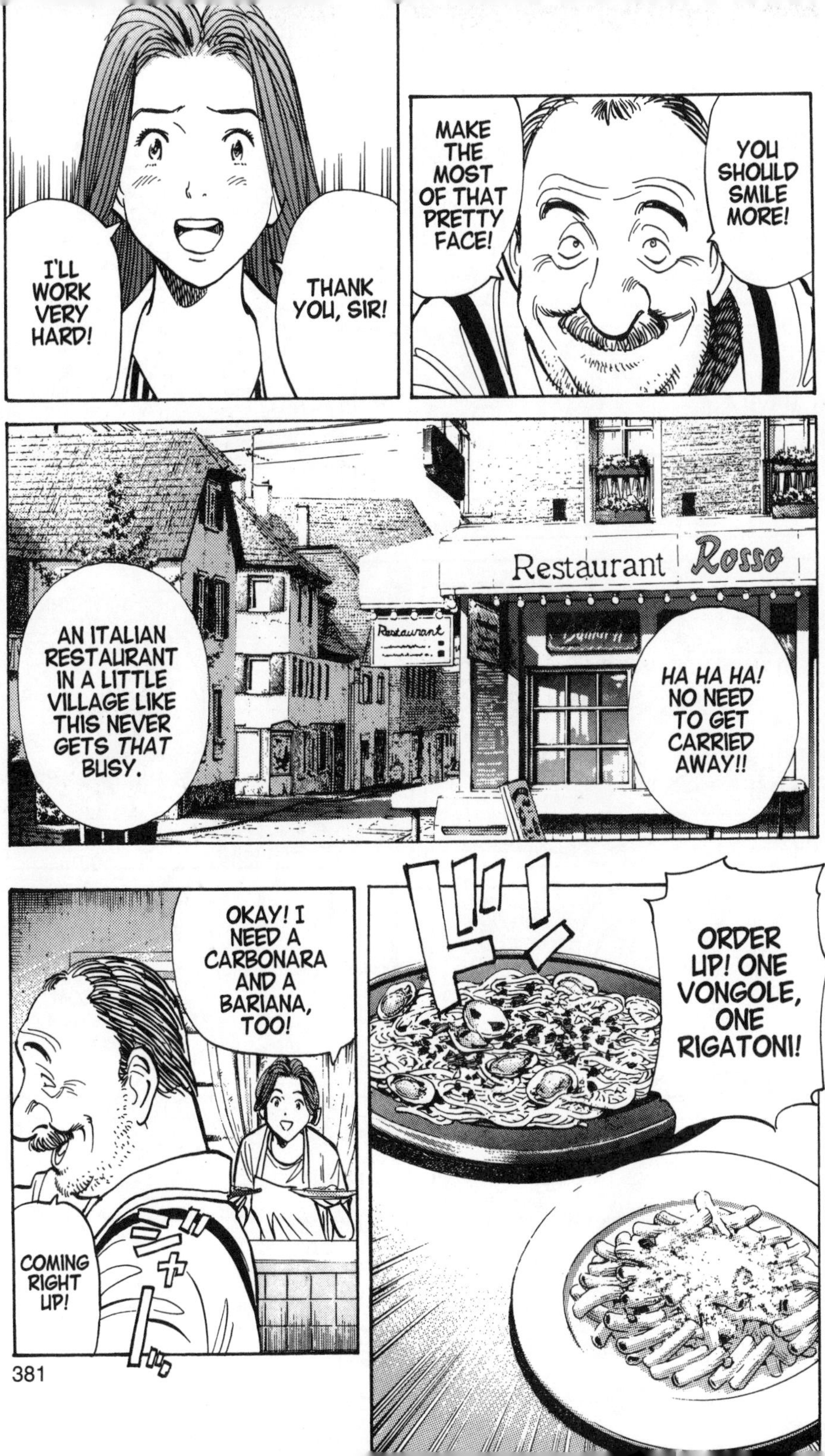
YOU SHOULD SMILE MORE!
MAKE THE MOST OF THAT PRETTY FACE!
THANK YOU, SIR!
I'LL WORK VERY HARD!
Restaurant Rosso
HA HA HA! NO NEED TO GET CARRIED AWAY!!
AN ITALIAN RESTAURANT IN A LITTLE VILLAGE LIKE THIS NEVER GETS *THAT* BUSY.
Restaurant
ORDER UP! ONE VONGOLE, ONE RIGATONI!
OKAY! I NEED A CARBONARA AND A BARIANA, TOO!
COMING RIGHT UP!

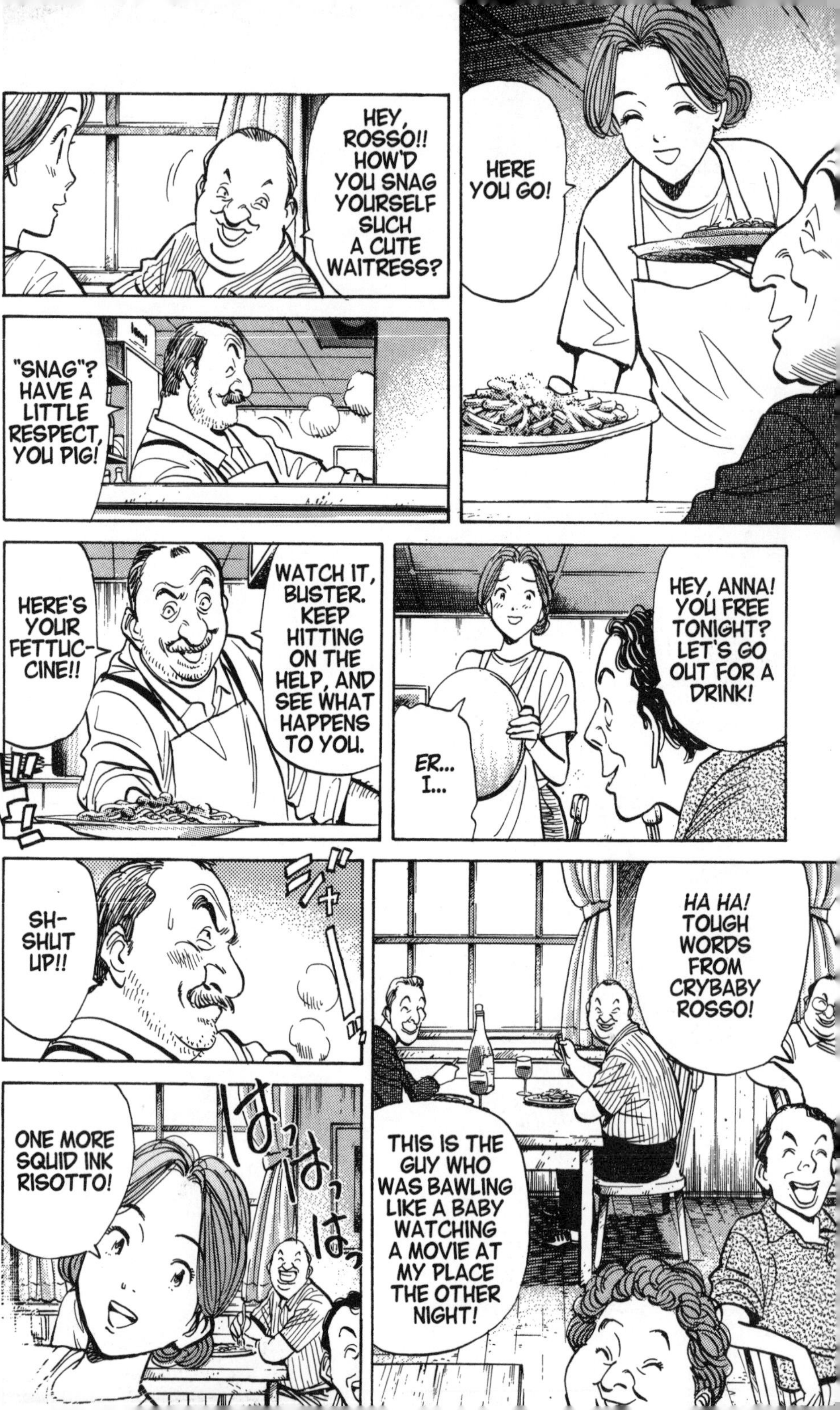
HERE YOU GO!
HEY, ROSSO!! HOW'D YOU SNAG YOURSELF SUCH A CUTE WAITRESS?
"SNAG"? HAVE A LITTLE RESPECT, YOU PIG!
HEY, ANNA! YOU FREE TONIGHT? LET'S GO OUT FOR A DRINK!
ER... I...
WATCH IT, BUSTER. KEEP HITTING ON THE HELP, AND SEE WHAT HAPPENS TO YOU.
HERE'S YOUR FETTUC-CINE!!
HA HA! TOUGH WORDS FROM CRYBABY ROSSO!
THIS IS THE GUY WHO WAS BAWLING LIKE A BABY WATCHING A MOVIE AT MY PLACE THE OTHER NIGHT!
SH-SHUT UP!!
ジャーッ
ONE MORE SQUID INK RISOTTO!
はっはっはっ

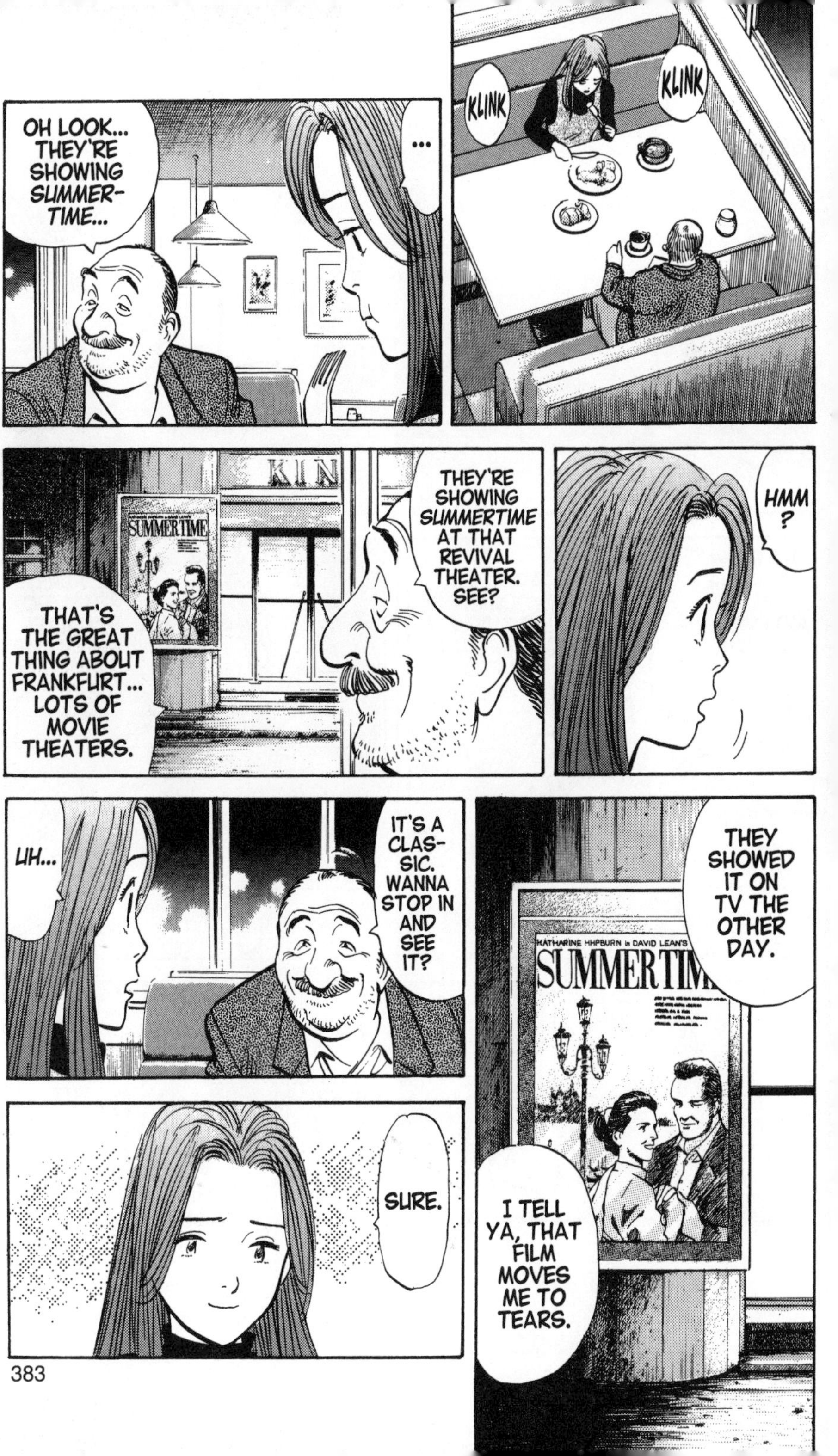
KLINK
KLINK
...
OH LOOK... THEY'RE SHOWING SUMMERTIME...
HMM?
THEY'RE SHOWING SUMMERTIME AT THAT REVIVAL THEATER. SEE?
KIN
SUMMERTIME
THAT'S THE GREAT THING ABOUT FRANKFURT... LOTS OF MOVIE THEATERS.
THEY SHOWED IT ON TV THE OTHER DAY.
KATHARINE HHPBURN in DAVID LEAN'S
SUMMERTIM
I TELL YA, THAT FILM MOVES ME TO TEARS.
IT'S A CLASSIC. WANNA STOP IN AND SEE IT?
UH...
SURE.

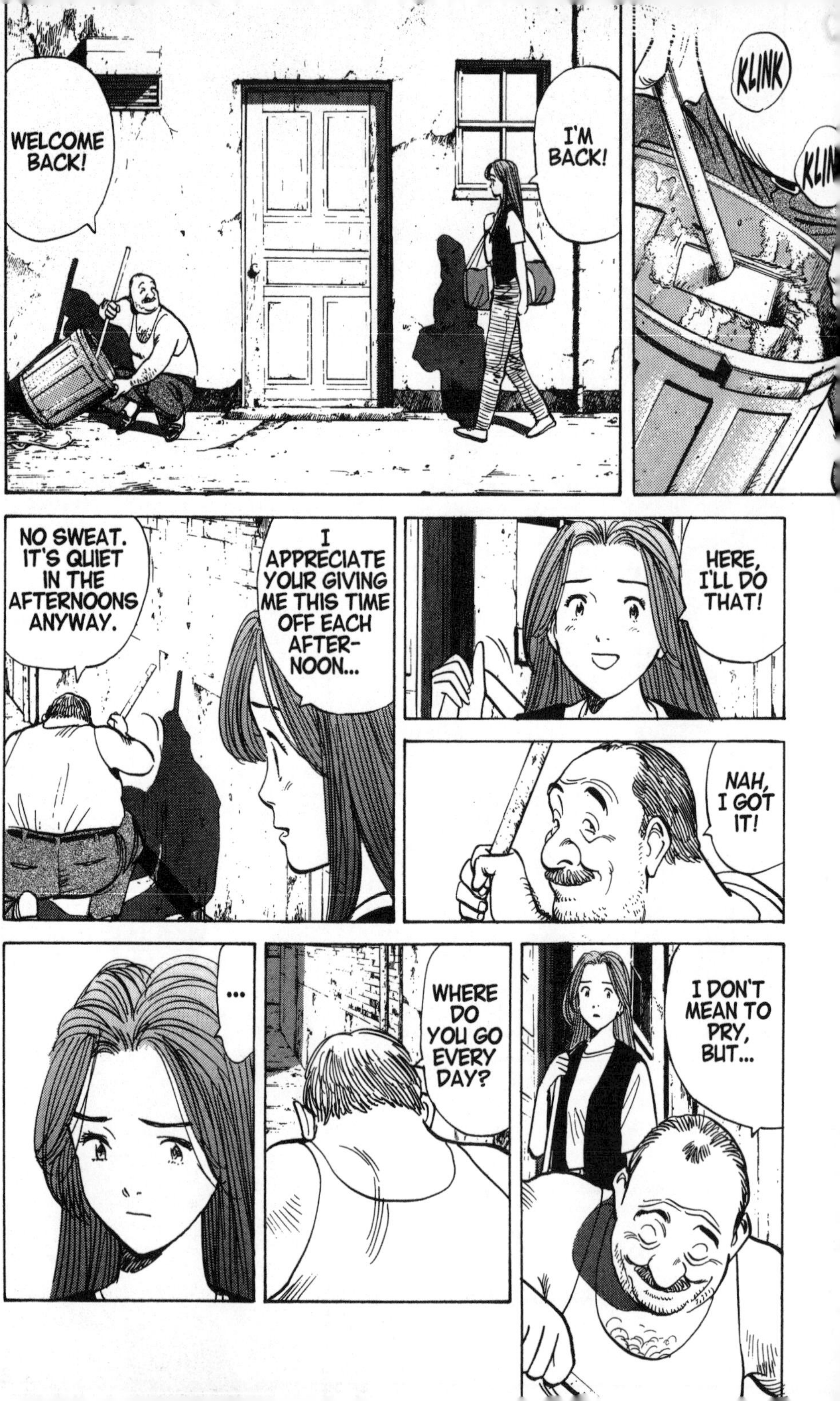
KLINK
KLIN
I'M BACK!
WELCOME BACK!
HERE, I'LL DO THAT!
NAH, I GOT IT!
I APPRECIATE YOUR GIVING ME THIS TIME OFF EACH AFTER-NOON...
NO SWEAT. IT'S QUIET IN THE AFTERNOONS ANYWAY.
I DON'T MEAN TO PRY, BUT...
WHERE DO YOU GO EVERY DAY?
...

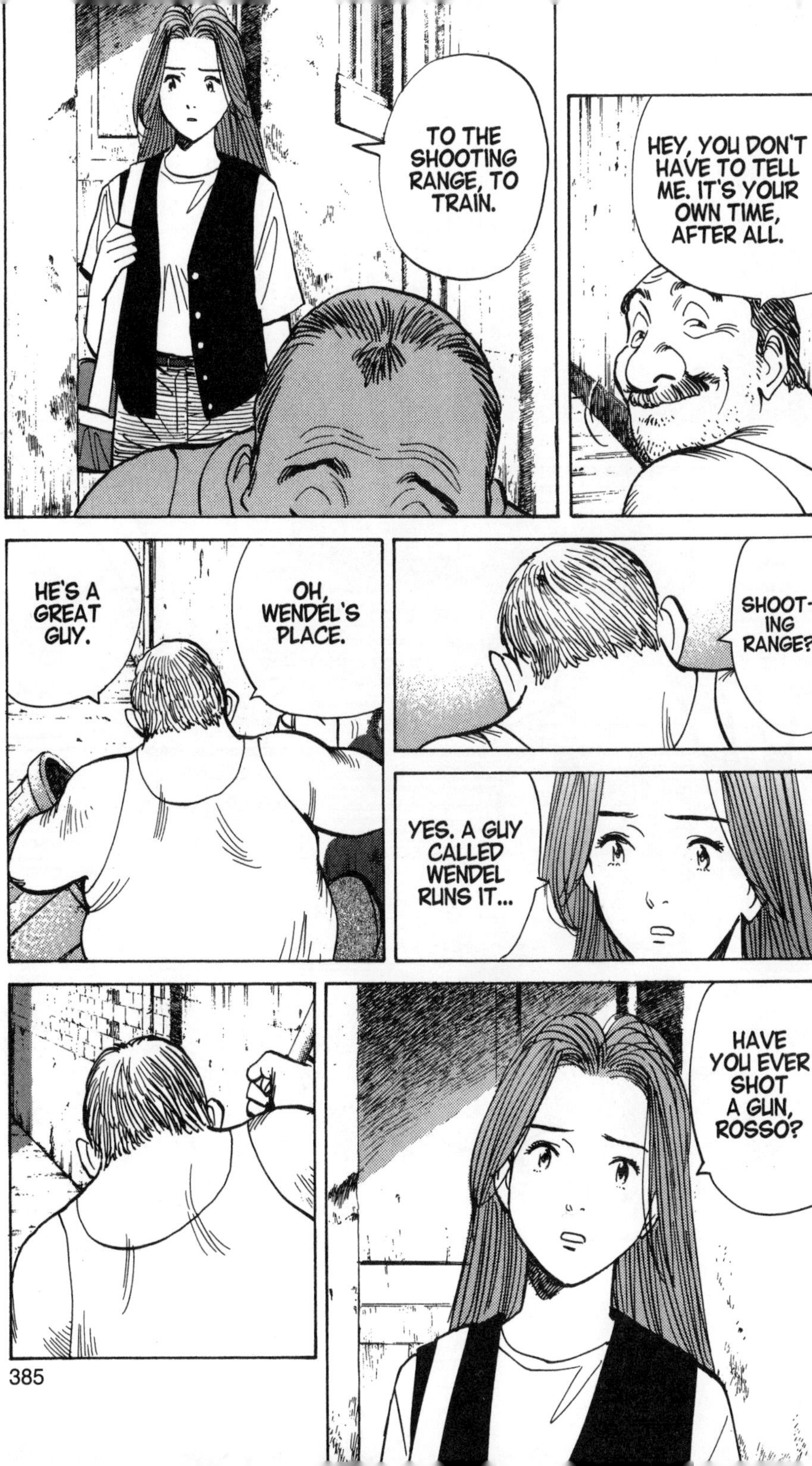
HEY, YOU DON'T HAVE TO TELL ME. IT'S YOUR OWN TIME, AFTER ALL.
TO THE SHOOTING RANGE, TO TRAIN.
SHOOT-ING RANGE?
YES. A GUY CALLED WENDEL RUNS IT...
OH, WENDEL'S PLACE.
HE'S A GREAT GUY.
HAVE YOU EVER SHOT A GUN, ROSSO?

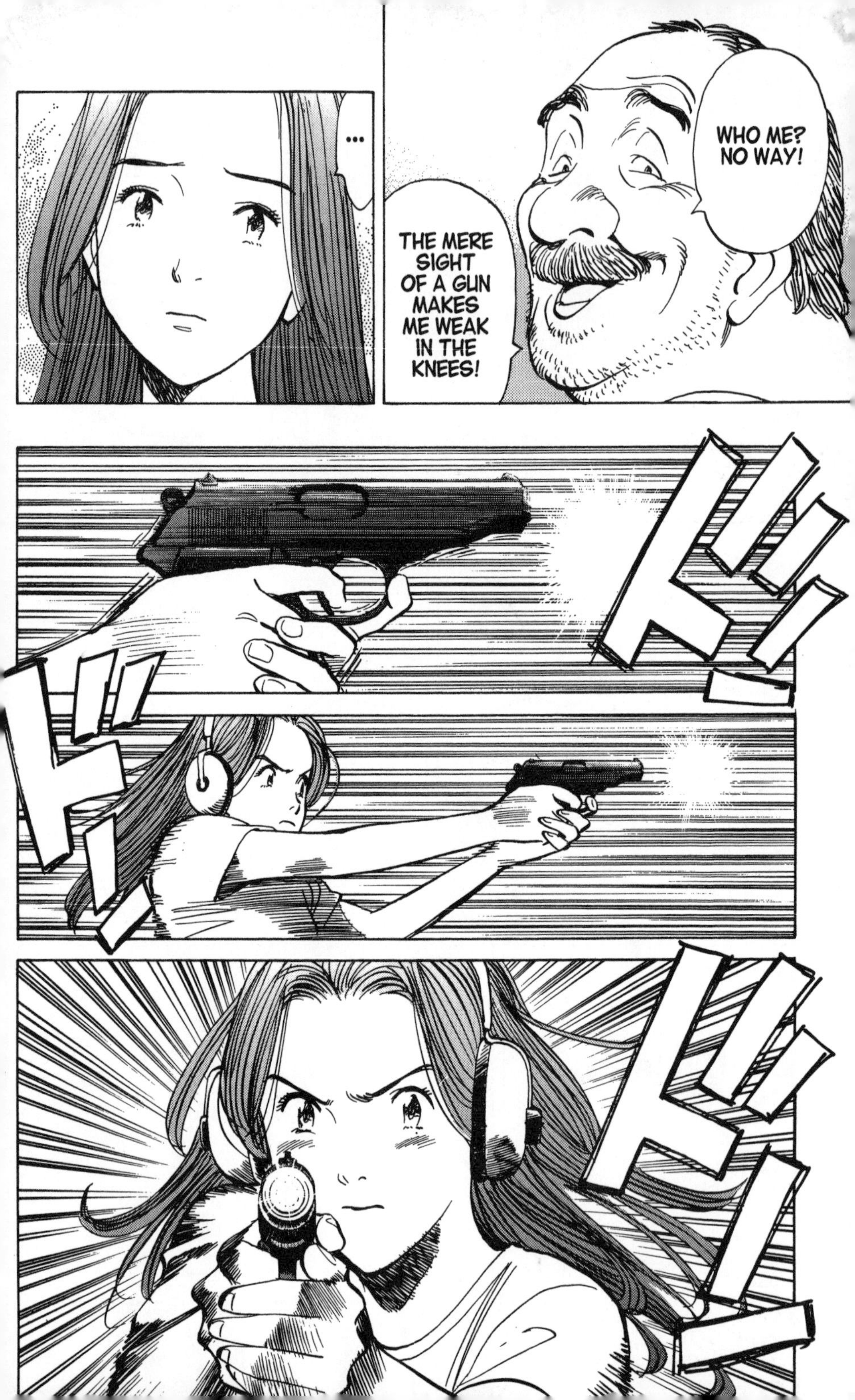
WHO ME? NO WAY!
THE MERE SIGHT OF A GUN MAKES ME WEAK IN THE KNEES!
...
ドド
ドド
ドド

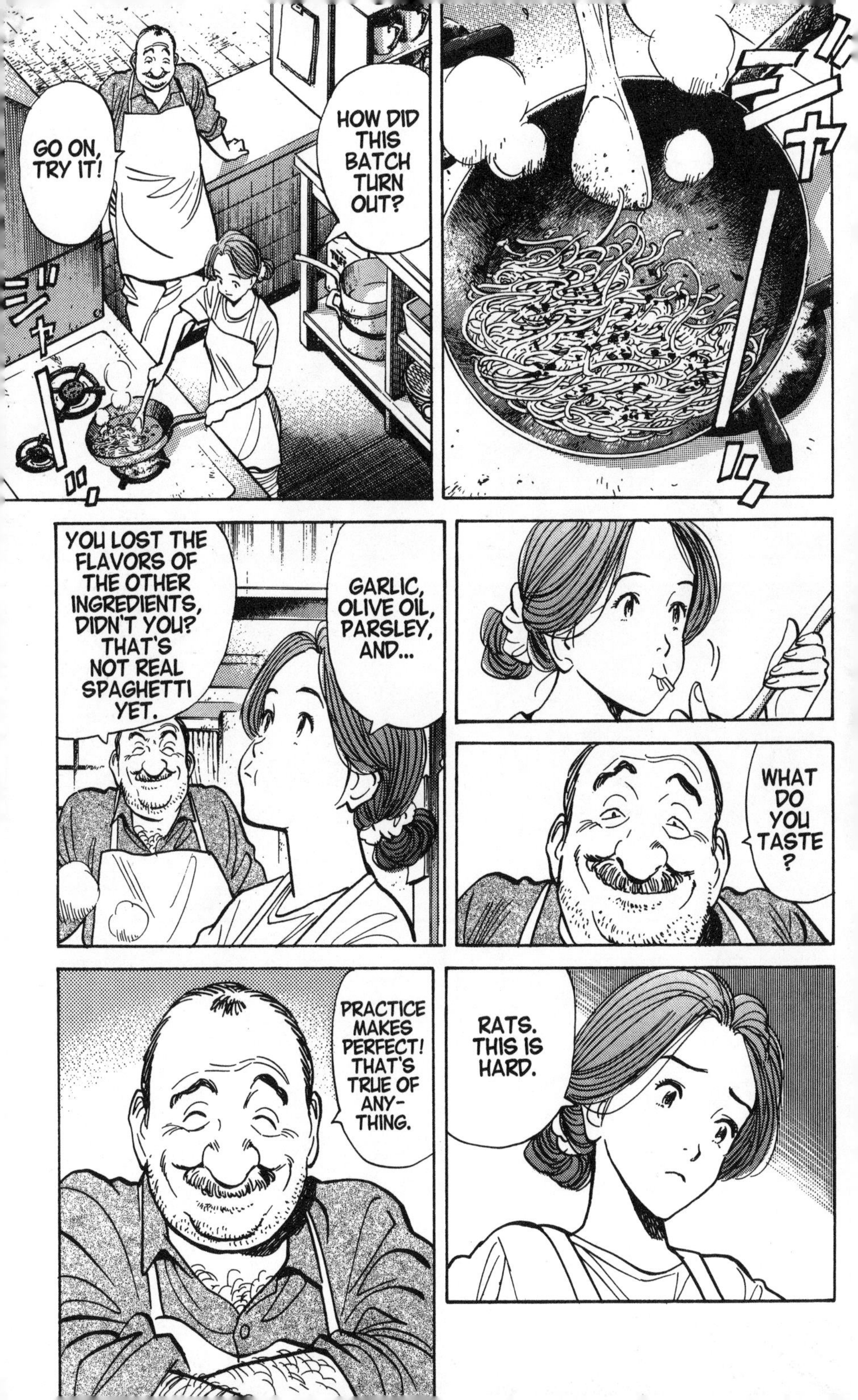
HOW DID THIS BATCH TURN OUT?
GO ON, TRY IT!
WHAT DO YOU TASTE?
GARLIC, OLIVE OIL, PARSLEY, AND...
YOU LOST THE FLAVORS OF THE OTHER INGREDIENTS, DIDN'T YOU? THAT'S NOT REAL SPAGHETTI YET.
RATS. THIS IS HARD.
PRACTICE MAKES PERFECT! THAT'S TRUE OF ANY-THING.

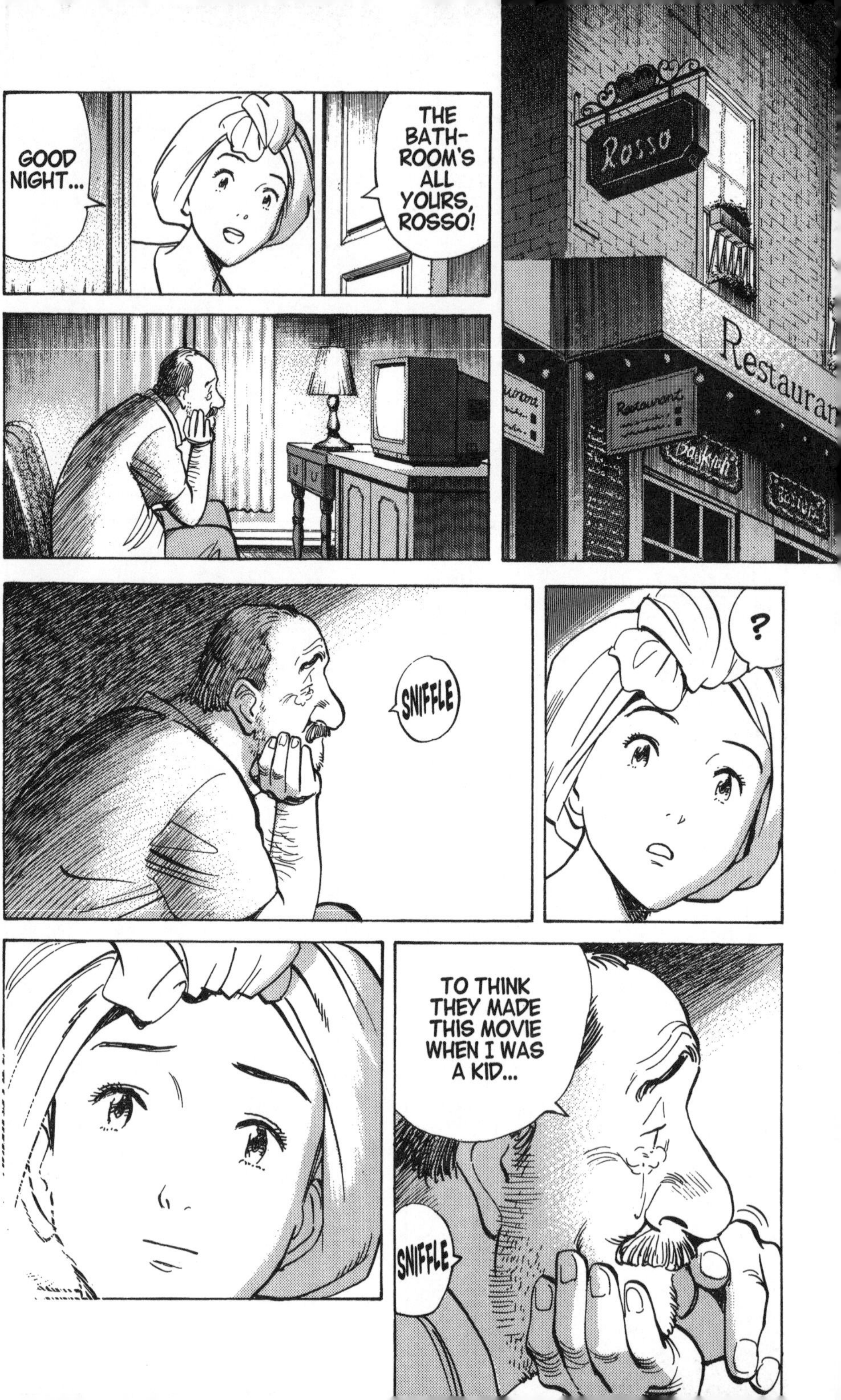
Rosso
Restaurant
Restaurant
THE BATH-ROOM'S ALL YOURS, ROSSO!
GOOD NIGHT...
?
SNIFFLE
TO THINK THEY MADE THIS MOVIE WHEN I WAS A KID...
SNIFFLE

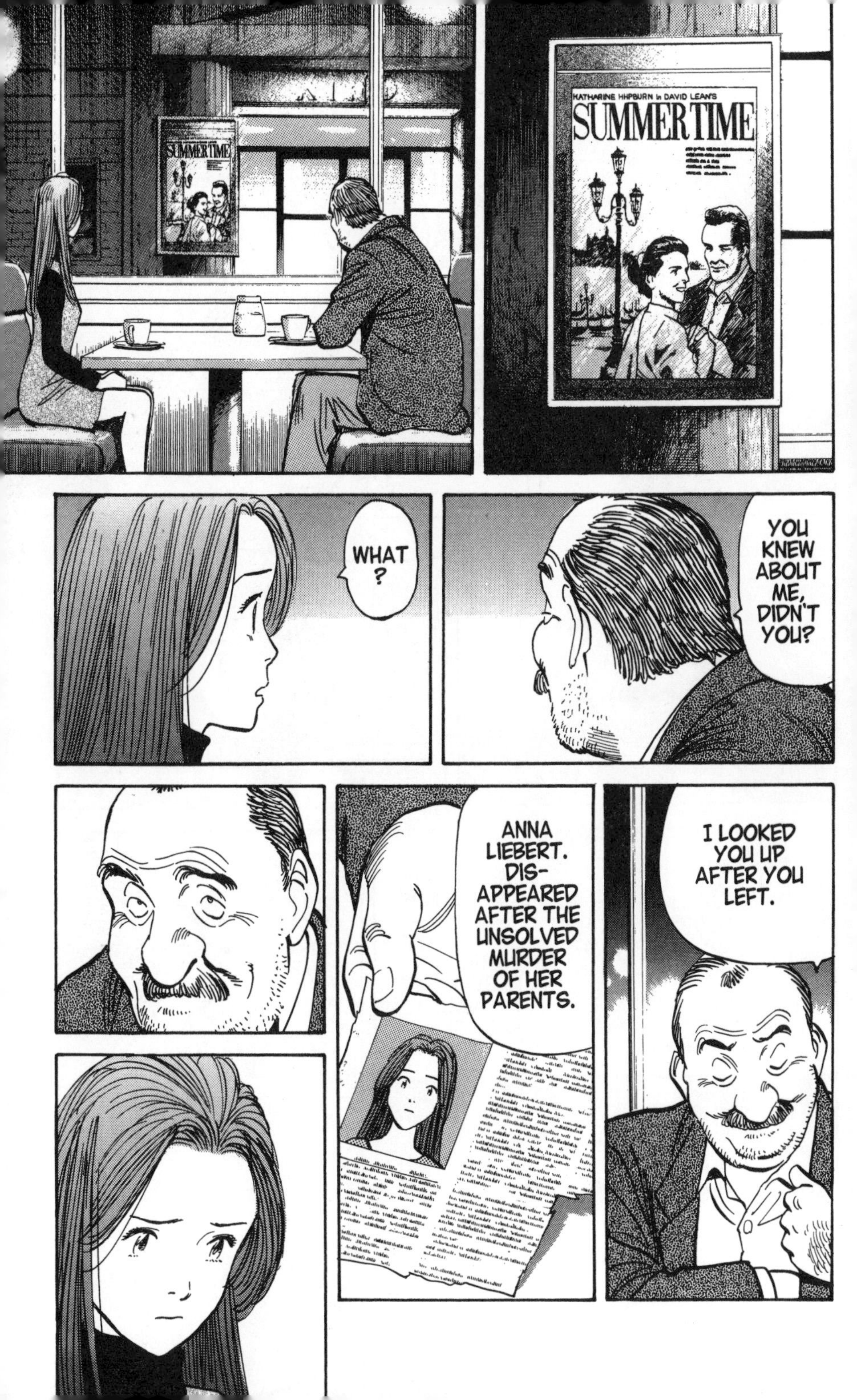
KATHARINE HHPBURN in DAVID LEAN'S
SUMMERTIME
SUMMERTIME
YOU KNEW ABOUT ME, DIDN'T YOU?
WHAT?
I LOOKED YOU UP AFTER YOU LEFT.
ANNA LIEBERT. DIS-APPEARED AFTER THE UNSOLVED MURDER OF HER PARENTS.

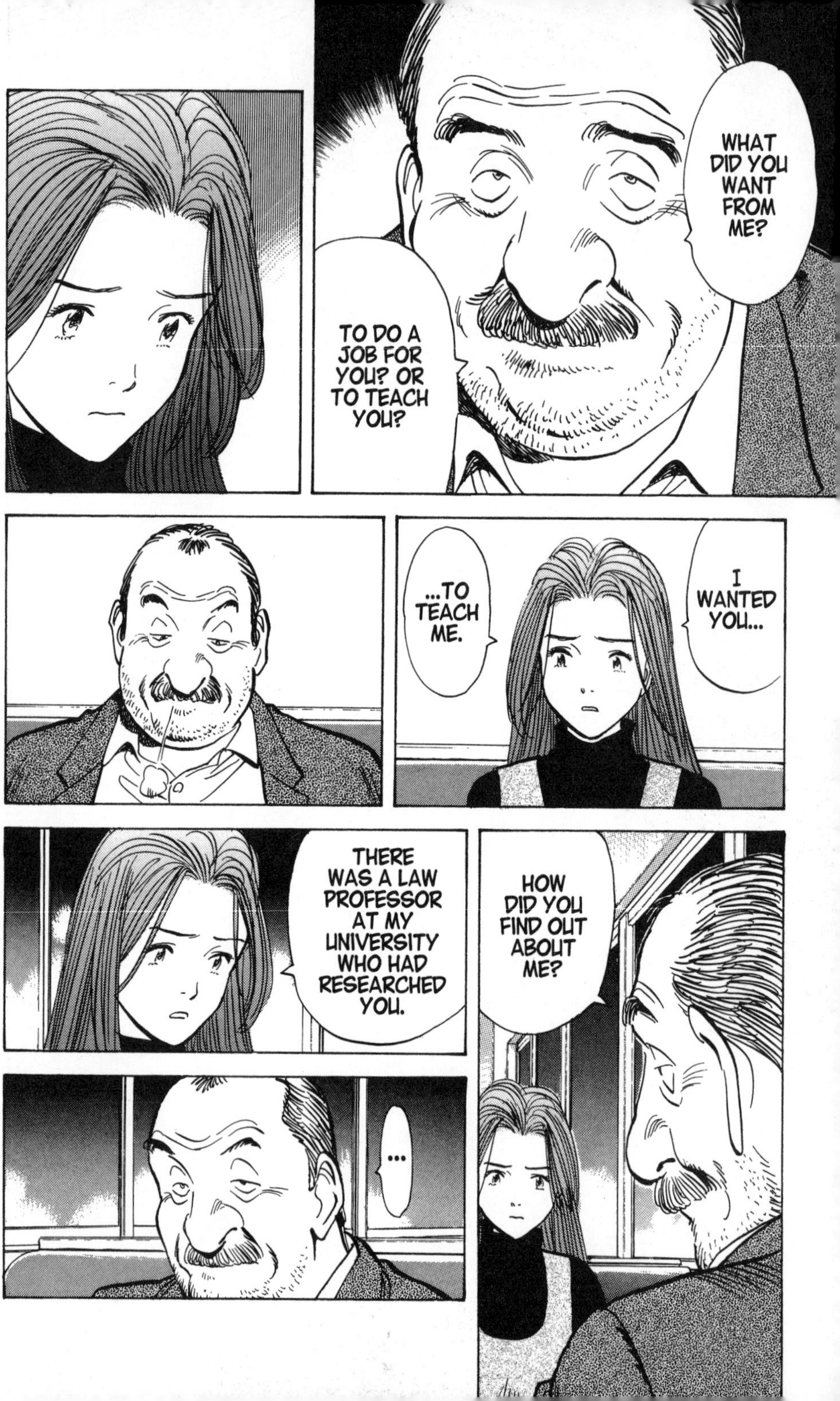
WHAT DID YOU WANT FROM ME?
TO DO A JOB FOR YOU? OR TO TEACH YOU?
I WANTED YOU...
...TO TEACH ME.
HOW DID YOU FIND OUT ABOUT ME?
THERE WAS A LAW PROFESSOR AT MY UNIVERSITY WHO HAD RESEARCHED YOU.
...

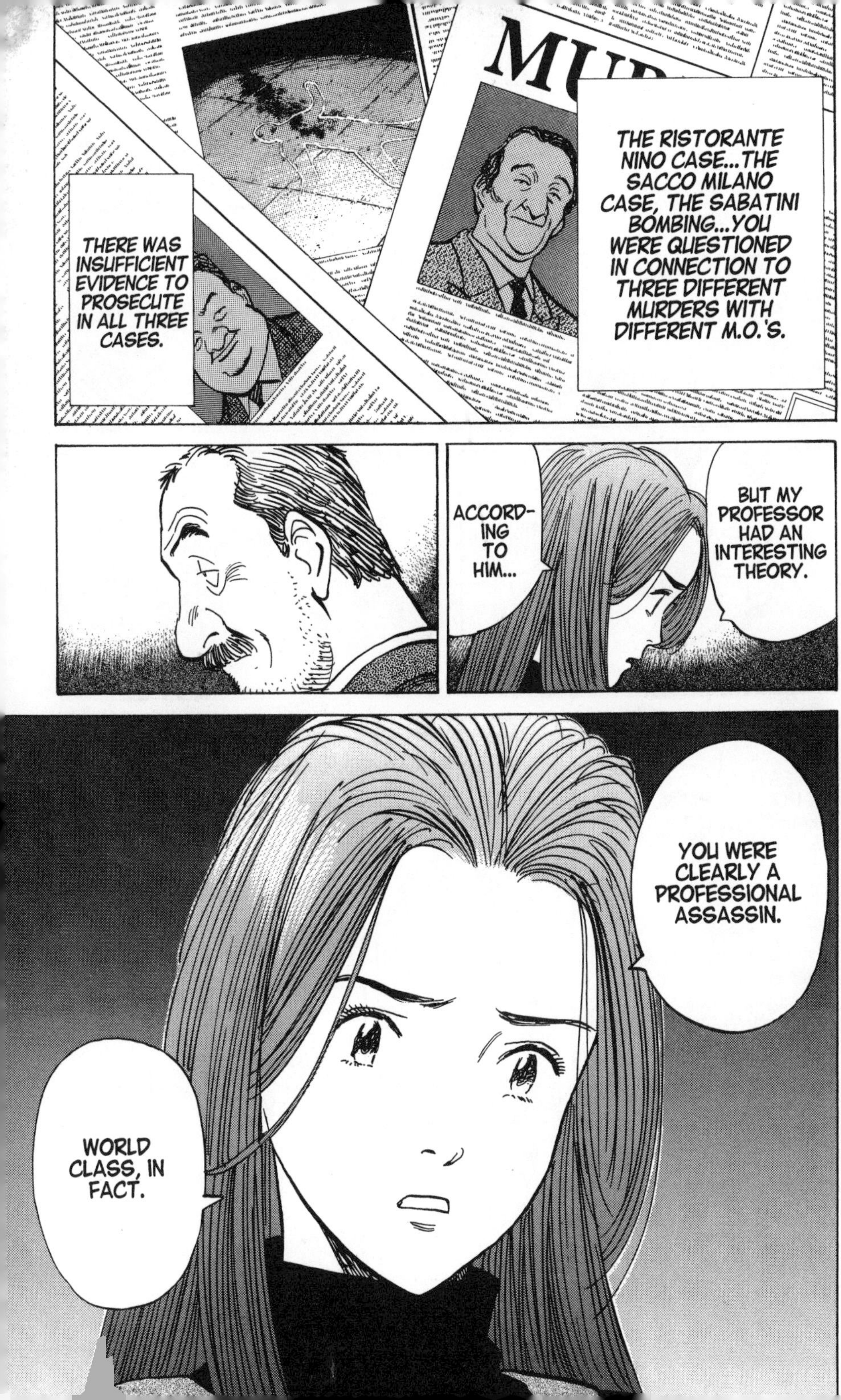
THE RISTORANTE NINO CASE...THE SACCO MILANO CASE, THE SABATINI BOMBING...YOU WERE QUESTIONED IN CONNECTION TO THREE DIFFERENT MURDERS WITH DIFFERENT M.O.'S.
THERE WAS INSUFFICIENT EVIDENCE TO PROSECUTE IN ALL THREE CASES.
BUT MY PROFESSOR HAD AN INTERESTING THEORY.
ACCORDING TO HIM...
YOU WERE CLEARLY A PROFESSIONAL ASSASSIN.
WORLD CLASS, IN FACT.

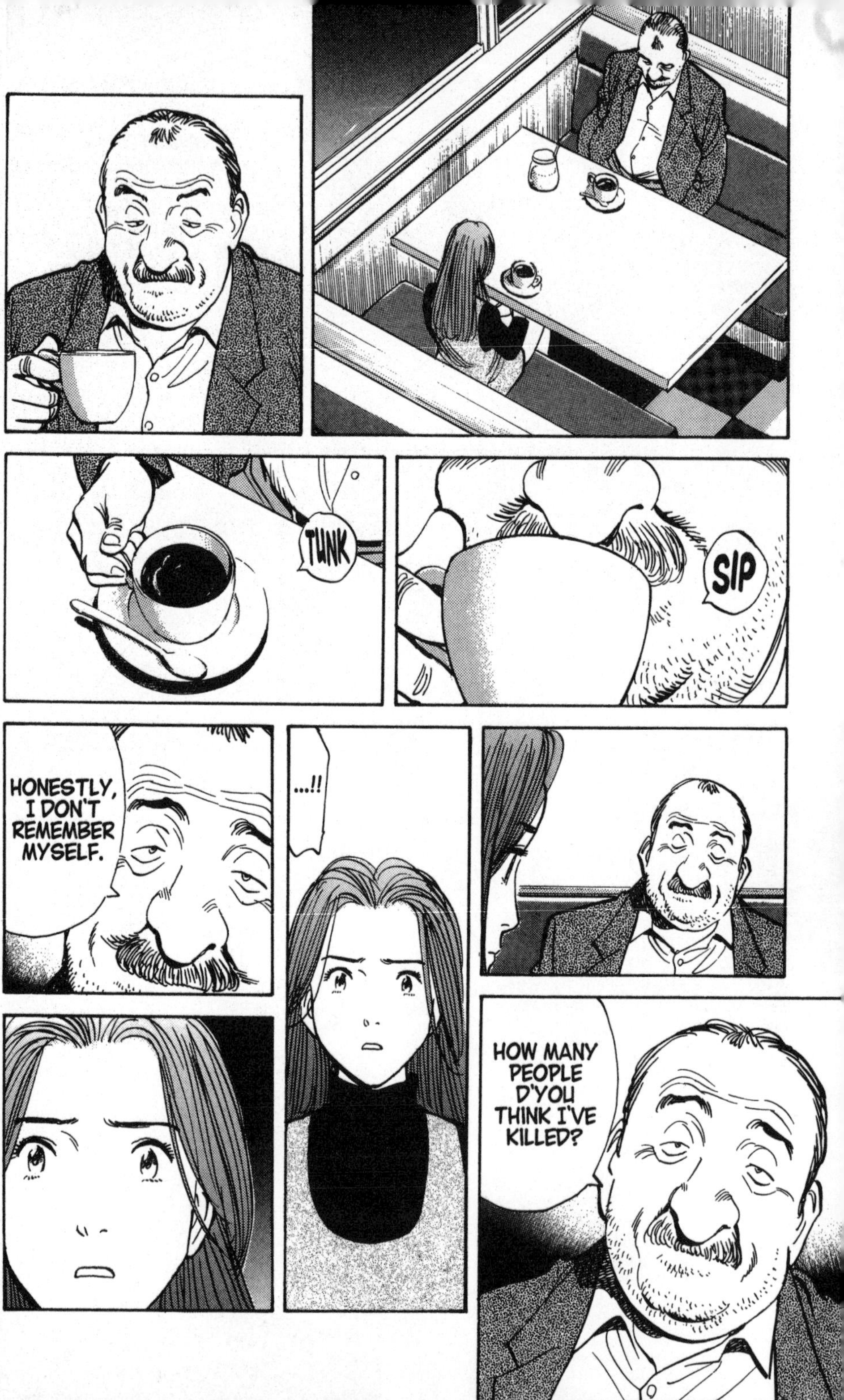
SIP
TUNK
HOW MANY PEOPLE D'YOU THINK I'VE KILLED?
...!!
HONESTLY, I DON'T REMEMBER MYSELF.

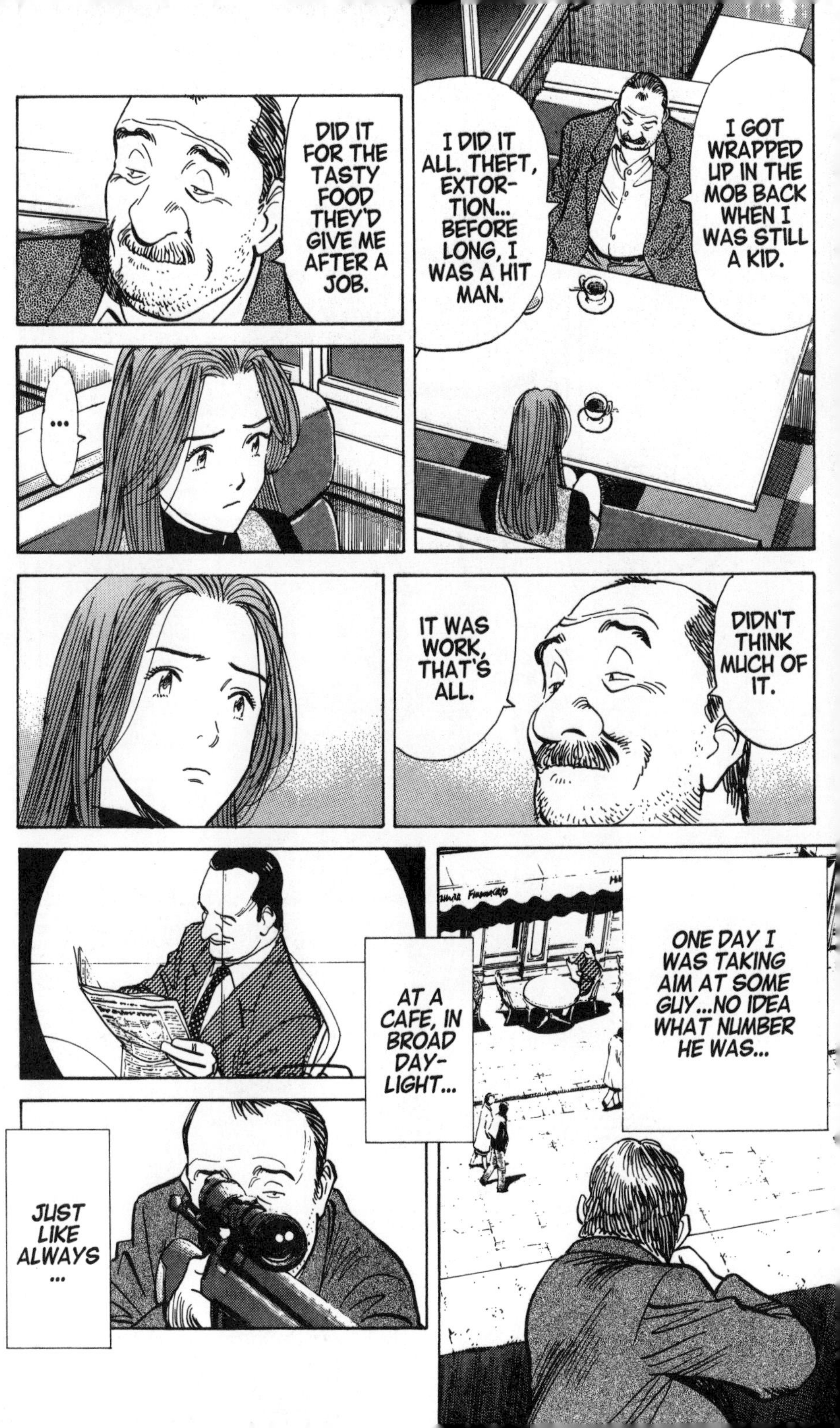
I GOT WRAPPED UP IN THE MOB BACK WHEN I WAS STILL A KID.
I DID IT ALL. THEFT, EXTOR-TION... BEFORE LONG, I WAS A HIT MAN.
DID IT FOR THE TASTY FOOD THEY'D GIVE ME AFTER A JOB.
...
DIDN'T THINK MUCH OF IT.
IT WAS WORK, THAT'S ALL.
ONE DAY I WAS TAKING AIM AT SOME GUY...NO IDEA WHAT NUMBER HE WAS...
AT A CAFE, IN BROAD DAY-LIGHT...
JUST LIKE ALWAYS...

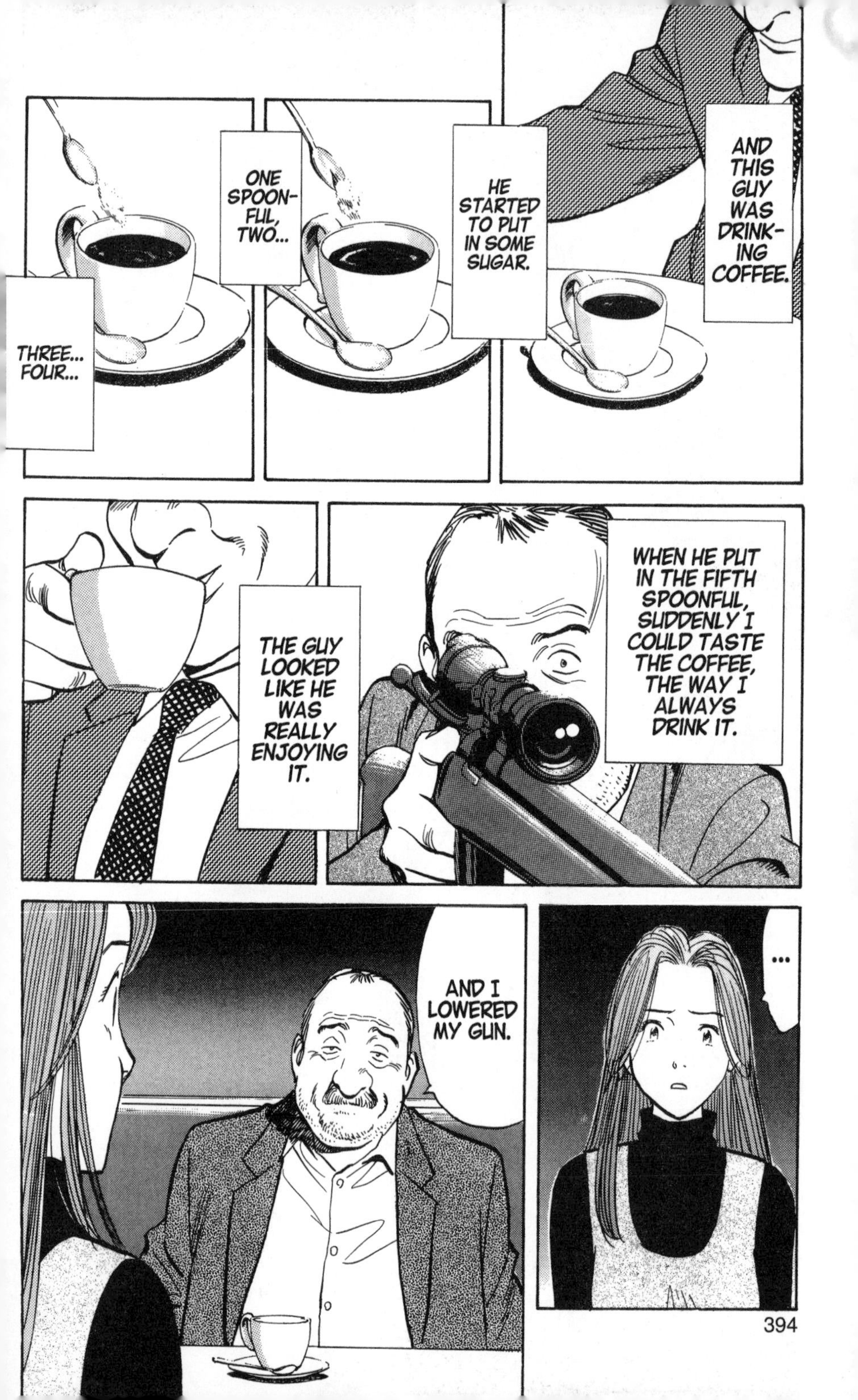

AND THIS GUY WAS DRINK-ING COFFEE.
HE STARTED TO PUT IN SOME SUGAR.
ONE SPOON-FUL, TWO...
THREE... FOUR...
WHEN HE PUT IN THE FIFTH SPOONFUL, SUDDENLY I COULD TASTE THE COFFEE, THE WAY I ALWAYS DRINK IT.
THE GUY LOOKED LIKE HE WAS REALLY ENJOYING IT.
...
AND I LOWERED MY GUN.

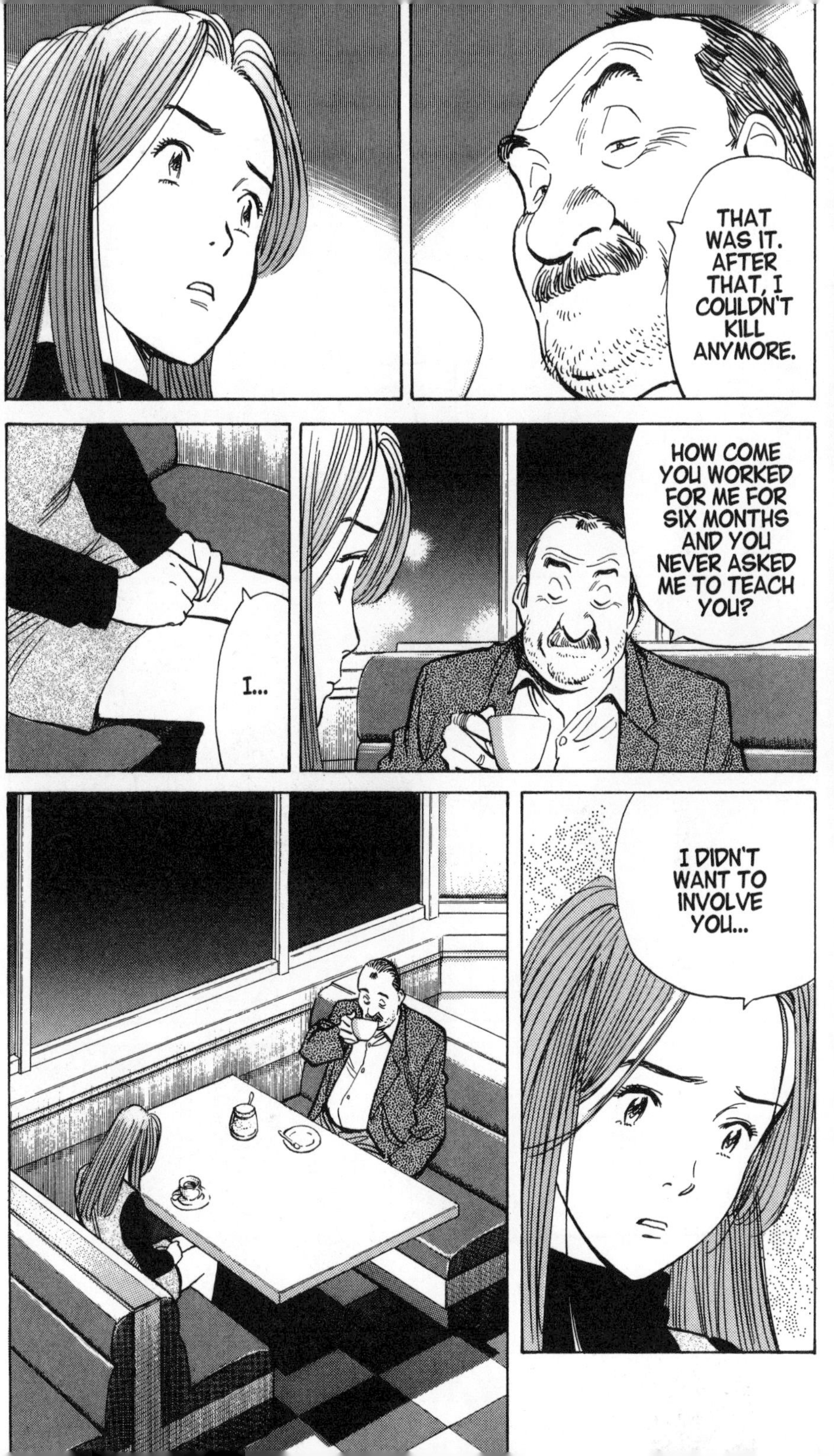
THAT WAS IT. AFTER THAT, I COULDN'T KILL ANYMORE.
HOW COME YOU WORKED FOR ME FOR SIX MONTHS AND YOU NEVER ASKED ME TO TEACH YOU?
I...
I DIDN'T WANT TO INVOLVE YOU...

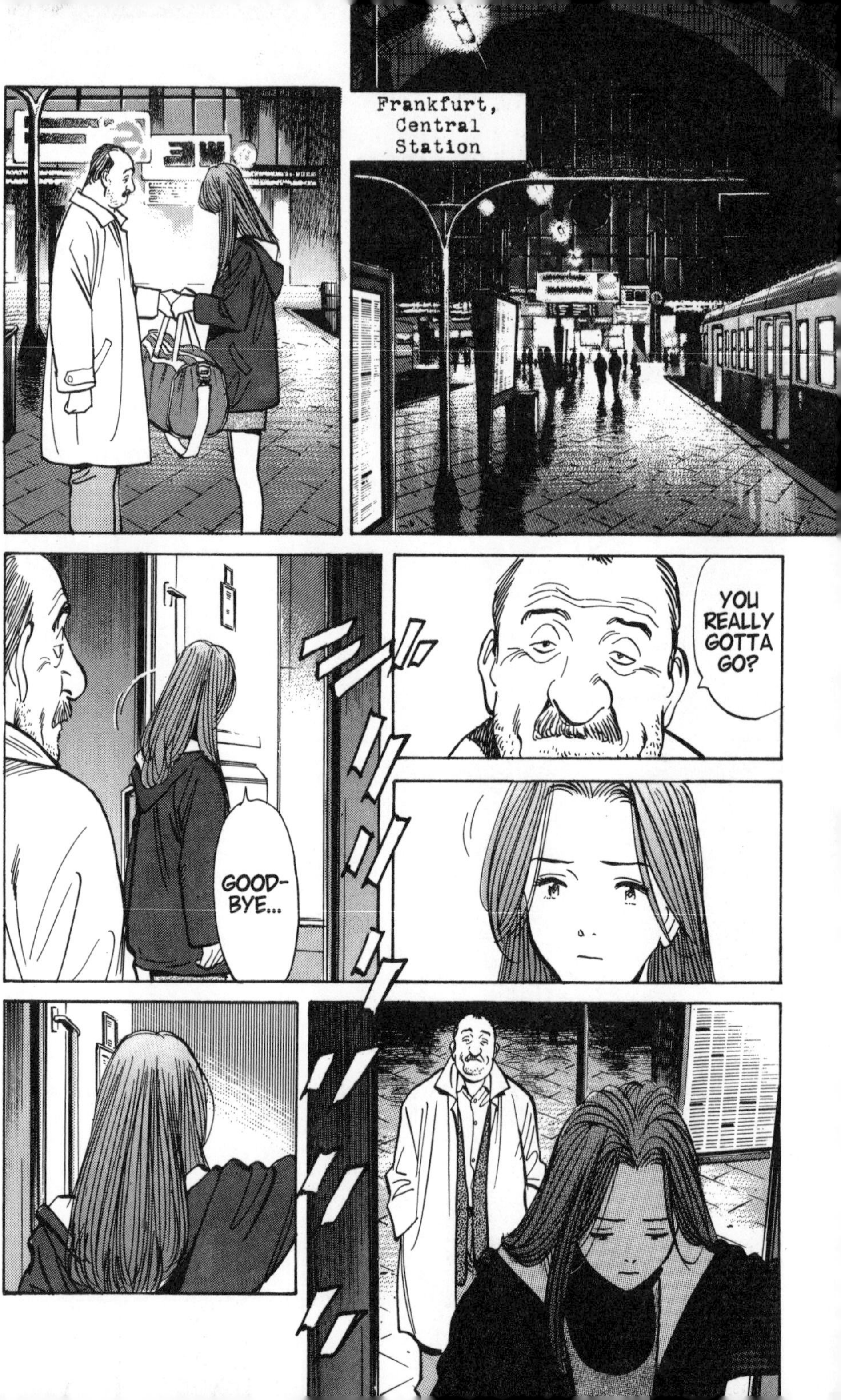
Frankfurt, Central Station
YOU REALLY GOTTA GO?
GOOD-BYE...

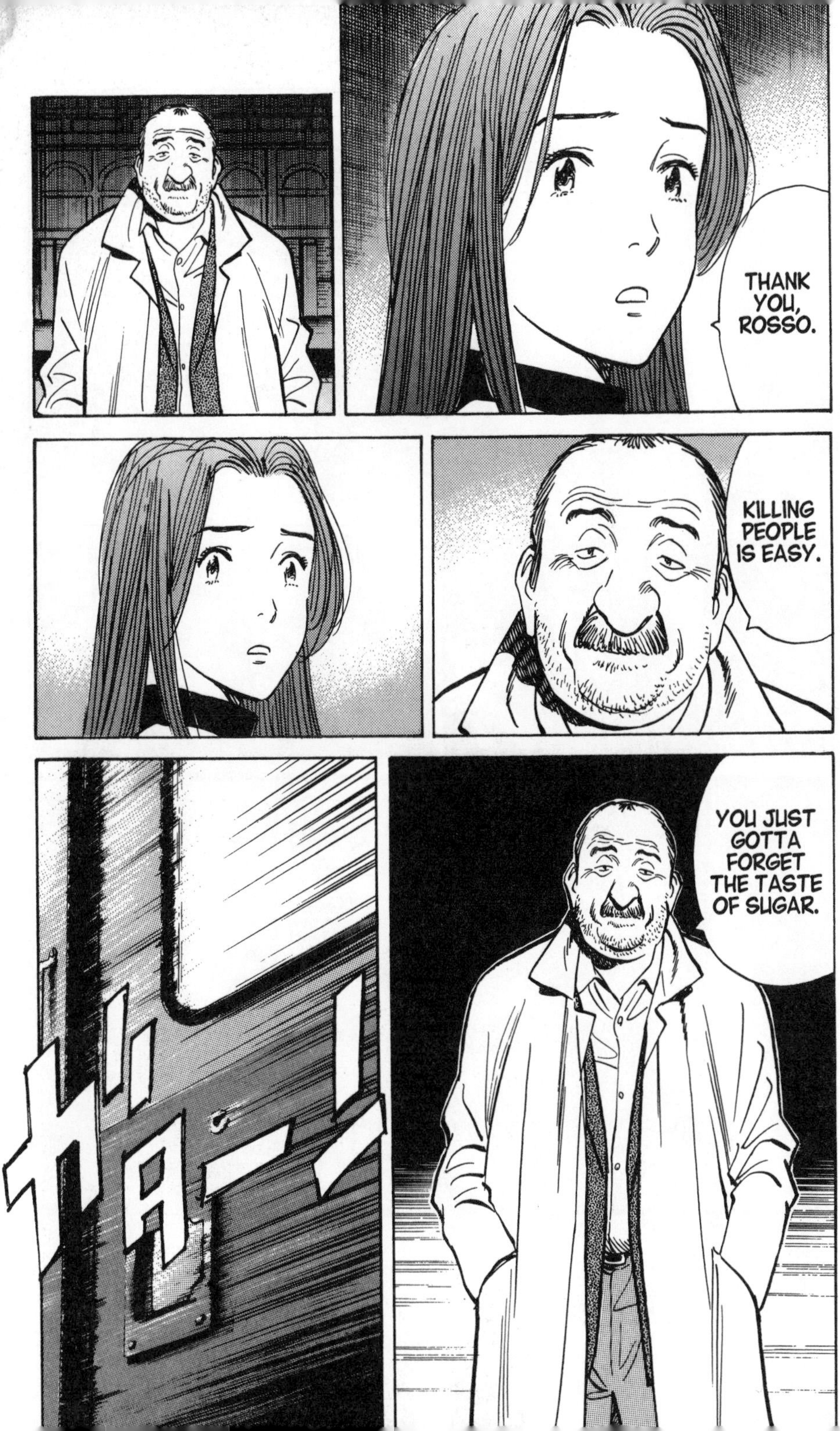
THANK YOU, ROSSO.
KILLING PEOPLE IS EASY.
YOU JUST GOTTA FORGET THE TASTE OF SUGAR.
ガターン

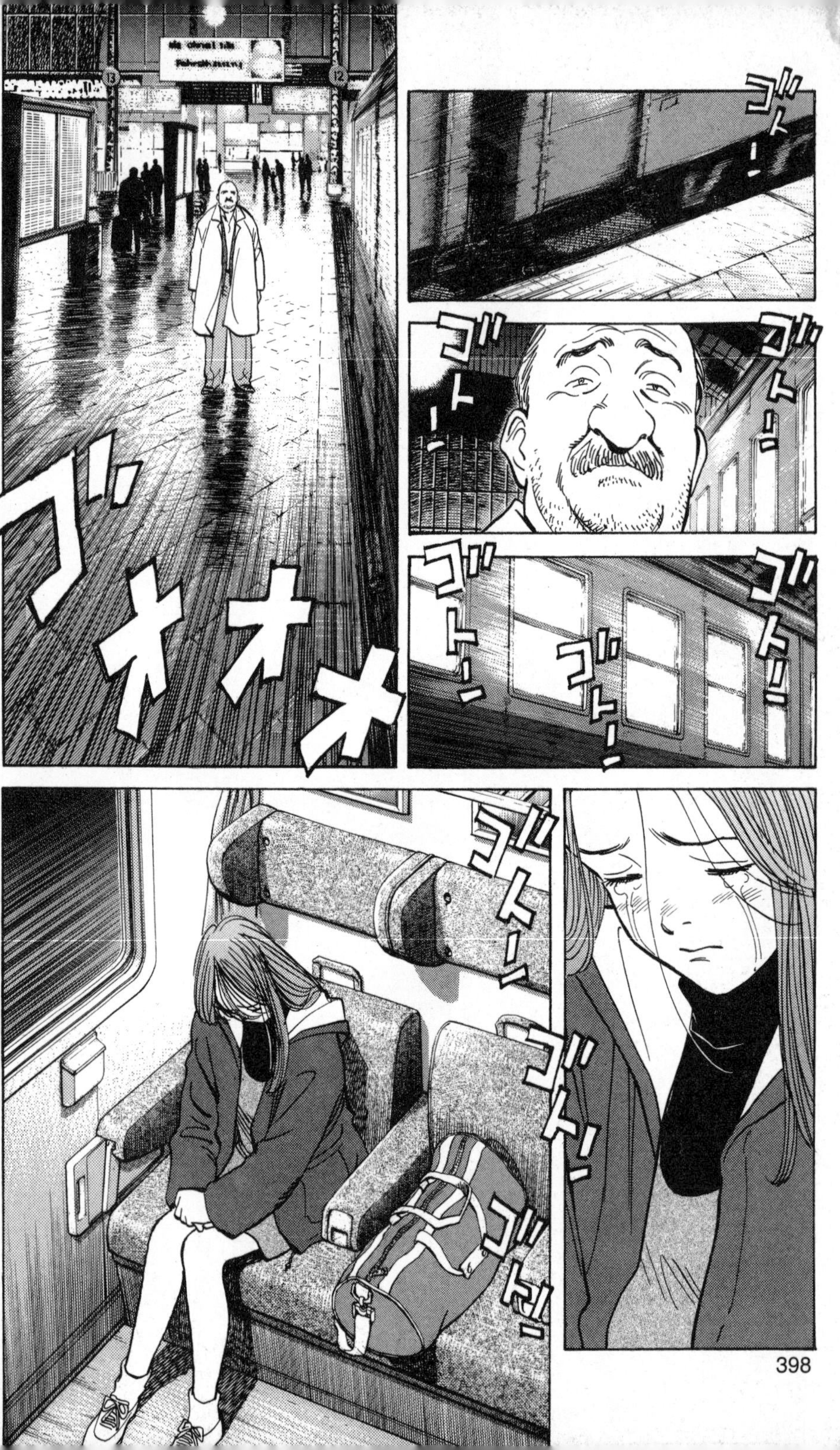
ゴトーン
ゴトーン
ゴトーン
ゴトン
ゴトーン
ゴトーン
ゴオオオ
ゴトーン
ゴトン
ゴトン

MONSTER — VOLUME 2 — END

Naoki Urasawa

Naoki Urasawa's career as a manga artist spans more than twenty years and has firmly established him as one of the true manga masters of Japan. Born in Tokyo in 1960, Urasawa debuted with *BETA!* in 1983 and hasn't stopped his impressive output since. Well-versed in a variety of genres, Urasawa's oeuvre encompasses a multitude of different subjects, such as a romantic comedy (*Yawara! A Fashionable Judo Girl*), a suspenseful human drama about a former mercenary (*Pineapple ARMY*; story by Kazuya Kudo), a captivating psychological suspense story (*Monster*), a sci-fi adventure manga (*20th Century Boys*), and a modern reinterpretation of the work of the God of Manga, Osamu Tezuka (*Pluto: Urasawa × Tezuka*; co-authored with Takashi Nagasaki, supervised by Macoto Tezka, and with the cooperation of Tezuka Productions). Many of his books have spawned popular animated and live-action TV programs and films, and 2008 saw the theatrical release of the first of three live-action Japanese films based on *20th Century Boys*.

No stranger to accolades and awards, Urasawa received the 2011 and 2013 Eisner Award for Best U.S. Edition of International Material—Asia, and is a three-time recipient of the prestigious Shogakukan Manga Award, a two-time recipient of the Osamu Tezuka Cultural Prize, and also received the Kodansha Manga Award. Urasawa has also become involved in the world of academia, and in 2008 accepted a guest teaching post at Nagoya Zokei University, where he teaches courses in, of course, manga.

204.1 – kshh (zaa: rain)
204.5 – blam (don: gunshot)
205.1-2 – blam (don: gunshot)
206.1 – kshh (zaa: rain)
207.2 – kshh (zaa: rain)
209.3-4 – kshh (zaa: rain)
215.1-3 – tak (ka: footsteps)
216.4 – tak (ka: footsteps)
216.6 – kchak (ban: bursting through door)
220.1-2 – whap (ba: blow)
220.3 – vwap (ga: grabbing arm)
220.5 – wham (zutan: slamming)
220.6 – fwap fwap (ban ban: tapping out)
221.1 – wsh (za: quick movement)
221.2-3 – clappa clappa (pachi pachi: clapping)
222.5-7 – whap (ba: blow)
223.1-3 – brrrm (ba ba: engine)
232.1-2 – chomp chomp (ga ga: eating)
238.2 – tmp (za: footstep)
239.1 – brrrm (bwoo: engine)
239.1 – honk (paah: honking)
239.4 – honk (paah: honking)
247.3 – kchak (batan: door slamming)
262.4 – brrrm (ba ba: engine)
263.8 – shff (za: movement)
264.2 – shff (za: movement)
269.4 – kchak (batan: door slamming)
274.6 – whud whud (dosa dosa: thudding)
275.1 – whud (dosa: thudding)
275.8 – kchak (batan: door slamming)
283.2 – tak tak (dota dota: running)
283.3 – kchak (gacha: door opening)
283.6 – whsh (da: quick movement)
285.1 – mnch mnch (hagu hagu: chomping)
294.6 – shff (za: movement)
296.1 – brmm (baa: motor)
300.5 – brmm (baa: motor)
300.7 – shp (za: walking)
302.2 – kchak (batan: door slamming)
302.4 – bam bam (don don: thumping on door)
303.1 – bam bam (don don: thumping on door)
305.7 – chok (ga: catching keys)
305.8 – whsh (da: quick movement)
306.8 – whsh (da: quick movement)
312.7 – shp (za: movement)
313.4 – whsh (da: quick movement)
313.5 – fwhsh (ba: quick thrust)
313.6 – whud (do: thud)
314.4 – grab (ga: grab)
314.5 – whap (ba: throw)
314.6 – slam (da: impact)
314.7 – klink klunk (kan karan: clattering)
315.1 – yank (ga: yanking arm behind back)
315.7 – yoink (gi: tugging)
316.6 – tmp (da: running)
317.3 – tmp (da: running)
318.1 – vrmm (baa: engine)
319.5 – tmp (da: running)
321.1-2 – bam bam (don don: thumping on door)

322.1 – rattle (gacha: rattling door)
323.2 – kreak (gi: door hinges)
325.6-9 – whmp (gu: forceful pushing)
326.1-7 – whmp (gu: forceful pushing)
333.1 – tmp (da: running)
333.2 – klak (gacha: door latch)
333.5 – kreak (gi: door hinges)
333.6 – wham (ban: door slamming)
336.1 – swhoo (baa: fast movement)
337.4 – vrrmm (oon: car engine)
338.2 – swhoo (baa: fast movement)
339.4 – swhoo (baa: fast movement)
343.3 – dash (da: quick movement)
343.5 – whsh (da: quick movement)
344.1 – sploosh (dobashan: splash)
344.4 – fwshh (gooo: rushing water)
346.1-3 – zsh (za: footsteps in grass)
346.7 – shmp (dosa: setting down bag)
349.6 – zsh (za: footsteps in grass)
350.5 – kshh (zaa: downpour)
357.1 – yappa yappa (zawa zawa: clamor)
358.2 – whip (ba: fast movement)
359.2 – rring (RRRR: phone ringing)
359.3 – yappa yappa (wai wai: commotion)
361.4 – kchak (gacha: door opening)
363.2-6 – shp (za: footsteps in grass)
369.3 – voosh (faa: train whooshing past)
369.4 – ktunk ktunk (goton goton: wheels on tracks)
370.3 – ktunk ktunk (goton goton: wheels on tracks)
379.6 – tak (za: footsteps)
387.1 – klop (ka: footsteps)
387.2 – voosh (ba: fast movement)
389.4 – kreak (gi: kreak)
391.2 – rring (RRR: phone ringing)
391.5 – eeoo eeoo (paapoo paapoo: sirens)
391.6-7 – tmp tmp (za za: footsteps)
392.1 – tmp tmp (ka ka: footsteps)
394.1 – eeoo eeoo (paapoo paapoo: sirens)
395.3 – bumpa bumpa (gata goto: bumping along)
395.4 – ktunk ktunk (goto goto: bumping along)
395.6 – bumpa bumpa (gata goto: bumping along)
440.8 – kshh (zaaa: rain)
403.1-3 – thok thok (tatan tatan: jumping)
403.4 – klap klap (pan pan: clapping)
403.5 – fwap (pishi: rope hitting feet)
403.6 – klap klap (pan pan: clapping)
406.8 – kchak (batan: door shutting)
409.2-4 – voosh (za: fast movement)
412.5 – blam blam (ban ban: shots)
414.7 – fwsh (za: fast movement)
415.4 – fwsh (za: fast movement)
415.6 – whsh (ba: pulling away)
415.7 – grab (ga: grabbing shoulder)
416.6 – blam blam (ban ban: shots)
417.2 – blam blam (ban ban: shots)
417.3 – kshh (zaaa: rain)
418.7 – kshh (zaaa: rain)
421.5 – kshh (zaaa: rain)

Sound Effects Glossary

The sound effects in this edition of Monster have been preserved in their original Japanese format. To avoid additional lettering cluttering up the panels, a list of the sound effects (FX) is provided here. Each FX is listed by page and panel number, so for example 3.4 would mean the FX is on page 3 in panel 4.

3.4 – tak tak (ka ka: footsteps)
3.5 – shp (ga: clasping hands)
4.3 – shah (ka: sunlight streaming in)
22.3-6 – whmp (don: thumping)
23.1 – whmp (don: thumping)
26.2 – chomp chomp (hagu: eating)
27.2 – shaaa (zaaa: downpour)
27.3 – wee-oo (paa-poo: siren)
27.4 – skree (kii: breaks squealing)
29.3 – dash (da: running)
29.7 – slam (ba: bursting in)
31.1 – wham (da: bursting in)
32.1-2 – zsshh (zaaa: downpour)
33.1 – shaaa (zaaa: downpour)
33.2 – fwish fwish (shakon shakon: wipers)
34.6 – shoop (bamu: emerging from car)
39.7 – vwaa (paa: oncoming truck)
40.2 – vrmmm (gohh: zooming truck)
40.2 – skree (kikii: breaks squealing)
40.5 – vwam (gan: thumping)
41.2 – tmp (da: running)
41.5 – tak tak (ka ka: footsteps)
42.5 – tak (ka: footstep)
44.7 – kchak (batam: door shutting)
46.1 – soosh (zaaa: water rushing)
46-7 – kreak (gi: squeaking door hinges)
47-3 – chik (ka: light coming on)
50.3 – tak (ka: footsteps)
50.4 – wmp (pon: thumping on shoulder)
50.5-6 – tak (ka: footsteps)
52.2 – whmp (don: thumping)
52.4 – whmp (don: thumping)
55.2-3 – tak (ka: footsteps)
56.1 – kreak (gi: squeaking door hinges)
56.2 – wham (bamu: door slamming)
56.3 – chik (ka: light coming on)
63.7 – tak (ka: footsteps)
71.3 – tak (ka: footsteps)
73.3-4 – clappa clappa (pachi pachi: applause)
74.2-3 – clappa clappa (pachi pachi: applause)
74.4 – chatter chatter (wai wai: talking)
74.5 – ha ha ha (ha ha ha: laughter)
76.2 – Ooh! (waaa: exclamations)
76.2-3 – clappa clappa (pachi pachi: applause)
77.7 – clappa clappa (pachi pachi: applause)
79.7 – chatter chatter (wai wai: talking)
82.6 – thump (don: thumping fist)
98.2 – tak (da: footstep)
99.1- tak (da: footstep)
101.2 – yoink (ga: yanking)
103.6 – whump (don: shove)
103.7 – kchak (batan: door slamming)

105.1 – shf (ka: quick movement)
106.2 – kreak (gi: door squeaking)
106.7 – ka-bash (don garagan: crashing)
107.5 – kreak (gi: door squeaking)
109.5 – kreak (gi: door squeaking)
111.3 – wobble (yoro: staggering)
111.4 – kreak (gi: door squeaking)
113.2 – clamor clamor (wai wai: shouting voices)
114.1 – tmp tmp (do do: running)
114.4 – tak (da: footstep)
114.5 – yappa yappa (zawa zawa: commotion)
115.2 – tak (ka: footsteps)
116.3 – shove (don: collision)
117.3 – tak (da: footstep)
117.4 – tak tak (da da: footsteps)
117.5 – fwam (ba: bursting through door)
121.2 – zsh (za: quick movement)
121.5 – whsh (ba: quick movement)
123.1 – whak (za: quick movement)
129.4 – kchak (kacha: door opening)
138.2 – tak tak (ka ka: footsteps)
138.4 – tak (ka: footsteps)
139.3 – splish (basha: splashing)
143.2 – shf (ta: quick movement)
143.3 – shoo (hyoon: falling)
145.8 – fwoo (da: running)
147.4 – shah (ka: light coming on)
147.5 – shp (kyu: putting on gloves)
149.3 – tmp (da: running)
150.1 – brmm (ooo: car's engine)
150.4-8 – skreee (gyagyagya: breaks squealing)
150.6 – vwam (don: impact)
151.3 – yappa yappa (zawa zawa: commotion)
152.2-3 – tak tak (ka ka: footsteps)
153.5 – voosh (zaa: fast movement)
153.6 – kchak (bamu: door shutting)
153.7 – tak (ka: footsteps)
157.6 – kchak (batan: door closing)
158.2 – shah (ka: light coming on)
169.1 – kchak (batan: door closing)
175.3-7 – quiver quiver (kata kata: shivering)
176.1 – quiver quiver (kata kata: shivering)
179.1 – kreak (gi: door opening)
181.2 – tmp (da: running)
181.8 – whsh (ba: quick movement)
182.1 – whsh (ba: quick movement)
182.4 – krash (gashan: clock smashing)
182.5 – tmp (da: running)
183.2 – tmp (da: running)
183.6 – kang kang (kan kan: running down stairs)
184.3 – whsh (ta: turning)
203.1 – kshh (zaa: rain)

NAOKI URASAWA Volume.2

MONSTER

Perfect Edition

MONSTER
Volume 2
VIZ Signature Edition

Story & Art by NAOKI URASAWA
Story Coproduced with TAKASHI NAGASAKI

Translation & English Adaptation/Camellia Nieh
Lettering/Steve Dutro
Cover & Interior Design/King Clovis
Editor/Mike Montesa

MONSTER KANZENBAN Vol.2
by Naoki URASAWA/Studio Nuts
Story coproduced with Takashi NAGASAKI
© 2008 Naoki URASAWA/Studio Nuts
All rights reserved.
Original Japanese edition published by SHOGAKUKAN.
English translation rights in the United States of America, Canada, United Kingdom,
Ireland, Australia and New Zealand arranged with SHOGAKUKAN.
Original Art Direction by Kazuo UMINO
Original cover design by Mikiyo KOBAYASHI + Bay Bridge Studio

Printed in the U.S.A.

Published by VIZ Media, LLC
P.O. Box 77010
San Francisco, CA 94107

10 9 8 7 6 5 4 3 2 1
First printing, October 2014

www.viz.com

VIZ SIGNATURE